Less managing. More teaching. Greater learning.

INSTRUCTORS...

Would you like your **students** to show up for class more **prepared**? *(Let's face it, class is much more fun if everyone is engaged and prepared...)*

Want ready-made application-level **interactive assignments**, student progress reporting, and auto-assignment grading? *(Less time grading means more time teaching...)*

Want an **instant view of student or class performance** relative to learning objectives? *(No more wondering if students understand...)*

Need to **collect data and generate reports** required for administration or accreditation? *(Say goodbye to manually tracking student learning outcomes...)*

Want to **record and post your lectures** for students to view online?

With **McGraw-Hill's** *Connect*™ *Plus International Business,*

INSTRUCTORS GET:

- Interactive Applications – **book-specific interactive assignments** that require students to APPLY what they've learned.

- Simple **assignment management,** allowing you to spend more time teaching.

- **Auto-graded** assignments, quizzes, and tests.

- **Detailed Visual Reporting** where student and section results can be viewed and analyzed.

- Sophisticated **online testing** capability.

- A **filtering and reporting** function that allows you to easily assign and report on materials that are correlated to accreditation standards, learning outcomes, and Bloom's taxonomy.

- An easy-to-use **lecture capture** tool.

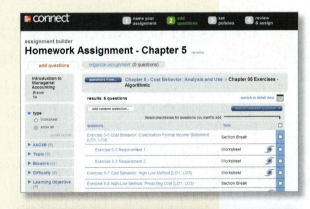

Want an online, **searchable version** of your textbook?

Wish your textbook could be **available online** while you're doing your assignments?

 ***Connect*™ *Plus International Business* eBook**

If you choose to use *Connect*™ *Plus International Business*, you have an affordable and searchable online version of your book integrated with your other online tools.

***Connect*™ *Plus International Business* eBook offers features like:**

- Topic search
- Direct links from assignments
- Adjustable text size
- Jump to page number
- Print by section

 Want to get more **value** from your textbook purchase?

Think learning international business should be a bit more **interesting**?

 Check out the STUDENT RESOURCES section under the *Connect*™ Library tab.

Here you'll find a wealth of resources designed to help you achieve your goals in the course. You'll find things like **quizzes, PowerPoints, and Internet activities** to help you study. Every student has different needs, so explore the STUDENT RESOURCES to find the materials best suited to you.

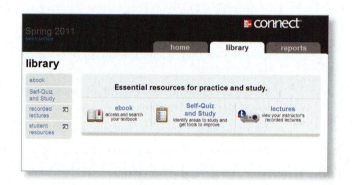

international
business

J. Michael Geringer
CALIFORNIA POLYTECHNIC UNIVERSITY

Michael S. Minor
UNIVERSITY OF TEXAS-PAN AMERICAN

Jeanne M. McNett
ASSUMPTION COLLEGE

international business

VICE PRESIDENT AND EDITOR-IN-CHIEF	**BRENT GORDON**
EDITORIAL DIRECTOR	**PAUL DUCHAM**
EXECUTIVE EDITOR	**JOHN WEIMEISTER**
EXECUTIVE DIRECTOR OF DEVELOPMENT	**ANN TORBERT**
DEVELOPMENT EDITOR	**MEGAN RICHTER**
VICE PRESIDENT AND DIRECTOR OF MARKETING	**ROBIN J. ZWETTLER**
MARKETING MANAGER	**DONIELLE XU**
VICE PRESIDENT OF EDITING, DESIGN, AND PRODUCTION	**SESHA BOLISETTY**
LEAD PROJECT MANAGER	**CHRISTINE A. VAUGHAN**
SENIOR BUYER	**CAROL A. BIELSKI**
SENIOR DESIGNER	**MARY KAZAK SANDER**
PHOTO RESEARCH COORDINATOR	**JOANNE MENNEMEIER**
SENIOR MEDIA PROJECT MANAGER	**GREG BATES**
MEDIA PROJECT MANAGER	**CATHY L. TEPPER**
COVER IMAGE	**© CHAD ANDERSON**
BACK COVER IMAGE	**© JOHN CUMMING**
TYPEFACE	**10/12 MINION PRO REGULAR**
COMPOSITOR	**LASERWORDS PRIVATE LIMITED**
PRINTER	**QUAD/GRAPHICS**

M: INTERNATIONAL BUSINESS

Published by McGraw-Hill/Irwin, a business unit of The McGraw-Hill Companies, Inc., 1221 Avenue of the Americas, New York, NY, 10020.

Some ancillaries, including electronic and print components, may not be available to customers outside the United States.

This book is printed on acid-free paper.

1 2 3 4 5 6 7 8 9 0 QDB/QDB 1 0 9 8 7 6 5 4 3 2 1

ISBN 978-0-07-802937-0
MHID 0-07-802937-6

Library of Congress Control Number 2010938656

www.mhhe.com

brief contents

contents

CHAPTER 11   ORGANIZATIONAL DESIGN AND CONTROL 182

CHAPTER 12   ASSESSING INTERNATIONAL MARKETS 200

CHAPTER 17 INTERNATIONAL ACCOUNTING AND FINANCIAL MANAGEMENT 278

international business

coming up

The world we share is becoming increasingly interconnected in complex and interesting ways. Section One describes the nature and scope of international business and introduces the three environments in which international business managers must operate. How well they perform in their undertakings depends in great measure on their understanding of domestic, international, and foreign environments.

Chapter 1 discusses what international business is and also presents the concepts of the three environments and their forces. From the history of international business, we learn that international firms have been in existence for centuries, but that present-day global companies–characterized by explosive growth and closer central control of foreign operations–are markedly different from their predecessors. We discuss what is driving globalization of business and why firms go abroad, and examine the debate about pros and cons of globalization of business. We also examine the seven dimensions along which managers can globalize if they take their companies international.

In Chapter 2, information is presented to help you comprehend the dynamic growth and the magnitude of both international trade and foreign investment. We also provide an overview of the major theories of international trade and investment. A basic understanding of this material will help explain the actions already taken by managers and by government officials and provide insight into what they plan to do in the future.

Chapter 3 discusses institutions that operate in the international environment and that may affect international businesses in fundamental ways. International institutions can be both a help and a hindrance to businesses, and the international institutions and agreements discussed in this chapter are organizations of governments, along with some private organizations, whose main purpose is political, economic, or a combination of the two. Some of these organizations have large amounts of power (such as the European Union), and others have less power, but all are important to business. ■

up

THE NATURE OF INTERNATIONAL BUSINESS

section one
THE NATURE OF INTERNATIONAL BUSINESS

section two
INTERNATIONAL ENVORONMENTAL FORCES

section three
THE ORGANIZATIONAL ENVIRONMENT

the challenging world of
international business

"In the past, complex international transactions were the domain of diplomats and international policy and business experts. Today a converging set of powerful economic, technological, demographic and geopolitical trends will demand that all citizens, not just the elite, have that kind of global fluency. Knowledge of the world is no longer a luxury, it is a necessity."

—Nicholas Platt, president emeritus of the Asia Society

chapter one

To think about how you are involved in the global economy, think back to how you began your own day. After you awoke, you may have looked at your Casio watch for the time, checked your Samsung cell phone for messages, and turned on your Toshiba TV for the news and weather while you showered. After drying your hair with a Conair dryer, maybe you slipped into some Diesel jeans, quickly swallowed some Dannon yogurt and a glass of Mott's apple juice, brushed your teeth with Close-Up toothpaste, and drove off to class in your Honda with its Firestone tires and a tank full of Shell gasoline. Meanwhile, on the other side of the world, a group of Nike-clad Japanese students may be turning off their H-P computers after watching videos on YouTube.com and debating whether they should stop for hamburgers and Cokes at McDonald's or coffee at Starbucks. As they leave, they place their books and other materials into their JanSport backpacks, put on their North Face jackets and Oakley sunglasses, and turn on their iPods.

LEARNING OBJECTIVES

After reading this chapter, you should be able to:

LO1 Understand what international business is and why it is important.

LO2 Comprehend why and how international business differs from domestic business.

LO3 Appreciate that international business has a long and important history in the world's development.

LO4 Appreciate the dramatic internationalization of markets.

LO5 Understand the five kinds of drivers, all based on change, that are leading firms to internationalize their operations.

LO6 Recognize the key arguments for and against the globalization of business.

LO7 Explain the reasons for entering foreign markets.

LO8 Recognize that globalization of an international firm occurs over at least seven dimensions and that a company can be partially global in some dimensions and completely global in others.

What do you and the Japanese students have in common? You are all consuming products made by *foreign-owned companies*. This is international business.

All that you have read so far points to one salient fact: *all managers need to have a basic knowledge of international business to be able to meet the challenge of global competition.* Acquiring this knowledge consists, in part, of learning the special terminology of international business, an important function, as you already know, of every introductory course. To assist you in learning the international business "language," we've included a glossary at the end of the book and listed the most important terms at the end of each chapter. They also appear in bold print where they are first used in the text, with their definitions in the margin.

LO1   Understand what international business is and why it is important.

WHAT IS INTERNATIONAL BUSINESS?

Because international business is a relatively new discipline and is extremely dynamic, you will find that the definitions of a number of terms vary among users. To avoid confusion due to the range of different definitions of terms in international business, in this text we will employ the definitions listed below, which are generally accepted by managers:

1. **International business** is business whose activities are carried out across national borders. This definition includes not only international trade and foreign manufacturing but also the growing service industry in areas such as transportation, tourism, advertising, construction, retailing, wholesaling, and mass communications.

2. **Foreign business** denotes the operations of a company outside its home or domestic market; many refer to this as business conducted within a foreign country. This term sometimes is used interchangeably with *international*

business by some writers, although that will not be the practice in this book.

3. A **multidomestic company (MDC)** is an organization with multicountry affiliates, each of which formulates its own business strategy based on perceived market differences.

4. A **global company (GC)** is an organization that attempts to standardize and integrate operations worldwide in most or all functional areas.

5. An **international company (IC)** is a global or multidomestic company.

Although we primarily use the terms *global, multidomestic,* and *international* firms or companies, at times we may use *multinational enterprise (MNE)* or *multinational company (MNC)* interchangeably with *international company (IC),* inasmuch as both terms are employed in the literature and in practice.

Although you may find those who consider *multinational corporation* to be synonymous with *multinational enterprise* and *transnational corporation,*[1] the United Nations and the governments of many developing nations use *transnational* instead of *multinational* to describe any firm doing business in more than one country. The specialized agency, the United Nations Conference on Trade and Development (UNCTAD), for example, employs the following definition: "A transnational corporation is generally regarded as an enterprise comprising entities in more than one country which operate under a system of decision making that permits coherent policies and a common strategy. The entities are so linked, by ownership or otherwise, that one or more of them may be able to exercise a significant influence over the others and, in particular, to share knowledge, resources and responsibilities with the others."[2] More recently, some academic writers have employed the term *transnational* for a company that combines the characteristics of global and multinational firms: (1) trying to achieve economies of scale through global integration of its functional areas and at the same time (2) being highly responsive to different local environments (a newer name is *multicultural multinational*).[3]

WHAT IS DIFFERENT ABOUT INTERNATIONAL BUSINESS?

International business differs from domestic business in that a firm operating across borders must deal with the forces of three kinds of environments—domestic, foreign, and international. In contrast, a firm whose business activities are carried out within the borders of one country needs to be concerned essentially with only the domestic environment. However, no domestic firm is entirely free from foreign or international environmental forces because the possibility of having to face competition from foreign imports or from foreign competitors that set up operations in its own market is always present. Let us first examine these forces and then see how they operate in the three environments.

Influence of External and Internal Environmental Forces

The term **environment** as used here means all the forces influencing the life and development of the firm. The forces themselves can be classified as *external* or *internal*. The external

4. *Socioeconomic:* characteristics and distribution of the human population.

5. *Financial:* variables such as interest rates, inflation rates, and taxation.

6. *Legal:* the many foreign and domestic laws governing how international firms must operate.

7. *Physical:* elements of nature such as topography, climate, and natural resources.

8. *Political:* elements of nations' political climates such as nationalism, forms of government, and international organizations.

9. *Sociocultural:* elements of culture (such as attitudes, beliefs, and opinions) important to international managers.

10. *Labor:* composition, skills, and attitudes of labor.

11. *Technological:* the technical skills and equipment that affect how resources are converted to products.

The elements over which management does have some control are the internal forces, such as the factors of production (capital, raw materials, and people) and the activities of the organization (personnel, finance, production, and marketing). These are the **controllable forces** management must administer in order to adapt to changes in the uncontrollable

environment All the forces surrounding and influencing the life and development of the firm

uncontrollable forces External forces over which management has no direct control, although it can exert an influence

controllable forces Internal forces that management administers to adapt to changes in the uncontrollable forces

> ## ONE CHANGE IN THE POLITICAL FORCES—THE EXPANSION OF THE EUROPEAN UNION (EU) IN 2007—AFFECTED ALL THE CONTROLLABLE FORCES OF FIRMS WORLDWIDE THAT DO BUSINESS IN OR WITH THE 27 EU MEMBER-NATIONS.

forces are commonly called **uncontrollable forces.** Management has no direct control over them, although it can exert influence–such as lobbying for a change in a law and heavily promoting a new product that requires a change in a cultural attitude. External forces consist of the following:

1. *Competitive:* kinds and numbers of competitors, their locations, and their activities.

2. *Distributive:* national and international agencies available for distributing goods and services.

3. *Economic:* variables (such as gross national product [GNP], unit labor cost, and personal consumption expenditure) that influence a firm's ability to do business.

environmental variables. Look at how one change in the political forces—the expansion of the European Union (EU) in 2007—affected all the controllable forces of firms worldwide that do business in or with the 27 EU member-nations. Suddenly these firms had to examine their business practices and change those affected by this new expansion. For example, some European concerns and foreign subsidiaries in the EU relocated parts of their operations to other nations in the Union to exploit the lower wages there. Some American and Asian companies set up production in one of the member-countries to supply this giant free trade area. By doing this, they avoid paying import duties on products coming from their home countries.

domestic environment All the uncontrollable forces originating in the home country that surround and influence the firm's life and development

foreign environment All the uncontrollable forces originating outside the home country that surround and influence the firm

international environment Interaction between domestic and foreign environmental forces or between sets of foreign environmental forces

The Domestic Environment

The **domestic environment** is all the uncontrollable forces originating in the home country that influence the life and development of the firm. Obviously, these are the forces with which managers are most familiar. Being domestic forces, however, does not preclude their affecting foreign operations. For example, if the home country is suffering from a shortage of foreign currency, the government may place restrictions on overseas investment to reduce its outflow. As a result, managers of multinationals find that they cannot expand overseas facilities as they would like to do. In another instance from real life, a labor union striking the home-based plants learned that management was supplying parts from its foreign subsidiaries. The strikers contacted the foreign unions, which pledged not to work overtime to supply what the struck plants could not. The impact of this domestic environmental force was felt overseas as well as at home.

the Argentine government ordered the Argentine subsidiary to fill the order. The Argentine government said that Argentine companies, of which the subsidiary was one, did not answer to the demands of a foreign government. The Argentine management of the subsidiary was in a quandary. Finally, headquarters relented and permitted its Argentine subsidiary to fill the order.

Forces Can Be Difficult to Assess
Another problem with foreign forces is that they are frequently difficult to assess. This is especially true of legal and political forces. A highly nationalistic law may be passed to appease a section of the local population. To all outward appearances, the government may appear to be against foreign investment; yet pragmatic leaders may actually encourage it. A good example is Mexico, which until 1988 had a law prohibiting foreigners from owning a majority interest in a Mexican company. However, a clause permitted exceptions "if the investment contributes to the welfare of the nation." IBM, Eaton, and others were successful in obtaining permission to establish a wholly owned subsidiary under this clause.

The Forces Are Interrelated
In the chapters that follow, it will be evident that the forces are often interrelated. This in itself is not a novelty because the same situation confronts a domestic manager. On the foreign scene, however, the kinds of interaction that occur and the outcomes may differ. For instance, the combination of high-cost capital and

> ## BARRIERS TO THE FREE MOVEMENT OF A NATION'S PEOPLE, SUCH AS MOUNTAIN RANGES AND DESERTS, HELP MAINTAIN POCKETS OF DISTINCT CULTURES WITHIN A COUNTRY.

The Foreign Environment

The forces in the **foreign environment** are the same as those in the domestic environment except that they occur outside the firm's home country. However, they operate differently for several reasons, including those provided here.

Forces Have Different Values
Even though the kinds of forces in the two environments are identical, their values often differ widely, and at times they are completely opposed to each other. A classic example of diametrically opposed political-force values and the bewilderment they create for multinational managers involves the American export embargo on shipments of most goods to Cuba. This embargo meant that Cuba could not buy buses from a U.S. manufacturer. To circumvent the embargo, the Cuban government ordered the buses from the American firm's Argentine subsidiary. When word came from the firm's American headquarters that the order should not be filled because of the American embargo,

an abundance of unskilled labor in many developing countries may lead to the use of a lower level of technology than would be employed in the more industrialized nations. In other words, given a choice between installing costly, specialized machinery needing few workers and installing less expensive, general-purpose machinery requiring a larger labor force, management will frequently choose the latter when faced with high interest rates and a large pool of available workers. Another example is the interaction between physical and sociocultural forces. Barriers to the free movement of a nation's people, such as mountain ranges and deserts, help maintain pockets of distinct cultures within a country, and this has an effect on decision making.

The International Environment

The **international environment** consists of the interactions (1) between the domestic environmental forces and the foreign environmental forces and (2) between the foreign environmental forces of two countries when an affiliate in one country does business with customers in another. This agrees with the definition of international business: business that involves the crossing of national borders.

For example, personnel at the headquarters of a multidomestic or global company work in the international environment if they are involved in any way with another nation, whereas those in a foreign subsidiary do not unless they too are engaged in international business through exporting or the management of other affiliates. In other words, a sales manager of Nokia's China operations does not work in the international environment if he or she sells cellular phones only in China. If Nokia's China operations export cell phones to Thailand, then the sales manager is affected by forces of both the domestic environment of China and the foreign environment of Thailand and therefore is working in the international environment. International organizations whose actions affect the international environment are also properly part of it. These organizations include (1) worldwide bodies (e.g., World Bank), (2) regional economic

some managers will ascribe to others their own preferences and reactions. Thus, a foreign production manager, facing a backlog of orders, may offer her workers extra pay for overtime. When they fail to show up, the manager is perplexed: "Back home they always want to earn more money." This manager has failed to understand that the workers prefer time off to more money. This unconscious reference to the manager's own cultural values, called the **self-reference criterion,** is probably the biggest cause of international business blunders. Successful managers are careful to examine a problem in terms of the local cultural traits as well as their own.

> **self-reference criterion** Unconscious reference to one's own cultural values when judging behaviors of others in a new and different environment

LO3 Appreciate that international business has a long and important history in the world's development.

["The self-reference criterion is probably the biggest cause of international business blunders."]

groupings of nations (e.g., North American Free Trade Agreement, European Union), and (3) organizations bound by industry agreements (e.g., Organization of Petroleum Exporting Countries).

Decision Making Is More Complex Those who work in the international environment find that decision making is more complex than it is in a purely domestic environment. Consider managers in a home office who must make decisions affecting subsidiaries in just 10 different countries (many ICs are in 20 or more countries). They not only must take into account the domestic forces but also must evaluate the influence of 10 foreign national environments. Instead of having to consider the effects of a single set of 10 forces, as do their domestic counterparts, they have to contend with 10 sets of 10 forces, *both individually and collectively,* because there may be some interaction.

For example, if management agrees to labor's demands at one foreign subsidiary, chances are it will have to offer a similar settlement at another subsidiary because of the tendency of unions to exchange information across borders. Furthermore, as we shall observe throughout this text, not only are there many sets of forces, but there are also extreme differences among them.

Self-Reference Criterion Another common cause of the added complexity of foreign environments is managers' unfamiliarity with other cultures. To make matters worse,

A BRIEF HISTORY OF INTERNATIONAL BUSINESS

While international business as a discipline is relatively new, as a business practice it is not, so let's briefly explore the history of international business.

Well before the time of Christ, Phoenician and Greek merchants were sending representatives abroad to sell their goods. Subsequently, a vast expansion of agricultural and industrial production in China stimulated the emergence of an internationally integrated trading system. The saying that "all roads lead to China" had relevance within the international trade system, as China was the world's leading manufacturing country for about 1,800 years, until it was replaced by Britain in about 1840.

The impact of the emerging international trading system was extensive. Politics, the arts, agriculture, industry, and other sectors of human life were profoundly influenced by the goods and ideas that came with trade. Public health was also affected. An interesting precursor to contemporary concerns about global health epidemics, such as severe acute respiratory syndrome (SARS) and the so-called "swine flu," was international trade's association with the spread of the plague, one of the worst natural disasters in history. Believed to have originated in Asia, the

> THE RISE OF THE OTTOMAN EMPIRE BEFORE 1300, ULTIMATELY SPANNING EUROPE, NORTH AFRICA, AND THE MIDDLE EAST, PROFOUNDLY INFLUENCED THE EMERGING TRADE ROUTES FOR PEOPLE, GOODS, MONEY, ANIMALS, AND MICROORGANISMS.

plague moved west with traders and soldiers, carried by oriental rat fleas that lived on rodents that stowed away on ships and caravans. Called the Black Death in Europe and repeated in waves from the mid-1300s through the 1500s, the plague ravaged cities, caused widespread hysteria, and killed one-quarter of China's people and one-third of the population of Europe.[4]

The rise of the Ottoman Empire before 1300, ultimately spanning Europe, North Africa, and the Middle East, profoundly influenced the emerging trade routes for people, goods, money, animals, and microorganisms that spanned from England to China, across the Mediterranean and Northern Africa, and through Central Asia and the Indian Ocean region. The powerful central location of the Ottomans within this trading web had the effect of raising the cost of Asian trade for the Europeans. This spawned a search for sea routes to Asia, including expeditions that discovered the Americas.

In 1600, Great Britain's British East India Company, a newly formed trading firm, began to establish foreign branches throughout Asia, an action soon followed by many of the other European nations intent on exploiting trade opportunities for national advantage, including Portugal, the Netherlands, and France. In 1602, the Dutch East India Company was formed to carry out colonial activities in Asia and to open ocean trade routes to the East. The first company to issue stock, it is also frequently identified as the world's first multinational corporation.[5] By the end of the 1600s, ships commissioned by European trading companies regularly traveled to Asia via an interconnected Atlantic, Indian, and Pacific Ocean system of government-protected trade routes. Their goal was to acquire goods for sale or resale within various Asian markets and ultimately to return to Europe with valuable cargoes of cloth, spices, and other goods that would yield significant profits for investors. The 17th and 18th centuries have frequently been termed the "age of mercantilism" because the power of nations depended directly on the sponsorship and control of merchant capital, which expanded under the direct subsidization and protection of national governments. The concept of mercantilism is discussed in Chapter 2.

A number of multinational companies existed in the late 1800s. One of the first American companies to own foreign production facilities, have worldwide distribution networks, and market its products under global brands was Singer Sewing Machine. In 1868, it built a factory in Scotland and, by 1880, the company had become a global organization with an outstanding international sales organization and several overseas manufacturing plants. Other firms, such as J&P Coats (United Kingdom) and Ford Motor Company, soon followed, and by

1914, at least 37 American companies had production facilities in two or more overseas locations.[6] Interestingly, and quite a contrast to today's situation, in the 1920s *all* cars sold in Japan were made in the United States by Ford and General Motors and sent to Japan in knocked-down kits to be assembled locally. European companies were also moving overseas. For example, Friedrich Bayer purchased an interest in a New York plant in 1865, two years after setting up his plant in Germany. Then, because of high import duties in his overseas markets, he proceeded to establish plants in Russia (1876), France (1882), and Belgium (1908).[7]

As you have just read, multinational firms existed well before World War I, and the level of intracompany trade of multinationals in 1930, as a percentage of overall world trade, may have exceeded the proportion at the end of the 20th century.[8] Yet only in recent years have multinationals become the object of much discussion and investigation, especially concerning the increasing globalization of their operations.

LO4 **Appreciate** the dramatic internationalization of markets.

GROWTH OF INTERNATIONAL FIRMS AND INTERNATIONAL BUSINESS

The size and the number of U.S. and foreign international concerns have been increasing rapidly in recent years, as have the levels of foreign direct investment (FDI) and exporting.

Expanding Number of International Companies

UNCTAD, the United Nations agency in charge of all matters relating to FDI and international corporations, estimates that there are 64,000 transnational corporations with international production activities. These transnationals have approximately 866,000 foreign affiliates that collectively employ more than 53 million people (versus only 19 million two decades ago). These transnationals account for approximately 25 percent of total global output and two-thirds of world trade. Foreign affiliates' sales have grown about 700 percent in the past 20 years.[9]

As a result of this expansion, the subsidiaries of foreign companies have become increasingly important in the industrial and economic life of many nations, developed and developing. This situation is in sharp contrast to the one that existed when the dominant economic interests were in the hands of local citizens. The expanding importance of foreign-owned firms in local economies came to be viewed by a number of governments as a threat to their autonomy. However, there has been a marked liberalization of government policies and attitudes toward foreign investment in both developed and developing nations since the early 1980s. Many government leaders know that local firms must obtain modern commercial technology in the form of direct investment, purchase of capital goods, and the right to use the international company's expertise if they are to be competitive in world markets.

Despite this change in attitude, there are still critics of large global firms who cite such statistics as the following to "prove" that host governments are powerless before them: In 2008, only 19 nations had gross national incomes (GNIs) greater than the total annual sales of Royal Dutch Shell, the company with the greatest level of sales in the world.[10] Further, when nations and corporations are ranked by GNI and total sales, respectively, nearly half of the first 100 on the list are corporations. However, a nation's GNI and a company's sales are not directly comparable because GNI is a measure of value added, not sales. If a nation's total sales were computed, the result would be far greater than its GNI because there would be triple and quadruple counting. For example, suppose a steel manufacturer sells steel wire to a tire company, which uses it to build tires. Then the tire company sells the tires to automakers, which mount them on their automobiles, which they in turn sell to the public. Sales of the wire would be counted three times. However, in calculating GNI, governments merely sum the values added in each transaction, which is the difference between the sales of the company and the costs of materials bought outside the company. If company sales were measured by value added, Shell's revenues of $458 billion would have been $63 billion on a value-added basis.[11] While Shell's sales are about the same as Poland's GNI, when both the economy and the company are measured by the value added, Poland's economy is more than seven times the size of Shell.

A firm's size may at times give it bargaining power, as in the case of a government that wants a firm to set up a subsidiary because of the employment it will offer and the purchases it will make from other firms in that country. Yet, regardless of the parent firm's size, each subsidiary is a local company that must comply with the laws in the country in which it is located. If it does not, it can be subject to legal action or even government seizure.

> "The subsidiaries of foreign companies have become increasingly important in the industrial and economic life of many nations."

Foreign Direct Investment and Exporting Are Growing Rapidly

One variable commonly used to measure where and how fast internationalization is taking place is the increase in total foreign direct investment. **Foreign direct investment (FDI)** refers to direct investments in equipment, structures, and organizations in a foreign country at a level that is sufficient to obtain significant management control. It does not include mere foreign investment in stock markets. The world stock of outward FDI was $16.2 *trillion* in 2008, which was 9 times larger than what it was 18 years earlier, in 1990.[12]

Of course, a substantial amount of international business involves exporting rather than FDI. **Exporting** is the transportation of any domestic good or service to a destination outside a country or region. It is the opposite of **importing,** which is the transportation of any good or service into a country or region, from a foreign origination point. Merchandise exports have grown faster than world output in nearly each of the past 60 years. World merchandise exports grew from $2.0 trillion in 1980 to $3.45 trillion in 1990, $6.46 trillion in 2000, and $16.1 trillion in 2008, before declining to $12.5 trillion during the global recession in 2009. This represents an eightfold increase from 1980 to 2008, and with 2008 exports being 250 percent of the figure for 2000.[13] The level of service exports worldwide grew even more during this time, from $365 billion in 1980 to $781 billion in 1990, $1.48 trillion in 2000, and $3.80 trillion in 2008, before declining to $3.31 trillion in 2009. This represented more than a tenfold increase between 1980 and 2008.[14] Trends regarding FDI and exporting, along with theories that help explain the level and location of exports and FDI, are discussed in Chapter 2. Figure 1.1 shows the growth in FDI and in services and merchandise exports from 1980 to 2009.

What Is Driving the Globalization of Business?

Although globalization is discussed everywhere—television shows, Internet chat rooms, political demonstrations, parliaments, management boardrooms, and labor union

foreign direct investment (FDI) Direct investments in equipment, structures, and organizations in a foreign country at a level that is sufficient to obtain significant management control; does not include mere foreign investment in stock markets

exporting The transportation of any domestic good or service to a destination outside a country or region

importing The transportation of any good or service into a country or region, from a foreign origination point

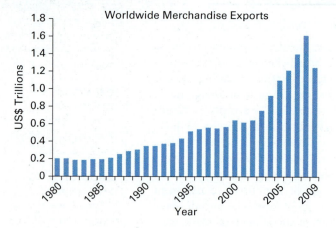

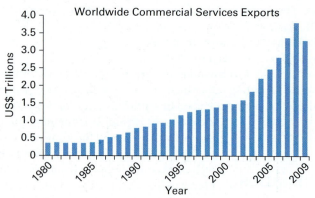

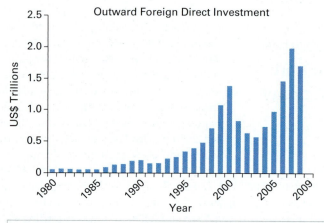

▲ **FIGURE 1.1**
World Merchandise Exports, Commercial Services Exports, and Outward Foreign Direct Investment, 1980-2009 (US$ trillions)

Sources: United Nations Conference on Trade and Development (UNCTAD), "FDI stock, by region and economy, 1990, 2000, 2008," *World Investment Report 2009* (New York: United Nations, 2009), p. 251; "Total Merchandise Trade," World Trade Organization, http://stat.wto.org/StatisticalProgram/WsdbExport.aspx?Language=E (May 2, 2010); and "Trade in Commercial Services," World Trade Organization, http://stat.wto.org/StatisticalProgram/WSDBStatProgramSeries.aspx?Language=E (May 2, 2010).

meetings—so far it has no widely accepted definition. In fact, its definition continues to broaden. Now, for example, social scientists discuss the political, social, environmental, historical, geographic, and even cultural implications of globalization.[15] Some also speak of technological globalization, political globalization, and the like.

WHAT IS GLOBALIZATION?

The most common definition and the one used in international business is that of **economic globalization**—the tendency toward an international integration of goods, technology, information, labor, and capital, or the process of making this integration happen. The term *globalization* was first coined by Theodore Levitt in a *Harvard Business Review* article in which he maintained that new technologies had "proletarianized" communication, transport, and travel, creating worldwide markets for standardized consumer products at lower prices. He maintained that the future belonged to global corporations that did not cater to local differences in taste but, instead, adopted strategies that operated "as if the entire world (or major regions of it) were a single entity; [such an organization] sells the same things in the same way everywhere."[16]

LO5 Understand the five kinds of drivers, all based on change, which are leading firms to internationalize their operations.

THE DRIVERS OF GLOBALIZATION

Five major kinds of drivers, all based on change, are leading international firms to globalize their operations: (1) political, (2) technological, (3) market, (4) cost, and (5) competitive.

Political There is a trend toward the unification and socialization of the global community. Preferential trading arrangements, such as the North American Free Trade Agreement and the European Union, that group several nations into a single market have presented firms with significant marketing opportunities. Many firms have moved swiftly to gain access to the combined markets of these trading partners, either through exporting or by producing in the area.

Two other aspects of this trend are contributing to the globalization of business operations: (1) the progressive reduction of barriers to trade and foreign investment by most governments, which is hastening the opening of new markets by international firms that are both exporting to them and building production facilities in them, and (2) the privatization of much of the industry in formerly communist nations and the opening of their economies to global competition.

Technological Advances in computers and communications technology are permitting an increased flow of ideas and information across borders, enabling customers to learn about foreign goods. Cable and satellite TV systems in Europe and Asia, for example, allow an advertiser to reach numerous countries simultaneously, thus creating regional and sometimes global demand. Global communications networks enable manufacturing personnel to coordinate production and design functions worldwide so that plants in many parts of the world may be working on the same product.

The Internet and network computing enable small companies to compete globally because they make possible the rapid flow of information regardless of the physical location of the buyer and seller. Internet videoconferencing allows sellers to demonstrate their products to prospective buyers all over the world without the need to travel. It also permits international companies to hold corporate meetings between managers from headquarters and overseas subsidiaries without expensive, time-consuming travel. In addition, communicating by e-mail on the Internet is faster and more reliable than using postal mail and much less expensive than using a fax machine. Both Internet uses have given home office managers greater confidence in their ability to direct overseas operations.

Market As companies globalize, they also become global customers. When Nokia announced its intention to set up a cell phone assembly plant in Chennai, India, suppliers of key components quickly confirmed that they would also establish plants adjacent to Nokia's facilities in order to avoid having a competitor capture the business. Likewise, for years, advertising agencies established offices in foreign markets when their major clients entered those markets to avoid having a competitor steal the accounts.

Finding the home market saturated also sends companies into foreign markets. According to a recent Dow Jones survey of the world's largest companies, 84 percent of the respondents expect that international markets will generate most of their growth in the next five years.[17] Indeed, the United States has only about 5 percent of the world's population, so the vast proportion of most companies' potential customers are located elsewhere.

Cost Economies of scale to reduce unit costs are a common management goal. One means of achieving them is to globalize product lines to reduce development, production, and inventory costs. Management can also move production or other parts of the company's value chain to countries where costs are lower. Dramatic reductions in the cost of generating and transmitting information due to innovations in computing and telecommunications, as well as the decline in transportation costs, have facilitated this trend toward relocating activities worldwide.

Competitive Competition continues to increase in intensity. New firms, many from newly industrialized and

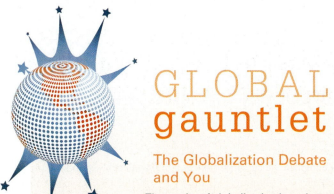

GLOBAL gauntlet

The Globalization Debate and You

The merits of globalization have been the subject of many heated debates in recent years. There have been extensive public protests about globalization and the liberalization of international trade at World Trade Organization meetings and at other gatherings of international organizations and leaders. The debate is, in many respects, waged by diametrically opposed groups with extremely different views regarding the consequences of globalization. Sifting through the propaganda and hyperbole spouted by both sides is a challenge. However, it is important to recognize the various perspectives on globalization, as their arguments can generate appeal (or rejection) both intellectually and emotionally. The contributions of free trade and globalization to dramatic reductions in worldwide poverty are contrasted with anecdotal stories of people losing their livelihoods under the growing power of multinationals. Likewise, increases in service sector employment are contrasted against losses in high-paying manufacturing jobs.

developing countries, have entered world markets in automobiles, computers, and electronics, for example. Another competitive driving force for globalization is the fact that companies are defending their home markets from competitors by entering the competitors' home markets to distract them. Many firms that would not have entered a single country because it lacked sufficient market size have established plants in the comparatively larger trading groups (European Union, Association of Southeast Asian Nation [ASEAN], Mercosur). It is one thing to be shut out of Belgium, but it is another to be excluded from all Europe.

The result of this rush to globalization has been an explosive growth in international business. Many of the issues associated with globalization are highly complex, and there is no single measure of globalization or of integration within the world economy. Each element of global integration can have different effects. Following are some of the arguments for and against the globalization process and its outcomes.

> ## " EXPANDING TRADE BY COLLECTIVELY REDUCING BARRIERS IS THE MOST POWERFUL TOOL THAT COUNTRIES, WORKING TOGETHER, CAN DEPLOY TO REDUCE POVERTY AND RAISE LIVING STANDARDS. "
>
> —Horst Kohler and James Wolfensohn

LO6 Recognize the key arguments for and against the globalization of business.

Arguments Supporting Globalization[18]

Free Trade Enhances Socioeconomic Development

That free trade is the best strategy for advancing the world's economic development is one of the few propositions on which almost all economists agree, not only because it is theoretically compelling but also because it has been demonstrated in practice. Data have shown a clear and definitive link between liberalization of trade and economic growth.[19] On a wide range of measures—poverty, education, health, and life expectancy—more people have become better off at a faster pace in the past 60 years than at any other time in history. Evidence is strong regarding the dramatic decline in both the proportion and the absolute number of destitute people. The World Development Indicators from the World Bank show that the number of people in extreme poverty fell from 1.5 billion in 1981 to 1.1 billion in 2001. Measured as a proportion of the population in developing countries, the decline was from 39.5 percent in 1981 to 21.3 percent in 2001. Between 1981 and 1999, the proportion of people in the East Asia and Pacific region living on less than $1 a day fell from 56 to 16 percent. In China, it plummeted from 61 to 17 percent. The proportion of

people living in nations with daily food supplies under 2,200 calories per capita has declined from 56 percent in the mid-1960s to less than 10 percent. Life expectancy in the developing world has nearly doubled since World War II, and infant mortality has decreased in all of the developing regions of the world. The proportion of children in the labor force fell from 24 percent in 1960 to 10 percent in 2000. Global literacy grew from 52 percent in 1950 to 81 percent in 1999, and on average the more globally integrated countries spend more on public education, especially in developing countries. Citizens from more globally integrated countries have greater levels of civil liberties and political rights. Within a generation's time, there has been an enormous improvement in the human condition, and every one of the development success stories was based on export-led growth facilitated by the liberalization of trade.

Of course, countries can reject globalization, and some have, including Myanmar, the Democratic Republic of Congo, Sierra Leone, Rwanda, Madagascar, Guinea-Bissau, Algeria, the Republic of Congo, Burundi, Albania, Syria, and Ukraine. They are among the most impoverished countries in the world. As an article in the *Financial Times* puts it, "They are victims of their refusal to globalize."[20]

Free Trade Promotes More and Better Jobs

Expanded trade is also linked with the creation of more and better jobs. Over the past two decades—a period of immense technological change and growth in trade—around 40 million more jobs were created than were destroyed in the United States. It is true that when a country opens to trade, just as when new technologies are developed, some of its sectors may not be competitive. Companies may go out of business, and some jobs will be lost. But trade creates new jobs, and these tend to be better than the old ones. The key is not to block change but, instead, to manage the costs of trade adjustment and to support the transition of workers to more competitive employment.

Concerns with Globalization[21]

Those expressing concern with globalization have come from a range of sectors of society, and they express a correspondingly diverse set of concerns. Some fundamentally oppose the very process and outcomes of globalization on ideological grounds, while others may merely be concerned about finding ways to better manage globalization processes and the resulting outcomes. Some of the opponents' concerns may be viewed as naïve or clearly inconsistent with the preponderance of evidence. Other challenges to globalization may have theoretic merit or other supporting evidence and

Demonstrators at a World Trade Organization meeting.

WE'RE NOT AGAINST TRADE; WE WANT TRADE RULES THAT ALLOW AMERICANS TO COMPETE FAIRLY IN THE MARKETPLACE. THE RECORD IS CLEAR: CURRENT TRADE POLICY ISN'T WORKING. IT HAS LED TO TREMENDOUS JOB LOSS AND HUMAN RIGHTS ABUSES. THE [PROPOSED] FTAA [FREE TRADE AREA OF THE AMERICAS] WILL LEAVE PLANT CLOSINGS, TRASHED ENVIRONMENTS AND SWEATSHOPS IN ITS WAKE.

—Richard Trumka, secretary-treasurer, AFL-CIO "

certainly may be worthy of discussion and the fostering of substantive change.

Although perspectives on the globalization debate may in many respects depend on one's values and ideology, thus further compounding efforts to reach a mutually agreed-on resolution, let us first ask this question: what are some of the primary concerns of the opponents of globalization? While many of the antiglobalizers concede that globalization "increases the size of the pie," they also claim that it has been accompanied by a broad array of injurious social implications. Among their concerns, let us briefly examine three primary ones here: (1) that globalization has produced uneven results across nations and people, (2) that globalization has had deleterious effects on labor and labor standards, and (3) that globalization has contributed to a decline in environmental and health conditions.

Globalization Has Produced Uneven Results across Nations and People
In stark contrast to the positive picture presented by supporters of globalization, opponents describe the painful impact of foreign investment and trade liberalization on the people of the world. Far from everyone has been a winner, they say. The promise of export-led growth has failed to materialize in several places. For example, most of Latin America has failed to replicate Asia's success despite efforts to liberalize, privatize, and deregulate its economies, with results ranging from disappointment in Mexico to catastrophe in Argentina. Similarly, efforts in sub-Saharan Africa have produced only limited benefits, and the share of the population living in extreme poverty there rose from 42 to 47 percent between 1981 and 2001. Open world markets, it seems, may offer the possibility of economic development—but the recipe is neither easy in its implementation nor universal in its outcomes.

Many opponents of globalization have claimed that there is a huge gap between the world's rich and poor and that globalization has caused that gap to increase. That there is a gap between rich and poor is unquestionable, but the evidence is perhaps not so clear regarding the charge that globalization has increased this inequality. Although Martin Wolf's analysis shows that income inequality has not risen in most developing countries that have integrated with the world economy, it does show that inequality has increased in some places, most notably in China. Inequality has risen in some high-income countries as well, but he attributes that more to the nature of technological change than to globalization. When income data are adjusted to reflect relative purchasing power, the inequality in income between poor and rich nations diminishes. Wolf also notes that while globalization of trade and investment is an enabler to improved income and living standards, the results may vary if obstacles exist such as poor governance or excessive borrowing.[22]

Globalization Has Had Deleterious Effects on Labor and Labor Standards
The issue of the impact of globalization on labor standards has become an oft-mentioned concern of workers in the United States and other nations. With trade liberalization through the World Trade Organization and increased mobility of capital, measures to keep a country's industries within its borders have been reduced, and companies have an easier time divesting their interests in one country and moving to another. Workers in developed countries frequently voice concerns that their jobs will migrate to developing nations where there are lower standards, and thus lower costs, leading to the infamous "race to the bottom," where developed nations with more rigorous labor standards become disadvantaged. Indeed, the Labor Secretariat for the North American Free Trade Agreement (NAFTA) commissioned a report that found more than half of firms surveyed used threats to close U.S. operations as a tool to fight union-organizing efforts. Since NAFTA's inception and the subsequent reduction in trade and investment barriers, these threats have become more plausible. As reported by Alan Tonelson, "In fact, more than 10 percent of employers studied . . . 'directly threatened to move to Mexico,' and 15 percent of firms, when forced to bargain with a union, actually closed part or all of a factory—triple the rate found in the late 1980s, before NAFTA."[23]

The concern can run both ways, however. Although labor standards in developing countries are usually lower than in industrialized countries, they are rising—and evidence shows that multinationals investing in host nations pay higher wages, create new jobs at a faster rate, and spend more on R&D than do local firms. Developing countries may also view the imposition of more demanding labor standards within their borders as a barrier to free trade. They may feel that lower-cost labor constitutes their competitive advantage and that if they are forced to implement more stringent labor standards, then companies may no longer have an incentive to set up operations in their countries, damaging their prospects for improved economic development. As the authors of *Globaphobia* ask, "Is it humane for the United States to refuse to trade with these countries because their labor standards are not as high as we would prefer? The consequence of taking this position is that many third-world workers will have no jobs at all, or must take jobs that pay even lower wages and have even worse working conditions than those currently available in the export-oriented sector."[24] A study by the Carnegie Endowment for International Peace found that Mexico's agricultural sector, which provides most of the country's employment, had lost 1.3 million jobs in the first decade since NAFTA was implemented. In addition, far from diminishing under NAFTA, the flow of impoverished Mexicans into the United States has risen dramatically, the study says.[25]

Globalization Has Contributed to a Decline in Environmental and Health Conditions Regarding concerns of antiglobalization forces that globalization contributes to declining environmental standards, former president Zedillo of Mexico stated, "Economic integration tends to favor, not worsen the environment. Since trade favors economic growth, it brings about at least part of the necessary means to preserve the environment. The better off people are, the more they demand a clean environment. Furthermore, it is not uncommon that employment opportunities in export activities encourage people to give up highly polluting marginal occupations." Yet a difficulty caused by the North American Free Trade Agreement and the maquiladora program that began before NAFTA has been the substantial increases in ground, water, and air pollution along the Mexico–U.S. border. Damage to the environment has been caused by the many new production facilities and the movement of thousands of Mexicans to that area to work in them. In addition, some health and environmental issues extend beyond the scope of trade agreements. Some of NAFTA's rules on trade in services may cause governments to weaken environmental standards for sometimes hazardous industries like logging, trucking, water supply, and real estate development. For example, to comply with NAFTA's rules on trade in services, the Bush administration waived U.S. clean air standards in order to allow trucks based in Mexico to haul freight on U.S. highways. Globalization opponents argue that this could increase air pollution and associated health concerns in border states, as the aging Mexican truck fleet pollutes more than similar U.S. trucks and these vehicles do not use the cleaner fuels required in the United States. Protesters have also claimed that, under liberalized rules regarding the globalization of trade and investment, businesses have an incentive to move their highly polluting activities to nations that have the least rigorous environmental regulations or a lower risk of liability associated with operations that can create environmental or health-related problems. On the other hand, the economic growth fostered by globalization can help generate and distribute additional resources for protecting the environment, and improved trade and investment can enhance the exchange of more environmentally friendly technologies and best practices, particularly within developing nations.

As you read the preceding synopsis of the complex issues and arguments of supporters and opponents of globalization, are you convinced one way or the other? Is there a way the debate can move beyond a simplistic argument for or against globalization and toward how best to strengthen the working of the global economy in order to enhance the welfare of the world and its inhabitants?

LO7 **Explain** the reasons for entering foreign markets.

MOTIVES FOR ENTERING FOREIGN MARKETS

Now let us briefly examine the reasons international firms enter foreign markets, which are all linked to either (1) the desire to increase profits and sales or (2) the desire to protect these profits and sales from being eroded by competitors.

Increase Profits and Sales

Enter New Markets Managers are always under pressure to increase the sales and profits of their firms, and when they face a mature, saturated market at home, they begin to search for new markets outside the home country. They find that (1) markets with a rising gross domestic product (GDP) per capita and population growth appear to be viable candidates for their operations and (2) the economies of some nations where they are not doing business are growing at a considerably faster rate than is the economy of their own market.

New Market Creation As we will discuss in Chapter 12, there are many ways in which potential new markets can be identified and assessed. Sources of potential market size and overall market growth rate can be found in publications such as the annual *Human Development Report* of the United Nations Development Program (http://hdr.undp.org/en/). Reviewing data in such reports will reveal great variety in growth rates among countries when ranked by variables such as GDP (gross domestic product) per capita.

Data from sources such as the *Human Development Report* indicate that from a macro perspective, markets around the world are growing. However, this does not mean that equally good opportunities exist for all kinds of business. Perhaps surprisingly, economic growth in a nation causes markets for some products to be lost forever while, simultaneously, markets for other products are being created. Take the case of a country in the initial stage of development. With little local manufacturing, it is a good market for exporters of consumer goods. As economic development continues, however, managers see profit-making opportunities in (1) producing locally the kinds of consumer goods that require simple technology or (2) assembling from imported parts the products that demand a more advanced technology. Given the tendency of governments to protect local industry, the importation of goods being produced in that country will normally be prohibited or discouraged through taxes, tariffs, or other means once local production of those goods has been established. Thus, exporters of easy-to-manufacture consumer goods, such as paint, adhesives, toiletries, clothing, and almost anything made of plastic, will begin to lose this market, which

Improved Communications

This might be considered a supportive reason for opening up new markets overseas, because certainly the ability to communicate rapidly and less expensively with customers and subordinates by electronic mail, wireless and wired telephones, and videoconferencing has given managers confidence in their ability to control foreign operations. Advances in computer-based communications are allowing virtual integration, which permits firms to become more physically fragmented as they search the world for lower-cost inputs. For example, good, relatively inexpensive international communication enables large insurance, banking, software, and other firms to "body shop," that is, transmit computer-oriented tasks worldwide to a cheap but skilled labor force. The clients of numerous Indian software companies are in the United States. A few years ago, software teams were required to fly back and forth between the two countries. Now, at the end of the day, customers in the United States e-mail their problems to India. The Indians then work on the solutions and have them back in the United States before the Americans have had breakfast the next day. For their work, Indian software engineers often receive only 15 to 20 percent as much pay as do their American counterparts.

> "83 of the 182 countries . . . for which data were available (46 percent) had average annual GDP per capita growth rates that were higher than the U.S. growth rate."

now becomes a new market for producers of the inputs to these "infant industries."

Faster-Growing Markets

Not only are new foreign markets appearing, but many of them are growing at a faster rate than is the home market. A firm looking for a market large enough to support the local production of appliances or machinery, for example, might be attracted by the wealth, growth, and population size of Japan and Spain. When you examine the low GDP per capita and negative growth rates of many of the African nations, you realize why foreign direct investment in that entire continent is so low. Clearly, market analysts will investigate other factors, such as the legal and political situations (discussed in Chapters 6 and 7), but an examination of variables such as those contained in the *Human Development Report* mentioned earlier is a good place to start. Interestingly, 83 of the 182 countries in the 2009 *Human Development Report* for which data were available (46 percent) had average annual GDP per capita growth rates that were higher than the U.S. growth rate for the period 1990–2007.[26]

Obtain Greater Profits

As you know, greater profits may be obtained by either increasing total revenue or decreasing the cost of goods sold, and often conditions are such that a firm can do both.

Greater Revenue

Rarely will all of a firm's domestic competitors be in every foreign market in which it is located. Where there is less competition, the firm may be able to obtain a better price for its goods or services. Increasingly, firms are also obtaining greater revenue by simultaneously introducing products in foreign markets and in their domestic markets as they move toward greater globalization of their operations. This can result in greater sales volume while lowering the cost of the goods sold.

Lower Cost of Goods Sold

Going abroad, whether by exporting or by producing overseas, can frequently lower the cost of goods sold. Increasing total sales by exporting not only will reduce research and development (R&D) costs per unit but also will make other economies of scale possible. Another factor that can positively affect the cost of goods sold is the inducements—such as reduced taxes or subsidies for R&D—that some governments offer to attract new investment.

Higher Overseas Profits as an Investment Motive

There is no question that greater profits on overseas investments has been a strong motive for going abroad. *Business International,* for example, reported that 90 percent of 140 Fortune 500 companies surveyed had achieved higher profitability on foreign than on domestic assets. One study of the 100 largest multinationals showed that only 18 of them earned more than 50 percent of their revenue overseas, but 33 earned more than 50 percent of their profits from foreign operations.

Let's now look at some reasons for going abroad that are more related to the protection of present markets, profits, and sales.

Protect Markets, Profits, and Sales

Protect Domestic Market by Following Customers Overseas

Frequently, a firm will go abroad to protect its home market. Service companies (e.g., accounting, advertising, marketing research, banking, law) will establish

moving part or all of its production facilities to the countries from which its competition is coming, it can enjoy such advantages as less costly labor, raw materials, and energy. Managers may decide to produce certain components abroad and assemble them in the home country, or, if the final product requires considerable labor in the final assembly, it may send the components overseas for this activity. Many nations, especially developing countries, offer export processing zones in which firms, mostly foreign manufacturers, enjoy almost complete absence of taxation and regulation of materials brought into the zones for processing and subsequent re-export.

Protect Foreign Markets

Changing the method of going abroad from exporting to overseas production is often necessary to protect foreign markets. Managers of a firm supplying a profitable overseas market via exports may begin to note some ominous signs that this market is being threatened.

Lack of Foreign Exchange

One of the first signs is a delay in payment by the importers. The importers may have sufficient local currency but may be facing delays in buying foreign exchange (currency) from the government's central bank. The credit manager in the exporting firm, by checking with his

> In examining the country's balance of payments, the financial manager may find that the company's export revenue has declined while the import volume remains high.

foreign operations in markets where their principal accounts are located to prevent competitors from gaining access to those accounts. They know that once a competitor has been able to demonstrate to top management what it can do by servicing a foreign subsidiary, it may be able to take over the entire account. Similarly, suppliers to original equipment manufacturers (e.g., battery manufacturers supplying automobile producers) often follow their large customers. These suppliers have an added advantage in that they are moving into new markets with a guaranteed customer base.

Attack in Competitor's Home Market

Occasionally, a firm will set up an operation in the home country of a major competitor with the idea of keeping the competitor so occupied defending that market that it will have less energy to compete in the firm's home country.

Using Foreign Production to Lower Costs

A company may go abroad to protect its domestic market when it faces competition from lower-priced foreign imports. By

or her bank and other exporters, learns that this condition is becoming endemic—a reliable sign that the country is facing a lack of foreign exchange. In examining the country's balance of payments, the financial manager may find that the company's export revenue has declined while the import volume remains high. Experienced exporters know that import and foreign exchange controls are in the offing and that there is a good chance of losing the market, especially if they sell consumer products. In times of foreign exchange scarcity, governments will invariably give priority to the importation of raw materials and capital goods.

If the advantages of making the investment outweigh the disadvantages, the company may decide to protect this market by producing locally. Managers know that once the company has a plant in the country, the government will do its utmost to provide foreign exchange for raw materials to keep the plant, a source of employment, in operation. Because imports of competing products are prohibited, the only competition, if any, will have to come from other local manufacturers.

Local Production by Competitors Lack of foreign exchange is not the only reason a company might change from exporting to manufacturing in a market. For instance, while a firm may enjoy a growing export business and prompt payments, it still may be forced to set up a plant in the market if competitors have also noticed their export volumes will support local production. If a competing firm moves to put up a factory in the market, management must decide rapidly whether to follow suit or risk losing the market forever. Managers know that many governments, especially those in developing nations, not only will prohibit further imports once the product is produced in the country but also will permit only two or three companies to enter so as to maintain a sufficient market for these local firms.

Downstream Markets

A number of Organization of Petroleum Exporting Countries (OPEC) nations have invested in refining and marketing outlets, such as filling stations and heating-oil distributors, to guarantee a market for their crude oil at more favorable prices. Petróleos de Venezuela, owner of Citgo, is one of the largest foreign investors in the United States.

Protectionism When a government sees that local industry is threatened by imports, it may erect import barriers to stop or reduce these imports. Even threats to do this can be sufficient to induce the exporter to invest in production facilities in the importing country.

Guarantee Supply of Raw Materials Few developed nations possess sufficient domestic supplies of raw materials. Japan and Europe are almost totally dependent on foreign sources for many important materials, and even the United States depends on imports for more than half of its consumption of aluminum, chromium, manganese, nickel, tin, and zinc. To ensure a continuous supply, manufacturers in the industrialized countries are being forced to invest, primarily in the developing nations where most new deposits are being discovered.

Acquire Technology and Management Know-How A reason often cited by foreign firms for investing in the United States is the acquisition of technology and management know-how. Nippon Mining, for example, a Japanese copper mining company, came to Illinois and paid $1 billion for Gould Inc. to acquire technology leadership and market share in producing the copper foil used in printed circuit boards for electronics products.

Geographic Diversification Many companies have chosen geographic diversification as a means of maintaining stable sales and earnings when the domestic economy or their industry goes into a slump, since the industry or the other economies may still be at their peak in other parts of the world.

Satisfy Management's Desire for Expansion The faster growth mentioned previously helps fulfill management's desire for expansion. Stockholders and financial analysts also expect firms to continue to grow, and those companies operating only in the domestic market have found it increasingly difficult to meet that expectation. As a result, many firms have expanded into foreign markets. This, of course, is what companies based in small countries, such as Nestlé (Switzerland) and Nokia (Finland), discovered decades ago.

LO8 Recognize that globalization of an international firm occurs over at least seven dimensions and that a company can be partially global in some dimensions and completely global in others.

THE SEVEN DIMENSIONS FOR GLOBALIZING A BUSINESS

In organizing their international activities, there are at least seven dimensions along which management can globalize (standardize): (1) product, (2) markets, (3) promotion,

Explore International Job Opportunities

If you are considering an international career but not sure where to look to find one, there are numerous websites with Internet listings for private industry and government jobs. The website for this book, **www.mhhe.com/geringerM**, includes a broad range of sites, such as the following:

- The *Riley Guide* has hundreds of worldwide listings for companies and governments. The Targeting and Research section has information on Business and Employer Research and Living and Working Overseas: **www.rileyguide.com**

- *GoingGlobal.com* offers a wide range of information on international careers, international job search resources, job opportunities worldwide, and information to help build your international career: **http://www.goinglobal.com/HotTopics.asp**

- *Expertise in Labour Mobility* (ELM) is a knowledge provider on international work issues for companies and individuals entering the global workplace. ELM's "Looking for work in . . ." guides cover 40 countries and are "must have" tools for everybody involved in securing a job abroad: **http://www.labourmobility.com**

- *Escape Artist* provides a broad range of international job postings as well as related reference materials: **http://www.escapeartist.com/jobs/overseas1.htm**

- *International Jobs Center* provides extensive international business and international development job postings: **http://www.internationaljobs.org/**

- *Jobs Abroad* supplies listings for jobs in many nations of the world, along with other resources: **http://www.jobsabroad.com/**

- *International Careers and Jobs by Profession* provides resources for work abroad, study abroad, volunteering abroad, and international travel: **http://www.transitionsabroad.com/listings/work/careers/-keywebsitesprofessionspecific.shtml**

- *Partnerjob.com* facilitates the geographic mobility of members' employees by helping find jobs for those employees' spouses and partners at their new location: **http://www.partnerjob.com/**

Look For International Internship Opportunities While You Are Still in School

- *Internships Abroad* is an internship program offered through Ohio University for internships in the United Nations, in the U.S. Department of State, and in over 65 countries: **www.ohiou.edu/studyabroad/internships.htm**

- *U.S. Department of Commerce* has various intern programs. For example, Student Employment Opportunities covers a broad range of student employment and internship opportunities: **www.ohrm.os.doc.gov**

- *U.S. Department of State* holds oral prep sessions all across the United States and Asia to assist candidates for the Foreign Service oral exam. It also offers an extremely helpful description of Student Employment Programs with good information on how to apply for them: **www.careers.state.gov/index.html**

- *Organization of American States* offers a program designed for juniors, seniors, and graduate students at the university level to allow them to work within their fields of study. They must have at least a 3.0 GPA and command of two of the four official languages: English, Portuguese, Spanish, and French. The program has three sessions during the year: Fall, Winter-Spring, and Summer: **www.oas.org/EN/PINFO/HR/gen_information.htm**

Set Realistic Job and Career Objectives for Your First International Job

More than likely, your first job in international business will NOT come with a business class airline ticket to Shanghai, Paris, or Rio de Janeiro and a "sky's the limit" expense account. More realistically, it will come with a desk, computer, FAX machine, e-mail, and smartphone (e.g., Blackberry, iPhone). Many entry-level jobs in international business involve import/export documentation to move shipments across international borders, tracking shipments by boat, plane, train and truck, following sales to make sure orders and payments are received, as well as dealing with foreign customers by phone, FAX, and e-mail. Is this the glamour of international business? Probably not. But it is business, and it is international, and it does put your career track in the international arena, which is where you need to be to start your international business career. However, some entry-level jobs in many SMEs will involve short international visits to client meetings, conferences, trade shows, or corporate meetings in international locations. In addition to your willingness to take that all important entry-level international job and work to be successful at it, here are several other suggestions to build your international career:

- Inform your boss and your company's Human Resources Department about your interest in a career in international business.

- Join several international business trade associations in your city and regularly attend their meetings:

  - *International Chamber of Commerce*—**http://www.iccwbo.org/**

  - *International Association of Business Communicators* (IABC)—**http://www.iabc.com/**

  - *International Trade Association of the U.S. Department of Commerce* seminars and workshops—**http://trade.gov/index.asp**

  - *Federation of International Trade Associations* (FITA) offers a directory of international trade associations by specialty with locations—**www.fita.org**

  - Your state's *Department of Commerce or Economic Development* offers workshops and seminars on international trade.

  By attending these meetings, you will network and get to know their members so they get to know you and learn about your interest in a career in international business.

- Read international business publications and listen to international news and business broadcasts so you are current with issues, trends, and practices in international trade. Here are several:

  - *World Trade* (this is free)—**http://www.worldtrademag.com/**

  - *International Trade Update*—published monthly by the International Trade Association of the U.S. Department of Commerce—**http://trade.gov/press/publications/newsletters/ita_0506/index_0506.asp**

- *International Herald Tribune*—**www.iht.com/**

- *Financial Times*—**www.ft.com**

- *The Economist*—**www.economist.com**

- *Reuters*—**www.reuters.com**

- *BBC*—**www.bbc.co.uk**

- Find a mentor to teach, guide, and assist you in building your international business career.

- Be ready to travel internationally at a moment's notice—hold a valid passport.

- Since not all international jobs are in business, explore the possibilities and you just might be surprised with the range of international opportunities available to you.

Alternatives for Working Globally—Consider International Jobs and Careers Other than in Business

The first thought that typically comes to mind when you hear "International Careers" is a job in the corporate world working for a Fortune 500 firm that services international markets and has a global reputation. This is not the only track into an international career. There are many outstanding international career opportunities for people with desirable interpersonal and language skills that are not in mainstream business but may require basic business expertise. Explore these options to become a part of the global workforce:

- Travel, Tourism & Hospitality—a major international industry found in virtually every country of the world.

- Engineering, Information Technology and Computer Science—experiencing major worldwide growth

- Health Professions and Health Care Management

- Translation and Language Teaching Abroad

- The Fine and Performing Arts

- Architecture

- Environmental and Natural Resource Management

- International Chambers of Commerce

- Foreign Trade Divisions of State Offices of Economic Development

- The United States Government

  - U.S. Counselor Service

  - Foreign Service—U.S. State Department

  - The Central Intelligence Agency and the National Security Agency

  - The Agency for International Development (AID)

  - The Export-Import Bank

  - The International Trade Commission

  - U.S. Information Agency

  - The Peace Corps

- International Education Exchange—teach abroad

- Volunteer and Social Service Agencies

The skills and experiences offered by any of these career options are highly sought after and readily transferable between the public and the private sector.

---

(4) where value is added to the product, (5) competitive strategy, (6) use of non-home-country personnel, and (7) extent of global ownership in the firm. The possibilities range from zero standardization (multidomestic) to standardization along all seven dimensions (completely global). The challenge for company managers is to determine how far the firm should go with each one. Usually the amount of globalization will vary among the dimensions. For example, promotional activities for washing machines might be standardized to a great extent: people use them to get their clothes clean. However, for economic reasons, in poorer countries the machines must be simpler and less costly and, therefore, the product is not standardized worldwide. We return to this topic in various parts of the text, particularly in Chapter 10.

ORGANIZATION OF THIS BOOK

After describing the nature of international business and the institutions associated with it in Section One, we analyze several of the key uncontrollable forces that make up the foreign and domestic environments and illustrate their effect on management functions in Section Two. In Section Three, we reverse the procedure and deal with the management functions, demonstrating how they are influenced by the uncontrollable forces.

A solid understanding of the business concepts and techniques employed in the United States and other advanced industrial nations is a requisite for success in international business. However, because transactions take place across national borders, three environments—domestic, foreign, and international—may be involved instead of just one. Thus, in international business, the international manager has three choices in deciding what to do with a concept or a technique employed in domestic operations: (1) transfer it intact, (2) adapt it to local conditions, or (3) not use it overseas. International managers who have discovered that there are differences in the environmental forces are better prepared to decide which option to follow. To be sure, no one can be an expert on all these forces for all nations, but just knowing that differences may exist will cause people to "work with their antennas extended." In other words, when they enter international business, they will know they must look out for important variations in many of the forces that they take as given in the domestic environment. It is to the study of these three environments that this text is directed. ■

CHECK IT OUT!

mhhe.com/GeringerM

for study materials
including quizzes,
iPod downloads,
and video

chapter two

"My policy has been, and will continue to be, while I have the honor to remain in the administration of the government, to be upon friendly terms with, but independent of, all the nations of the earth. To share in the broils of none. To fulfil our own engagements. To supply the wants, and be carriers for them all: Being thoroughly convinced that it is our policy and interest to do so."

—George Washington

international trade + investment

nternational trade and investment have become fundamental to most people's lives. For example, much of the food we eat, the clothes we wear, the vehicles we drive, and the electronic goods that we use for work and pleasure are produced in other nations. Many of our jobs are dependent on exports, imports, or foreign investment. In this chapter, we examine (1) *international trade,* which includes exports and imports, and (2) *foreign direct investment,* which international companies must make to establish and expand their overseas operations. We will briefly examine key trends and traits of international trade and investment across the globe, and we will also present an overview of some of the most prominent theories that have been developed to explain the incidence and level of international trade and investment.

LEARNING OBJECTIVES

After reading this chapter, you should be able to:

LO1 **Appreciate** the magnitude of international trade and how it has grown.

LO2 **Identify** the direction of trade, or who trades with whom, and trends in such trade.

LO3 **Explain** the theories that attempt to explain why certain goods are traded internationally.

LO4 **Explain** the size, growth, and direction of foreign direct investment

LO5 **Explain** some of the theories of foreign direct investment.

The following discussion of international trade first examines the volume of trade, including which nations account for the largest volume of the world's exports and imports. We then discuss the direction of trade and the trend toward increased regionalization of international trade. We examine the issue of major trading partners and their relevance for managers, and then we finish this section of the chapter by discussing several leading theories that help to explain international trade.

LO1 Appreciate the magnitude of international trade and how it has grown.

INTERNATIONAL TRADE

Volume of International Trade

In 1990, a milestone was reached when the volume of international trade in goods and services measured in current dollars surpassed $4 trillion. By 2008, exports of goods and services had nearly quintupled, exceeding $19.5 trillion.[1] The dollar value of total world exports was greater than the gross national product of every nation in the world except the United States. One-fourth of everything grown or made in the world is now exported, another measure of the significance of international trade. Figure 2.1 illustrates the combined level of goods and

services exports and imports as a percentage of gross domestic product for various nations. As can be seen, international trade has become a critical factor in the economic activity of many, if not most, of the countries of the world.

Of the $19.5 trillion in international trade in goods and services in 2008, exports of merchandise were $15.8 trillion, nearly five times what they had been 18 years earlier. While smaller in absolute terms, worldwide trade in services, at over $3.7 trillion, has grown faster since 1980 than has trade in merchandise. The volume of world trade in services had reached a level that was more than 10 times what it had been in 1980.

How even has this growth in trade been? Have some nations fared better than others? Although the absolute value of their merchandise exports increased, the proportion of exports coming from the regions of North America, Latin America, Africa, and the Middle East decreased between 1980 and 2008. For example, the level of exports from Africa grew by over 250 percent from 1980 to 2008, yet the region's proportion of overall world merchandise exports declined by half. In contrast, the proportion of merchandise exports from Asia increased by approximately 90 percent between 1980 and 2008, with China accounting for nearly two-thirds of that increase. Although the European Union increased its proportion of world trade, the increase is attributable to the expansion of the EU to 27 member-countries.

The results for services exports share some similarity with merchandise exports. The extensive growth in the level of overall worldwide trade in services means that all of the regions and essentially all of the primary nations have experienced an absolute increase in the dollar volume of services exports. The proportion of world exports of commercial services accounted for by Latin America, the European Union, Africa, and the Middle East has evidenced an overall decline since 1980. However, the United States' proportion of services exports has risen by over 32 percent from 1980 to 2008. Asia has also been increasing its proportion of services exports at an even greater rate.

The rapid expansion of world exports since 1980 demonstrates that the opportunity to increase sales by exporting is a viable growth strategy and one that can benefit the exporting nations through the creation of jobs. At the same time, however, the export growth of individual nations should be a warning to managers that they must be prepared to meet increased competition from exports to their own domestic markets. The proportion of manufacturing value added that is located in developed countries has declined across most industrial sectors between 1995 and 2010, with the largest portion of that decline occurring since 2000.[2] Correspondingly,

▼**FIGURE 2.1** Merchandise and Services Trade as a Percentage of Gross Domestic Product

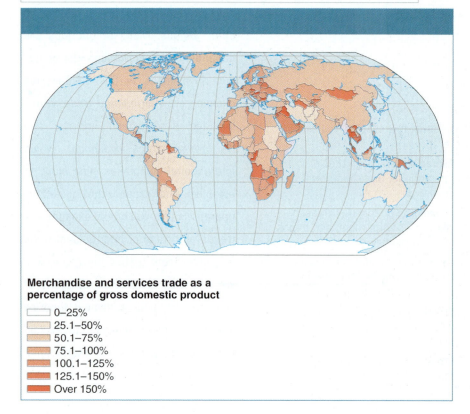

Merchandise and services trade as a percentage of gross domestic product

- 0–25%
- 25.1–50%
- 50.1–75%
- 75.1–100%
- 100.1–125%
- 125.1–150%
- Over 150%

APPROXIMATELY 70 PERCENT OF EXPORTS FROM DEVELOPED ECONOMIES GO TO OTHER INDUSTRIALIZED NATIONS, NOT TO DEVELOPING COUNTRIES.

developing countries' share of value added has been increasing during this time, although the location of value-adding activities has been changing substantially. For example, while Africa and Latin America have not added appreciably to their proportion of worldwide manufacturing value added, the proportion generated by South and East Asia has quadrupled since 1980. These trends have important implications for managers in terms of not merely where there may be new markets (e.g., for machine tools or other capital goods used by expanding manufacturing sectors) but also where competition in manufacturing may be intensifying or where new sources of export competition might emerge.

Which Nations Account for the Most Exports and Imports?

Which nations are responsible for the large and growing levels of merchandise and services trade that we have seen worldwide? Table 2.1 presents the world's 10 largest nations in terms of exports and imports of merchandise and of services. As you can see, the largest exporters and importers of merchandise are generally developed countries, although China ranks in the top 5 on each list. These 10 largest exporters and importers collectively account for over half of all exports and imports for each of merchandise and services.

LO2 **Identify** the direction of trade, or who trades with whom, and trends in such trade.

DIRECTION OF TRADE

What are the destinations of these merchandise exports? If you have never examined trade flows, you may think that international trade consists mainly of manufactured goods exported by the industrialized nations to the developing nations in return for raw materials. However, this is only partially correct. While more than half the exports from developing nations do go to developed countries, this proportion has been declining over the past 35 years, from 72 percent in 1970 to about 50 percent in 2009.[3] Also, approximately 70 percent of exports from developed economies go to other industrialized nations, not to developing countries.

The direction of trade frequently changes over time among nations or regions of the world. The development of expanded regional trade agreements (discussed in Chapter 3), such as the Association of Southeast Asian Nations (ASEAN), Mercosur in South America, and the EU, can substantially alter the level and proportion of trade flows within and across regions. For example, most of Canada's exports go to the United States and

▼ **TABLE 2.1** 10 Leading Exporters and Importers in World Merchandise and Service Trade, 2009 (billions of dollars)

Merchandise Exporters			Merchandise Importers			Service Exporters			Service Importers		
Rank	Nation	Value	Rank	Nation	Value	Rank	Nation	Value	Rank	Nation	Value
1	China	$1,194	1	United States	$1,604	1	United States	$470	1	United States	$331
2	Germany	1,121	2	China	1,006	2	United Kingdom	240	2	Germany	255
3	United States	995	3	Germany	931	3	Germany	215	3	United Kingdom	160
4	Japan	516	4	France	551	4	France	140	4	China	158
5	France	457	5	Japan	551	5	China	129	5	Japan	146
6	Netherlands	398	6	United Kingdom	480	6	Japan	124	6	France	124
7	Italy	369	7	Netherlands	446	7	Spain	122	7	Italy	114
8	South Korea	355	8	Italy	410	8	Italy	101	8	Ireland	104
9	United Kingdom	351	9	Hong Kong	353	9	Ireland	95	9	Netherlands	87
10	Hong Kong	317	10	Belgium	351	10	Netherlands	92	10	Spain	87

Sources: Central Intelligence Agency, *The World Factbook* (Washington, D.C.: CIA, 2010), https://www.cia.gov/library/publications/the-world-factbook/rankorder/2078rank.html; and World Trade Organization, "Trade to Expand by 9.5% in 2010 after a Dismal 2009, WTO Reports," March 26, 2010, http://www.wto.org/english/news_e/pres10_e/pr598_e.htm (May 15, 2010).

more than 20 percent of American exports go to Canada, mainly as a result of the North American Free Trade Agreement and prior bilateral free trade treaties between these two nations.[4] The $129 billion value of U.S. exports to Mexico in 2009 was almost four times the level in 1991.[5] The proportion of their total exports that Mexico, Canada, and the United States sent to one of their two partners in NAFTA totaled 49.8 percent in 2008.[6] Similarly, the proportion of overall exports accounted for by members of the regional trade agreement totaled 67 percent for the European Union, 25 percent for ASEAN, and 15 percent for Mercosur. Overall, there are more than 200 regional trade agreements in operation worldwide and the share of world trade accounted for by members of these agreements increased from 37 percent in 1980 to more than 70 percent by 2009.

It appears that the American exporters have made major inroads in developing country markets, which in turn are selling more to the United States. This is due in part to their increasing ability to export manufactured goods and the growing intracompany trade among international companies' affiliates. The fact that members of trade groups are increasingly selling more to each other is a development that will influence international companies' choices of locations for their plants and other operations.

MAJOR TRADING PARTNERS: THEIR RELEVANCE FOR MANAGERS

An analysis of the major trading partners of a firm's home country and those of the nations where it has affiliates that export can provide valuable insights to management. Among the advantages to focusing attention on a nation that is already a sizable purchaser of goods coming from the would-be exporter's country are:

1. The business climate in the importing nation is relatively favorable.

2. Export and import regulations are not insurmountable.

3. There should be no strong cultural objections to buying that nation's goods.

4. Satisfactory transportation facilities have already been established.

5. Import channel members (merchants, banks, and customs brokers) are experienced in handling import shipments from the exporter's area.

6. Foreign exchange to pay for the exports is available.

7. The government of a trading partner may be applying pressure on importers to buy from countries that are good customers for that nation's exports. We have seen the efforts of the Japanese, Korean, and Taiwanese governments to persuade their citizens to buy more American goods. They have also sent buying missions to the United States.

Major Trading Partners of the United States

Table 2.2 shows the major trading partners of the United States. The data indicate that the United States, an industrialized nation, generally follows the tendency we found earlier; that is, developed nations trade with one another. Mexico and Canada are major trading partners in great part because they share a common border with the United States. Freight charges are lower, delivery times are shorter, and contacts between buyers and sellers are easier and less expensive. Being joined with the United States in the North American Free Trade Agreement helps ensure that the three nations' mutual importance as trading partners will remain strong.

Of the top 15 nations that the United States imports from, 9 of these nations have remained on the list over the past 45 years, including Canada, Mexico, Japan, Germany, the United Kingdom, Italy, France, Venezuela, and Brazil. However, each nation's ranking has changed over time, and some new nations have been added to replace other nations that have become relatively less important as trade partners. Nations from East and Southeast Asia, besides long-term trade partner Japan, have become increasingly important trade partners in recent years. China, Hong Kong, Singapore, South Korea, Taiwan, and Malaysia are supplying the United States with huge quantities of electronic products and components as well as a variety of largely labor-intensive manufactured goods, many of which are

▼ **TABLE 2.2** Major Trading Partners of the United States, 2009 ($ billions)

Exports			Imports		
Rank	Country	Value	Rank	Country	Value
1	Canada	$205	1	China	$296
2	Mexico	129	2	Canada	225
3	China	70	3	Mexico	177
4	Japan	51	4	Japan	96
5	United Kingdom	46	5	Germany	71
6	Germany	43	6	United Kingdom	47
7	Netherlands	32	7	South Korea	39
8	South Korea	29	8	France	34
9	France	27	9	Taiwan	28
10	Brazil	26	10	Venezuela	28
11	Singapore	22	11	Ireland	28
12	Belgium	22	12	Italy	26
13	Hong Kong	21	13	Malaysia	23
14	Australia	20	14	Saudi Arabia	22
15	Taiwan	18	15	India	21

Source: "Top U.S. Trade Partners," Department of Commerce International Trade Administration, http://ita.doc.gov/td/industry/otea/ttp/Top_Trade_Partners.pdf (May 15, 2010).

produced by affiliates of American international companies. Between 1991 and 2009, China rose from sixth to first place in exports to the United States and it also moved up to third place as an importer of U.S. goods (although the $70 billion level of Chinese imports was only 23 percent of the level of exports it sent to the United States).

Many of the same Asian countries appear as importers of American goods as well because (1) their rising standards of living enable their people to afford more imported products, and the countries' export earnings provide the foreign exchange to pay for them; (2) they are purchasing large amounts of capital goods to further their industrial expansion; (3) they are importing raw materials and components that will be assembled into subassemblies or finished goods that will subsequently be exported, often to the United States; and (4) their governments, pressured by the American government to lower their trade surpluses with the United States, have sent buying missions to this country to look for products to import.

The analysis of foreign trade that we have described would be helpful to anyone just starting to search outside the home market for new business opportunities. The preliminary steps of (1) studying the general growth and direction of trade and (2) analyzing major trading partners would provide an idea of where the trading activity is. What kinds of products do these countries import from the United States? The International Trade Administration of the U.S. Department of Commerce maintains a site on the Internet with downloadable files of trade statistics. One entry, "Foreign Trade Highlights" (http://www.trade.gov/td/industry/otea/usfth/), contains more than 100 tables of goods and services, including one that reports on the top U.S. exports to and imports from its 80 largest trading partners. There are also tables on the Commerce Department's Export.gov website that list imports and exports from a range of different industries. These tables present multiyear data on levels of imports and exports between the United States and the other countries of the world, providing an idea of the size and potential attractiveness of various sectors.[7]

We have seen that the volume of international trade is large, growing, and critical to the economic performance of most nations. But why does this trade occur, both overall and between particular nations? To answer this question, we will briefly examine several of the leading theories of international trade. Understanding these theories is essential for international managers, because they frequently will be dealing with government officials trained in economics and must therefore be prepared to speak their language. When presenting plans requiring governmental approval, managers must take care that the plans are economically sound, because they are almost certain to be studied by economists and will often need to be approved by them. Marketers proposing large projects to government planners must be aware that the key determinant now is economic efficiency rather than mere financial soundness.[8] Moreover, knowledge of economic concepts in the areas of international trade and investment frequently provides insight into future government action.

LO3 **Explain** the theories that attempt to explain why certain goods are traded internationally.

EXPLAINING TRADE: INTERNATIONAL TRADE THEORIES

Why do nations trade? This question and the equally important proposition of predicting the direction, composition, and volume of goods traded are what international trade theory attempts to address. Interestingly, as is the case with numerous economic writings, the first formulation of international trade theory was politically motivated. Adam Smith, incensed by government intervention and control over both domestic and foreign trade, published *An Inquiry into the Nature and Causes of the Wealth of Nations* (1776), in which he tried to destroy the mercantilist philosophy.

Mercantilism

Mercantilism, the economic philosophy Smith attacked, evolved in Europe between the 16th and 18th centuries. A complex political and economic arrangement, mercantilism traditionally has been interpreted as viewing the accumulation of precious metals as an activity essential to a nation's welfare. These metals were, in the mercantilists' view, the only source of wealth. Because England had no mines, the mercantilists looked to international trade to supply gold and silver.

Container ship docked in port.

The government established economic policies that promoted exports and stifled imports, resulting in a trade surplus to be paid for in gold and silver. Import restrictions such as import duties reduced imports, while government subsidies to exporters increased exports. Those acts created a trade surplus, in addition to protecting jobs within the mercantilist nation. Of course, another outcome of mercantilism was the generation of benefits for certain economic groups, such as domestic merchants, artisans, and shippers, albeit at a cost to other groups such as consumers and emerging industrialists.

Although the mercantilist era ended in the late 1700s, its arguments live on. Many people still argue that exports are "good" for a country because they create jobs, while imports are "bad" because they transfer jobs from the country to other nations. This view essentially sees trade as a zero-sum activity, where one party must lose in order for another to gain. Similarly, a "favorable" trade balance still means that a nation exports more goods and services than it imports. In balance-of-payments accounting, an export that brings dollars to the country is called *positive*, but imports that cause dollar outflow are labeled *negative*.

In the United States and Europe, as well as many emerging markets in Asia, many managers believe that China remains a present-day "fortress of mercantilism" that raises barriers to imported goods while giving Chinese exporters an unfair advantage. Despite impressive economic growth and burgeoning trade surpluses, Chinese authorities have resisted efforts to revalue their currency, instead continuing to hold their currency, the yuan, within a tight trading range relative to the U.S. dollar. By limiting the extent to which the yuan can appreciate in value, the Chinese authorities have been accused of engaging in mercantilist behavior because they help the international cost-competitiveness of Chinese companies relative to that of companies from the United States and other nations. One study argues that 40 percent of the price advantage of companies from China is due to mercantilist policies of China's central government, including an undervalued currency, export subsidies, and lax regulatory oversight.[9]

Theory of Absolute Advantage

Adam Smith argued against mercantilism by claiming that market forces, not government controls, should determine the direction, volume, and composition of international trade. He argued that under free, unregulated trade, each nation should specialize in producing those goods it could produce most efficiently (for which it had an **absolute advantage,** either natural or acquired). Some of these goods would be exported to pay for imports of goods that could be produced more efficiently elsewhere. Smith showed by his example of absolute advantage that both nations would gain from trade.

An Example

Assume that a world of two countries and two products has perfect competition and no transportation costs. Suppose that in the United States and China (a) one unit of input (combination of land, labor, and capital) can produce the quantities of soybeans and cloth listed in the following table, (b) each nation has two input units it can use to produce either soybeans or cloth, and (c) each country uses one unit of input to produce each product. If neither country imports or exports, the quantities shown in the table are also those that are available for local consumption. The total output of both nations is 4 tons of soybeans and 6 bolts of cloth.

Commodity	United States	China	Total Output
Tons of soybeans	3	1	4
Bolts of cloth	2	4	6

In the United States, 3 tons of soybeans or 2 bolts of cloth can be produced with one unit of output. Therefore, 3 tons of soybeans should have the same price as 2 bolts of cloth. In China, however, because only 1 ton of soybeans can be produced with the input unit that can produce 4 bolts of cloth, 1 ton of soybeans should cost as much as 4 bolts of cloth.

The United States has an absolute advantage in soybean production (3 to 1). China's absolute advantage is in cloth making (4 to 2). Will anyone anywhere give the Chinese cloth maker more than 1 ton of soybeans for 4 bolts of cloth? According to the example, all American soybean producers should because they can get only 2 bolts of cloth for 3 tons of soybeans at home. Similarly, Chinese cloth makers, once they learn that they can obtain more than 1 ton of soybeans for every 4 bolts of cloth in the United States, will be eager to trade Chinese cloth for American soybeans.

Each Country Specializes

Suppose each nation decides to use its resources to produce only the product at which it is more efficient. The following table shows each nation's output. Note that with the same quantity of input units, the total output is now greater.

Commodity	United States	China	Total Output
Tons of soybeans	6	0	6
Bolts of cloth	0	8	8

Terms of Trade (Ratio of International Prices)

With specialization, now the total production of both goods is greater, but to consume both products, the two countries must trade some of their surplus. What are the limits within which both countries are willing to trade? Clearly, the Chinese cloth makers will trade some of their cloth for soybeans if they can get more than the 1 ton of soybeans that they get for 4 bolts of cloth in China. Likewise, the American soybean growers will trade their soybeans for Chinese cloth if they get a bolt of cloth for less than the 1.5 tons of soybeans it costs them in the United States.

If the two nations take the midpoint of the two trading limits so that each shares equally in the benefits of trade, they will agree to swap 1.33 bolts of cloth for 1 ton of soybeans. Both will gain from specialization because each now has the following quantities:

Commodity	United States	China	Total Output
Tons of soybeans	3	3	6
Bolts of cloth	4	4	8

Gains from Specialization and Trade
Because each nation specialized in producing the product at which it was more efficient and then traded its surplus for goods that it could not produce as efficiently, both nations benefited. China gained 2 more tons of soybeans and the United States gained 2 more bolts of cloth.

Although Adam Smith's logic helped to convince many governments to dismantle trade barriers and encourage increased international trade, it failed to calm concerns of those whose countries lacked any absolute advantage. What if one country has an absolute advantage in the production of both soybeans and cloth? Will there still be a basis for trade?

Theory of Comparative Advantage

David Ricardo demonstrated in 1817 that even though one nation held an absolute advantage over another in the production of each of two different goods, international trade could still create benefit for each country (thus representing a positive-sum game, or one in which both countries "win" from engaging in trade). The only limitation to such benefit-creating trade is that the less efficient nation cannot be *equally* less efficient in the production of both goods.[10] To illustrate how this can occur, let us slightly change our first example so that now China has an absolute advantage in producing *both* soybeans and cloth. Note that compared with China, the United States is less inefficient in producing soybeans than in manufacturing cloth. Therefore, it has a **comparative advantage** in producing soybeans.

Commodity	United States	China	Total Output
Tons of soybeans	4	5	9
Bolts of cloth	2	5	7

Each Country Specializes
If each country specializes in what it does best, its output will be as follows:

Commodity	United States	China	Total Output
Tons of soybeans	8	0	8
Bolts of cloth	0	10	10

Terms of Trade
In this case, the terms of trade will be somewhere between the pretrade price ratios of 1 ton of soybeans for 1 bolt of cloth that Chinese soybean growers must pay in China and the 1/2 bolt of cloth that American cloth makers must pay for 1 ton of American soybeans.

Let us assume that the traders agree on an exchange rate of 3/4 bolt of cloth for 1 ton of soybeans. Both will gain from this exchange and specialization, as the following table shows:

Commodity	United States	China
Tons of soybeans	4	4
Bolts of cloth	3	7

Note that this trade left China with 2 surplus bolts of cloth and 1 less ton of soybeans than it had before specializing. America has the same quantity of soybeans and 1 more bolt of cloth. However, the Chinese cloth manufacturers should be able to trade 1 bolt of surplus cloth for at least 1 ton of soybeans elsewhere. Then the final result will be as follows:

Commodity	United States	China
Tons of soybeans	4	5 +
Bolts of cloth	3	6

Gains from Specialization and Trade
Gains from specialization and trade in this case are 1 additional bolt of cloth for each of the United States and China, and about 1 more ton of soybeans for China.

This simple concept of comparative advantage serves as a basis for international trade, even when one nation has an advantage over another in the production of each of the goods being traded. We have presented the theory of comparative advantage without mentioning money; however, a nation's comparative advantage can be affected by differences between the costs of production factors in that country's currency and their costs in other currencies. As we shall see in the next section, money can change the direction of trade.

How Money Can Change the Direction of Trade

Suppose the total cost of land, labor, and capital to produce the daily output of soybeans or cloth in the example on absolute advantage is $10,000 in the United States and 80,000 yuan in China. The cost per unit is as follows:

Price per Unit		
Commodity	United States	China
Ton of soybeans	$10,000/3 = $3,333/ton	80,000 yuan/1 = 80,000 yuan/ton
Bolt of cloth	$10,000/2 = $5,000/bolt	80,000 yuan/4 = 20,000 yuan/bolt

comparative advantage Theory that a nation having absolute disadvantages in the production of two goods with respect to another nation has a comparative or relative advantage in the production of the good in which its absolute disadvantage is less

To determine whether it is more advantageous to buy locally or to import, the traders need to know the prices in their own currencies. To convert from foreign to domestic currency, they use the *exchange rate*.

Exchange Rate

The **exchange rate** is the price of one currency stated in terms of the other. If the prevailing rate is $1 = 8 yuan, then 1 yuan must be worth 0.125 dollar.* Using the exchange rate of $1 = 8 yuan, the prices in the preceding example appear to the U.S. trader as follows:

Price per Unit (dollars)		
Commodity	United States	China
Ton of soybeans	$3,333	$10,000
Bolt of cloth	$5,000	$ 2,500

The American soybean producers can earn $6,667 more per ton by exporting soybeans to China than they can by selling locally,[†] but can the Chinese cloth makers gain by exporting to the United States? To find out, they must convert the American prices to Chinese yuan.

Price per Unit (yuan)		
Commodity	United States	China
Ton of soybeans	26,664 yuan	80,000 yuan
Bolt of cloth	40,000 yuan	20,000 yuan

It is apparent that the Chinese cloth makers will export cloth to the United States because they can sell at the higher price of 40,000 yuan per bolt. The American cloth makers, however, will need some very strong sales arguments to sell in the United States if they are to overcome the $2,500 price differential.

Influence of Exchange Rate

Soybeans to China and cloth to the United States will be the direction of trade as long as the exchange rate remains around $1 = 8 yuan. But if the dollar strengthens to $1 = 24 yuan, American soybeans will cost as much in yuan as do Chinese soybeans, and importation will cease. On the other hand, should the dollar weaken to $1 = 4 yuan, then 1 bolt of Chinese cloth will cost $5,000 to American traders, and they will have little reason to import. This example suggests that a nation can attempt to regain competitiveness in world markets through **currency devaluation** (lowering its price in terms of other

currencies). Note that in many but by no means all cases, this action can leave domestic prices largely unchanged. This issue will be discussed further in Chapter 8.

Some Newer Explanations for the Direction of Trade

The international trade theory we have been discussing was essentially the only theoretical explanation of trade available to us until the second half of the 20th century. Since that time, however, several other possible explanations for international trade have been developed.

Differences in Resource Endowments

Some countries have an abundance of resources, when compared to the endowments of other nations. For example, the United States has a large supply of fertile farmland, Chile has abundant supplies of copper, and Saudi Arabia has extensive amounts of crude oil. These differences in endowments can result in differences across countries in the opportunity cost of producing these resources. As a result, countries are likely to export those products that are less expensive for them to produce, and to import products that are either unavailable domestically or that can be produced more cheaply in other nations. Theory based on differences in resource endowments would suggest that developed countries would be more likely to trade with developing countries, which have very different factor endowments, rather than with other developed countries that would have similar factor endowments. This theory can adequately explain international trade in primary products.

Overlapping Demand

In contrast to resource endowment–based theory, Swedish economist Stefan Linder theorized that customers' tastes are strongly affected by income levels, and therefore a nation's income per capita level determines the kinds of goods its people will demand. Because an entrepreneur will produce goods to meet this demand, the kinds of products manufactured reflect the country's level of income per capita. Goods produced for domestic consumption will eventually be exported, due to similarity of income levels and therefore demand in other countries.

The theory of overlapping demand thus deduces that international trade in manufactured goods will be greater between nations with similar levels of per capita income than between those with dissimilar levels of per capita income, the very situation observed in our review of trade data earlier in this chapter. Even though two developed countries may have similar factor endowments, which under

> **Several other possible explanations for international trade have been developed.**

---

*If $1 = 8 yuan, to find the value of 1 yuan in dollars, divide both sides of the equation by 8. Then 1 yuan = 1/8 = $0.125.

†For example, to calculate this figure, you would multiply the American price of $3,333 per ton of soybeans times 8 yuan per dollar, yielding a price of 26,664 yuan per ton.

the resource endowment theory would result in limited trade between them, these nations still can have a large volume of trade with each other. The goods that will be traded are those for which there is an *overlapping demand* (consumers in both countries are demanding the same good).[11] For example, if an American company such as Apple invents a sophisticated cell phone with advanced features for its home market, the best export opportunities for this phone will be in other advanced nations such as Japan and western European countries, even if these countries have their own domestic producers of cell phones. Note that the theory of overlapping demand differs from the theory of comparative advantage in that it does not specify in which direction a given good will go. In fact, this intraindustry trade occurs because of *product differentiation*; for example, Apple exports its cell phones to Europe and Japan and Sony-Ericsson exports cell phones to the United States, because consumers in these different markets perceive a difference in the brands.

National Competitive Advantage from Regional Clusters

National competitiveness involves a nation's ability to design, produce, distribute, or service products within an international trading context while earning increasing returns on its resources. A nation's ability to achieve sustained international success within a particular industry may be explained by variables other than the factors of production on which the theories of comparative advantage and resource endowment are based. For example, Alfred Marshall's seminal work on economic theory helped to explain why, in many industries, firms tend to cluster together on a geographic basis.[12] He suggested that geographic clusters appeared for three reasons: (1) advantages associated with pooling of a common labor force so that staffing requirements can be met quickly, even with unexpected fluctuations in demand; (2) gains from the development of specialized local suppliers whose operations and skills can be coordinated with the needs of the buyers; and (3) benefits that result within the geographic region from the sharing of technological information and corresponding enhancement of the rate of innovation.

Michael Porter, an economics professor at Harvard, extended the work of Marshall.[13] His Diamond Model of national advantage claims that four kinds of variables will have an impact on the ability of the local firms in 1 country to utilize the country's resources to gain a competitive advantage:

1. *Demand conditions:* the nature, rather than merely the size, of the domestic demand. If a firm's customers are sophisticated and demanding, it will strive to produce high-quality and innovative products and, in doing so, will obtain a global competitive advantage over companies located where domestic pressure is less. This might have been the case in the past, when international firms introduced their new products in home markets first (a condition of the international product life cycle theory), but as more firms introduce new products globally, this variable will lose importance.

2. *Factor conditions:* level and composition of factors of production. Porter distinguishes between the basic factor endowments and the advanced factors (a nation's infrastructure, such as telecommunications and transportation systems, or university research institutes). He also distinguishes between created factors (e.g., from investments made by individuals, companies, or governments) and inherited factors (e.g., natural resources, location). Lack of natural endowments has caused nations to invest in the creation of the advanced factors, such as education of its work force, free ports, and advanced communications systems, to enable their industries to be competitive globally. Various Caribbean nations have upgraded their communications systems to attract banking and other service companies that have little dependence on the basic factors of production.

3. *Related and supporting industries:* suppliers and industry support services. For decades, firms in an industry with their suppliers, the suppliers' suppliers, and so forth, have tended to form a cluster in a given location, often without any apparent initial reason. Yet these related and supporting industries serve as an important foundation for competitive success by providing a network of suppliers, subcontractors, and a commercial infrastructure. For example, the San Francisco Bay Area has a range of related and supporting industries for the personal computer industry. These include research, design, production, or service operations of such suppliers as semiconductor designers, semiconductor manufacturers, technologically savvy venture capitalists, and intellectual property rights lawyers, as well as related industries such as scientific equipment, electronics (e.g., MP3 players, "smart" phones such as the iPhone), telecommunications equipment, software developers, and a wide range of Internet-related companies.[14]

4. *Firm strategy, structure, and rivalry:* the extent of domestic competition, the existence of barriers to entry, and the firms' management style and organization. Porter states that companies subject to heavy competition in their domestic markets are constantly striving to improve their efficiency and innovativeness, which makes them more competitive internationally. For decades, firms in oligopolistic industries have carefully watched their competitors' every move and have even entered foreign markets because their competitors had gone there. For example, Japanese automakers such as Toyota, Honda, Nissan, and Mitsubishi have competed vigorously with each other for decades in their domestic marketplace, constantly pressuring each other to improve the quality and performance of their products or else risk the loss of market share. This vigorous competition has enabled these firms to develop world-leading capabilities in auto design and manufacturing. As soon as one of these companies ventures forth into a new international market such as the United States, Europe, or Southeast Asia for the sale or manufacturing of autos, the competitors tend to be close behind in order to avoid a decline in their relative international competitiveness.

In addition to these four variables, Porter claimed that competitiveness could be affected by government and chance. For example, competitiveness may be influenced through government policies such as incentives, subsidies, temporary protection from foreign competitors, or infrastructure development, or through random events such as the location and timing of research breakthroughs or luck.

Porter argues that these factors are fundamentally interrelated, creating a "virtuous circle" of resource generation and application, as well as responsiveness in meeting the demands of customers, as depicted in Figure 2.2.

Summary of International Trade Theory

International trade occurs primarily because of relative price differences among nations. These differences stem from differences in production costs, which result from:

1. Differences in the endowments of the factors of production.

2. Differences in the levels of technology that determine the factor intensities used.

3. Differences in the efficiencies with which these factor intensities are utilized.

4. Foreign exchange rates.

However, taste differences, a demand variable, can reverse the direction of trade predicted by the theory.

International trade theory shows that nations will attain a higher level of living by specializing in goods for which they possess a comparative advantage and importing those for which they have a comparative disadvantage. Generally, trade restrictions that stop this free flow of goods will harm a nation's welfare. Chapter 6's discussion of political forces examines a broad range of arguments that have been presented in support of restrictions on international trade of goods and services.

The topic we have been examining—international trade—exists because firms export. As you know, however, exporting is only one aspect of international business. Another—overseas production—requires foreign investment, the topic of the next section.

LO4 Explain the size, growth, and direction of foreign direct investment

FOREIGN INVESTMENT

Foreign investment can be divided into two components: **portfolio investment,** which is the purchase of stocks and bonds solely for the purpose of obtaining a return on the funds invested, and **direct investment,** by which the investors participate in the management of the firm in addition to receiving a return on their money. The distinction between these two components has begun to blur, particularly with the growing size and number of international mergers, acquisitions, and alliances in recent years. For example, investments by a foreign investor in the stock of a domestic company generally are treated as direct investment when the investor's equity participation ratio is 10 percent or more. In contrast, deals that do not result in the foreign investor's obtaining at least 10 percent of the shareholdings are classified as portfolio investments. With the increasing pace of business globalization, it is not uncommon for companies to form strategic relationships with firms from other nations in order to pool resources (such as manufacturing, marketing, and technology and other know-how) while still keeping their equity participation below 10 percent. Financing from foreign venture capitalists also tends to be treated as a portfolio investment, although these investors frequently become actively involved in the target company's business operations, with the goal of ultimately realizing substantial capital gains when the target company goes public.

Portfolio Investment

Although portfolio investors are not directly concerned with the control of a firm, they invest immense amounts in stocks and bonds from other countries. For example, data from the Department of Commerce show that persons residing outside the United States owned American stocks and bonds other than U.S. Treasury securities with a value of $6.2 billion in 2007 (including $2.9 billion in corporate stocks), more than four times the corresponding level in 1997.[15] The very substantial proportion of the increase in the valuation of American stock held by persons residing outside this country is associated with the large number and scale of acquisitions of U.S. companies by foreign companies.

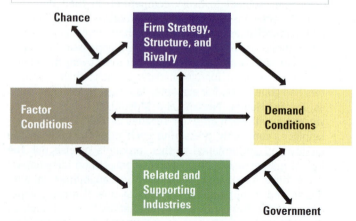

▼ **FIGURE 2.2** Variables Affecting Competitive Advantage: Porter's Diamond

Source: Reprinted by permission of the *Harvard Business Review.* "The Competitive Advantage of Nations" by Michael E. Porter, March–April 1990, p. 77. Copyright © 1990 by the President and Fellows of Harvard College, all rights reserved.

Americans, by contrast, owned $6.8 billion in foreign securities in 2007, which was 380 percent of the corresponding level for 1997.[16] Of the foreign securities held by Americans in 2007, $5.2 billion was in corporate stocks. This increase reflects net U.S. purchases of foreign stocks, acquisitions of foreign companies by U.S. companies, and price appreciation in many foreign stocks. As you can see, foreign portfolio investment is sizable and will continue to grow as more international firms list their bonds and equities on foreign exchanges.

Foreign Direct Investment

The following discussion examines the volume, level, and direction of foreign direct investment, and the influence of international trade on foreign direct investment. This section discusses the overall level of foreign direct investment, as well as annual outflows and inflows of FDI.

The Outstanding Stock of FDI The *book value*—or the value of the total outstanding stock—of all foreign direct investment (FDI) worldwide was $16.2 trillion at the end of 2008.[17] Individuals and corporations from the United States had $3.2 trillion invested abroad, which was more than double the FDI of the next-largest investor, the United Kingdom. The proportion of FDI accounted for by the United States declined by nearly 46 percent between 1980 and 2008, however, from 36 to less than 20 percent. During the same time period, the proportion of FDI accounted for by the European Union increased by nearly 40 percent, from 36 to 50 percent, although a portion of that increase was due to the inclusion of additional member-countries in the EU calculations. Japan's proportion of FDI declined from 12 percent in 1990 to 4 percent in 2008. Reflecting their continued economic development, developing countries have dramatically increased their share of FDI stock, from 1 percent in 1980 to nearly 15 percent in 2008. Figure 2.3 highlights the rate of growth of FDI stock for selected nations and regions, particularly the M-BRIC emerging market economies, that is, Mexico, Brazil, Russia, India, and China.

An important development in the level of worldwide FDI is the emergence of what has been called the "bamboo network" of ethnic Chinese family businesses based outside of China. The 500 largest public companies in Asia that are controlled by overseas Chinese investors have more than $1 trillion in total assets, and this figure excludes these families' privately owned companies.[18] Ethnic

Chinese are reported to be the largest cross-border investors in Malaysia, Thailand, Indonesia, Vietnam, the Philippines, and Hong Kong, and they are a major source of investment capital flowing into the Chinese mainland. Another important development is the emergence of sovereign wealth funds, which are state-owned investment funds primarily from countries with either extensive commodity exports (e.g., petroleum) or trade surpluses. These funds were estimated to control approximately $3.8 trillion in assets in 2009, with that amount projected to increase to as much as $10 trillion by 2013.[19] Some observers are concerned not merely with the level of assets controlled by these funds, but also the potential for sometimes secretive state-owned investment funds to make decisions based at least partly on political or other noncommercial criteria.

Annual Outflows of FDI Annual FDI outflows (the amount invested each year into other nations) hit a historical high in 2000—$1.2 trillion, more than 250 percent of the level in 1997.[20] However, the slowdown that began to hit most of the world's economies in late 2000 resulted in a subsequent decline in the overall level of annual FDI flows. By 2002, the total was only $647 billion, only about 54 percent of the 2000 figure. Outflows subsequently increased, reaching $2.1 trillion in 2007 before declining again to $1.9 trillion during the economic downturn of 2008.

The overall volume of outward FDI from developing nations increased by approximately 700 percent by 2008 compared to

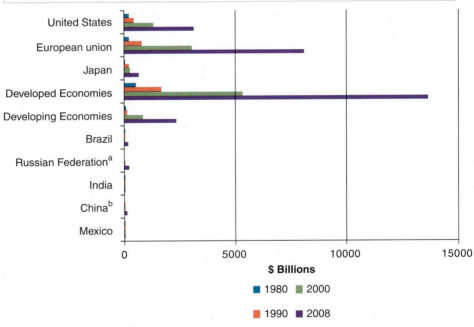

▼ FIGURE 2.3 Stocks of Outward Foreign Direct Investment, Selected Countries and Categories, 1980, 1990, 2000, and 2008 ($ billions)

■ 1980 ■ 2000
■ 1990 ■ 2008

[a]Data not available for 1980 and 1990.

[b]Data not available for 1980.

Source: Various "Country Fact Sheets," *World Investment Report 2001,* United Nations Conference on Trade and Development, Geneva, October 2001; and *World Investment Report 2009,* United Nations Conference on Trade and Development, Geneva, unctad.org/en/docs/wir2009_en.pdf (May 15, 2010).

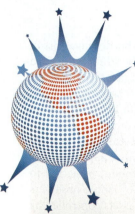

GLOBAL gauntlet

Comparative Advantage and Offshoring of Service Jobs from the United States to India

India, a nation with approximately 1 billion people, has relatively few other resources compared with developed nations. Therefore, it should have a comparative advantage in production of goods or services that require large amounts of labor and relatively little capital. However, India has an additional comparative advantage because many of its citizens speak English (which is taught in many Indian schools and universities rather than using one of the other 18 major languages and 844 dialects spoken in the country). Thus, labor has a relatively low price due to the large Indian workforce (about 450 million, with nearly 10 million additional people entering the workforce each year), high levels of unemployment or underemployment (officially an unemployment rate of 8 percent, but a poverty rate that exceeds 20 percent), and a large proportion of rural and unskilled workers (about 2 percent of Indians own a computer, inhibiting the development of computer-based skill sets). As Internet and cellular telephone communications continue to become less expensive, India increasingly is using its English-speaking pool of labor to export services—such as software engineering, telemarketing, reviews of credit or mortgage applications, preparation or review of legal documents, analysis of blood tests and other medical services, and claims processing—to foreign companies and their customers, a process known as offshoring.

The Indian IT industry generated revenues nearly 5 percent of India's GDP, and the overall size of this sector is projected to grow to $175 billion in revenues by 2010 as a result of factors such as declining computer prices, new tax incentives, and the Indian government's efforts to connect the country's extensive and isolated rural areas with the outside world. Fortune 500 companies such as Amazon.com, IBM, and American Express, as well as a range of more moderate-sized firms, have already offshored millions of jobs. By 2015, it has been estimated that 3.4 million U.S. jobs, representing $136 billion in wages, will have been offshored, and India is well positioned to capture much of

this business. According to Noshir Kaka of the consulting firm McKinsey, "This industry can do for India what automobiles did for Japan and oil for Saudi Arabia."

For example, more than 500,000 U.S. individual and corporate tax returns were estimated to have been prepared in India in 2009. Documents obtained from taxpayers are scanned and shipped electronically to India, where forms are completed and sent back to the United States to be examined, approved, and signed by an American accountant. While a U.S. tax preparer might cost more than $3,000 per month during the peak tax season, a comparable Indian worker might cost less than $300. There is no requirement that the taxpayer be informed that the tax work is done abroad, and most accounting firms charge the same fees as those charged if the job is done by accountants in the United States, thus helping to boost profitability.

Companies in financial services and insurance have also been actively pursuing offshoring. More than 80 percent of global financial services companies have an offshore facility, and the range of services being offshored is rapidly being broadened. "Offshoring has released a new competitive dynamic. Larger firms are driving change across the financial services industry and using offshoring to open up a competitive advantage over their smaller rivals," said Chris Gentle of the professional services firm Deloitte. "Offshoring is fundamentally changing the way financial institutions do business, creating a global division of labor that demands new operating models, new structures and new management skills."

"This is a global industry in the throes of flux. It is a sector where [Indian companies] are rewriting the rules of the game. That is the difference that has become apparent and increasingly accepted," says Nandan Nilekani, CEO of the rapidly expanding Indian company Infosys Technologies. The basis for this change, he says, is the "global delivery model" being pioneered in India and replicated in other low-cost nations. In the IT sector, for example, a plentiful supply of Indian software engineers can work on projects "offshore," delivering the finished product to clients "on site" in the United States. "Our business innovation is forcing rivals to redesign the way they do things."

This disruptive change is threatening to transform the business models in operation across a broad range of industries. Although many people think of low-skill jobs like telemarketing and call centers when they think of outsourcing to India, the sophistication and skill levels associated with processes being outsourced are rising rapidly. A big driver for this trend is the abundance of qualified personnel in India. A NASSCOM-McKinsey study found that India has 28 percent of the overall supply of skilled services personnel in low-cost nations, and these potential employees remain amazingly inexpensive. According to the Boston Consulting Group, an Indian IT engineer earns a typical annual salary of $5,000 and one with a master's degree in business earns $7,500—about one-tenth the level of their American counterparts, although salary inflation is starting to reduce that gap.

Services represent 60 percent of the U.S. economy and employ up to 80 percent of American workers, so it is not surprising that the offshoring of service jobs has generated concerns across a broad spectrum of society. John Steadman, president of the Institute of Electrical and Electronics Engineers, cautioned, "If we continue to offshore high-skilled professional jobs, the U.S. risks surrendering its leading role in innovation." Andrew Grove, former Chairman of Intel Corp., warned that "it's a very valid question" whether the United States could lose its dominance in information technology as a result of this trend, as it did in electronics manufacturing. Responding to the outsourcing to an Indian firm of calls from New Jersey welfare recipients about their benefits, state senator Shirley Turner said, "I was outraged. Here we are in New Jersey, as we are in every state, requiring welfare recipients to go to work. And yet, we were sending these jobs overseas . . . so that corporations can make more money." She noted that unemployed people do not pay taxes, and the loss of these tax revenues exacerbates budget deficits. Ironically, widespread publicity regarding concerns about offshoring may have hastened the trend by making more companies aware of the possible cost savings from such undertakings.

On the other hand, some have argued that offshoring will help to strengthen American industry and the economy as a whole.

> **If we continue to offshore high-skilled professional jobs, the U.S. risks surrendering its leading role in innovation.**

Outsourcing is not necessarily a zero-sum game, where one Indian worker substitutes for one American worker. When American firms hire lower-cost labor abroad, they often must hire other workers to complement the increased level of foreign labor. Overseas expansion can also cause companies to modify the scope of activities undertaken in the United States, placing increasing emphasis on higher-value-added activities rather than the lower-skill positions that have been offshored. Shifting work to lower-cost locations abroad has the potential to lower prices in the United States, thus raising the purchasing power of American consumers, enhancing consumer spending and economic activity, and thereby creating more jobs. As *The Wall Street Journal* editorialized, "The world economy is a dynamic enterprise. Jobs created overseas generate jobs at home. Not just more jobs for Americans, but higher-skilled and better paying ones. At the same time, trade offers consumers a greater quantity and variety of goods and services for lower prices. David Ricardo lives."

Sources: Business Monitor International, *The India Information Technology Report 2008* (London: Business Monitor International, 2008), http://www.businessmonitor.com/it/india.html (May 15, 2010); Meg Fletcher, "Moving Services Offshore," *Business Insurance,* June 2006, pp. 16–17; Joanna Slater, "In India, a Job Paradox," *The Wall Street Journal,* May 5, 2004, p. A12; Julie Gallagher, "Redefining the Business Case for Offshore Outsourcing," *Insurance & Technology,* April 2002, pp. A5, A8–A9; Khozem Merchant, "The Future on India's Shores," *Financial Times,* April 21, 2004, p. 8; "Outsourcing 101," *The Wall Street Journal,* May 27, 2004, p. A20; Rebecca Paley, "Fighting for the Down and Out(sourced)," *Mother Jones,* May/June 2004, pp. 20–21; Manjeet Kripalani and Pete Engardio, "The Rise of India," *BusinessWeek,* December 8, 2003, pp. 66–76; Robert Orr, "Offshoring Opens Gap in Financial Services Race," *Financial Times,* June 29, 2004, p. 9; SourcingNotes, "Offshoring Tax Returns Preparation to India," http://www.sourcingnotes.com/content/view/197/54/ (May 15, 2010); and Heather Timmons, "India Feels Less Vulnerable as Outsourcing Presses On," *New York Times,* June 2, 2009, http://www.nytimes.com/2009/06/03/business/global/03outsource.html (May 15, 2010).

its average from 1985 to 1995, and the proportion of worldwide outward FDI that comes from developing nations increased from under 11 percent from 1985 to 1995 to 16 percent in 2008. Despite this increase, the vast proportion of outward FDI, more than 81 percent in 2008, still originates from the developed countries. The United States and the EU have been accounting for the largest share of worldwide FDI, 62 percent in 2008. The United States had been the leading source of FDI outflows through most of the 1990s and 2000s, although the proportion of worldwide outward FDI accounted for by the United States declined from an average of 21 percent in 1985–1996 to 17

percent for 2006–2008. American FDI outflows of $312 billion in 2008 exceeded the outflows of the second-largest source of FDI, France, by 42 percent. The European Union's proportion of outward FDI grew from an average of around 47 percent in 1985–1997 to a peak of 75 percent by 2000, before subsequently declining to 50 percent of global outward FDI from 2006–2008.

Much of this outward FDI has been associated with mergers and acquisitions. For example, historically, approximately two-thirds of the value of corporate investments made in the United States from abroad have been spent to acquire going companies rather than to establish new ones (similarly, the majority of American investments into foreign markets have gone to the acquisition of going companies). A number of reasons are responsible for this fact: (1) corporate restructuring in the United States caused management to put on the market businesses or other assets that either did not meet management's profit standards or were considered to be unrelated to the company's main business; (2) foreign companies wanted to gain rapid access in the United States to advanced technology, especially in computers and communications; (3) management of foreign firms felt that entrance into the large and prosperous American market could be more successful if they acquired known brand names rather than spending the time and money to promote new, unknown ones; and (4) increased international competitive pressures, including the pursuit of improved economies of scale, has led to restructuring and consolidation in many industries, and the acquisition of companies in major markets such as the United States has been a by-product of these industrial trends.

Annual Inflows of FDI In which countries are investments being made, and where do the investments come from? The industrialized nations invest primarily in one another, just as they trade more with one another. An average of nearly 70 percent of annual FDI investments have been going into developed countries in recent years, although the proportion has

substantially during the past two decades. The proportion of worldwide inward FDI flows that have gone to Latin America declined from 16.5 percent in 1996 to less than 7 percent for 2000 and 8.5 percent for 2006. For Asia as a whole, total inflows to the region rose to a record $388 billion in 2008, nearly 1,300 percent of the average inward investments during 1985–1995. Asia accounted for over 44 percent of all investments not directed to the United States and the European Union in 2008. A particularly important trend is the proportion of Asian FDI that has been directed to China and its territories. Their combined proportion of Asian FDI was 43 percent from 2006 to 2008, and it appears that some of the FDI previously directed toward other Asian nations might have been redirected toward these Chinese investments.

Level and Direction of FDI Even though it is impossible to make an accurate determination of the present value of foreign investments, we can get an idea of the rate and amounts of such investments and of the places in which they are being made. This is the kind of information that interests managers and government leaders. It is analogous to what is sought in the analysis of international trade. If a nation is continuing to receive appreciable amounts of foreign investment, its investment climate must be favorable. This means that

> **"** An average of nearly 70 percent of annual FDI investments have been going into developed countries in recent years **"**

fallen from more than 79 percent in 1996 to 57 percent by 2008.[21] The United States and the EU accounted for an average of more than 60 percent of all inward FDI from 1985 to 2004, exceeding 80 percent in 1999 and 2000, before declining to 49 percent by 2008. As noted earlier, much of this inward investment has gone to mergers and acquisitions made by companies whose businesses are confronting competition and consolidation globally. Japan has not been a significant recipient of inward FDI, averaging less than 1 percent of worldwide FDI from 1985 to 2008.

Worldwide, the developing countries as a whole obtained a 70 percent increase in the level of FDI for 2000 versus 1996, and a further 220 percent increase by 2008. Although the overall dollar value of FDI going to developing countries has been increasing substantially in recent years, the proportion of FDI funds going to these nations has fluctuated substantially. The average from 1985 to 1995 was 28 percent, rising to more than 52 percent in 1996, declining to less than 18 percent in 2000, and then rising again to 37 percent in 2008. African nations have participated relatively little in the growing flow of inward FDI, accounting for an average of less than 3 percent of all inflows from 1985 to 2008. The small nation of Singapore (population 3 million) received approximately as much foreign investment as the entire African continent did during this time. In Latin America, annual FDI inflows have fluctuated

the political forces of the foreign environment are relatively attractive and that the opportunity to earn a profit is greater there than elsewhere. Other reasons for investing exist, to be sure; however, if the preceding factors are absent, foreign investment is not likely to occur.

ARE ECONOMIC AND SOCIAL DEVELOPMENT AFFECTED BY TRADE AND INVESTMENT?

All economies are increasingly open in today's economic environment of globalization. Trade plays a vital role in shaping economic and social performance and prospects of countries around the world, especially those of developing countries. No country has grown without trade. However, the contribution of trade to development depends a great deal on the context in which it works and the objectives it serves.[22]

This quote is the way the United Nations Conference on Trade and Development (UNCTAD) began its groundbreaking report examining international trade and developing countries.

International trade clearly has an important role in influencing nations' economic and social performance in a world of globalization. This role is even more fundamental in the case of developing countries. Yet the mere expansion of trade does not guarantee improvement for a country and its people. Rather, it is essential that trade performance be viewed in the context of its effects on employment levels, economic growth, development, and an improvement in the overall human condition.

To assist in efforts to ensure that trade plays a full and constructive role in enhancing growth and development, UNCTAD launched an ambitious initiative that included the Trade and Development Index (TDI), a tool designed to assist efforts "to systematically monitor the trade and development performance of developing countries with a view to facilitating national and international policies and strategies that would ensure that trade serves as a key instrument of development." By capturing the interactions among a range of institutional, structural, financial, trade and development factors underlying trade and development, the TDI attempts to provide a quantitative indication of a nation's trade and development performance. Although UNCTAD created the TDI primarily for assessing performance in developing nations, to facilitate comparisons and insight, it also constructed the TDI for developed countries and for newly industrializing countries. Overall, 123 countries were evaluated. The 20 top- and bottom-ranked countries are listed in Table 2.3.[23]

The average score for developed countries was 640, versus 467 for developing countries and 395 for the least developed countries. Seven major emerging economies (Brazil, Russia, India, China, Mexico, South Korea, and South Africa), which account for 45 percent of the world's population and more than 26 percent of global exports of goods and services, had an average TDI score of 509, and they have all evidenced increasing TDI scores. This indicates that the gap in development can be shrunk—and has been in the case of several nations. Overall, compared with developed countries, developing countries evidence a continuing lag in such areas as physical infrastructure, human capital, financial intermediation, institutional quality, economic and social well-being, and trade performance.

The initial TDI evaluation revealed that the 30 highest-ranked nations were all developed countries, except for Singapore (#5), South Korea (#21), China (#25), Malaysia (#27), and Thailand (#29). This result is interpreted as evidence that few developing nations have been able to come close to the developed countries in terms of their trade and development performance. Nine of the bottom 10 nations are sub-Saharan African countries, accentuating the severity of the trade and development problems confronting sub-Saharan Africa and least developed nations in general. The best regional performance among developing nations was that of the countries of the East Asia and Pacific region, followed by the Middle East and North Africa region and the Latin America and Caribbean region. The regions of South Asia and of sub-Saharan Africa significantly lagged behind the other three regional groups in terms of their TDI scores.

A critical factor contributing to high TDI scores is trade liberalization. The importance of this factor is highest for countries with lower TDI scores, and vice versa. This suggests that the extent of trade liberalization has much greater importance for developing countries, and especially the least developed countries, than for developed nations. In general, over the longer term and in the absence of externalities or market failures, trade liberalization is an effective policy promoting development. However, efforts to liberalize too rapidly can also result in short-term adjustment problems.

▼ **TABLE 2.3** Top and Bottom Ranked Countries on the Trade and Development Index, 2006

Top-Ranked Countries			Bottom-Ranked Countries		
Rank	Country	TDI Score	Rank	Country	TDI Score
1	United States	743	103	Zimbabwe	395
				Pakistan	395
2	Germany	696	105	Syrian Arab Republic	392
3	Denmark	691		Chad	392
4	United Kingdom	682	107	Côte d'Ivoire	387
5	Singapore	675		Mauritania	387
6	Japan	668	109	Burkina Faso	386
	Sweden	668	110	Benin	384
8	France	664	111	Burundi	382
	Norway	664	112	Central African Republic	381
10	Canada	650		Zambia	381
	Switzerland	650	114	Ethiopia	379
12	Belgium	642	115	Cameroon	373
	Iceland	642	116	Guinea	372
14	Finland	636	117	Yemen	370
15	Ireland	630	118	Angola	364
16	Australia	628		Democratic Rep. of Congo	364
17	Austria	627	120	Niger	362
18	New Zealand	623	121	Nigeria	350
19	Spain	619	122	Guinea-Bissau	339
20	Israel	610	123	Sudan	326

Source: UNCTAD, *Developing Countries in International Trade 2007: Trade and Development Index* (New York: United Nations, 2007), http://www.unctad.org/Templates/Page.asp?intItemID54388&lang51 (May 15, 2010).

Both external and internal factors were found to influence a nation's export performance. External factors include market access conditions (e.g., transportation costs, geography, physical infrastructure, trade barriers, competition) and other factors that influence demand for imports. Internal factors include supply-side conditions within a nation (e.g., raw materials, labor and capital costs, access to technology, economic policy, institutional environment). A country's extent of market access is particularly important, because limitations on access for foreign markets are a major cause of poor export performance.

Foreign direct investment (FDI) was found to have a significant and positive impact on export performance across all of the nations studied and for every time period studied. FDI has a key role in influencing the composition of exports, including the technological content and the development of export supply capacity, and especially in knowledge-based industries. The impact of FDI is strongest for the two poorest-performing groups of exporters and at their early stages of export development.

UNCTAD emphasized that merely improving trade factors, such as liberalizing the trade environment, will yield only marginal benefits for a nation unless these efforts are done in conjunction with a focus on other factors associated with development and poverty reduction. There is a strong need for integration and consistency between trade policy and other social, political, and economic undertakings. For example, nations must act simultaneously both on domestic capacity to supply goods and services and on access to foreign markets in order to produce strong performance. At early stages of development, important factors influencing domestic supply capacity include transportation infrastructure and macroeconomic stability.

Does Trade Lead to FDI?

Historically, foreign direct investment has followed foreign trade. One reason is that engaging in foreign trade is typically less costly and less risky than making a direct investment into foreign markets. Also, management can expand the business in small increments rather than through the considerably greater amounts of investment and market size that a foreign production facility requires. Typically, a firm would use domestic or foreign agents to export. As the export business increased, the firm would set up an export department and perhaps hire sales representatives to live in overseas markets. The firm might even establish its own sales company to import in its own name.

Meanwhile, managers would watch the total market size closely because they would know that their competitors were making similar studies. Generally, because the local market would not be large enough to support local production by all the firms exporting to it, the situation would become one of seeing who could begin manufacturing there first. Experienced managers know that governments often limit the number of local firms making a given product so that those that do set up local operations will be assured of having a profitable and continuing business. This is especially important to developing countries that are dependent on foreign investment to provide jobs and tax revenue.

This sort of linear path to market expansion that we have just discussed is one that many international firms have taken and still take today. However, the new business environment of fewer government barriers to trade, increased competition from globalizing firms, and new production and communications technology is causing many international firms to disperse the activities of their production systems to locations close to available resources. They then integrate the entire production process either regionally or globally. As a result, the decision about where to locate may be either an FDI or a trade decision, illustrating just how closely FDI and trade are interlinked.

LO5 **Explain** some of the theories of foreign direct investment.

EXPLAINING FDI: THEORIES OF INTERNATIONAL INVESTMENT

This section examines several of the leading theories of foreign direct investment, which comprises both ownership and control of international investments involving real or physical assets such as plants and other facilities, rather than theories regarding other types of international investment such as portfolios of stocks, bonds, or other forms of debt. Foreign direct investment involves the establishment of production or other facilities abroad, either through greenfield investment (the establishment of new facilities from the ground up) or cross-border acquisition (the purchase of an existing business in another nation). It is usually assumed that strategic motives will be the driving force for decisions to invest abroad, driven by desire to find new markets, access raw materials, achieve production efficiencies, gain access to new technologies or managerial expertise, enhance political safety of the firm's operations, or respond to competitive or other pressures in the external environment.[24]

Monopolistic Advantage Theory

The modern **monopolistic advantage theory** stems from research showing that foreign direct investment occurs largely in oligopolistic industries rather than in industries operating under near-perfect competition. This means that the firms in these industries must possess advantages not available to local firms in order to overcome liabilities associated with being a foreigner—such as lack of knowledge about local market conditions, increased costs of operating at a distance, or differences in culture, language, laws and regulations, or institutions—that cause a foreign company to be at a disadvantage against local firms. Under this perspective, the advantages must be economies of scale, superior technology, or superior knowledge in marketing, management, or finance. Foreign direct investment takes place because of these product and factor market imperfections, which enable the multinational enterprise to operate more profitably in foreign markets than can local competitors.[25]

Internalization Theory

The **internalization theory** suggests that a firm may have superior knowledge, but due to inefficiency in external markets (i.e., transaction costs), the firm may obtain a higher price for that knowledge by using the knowledge itself rather than by selling it in the open market. By investing in foreign subsidiaries for activities such as supply, production, or distribution, rather than licensing, the company is able to send the knowledge across borders while maintaining it within the firm. The expected result is the firm's ability to realize a superior return on the investment made to produce this knowledge, particularly as the knowledge is embodied in various products or services that are sold to customers.[26]

Dynamic Capabilities

The dynamic capability perspective argues that ownership of specific knowledge or resources is necessary, but not sufficient, for achieving success in international FDI. The firm must also be able to effectively create and exploit dynamic capabilities for quality and/or quantity-based deployment, and these

monopolistic advantage theory Theory that foreign direct investment is made by firms in oligopolistic industries possessing technical and other advantages over indigenous firms

internalization theory The concept that to obtain a higher return on its investment, a firm will transfer its superior knowledge to a foreign subsidiary rather than sell it in the open market

eclectic theory of international production Theory that for a firm to invest overseas, it must have three kinds of advantages: ownership specific, internalization, and location specific

capabilities must be transferable to international environments in order to produce competitive advantage. Companies typically develop centers of excellence in order to develop distinctive competencies that will be subsequently applied to their investments within the host countries.

Eclectic Theory of International Production

The eclectic theory, which combines elements of some of those we have discussed, is the most widely cited and accepted theory of FDI currently. Developed by Dunning, the **eclectic theory of international production** attempts to provide an overall framework for explaining why firms choose to

CU in ib

Kerry Thwing on Developing a Foundation in the International Area

The daughter of a travel agent, I was exposed to the "travel bug" as a baby. Ever since I can remember, my mother would plan yearly family vacations. Travel became a part of my life and I would look forward to the adventures and experiences that would come with each trip. I was sixteen when I decided to set out on my first international solo excursion. I participated in a student exchange program to France, staying with a family in Cognac for a month and exploring Paris for a week. My life would not be the same had I chosen to stay home instead of taking a chance and leaving my comfort zone for this solo adventure. During that month abroad, I learned so much about myself and about others. I came home a wiser, more confident person. Now the travel bug had bitten me officially.

In college, I participated in three study abroad programs. My first year, I traveled to South America via a training ship as part of the Cal Poly at Sea study abroad program. We made port in Mexico, Chile, Peru, and Costa Rica. Then the summer of my second year, I studied in London, England. Finally, my fourth and final year at university, I studied in Adelaide, Australia. Though the ultimate purpose of these excursions was to complete the courses needed for my bachelor's degree in business administration, I learned so much more and such different things than I ever could have from a textbook or lecture. Travel can provide the ultimate education. Nothing can compare to the experience of leaving your comfort zone and observing your actions and the actions of others in a different environment.

Through international travel, not only will you learn about different cultures and values around the world, you will also learn many things about yourself. You can discover what you are truly capable of and you may be quite surprised by what you find. During my travels, there were many instances when things did not go as planned, but it is those times that are the most memorable for me. I was always pleasantly surprised by my ability to adapt and problem solve when put in a difficult situation. This is a skill that I learned

through travel, and it has proven useful in many aspects of my life.

However, my favorite aspect of travel is the people that I have met, the connections to others that I have made. Throughout my time abroad, I have gained many great friends on a global scale. In fact, the majority of the relationships I have cultivated are related to my study abroad programs. It is important, especially when going with your friends to study abroad, to branch out and meet the locals. Not only will they be able to tell you about the city you are visiting, they will also teach you about the culture and may even become your new friends.

If I could give any piece of advice, I would say to take any chance you can to travel and experience new things. The only regrets I have are the opportunities that I did not take advantage of. In addition, take every chance you can *now* because you never know what will happen in the future. Personally, I decided to take the opportunity to return to Adelaide to complete my postgraduate education. I am currently residing in Adelaide and planning my next excursion abroad. I would encourage you to do the same as I do: explore every chance you can to spend time abroad.

engage in FDI rather than serve foreign markets through alternatives such as exporting, licensing, management contracts, joint ventures, or strategic alliances. This theory maintains that if a firm is going to invest in production facilities overseas, it must have three kinds of advantages:

1. *Ownership specific.* This is the extent to which a firm has or can develop a firm-specific advantage through ownership of tangible and intangible assets that are not available to other firms and can be transferred abroad. The three basic types of tangible or intangible ownership-specific advantages include knowledge or technology, economies of scale or scope, and monopolistic advantages associated with unique access to critical inputs or outputs. The advantage generates lower costs and/or higher revenues that will offset the added costs of operating at a distance within a foreign location.

2. *Location specific.* A foreign market must have specific characteristics, of an economic, social, or political nature (e.g., market size, tariff or nontariff barriers, or transport costs), that will permit the firm to profitably exploit its firm-specific advantages by locating to that market rather than from serving the market through exports.

3. *Internalization.* Firms have various alternatives for entering foreign markets, ranging from arm's-length market transactions to the use of hierarchy via a wholly owned subsidiary, as we will discuss in Chapter 13. It is in the firm's best interests to exploit its ownership-specific advantages through internalization in those situations where either the market does not exist or it functions inefficiently, causing the transaction costs of using market-based (arm's-length) options to be too high.

Because of the names of these three types of advantages that a firm must have, the eclectic theory of international production is sometimes referred to as the *OLI model.* This theory provides an explanation for an international firm's choice of its overseas production facilities. The firm must have both location and ownership advantages to invest in a foreign plant. It will invest where it is most profitable to internalize its monopolistic advantage.[27,28] These investments can be proactive, being strategically anticipated and controlled in advance by the firm's management team, or reactive, in response to the discovery of market imperfections.

There is one commonality to nearly all of these theories that is supported by empirical tests—the major part of direct foreign investment is made by large, research-intensive firms in oligopolistic industries. Also, all these theories offer reasons companies find it *profitable* to invest overseas. However, as we stated in Chapter 1, all motives can be linked in some way to the desire to increase or protect not only profits but also *sales* and *markets.* ◼

chapter three

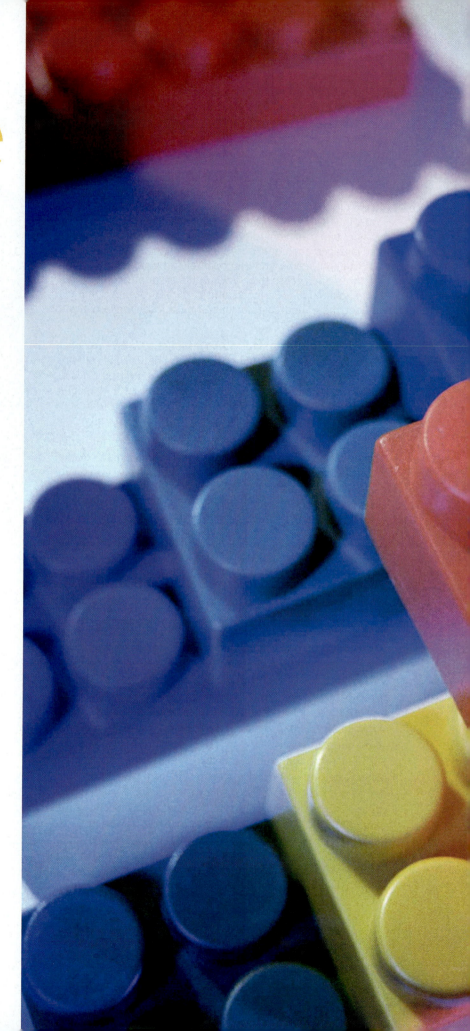

" Every institution not only carries within it the seeds of its own dissolution, but prepares the way for its most hated rival."

—Dean William R. Inge, 1860–1954, Dean of St Paul's, London

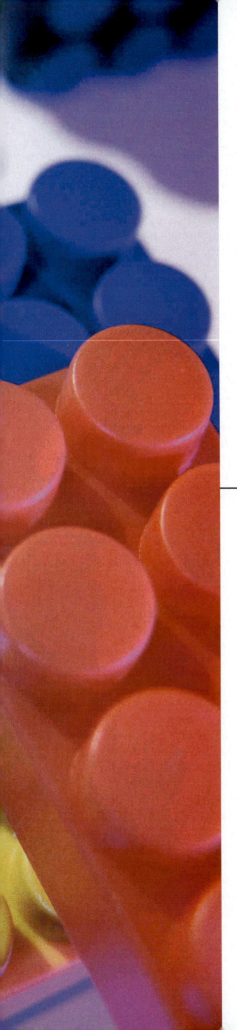

international institutions
from an international business perspective

We begin this chapter by examining the institutions that are most important to the international manager, moving from those that focus on global cooperation (such as the United Nations, the World Trade Organization, and the International Monetary Fund) to those whose concerns are mainly regional (such as regional trade alliances). We begin with a focus on what institutions are and how they influence the firm.

LO1 Explain the importance of international institutions to business decision makers and their firms.

WHAT ARE INSTITUTIONS AND WHY ARE THEY USEFUL?

Institutions are organizations constructed by a group, society, or culture to achieve a common goal that function to "provide stability and meaning to social life."[1] A contemporary understanding of institutions suggests that they are a collection of norms that "regulate the relations of individuals to each other."[2] That is, institutions are socially constructed—a group, society, or culture constructs them—and they limit behavior. This approach to understanding institutions, called **new institutional theory,** suggests that

firm's behavior when it wants to execute a merger or acquisition, even if the companies involved in the proposed transaction are not European, because if the merged business wants to sell into the EU, its merger or acquisition requires EU approval. The EU can also mandate product composition and computer code openness, as Microsoft has learned in regard to bundling software and sharing code. Formal institutions, then, function to constrain and regulate the firm's behavior through rules, laws, and sanctions—all mechanisms that enforce or coerce compliance. Firms comply with the rules of formal institutions because to do so makes sense; expedience is the basis of firm compliance.

While formal institutions use laws and regulations to gain compliance, informal institutions rely on norms, values, customs, and ideologies to mold behavior. There are two types of informal institutions, normative and cognitive. *Normative* informal institutions establish standards, "propagate principles, and broadly represent 'humanity.'"[5] Examples are professional organizations and nongovernmental organizations (NGOs) that influence behavior through shared norms and values. The United Nations is also an informal normative institution. Behavior is influenced through shared norms; compliance is built on social obligation.

The final type of informal institution, the *cognitive,* is of tremendous importance to the international manager. It uses

> **MORE THAN EVER BEFORE IN HUMAN HISTORY, WE SHARE A COMMON DESTINY. WE CAN MASTER IT ONLY IF WE FACE IT TOGETHER. AND THAT, MY FRIENDS, IS WHY WE HAVE THE UNITED NATIONS.**
>
> —Kofi Annan, former Secretary General of United Nations

from a business point of view, institutions may be understood as organized collections of basic rules and unwritten codes of conduct that limit and direct the decisions firms can make. A *rules of the game* image captures this view of institutions as they strive to reduce uncertainty in the firm's external environment.[3]

Institutions influence behavior in several ways. **Formal institutions** operate through laws and regulations, while **informal institutions** use norms, values, customs and ideologies.[4] Formal institutions, such as national governments, are major rule-setters, especially in their geographical areas, but in some cases, far beyond their borders. Think of the power and the explicit rules of the European Union or of the United States tax authorities. The European Union's Directorate General for Competition is a body that influences the international

shared ideas to define reality by means of conceptual frameworks or schema. These conceptual informal institutions are often less explicit or tangible and obvious to the non-native than are the formal institutions or informal normative institutions, since ideas are invisible. Examples are found in the contrast between the Japanese and American supplier relationship and the Chinese concept of *guanxi.*

Supplier relationships contrast greatly between Japan and the United States. Remember our earlier image for institutions as setting the rules of the game? The "supplier game" in Japan calls for the supplier to build a relationship with the potential buyer; such a relationship allows the firm to build knowledge about the reliability of the supplier, which is most important. Price, then, is likely to not be an early determinant of the buy decision in Japan. In contrast, in supplier relationships in the United States, the game is thought of differently. Price plays a more prominent initial role. Note, too, that the cultural custom in the United States is to share drinks *after* the deal is sealed, while this happens *before* the deal is structured in Japan, as a way to build the relationship, and continues during and after. None of these culture-based frameworks that constitute the supplier process is formalized, yet these assumptions about the right way to negotiate with suppliers are institutionalized and operate to limit behavior choices and reduce uncertainty for the supplier and buyer in both Japan and the United States.

Guanxi, a Chinese institution that describes a type of relationship similar to a combination of social capital and mentoring, is another example of an informal institution. *Guanxi* relationships carry obligations that may be stronger than civic responsibilities and rational understandings of business situations.

These examples illustrate that informal institutions, which consist of voluntary agreements or a set of shared assumptions, a bit like the mind's software,[6] exert a powerful influence on the choices open to the firm in international activities. Note, too, that in developing economies, informal institutions tend to play a greater role than in developed economies. One way to think of this is that the informal institutions emerge to bring added order to the chaotic, unstructured environment in the developing economy, which lacks well-developed formal institutions. Figure 3.1 describes institutions in more detail.[7]

To illustrate the importance of strong international institutions, think about the roles of the United States and China on the global stage, one a superpower, the other a rapidly developing nation preparing for a major global role. Martin Wolfe, chief economist at the *Financial Times,* notes that both nations are fated to cooperate.[8] Yet look at their differences: as Wolfe points out, one is a democracy, the other an autocracy; one is "a child of the enlightenment," the other an agrarian empire. Although working together will not be easy for either, international institutions such as the United Nations and the World Trade Organization encourage such efforts and make them more likely to succeed by developing multilateral solutions, in which all member nations cooperate. For individual nations, agreeing to abide by a mutually negotiated UN resolution or a World Trade Organization rule is much more acceptable than agreeing to a bilateral negotiation, which tends to be zero-sum, with a winner and a loser, and in which power and prestige are at stake. There is no humiliation at stake with a negotiated UN resolution that applies to all nations' behavior.

FIGURE 3.1
Institutions: Characteristics

	Institution type:	Formal	Informal	
	Social agreement is:	**Regulative**	**Normative**	**Cognitive**
Attributes	**Compliance based on**	Expedience	Social obligation	Predisposition (taken for granted)
	Institutionalization based on	Coercion	Norms	Imitation
	Logic based on	Means to an end	Appropriateness	Conformance, orthodoxy
	Legitimacy based on	Legal enforcement	Moral governance	Cultural support, concept correctness
	Indicators/ Evidence	Rules, laws, sanctions,	Certification, accreditation	Prevalence, similarity

Source: J. McNett after W. R. Scott (1995) p. 10.

United Nations (UN)
192-member organization dedicated to the promotion of peace and stability of the world

LO2 Outline the United Nations as an institution and its relevance to international business.

THE UNITED NATIONS

The **United Nations (UN)** is probably the best-known worldwide organization. Its 192 member-nations are dedicated to the promotion of peace and global stability. Many of its activities relate directly to business and to possible actions of the firm. For example, the UN is responsible for many international agreements that directly affect commercial relationships, including much of the body of international law. In addition, as a stabilizing force in the world economy, the UN contributes to the conditions under which international business is conducted. Because the UN operates with voluntary agreements, it is largely an informal institution. Here are some areas in which the UN plays a significant role for international business:

- UN agreements set technical standards and norms. These standards and norms function as the "soft infrastructure" for the global economy. The United Nations Center for Trade Facilitation and Electronic Business (UN/CEFACT) has standardized trade documents and developed standards for electronic data exchange.
- UN efforts prepare the ground for investment in emerging economies through a focus on areas necessary to development such as health, education, governance, and political stability. The United Nations Educational, Scientific and Cultural Organization (UNESCO) actively promotes literacy for the world's 860 million adults and 113 million children who cannot read and write.
- Various UN agencies address the downsides of globalization, such as terrorism, crime, drugs, and arms traffic. Treaties focused on areas of terrorism such as the taking of hostages have been developed so that agreed-upon responses among UN members exist.

Economic and Social Council (ECOSOC) UN body concerned with economic and social issues such as trade, development, education, and human rights

General Assembly Deliberative body of the UN made up of all member-nations, each with one vote regardless of size, wealth, or power

Security Council Main peacekeeping body of the UN, composed of 15 members including 5 permanent members

- UN efforts to seek solutions to global environmental problems include the work of the UN Environment Programme (UNEP), the agency that laid the groundwork for the Climate Change Convention, leading to the Kyoto Protocol to reduce greenhouse gases. The UNEP has developed many initiatives that support sustainable business practices.

- The UN addresses education and health issues that require global-level solutions arrived at in partnership with businesses, through the Global Compact, an effort to partner private industry with groups in developing nations.

- The UN promotes social justice and human and labor rights. Central to these concerns is the UN Economic and Social Council.

- International Telecommunication Union allotment of frequencies keeps the air waves from becoming hopelessly clogged, and thus avoids interference among radio transmissions.

- Data collected and redistributed from member states by the World Meteorological Organization make possible worldwide and country-specific weather forecasts.

- The UN Sales Convention and the UN Convention on the Carriage of Goods by Sea help to establish rights and obligations for buyers and sellers in international commercial transactions.[10]

UN Organization

The work of the United Nations is carried out through five active bodies, called *organs* in UN terminology. All UN member-nations are members of the **General Assembly,** the main deliberative body in which each nation has one vote regardless of its size, wealth, or power. The General Assembly acts by adopting resolutions that express the will of the member-nations. General Assembly decisions are normative and carry the heavy weight of world opinion, yet they have no legally binding force for governments or citizens in the member-nations.

> " This organization [the United Nations] is created to prevent you from going to hell. It isn't created to take you to heaven. "
>
> —Henry Cabot Lodge Jr.

- Efforts of the UN build the cornerstones of an interdependent world: trust and shared values. The Global Compact provides a framework for businesses that are committed to aligning their operations and strategies with 10 universally accepted principles in the areas of human rights, labor, the environment and anticorruption. This is one example of UN efforts to build trust and shared values.[9]

The impact of the UN on the conduct of business can be extremely specific, because UN committees negotiate the global "rules of the game" for the international exchanges of goods, services, money, and information.

- When ships sail freely across the seas and through international straits, they are protected by rules legitimized in UN conferences.

- Commercial airlines have the right to fly across borders, and to land in case of emergency, due to agreements negotiated by the International Civil Aviation Organization, part of the UN system.

- The World Health Organization sets criteria for pharmaceutical quality and standardizes drug names.

- Universal Postal Union protocols prevent losses and allow the mail to move across borders.

The UN **Security Council** has responsibility for maintaining international peace and security. Membership is five permanent members—China, France, the Russian Federation, the United Kingdom, and the United States—each having veto power, and 10 nonpermanent members elected by the General

Members of the UN Security Council in session.

Assembly and representing specific regions to ensure every area is represented. Presently the Security Council's peacekeeping operations are active in 16 locations in Africa, the Americas, Europe, Asia and the Pacific, and the Middle East.[11]

The **Economic and Social Council (ECOSOC)** is concerned with economic and social issues, including trade, transport, industrialization, economic development, population growth, children, housing, women's rights, racial discrimination, illegal drugs, crime, social welfare, youth, the human environment, and food. ECOSOC makes recommendations on how to improve education and health conditions and promotes respect for and observation of the human rights and freedom of people everywhere.

The **International Court of Justice (ICJ),** also known as the *World Court,* makes legal decisions involving disputes between national governments and gives advisory opinions. Because only nations litigate before the court, governments often intervene on behalf of corporations and individuals in their countries. Even though the court has worldwide jurisdiction to hear disputes between governments, it hears relatively few cases. There are presently two cases being heard and 15 cases pending.[12] The ICJ has 15 judges, who come from 15 different countries and serve nine-year terms, appointed by majorities of the General Assembly and the Security Council.

The **Secretariat,** headed by the secretary-general of the United Nations, is the UN's staff. The secretary-general is appointed by the General Assembly on the recommendation of the Security Council for a five-year renewable term. The eighth secretary-general, Ban Ki-Moon of Korea, began his first term in 2007. About 40,000 people from around the world make up the UN Secretariat staff.

> " Modification of the vote allocation is under way, though, so that low-income nations can play an increased role in UN decision making. "

L03 Describe the purposes of the two global monetary institutions, the IMF and the World Bank

INTERNATIONAL MONETARY INSTITUTIONS

There are two global monetary institutions, the International Monetary Fund and the World Bank, both established at the Bretton Woods conference, called by the UN in 1944, near the end World War II. **Bretton Woods** is significant because it resulted in the world's first negotiated agreement among independent nations to support trade through monetary institutions. These meetings set up the **International Monetary Fund (IMF)** to establish rules for international monetary policies and their enforcement and the **World Bank** to lend money for development projects.

International Monetary Fund

The premise of the International Monetary Fund, which operates as a collaboration of nations, is that the common interest of all nations in a workable international monetary system far transcends their conflicting national interests.[13] The IMF promotes international monetary cooperation, including orderly exchange arrangements and payments systems, and makes funds available for balance-of-payments corrections. Each of the 186 members contributes funds, known as *quotas,* determined by the nation's relative size in the world economy. The aggregate quotas, which as of September 2009 totaled $558.9 billion, form a pool of money from which the IMF can lend. The quota also is used to determine how much a nation can borrow from the IMF and how many votes it has.[14] The United States has 16.77 percent of the total votes, while Germany has 5.88 percent, China 3.66, and Japan 6.02. Modification of the vote allocation is under way, though, so that low-income nations can play an increased role in UN decision making. Although the IMF deals solely with governments, its policies and actions have a profound impact on business worldwide because they set the monetary framework for trade.[15]

IMF and Exchange Rates

The IMF Articles of Agreement, which took effect in 1945, set up fixed exchange rates among member-nations' currencies, with **par value** based on gold and the U.S. dollar, which was valued at $35 per ounce of gold. Previously, the gold standard, which had used gold as the common denominator among currencies, had undergone severe pressure, including the Great Depression (1929–1933). To illustrate the Bretton Woods system, the British pound's par value was set at US$2.40, the French franc's at US$0.18, and the German mark's at US$0.2732. There was an understanding that the U.S. government would redeem dollars for gold and that the dollar was the

World Bank Institution that focuses on funding development projects to reduce poverty

only currency to be redeemable for gold. This new system, which lasted from 1944 to 1971, was a dollar-based gold exchange standard. Through it, the U.S. dollar became both a means of international payment and a reserve currency. Later, we will discuss the effects of this arrangement on the U.S. economy and how the currency exchange rate system has evolved. In 1971, President Nixon took the United States off the gold standard by literally closing the gold window at the U.S. Treasury, where people would queue to exchange currency for gold. As the IMF struggles today with core issues related to its purpose in a changing world, some economists think that exchange rates may be an area for renewed IMF focus.

The World Bank

The **World Bank** was established along with the IMF at the Bretton Woods meeting in order to address development issues. Organized into two major and three smaller institutions, it functions as a nonprofit cooperative for its 186 member-nations, able to pass on its ability to borrow funds at low rates to developing nations. The World Bank Group's two major institutions are the International Bank for Reconstruction and Development (IBRD), also known simply as the World Bank, and the International Development Association

(IDA). Both loan to countries to support their development, the IBRD to middle income (GDP per head from $1,000 to $10,000) and creditworthy poor nations, and IDA to the poorer nations. In 2009, IBRD and IDA along with smaller institutions of the World Bank lent or provided loan guarantees of $58.8 billion to 767 projects designed to develop infrastructure, health and education, and other areas connected to development.[16] The World Bank interactive map at http://geo .worldbank.org/ has map, satellite, and hybrid views of World Bank projects. More information about the IMF, including a communiqué on the financial crisis in developed nations, can be found at www.imf.org.

The other three institutions that participate in the World Bank Group are the International Finance Corporation (IFC), which invests in companies and financial institutions in developing countries to build domestic capital markets so that local entrepreneurs have access to funding; the Multilateral Investment Guarantee Agency (MIGA), which guarantees private sector investment in developing countries through political risk insurance, technical assistance, and dispute mediation; and the International Centre for the Settlement of Investment Disputes (ICSID), which helps to resolve disputes between governments and foreign investors, and, in that way, helps build foreign direct investment.

The call for an additional bank, a World Education Bank, to fund education in all countries that ask for help was made

▼FIGURE 3.2
World Bank Lending by Region, Theme and Sector

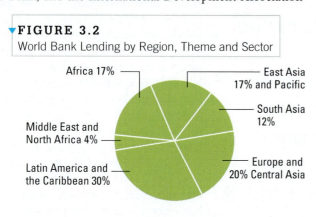

(a) IBRD and IDA Lending by Region, Fiscal 2009

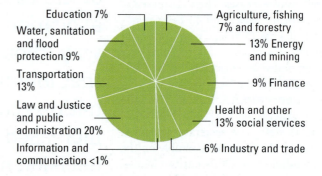

(b) IBRD and IDA Lending by Sector, Fiscal 2009

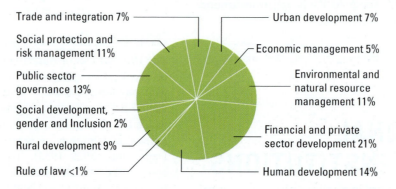

(c) IBRD and IDA Lending by Theme, Fiscal 2009

Source: http://www.worldbank.org

by the former British ambassador to the United States, Sir David Manning, in the *Financial Times* on March 3, 2008. He argued that many developing countries cannot afford to set up even primary schools, let alone the programs needed to train teachers. His rationale is that education is no longer simply a development issue; it has become a critical security and foreign policy issue for the developed nations. Those who receive no public-funded education are primary targets for extremist groups that set up schools preaching hatred.

Such a bank, though, would be for all countries, because all countries have serious educational problems. Big cities in the developed world could access the bank to make up for funding not provided by their national and local governments. The bank would be a global public–private partnership in which foundations and international businesses could play vital roles. Such collaborative efforts could change the future of millions of people. Such a bank could reduce the appeal of private, hate-mongering educational efforts and would be good for the

WTO currently has 153 members, all of whom sign on to every WTO agreement.

WTO Principles

In WTO negotiations, members have established five basic principles, norms on which the global trade system rests:[18]

World Trade Organization (WTO) An international organization that deals with rules of trade between nations

Doha Development Agenda WTO extended conference on trade

1. *Trade without discrimination.* This is the most-favored nation (MFN) principle, and it requires that nations treat all WTO members equally. If one nation grants another nation a special trade deal, that deal has to be extended to all WTO members. Another aspect of nondiscrimination is that foreigners and locals should be treated equally. This means that imported goods, once they are in the market, should not face discrimination.

> " **THE NATIONS MUST BE ORGANIZED INTERNATIONALLY AND INDUCED TO ENTER INTO PARTNERSHIP, SUBORDINATING IN SOME MEASURE NATIONAL SOVEREIGNTY TO WORLDWIDE INSTITUTIONS AND OBLIGATIONS.** "
>
> —Arthur Henderson

countries involved, good for the work forces available to international businesses, and good for the many individuals who would be helped by a primary education.[17]

LO4 Discuss the purpose of the World Trade Organization and its impact on international business.

WORLD TRADE ORGANIZATION

The **World Trade Organization (WTO)** is the only global international organization designed to establish and help implement rules of trade between nations. Since its beginning in 1995, the WTO's goal has been to reduce or eliminate trade barriers and restrictions worldwide to help producers of goods and services, exporters, and importers conduct their business by reducing costs. The WTO, a rules-based, member-driven organization with decisions negotiated by all the member governments, negotiates agreements to establish rules for equitable trade that limit the possible actions governments may take in their trade relationships, and thereby increase trade flows. The

2. *Freer trade, gradually, through negotiation.* Lower trade barriers encourage trade growth. WTO agreements establish "progressive liberalization" through gradual changes. Developing economies are given longer to make adjustments.

3. *Predictability, through binding and transparency.* Predictability helps businesses know what the real costs will be. The WTO operates with tariff "bindings," or agreements to not raise a specific tariff over a given time. Such promises are as good as lowering a tariff because they give businesspeople realistic data. Transparency, making trade rules as clear and accessible as possible, also helps businesspeople anticipate a stable future.

4. *Promoting fair competition.* Although many describe the WTO as a "free trade" organization, and it certainly does work toward trade liberalization, the WTO also realizes that trade relationships among nations can be exceedingly complex. Many WTO agreements support fair competition in agriculture, services, and intellectual property, discouraging subsidies and the dumping of products at prices below the cost of their manufacture.

5. *Encouraging development and economic reform.* Three-quarters of WTO members are developing economies and those transitioning to market economies. These nations are active in the WTO's current **Doha Development Agenda**

or extended conference. One of Doha's goals is that developed countries provide market access to goods from the very least developed countries and increase technical assistance for them. Developed countries have started to allow duty-free and quota-free imports for many products from the least developed countries, but agriculture remains a difficult area in which to build agreement.

At 2001 WTO talks in Doha, Qatar, member governments agreed to launch a new agenda and to work on trade-related issues between developed and developing economies. The WTO membership has recognized that developing nations face constraints that limit their ability to benefit from the WTO trading system, especially on issues around trade in textiles, clothing, agriculture, and fish. The WTO has recently initiated an aid program, the Aid for Trade initiative, to provide assistance to WTO members for infrastructure, technical support, and productive capacity—three areas that affect a developing

violations legendary in India, China, and Brazil. The WTO has negotiated a basic agreement that property rights should not take precedence over public health. Any country that adopts TRIPS will have the right to copy drugs patented before 1995. The WTO has also established a system of compulsory licensing that mandates that copyright holders license producers in developing countries. From 1972 to 2005, India did not have property rights protection for pharmaceuticals, which led to a huge generic drugs export market. India's joining the WTO agreement has provided patent protection for pharmaceuticals there while at the same time ensuring that its citizens have access to health care.

There is no disagreement among WTO members that the benefits of liberalized trade have, so far, been uneven. The opening of borders, new trade agreements, and other achievements of the WTO have not resulted in equal benefits for poorer nations. Instead, according to the World Commission on the Social Effects of Globalization, an International Labour Organization UN study group, the uneven benefits of globalization are building a growing divide between rich and poor among countries, as well as within countries. Globalization, it suggests,

> **"One of Doha's goals is that developed countries provide market access to goods from the very least developed countries and increase technical assistance for them."**

nation's ability to gain from trade agreements. In 2008, Aid for Trade received approval from all WTO members. Yet the Doha Development Agenda has seen discord on many other issues connected to the trading needs of developing nations. Talks held in 2003 in Cancun, Mexico, collapsed when delegates from developing nations in Africa, the Caribbean, and Asia left the meeting over disagreement with the developed nations over agricultural issues. Twenty-one nations banded together to make the case that the agricultural subsidies wealthy nations pay to their own farmers undermine poor farmers around the world. In June 2004, the WTO delegates agreed to debate a proposal from the developing nations calling for the reduction and elimination of agricultural tariffs. Then in 2005, Brazil successfully sued the United States in the WTO over cotton subsidies. The United States and the EU have each agreed in principle to reduce agricultural subsidies. Ongoing Doha discussions are scheduled for 2010.

In addition to agriculture, property rights remain a difficult negotiation area for WTO members. Their discussion of **trade-related intellectual property rights (TRIPS)** has so far led to agreement on 20-year patents and 50-year copyrights. Intellectual property rights violations are endemic in several industries, such as music, software, and pharmaceuticals, and tend to occur in a small group of developing countries, with music and software piracy rampant in China and pharmaceutical patent

"is at a turning point and international institutions need to address social inequities as well as other consequences of open borders."[19]

Although there are many issues of concern for WTO members, including farmers, women, and entrepreneurs trying to build success in developing economies, two bright spots are China and India, which together account for one-third of the global population. In both countries, absolute poverty has declined as a result of increased trade. The future growth of world trade and the economic health of developed nations depend on getting globalization right so that all participants benefit from trade, just as a rising tide lifts all boats. New markets, an educated workforce, economic growth, and political stability in emerging nations are all important for international business.[20]

Recently, in part because WTO progress on trade liberalization and addressing the inequities of globalization has been slow, regional trade agreements have grown, to fill in the gap. The WTO reports that in 2010, more than 400 regional trade agreements take effect.[21] Such agreements as the European Union and the North American Free Trade Agreement may weaken the WTO, because they disrupt or limit the trade of excluded nations. Since most of these trade agreements are among developed nations, the impact on developing nations could be substantial. We now look at these trade agreements, beginning with the process of economic integration.

free trade area (FTA) Area in which tariffs among members have been eliminated, but members keep their external tariffs

customs union Collaboration that adds common external tariffs to an FTA

common market Customs union that includes mobility of services, people, and capital within the union

complete economic integration Integration on economic and political levels

LO5 Identify the levels of economic integration

ECONOMIC INTEGRATION AGREEMENTS

Often, economic cooperation begins with an agreement to have a free trade area, such as the North American Free Trade Agreement among Canada, Mexico and the United States. In a **free trade area (FTA),** tariffs are abolished among the members, but each member-nation maintains its own external tariffs, those to countries in the rest of the world. So members have free trade among themselves but have their own trade restrictions with nonmember nations. Within the FTA, restrictions generally remain on the movement of services (such as accounting, insurance, and legal services), people (labor), and capital. Table 3.1 compares the relative sizes of the major trading blocs and trading nations.

The FTA often develops into a **customs union,** an agreement that adds common external tariffs to the FTA. Examples are the Southern African Customs Union (SACU), with membership of South Africa, Lesotho, Namibia, Swaziland, and Botswana; the Common Market of the South (Mercosur or Mercosul), with membership of Argentina, Brazil, Paraguay, and Uruguay; and the Andean Community (Peru, Ecuador, Bolivia, and Colombia).

The next level of economic integration is a **common market,** created when a customs union lifts restrictions on the mobility of services, people, and capital among the member-nations. Mercosur plans to develop in this direction. A common market is essentially a single market, so all of the barriers to trade, such as standards, borders, and taxes become common. To achieve this level of economic integration, common market members establish common economic policies, an achievement that requires a great deal of political will.

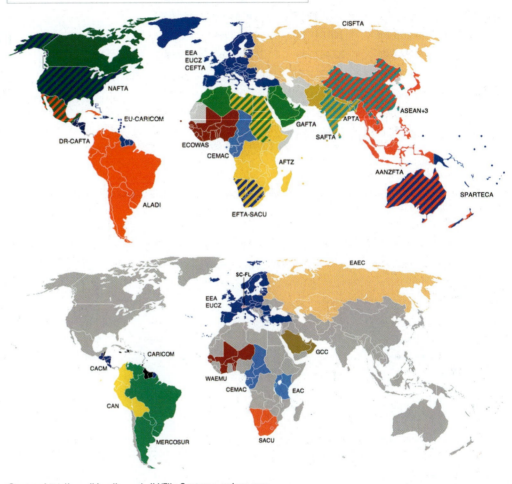

▼**FIGURE 3.3** Free Trade Areas and Customs Unions

Source: http://en.wikipedia.org/wiki/File:Customs_unions.png

Eventually the common market agreement may move toward an agreement for **complete economic integration,** as has happened with the EU. Such integration involves a high degree of political integration, which requires member-nations to surrender important elements of their sovereignty. For example, in the EU a central bureaucracy is responsible for coordinating and harmonizing tax rates, labor systems, education systems, and other social and legal systems for all EU members, while the European Central Bank develops monetary policy. A single currency, the euro, has been established to replace member-nations' currencies and is used in 16 of the member states.

Trading blocs such as FTAs and common markets impact the international firm due both to the cost reductions they bring to

▼ **TABLE 3.1** Regional Trading Blocs and Major Trading Nations

Regional Bloc	Area (sq km)	Population	GDP (US$)*	GDP per Capita**	Members
EU	3,976,372	491,582,852	$14.52 trillion	32,700	27
NAFTA	21,783,895	451,911,210	17.01 trillion	35,491	3
China	9,596,960	1,338,612,968	8.767 trillion	6,500	—
India	3,287,590	1,156,897,766	23.548 trillion	3,100	—
Russia	17,075,200	140,041,247	2.103 trillion	15,200	—
Canada	9,984,670	33,487,208	1.287 trillion	38,400	—
Mexico	1,972,550	111,211,789	1.473 trillion	13,200	—
ASEAN	4,464,322	583,651,000	1.504 trillion*	5,252.7	10
United States	9,826,675	307,212,213	14.25 trillion	46,400	—
World	510.072 million	6,790,062,216	57.53 trillion (GWP, est. 2009)	10,500 (2009, est.)	

*Purchasing power parity values, except ASEAN;

**nominal, not PPP

Sources: *CIA Factbook,* 2010, www.cia.gov/cia/publications/factbook/; ASEAN Trade Database, October 2009, www.asean.org.

▼ **FIGURE 3.4** Regional Trade Agreements in Central and South America

- Andean Community
- Central American Free Trade Zone + Dominican Republic, United States
- Mercosur
- None

those inside the integrated area, through reductions in tariffs, quotas, and other trade barriers, and to the cost increases they bring to those firms outside the trading bloc. See again Table 3.1 for relative sizes of the major trading blocs and trading nations.

EXAMPLES OF ECONOMIC INTEGRATION AGREEMENTS

The **North American Free Trade Agreement (NAFTA)** created a free trade area among Canada, Mexico, and the United States that came into existence on January 1, 1994. Since its establishment, NAFTA has paved the way for strong economic growth and prosperity based on liberalized trade among the three members.[22] Through NAFTA, the three countries have created one of the world's largest free trade zones—one of the most powerful productive forces in the global economy. Trade in North America is now virtually tariff-free. The last trade area to have tariffs dropped was U.S. corn exports into Mexico, where the many small farmers have had transitional protection from U.S. corn imports.[23]

African countries have formed regional trade groups to promote economic growth throughout the continent. Most African countries, though, have their main trade relationships with developed countries, in many cases with former colonial powers. Except for South Africa, African economies are small and underdeveloped, and governments face daunting challenges: infrastructure development; public health needs connected to HIV/AIDS, tuberculosis, and malaria; corruption; and insurgencies and civil wars. The unstable environment is not conducive to economic growth, yet the collaborations persevere. Five of these groups are the *Economic Community of West African States (ECOWAS)*, the *Common Market for Eastern and Southern Africa (COMESA)*, the *Southern African Development Community (SADC)*, the *African Free Trade Zone (AFTZ)*, and the *African Union (AU)*.

Mercosur (Spanish) or *Mercosul* (Portuguese) is an acronym for the Common Market of the South, whose members are Argentina, Brazil, Paraguay, and Uruguay. Their goal is a common market and their alliance has made progress. Most trade within Mercosur

▼**FIGURE 3.5** ASEAN Members

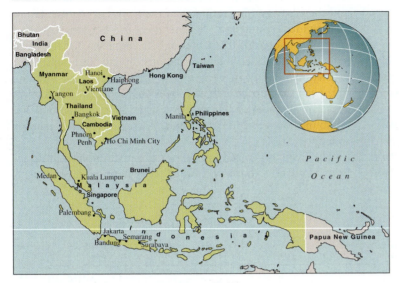

● Members of Association of Southeast Asian Nations (ASEAN).

Source: Association of Southeast Asian Nations.

is tariff-free, and members have adopted a common external tariff on most products.

The Central American Free Trade Agreement (DR-CAFTA) includes the United States, Guatemala, Honduras, Nicaragua, and El Salvador, Costa Rica and the Dominican Republic. Although there is criticism of DR-CAFTA because it is asymmetrical (the aggregate GDP of the Central American members is equal to around .5 percent of the U.S. GDP), trade figures report substantial growth in the DR-CAFTA economies, a solid portion of which is attributable to the influence of this free trade area.[24] Other Central and South American trade agreements include the Andean Community (CAN), whose members are Colombia, Peru, Ecuador, and Bolivia. Venezuela decided in 2006 to withdraw from the Andean Community.

In Asia, the Association of Southeast Asian Nations (ASEAN) was formed to foster peaceful relations among members and offer mutual protection against the growth of communism in their region. This political cooperation has led to some economic cooperation.[25] Since Southeast Asia is one of the fastest-developing and most dynamic economic regions in the world, ASEAN (Brunei, Cambodia, Indonesia, Laos, Malaysia, Myanmar [formerly Burma], the Philippines, Singapore, Thailand, and Vietnam) has increasing significance. ASEAN's initial agreement to noninterference in each other's internal affairs has allowed them to overcome conflict among themselves and to build the cohesion and mutual values needed for a common market. ASEAN+3 adds China, Japan and South Korea to foster Asian cooperation and financial stability.

The European Union, which we look at next, has developed from a customs union to a common market and then beyond,

with added political integration. Our review looks at the EU's development, then its basic organization, and finally, its impact.

L06 Discuss the EU and its impact.

THE EUROPEAN UNION

EU Development

Left in a shambles by World War II, Europeans faced rebuilding their society aware that previous economic and political systems had failed them. Out of this awareness slowly developed a willingness to relinquish some aspects of national sovereignty for the greater economic and political good. French foreign minister Robert Schuman began the process with the integration of the coal and steel industries into a common market in 1950, the European Coal and Steel Community (ECSC). The initial six members—Belgium, West Germany, France, Italy, Luxembourg, and the Netherlands—signed the Treaty of Rome in 1957, which established a common market among the six members. By 1967, this core group had established the European Community (EC), with a European Parliament, a European Commission, and a Council of Ministers. Then, in 1993, the EC members signed the Maastricht Treaty, which established the **European Union (EU),** with three areas of integration: the economic community, foreign policy, and domestic affairs. Denmark, Ireland, and the United Kingdom joined the EU's six founding members in 1973, followed by Greece in 1981; Spain and Portugal in 1986; and Austria, Finland, and Sweden in 1995. The European Union welcomed 10 new countries in 2004: Cyprus, the Czech Republic, Estonia, Hungary, Latvia, Lithuania, Malta, Poland, Slovakia, and Slovenia. In 2007, Bulgaria and Romania joined. Presently there are three candidate countries: Croatia, the former Yugoslav Republic of Macedonia, and Turkey—all of which have been approved for accession with entry dates still to be set, and Serbia is in talks to join the candidates. Today the European Union's 27 member-countries constitute most of the economic, industrial, and population strengths of Europe.[26] The population of the EU is 500 million people, about 60 percent larger than that of the United States. The EU has 7.3 percent of the world's population, and its trade with the rest of the world makes up 20 percent of global imports and exports.[27] Notable are the Western European countries that have rejected membership in the EU, Switzerland and Norway, both of which made the decision not to join based on national

European Monetary Union (EMU) or Economic and Monetary Union EU group that established use of the euro in the 16-country euro zone

elections. Figure 3.6 shows a map of the present EU.

The EU is a supranational body that has become a regional government. With passage of the Lisbon Treaty, which came into effect in 2009, the EU has modernized its institutions, made them more democratic, and moved forward with integration in the areas of foreign affairs, security, and justice. The **European Monetary Union (EMU), or Economic and Monetary Union,** as it is known in Europe, already has established a common currency used in 16 of the EU member-countries. The euro (€) is also used widely as a reserve currency, as an alternative to the dollar. Recently, the European commissioner for economic and monetary affairs called for EU representation at the IMF and the G20 as a bloc rather than their present representation as individual countries.[28] EU members use EU passports and can move and work freely among EU countries, for the most part; the EU can tax member-nations directly and implement legislation directly in each of the member-nations; and the European Court of Justice has power to impose fines and other sanctions on individuals, companies, and member-nations that are found to violate EU agreements. A regional government is well under way.

The EU is organized into nine main institutions with functions similar to those performed by a national government.

▼**FIGURE 3.6**
European Union: Current Member-Nations and Candidate Nations

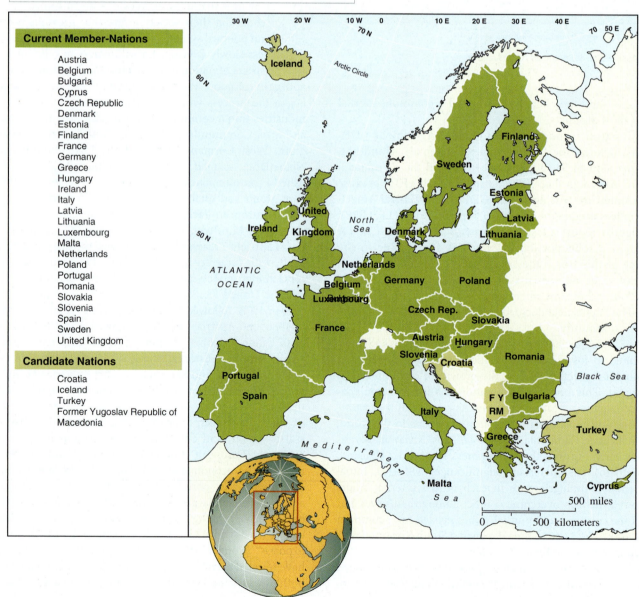

Current Member-Nations

Austria
Belgium
Bulgaria
Cyprus
Czech Republic
Denmark
Estonia
Finland
France
Germany
Greece
Hungary
Ireland
Italy
Latvia
Lithuania
Luxembourg
Malta
Netherlands
Poland
Portugal
Romania
Slovakia
Slovenia
Spain
Sweden
United Kingdom

Candidate Nations

Croatia
Iceland
Turkey
Former Yugoslav Republic of Macedonia

Source: European Union, http://europa.eu/abc/maps/index_en.htm, February 2, 2010 © European Commission

The **European Parliament** represents the people of Europe and is elected from member-states. Its sessions are available live at www.europarl.europa.eu. The **Council of the European Union** represents the member-states and is the primary policy-setting institution of the EU. When the Council meets, the minister who represents the specific area being discussed serves as the representative of the member-nation. When financial matters are discussed, for example, the finance ministers of all member-nations are present. Council decisions are supranational and are set forth in regulations and directives. Recent directives deal with foreign policy issues (terrorism, weapons of mass destruction control, Burma/Myanmar) and issues of health and safety (flu tracking and precautions, disaster planning, workplace safety equipment, computer use rules,

European Parliament EU legislative body whose members are popularly elected from member-nations

Council of the European Union The EU's primary policy-setting institution

CU in IB

Lin Chiang Builds his International Career

Lin Chiang graduated from Fontbonne College, St. Louis, Missouri, with an MBA in international business. His undergraduate work was done in accounting, statistics, and business in Taiwan. Lin is lucky, because Taiwan's economic dependence on foreign trade meant that he could begin working directly in the international arena once he finished his education. In contrast, many Americans can expect to spend a year or two with their company before they move into international responsibilities.

Lin is an international marketing manager in the Photonics Division of Universal Microelectronics Co., Ltd. (UMEC), headquartered in Taichung, Taiwan, R.O.C. UMEC is an ISO-9001/140001, QS-9000 certified company and one of the world's leading manufacturers in the area of photonics products, including fiber-optic active and passive components, CATV integrated systems, magnetic components, power supplies, telecommunication products, and OEM assemblies. More than 80 percent of their production is for export into world markets. UMEC has branch offices in Taipei, Taiwan; ShenZenh, China; Hong Kong; Los Angeles, California; Minneapolis, Minnesota; Germany; and Italy. UMEC factories are located in Taichung, Taiwan, and in ShenZeng and Ningbo, China. Lin's work for the firm takes him to Japan, China, Thailand, Sweden, Denmark, Holland, Germany, Italy, France, the UK, and 23 U.S. cities.

> " Note that, in this sense, background in the liberal arts can be a significant strength. "

Lin's advice on how to get a job in international business is to educate yourself for global business. "It is not difficult to get a job in international business. You only have to get a degree (in international business) or a related degree or related knowledge. Have language skills. English is the most popular language and Chinese is getting important. If you can understand both English and Chinese you can communicate with almost two-thirds of the people in the world." So the first step is to prepare yourself through education, including languages. Even a semester of Mandarin is helpful. Essentially, Lin is suggesting that during your education, you have the opportunity to build a global mindset, a cosmopolitan openness to diversity combined with an ability to synthesize across this diversity. He further suggests that you know about sports, music and art, and understand the culture in which you want to do business. Note that, in this sense, background in the liberal arts can be a significant strength.

Here are a few international institutions that provide career opportunities you might investigate: IMF (www.imf.org), the World Bank (www.worldbank.org), the World Trade Organization (www.wto.org), and the United Nations (www.un.org). This is just a beginning; you can add nongovernmental organizations (NGOs), governmental organizations such as the State Department or foreign service, and security and military organizations. Northwestern University compiles a directory of international institutions you might find a good source of additional career opportunities. See www.library.northwestern.edu/govpub/resource/. . ./igo.html

and environmental safety for workers). The **European Commission** administers the daily operations of the EU. It consists of 27 commissioners, one from each member-nation. Commission members are nominated by their countries, appointed by the Commission president-elect, and then approved by a vote of the European Parliament.

The remaining six EU institutions focus on financial and social issues. The *Court of Auditors* is the financial conscience of the EU. It reviews the spending of EU funds to make certain the spending is legal and for the intended purpose. EU funding is tax-based and includes the value-added tax (VAT), customs duties, and other fees paid by member-states. The *European Economic and Social Committee (EESC)* is an advisory and consultative body of specialists in areas of occupational and social interest. The 344 members are nominated by national governments to serve four-year terms to represent employers, employees, and other social interests. The *Committee of the Regions (CoR)* is a consultative group that represents local viewpoints on issues such as transportation, education, and health. The CoR ensures that the EU continues its commitment to four levels of participation: local, regional, national, and European. The *European Investment Bank* finances projects promoting EU objectives. The **European Central Bank (ECB)** manages the euro to ensure the price stability of European markets, largely by managing interest rates. It makes decisions independent of

Flag of the European Union.

27 nations have scrapped more than 60 million customs and tax formalities at their shared borders. It is the world's largest trading economy, a large source of FDI outflows, and the source of approximately 26 percent of the world's total output. The introduction of the euro is one of the most significant achievements of the EU.

These EU successes significantly impact the conduct of business in several different ways. In some areas, such as the use of a common currency and common import processes, the cost of doing business within the EU has been reduced. A significant number of EU regulations have major impact in the United States, Japan, China, and elsewhere, because of the EU's size and importance as a trading partner. EU standards tend to be advanced, especially in ecology and sustainability requirements. For example, in an effort to prevent electronic equipment waste, the EU requires recycling of at least 50 percent of all equipment, including cell phones, computers, household

> "If foreign companies want access to the EU market, they must conduct business by the European Union's rules, often at the global level as well as within the EU."

member governments. The **European Court of Justice (ECJ)** decides cases arising under the Treaty of Rome and subsequent agreements. On EU matters, its authority supersedes that of the member-nations' national courts. The influence of the ECJ is growing steadily as it decides an increasing number of cases.

The EU's Impact on International Business

The EU is a major world political and economic force. Its directives have superseded 27 sets of national rules and harmonized hundreds of thousands of national standards, labeling laws, testing procedures, and consumer protection measures covering everything from toys to food, stock brokering to teaching. The

appliances, and televisions. It requires 80 percent recovery by weight for larger appliances, 75 percent for IT and telecommunications equipment, and 70 percent for small appliances. In addition, the manufacturers are required to provide collection for the waste that is not from private households. We may expect even more progress with continued European integration.

Microsoft is an example of a company whose business practices have been substantially influenced by the EU. In 2004, the European Commission ordered the company to pay €497 million, share its software code with competitors, and offer an unbundled version of the Windows operating system. Microsoft complied. Then, in 2005, the EU ruled that Microsoft would be fined $2.37 million per day if the software code it provided competitors didn't have better documentation. In 2008, the EU imposed a $1.35 billion fine, because Microsoft had not complied fully with its 2004 order to share code. The point is clear: if foreign companies want access to the EU market, they must conduct business by the European Union's rules, often at the global level as well as within the EU.

This chapter has reviewed institutions and focused on their importance to managers engaged in IB. Next we address the environmental forces to which the international manager has to adjust, beginning with sociocultural forces. ■

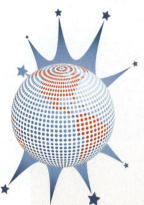

GLOBAL gauntlet

Do International Institutions Weaken the Nation-State?

One of the major forces of opposition to global institutions such as we have reviewed in this chapter are groups concerned with their nation's sovereignty, briefly understood as the authority of their nation to govern itself. Many groups hold that supranational agreements are an assault on the nation's independence. Their concern is that, for example, United Nations treaties and conventions would weaken the power of their nation to make its own decisions. A specific example of this is found in the U.S. refusal to ratify the UN Convention on the Rights of the Child, which would, the claim is, hold international law over state and federal laws protecting the rights of parents to make decisions related to their children's upbringing and education. The Kyoto Protocol on Climate Change is another example. The argument here is that such an international agreement on emissions would modify the power of the state and federal government to regulate in this area. Ratification of foreign treaties and agreements requires a two-thirds vote in the Senate. One of the counter-arguments to the sovereignty position is that the benefits gained from joining in such supranational agreements far outweigh their trade-offs. This is especially the case with issues whose limits do not fall on international borders, such as climate change and pollution. What do you think?

coming  up

I n Chapter 1, we stated that many practices followed at home can be transferred intact to other countries. However, we also mentioned that, because of the differences in environmental forces, some ways of doing business must be adapted to local conditions or changed completely.

In Section Two, we examine these forces to see how they differ from those we encounter at home. We begin Section Two with Chapter 4, which discusses cultural forces and points out that the variety of attitudes and values among cultures affects managers of all the business functions in ways that can require them to behave differently than they would have done at home. Next we look at the physical forces—location, topography, and climate, along with natural resources and environmental sustainability (Chapter 5).

In Chapter 6, we explore socioeconomic and political forces, including the underground economy, nationalism and terrorism. Then, in Chapter 7, we look at legal forces, an additional set of constraints within which firms must operate.

Our discussion then moves to the international monetary system and financial forces in Chapter 8. Topics here include currency exchange risks, currency exchange controls, taxation and inflation, and the balance of payments accounts. Finally, in Chapter 9, we look at the labor force, its composition, skills, and attitudes. ■

INTERNATIONAL ENVIRONMENTAL FORCES

"Speaking about cultural differences among Europeans . . . it is no good focusing on similarities and common interests and hoping things will work out. We have to recognize the differences and work with them."

—Dr. Allan Hjorth, Copenhagen Business School, trainer in cross-cultural behavior

sociocultural
forces

four

The national characteristics of culture we encounter in our discussions are generalizations. They are broadly true, but there are always exceptions. Furthermore, characteristics or characterizations may change over time. The Scandinavians were considered by a 10th-century writer to be "the filthiest race God ever created," and a noted 18th-century writer was amazed at the lack of German military spirit and how easygoing Germans were compared to the French.[1] We begin our discussion of the significance of culture for international businesspeople with a review of culture's definition.

LEARNING OBJECTIVES

After reading this chapter, you should be able to:

LO1 Describe what culture is.

LO2 Explain the significance of culture differences for international business.

LO3 Describe Hall's concept of high and low context.

LO4 Describe Hofstede's framework.

LO5 Outline Trompenaars' dimensions.

LO6 Discuss the sociocultural aspects of culture as a phenomenon.

L01   Describe what culture is.

WHAT IS CULTURE?

Although there are many useful definitions of culture, most anthropologists view culture as the *sum total of the beliefs, rules, techniques, institutions, and artifacts that characterize human populations.*[2] In other words, culture consists of the "individual worldviews, social rules, and interpersonal dynamics characterizing a group of people set in a particular time and place."[3] Most anthropologists also agree that:

1. Culture is *learned;* we are not born with a culture.

2. The various aspects of culture are *interrelated.*

3. Culture is *shared, patterned, and mutually constructed through social interaction.*

4. Culture *defines the boundaries* of different groups.[4]

a lifetime in a culture, or (2) undergo an extensive training program that covers the main characteristics of a culture, including the language. Such a program is much more than a briefing on a country's customs. It is a study of what culture is and what it does, building an understanding of the various ways in which human behavior has been institutionalized in the country.[7]

To be successful in their relationships with people in other countries, international businesspeople need to be students of culture. They need factual knowledge, which is relatively easy to obtain, but they must also become sensitive to cultural differences, and this type of knowledge is more difficult to obtain, as Hall's observation suggests. Most newcomers to international business do not have the opportunities Hall recommends. They need to hit the ground running, so to speak, and can rarely afford the time necessary for in-depth study of new cultures. They can, however, take the important first step of realizing that there *are* other cultures. In this chapter we point out some of the important areas of sociocultural difference that concern businesspeople. We hope that you will remember that there are cultural differences for which you must look, and

> ## "Culture is a little like dropping an Alka-Seltzer into a glass—you don't see it, but somehow it does something."
> —Hans Magnus Enzensberger

Society is composed of people living within their cultural frameworks, so, to understand a specific society, how it works, what its norms and values are, we need to understand its culture. Yet culture cannot be directly observed; we learn about it by observing the social world in which it exists. Because of their close linkage, anthropologists often combine the terms *social* and *cultural* into the term **sociocultural,**[5] and we follow their practice.

When people work in societies and cultures different from their own, they have to communicate across cultural borders, with cultures they may not understand. A failure to communicate across one cultural border is problematic; such problems are magnified with the multiple cultures of a firm's foreign markets. In addition, most societies consider their culture superior to all others (**ethnocentricity**).[6] You can see that any attempt to introduce one's own approach in a business environment (the "German way" or the "American way") may be met with stubborn resistance.

How do international businesspeople learn to live with, work in, and meet business goals in other cultures? The first step is to realize that the cultures are different from their own. Then they need to learn the characteristics of those cultures so that they may adapt to them. The anthropologist E. T. Hall claims this can be accomplished in only two ways: (1) spend

that you will seek out opportunities to build your knowledge of other cultures.

The concept of culture is broad; it includes everything. Ethnologists break their study of culture into focused areas such as aesthetics, attitudes and beliefs, religion, material culture, language, societal organization, education, legal characteristics, and political structures. We will look at several of these specific areas going forward. First, though, we review the significance of culture for business and explore several frameworks international managers find useful to build their understanding of other cultures.

L02   Explain the significance of culture differences for international business.

CULTURE AFFECTS ALL BUSINESS FUNCTIONS

Everything we do is influenced by culture, and most of us realize that about other cultures, but not always about our own. Thinking about how national cultural differences can affect the functional areas of a business with an international presence is a good place to begin our focus on culture.

Marketing

In marketing, the wide variation across cultures in attitudes and values requires that many firms use different marketing mixes in different markets. To develop effective marketing campaigns, the marketer has to understand the foreign market the firm is selling into, and the understanding has to be at a subtle level. The closer the marketer can come to understanding how potential purchasers in the target market give meaning to what occurs in their worlds and how they think their worlds should be, the better. Many businesses have made costly mistakes with product introductions into foreign markets, in physical property design, inappropriate copy for advertisements, and pricing. Through these errors, they learn the importance of understanding their markets, even though acquiring knowledge about a new culture is both time-consuming and expensive. Major misunderstandings in marketing due to cultural misunderstandings abound, and you can read about some of them at a website on which an international marketing consultant tracks and reports on them: www.deborahswallow.com/2009/08/20/cross-cultural-marketing-blunders/.

> "Through these errors, they learn the importance of understanding their markets."

Human Resources

Sociocultural values play key roles in motivation and evaluation of employees. In some cultures, individual effort is rewarded, while in others, group effort is more highly valued. Other values that come into play often connect to attitudes toward status. Is social status something we earn, through achievements, what we do, or is it a result of our family's social position, who we are? For example, Americans, who expect to be promoted based on their accomplishments, often are surprised to learn what a significant role schooling in the "right" institutions and family background play in this process in Great Britain. Personnel problems can result from differences in attitudes toward authority, another sociocultural variable. Is the manager the *patron,* an authoritarian figure responsible for their employees' welfare? Or is the manager one among equals? Is the control process of an annual review widely seen as a way to credit the employee's work and help the employee grow, or a way to exact higher labor output from the worker?

Production

Production managers have found that attitudes toward change can seriously influence the acceptance of new production methods. Plant layout is also influenced by culture. The assembly line is the product of minds socialized in a linear culture in which the task receives primary focus, not the social relationship. In procurement, sociocultural norms and rules structure the way the firm acquires resources. In Japan, procurement often exists in a web of social relationships and friendships, whereas in the United States, transparency and price frequently drive the process.

Accounting and Finance

A culture's accounting controls directly relate to the culture's assumptions about the basic nature of people. Are the controls tight throughout the organization, perhaps suggesting low levels of trust at cultural levels, or loose, suggesting that the culture assumes people will act honestly, even when they are not closely monitored? Are the controls formal, gaining compliance through rules and sanctions, or informal, gaining compliance through social norms (Chapter 3)? Treasurers realize the strength of the sociocultural forces when, armed with excellent balance sheets, they approach local banks, only to find that the banks in some cultures attach far more importance to who they are than to how strong their companies are or how strong they appear to be on paper. Also, in some cultures financial statements are notoriously unreliable, as the local culture allows creative accounting to keep the tax man away.

Preferred Leadership Styles

Leadership traits vary by culture, as well. Is the usual relationship between leader and followers hierarchical or more lateral? Is the leadership model paternalistic? Heroic? Does the ideal leader come up through the ranks, or is the ideal leader someone placed in the leadership position due to family or status? The function of leadership also may be understood differently, depending on culture. Does leadership integrate a group of people or is it to provide direction for a collection of individuals?

FRAMEWORKS TO COMPARE CULTURES

We have seen that sociocultural forces are important to international business. Increasingly, one useful way managers build a quick sense of a culture is to use a framework. These frameworks help managers build ways to understand behavior patterns across cultural borders. As we review these frameworks, remember that their use is comparative: our own culture functions as an implicit reference point.

The studies of national-level differences in values on which the frameworks are based include work by Kluckhohn and Strodtbeck,[8] Hall,[9] House,[10] Hofstede,[11] and Trompenaars.[12] Here we briefly look at three of these: Hall's, Hofstede's, and Trompenaars'. Hall's theoretical framework is simple and yet powerful; Hofstede's dimensions are empirically derived and have received significant attention; and Trompenaars' work integrates concepts that are derived from the social sciences.

context The relevant environment

monochronic Having to do with linear time, sequential activities

polychronic Having to do with simultaneous activities, multi-tasking

LO3 Describe Hall's concept of high and low context.

Hall's High and Low Context

Hall offers a classification of cultures based upon communication styles and, specifically, on the role that **context** plays in the communication patterns. The context of the communication act is the relevant environment beyond the explicit communication. For example, part of context may be the speaker's body language, place in the room, and who speaks before and after the speaker.

Hall suggests that in high context (HC), the communication tends to be implicit and indirect. Context plays an exceedingly strong role, actually carrying much of the meaning. In these cultures, such as Japan, China, Latin American and Middle Eastern countries, communication is more subtle and inferred. (See Figure 4.1.)

In contrast, Hall notes that people in low context cultures have explicit communication patterns. They do not rely so greatly on the context of the communication. The explicit communicator is direct and unambiguous: What you say is what you mean. In North America, communication tends to be low context (LC), direct and to-the-point. In LC cultures, to "tell it like it is" is understood to be a positive trait. Figure 4.2 shows examples of HC and LC cultures, along with examples of the concept applied to occupations.

To look at the social dimensions of Hall's framework, in LC cultures, people tend to have many connections that endure for short time periods. Because the stored mutual history is minimal, explicit communication ensures that the intended meaning is communicated. In HC culture societies, people have close connections over a long period of time, so much of the meaning is already known because it resides in the context. Figure 4.1 shows these communication relationships and further describes behaviors connected with these two communication patterns.

Hall's work also suggests that LC cultures tend to be **monochronic,** with time characterized as linear, tangible, and divisible into blocks, consistent with the economic approach to time.[13] Monochronic time emphasizes planning and the establishment of schedules, with significant energy put into the maintenance of established schedules. In contrast, HC cultures tend to be **polychronic.** That is, two or more activities are carried out within the same clock block; switching among activities can be both desirable and productive. We think of this as multi-tasking.[14]

LO4 Review Hofstede's framework.

Hofstede's Five Dimensions

Hofstede is a Dutch business researcher and consultant trained in anthropology. He developed his framework from surveys he administered to global IBM employees in the late

▼**FIGURE 4.1**
High and Low Context Attributes

High Context

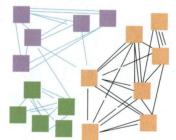

- Less verbally explicit communication, less written/formal information
- More internalized understandings of what is communicated
- Multiple cross-cutting ties and intersections with others
- Long term relationships
- Strong boundaries—insider/outsider
- Knowledge is situational, relational
- Decisions and activities focus around personal face-to-face relationships, often around a central authority person

Low Context

- Rule oriented, people play by external rules
- More knowledge is codified, public, external, and accessible.
- Sequencing, separation—of time, of space, of activities, of relationships
- More interpersonal connections of shorter duration
- Knowledge is more often transferable
- Task-centered. Decisions and activities focus around what needs to be done, division of responsibilities.

Source: Modified from www.culture-at-work.com/highlow.html (accessed June 5, 2010)

1960s, augmenting them later, and the framework is concerned primarily with work values.[15] With his early work, he developed four dimensions with which to classify the survey data that underlie and differentiate cultures: individualism-collectivism, power distance, uncertainty avoidance, and masculinity-femininity. In collaboration with researchers in Asia, he later added a fifth dimension, long-term orientation, having recognized that his earlier work represented a Western perspective. This fifth dimension is sometimes referred to as Confucian Dynamism. His initial data base had not included Asian cultures in which IBM had had less exposure at the time. These five dimensions provide managers with a way to understand how cultural differences affect organizations and management methods. They also assist in showing that management skills are culturally specific; that is, "a management technique or philosophy that is appropriate in one national culture is not necessarily appropriate in another."[16] Now to the dimensions.

Individualism-Collectivism[17]

The individualism-collectivism dimension measures the degree to which people in the culture are integrated into groups. People in highly *collectivistic* cultures belong to strong, cohesive in-groups that look after them in exchange for loyalty. The force of this dimension can be illustrated with the Japanese saying: "the nail that sticks up gets hammered down." In contrast, people in highly *individualistic* cultures are more loosely connected and look after themselves and their immediate family. The United States is highly individualistic; the culture rewards independence; the education system rewards outstanding individuals. This dimension plays out strongly in employee motivation and decision making. Countries with predominantly individualist cultures are the United States, Canada, the United Kingdom, Australia, the Netherlands, New Zealand, Sweden, France, and Germany. Cultures that are collectivist include Guatemala, Ecuador, Panama, Indonesia, Pakistan, Taiwan, China, Japan, and West and East African countries.

High Context	High Context
Japanese	
Chinese	Human resources
Arab	Marketing/Sales
Greek	Management
Mexican	
Spanish	Manufacturing
Italian	Products
French	R&D
French Canadian	
English	Technical
English Canadian	Information Systems
American (US)	
Scandanavian	Engineers
German	Finance
German-Swiss	
Low Context	Low Context

Power Distance

Power distance is the extent to which members of a society expect and accept power to be distributed unequally. Power distance is similar to inequality, but defined from below, not from above. The dimension suggests that a society's level of inequality is endorsed by followers as well as by leaders. In large-power-distance societies, seniority, age, rank and title are important. People will want directions, and formality is emphasized. In a small-power-distance environment, a consultative style of leadership predominates, informality tends to be the norm, and there is equal distance among people. For example, just about everyone in the United States self-identifies as middle-class. Examples of large-power-distance cultures are Malaysia, Guatemala, Panama, Philippines, Arab countries, India, West African countries, and Singapore. Examples of small-power-distance countries include Austria, Israel, Denmark, New Zealand, Republic of Ireland, Sweden, Norway, Canada, United States, and Germany.

Long-Term Orientation Characteristics	Short-Term Orientation Characteristics
Social order	Personal survival/security
Hierarchical relationships	Personal respect/dignity
Collective face-saving	Individual face-saving
Long-term planning	Short- to medium-term planning
Thrift-centered	Spending-centered
Long-term outcomes	Short- to medium-term outcomes
Examples	**Examples**
China	Pakistan
Hong Kong	Nigeria
Taiwan	Philippines
Japan	Canada
South Korea	Zimbabwe
India	United Kingdom
Brazil	United States
Singapore	Germany

▼ TABLE 4.2 Selected Scores for Hofstede's Cultural Dimensions

Country	Power Distance	Uncertainty Avoidance	Individualism	Masculinity	Long-Term orientation*
Mexico	81	82	30	69	
Venezuela	81	76	12	73	
Colombia	64	80	13	64	
Peru	90	87	16	42	
Chile	63	86	23	28	
Portugal	63	104	27	31	
China	80	30	20	66	118
Japan	52	92	46	95	80
United States	50	46	91	62	29
Australia	49	51	90	61	31
South Africa (SAF)	49	49	65	63	
New Zealand	45	49	79	58	30
Canada	39	48	80	52	23
United Kingdom	35	35	89	66	25
Ireland	28	35	70	68	

*Data for long-term orientation have not been collected for many countries yet, so these are blank.
Source: Geert Hofstede, "Cultural Dimensions in Management and Planning," *Asia Pacific Journal of Management,* January 1984, p. 83.

Uncertainty Avoidance *Uncertainty avoidance* describes a society's comfort with uncertainty. Hofstede points out that this dimension "ultimately refers to man's search for Truth" because it describes the extent a culture programs its members to feel either uncomfortable or comfortable in unstructured situations. Cultures that avoid uncertainty try to minimize the possibility of such situations by "strict laws and rules, safety and security measures." Strong uncertainty avoidance cultures resist change, including career change and organizational change, expect clear procedures, and preserve the status quo. Weak uncertainty avoidance cultures see conflict as having positive aspects, expect innovation, encourage risk taking, and reward career change. Examples of strong uncertainty avoidance cultures are Greece, Portugal, Guatemala, Uruguay, Japan, France, Spain, South Korea. Examples of weak uncertainty avoidance cultures include Singapore, Jamaica, Denmark, Sweden, Hong Kong, United States, Canada, Norway, and Australia.

Masculinity-Femininity The *masculinity-femininity* dimension describes the distribution of roles between the genders. Hofstede's data indicate that "women's roles across cultures differ less than do men's, and that men's values among countries vary considerably, from very assertive and competitive and maximally different from women's values on the one side, to modest and caring and similar to women's values on the other." The assertive pole is masculine, and the caring one feminine. "The women in feminine countries have the same modest, caring values as the men; in the masculine countries they are somewhat assertive and competitive, but not as much as the men, so that these countries show a gap between men's values and women's values." Note that this dimension is about *the gap between* men's and women's roles in the culture. In a feminine culture, there is relatively less variation between male and female roles, which suggests that leadership and decision-making roles would be equally open to men and women. Quality of work life is important, people work in order to live, and environmental issues matter from a business perspective. In a masculine culture, male roles are more likely to be task focused and female roles relationship focused, achievements are emphasized, economic growth is central, people live in order to work, and business performance is the primary goal. Examples of masculine cultures include Japan, Austria,

Venezuela, Italy, Mexico, and the Philippines. Examples of feminine cultures include Sweden, Norway, the Netherlands, Denmark, Costa Rica, and Finland. A word of caution: to think that feminine cultures are not concerned with production and business success, just think of the globally successful Scandinavian firms in order to correct your misapprehension: Ikea, Nokia, Lego, Volvo, Ericsson, H&M, Bang & Olufson, and Carlsberg begin the list.

Long-Term Orientation/ Confucian Dynamism[19]
This dimension came from a study among students in 23 countries around the world, using a questionnaire designed by Chinese scholars. Hofstede describes it as dealing with Virtue regardless of Truth, that is, the level to which people in the culture will persevere to overcome obstacles they cannot overcome with will or strength. In long-term-oriented societies, people value actions and attitudes that affect the future: persistence/perseverance, thrift, saving face at the group level, and shame. In short-term-oriented societies, values connected to the present and past are stronger: respect for tradition, fulfilling social obligations, high consumption patterns, and protecting face at the individual level. Because this dimension is often misinterpreted, a brief chart is shown in Table 4.1.

Table 4.2 presents the scores for Hofstede's five dimensions for about one-third of the countries in his sample.

Figure 4.3 plots the scores for selected nations on the power-distance and uncertainty-avoidance dimensions. The Latin American countries in the second quadrant had high power distance and strong uncertainty avoidance. These scores suggest that lines of communication in organizations in these countries will be vertical, employees will prefer directive management styles, and risk taking will be avoided. By clearly defining roles and procedures, the organizations are very predictable. The Anglo nations in the fourth quadrant had small power distance and weak uncertainty avoidance. Organizations in these countries are characterized by less

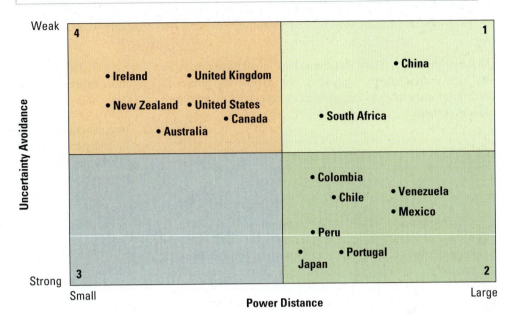

▼ **FIGURE 4.3** Plot of Selected Nations on Power Distance and Uncertainty Avoidance

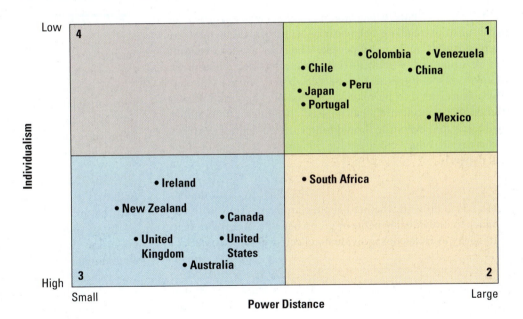

▼ **FIGURE 4.4** Plot of Selected Nations on Individualism and Power Distance

formal controls and fewer layers of management, along with more participative leadership styles. Relationships tend to be informal. Note, too, that Japan and China have quite different scores.

The scores for individualism and power distance are plotted in Figure 4.4. The Latin and Asian countries (first quadrant) scored relatively high on power distance and weak on individualism. Employees tend to expect their organizations to look after them and defend their interests. They expect close supervision and managers who act paternally. On the other hand, people in the Anglo countries (third quadrant) have small power distance and high individualism, suggesting that they would prefer to do things for themselves and would not expect organizations to look after them.

LO5 Outline Trompenaars' dimensions.

Trompenaars' Seven Dimensions

Fons Trompenaars, trained as an economist, is also Dutch. His seven-dimension framework for understanding culture is derived from the social sciences, and his initial data are from 47 countries, later greatly expanded in collaboration with Hampden-Turner. The first five dimensions address the culture's patterns for relationships among people, and the final two have to do with time and nature.[20]

Universalism vs. Particularism (rules vs. relationships)
This dimension addresses whether rules or relationships regulate behaviors. A culture's values that are **universalist** apply to all people. The rules are for everyone in all situations. **Particularist** values consider the context. Universalist cultures tend to be rules-based, while particularist cultures tend to be relationship-based. The United States tends to be moderately rules-based (in ethics, for example, we think that everyone should follow the guidelines or rules), whereas in other cultures, the judgment is situational—it all depends.

Individualism vs. Communitarianism
This dimension has to do with whether people plan their actions with reference to individual benefits or group benefits. You will note its similarity to Hofstede's individual-collectivism dimension.

Neutral vs. Affective (unemotional vs. emotional)
This dimension describes the culture's rules for display of emotions. People in neutral cultures tend to withhold emotional expression, while people in affective cultures are much more expressive.

Specific vs. Diffuse
The specific-diffuse dimension distinguishes among cultures based on the social patterns for public and private life. In specific cultures, there is a small private life that is kept private, with a large public life, with many relationships that may be brief. In a diffuse culture, there is a large private life and a smaller public life that is more difficult to enter. In a diffuse culture, there is no clear distinction between work life and private life.

Achievement vs. Ascription
This dimension focuses on the basis of social status and reward, with status being related to either who a person is or what a person does. Ascription cultures consider who a person is by family lineage or age, or other attributes. Achievement cultures are meritocracies that reward what you do. In the United States, for example, achievement is the primary determinant of social status. This dimension may be especially helpful with staffing and interpersonal dynamics.

Attitudes toward Time
Trompenaars' time dimension has two aspects. The first is where the primary focus exists, on the past, the present, or the future. Past-focused cultures use history as a lens to view the present. Present-focused cultures focus on what is happening now. Future-oriented cultures plan, anticipate, and see a better world evolving. The second aspect to the time dimension is whether actions are sequential (linear) or synchronous (polychronic).

Attitudes toward the Environment
Our relationship with nature is the basis of this dimension. Are we in harmony with nature or does our understanding of the natural order of things (our culture) suggest that we control nature? North American Anglo cultures tend to assume that they are meant to dominate nature. This can-do attitude does not allow natural obstacles such as oceans and mountains get in the way of progress. Other cultures may be more inclined to seek harmony with nature rather than to dominate it. The impact of

> We need to recognize the limitations of these frameworks and use them to help us understand the complex reality we face, not to limit our perceptions.

FIGURE 4.5
Examples of Country Rankings on Trompenaars' Dimensions

China

Dimension		
Universal --X-----	Particularist
Individualist ------------------------------------- X --------	Collectivist
Neutral--X-------------	Affective
Specific--- X ---	Diffuse
Achievement---X---	Ascription

Mexico

Dimension		
Universal --------------------------------- X -----------------	Particularist
Individualist ------------- X ---------------------------------	Collectivist
Neutral--X--	Affective
Specific------------------------------------ X --------------------	Diffuse
Achievement------- X ---------------------------------------	Ascription

United States

Dimension		
Universal --- X--	Particularist
Individualist -- X ---------------------------------------	Collectivist
Neutral--X-----------------	Affective
Specific------------- X --------------------------------	Diffuse
Achievement--X--	Ascription

this dimension influences obvious areas such as infrastructure development, and also ways people think about obstacles in the external world. Do they adjust or reconfigure?

Figure 4.5 illustrates an application of Trompenaars' dimensions to China, Mexico, and the United States.

As we conclude this review of culture frameworks, a few words of caution about how to use them is in order: the data of both Hofstede and Trompenaars are a normal distribution within a national culture of the specific value dimension. The specific score of each dimension represents its mean for each country, the central tendency. So you will find people in the culture at all points on the distribution curve. The dimensions suggest that people from a specific culture think and behave in a certain way. Such generalizations are at best sophisticated stereotypes of the complex culture we are trying to understand.[21] This is an important caution. Remember, too, that these data have been analyzed on a national level and do not recognize the existence of subcultures. Cultural frameworks are useful tools, but we need to recognize the limitations of these frameworks and use them to help us understand the complex reality we face, not to limit our perceptions.

aesthetics A culture's sense of beauty and good taste

material culture or artifacts All human-made objects; concerned with *how* people make things (technology) and *who* makes *what* and *why* (economics)

L06 Discuss the sociocultural aspects of culture as a phenomenon.

SOCIOCULTURAL ASPECTS OF CULTURE

Now that we have discussed what culture is, its importance to international business managers, and the frameworks available to help build our understanding of specific cultures, we focus on some of the sociocultural aspects of cultural variation, that is, how a society's culture manifests or shows itself, through aesthetics, religion, material culture, language, and social organization and a special, albeit brief, focus on gift giving.

Aesthetics

Aesthetics describe a culture's sense of beauty and taste and is expressed in its art, drama, music, folklore, and dance.

Art Of particular interest to international businesspeople are art, color, and form because of their symbolic meanings. For example, colors carry different meanings in different cultures. The color of mourning is black in the United States and Mexico, black and white in the Far East, and purple in Brazil. Green is a propitious color in the Islamic world, and any ad or package featuring green is looked at favorably there.

Aesthetics apply to our ideas about our bodies and their physical beauty, as well. The view of an ideal weight differs markedly across cultures. Often, in richer countries, the better-off are thinner, while in poorer countries, the poorer are thinner. In Japan, sumo athletes are obese, and in some areas of Nigeria, girls enter "fattening rooms" to bulk up. Tattoos are another aspect of body aesthetic value differences across cultures. In some cultures, they are seen as beauty-enhancing, while in others, a desecration. The oldest preserved human, the Iceman found between Austria and Italy, is tattooed. In an interesting reversal, at one time in Japan, criminals were tattooed by authorities as a way to identify them, a negative meaning. Today, the Yakuza tattoo themselves to establish their in-group identity.

Music and Folklore Musical tastes vary across cultures, and, although commercials with music are generally popular worldwide, the marketer must know what kind of music each market prefers. Thus, a commercial that used a ballad in the United States might be better received if accompanied by the tune of a bolero in Mexico or a samba in Brazil.

A culture's folklore can disclose much about a society's way of life. The incorrect use of folklore can sometimes cost the firm a share of the market. For example, associating a product with

the cowboy would not obtain the same results in Chile or Argentina as in the United States, because in those countries the cowboy is a far less romantic figure—it is just a job. On the other hand, Smirnoff's use of an image of late revolutionary leader Ernesto "Che" Guevara in an advertisement for spicy vodka sparked controversy in Cuba, where Guevara is a national hero.[22] In many areas, especially where nationalistic feeling is strong, local firms have been able to compete successfully with foreign affiliates by making use of indigenous folklore in the form of slogans and proverbs.

Religion

Religion, an important component of culture, is responsible for many of the attitudes and beliefs affecting human behavior. A knowledge of the basic tenets of the religions of your markets will be useful as you build your understanding of those cultures. Knowledge of the local religion will also help you to communicate your respect for the culture. Figure 4.6 shows the world's major religions.

Material Culture

Material culture or artifacts are all the human-made objects of a culture; people who study material culture are concerned with *how* people make things (technology) and *who* makes *what* and *why* (economics). Every culture has certain parts of its material culture of which it is especially proud. Some awareness of these objects and the meaning they have for people in the culture can communicate interest in the culture.

Language

Probably the most apparent cultural distinction that the newcomer to international business perceives is in the means of communication. Differences in the spoken language are readily discernible, and after a short period in the new culture, it becomes apparent that there are variations in the unspoken language as well. Language is an important key to a culture, and without it, people find themselves locked out of all but a culture's perimeter. As illustrated in Chapter 5, spoken languages demarcate cultures just as physical barriers do. In fact, nothing equals the spoken language for distinguishing one culture from another.

Even though many businesspeople speak English, when they buy, they often want to do business in their own language. The foreign seller who speaks the local language has a competitive edge. Figure 4.7 shows a map of the major languages of the world.

Nonverbal communication, or the unspoken language, can often tell businesspeople something that the spoken language does not—if they can understand it. High context cultures tend to use unspoken language more intensively than do low context cultures and thus, people in HC cultures often have developed advanced "reading ability" of unspoken language. Because context plays such an important role in their home culture, they are aware of this medium. Eye contact, posture, and subtle facial expressions are all cues on which HC cultures rely.

Gestures are a common form of cross-cultural communication, yet they vary from one region to another. For instance, Americans and most Europeans understand the thumbs-up gesture to mean "all right," but in southern Italy and Greece, it transmits a vulgar message. Similarly, making a circle the "OK" sign, with the thumb and the forefinger is friendly in the United States, but it means "you're worth nothing" in France and Belgium and is vulgar in Greece and Turkey.

The unspoken language also includes aspects of work spaces. In the United States, an office door that is closed suggests a request for privacy; the normal position of the door is open. Germans regularly keep their doors closed. Hall suggests that the closed door does not mean that the person behind it wants no visitors but only that he or she considers open doors to be sloppy and disorderly.[23] Office size and location can mean different things in different cultures. In the United States, the higher the status of the executive, the larger and more secluded the office, but in the Arab world, the company president may be in a small, crowded office. In Japan, the senior person is likely to be closest to the center of the room, and the least valuable places on an office floor are by the windows. The French also locate important department heads in the center of activities, with their assistants located outward on radii from this center.

Conversational distances, the space between people in a conversation, tend to vary across cultural borders, as well. For example, they tend to be much smaller in the Middle East than in Anglo cultures. Conversational distances vary by gender as well, and comfortable distance may also vary by the degree of familiarity of the parties involved.

Special Focus: Gift Giving

Gift giving is an important aspect of every international manager's life, and a confusing aspect for many. In all cultures, some sort of entertainment outside of office hours and the exchange of gifts are part of the process of getting better acquainted. In high context cultures and cultures with large power distance,

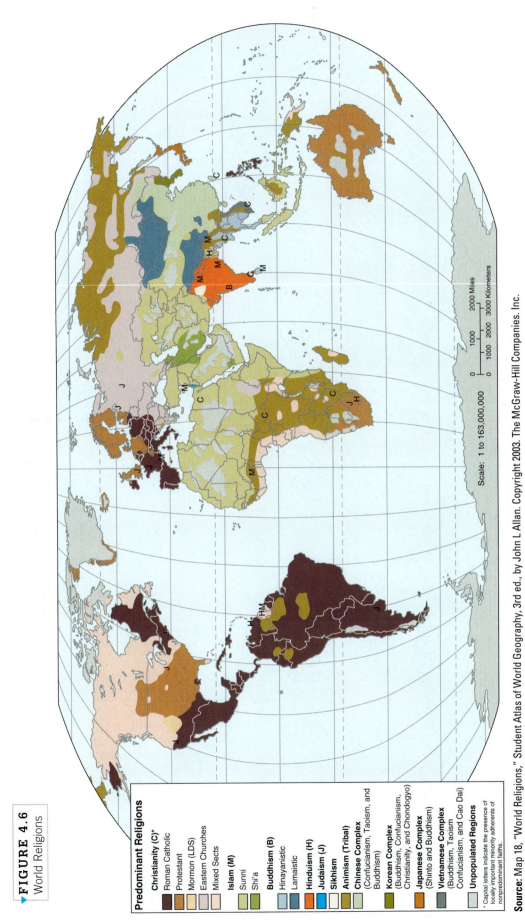

FIGURE 4.6
World Religions

Predominant Religions

Christianity (C)*
Roman Catholic
Protestant
Mormon (LDS)
Eastern Churches
Mixed Sects

Islam (M)
Sunni
Shi'a

Buddhism (B)
Hinayanistic
Lamaistic

Hinduism (H)

Judaism (J)

Sikhism

Animism (Tribal)

Chinese Complex
(Confucianism, Taoism, and
Buddhism)

Korean Complex
(Buddhism, Confucianism,
Christianity, and Chondogyo)

Japanese Complex
(Shinto and Buddhism)

Vietnamese Complex
(Buddhism, Taoism
Confucianism, and Cao Dai)

Unpopulated Regions

* Capital letters indicate the presence of
locally important minority adherents of
nonpredominant faiths.

Scale: 1 to 163,000,000

0   1000   2000 Miles
0   1000 2000 3000 Kilometers

Source: Map 18, "World Religions," *Student Atlas of World Geography,* 3rd ed., by John L Allan. Copyright 2003. The McGraw-Hill Companies. Inc.

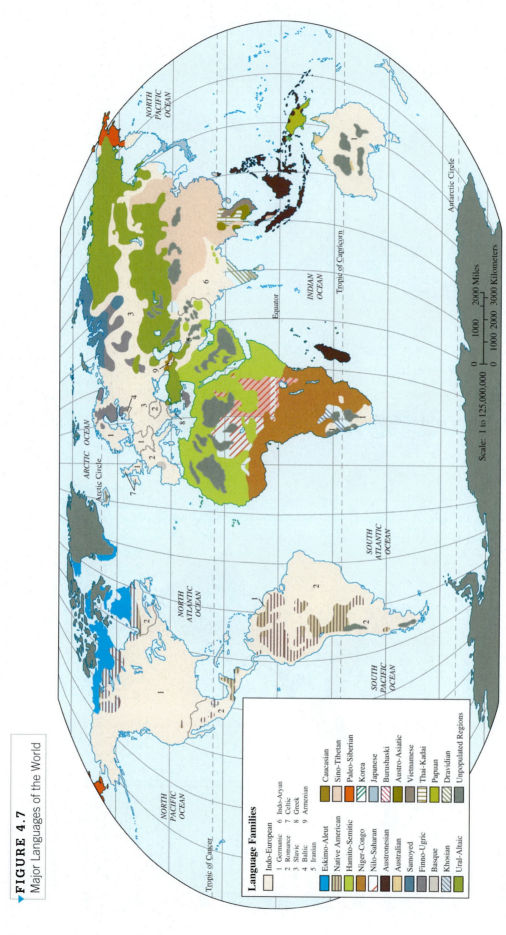

▶ **FIGURE 4.7**
Major Languages of the World

Language Families

Indo-European
1 Germanic   6 Indo-Aryan
2 Romance   7 Celtic
3 Slavic   8 Greek
4 Baltic   9 Armenian
5 Iranian

Eskimo-Aleut
Native American
Hamito-Semitic
Niger-Congo
Nilo-Saharan
Austronesian
Australian
Samoyed
Finno-Ugric
Basque
Khosian
Ural-Altaic

Caucasian
Sino-Tibetan
Paleo-Siberian
Korea
Japanese
Burushaski
Austro-Asiatic
Vietnamese
Thai-Kadai
Papuan
Dravidian
Unpopulated Regions

Scale: 1 to 125,000,000

0   1000   2000 Miles
0 1000 2000 3000 Kilometers

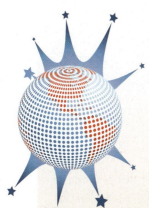
the etiquette for gift giving is markedly different than in low context cultures and cultures with small power distance.

The first point about gifts is to figure out what constitutes an acceptable gift in the culture and what the role of gift giving is. In Japan, for example, one never gives an unwrapped gift or visits a Japanese home empty-handed. A gift is presented with the comment that it is only a trifle, which implies that the humble social position of the giver does not permit giving a gift in keeping with the high status of the recipient. The recipient, in turn, will not open the gift in front of the giver to spare him/her any embarrassment. Gift giving in Japan has the intention to convey thoughtfulness and consideration for the receiver, who over time builds up trust and confidence in the giver.

Every country will have an etiquette and set of implicit rules around the giving of gifts: their timing, their value, how they are presented. Know what these are.[24] Many organizations have policies related to gift giving designed to separate this cultural pattern from bribery or extortion, so managers will want to keep their organization's guidelines in mind.

institutions, based on the conditions of their formation: *kinship* and *free association*.

The family is the basic unit of institutions based on kinship. Unlike the American family, which is generally composed of the parents and their children, families in many nations are extended to include all relatives by blood and by marriage. Many of these cultures will be high context. For the foreign firm, this extended family is a source of employees and business connections. The trust that people place in their relatives may motivate them to buy from a supplier owned by their cousin's cousin, even though the price is higher. Local personnel managers may fill the best jobs with family members, regardless of qualifications. Although the extended family is large, each member's feeling of responsibility to it is strong.

Associations not based on kinship may be formed by age, gender, or common interest.[25] These groups are important for marketers to understand, since their rules and organization are likely to differ across cultural borders. Consumer organizations, for example, have forced firms to change their products,

> ❝ A new kind of association has emerged with Facebook and other social networks, with their own unwritten cultural rules. ❞

Societal Organization

Every society structures its social relationships, and these patterned arrangements of relationships define an important aspect of culture. There are two main classes of social

promotion, and prices. A new kind of association has emerged with Facebook and other social networks, with their own unwritten cultural rules. They may have a significant influence on firms.

cu in ib

Mallory Wedeking: Attitude Is Everything!

Mallory Wedeking has studied and worked in Uganda and Rwanda. When asked to give advice to students studying international business and wondering if it is for them, she has some very interesting observations. Here are her comments:

My concentration in school is entrepreneurship and my career goals are to pursue a career in business in the context of International Development. I became interested in International Business when I first traveled after I graduated high school. Interacting with different cultures and different lifestyles inspired in me creativity and a desire to learn. I craved the excitement and added texture to doing business in an international context.

The most influential time abroad I have experienced would be the four months I studied in Uganda and Rwanda, two countries located in East Africa. While I was there, in addition to studying, I was also able to do an internship through the non-profit Food for the Hungry. My duties in the internship involved working with a rural village in Eastern Africa to help foster economic development and financial responsibility within the community.

I chose this location because I desired to expand my knowledge and cultural awareness beyond that of the Western, developed world. Obviously, I knew I was going to experience a much broader cultural gap than I had in Europe and was nervous about the transition. I briefly familiarized myself with the culture (which would definitely be necessary in more formal cross-cultural interactions), but most of the cultural awareness, including "Dos" and "Don'ts," I learned along the way. I learned early on that mistakes were unavoidable and that the attitude in which you deal with them is what matters.

Learning another culture is truly a humbling experience. Along those lines, if I had to give anyone advice in working abroad, I would have to say that attitude is everything. Cultural miscommunications will happen no matter how much you prepare ahead of time. I do not think I would have been able to learn in the capacity that I did if I wasn't able to get back up on my feet (literally, in some cases) and keep moving forward. Also, I would recommend understanding the phases of culture shock and being able to properly identify where you are in order to deal with your current feelings and emotions. There is a tendency at certain points of culture shock to retreat from the culture and surround yourself with only things familiar and comfortable. I experienced this feeling two months into my stay abroad, often retreating with my fellow American students and watching movies like Ferris Bueller's Day Off or Star Wars. I had to force myself to continue interacting with the Ugandan people, against all my other desires.

Surprisingly, I found that returning to the United States was a much more difficult cultural adjustment than arriving in East Africa. One reason was because I had not expected that my home for twenty years of my life could feel overwhelming and unfamiliar. It took about six months to completely feel comfortable here again. I learned that the process cannot be rushed, and it is important to give yourself time to really absorb everything you learned while abroad. You shouldn't expect or want yourself to be the same exact person you were before you left.

My greatest enjoyment while I was working abroad was finding different ways to connect with people. I realized that though we were worlds apart culturally, not to mention mileage, there were so many ways we could relate to each other, especially through song and dance. Emphasizing the things you have in common, rather than the differences (which easily outnumber the commonalities), is so important in learning to relate with one another. After all, we are all human, and that's a huge thing in common!

I would highly recommend working internationally. The daily surprises keep things interesting and teach you invaluable qualities and skills. Even traveling for pleasure purposes or studying abroad teaches you skills such as being adaptable, thinking and making decisions quickly, learning on the go and developing advanced communication skills, all of which are extremely desirable to employers.

In Chapter 4, we have looked at what culture is and its significance for international business, reviewed three of the most useful cultural dimension frameworks, and addressed some of the more significant sociocultural aspects of societies, including aesthetics, religion, material culture, and language. Moving forward to other external forces that managers must address and over which they have limited control, please remember that all of these forces are influenced by culture. You might think of culture as a collection of rules, many of them unwritten, that social groups use to solve their problems and differentiate themselves from one another. Understanding culture at a significant level provides international managers with a rich way to build understanding, and possibly value, across cultural borders. ■

CHECK IT OUT!

mhhe.com/GeringerM

for study materials
including quizzes,
iPod downloads,
and video

chapter five

"Climate change may prove to be the most important business issue of the 21st century. Managers who wish to be responsible to shareholders and the broader community must be prepared to face the challenges and opportunities presented by our shifting climate. Trillions of dollars, millions of lives, thousands of species—infinite solutions."

—Stanford University's Graduate School of Business,
The MBA's Climate Change Primer

natural resources
+environmental sustainability

The scope of *natural resources* is quite broad. We begin with a consideration of the geographic basics, location, topography, and climate, and then continue with a focus on the major natural resources of energy and nonfuel minerals. Our consideration of natural resources leads directly to concerns about their stewardship. The final section addresses those issues through a focus on environmental sustainability.

LEARNING OBJECTIVES

After reading this chapter, you should be able to:

LO1 Describe how geographical features of a country or region create contextual differences that contribute to economic, cultural, political, and social conditions important to international business.

LO2 Outline the nonrenewable and renewable energy options available and their broad business implications.

LO3 Describe the concept of environmental sustainability and its potential influence on business.

LO4 Explain the major characteristics of sustainable business.

LO5 Discuss the utility of the stakeholder model for sustainable business.

LO1 **Describe** how geographical features of a country or region create contextual differences that contribute to economic, cultural, political, and social conditions important to international business.

GEOGRAPHY

Switzerland is a good example to illustrate how geography—location, topography, climate, and natural resources—can have a profound impact on the way people organize their activities. Here we explore how the physical environment provides the basic context for our economic lives. Think about Swiss watches, chocolates, cheese, precision machinery, and pharmaceuticals. What they have in common is their high value per kilo and their quality. Switzerland has a mountainous terrain, is near the heavily populated lowlands of western Europe, yet separated by the Alps, and lacks mineral resources. Yet Switzerland has developed creative ways to overcome this lack of local raw materials and the high transportation costs, their endowment disadvantages. The Swiss import small amounts of raw materials, add high value to them, and export a lightweight, skillfully crafted finished product. For watches, they import high quality Swedish steel costing 40 cents per ounce and convert it to watch movements selling for $60 per ounce. Because of their low weight, the cost of transporting these movements to market is minimal. Precision machinery and pharmaceuticals are other products that minimize the need for importing bulky raw materials. Swiss dairies do to milk what the watchmakers do to the steel—convert it via processing to concentrated, high-value products: cheese and chocolates that compete on the basis of reputation and quality.[1]

We consider the physical elements of a location as largely uncontrollable forces because, much like the foreign environmental forces we discussed earlier, they are the givens around which managers must adjust their strategies as they make efforts to compensate for differences in these forces among markets. An additional way to explain the importance of the environment and natural resources is to examine Michael Porter's diamond (see Figure 5.1), a model developed to explain differing levels of success among the many national players in world markets.[2]

COMPETITIVE ADVANTAGE: PORTER'S DIAMOND

Porter's diamond model, as explained in Chapter 2, considers four aspects of a country's economic environment that affect its competitive position: factor conditions, related and supporting industries, demand conditions, and firm strategy, structure, and rivalry. Porter suggests that competitively successful countries are the ones that have the most favorable diamonds. The geographic attributes of a country are a core part of its basic factor conditions, inherited assets, over which the country has either no or quite limited control, such as topography, climate, and natural resources. Porter distinguishes between *basic factors,* those that a country inherits, such as the mountains and lack of natural resources for the Swiss, and *advanced factors,* those a country can readily mold, such as the labor force and infrastructure. He makes the interesting point that local disadvantages in factor conditions can be recognized as advantages and become a force for innovation. His thinking is that adverse conditions such as local terrain and climate or scarce raw materials at the basic-factor level, or labor shortages at the advanced-factor level, force firms to develop new methods, and this innovation may lead to a national competitive advantage. Hence, awareness of a nation's factor conditions is important for the international firm.

Going back to the Swiss example of high-value-added concentrated goods, the Swiss have developed expertise areas that take into account their geography, in this case, mostly constraints (basic factors), by developing advanced-factor conditions that recognize and incorporate their basic, inherited conditions. The Swiss have built an educated, skilled, and specialized workforce; they protect agriculture against foreign competition; they pursue neutrality, thus keeping trade relationships open; they have established a reliable transportation system that overcomes their topographical challenges; and they have encouraged high levels of savings, so they can draw on both domestic and foreign savings in Switzerland.

▼**FIGURE 5.1**
Variables Affecting Competitive Advantage: Porter's Diamond

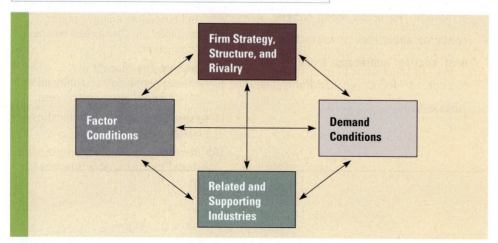

Source: Reprinted by permission of the *Harvard Business Review.* "The Competitive Advantage of Nations" by Michael E. Porter, March–April 1990, p. 77. Copyright © 1990 by The President and Fellows of Harvard College; all rights reserved.

Switzerland has taken a strategic approach to developing its resources by drawing on its basic endowments, limiting though they may seem, and building its advanced endowments. This approach has led to the Swiss competitive advantage in the areas of watches, precision machinery, chocolate, pharmaceuticals, and cheese, among others.

LOCATION: POLITICAL AND TRADE RELATIONSHIPS

Where a country is located, who its neighbors are, and how its capital and major cities are situated are also basic factor conditions. How they contribute to the way a country builds its competitive advantage should be part of the general knowledge of international businesspeople. Location helps explain many of a country's political and trade relationships, as the following focus on Austria will illustrate. While we look at one country to illustrate the relationships among location, politics and trade, remember that every country will have its own set of such relationships.

At the height of the Cold War, Austria's location enabled that country to be a political bridge between the noncommunist nations of the West and the communist nations of the East (see Figure 5.2). In addition, Austria's political neutrality made it a popular location for the offices of international firms servicing eastern European operations. Furthermore, because Austria had led the Austro-Hungarian Empire until 1918, the Austrians were completely familiar with the cultures and practices of those neighboring countries to which they had once been joined. Finally, Vienna, Austria's capital, was close to both the former Czechoslovakia (today the Czech Republic and Slovakia) and

Hungary. Austria took advantage of its location to (1) increase trade with the East, (2) become the principal financial intermediary between the two regions, and (3) strengthen its role as the regional headquarters for international businesses operating in Eastern Europe.

In 1991, when the collapse of the Soviet bloc (COMECON, consisting of Bulgaria, Czechoslovakia, East Germany, Hungary, Romania, Poland, the Soviet Union, Cuba, Mongolia, and Vietnam) forced eastern European enterprises to reorient their trade toward the West, their location and relationships allowed Austrian entrepreneurs to capture an important share of the Western nations' exports to the East.

Geographical proximity is often a major reason for trade between nations and plays a role in the formation of trading groups, as well. With proximity, knowledge of the country is likely, delivery faster, freight costs lower, and service costs lower, too. The major trading partners of the United States—Canada and Mexico—lie on its borders. Geographical proximity is evident in the formation of trading groups such as the EU, Mercosur, ASEAN and NAFTA. Proximity also helps to explain why Japan is China's largest source of imports and its largest trading partner.[3]

TOPOGRAPHY

Surface features such as mountains, plains, deserts, and bodies of water contribute to differences in economies, cultures, politics, and social structures, both in nations and in regions of a single country. These topographic features, the features on the land's surface, can both hinder and aid physical distribution. They also may require that products be altered. For example, the effects of altitude on food products require a change in baking instructions at heights above 3,000 feet. Internal combustion engines begin to lose power at 5,000 feet, which may require the manufacturer of gasoline-powered machinery to use larger engines. Because topography contributes to the factor conditions of a given location, we examine its major components: mountains, plains, deserts, and bodies of water.

Mountains are barriers that tend to separate and impede exchange and interaction, whereas level areas (plains and plateaus) facilitate them, unless climate makes exchange unlikely, as in the Sahara and Gobi deserts. The extent to which mountains serve as barriers depends on their massiveness, ruggedness, and transecting valleys. One example of such a barrier is the Himalaya Mountains. Travel across them is so difficult that transportation between India and China is by air or sea rather than overland. The contrast between the cultures of the Indo-Malayan people living to the south of the mountains and those of the Chinese living to the north is evidence of the Himalayas' effectiveness as a barrier. Another example of the influence of mountain barriers is found in Afghanistan, where mountains dominate the landscape, running northeast to southwest through the

▼**FIGURE 5.2**
Austria and Her Neighbors: A Cold War Map

The Central Asian Hindu Kush runs from north central Pakistan through eastern and central Afghanistan.

center of the country, including the Hindukush ("Hindu Killer") area. More than 40 percent of Afghanistan lies above 6,000 feet.[4] For comparison, there are only two peaks east of the Mississippi in the United States that hit 6,000 feet, Mt. Mitchell in North Carolina and Mt. Washington in New Hampshire. In Afghanistan, high passes transect the mountains, creating a network for caravans. There are at least 10 major ethnic groups and 33 languages spoken in Afghanistan,[5] evidence of the ability of mountain ranges to separate populations. Figure 5.3 illustrates Afghanistan's topography. In similar fashion, the Alps, Carpathians, Balkans, and Pyrenees have long separated the Mediterranean cultures from those of northern Europe.

Nations whose mountain ranges divide them into smaller regional areas, such as Afghanistan and Switzerland, pose a challenge to businesspeople in the form of regional markets, each with its own distinctive industries, climate, culture, dialect, and sometimes even language. In addition to Afghanistan and Switzerland, Spain, China, and Colombia present the challenge of mountain ranges. In Spain, Catalonia and the Basque country (see Figure 5.4) have separate languages, Catalan and Euskara, along with sizable minorities that wish to secede from Spain to form a separate nation. Although the Basques and the Catalans can speak Spanish, when they are among themselves they use their own languages, which are unintelligible to other Spaniards. This creates the sort of

▼**FIGURE 5.3**
Map of Afghanistan Mountains

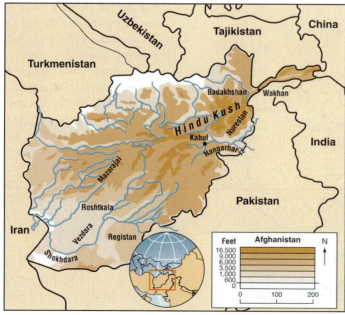

The green wall of China, here in Taipusi, Inner Mongolia, has been planted to fend off the encroaching Gobi desert.

▼ **FIGURE 5.4** Map of Spain

German   French   Italian   Romansh

problems that are found wherever there are language differences. In Catalonia and the Basque country, Spanish-speaking managers do not attain the empathy with their local employees that they do in other parts of Spain, and sales representatives who speak the local language are more effective. These language differences increase promotional costs if, to be more effective, companies choose to prepare their material in Euskara, Catalan, and Spanish.[6] Figure 5.5 shows the language borders of Switzerland.

In China, dozens of languages, each having many dialects, developed in villages separated by mountains. This language diversity caused communication problems that hindered economic development until the government decreed Mandarin, known in China as *Putonghua,* to be the official language in 1956. Today, though, many dialects persist. The written language is shared among the many language groups, but spoken language is virtually incomprehensible across language borders. Compare the Chinese language map in Figure 5.6 to the topographical map to see that language areas and topography correspond.

In Colombia, three ranges of the Andes run like spines from north to south to divide Colombia into four separate markets,

each with its own culture and dialects (see Figure 5.7). Depending on the product, marketers may need to create four distinct promotional mixes. In addition, Colombia has a range of climates due to the great differences in altitude throughout habitable parts of the country. The variation from hot and humid at sea level in Barranquilla to cold and dry in Bogotá creates production and inventory challenges for a manufacturer that must produce a distinct product and package for each climate zone.

Deserts and tropical forests also separate markets, increase the cost of transportation, and create concentrations of population. More than one-third of the earth's surface consists of arid and semiarid regions located either on the coasts, where the winds blow away from the land, or in the interior, where mountains or long distances cause the winds to lose their moisture before reaching these regions. Every continent has them, and every western coast between 20 and 30 degrees north or south of the equator is dry. Only in latitudes where there is a major source of water, as in Egypt, is there a concentration of population. Nowhere is the relationship between water supply and population concentration better illustrated than in Australia, a continent the size of the continental United States but with only 20.7 million inhabitants,

FIGURE 5.6 Topographical and Language Maps of China

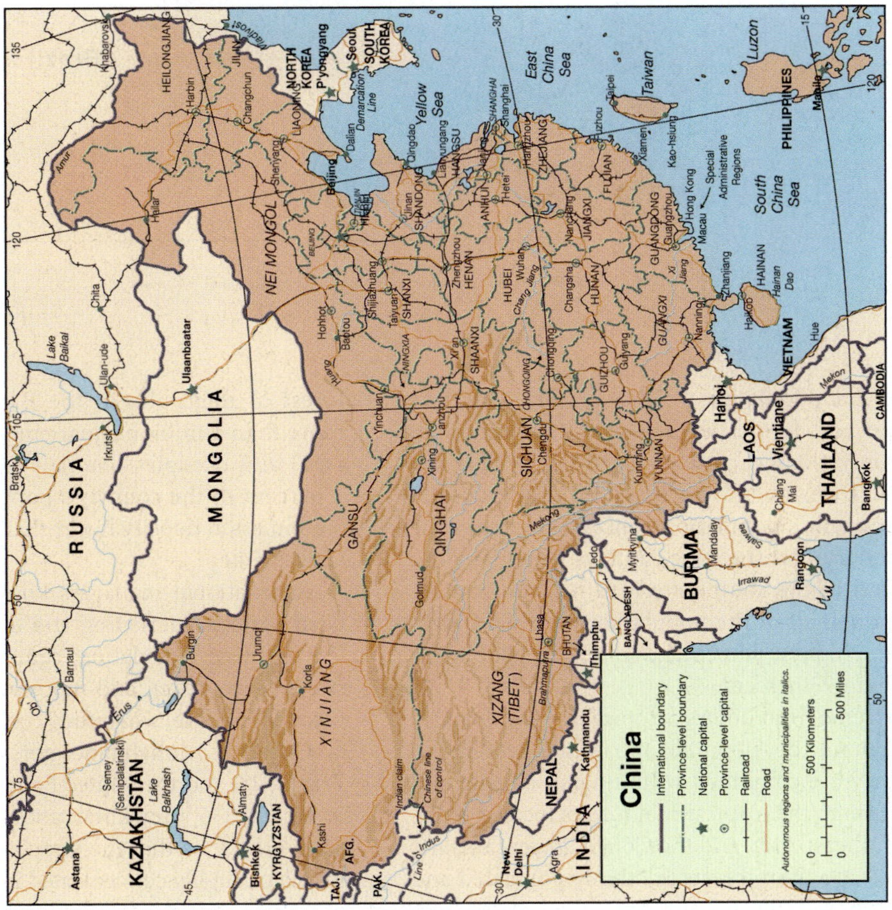

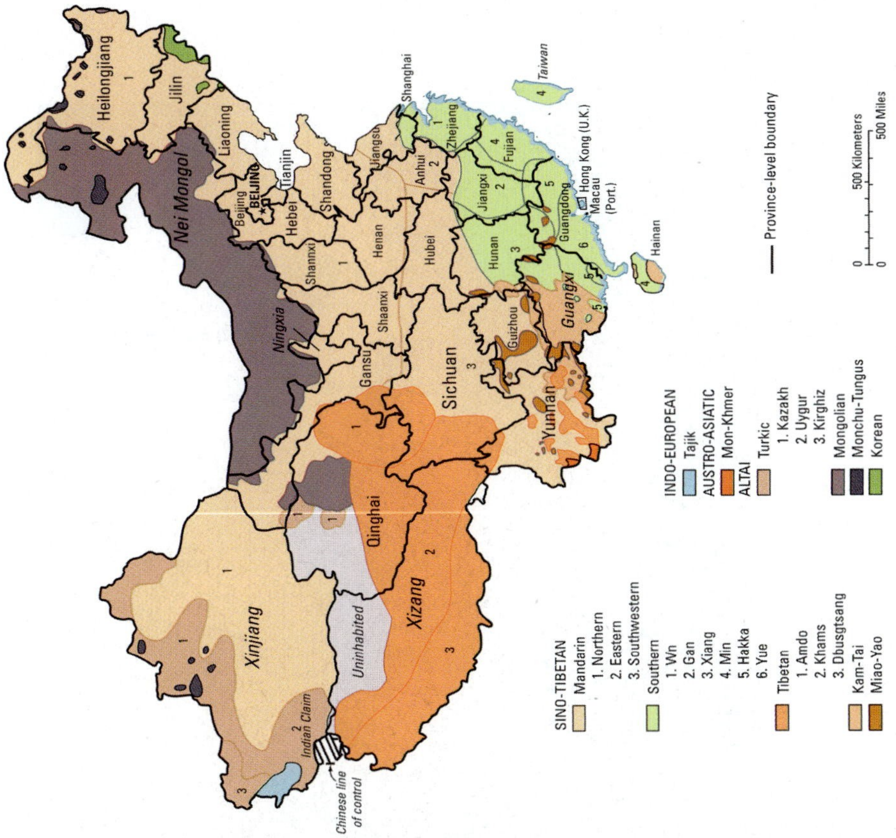

Language map legend:

SINO-TIBETAN

Mandarin
1. Northern
2. Eastern
3. Southwestern

Southern
1. Wu
2. Gan
3. Xiang
4. Min
5. Hakka
6. Yue

Tibetan
1. Amdo
2. Khams
3. Dbusgtsang

Kam-Tai

Miao-Yao

INDO-EUROPEAN
Tajik

AUSTRO-ASIATIC
Mon-Khmer

ALTAI
Turkic
1. Kazakh
2. Uygur
3. Kirghiz

Mongolian

Monchu-Tungus

Korean

— Province-level boundary

500 Kilometers
500 Miles

Topographical map legend:

China

— International boundary
— Province-level boundary
★ National capital
◉ Province-level capital
╫ Railroad
— Road

Autonomous regions and municipalities in italics.

500 Kilometers
500 Miles

▼**FIGURE 5.7**
Map of Colombia

Colombia
—— Department, Intendencia and Comisar'a Boundaries   ● Elevations above 14,000 meters

in contrast to the U.S. population of 304 million. Australia's coastline is humid and fertile, whereas the huge center of the country is mainly a desert closely resembling the Sahara. Figure 5.8 illustrates this by a focus on land use. Because of its topography, Australia's population concentrates along the coastal areas in and around the state capitals, which are also major seaports, and in the southeastern fifth of the nation, where more than one-half of the population lives. This gives Australia one of the highest percentages of urban population in the world, at about 93 percent.

At the other extreme from deserts, tropical rain forests also are a barrier to economic development and human settlement, especially when they are combined with a harsh climate and poor soil. This occurs in the tropical rain forests located in the Amazon basin, Southeast Asia, and the Congo. Except in parts of West Africa and Java, rain forests are thinly populated and little developed economically. For example, the greatest rain

forest of them all—in the Brazilian Amazon basin—covers more than 1 million square miles (one-fourth of the U.S. land area) and occupies one-half of Brazil; it is inhabited by just 4 percent of the country's population. Only true deserts have a population density lower than the Amazon's one person per square mile.

International managers know that in more densely populated nations, marketing and distributing their products costs less because population centers are closer, communication systems are better, and more people are available for employment. Therefore, when they compare population densities such as Canada's 3 inhabitants per square kilometer, Australia's 3, Brazil's 23, and the United States' 33 with the Netherlands' 401 or Japan's 336, they know not to draw the wrong conclusions.[7] They are aware that the populations in Canada, Australia, and Brazil are highly concentrated in a relatively small area, because of deserts and tropical rain forests.

▼ FIGURE 5.8 Map of Australia

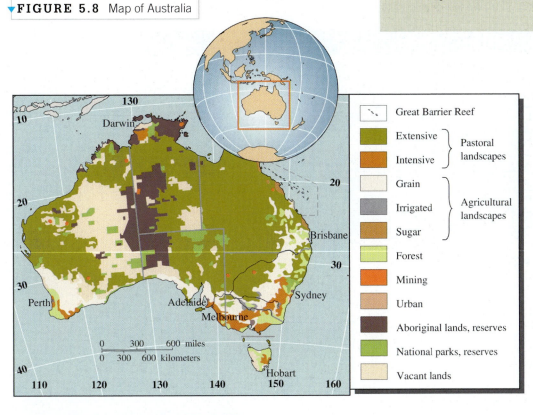

Great Barrier Reef

Extensive } Pastoral
Intensive } landscapes

Grain }
Irrigated } Agricultural
Sugar } landscapes

Forest

Mining

Urban

Aboriginal lands, reserves

National parks, reserves

Vacant lands

BODIES OF WATER

Bodies of water, unlike mountains, deserts, and tropical forests, attract people and facilitate transportation. Water, an important natural resource, is necessary for life and critical for industry, yet invisible to most consumers when used in agriculture and manufacturing. As much as 2,400 liters are used to produce one hamburger, while 11,000 liters can be used in the production of a pair of jeans.[8] A world population map clearly shows that bodies of water have attracted more people than have areas remote from water (see Figure 5.9). Densely populated regions coincide with rivers, lakes, and seacoasts. Although water is an abundant natural resource, its abundance is not reflected in patterns of water distribution. In general, the poor lack access to clean water. As an example, in the slums of Dar es Salaam, Tanzania's largest city, 1,000 liters of water could cost $8. The same amount in the wealthy areas of the same city would cost $.34, and $.68 in the United States, according to the not-for-profit WaterAid.[9]

One significant feature associated with bodies of water is the **inland waterway,** significant because it provides inexpensive access to interior markets. Before the construction of railways, water transport was the only economically practical carrier for bulk goods moving over long distances. Water transport increased even after the building of railroads; and today, in every continent except Australia, which has no inland waterways, extensive use is still made of water transportation. The importance of waterways relative to railroads, however, has diminished everywhere with one exception—Europe's **Rhine waterway,** the world's most important inland waterway system.

To illustrate the Rhine's significance: one-half of Switzerland's exports and nearly three-fourths of its imports pass through the city of Basel, the Swiss inland port. (See Figure 5.10.) From ancient times, shipments have moved between the Netherlands, Belgium, Germany, France, Austria, Liechtenstein, and Switzerland by means of the Rhine and its connecting waterways. The Rhine-Main-Danube Canal, completed in 1992, creates access from the Netherlands and the North Sea through 15 countries to the Black Sea. From there, shipments can continue to Moscow over the interconnected system of the Volga and Don rivers. Increasingly, firms have been turning to the Rhine waterway as an environmentally friendly alternative to road transportation.

A review of major inland waterways includes, in South America, the Amazon and its tributaries, which offer some 57,000 kilometers of navigable waterways during the flood season (see Figure 5.11). In Asia, the major waterways are the Yangtze (China), the Ganges (India), and the Indus (Pakistan). Rivers are especially important in China because water is the

Cargo ships passing through Germany on Europe's main transportation artery, the Rhine waterway.

▼FIGURE 5.9 World Population Map

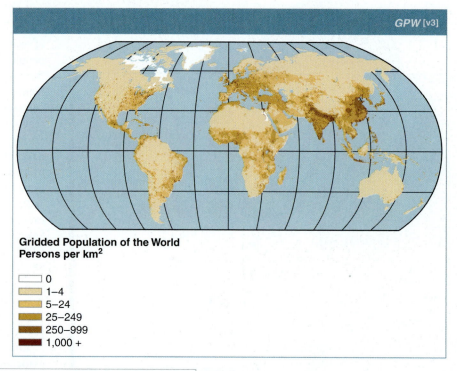

**Gridded Population of the World
Persons per km²**

☐	0
☐	1–4
☐	5–24
☐	25–249
☐	250–999
☐	1,000 +

▼FIGURE 5.10 Map of Rhine-Main-Danube Canal

Source: Center for International Earth Science Information Network (CIESIN), Columbia University, and Centro International de Agricultura Tropical (CIAT), used by permission, http://ciesin.columbia/edu/gpw.

FIGURE 5.11 Map of Amazon River

Source: https://www.cia.gov/library/publications/the-world-factbook/maps/maptemplate_br.html

CLIMATE

Climate (temperature, precipitation, and wind) is important because it sets the limits on what people can do, physically and economically. Where the climate is harsh, there are few human settlements, but where it is permissive, there tends to be population density. However, climate is not deterministic—it allows certain developments to occur, but it does not cause them. In terms of Porter's diamond, although climate is an inherited asset as a factor condition, technology can be applied to modify its impact. Similar climates occur in similar latitudes and continental positions, and the more water-dominated an area, the more moderate its climate.

We should mention in our discussion of climate that for centuries, some writers have used climatic differences to explain differences in human and economic development. This explanation, known as the North-South divide, suggests that the greatest economic and intellectual development has occurred in the temperate climates of northern Europe and the United States because the less temperate climates limit human energy and mental powers.[10] However, businesspeople must not be taken in by such ethnocentric reasoning that fails to explain the difference in the level of technology employed in the 1600s by the inhabitants of northeastern North America and northern Europe. Clearly other factors, such as the Industrial Revolution, population size, and location, have contributed to the North-South development differences. Jared Diamond's Pulitzer Prize–winning *Guns, Germs, and Steel: The Fates of Human Societies* explores the basis of these factors.[11] Diamond argues that the gaps in technology among human societies are caused by environmental differences amplified by feedback loops and that these differences do not lead to intellectual or moral superiority. World Bank studies have shown that many of the factors responsible for underdevelopment in tropical nations are present because of the tropical climate: continuous heat and the lack of winter temperatures offer no constraints for reproduction and growth of weeds, insects, viruses, birds, and parasites, and this results in destroyed crops, dead cattle, and people infected with debilitating diseases.[12] Techniques are becoming available to control pests and parasites, and once this is accomplished, the very characteristics that are now detrimental to tropical Africa will give it advantages over the temperate zones in agriculture. The resulting income would create a market in tropical Africa that could easily surpass that

least expensive, and often the only, means of moving industrial raw materials to the manufacturing centers. The United States depends heavily on two waterways, the Great Lakes–St. Lawrence and the Mississippi.

Historically, navigable waterways with connections to the ocean have been important because they have permitted the low-cost transportation of goods and people from a country's coast to its interior, and today they are the only means of access from the coasts of many developing nations. In Africa, where 14 of the world's 20 landlocked developing countries are located, access to the coast is a major issue. Governments must construct costly, long truck routes and extensive feeder networks for relatively low volumes of traffic. Furthermore, governments in countries with coastlines through which the imports and exports of the landlocked nations must pass are in a position to exert considerable political influence. An example of this is found with the Mercosur governments of Argentina, Brazil, Paraguay and Uruguay and the Parana and Paraguay Rivers Trade Corridor, which connects the landlocked interior of South America with seaports, as illustrated in Figure 5.12. Struggles for outlets to the sea still exist as important political and economic factors.

natural resources Anything supplied by nature on which people depend

nonrenewable energy sources The principal nonrenewable energy sources are the fossil fuels—petroleum, coal, and natural gas—and nuclear power

of the Middle East. As a parallel example, we might recall the huge development shift from the northern to the southern U.S. states, supported as it was by two technological innovations, DDT for malaria and air conditioning.

Location, topography, and climate form the basic, inherited context for business ventures. Try as the Swiss might to alter things, Switzerland is likely to continue to be a mountainous country with long, snowy winters on a heavily populated plain at the foot of the Alps. Of course, people may undertake massive modifications: Holland, situated below the North Sea level, has protected itself through a system of dykes. Singapore has greatly increased its landmass by reclaiming land from the surrounding sea, as have the Japanese in their landfill expansion into Tokyo Harbor. Such modification of an inherited factor illustrates Porter's idea of changing a disadvantage to an advantage. Yet for the most part, location, topography, and climate tend to be permanent facts. In contrast, natural resources, our next focus, present businesspeople with sources of raw materials that, unlike location, topography and climate, are extractable and malleable.

LO2 Outline the nonrenewable and renewable energy options available and their broad business implications.

▼ **FIGURE 5.12** Map of Paraná-Paraguay Rivers Trade Corridor

Trade corridor

0   150   300 Miles

0   150   300 Kilometers

NATURAL RESOURCES

What are **natural resources?** For our purposes, they are anything supplied by nature on which people depend. The principal natural resources important to business productive capacity are energy and nonfuel minerals. The final section of this chapter addresses their sustainability.

Energy

Natural resources that are sources for energy are either nonrenewable or renewable. The nonrenewable sources are fossil fuels, including petroleum, coal, and natural gas; once we use them, their supplies are depleted. Nuclear energy is also nonrenewable, but on a quite different scale than are the fossil fuels. Among renewable energy sources are hydroelectric, wind, solar, geothermal, waves, tides, biomass, and ocean thermal energy conversion. Figure 5.13 illustrates the evolution of the world's marketed energy supply by fuel from 1980 to 2030. You can see that nonrenewables have dominated the market. We look first at these major **nonrenewable energy sources** and then at the renewable sources.

Petroleum Petroleum, or crude oil, has been a cheap source of energy and a raw material for plastics, fertilizers, and other industrial applications. The world is running out of oil, but when is uncertain. Fifty years at current consumption rates seems an optimistic estimate.[13] In addition to depleted oil supplies, there are also above-ground issues that will drive up the cost of petroleum.[14] Another factor that influences petroleum availability is that the easy sources have already been tapped, and now the reserves that are more difficult to harvest

▼ **FIGURE 5.13**
World Marketed Energy Use by Fuel Type, 1980–2030

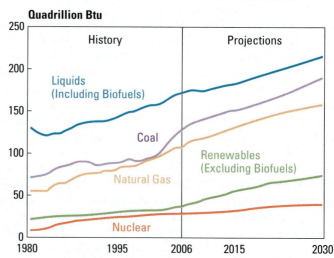

Sources: History: Energy Information Administration (EIA), *International Energy Annual 2006* (June–December 2008), web site www.eia.doe.gov/iea. **Projections:** EIA, World Energy Projections Plus (2009).

will need to be used. Estimates of these reserves change for a number of reasons:

- New discoveries continue to be made in proven fields with the aid of improved prospecting equipment.

- Governments open up their countries to exploration and production.

- Improved techniques such as steam and hot water injection enable producers to obtain greater output from wells already in operation, and put new areas into operation.

- Automated, less expensive equipment lowers drilling costs; for instance, wellheads located on the ocean floor can replace expensive offshore platforms. This innovation allows a company to profitably work smaller-sized discoveries that otherwise it would not touch.

Nevertheless, there is no doubt that we face a serious dependency issue with oil. A group of oil industry professionals, the Association for the Study of Peak Oil and Gas, points out that we are probably in the peak production time period right now,[15] and their critical question is: how long do we have to make adjustments before the price of oil becomes prohibitive?

The U.S. Energy Information Administration projects that world energy consumption will continue to increase through 2035, with dramatic increases in developing countries such as China and India as they industrialize.[16] Figure 5.14 illustrates marketed or sold energy use by region.

Oil is projected to remain the world's dominant energy source in this period, with reductions seen after 2020. Present production is around 72 million barrels per day.[17] Some industry analysts suggest that oil production peaked in 2008 at 75 million barrels per day and has begun a steady decline. The United States Energy Information Administration's projections also suggest a slow decline going forward. Table 5.1 shows the greatest oil reserves by country, and then Figures 5.15 and 5.16 show these reserves categorized by investment risk and political risk. Note that, increasingly, oil reserves are controlled by governments that limit the access of the major oil companies.

The unconventional sources of petroleum whose attractiveness increases as conventional sources are depleted include oil sands, oil-bearing shale, coal, and natural gas. In addition to being a source for petroleum, the last two are also used to generate energy on their own. As the price of oil rises and technologies develop, unconventional oil development from oil sands and other sources of oil that is not easily recoverable will increase. These sources are often grouped together as **heavy oil,** and are seen as the future for oil companies. The major oil sands are located in Canada (Athabasca, in Alberta), Venezuela, and the Republic of Congo. The sands contain bitumin, a tarlike crude oil, and place Canada first in heavy oil reserves and second only to Saudi Arabia in overall proven reserves.[18]

FIGURE 5.14
Marketed Energy Use by Region

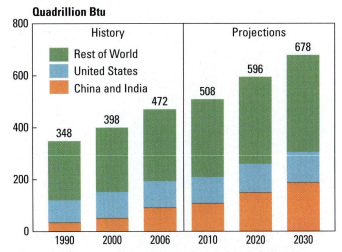

Sources: History: Energy Information Administration (EIA), *International Energy Annual 2006* (June–December 2008), web site www.eia.doe.gov/iea. **Projections:** EIA, World Energy Projections Plus (2009).

TABLE 5.1 World Oil Reserves by Country as of January 2010, Top 14

Rank	Country	Proved Reserves (billions of barrels)	Reserve to Production Ratio	Share of World Production*
1	Saudi Arabia	267	72 years	10.2%
2	Canada	179	149	3.3
3	Iran	138	95	4.0
4	Iraq	115	150	2.1
5	Kuwait	104	110	2.6
6	United Arab Emirates	98	88	2.9
7	Venezuela	87	107	2.7
8	Russia	60	17	9.9
9	Libya	41	66	1.7
10	Nigeria	36	41	2.4
11	Kazakhstan	30	59	1.4
12	United States	21	8	7.5
13	China	16	11	3.9
14	Qatar	15	46	0.9

*Energy Information Administration, http://www.eia.doe.gov/emeu/international/oilproduction.html (accessed February 20, 2010).

Oil-bearing **shale** is fine-grained sedimentary rock that yields 25 liters or more of liquid hydrocarbons per ton of rock when heated to 500°C, whose largest known source is the three-state area of Utah, Colorado, and Wyoming, in the United States. Oil shale has remained underdeveloped because of the

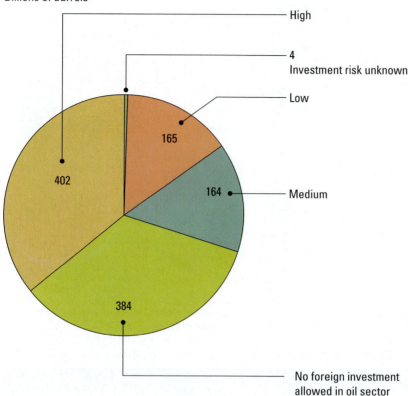

▼ **FIGURE 5.15**
Worldwide Proven Oil Reserves by Investment Risk

Billions of barrels

High

4
Investment risk unknown

Low

165

164 — Medium

402

384

No foreign investment
allowed in oil sector

Source: www.gao.gov/new.items/d07283.pdf.

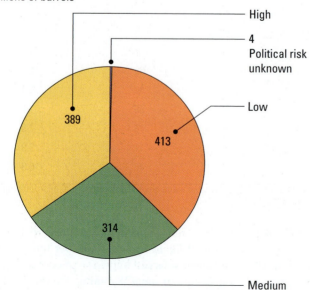

▼ **FIGURE 5.16**
Worldwide Proven Oil Reserves by Political Risk

Billions of barrels

High

4
Political risk
unknown

Low

389

413

314

Medium

Source: www.gao.gov/new.items/d07283.pdf.

availability of less expensive conventional oil, the environmental problems of waste rock disposal, and the great quantities of water needed for processing. Recent technological advances along with oil price increases make oil recovered with minimal environmental impact from shale economically feasible, although Greenpeace and other environmental groups have campaigned against oil shale projects, claiming that extracting the oil from shale creates four times the greenhouse impact as does extracting conventionally drilled oil, and that investing in the development of more nonrenewable energy sources, when we know that eventually we have to switch to renewable energy sources, doesn't make sense. Yet, as conventional sources of oil become depleted, these synthetic petroleum sources such as oil sands and oil-bearing shale have become more useful.

Coal and natural gas can also be converted to oil through a complex chemical process. During the South Africa apartheid boycotts in the 1980s, when oil exporters refused to sell South Africa oil, the South African government commercialized the German-developed Fischer-Tropsch process to obtain oil from coal through a catalyzed chemical reaction. Coal is put under pressure at high temperature and is converted to crude gas. After cooling and purification, the gas passes through a conversion process that produces high-value chemical components and synthetic oil.[19] A similar process can be used with natural gas. Chevron has a joint venture with Sasol, the innovative South African petrochemical company, for worldwide use of its gas-to-liquid (GTL) technology. Sasol has projects in Qatar, Gabon, Mozambique, Nigeria, Germany, China, India, and the United States. The U.S. military, the country's largest consumer of oil, is using alternatives such as synthetic oil and encouraging their development. The Air Force

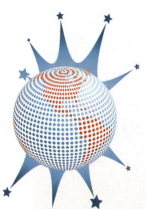

GLOBAL gauntlet

How Immediate Is the Fossil Fuel Crisis?

How do we know when our oil reserves have reached their midpoint and are starting to decline?

The answer to that important question is a critical point of contention, a bit like figuring out when we've fished the next-to-the-last fish from the ocean. You don't know for sure until it has happened. Specialists are divided and of many, even contradictory, judgments and predictions. Goldman Sachs analysts and OPEC officials themselves have said that the price of oil could hit $200 a barrel within two years. One school of analysts argues that oil production has already reached its peak and is on the decline. The peak oil theory, developed by Marion Hubbert, a geologist for Shell, holds that oil's decline will follow a bell curve. This terminal decline, fringe analysts warn, would bring us out of our cars and our economy to a standstill. Chaos would ensue. The time has come to stash in survival guides and freeze-dried food, to get ready for the economic collapse.

Increasingly this evidence is reaching people beyond the eccentric fringe so that regular citizens are becoming concerned about their carbon footprint. The largest proven oil reserves are in Saudi Arabia, and we know little of what is actually happening there. Satellite reconnaissance might suggest that the Saudis are having to push harder to get more out of the world's largest field, Ghawar. After all, Ghawar has been a major source of energy for our fossil-fuel economy for 75 years. Matthew Simmons, author of *Desert: The Coming Saudi Oil Shock and the World Economy,* has reviewed outputs of the world's oilfields, noting that 20 percent of the world's oil consumption is sourced from old fields, and no new fields in their league have been discovered in almost 30 years. In addition, many of the producers face political unrest and nationalism in countries with sizable reserves: Nigeria, Russia, Iran, Iraq, and Venezuela among them.

There is a brighter point of view. Cambridge Energy Research Associates suggests that no decline in ability to produce oil would occur before 2030. Guy Caruso, head of the U.S. government's Energy Information Administration, has faith in the market to drive consumer behavior, government policy, and innovation. He thinks that the primary risk is not reserves, but above-the-ground political issues.

Developed world consumption, especially in the United States, will face challenges as India and China draw from the same supplies to build their economies. People realize that the price of oil is destined to rise and that they have to adjust to these realities. To many in the United States, conservation and the development of renewable resources look like a reasonable path, much more so than five years ago. Conservation and a call for renewable energy sources is becoming mainstream. Colleges have green dorms where residents recycle and reduce their energy consumption. Recycling has become commonplace in most areas. Towns are erecting wind power and solar farms to meet their municipal needs. And SUV gas guzzlers, one of the valued American indulgences, are becoming burdensome beyond their value.

Increased gas efficiency in our vehicles, improved domestic oil supply, including untapped reserves, deep sea drilling, the application of new technologies to coal, and the increase of ethanol production are ways to address the oil scarcity/unavailability issue in the United States. (True, increased production of ethanol reduces food production at a time when there are worldwide food shortages and food prices are rising dramatically. So the question, "Does a developed country have a moral duty to produce food over fuel crops when hunger is a global issue?" may arise.)

What's your best thinking on how immediate the fossil fuel crisis may be? Is it immediate, or do we have another good 50 to 100 years to figure out our transition to new energy sources?[20]

plans to buy 25 percent of its jet fuel from synthetic sources by 2016, and the Pentagon is actively exploring the use of synthetic fuels throughout the Defense Department.[21]

Nuclear Power Nuclear power was predicted to be on its way out because waste material storage is problematic and accidents at the plants can be dangerous over large distances, as we learned from Chernobyl, the 1986 Ukrainian nuclear disaster.[22] Yet nuclear power plants generate little pollution in their normal operation, so as the price of oil rises and new designs are available, nuclear power use has increased. Fewer nuclear plants are being retired, and those in service are being used at higher capacity. Higher nuclear growth is expected in developing countries, where most of the reactors under

> IF EVERYONE IN THE WORLD ENJOYED THE SAME LEVEL OF NATURAL RESOURCE CONSUMPTION AS A TYPICAL UK CITIZEN, WE WOULD NEED THREE PLANETS TO SUPPORT US. THIS [APPROACH TO FOSSIL FUEL ENERGY CONSUMPTION] IS CLEARLY UNSUSTAINABLE.
>
> —www.bioregional.com

construction are located. China, India and Russia have ambitious nuclear plants coming on-line or under construction. The International Atomic Energy Agency (IAEA) lists 56 nuclear plants under construction, the majority in China (21), Russia (9), Korea (6), and India (5).[23] (See Figure 5.17.) China has 11 plants in operation, 20 under construction, and is committed to a sixfold increase by 2020.[24] The U.S. Nuclear Energy Institute reports that more than 30 nuclear power plant licenses are being actively pursued in the United States, although there is significant concern about safety issues.[25] In addition, France has turned heavily to nuclear generation while making a concerted effort to curb fossil fuel consumption and develop a strategic energy security policy. France produces 75 percent of its electricity by nuclear power and has one of the lowest rates of greenhouse gas emissions in the industrialized world.[26] Strong commitment to nuclear power has enabled France to go from a net importer of electricity to the world's largest exporter. If the price of oil stays high, nuclear power is likely to continue to grow from its present 15 percent share of the world's electricity grid. Despite the dangers of spent fuel storage and radiation, nuclear energy has very low carbon emissions, and its use also contributes to energy self-sufficiency, as is the case with France.

Coal Coal, much like nuclear power, was predicted to be on its decline as an energy source, largely because it pollutes heavily, but just the opposite is the case: coal's consumption is projected to increase 49 percent through 2030, largely due to increases in China and India. However, because other fuel sources are developing at a faster pace than is coal, its share of world primary energy consumption is projected to increase only slightly, from 26 percent in 2004 to a projected 28 percent in 2030.[27] Non-OECD member countries in Asia, the largest of which are China and India, are projected to account for 94 percent of the expected global increase in the use of coal through 2030.[28] The United States has coal reserves to last 134 years at current consumption rates, which puts the United States at the top of countries with substantial recoverable coal reserves.[29] Russia, China, India and Australia follow. (See Figure 5.18.)

Unfortunately, burning coal frequently creates emissions that are directly responsible for global warming, although there are clean coal technologies being developed. They promise to reduce emissions from coal-fired plants, one by venting the emissions deep into the ground, another by pulverizing the coal before it is burned, and still another that uses the South African conversion process to change the coal to a gas before it is burned.

▼**FIGURE 5.17**
World Nuclear Generating Capacity by Region, 2006, 2013, and 2030

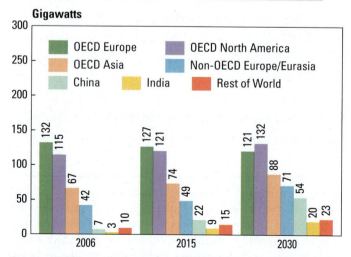

Sources: 2006: Energy Information Administration (EIA), *International Energy Annual 2006* (June–December 2008), web site www.eia.doe.gov/iea. **2015 and 2030:** EIA, World Energy Projections Plus (2009).

▼**FIGURE 5.18**
Coal Consumption in Selected World Regions, 1980–2030

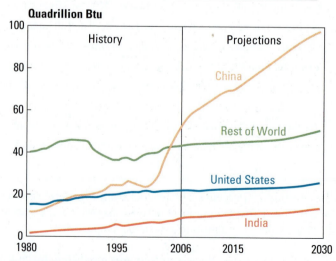

Sources: History: Energy Information Administration (EIA), *International Energy Annual 2006* (June–December 2008), web site www.eia.doe.gov/iea. **Projections:** EIA, World Energy Projections Plus (2009).

Through their use of coal, China, India, and the United States contribute greatly to greenhouse gasses. In the United States, the Environmental Protection Agency ruled in December 2009 that greenhouse gases threaten public health, so now the federal government can enact regulation of tailpipe and smokestack emissions. The **Kyoto Protocol,** the United Nations Framework Convention on Climate Change, calls for nations to work together to reduce global warming by reducing their emissions of the gasses that contribute to it, carbon dioxide first among them. To date, the United States is the only industrialized country that has signed and not ratified the Kyoto Protocol.

Natural Gas

Natural gas is the cleanest burning among the fossil fuels, its greenhouse gas emissions significantly less than with oil or coal. This increased burning efficiency means gas has much lower contributions to acid rain, solid waste and water pollution than do other fossil fuels. As oil prices increase, natural gas consumption is expected to increase as a substitute fuel, with a 47 percent projected increase through 2030.

Renewable Energy Sources

Everyone accepts that one day renewable energy sources will replace fossil fuels, either because the price of nonrenewable energy sources will become too high relative to the cost of developing sustainable renewable sources or because the sources themselves will be depleted. In addition, there is growing concern about the impact of carbon emissions produced by coal and oil on climate change. There are at least eight renewable alternative energy sources: hydroelectric, solar, wind, geothermal, waves, tides, biomass fuels such as ethanol, and ocean thermal energy conversion. (See Figure 5.19.)

None of these is available everywhere, but all appear to have applications under appropriate conditions. There is growth in all areas of renewable energy sources. For the first time, growth in the renewable sector outpaced growth in the nonrenewable sector in both the European Union and the United States.[30] Total global power capacity from new renewable energy sources was up 16 percent, spurred on by two basic drivers, climate change and energy security. Wind power has achieved a 31 percent growth rate in 2009 alone, with growth in China over 100 percent, for the fourth year in a row.[31] The fastest growing renewable energy source is solar, specifically, photovoltaics (PV), with a 70 percent increase over 2008. Much of this growth is represented by homes with PV solar panels mounted on their roofs. Geothermal growth moved forward, especially in the United States. As Figure 5.20 suggests, renewable energy is still a small portion of the world's energy supply, yet it is a growing part. Figure 5.21 illustrates financial new investment in sustainable energy from 2002 through 2008.

Biomass is a category of renewable energy fuels based on photosynthesis, the process through which plants transform the sun's energy into chemical energy. Ethanol is a biomass fuel and,

Kyoto Protocol
United Nations Framework Convention on Climate Change, which calls for nations to reduce global warming by reducing their emissions of the gasses that contribute to it

biomass A category of fuels whose energy source is photosynthesis, through which plants transform the sun's energy into chemical energy; sources include corn, sugarcane, wheat

▼**FIGURE 5.19**
Renewable Power Capacities, Developing World, EU and Top Six Countries

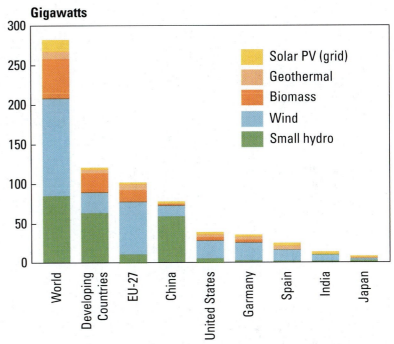

Source: www.ren21.net/globalstatusreport/g2009.asp.

▼**FIGURE 5.20**
World Electricity Generation by Fuel, 2006–2030

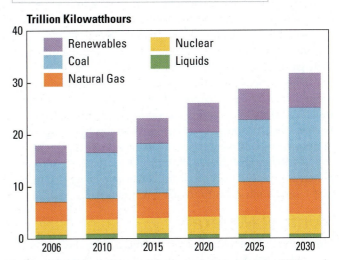

Sources: 2006: Derived from Energy Information Administration (EIA), *International Energy Annual 2006* (June–December 2008), web site www.eia.doe.gov/iea. **Projections:** EIA, World Energy Projections Plus (2009).

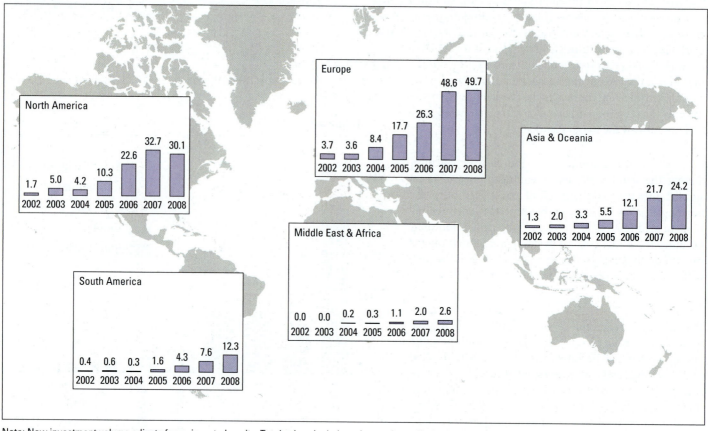

Note: New investment volume adjusts for re-invested equity. Total values include estimates for undisclosed deals
Source: New Energy Finance, UNEP SEFI

coincidentally, the source of alcohol in alcoholic beverages. Its use has risen as the cost of oil has increased beyond ethanol's production cost. Since ethanol burns cleaner than does gasoline, its use also reduces carbon emissions. The sources of ethanol are diverse, with corn, wheat, and sugarcane among the most popular. Brazil leads the world in biomass fuel, meeting 40 percent of its gasoline demand with ethanol produced from sugarcane. Brazil has also pioneered the concept of flexible-fuel vehicles and has added 25 percent ethanol to fuel sold there. Cellulose to ethanol technology to generate ethanol from agricultural waste such as corncobs is in the project demonstration phase. Figure 5.21 displays new investment in sustainable power by region. In addition, the Renewable Energy Policy Network for the 21st Century has an interactive map of global renewable energy sources by sector and country at http://www.ren21.net/map/.

Nonfuel Minerals

Although much of the world's attention to natural resources has centered on the discovery and development of new and cleaner energy sources, there are some mineral natural resources about which governments and industry need to think strategically.

Nonfuel minerals are used in all areas of modern living, from house construction to the manufacture of computers and motor vehicles. Chrome and manganese are indispensable for hardening steel; platinum is a vital catalytic agent in the oil-refining process and is used in automotive catalytic converters; vanadium is used in forming aerospace titanium alloys and in producing sulfuric acid. Table 5.2 illustrates the main sources of mineral imports into the United States.

We have reviewed major natural resources, the factor conditions on which all business rests. These resources are what we have to work with. Now we move to the more challenging issue of how we work with what we have, how we use these resources. Currently we face two energy crises. The first has to do with the eventual depletion of nonrenewable fossil fuels. The second energy crisis is driven by climate change, and its resolution requires global cooperation.[32] The triggers for climate change lie in emissions from the same carbon-based fuels whose limited supply contributes to the first crisis. One response to both of these crises would be to develop clean energy sources. We consider business and environmentally sustainable approaches next.

▼ **TABLE 5.2** U.S. Minerals Ranked by Net Import Reliance, 2009

Commodity	Percent	Major Sources (2005–08[1])
Arsenic (trioxide)	100	China, Morocco, Belgium, Hong Kong
Asbestos	100	Canada
Bauxite and Alumina	100	Jamaica, Guinea, Brazil, Australia
Cesium	100	Canada
Fluorspar	100	China, Mexico, South Africa
Graphite (natural)	100	China, Mexico, Canada, Brazil
Indium	100	China, Japan, Canada, Belgium
Manganese	100	South Africa, Gabon, China, Australia
Mica, sheet (natural)	100	China, Brazil, Belgium, India
Niobium (columbium)	100	Brazil, Canada, Germany, Estonia
Quartz Crystal (Industrial)	100	China, Japan, Russia
Rare Earths	100	China, Japan, France, Russia
Rubidium	100	Canada
Strontium	100	Mexico, Germany
Tantalum	100	Australia, China, Brazil, Japan
Thallium	100	Russia, Germany, Netherlands
Thorium	100	United Kingdom, France, Canada
Vanadium	100	Czech Republic, Rep. of Korea, Canada, Austria
Yttrium	100	China, Japan, France
Gallium	99	Germany, Canada, China, Ukraine
Gemstones	99	Israel, India, Belgium, South Africa
Antimony	93	China, Mexico, Belgium
Bismuth	90	Belgium, China, United Kingdom, Mexico
Germanium	90	Belgium, China, Germany, Russia
Platinum	89	South Africa, Germany, United kingdom, Canada
Barite	80	China, India
Tin	80	Peru, Bolivia, China, Indonesia
Rhenium	79	Chile, Netherlands
Diamond (natural industrial stone)	78	Botswana, South Africa, Namibia, India
Stone (dimension)	78	Brazil, Italy, China, Turkey
Zinc	76	Canada, Peru, Mexico, Ireland
Cobalt	75	Norway, Russia, China, Canada
Potash	73	Canada, Belarus, Germany, Russia

Commodity	Percent	Major Sources (2005–08[1])
Titanium Mineral Concentrates	73	South Africa, Australia, Canada, Ukraine
Titanium (sponge)	67	Kazakhastan, Japan, China, Ukraine
Silver	63	Mexico, Canada, Peru, Chile
Tungsten	63	China, Germany, Canada, Bolivia
Peat	60	Canada
Palladium	47	Russia, South Africa, United Kingdom, Belgium
Nitrogen (fixed), Ammonia	40	Trinidad and Tobago, Canada, Russia, Ukraine
Chromium	39	South Africa, Kazakhstan, Russia
Vermiculite	39	China, South Africa
Garnet (industrial)	37	Australia, India, China, Canada
Diamond (dust, grit, and powder)	35	China, Ireland, Russia, Rep. of Korea
Magnesium Metal	35	Canada, Russia, Israel, China
Magnesium Compounds	28	China, Austia, Canada, Australia
Silicon (ferrosilicon)	27	China, Russia, Venezuela, Canada
Copper	24	Chile, Canada, Peru, Mexico
Perlite	21	Greece
Gypsum	19	Canada, Mexico, Spain
Salt	19	Canada, Chile, Mexico, Peru
Aluminum	18	Canada, Russia, Brazil, Venezuela
Nickel	18	Canada, Russia, Australia, Norway
Mica, scrap and flake (natural)	11	Canada, China, India, Finland
Cement	8	China, Canada, Republic of Korea, Thailand
Iron and Steel Slag	8	Japan, Canada, Italy, France
Iron and Steel	7	Canada, European Union, China, Mexico
Sulfur	4	Canada, Mexico, Venezuela
Pumice	3	Greece, Turkey, Iceland, Mexico
Beryllium	2	Kazakhastan, United Kingdom, Kenya, Ireland
Lime	2	Canada, Mexico
Stone (crushed)	2	Canada, Mexico, The Bahamas
Phosphate Rock	1	Morocco

Note: Excludes mineral fuels.

[1] In descending order of import share.

Source: USGS, *Mineral Commodity Summaries, 2010*
Updated: February 2010

ENVIRONMENTAL SUSTAINABILITY

The concept of sustainability has broad scope. *Sustainability* is about maintaining something, and that something might be the environment, society, the economy, people within the economy, or the organization.[33] By its very nature, sustainability is a systems concept. The thing we are trying to sustain (a business, a way of life, the natural world) exists within a larger system, and if that larger system is not sustained, the subsystem is unlikely to survive. For example, are the Everglades likely to be sustained if temperature and precipitation change significantly? As this example illustrates, the likelihood of a specific local geography or culture being sustained if the larger environment is not sustained is quite slim. In this way, sustainability is actually local and global at the same time; any location involves systems that are global.[34] France has controlled its greenhouse gas emissions by developing nuclear energy as the basis of its energy grid, yet greenhouse gas produced in the United States or China will affect people in France. **Environmental sustainability** is both local and global. Figure 5.22 illustrates this "act locally, think globally" truth of sustainability. It rests

on the commitment of business to operate without reducing the capacity of the environment to provide for future generations.[35]

Environmentally sustainable approaches involve taking care of the present needs of the business and the needs of future generations at the same time.[36] Such approaches usually consider the ecological, social, and economic systems in which a business functions, its natural world, social world, and economic world. In this section, we look at the characteristics of sustainable business practices and explore an application of the *stakeholder model* to sustainability.

LO4   **Explain** the major characteristics of sustainable business.

Characteristics of Environmentally Sustainable Business

There are three characteristics of evolving sustainable business practices that are widely agreed upon: limits, interdependence, and equity.[37] *Limits* have to do with the recognition that environmental resources are exhaustible. Water, soil, and air can become toxic, and their use needs to be informed by awareness of that danger. The current focus on greenhouse gasses and their contribution to global warming offers one example of limits. Let's assume as a given that control of emissions would be an ecologically responsible decision. A business that learns how to operate within the limits of the inevitable emissions controls early on in the adoption process would accrue first-mover advantages.

Interdependence describes the relationships among ecological, social, and economic systems. Action in one system affects the others. This interdependence can be seen in stark

▼**FIGURE 5.22**   Sustainability Is Local and Global

Ecological	Social	Economic	
Survival Sustainability			Global ↕ Local
Production of life support systems Prevention of species extinction	Capacity to solve serious problems	Subsistence	
Maintaining Quality of Life			Global ↕ Local
Maintenance of decent environmental quality	Maintenance of decent social quality (e.g., vibrant community life)	Maintenance of decent standard of living	
Improving Quality of Life			Global ↕ Local
Improving environmental quality	Improving social quality	Improving standard of living	

Source: Philip Sutton, www.green-innovations.asn.au/sustblty.htm.

dimensions in examples from the extractive industries. Mining operations in Papua (formerly Irian Jaya), Indonesia, have settled areas that had previously been the hunting grounds of indigenous hunter-gatherer tribes, among them the Kamoro and Amungme, causing considerable social stress. The mining operations involve some river and stream pollution from tailings, which can be, and in many cases have been, abated. The mining company, Freeport-McMoran, provides health care and education for the indigenous peoples in the area and appears to have made efforts to be a good citizen and a socially responsible neighbor. Yet the advancement the company brings is threatening the continued existence of the indigenous people, through development and education. Imagine the strains on a social system in which parents, wearing loin-cloths and using poisoned blow arrows to kill game, are living as traditional hunter-gatherers, while their children are being educated to cruise the Internet technologies and eat Western-style food. The interrelatedness of mining operations in this remote area and good corporate citizenship issues go beyond pollution and infringement of hunting grounds to complicated ethical and social issues related to development. The local social, economic, and ecological systems are all players whose sustainability is threatened in this situation. In less stark dimensions, filmmaker Michael Moore's eulogy to Flint, Michigan, *Roger and Me,* explores the economic, social, and ecological implications of GM's decision to move production out of Flint.

Equity in distribution suggests that for interdependence to work, there cannot be vast differences in the distribution of gains. Especially in a globalizing world where information is increasingly more open, vast inequities may lead to unrest and violence. An example of corporate challenges presented by lack of equity in distribution is found in Shell Oil's operations in southern Nigeria, which have been forced to shut down several times after raids by groups claiming to speak for the local Ijaw tribe. The tribe claims they have been "cheated of oil wealth pumped from their land by the central government and oil companies." Shell employees have undertaken work stoppages as part of demands for equitable pay, and Shell, along with Mobil, has been forced to cut production by 25 percent, in

a market of rising demand.[38] Political tensions related to equity in distribution have also informed Venezuela's and Bolivia's oil businesses.

Increasingly, companies will need to make decisions about setting limits on how their operations affect the environment. They will also encounter increased signs of the interdependence that exists among the social, economic, and ecological systems that form the context for their business. Equity in distribution is one of the ways that such interdependence can work. It requires a business model that allocates gain from the business's value creation to all actors in the context, under the principle that a rising tide raises all boats. Sam Palisano, CEO of IBM, has spoken about this new way of understanding business when he said that IBM wanted to end its colonial company model and move on to a truly globally integrated model where high levels of trust persist among all stakeholders.[39]

LO5 Discuss the utility of the stakeholder model for sustainable business.

The Stakeholder Model for Sustainable Business

The concept of sustainability is a complex one because it impacts all aspects of business decisions. Some of the areas that are most commonly involved are:

Alternative fuels	Office maintenance
Brownfield remediation	Pollution prevention
Corporate accountability	Social investing
Ecological development	Sustainable technology
Ecotourism	Transportation alternatives
Energy conservation	Waste reduction
Green building design	Water conservation

One model that offers a helpful framework for thinking about environmental sustainability in business is **stakeholder theory**.[40] Developed by R. Edward Freeman, this approach differs from the traditional input-process-output economic business model because it involves identification and consideration of the network of tensions caused by competing demands within which any business exists. The traditional economic model of business considers a far narrower scope of influences (employees, owners, and

relationships in the larger context and the responsibilities that develop from them. In stakeholder theory, profits are a *result* of value creation rather than the primary driver in the process, as in the economic model. Freeman points out that there are many companies whose operations are consistent with stakeholder theory, including Johnson & Johnson, eBay, Google, and Lincoln Electric.

To achieve this balance among competing tensions, the company sees itself in relation to its stakeholders, and then views itself in a social context to identify its purpose, principles, and responsibilities clearly, as Figure 5.23 illustrates. The company then addresses limits, interdependence, and equity of distribution,

> "The whole idea of compassion is based on a keen awareness of the interdependence of all these living beings, which are all part of one another, and all involved in one another.
>
> —Thomas Merton

suppliers) that are driven by the single goal of creating profits. Stakeholder theory forces a business to address *underlying values and principles*. It "pushes managers to be clear about how they want to do business, specifically, what kind of relationships they want and need to create with their stakeholders to deliver on their purpose."[41] Stakeholder theory also suggests that the tensions among the varying stakeholders in a business environment can be balanced. Business then becomes about

all in a societal context. One way to measure the company's activities in this larger context is the process of triple-bottom-line accounting. Here the company measures its social and environmental performance in addition to its traditional economic performance. For an example of triple-bottom-line reporting, see Freeport-McMoRan's accounting of its mining operations in Indonesia (www.fcx.com, especially the Sustainable Development Report and the videos). The company's public materials suggest it is using a stakeholder approach, increasing value, and contributing to the quality of life for its constituencies, including locals, while operating low-impact mining.

Interface, Inc., is another company that has made progress in incorporating sustainability into their basic business model. The manufacturer of the trendy modular carpeting Flor is notable because its product is spun from petroleum products. In its overview of sustainability, Interface is "greatly concerned about activities that destroy the vitality and restorative quality of the Earth. As a petrochemical dependent company, we feel it is essential that we correct our actions and encourage others to follow our lead. In the regrettable absence of multilateral governmental action, we commit to voluntary action."[42] (See Figure 5.24.)

Patagonia, the international outdoor gear company, is another company that has environmental sustainability at the core of its mission. In the 1970s, the climber Yvon Chouinard founded Patagonia with the goal of providing equipment for "clean climbing," that is, climbing that minimizes environmental impact: "Patagonia exists as a business to

▼**FIGURE 5.23**
The Company in a Societal Context

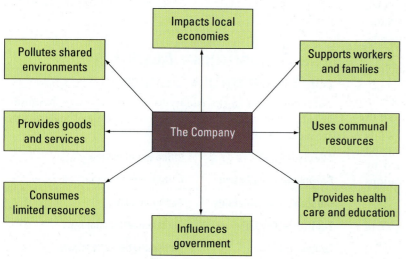

Source: "Your Company in a Societal Context," Slide 7 from Pathways PowerPoint presentation *Sustainability and Business,* World Resources Institute, http://pathways.wri.org/index.asp?Topic1 (accessed 2010).

FIGURE 5.24 Interface Metrics

(a) Cumulative Avoided Cost from Waste Elimination Activities

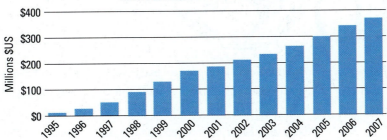

(b) Recycled and Biobased Raw Materials Used at Carpet Manufacturing Facilities

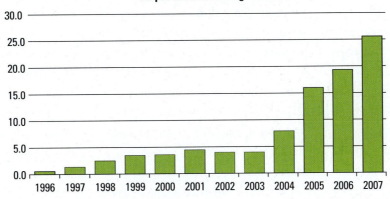

(c) Total Energy Consumption Profile in 2007

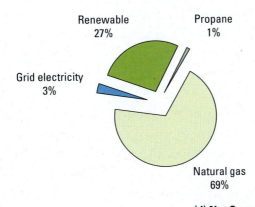

Renewable 27%

Propane 1%

Grid electricity 3%

Natural gas 69%

(d) Net Greenhouse Gas Emissions

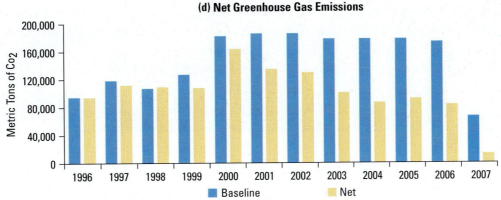

■ Baseline   ■ Net

Source: http://www.interfacesustainability.com/metrics.html.

CU in ib

Jacques Abelman: Cultural Immersion Provides Foundation for this Dutch Landscape Architect

Cultural immersion is critical for his development, says U.S. citizen Jacques Abelman, a landscape architect working in The Netherlands. He shares with you his observations on developing an international career:

I am currently living in Amsterdam and working in the field of landscape architecture and sustainable development. I have a background in fine arts and environmental science. During my undergraduate liberal arts education at Amherst College I was able to pursue the intellectual fields that interested me, and I find that although this was not a professional preparation for a specific field, the thinking skills I learned there have been instrumental in being able to function in a number of different professional contexts.

Ten years ago I left the United States to take a master's in design at The University of the Arts, London. I had not looked for a job before I left the U.S. The graduate program was my first introduction to life in a major city abroad, and I found that this was a big transition and quite stressful at times. But the number of opportunities I discovered in London soon allowed me to embark on a new professional trajectory. Because Europe is relatively compact, a job in London led to a job in Paris and eventually Amsterdam. The excitement and the challenge of adapting to life in each place, and in remarkably different cultural environments, has been very stimulating. Language and cultural differences require dedication and an extra layer of work. Dutch has been a challenging language to learn. But there is always a community of English speakers wherever I have gone and an "expat" scene. However, it is much more interesting to immerse yourself in the culture and through understanding more about the country and people you are with; you learn a lot more about yourself and your own skills. Europeans appreciate immensely foreigners taking the time to integrate into their culture, wherever it may be, and by doing that you can bring the best American qualities to bear in new situations. For example, moving forward to find the best solution in creative and ambitious ways . . . "thinking outside the box." The clichéd go-getter mentality is actually a huge asset. On the other hand, it takes time to learn how to translate our American mentalities into a new culture, to be able to "read" the cultural subtext that is always present in a situation. This is perhaps one of the major keys to being able to function effectively internationally.

My area of interest is sustainability, applied to fields of architecture and urbanism. My experiences led me to choose The Netherlands because my specific field, landscape architecture, is highly developed here. The Dutch have been designing and refining their landscape since the Middle Ages and have created successful models of high density sustainable cities. What is normal in Dutch cities often strikes foreigners as being quite remarkable, and what I am learning and doing here will allow me to export my knowledge abroad back to the United States and to other countries around the world. Sustainability is now present in almost every field imaginable in The Netherlands and highly supported by the government. New funding and research programs are constantly being developed and open up more possibilities for education and business. After living here for five years, I am considered to be a Dutch designer, and I benefit from the same opportunities as my native Dutch colleagues. Becoming a part of the design community here has been very rewarding, and I feel that I am still learning an immense amount. Having lived now in three different neighboring countries, all vastly different, has changed the way I see the world and enriched my life considerably.

inspire and implement solutions to the environmental crisis." Patagonia recognizes that the traditional approach to doing business, focusing on quarterly earnings and generally accepted accounting principles (GAAP), is not sustainable in that it is not complete. Such accounting does not account for negative externalities such as environmental degradation and social ills; thus, it creates an unrealistic view of economic performance; and it is bound to lead to an environmental crisis. Patagonia's "ecosystem model" for sustainability relies on the synergies between the environmental, social, and financial elements of a business. This synchronization creates a virtuous cycle: the company's environmental and social commitment attracts loyal customers and employees, which improves the financial performance of the firm, which facilitates further commitment, and so onward. Within such an approach, business can inspire solutions to the environmental crisis.[43] As Chouinard observed years ago, "No business can be done on a dead planet. A company that is taking the long view must accept that it has an obligation to minimize its impact on the natural environment."[44] On the production side, Patagonia uses recycled materials, both in its building construction and in its products. Plastic soda cans are the source of much of the fleece, and organic cotton is used exclusively. Patagonia also has introduced a program called the Footprint Chronicles that traces the ecological impact of the manufacture of select products, directly addressing the trade-offs global sourcing creates and evaluating the ecological impact of various sourcing decisions. This feature, designed to educate, avoids simplifying what is a complex set of issues and is a bit like listening in on an ethics class discussion. See "The Footprint Chronicles" at www.patagonia.com/web/us/contribution/patagonia .go?assetid=23429&ln=150/.

Chapter 5 has covered a lot of topics of importance to the international manager. We began with a focus on how location, topography, and climate can influence business, drawing on Porter's diamond model. We then looked at natural resources and moved on to look at environmental sustainability. ◼

chapter six

"
In politics stupidity is
not a handicap."

—Napoleon Bonaparte

political
+trade forces

In many ways, the political climate of a country in which a business operates is as important as the country's topography, its natural resources, and its climate. Hospitable, stable governments can encourage business investment and growth despite geographic or weather obstacles and a scarcity of natural resources. The opposite is equally true. Some areas of the world that are relatively blessed with natural resources and manageable topography and weather have been little developed because of government instability. Occasionally, a country's government is hostile to investment in its territory by foreign companies, even though they might provide capital, technology, and training for development of the country's resources and people.

This chapter provides an indication of the types of risks political forces pose to private business. As we shall see, some of the risks can stem from more than one political force. We also look at some of the ways international trade is heavily influenced by political forces.

LEARNING OBJECTIVES

After reading this chapter, you should be able to:

LO1 Discuss expropriation and privatization.

LO2 Explain the changing sources and reasons for terrorism and the methods and growing power of terrorists.

LO3 Evaluate the importance to business of government stability and policy continuity.

LO4 Explain country risk assessment by international business.

LO5 Discuss types of trade restrictions.

LO1 **Discuss** expropriation and privatization.

GOVERNMENT OWNERSHIP OF BUSINESS

One might assume that government ownership of the factors of production is found only in communist countries, but that assumption is not correct. For example, the 13 largest energy companies on earth are owned by governments. From country to country, there are wide differences in the industries that are government-owned and in the extent of government ownership.

Why Firms are Nationalized

Governments put their hands on firms for a number of reasons. Some of these reasons are (1) to extract more money from the firms, if the government suspects that the firms are concealing profits; (2) profitability—the government believes it can run the firms more efficiently and make more money; (3) ideology; (4) job preservation—to save jobs by putting dying industries on life-support systems; (5) because the government has pumped money into a firm or an industry, and control usually follows money; and (6) happenstance, as with the nationalization after World War II of German-owned firms in Europe.

Unfair Competition?

Where government-owned companies compete with privately owned companies, the private companies sometimes complain that the government companies have unfair advantages. Some of the complaints are that (1) government-owned companies can cut prices unfairly because they do not have to make profits, (2) they get cheaper financing, (3) they get government contracts, (4) they get export assistance, and (5) they can hold down wages with government assistance.

Another advantage state-owned companies enjoy over privately owned business comes in the form of direct subsidies: payments by the government to those companies. The EU Commission has been trying to discourage such subsidy payments. For years it has required annual financial reports from state-controlled companies as part of a crackdown on the subsidies that can distort competition.

PRIVATIZATION

Britain's former prime minister, Margaret Thatcher, was a leader of the **privatization** movement. During her years in office, Thatcher decreased state-owned companies from a 10 percent share of Britain's GNP to 3.9 percent. She sold more than 30 companies, raising some $65 billion. Similarly, from 1975 to 1989, Chile's Pinochet sold government stakes in more than 160 corporations and 16 banks and more than 3,600

agro-industrial plants, mines and real estate, not including the return of property expropriated during the previous government of Salvador Allende.

Privatization Anywhere

Privatization does not always involve ownership transfer from government to private entities. Activities previously conducted by the state may be contracted out, as Mozambique has contracted a British firm to run its customs administration and Thailand has private companies operating some of the passenger trains of its state-owned railroad.

Figure 6.1 shows privatization by geographic region. The percentages in the figure total 100 without reference to the United States; neither the U.S. government nor the individual state governments are participating substantially in the privatization trend.

GOVERNMENT PROTECTION

A historical function of government, whatever its ideology, has been the protection of the economic activities—farming, mining, manufacturing, and so forth—within its geographic area of control. These activities must be protected from attacks and destruction or robbery by bandits, revolutionaries, foreign invaders, or terrorists. In 1990, the Iraqi armed forces invaded Kuwait, quickly overwhelming the defenders of that smaller country.

The aftermath of this war demonstrates the influence of politics on business. In gratitude for American fighting in Desert Storm, Kuwait and other Gulf Cooperation Council countries—Saudi Arabia, Qatar, Bahrain, the United Arab Emirates, and Oman—bought some $36 billion of American arms. But in a 1997 competition to sell Kuwait 72 self-propelled howitzers, a Chinese company beat out an American company's widely considered superior versions. In private conversations, Kuwaiti officials said their reasons for buying Chinese had nothing to do with range, price, or accuracy and everything to

FIGURE 6.1
Privatizations by Region

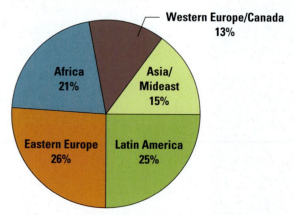

Source: "Privatization Worldwide Summary," prepared for the Trans-national Corporations and Management Division of the United Nations. Used here by permission of the author, Michael S. Minor.

do with politics. It seems China suggested it would withhold its support at the United Nations for extending trade sanctions against Iraq unless Kuwait gave the estimated $300 million order to the Chinese company. "Sometimes you get to a state when you feel you're being blackmailed," a senior Kuwaiti official said. "We lean toward the U.S. equipment, but we have to find a way to please the Chinese and not upset them in the Security Council."[1]

LO2   **Explain** the changing sources and reasons for terrorism and the methods and growing power of terrorists.

Terrorism

Since the 1970s, various groups have hijacked airplanes, shot and kidnapped individuals, and bombed people and objects. Al Qaeda is by no means the only terrorist organization in the world. Among the better-known groups involved in **terrorism** are the Irish Republican Army (IRA), Hamas, Hezballah, Abu Nidal and other Islamic fundamentalist groups, the Basque separatist movement (ETA), the Japanese Red Army, the German Red Army Faction, and various terrorist organizations in Latin America.

Countermeasures by Industry

Insurance to cover ransom payments, antiterrorist schools, and companies to handle negotiations with kidnappers have come into being. The insurance is called KRE (kidnap, ransom, and extortion), and it can pay for the ransom, the fees of specialist negotiators, the salary of the hostage, and counseling for the victim and the family. Fees for the security of CEOs can range up to $1.7 million per year for Larry Ellison, chairman of Oracle Corp., down to $239 for a home-alarm monitoring service for the chair of Valero Energy Corp.[4]

As kidnapping and extortion directed against businesses and governments have become common fund-raising and political techniques for terrorists, insurance against such acts has grown into a multimillion-dollar business. The world's largest kidnapping and extortion underwriting firm is located in London. The firm, Cassidy and Davis, says that it covers some 9,000 companies. Cassidy and Davis runs antiterrorism training courses for executives, with subjects ranging from defensive driving techniques—escape tactics and battering through blockades—

> ## " Sometimes you get to a state when you feel you're being blackmailed. . . "

Kidnapping for Ransom
Kidnapping is another weapon used by terrorists. The victims are held for ransom, frequently very large amounts, which provides an important source of funds for the terrorists. Estimates are that there are 8,000 to 10,000 ransom and kidnapping situations per year and that kidnappers take home up to $500 million. One firm engaged in corporate risk consulting notes that large ransoms can be physically daunting—$1 million in mixed $20 and $100 bills weighs about 66 pounds!

Paying Ransom Becomes Counterproductive
The hostage business is booming. A remarkable deal concluded in the Philippines explains why.

Libya's Colonel Muammar Qaddafi, trying to shake off that country's pariah status, bought the release of several Western hostages held by a band of Islamist bandits in the Philippines. The price was about $1 million each. The kidnappers evidently have learned two lessons: holding a few hostages keeps the army away, and grabbing more keeps the money rolling in. Within weeks after receiving the ransom money, the Philippine kidnappers had bought new weapons and a new speedboat with which to capture more people to sell.[2] As an illustration of the global reach of terrorism, the Philippine group is thought to have links with al Qaeda. It calls itself Abu Sayyaf.[3]

to crisis management. Country-by-country risk analyses are instantly available on international computer hookups.

Antiterrorist surveillance detection and evasive driving training are also available. International Training Inc. (ITI) teaches some 5,000 students each year how to frustrate would-be assassins and kidnappers. The students are company executives and high-wealth individuals. To enhance your chances of success with your driver's training, you can harden your automobile. For example, Carat Security Group offers multilayered ballistic glass, protected car floors, run-flat tires and protected fuel tanks for the automobiles of potential victims. It cites the recent violence in Mexico as a boon to the armored car industry.

Chemical and Biological Terrorism
In 1995, the Aum Shin Rikyo cult launched a nerve gas attack in the Tokyo subway that killed 12 people and injured 5,500, many of whom suffered severe nerve damage. A malfunction in the bomb delivery system is believed to have prevented thousands of additional casualties. Sarin was the nerve gas used in the Tokyo subway attack. Chemical information about sarin is available on the Internet, making threats possible from self-taught terrorists anywhere.

LO3   **Evaluate** the importance to business of government stability and policy continuity.

stability Characteristic of a government that maintains itself in power and whose fiscal, monetary, and political policies are predictable and not subject to sudden, radical changes

instability Characteristic of a government that cannot maintain itself in power or that makes sudden, unpredictable, or radical policy changes

country risk assessment (CRA) An evaluation, conducted by a bank or business, that assesses a country's economic situation and policies and its politics to determine how much risk exists of losing an investment or not being paid

GOVERNMENT STABILITY

Government **stability** can be defined in two ways. One can speak of either a government's ability to maintain itself in power, or the stability or permanence of a government's policies. It is safe to generalize that business prospers most when there is a stable government with permanent—or gradually changing—policies. **Instability** on the other hand is when a government cannot maintain itself in power or makes sudden, unpredictable, or radical policy changes. It is hard for business to flourish when government is unstable.

Stability and Instability: Examples and Results

Instability in Zimbabwe Zimbabwe was a relatively rich African country that was a net exporter of food. The Zimbabweans elected resistance leader Robert Mugabe as prime minister. In the 1990s he decided to seize land equipment from big farms and to redistribute it to small holders. People close to Mugabe were able to get the best of the land, but they have failed to work it and produce food.

There is now a severe food shortage, and the country depends on foreign aid. But the aid-donating countries have grown impatient with corruption and are cutting back their aid. It is also generally conceded that Mugabe stole the presidential election in 2008. The resulting instability caused a loss of confidence by potential foreign investors, so money, expertise, and technology are no longer coming in. Poverty and starvation are the lot of many Zimbabweans.

INTERNATIONAL COMPANIES

International business is not merely a passive victim of political forces. It can be a powerful force in the world political arena. About half of the world's 100 biggest economic units are firms, not nations.

International companies (ICs) repeatedly make decisions about where to invest, where to conduct research and development, and where to manufacture products. The country or area in which an investment is made or a laboratory, research facility, or manufacturing plant is located can benefit as jobs are created, new or improved technology becomes available, or products are produced that can be exported or substituted for imports.

Of course, the IC will seek the country and area in which it can operate most beneficially and profitably. It will negotiate with the national and local areas in which it is considering an investment or plant location in efforts to maximize benefits such as tax breaks, infrastructure improvements, and worker training programs.

The financial size of many ICs provides them with a strong negotiating position. And an IC's power need not rest solely on size. It can come from the possession of capital, technology, and management skills, plus the capability to deploy those resources around the world. An IC may have the processing, productive, distributive, and marketing abilities necessary for the successful utilization of raw materials or for the manufacture, distribution, and marketing of certain products. Those abilities are frequently not available in developing countries. Recognition of the desirability of IC investments is growing.[5] For example, China has operations in a wide variety of African states, such as oil exploration in Chad, the Congo and Guinea, and building projects in Ivory Coast, Nigeria and Angola.

LO4 Explain country risk assessment by international business.

COUNTRY RISK ASSESSMENT

The political events of recent years have caused firms to concentrate much more on country risk assessment (CRA). **Country risk assessment** is an evaluation, conducted by a bank or business, that assesses a country's economic situation and policies and its politics to determine how much risk exists of losing an investment. Because of recent turmoil, firms that had already done CRA updated and strengthened the function, and many other companies began to engage in the practice.

Types of Country Risks

Country risks are increasingly political in nature. Among them are wars, revolutions, and coups. Less dramatic, but nevertheless important for businesses, are government changes caused by election of a new government that may be hostile to private business and particularly to foreign-owned business.

The risks may be economic or financial. Countries may have persistent balance-of-payments deficits or high inflation rates. Repayment of loans may be questionable. Labor conditions may cause investors to pause. Labor productivity may be low, or labor unions may be militant. Laws may be changed in regard to such subjects as taxes, currency convertibility, tariffs, quotas, and labor permits. The chances for a fair trial in local courts must be assessed. And terrorism may be present. If it is, can the company protect its personnel and property?

- *Harvard Business Review*'s Global Risk Navigator
- Standard and Poor's Rating Group
- Moody's Investor Services.[6]

Instead of or in addition to using outside consultants, a number of firms have hired such experts as international business or political science professors or retired State Department, CIA, or military people.

LO5 Discuss basic types of trade restrictions.

> " In nearly every economic crisis, the root cause is political, not economic. "
>
> —Former Prime Minister Lee Kuan Yew of Singapore

Information Content for CRA

The types of information a firm will need to judge country risks vary according to the nature of its business and the length of time required for the investment, loan, or other involvement to yield a satisfactory return.

Nature of Business Consider the needs of a hotel company compared with those of mining companies. Sometimes variations exist between firms in the same industry or on a project-to-project basis also. The home country of the company may be a factor: does the host country bear a friendly attitude toward the home country or not?

Who Does Country Risk Assessing?

General or specific analyses, macro or micro analyses, and political, social, and economic analyses have been conducted for years. The Conference Board located bits and pieces of CRA being performed in various company departments—for example, the international division and the public affairs, finance, legal, economics, planning, and product-producing departments. Sometimes the people in one department were unaware that others in the company were similarly involved.

Outside consulting and publishing firms are another source of country risk analysis. As CRA has mushroomed in perceived importance, a number of such firms have been formed or have expanded. Some of the better-known outside consulting and publishing firms for CRA include:

- Business Environment Risk Intelligence (BERI) S.A.
- Control Risks Information Services
- Economist Intelligence Unit (EIU)
- Euromoney
- STRATFOR

TRADE RESTRICTIONS

Perhaps no foreign event (except fashion shows) is the subject of more writing by journalists than trade. For example, we are currently witnessing trade restrictions on rice, even as world food prices may increase as much as 40 percent. Infant industry arguments are being made in China; genetically modified and related food restrictions have appeared in Europe.

Arguments for Trade Restrictions

A number of arguments have traditionally been presented in support of efforts to restrict trade. We address several of the most common such arguments here, as well as associated rebuttal arguments.

National Defense The national defense argument for trade restrictions suggests that certain industries need protection from imports because they are vital to security and must be kept operating even though they are not competitive with foreign suppliers. For example, the U.S. shoe industry requested Congress to impose restrictions because growing reliance on imported footwear was "jeopardizing the national security of the United States." Speaking to the Armed Services Committee of the U.S. Congress, the president of the Footwear Industry of America stated: "In the event of war or other national emergency, it is unlikely that the domestic footwear industry could provide sufficient footwear for the military and civilian population. . . . Improper footwear can lead to needless casualties and turn sure victory into possible defeat." A Defense Department spokesman said he knew of no plan to investigate the prospects of a wartime shoe crisis. Furthermore, federal law already requires the armed forces to buy U.S.-made footwear exclusively.[7]

Critics of the defense argument claim it would be far more efficient for the government to subsidize a number of firms to maintain sufficient capacity for wartime use only. Moreover, a subsidy would clearly indicate to taxpayers the cost of maintaining these companies in the name of national security—something that some interests may not want known. Currently, most American ocean shipping companies receive government subsidies without which they could not remain in business because of the competition from foreign firms with lower operating costs. In this way, we have a merchant marine ready in case of hostility, and we know what this state of readiness costs us.

Sanctions to Punish Offending Nations

A related argument for imposing trade restrictions is to inflict economic damage on other nations in order to punish them or otherwise encourage them to modify behavior. A common approach is to pass legislation that prohibits trade with the "offending" nation.

But sanctions not only seldom achieve their goal of forcing change in the targeted country; they also tend to produce collateral economic damage in the nations applying them.[8] Eco-

A related argument concerns the protection of a "dying" industry, one threatened by an onslaught of imports that endangers the survival of domestic companies and the jobs they provide. Under this argument, it takes time to make the necessary adjustments to move labor and capital out of the industry and into other sectors. Protecting the industry from imports can therefore facilitate a smoother transition. This logic has been used in justifying protection for textiles and footwear in the United States and Europe. Other aid, such as subsidies for relocating to different geographic areas and for providing assistance to displaced workers, may also be part of the proposed solution.

Protect Domestic Jobs from Cheap Foreign Labor

Protectionists who use this argument usually compare lower foreign hourly wage rates to those paid in their home country. They conclude that foreign exporters can flood the home country's market with low-priced goods, and thus simultaneously eliminate jobs of home-country workers. The first fallacy of this argument is that wage costs are neither all of the production costs nor all of the labor costs, so a comparison merely based on relative hourly wages would be misleading.

> ## "The cost of subsidizing the American ethanol industry is estimated at $1 billion to $5 billion annually."

nomic sanctions during the 1990s may have cost the United States some $15 billion to $23 billion annually in exports, in addition to losses resulting from restrictions on foreign direct investment, capital flows, tourism, and other sources of income or output.[9]

Protect Infant (or Dying) Industry

Advocates for the protection of an infant industry may claim that in the long run the industry will have a comparative advantage but that firms need protection from imports until the required investment capital is obtained, the labor force is trained, production techniques are mastered, and economies of scale are achieved. Without the protection, advocates argue, a firm will not be able to survive because lower-cost imports from more mature foreign competitors will underprice it in its local market.

Efforts to protect emerging industries are not limited to developing nations, of course. For example, former Representative Ken Salazar of Colorado argued for the maintenance of a protective 54-cents-a-gallon import duty on foreign-produced ethanol, including imports from low-cost producer Brazil, in order to give "our infant industries a greater chance to grow." The cost of subsidizing the American ethanol industry is estimated at $1 billion to $5 billion annually.[10]

Second, the productivity per worker may be much greater in richer countries because of more capital per worker, superior management, and advanced technology. As a result, the labor cost component of the goods being produced could be lower even though wages are higher.

Scientific Tariff or Fair Competition

Supporters of this argument say they believe in fair competition. They simply want an import duty that will bring the cost of the imported goods up to the cost of the domestically produced article. This will eliminate any "unfair" advantage that a foreign competitor might have because of superior technology, lower raw material costs, lower taxes, or lower labor costs. It is not their intent to ban exports; they wish only to equalize the process for "fair" competition. If this were law, no doubt the rate of duty would be set to protect the least efficient producer, thereby enabling the more efficient domestic manufacturers to earn large profits. The efficient foreign producers would be penalized, and, of course, their comparative advantage would be nullified. The impact on consumers might also be viewed as unfair, since the import duty would result in an increase in the prices that they pay.

Retaliation

Representatives of an industry whose exports have had import restrictions placed on them by another

country may ask their government to retaliate with similar restrictions. An example of how retaliation begins is the ban by the European Union (EU) on imports of hormone-treated beef from the United States.

Dumping Retaliation also occurs for **dumping.** The WTO defines dumping as selling a product abroad for less than (1) the average cost of production in the exporting nation, (2) the market price in the exporting nation, or (3) the price to third countries. A manufacturer may dump products to sell excess production without disrupting prices in its domestic market, as a response to cyclical or seasonal factors (e.g., during an economic downturn or at the end of a fashion season), or as a way to raise market share. A manufacturer may also lower its export price to force the importing nation's domestic producers out of business, expecting to raise prices once that objective is accomplished. This is called *predatory dumping.*

The United States became the first country to prohibit dumping of foreign goods into its own market in 1916 (there is no U.S. law prohibiting American firms from dumping their goods abroad, though). Dumping is now within the domain of the WTO, which is the recipient of many related complaints through appeals by countries opposing the imposition of antidumping protections against their companies. Most governments retaliate when dumping is perceived to be harming local industry

New Types of Dumping There are at least five new kinds of dumping for which fair-trade lobbies consider sanctions to be justified in order to level the playing field for international trade. In reality, these special-interest groups calling for level playing fields are seeking to raise the production costs of their overseas competitors to protect local high-cost producers. The classes of dumping include:

1. *Social dumping*—unfair competition caused by firms, usually from developing nations with lower labor costs and poorer working conditions, which undermines social support systems, including worker benefits.

2. *Environmental dumping*—unfair competition caused by a country's lax environmental standards. It has been argued that globalization provides incentives to national governments to set weak environmental policies, particularly for industries whose plants can be relocated internationally.

3. *Financial services dumping*—unfair competition caused by a nation's low requirements for bank capital-asset ratios.

4. *Cultural dumping*—unfair competition caused by cultural barriers aiding local firms.

5. *Tax dumping*—unfair competition caused by differences in corporate tax rates or related special breaks. Slovakia was accused of tax dumping because its low corporate tax rate and generous incentive policies were perceived to give it an advantage over other European nations in attracting investment from multinationals.[11]

CU in ib

Ronny Cheng-Ruggeberg: Risk It!

I was born in Austin, Texas, but raised in Berkeley, California. Growing up, I traveled and moved around quite a bit, living in Arizona and Connecticut, and I frequently visited Austin to spend time at my father's famous restaurant, Chinatown. In my junior year of high school, I had planned to major in mechanical engineering, and I attended the National Student Leadership Conference at the University of Maryland–College Park to study engineering. I spent three months bored out of my mind sitting through those lectures on engineering, and that's when I realized that I needed more excitement in my life than theorems and calculus could provide.

This ultimately led to my decision to study international business and marketing at Cal Poly–San Luis Obispo and to eventually study abroad in Madrid, Spain.

While studying in Madrid, I traveled throughout Europe and have even made a return visit since then and visited many other cities and countries. I have also had the opportunity to do marketing work for a software company based out of Australia, and I am currently the channel marketing manager for a software company based out of Ireland. The best part of all of the international work and travel I have done has been the experiences. There's nothing more exciting than being able to climb up to the Acropolis in Athens, see a live bullfight in Madrid, or experience a soccer riot after a Real Madrid victory!

I have had quite a bit of international experience, and the best advice I can give is to keep an open mind, have a sense of humor, and learn from your mistakes. Don't go into another country with the mindset that your culture is right and theirs is wrong, because you won't enjoy yourself and you'll experience nothing but conflict. Whether it's work or day-to-day life, everybody makes mistakes, and what matters is how you react and learn from them. The faster you are able to laugh at any mistakes you make and learn, the easier it is to adapt to a new culture and environment. Working and traveling internationally can be the most rewarding experience, but you have to risk it to get the biscuit. You have to forget about any hang-ups you may have, because the greatest stories and accomplishments don't happen from sitting on your butt because you are too scared to go out and seek adventure.

Subsidies

Another cause of retaliation may be **subsidies** that a government makes to a domestic firm either to encourage exports or to help protect it from imports. Some examples are cash payments, government participation in ownership, low-cost loans to foreign buyers and exporters, and preferential tax treatment.

Competitors in importing nations frequently ask their governments to impose **countervailing duties** to offset the effects of a subsidy. In the United States, when the Department of Commerce receives a petition from an American firm claiming that imports from a particular country are subsidized, it first determines whether a subsidy actually was given. If so, Commerce imposes countervailing duties equal to the subsidy's amount.

result was a trade war that engulfed most of the world's economies. World trade plummeted from \$5.7 billion in 1929 to \$1.9 billion in 1932, unemployment skyrocketed, and the world entered a decade-long economic depression.

Official Prices

Official prices are included in the customs tariff of some nations. The official price guarantees that a certain minimum import duty will be paid irrespective of the actual invoice price. It thwarts a fairly common arrangement that numerous importers living in high-duty nations have with their foreign suppliers, whereby a false low invoice price is issued to reduce the amount of duty to be paid. The importer sends the difference between the false invoice price and the true price separately.

> "IMPOSITION OF TARIFFS CAN RESULT IN RETALIATION THAT IS HARMFUL RATHER THAN HELPFUL FOR A COUNTRY AND ITS WELL-BEING."

Tariff Barriers

Tariffs, or import duties, are taxes levied on imported goods primarily for the purpose of raising their selling price in the importing nation's market to reduce competition for domestic producers. A few smaller nations also use them to raise revenue on both imports and exports. Exports of commodities such as coffee and copper are commonly taxed in developing nations. However, imposition of tariffs can result in retaliation that is harmful rather than helpful for a country and its well-being.

For example, in the late 1920s, declining economic fortunes caused American farmers to lobby Congress for tariff protection on agricultural products. Over time, more domestic producers joined with agricultural interests, seeking their own protection from foreign competitors. The resulting legislative proposal increased tariffs for more than 20,000 items across a range of industries. The broad support for the legislation caused the Democratic and Progressive parties to join the Republicans on October 28, 1929, in supporting the Smoot-Hawley Tariff Act to establish some of the highest levels of tariffs ever imposed. That day the stock market crashed, falling 12 percent. In the following months, 34 foreign governments filed protests against Smoot-Hawley. Nevertheless, on June 17, 1930, President Herbert Hoover signed the bill. The

Variable Levy

One form of **variable levy,** which guarantees that the market price of the import will be the same as that of domestically produced goods, has been used by the EU for imported grains. Calculated daily, the duty level is set at the difference between world market prices and the support price for domestic producers.

Lower Duty for More Local Input

Import duties are set by many nations in such a way that they encourage local input. For example, the finished product ready for sale to the consumer may have a 70 percent duty. However, if the product is imported in bulk so that it must be packaged in the importing nation, the duty level may be 30 percent. To encourage some local production, the government may charge only a 10 percent duty on the semifinished inputs. These situations can provide opportunities for foreign manufacturers of low-technology products, such as toiletries, to get behind a high-tariff wall with very modest investments.

When tariffs are assessed at very low rates, they are sometimes referred to as *nuisance tariffs*. That is because importers are still required to go through the frequently lengthy process of paying these tariffs, even though their low levels may no longer serve their original intention, such as protecting domestic producers.

Nontariff Barriers

Nontariff barriers (NTBs) are all forms of discrimination against imports other than the import duties we have been examining. As nations reduced import duties, nontariff barriers assumed greater relative importance, and their use has been increasing. For example, government-required testing and certification requirements increased 600 percent between 1994 and 2004. NTBs can take many forms, including the quantitative and nonquantitative ones discussed next, and the additional costs they impose on producers and exporters help to discourage trade.

Quantitative One type of quantitative barrier is **quotas,** which set numerical limits for specific kinds of goods that a country will permit to be imported during a specified period. If the quota is *absolute,* once the specified amount has been imported, further importation for the rest of the period (usually a year) is prohibited. Quotas are generally *global;* that is, a total amount is fixed without regard to source. They may also be *allocated,* in which case the government of the importing nation assigns quantities to specific countries. The United States allocates quotas for specific tonnages of sugar to 40 nations.

Some producers have used transshipping to evade allocated quotas. In such cases, the finished goods are first shipped to a country with an unfilled quota, where the goods are labeled as products of that country, and then shipped to the quota-imposing nation. Prior to the ending of the Multi-Fiber Agreement in 2004 that limited textile imports from other nations, this deceptive labeling scheme was estimated to have brought $2 billion in illegal clothing imports from China into the United States annually. Gitano, for example, pled guilty to charges of

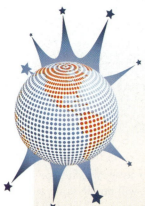

GLOBAL gauntlet

Chocolate, Coffee, and Fair Trade

When you last savored a bar of rich chocolate, a cup of hot cocoa, or a piece of chocolate cake or scoop of chocolate ice cream, did you know that you may have unwittingly been consuming a product made with child labor?

Chocolate, made from the fruit (cocoa bean) of the cacao tree, is one of the most-traded agricultural products in the world. About 70 percent of the world's cocoa is produced in West Africa. In practice, beans from different nations are usually mixed together during their exportation and transport to processing plants in the importing nations. So Hershey bars, Snickers, M&Ms, KitKats, Nestlé chocolates, fudge, hot chocolate—essentially all of these delicacies regularly enjoyed by hundreds of millions of consumers—will include cocoa from West

> "284,000 children were working in hazardous conditions on West African cocoa farms"

Africa, especially the Côte d'Ivoire (Ivory Coast), with about 43 percent of the world's total cocoa production.

Results of a survey on child labor in West Africa found that 284,000 children were working in hazardous conditions on West African cocoa farms, with the majority (200,000) working in Côte d'Ivoire. Nearly two-thirds of the child laborers were under the age of 14. Working conditions were described as slave-like, with 29 percent of the surveyed child workers in the Côte d'Ivoire indicating that "they were not free to leave their place of employment should they so wish." Many of these children had been brought into the cocoa-growing areas from distant regions of the Côte d'Ivoire or from poverty-stricken countries such as Burkina Faso, Mali, and Togo, often after being kidnapped. Some of the child laborers had been sold by their parents in the expectation that the child's earnings would be sent home. Although paid less than 60 percent of the rate of adult workers, children frequently worked for more than 12 hours per day, 6 days a week, and were regularly beaten. More than half of the children applied pesticides without protective gear. Only 34 percent of the children working on cocoa farms went to school, which was about half the level for children who were not working on cocoa farms.

These child laborers seemed to be trapped in a vicious cycle: they were forced into work either having been kidnapped or forced by economic circumstances faced by themselves and/or their families; they earned subsistence wages; and because most had not been to school and had minimal skills, their prospects for seeking other employment options were limited.

Fearing boycotts, trade sanctions, or certification and labeling requirements in key markets such as the United States and Europe, representatives from the chocolate industry attempted to develop a strategy for dealing with the problem. A protocol for the industry was developed that established a timetable for eliminating child labor and forced labor in the production of cocoa. A self-imposed deadline was set for establishing a viable monitoring and certification system: July 1, 2005.

In February 2005, several U.S. congressmen held a news conference in which they declared that they would not be buying chocolate for their wives for Valentine's Day because the candy had probably been made from cocoa produced in the Côte d'Ivoire with child slaves. Subsequently, after charging that the industry had failed to meet its self-imposed July 2005 deadline, the International Labor Rights Fund filed a lawsuit in federal court in Los Angeles against several international manufacturers of chocolate. The suit claimed that the manufacturers had ignored repeated, well-documented warnings about the exploitative use of child labor on cocoa farms in the Côte d'Ivoire.

But a number of companies have begun producing fair-trade-certified chocolate. Through observing a strict set of guidelines associated with fair-trade certification, these companies guarantee that a consumer of one of their chocolate products is "not an unwitting participant in this very inhumane situation." Fair-trade Labeling Organizations International, a consortium of fair-trade organizations from Canada, the United States, Japan, and 17 European nations, establishes certification standards. In the United States, Transfair USA is the sole

independent, third-party body for certifying fair-trade practices (www.transfair usa.org).

> "By providing a price floor, fair-trade practices protect Third World farmers from the ruinous fluctuations in commodity prices that result from free trade practices."

Fair-trade practices essentially involve international subsidies to farmers in developing countries, ensuring that farmers who are certified as engaging in fair-trade practices will receive a price for their produce that will at least cover their costs of production. By providing a price floor, fair-trade practices protect Third World farmers from the ruinous fluctuations in commodity prices that result from free trade practices. At the same time, fair-trade certification requires that farmers engage in appropriate social, labor, and environmental practices, such as paying livable wages and not using child or slave labor. In addition to the cocoa program, fair-trade certification programs have been implemented for a range of other products, such as coffee, bananas, and crafts.

Although still a nascent movement, sales of fair-trade certified products are growing. For example, Dunkin' Donuts sells only fair-trade coffee in its stores and Starbucks offers some fair-trade coffee. Will there be a similar result for chocolate? Already, about two dozen companies make fair-trade chocolate in the United States, including ClifBar, Cloud Nine, Newman's Own Organics, Kailua Candy Company, and Sweet Earth Organic Chocolates.

As a manager, do you feel that labor practices in another country should be a relevant consideration in international trade? Why or why not?

Sources: "Child Labor in the Cocoa Sector of West Africa," International Institute of Tropical Agriculture, August 2002, www.iita.org/news/cocoa.pdf (accessed August 2, 2006); "Combating Child Labour in Cocoa Growing," International Programme on the Elimination of Child Labour, Geneva, February 2005; "Cal Poly Professor Heading to Africa to Investigate Chocolate–Slave Labor Ties," www.calstate.edu/newsline/2005/n20050819slo1.shtml (accessed August 2, 2006); Sweet Earth Organic Chocolates, "Our Philosophy," www.sweetearthchocolates.com/level.itml/icOid/68 (accessed August 2, 2006); Tom Neuhaus, "A Luscious Exploration of 3 Fair-Trade-Certified Cocoa Cooperatives," *HopeDance Magazine,* www.hopedance.org/new/issues/47/article6.html (accessed August 2, 2006); "Fair-Trade Q&A," www.globalexchange.org/campaigns/fairtrade/fairtradeqa.html (accessed August 2, 2006); Samlanchith Chanthavong, "Chocolate and Slavery: Child Labor in Côte d'Ivoire," www.american.edu/TED/chocolate-slave.htm (accessed August 2, 2006); and Fair Trade, http://en.wikipedia.org/wiki/Fair_trade (accessed June 10, 2010).

voluntary export restraints (VERs)
Export quotas imposed by the exporting nation

orderly marketing arrangements
Formal agreements between exporting and importing countries that stipulate the import or export quotas each nation will have for a good

fraud for importing Chinese blouses labeled "Made in the Maldives Islands."

For many years there has been an agreement among nations against imposing quotas unilaterally on goods (except agricultural products). Therefore, governments have negotiated **voluntary export restraints (VERs)** with other countries (e.g., the Japanese government established a VER to restrict the number of automobiles that its manufacturers could export to the United States annually, and the Canadian government agreed to a VER to limit the amount of Canadian lumber to be exported to the United States).

Orderly Marketing Arrangements
Orderly marketing arrangements are VERs consisting of formal agreements between the governments of exporting and importing countries to restrict international competition and preserve some of the

Agricultural support programs are often promoted as being targeted toward protecting smaller farms and traditional rural economies. However, the largest 25 percent of farms receive 90 percent of the total level of agricultural support in the United States, 75 percent in Canada, 70 percent in the EU, and 68 percent in Japan.[12]

Government procurement policies are also trade barriers because they usually favor domestic producers and restrict purchases of imported goods by government agencies. Policies may also require that products purchased by government agencies have a stipulated minimum *local content.* Since the WTO Government Procurement Agreement went into effect, most nations have opened their government business to foreign bidders to comply with its requirements. However, as noted by the EU, the American government still has policies in place that may substantially interfere with international trade. For example, similar to practices in Canada and elsewhere in the world, the Buy America Act has a range of measures that either prohibit public sector organizations from purchasing from foreign suppliers of goods or services or hinder such purchases through mechanisms such as requirements for local content or the provision of advantageous pricing terms for American suppliers. The Department of Defense, which is the U.S. government's largest public procurement agency,

> ## "JAPAN PROHIBITS THE IMPORTATION OF CREAMY MUSTARD, LIGHT MAYONNAISE, OR FIGS CONTAINING POTASSIUM SORBATE, A FOOD ADDITIVE APPROVED BY NUMEROUS INTERNATIONAL FOOD BODIES AND ALLOWED BY THE JAPANESE IN 36 OTHER FOODS, PRIMARILY TRADITIONAL JAPANESE PRODUCTS."

national market for local producers. Usually, they stipulate the size of the export or import quotas that each nation will have for a particular good. The largest and oldest such arrangement was the Multi-Fiber Arrangement (MFA), which began in 1973 and regulated about 80 percent of the world's textile and clothing exports to the industrialized nations.

Nonquantitative Nontariff Barriers
Many international trade specialists claim that the most significant nontariff barriers are the nonquantitative type. Governments have tended to establish nontariff barriers to obtain the protection formerly afforded by import duties. A study of nonquantitative barriers revealed over 800 distinct forms, which may be classified under three major headings: (1) direct government participation in trade, (2) customs and other administrative procedures, and (3) standards.

1. *Direct government participation in trade.* The most common form of direct government participation is the subsidy. Besides protecting industries through subsidies, as was mentioned earlier, nearly all governments subsidize agriculture.

excludes foreign suppliers from many contracts. During the reconstruction efforts in Iraq after the 2003 invasion, for example, many of the major contracts could be granted only to American firms.[13]

2. *Customs and other administrative procedures.* These barriers cover a large variety of government policies and procedures that either discriminate against imports or favor exports. For example, in China, a product being imported may be subject to different rates of duty, depending on the port of entry and an arbitrary determination of the customs value. Because of this flexibility, customs charges often depend on negotiations between Chinese customs officials and managers. It is alleged that corruption is often involved.[14]

3. *Standards.* Both governmental and private standards to protect the health and safety of a nation's citizens certainly are desirable, but for years exporting firms have been plagued by many standards that are complex and discriminatory. For example, Canadian regulations treat products such as calcium-enriched orange juice as drugs and thus subject to special production and marketing requirements.[15] Japan prohibits the importation of creamy mustard, light mayonnaise,

or figs containing potassium sorbate, a food additive approved by numerous international food bodies and allowed by the Japanese in 36 other foods, primarily traditional Japanese products that are typically made only in Japan.[16] Kellogg Company makes four different versions of corn flakes at its European plants, because different nations have different standards regarding the vitamins that can be added to the cereal.

The European Parliament passed biotech food labeling requirements that impose mandatory traceability of genetically modified (GM) organisms and stringent labeling of foods that contain GM ingredients. The requirements include labels stating "This product is produced from GM organisms" and strict limits on mixing GM and non-GM ingredients in food exported to the EU. The United States is one of the world's leading producers and exporters of GM crops, with 75 percent of soybeans, 71 percent of cotton, and 34 percent of corn being GM. In the United States and Canada, 55–63 percent of customers see GM food as "bad," while this rises to 81 percent and 89 percent disapproving in Germany and France, respectively.[17]

Costs of Barriers to Trade

Trade restraints in the United States and other countries cost consumers tens of billions of dollars per year, while benefiting a relatively small number of companies in the protected sectors of the economy.

A recent study of just 20 product groups in protected industries showed that the average consumer cost per job saved was $231,289 per year. This means that consumers paid more than seven times the average annual compensation of manufacturing workers to preserve jobs through import constraints. Many of these sectors have been shielded from imports for 45 years or more. Studies done in other countries show similar results.[18] ■

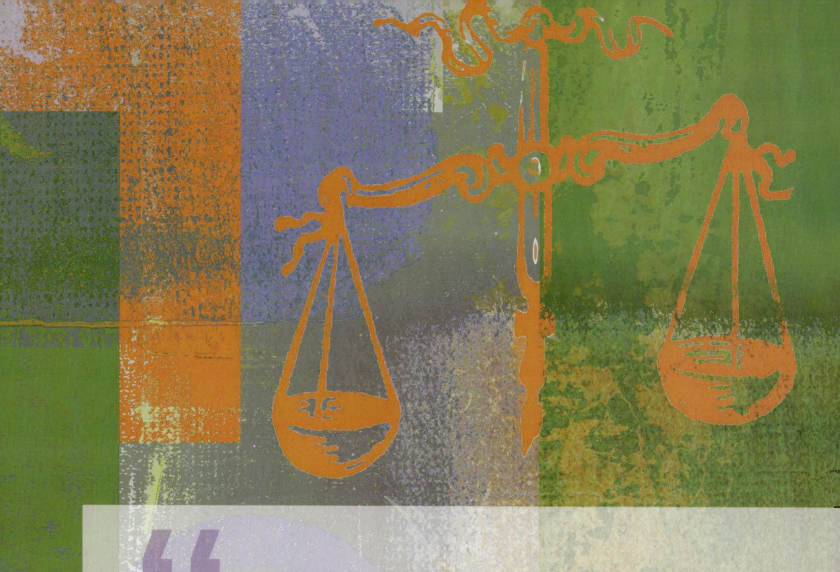

"The role which the Court [International Court of Justice] plays, through the power of justice and international law . . . is widely recognized and evidenced by the number of cases on the Court's docket. . . . It is not uncommon that these cases deal with issues concerning international peace and security. In performing its dispute resolution function, the Court, which embodies the principle of equality of all before the law, acts as a guardian of international law, and assures the maintenance of a coherent international legal order."

—Judge Shi Jiuyong, former president of the International Court of Justice, to the General Assembly of the United Nations, October 31, 2003

chapter seven

intellectual property +other legal forces

Participants in international business should understand the enormous breadth and depth of laws in various jurisdictions worldwide. Anyone studying legal forces affecting international business soon realizes that the variety of these forces complicate the task of understanding the laws.

While on the one hand businesses must be aware of laws in order to comply, on the other hand businesses also expect that laws will assist them when necessary. An issue of great concern to businesses that operate internationally is the stability of a host government and its legal system. When a business enters a country, the firm needs to know whether the country's host government will be able to protect the foreign business with an adequate legal system. The legal system must be able to enforce contracts and protect the basic rights of employees. In examining international legal forces, one must keep in mind that a stable government and an adequate court system are necessary to ensure a welcome environment for foreign businesses.

This chapter examines international law and looks at specific national laws that influence international business.

LEARNING OBJECTIVES

After reading this chapter, you should be able to:

LO1 **Discuss** the complexity of the legal forces that confront international business.

LO2 **Explain** the possibilities for international dispute settlement.

LO3 **Recognize** the need and methods to protect intellectual property.

LO4 **Explain** the risk of product liability legal actions.

LO5 **Discuss** some of the U.S. laws that affect international business operations.

treaties Agreements between countries, which may be bilateral (between two countries) or multilateral (involving more than two countries); also called *conventions, covenants, compacts,* or *protocols*

extraterritorial application of laws A country's attempt to apply its laws to foreigners or nonresidents and to acts and activities that take place outside its borders

LO1 Discuss the complexity of the legal forces that confront international business.

INTERNATIONAL LEGAL FORCES

Rule of Law

International businesspeople need to determine whether a country is governed by the rule of law. If a country's legal system is based on the rule of law, this encourages foreign investment because foreign businesses know that their interests will be protected. For example, Hong Kong has an advantage over

Extraterritoriality

Many countries, including the United States and members of the European Union, often attempt to enforce their laws outside their borders. This is referred to as **extraterritorial application of laws.** This attempt to enforce laws abroad is done not by force but through traditional legal means. For example, the U.S. government imposes taxes on U.S. citizens and U.S. permanent residents regardless of either the source of income or the residence of the taxpayer. If a U.S. citizen is living in Madrid and receives all of her income from Spanish sources, the United States will still expect the taxpayer to comply with U.S. tax laws. Likewise, when U.S. companies operate in other countries with U.S.-based personnel, the U.S. companies must comply with U.S. laws, including employment laws. Of course, these companies must also comply with the laws of the host country. Extraterritorial application of laws has been extended in many other areas including antitrust and environmental laws. Also, the Alien Tort Statute allows non-U.S. nationals to file lawsuits in U.S. courts for alleged violations of international law. In 2010, Coca-Cola was sued (in New York) for alleged violence against workers in Guatemala.

> "It is absolutely impossible for a foreign party to win a case against a Chinese party in a Chinese court.
>
> —Cao Siyuan, a Chinese commentator

Shanghai in attracting foreign investors because Hong Kong has a tradition of law adopted from British colonial days while Shanghai courts tend to favor Chinese litigants. This disparity in legal systems between the two cities is seen to give Hong Kong an advantage as a location for foreign firms.[1]

Sources of International Law

International law comes from several sources, the most important of which are bilateral and multilateral **treaties** between nations. Treaties are agreements between countries and may also be called *conventions, covenants, compacts,* or *protocols.* International organizations such as the United Nations have provided a forum for creation of many treaties. The UN has sponsored many conferences that have led to multinational agreements on a range of matters, including postal delivery and use of driver's licenses in other countries. Also, the International Court of Justice, an organ of the UN, creates international law when it decides disputes brought before it by member-nations.

Another source of international law is customary international law, which consists of international rules derived from customs and usage over centuries. An example of customary international law is the prohibition against genocide (there is also a specific international statute against genocide), or the immunity of visiting foreign heads of state.

LO2 Explain the possibilities for international dispute settlement.

INTERNATIONAL DISPUTE SETTLEMENT

Litigation

One of the major problems usually involved in cross-border litigation is the question of which jurisdiction's law should apply and where the litigation should occur. Each country (and each state in the United States) has elaborate laws for determining which law should apply and where litigation should occur. As with any other disputed matter, the final decision on these issues rests with the court. Occasionally, courts in two countries (or two states) will attempt to resolve the same dispute. Again, this is resolved by reference to the particular choice of law provisions and can be quite complicated. For this reason, it is prudent to include in contracts a choice-of-law clause and a choice-of-forum clause in the event of a dispute. A *choice-of-law clause* in a contract specifies which law will govern in the event of a dispute. For example, if there is a U.S. seller and an Australian buyer, the parties may agree that Australian law would govern any dispute. A *choice-of-forum clause* in a contract specifies where the dispute will be settled. For example, the parties in the preceding example may agree to have the dispute decided in California state courts in Los Angeles County, California.

Performance of Contracts

Whenever businesses enter into agreements with other businesses, the possibility exists that there may be problems getting the other side to perform its obligations. No worldwide court has the power to enforce its decrees. The worldwide courts that do exist, such as the UN's International Court of Justice, rely on the voluntary compliance of the parties before it. Each nation in the world is a sovereign nation and has its own rules for recognizing decrees and judgments from other nations.

When contracting parties are residents of a single country, the laws of that country govern contract performance and any disputes that arise between the parties. That country's courts have jurisdiction over the parties, and the courts' judgments are enforced in accordance with the country's procedures. When residents of two or more countries contract, those relatively easy solutions to dispute resolution are not available. Enforcing contracts that cross international lines is often quite complicated.

United Nations Solutions

When contract disputes arise between parties from two or more countries, which country's law is applicable? Many countries, including the United States, have ratified the UN Convention on the International Sale of Goods (CISG) to solve such problems.

The CISG established uniform legal rules to govern the formation of international sales contracts and the rights and obligations of the buyer and seller. The CISG applies automatically to all contracts for the sale of goods between traders from different countries that have ratified the CISG. This automatic application will take place unless the parties to the contract expressly exclude—opt out of—the CISG.

Private Solutions—Arbitration

As mentioned before, many people outside the United States dislike the U.S. court system. Likewise, many U.S. businesspeople dislike or at least fear litigation in other countries. For these reasons, international businesspeople often agree that any disputes will be resolved by arbitration, rather than by going to court in any country. **Arbitration** is a dispute resolution mechanism that is an alternative to litigation. Arbitration is usually quicker, less expensive, and more private than litigation, and it is usually binding on all parties. At least 30 organizations now administer international arbitrations, the best known of which may be the International Court of Arbitration of the International Chamber of Commerce in Paris. In addition, London and New York are centers of arbitration. Some organizations specialize in the type of arbitration cases they will consider. For example, the World Intellectual Property Organization (WIPO) Arbitration and Mediation Center handles technological, entertainment, and intellectual property disputes. In 2009 the Center settled a dispute between Research in Motion Ltd. and a private party over domain names using variations of the word BLACKBERRY. The International Centre for the Settlement of Investment Disputes specializes, logically, in investment disputes.

In summary, people and businesses may prefer arbitration for several reasons. They may be suspicious of foreign courts. Arbitration is generally faster than law courts, where cases are usually backlogged. Arbitration procedures are usually more informal than court procedures. Arbitration may be confidential, avoiding the perhaps unwelcome publicity accompanying an open court case. And generally it may be less expensive.

Other organizations are working toward a worldwide business law. For example, the 13 **Incoterms** of the International Chamber of Commerce and its Uniform Rules and Practice on Documentary Credits receive almost universal acceptance (new definitions of some Incoterms went into effect in 2011). (See Table 7.1 for examples of Incoterms.) The UN Commission on International Trade Law and the International Institute for the Unification of Private Law are doing much useful work. The Hague-Vishy Rules on Bills of Lading sponsored by the International Law Association have been adopted by a number of countries.[2]

Despite Legal Uncertainties, International Business Grows

Despite legal uncertainties of doing business in other countries, international business activities will increase in the future. For this reason, international businesspeople must be aware of the legal environment in which they find themselves. Legal systems

---

arbitration A process, agreed to by parties to a dispute in lieu of going to court, by which a neutral person or body makes a binding decision

Incoterms Universal trade terminology developed by the International Chamber of Commerce

---

▼ **TABLE 7.1** Examples of Incoterms

1. *FAS (free alongside ship—port of call).* The seller pays all the transportation and delivery expense up to the ship's side and clears the goods for export.

2. *CIF (cost, insurance, freight—foreign port).* The price includes the cost of the goods, insurance, and all transportation and miscellaneous charges to the named port of final destination.

3. *CFR (cost and freight—foreign port).* CFR is similar to CIF except that the buyer purchases the insurance, either because it can be obtained at a lower cost or because the buyer's government, to save foreign exchange, insists on use of a local insurance company.

4. *DAF (delivered at frontier).* The term *DAF* is often used by exporters to Canada and Mexico. The price covers all costs up to the border, where the shipment is delivered to the buyer's representative. The buyer's responsibility is to arrange for receiving the goods after they are cleared for export, carry them across the border, clear them for importation, and make delivery to the buyer.

vary significantly from country to country, and it is important to understand the differences. The assumptions one makes on the basis of the U.S. legal system may not apply in other countries.

LO3 Recognize the need and methods to protect intellectual property.

INTELLECTUAL PROPERTY

A *patent* is a government grant giving the inventor of a product or process the exclusive right to manufacture, exploit, use, and sell that invention or process. *Trademarks* and *trade names* are designs and names, often officially registered, by which merchants or manufacturers designate and differentiate their products. *Copyrights* are exclusive legal rights of authors, composers, creators of software, playwrights, artists, and publishers to publish and dispose of their works. *Trade secrets* are any information that a business wishes to hold confidential. All are referred to as **intellectual property.**

Trade secrets can be of great value, but each country deals with and protects them in its own fashion. The duration of protection differs, as do the products that may or may not be protected. Some countries permit the production process to be protected but not the product. International companies must study and comply with the laws of each country where they may want to manufacture, create, or sell products.

Patents

In the field of patents, the International Convention for the Protection of Industrial Property, sometimes referred to as the Paris Union, provides some degree of standardization. This convention is adhered to by 173 countries.

A major step toward the harmonization of patent treatment is the European Patent Organization (EPO). Through EPO, an applicant for a patent need file only one application in English, French, or German to be granted patent protection in all 27 EU member-states. Before the EPO, an applicant had to file in each country in the language of that country. Often multiple companies are involved. For example, the U.S. Supreme Court ruled in 2008 on a U.S. patent for computer chipsets, which South Korea's LG Electronics Inc. licensed to Intel Corp. When a Taiwan manufacturer used the chips, LG sued.

The prescription drug industry relies heavily on patents. Multinational pharmaceutical companies say they need years of patent protection to recoup expensive investments in research and development of new drug treatments. Pfizer Inc. has a blockbuster drug in Lipitor, an anti-cholesterol drug: Pfizer's revenue from Lipitor is about $13 billion per year. Pfizer's patent runs out in June 2011—so Pfizer negotiated an agreement with Indian generic-drug maker Ranbaxy Laboratories Ltd. to keep Ranbaxy's generic version off the U.S. market until November 2011. This extension for Pfizer is important, given that revenues average more than $1 billion per month.[3]

The World Intellectual Property Organization (WIPO) is a UN agency that administers 24 international intellectual property treaties. WIPO advises developing countries on such matters as running patent offices and drafting intellectual property legislation. Interest in intellectual property matters has been growing in developing countries. There is also another agreement called TRIPS, "trade-related aspects of intellectual property," that operates under the aegis of the World Trade Organization, as mentioned in Chapter 3. In addition, in 2007 the United States, European Union, Mexico, Japan, Switzerland, Australia, South Korea, and Canada began negotiations for ACTA, the Anti-Counterfeiting Trade Agreement. An official version of the draft agreement was published in 2010. Passage of the agreement may make it easier for border inspectors to search laptops for pirated contents, for example. Opponents allege that the ACTA would negatively affect the flow of information on the Internet.

At the UN, smaller nations have been mounting attacks on the exclusivity and length of patent protection. They want to shorten the protection periods from the current 15 to 20 years down to 5 years or even 30 months. But multinational companies are resisting the changes. They point out that the only incentives they have to spend the huge amounts required to develop new technology are periods of patent protection long enough to recoup their costs and make profits.

▼ **TABLE 7.2** The International Framework for IP Protection

Organization	Parent
World Intellectual Property Organization (WIPO)	UN
Trade Related Aspects of Intellectual Property (TRIPS)	WTO
Anti-Counterfeiting Trade Agreement (ACTA) (proposed)	Free-standing

An added dimension is the growth of so-called "patent trolls," who can be likened to modern-day highway robbers cashing in on loopholes in IP protection. These are lawyers and investors who buy patents that were mistakenly granted, mostly to failed companies. In one case, a patent troll claimed that a patent bought for about $50,000 was infringed by Intel's microprocessors and threatened to sue Intel for $7 billion in damages. This is a fascinating subworld populated not just by trolls but also patent pirates, patent thickets, and the like.

Trademarks

Trademarks can be a shape, a color or design (such as the Levi's small red tag on the left side of the rear pockets of its jeans), a catchy phrase, an abbreviation, or even a sound. Although blacksmiths who made swords in the Roman Empire may have been the first to use trademarks, Löwenbräu and Stella Artois claim use since the 14th century. Trademark protection varies from country to country, as does its duration, which may be from 10 to 20 years (with possible renewals). Such protection is covered by the Madrid Agreement of 1891 for most of the world, although there is also the General American Convention for Trademark and Commercial Protection for the Western Hemisphere. In addition, protection may be provided on a bilateral basis in friendship, commerce, and navigation treaties.

An important step in harmonizing the rules on trademarks was taken in 1988 when regulations for a European Union trademark law were drafted. A single European Trademark Office known as the Office of Harmonization in the Internal Market (OHIM) is responsible for the recognition and protection of proprietary marks in all EU countries, including trademarks belonging to companies based in non-EU member-countries.

Trade Names

Trade names (name of a business) are protected in all countries that adhere to the International Convention for the Protection of Industrial Property, which was mentioned earlier in connection with patents. Goods bearing illegal trademarks or trade names or false statements about their origin are subject to seizure upon importation into these countries.

Copyrights

Copyrights are protected under the Berne Convention of 1886, which is adhered to by 164 countries, the WIPO Copyright Treaty, and the TRIPS Agreement, to which all WTO members agree to abide.

STANDARDIZING LAWS AROUND THE WORLD

Many attempts have been made to standardize laws among various countries. To international business, the advantage of standardization is that business flows much better when there is a uniform set of rules. Worldwide harmonization is progressing slowly, though, in most areas. For now, businesspeople must confront the reality of differing standards.

In the tax area, there are tax conventions, or treaties, among nations. Each country tries to make each such treaty as similar as possible to the others, and so patterns and common provisions may be found among them.

In antitrust, the EU member-nations operate under Articles 81 and 82 of the Treaty of Rome, which are similar to the antitrust laws in the United States. In an unusual bilateral move, Germany and the United States signed an executive agreement on antitrust cooperation. This was the first attempt by national governments to cooperate on antitrust matters concerning firms operating in both countries. There have been proposals to create worldwide agreements on antitrust.

Some agreement exists in the field of international commercial arbitration, including enforcement of arbitration awards. If the disputed contract involves investment from one country into another, it can be submitted for arbitration by the International Center for Settlement of Investment Disputes at the World Bank. Chapter 3 covered a number of other UN-related organizations and other worldwide associations. Each of them has some harmonizing or standardizing effect on laws in the member-countries.

The UN Convention on the International Sale of Goods (CISG) provides some uniformity in international sales agreements for those parties who elect to use it. It has been signed by 74 states.

There have been attempts to make accounting and bankruptcy standards uniform worldwide. A Model Law on Cross-Border Insolvencies from UNCITRAL (UN Commission on International Trade Law) served as the basis for Chapter 15 of the U.S. Bankruptcy Code, for example.

Two standardizing organizations are the International Organization for Standardization (ISO) and the International Electrotechnical Commission (IEC). The IEC promotes standardization of measurement, materials, and equipment in almost every sphere of electrotechnology. The ISO recommends standards in other fields of technology. Most government and private purchasing around the world demands products that meet IEC or ISO specifications.

SOME SPECIFIC NATIONAL LEGAL FORCES

Competition Laws

Competition laws (known in the U.S. as antitrust laws) are intended to prevent inappropriately large concentrations of economic power, such as monopolies. Actions brought to enforce competition laws or antitrust laws usually involve government actions brought against business, but also may involve business actions against other businesses.

U.S. Laws and Attitudes Are Different—But the Differences Are Narrowing
The U.S. **antitrust laws** are strict and they are vigorously enforced. They are laws to prevent price fixing, market sharing, and business monopolies. The U.S. Department of Justice is charged with enforcing U.S. antitrust laws. Other countries, including the European Union, are becoming more active in the antitrust field. More than 80 countries now have antitrust laws. The EU Commission is responsible for enforcing EU competition policy. In addition to enforcing competition policy against businesses, the EU Commission also has the power to force EU member-governments to dismantle state monopolies that block progress toward an open, communitywide market.[4]

A number of important differences in antitrust laws, regulations, and practices exist between the United States, other nations, and the EU. One difference is the *per se* concept of the U.S. law. Under the U.S. laws, certain activities, such as price fixing, are said to be illegal "*per se.*" This means that they are illegal even though no injury or damage results from them. The EU Treaty of Rome articles dealing with restrictive trade practices do not contain the per se illegality concept of U.S. antitrust law. For example, a cartel that allows consumers a fair share of the benefits is legally acceptable in the EU. Also, the treaty is not violated by market dominance—only by misuse of that dominance to damage competitors or consumers.

The U.S. focus on antitrust legislation is concerned with the impact of the business deal on the consumer, while the EU is more concerned about the industry's competitive structure and thus pays attention to rivals' objections.[5] In Japan, antitrust legislation was introduced by the United States during its occupation of Japan after World War II. This legislation, the Japanese Anti-Monopoly Law, was modeled on U.S. antitrust law and did not harmonize well with the existing cooperative *zaibatsu* (conglomerates) the Japanese government had established. In fact, the Japanese approach to a rational development of the economy regarded antitrust measures as an impediment. However, with increasing foreign presence, Japanese companies have incorporated antitrust thinking into their strategies. Because the Japanese culture so values cooperation, this is a challenge, especially when it comes to cartels.[6]

Worldwide Application of U.S. Antitrust Laws
The U.S. government often attempts to enforce its antitrust laws extraterritorially. For example, in 1979, a grand jury in Washington, D.C., indicted three foreign-owned ocean shipping groups on charges of fixing prices without getting approval from the U.S. Federal Maritime Commission. The other governments, European and Japanese, protested bitterly, arguing (1) that shipping is international by definition, so the United States has no right to act unilaterally, and (2) that the alleged offenses were both legal and ethical practices outside the United States.[7] The U.S. Supreme Court has permitted overseas application of U.S. antitrust laws as recently as 2004.[8]

EU Extraterritorial Application of Its Competition Policy
Like the U.S. Department of Justice, the EU Commission has increasingly sought enforcement of its competition policy abroad when there is an effect on commerce within the EU. For example, the EU Commission had to give its approval before merger talks between America Online and Time Warner could proceed. Before its approval was given to the merger, AOL–Time Warner had to agree to sever all ties with the German media group Bertelsmann. The EU has also viewed Microsoft as anticompetitive and in 2008 fined the firm €899 million ($1.3 billion).[9]

Criminal Cases
U.S. antitrust laws contain both civil and criminal penalties.* A decision by the U.S. federal court of appeals held that criminal antitrust laws apply to foreign companies even if the conspiracy took place outside the United States. While earlier decisions had permitted U.S. antitrust laws to be used against foreign companies in civil cases, this decision, which was against Nippon Paper Industries, set the precedent that antitrust laws could be used also to get criminal convictions.

Proposal for Global Antitrust Approval
It is often difficult for international businesses to comply with the variety of antitrust laws worldwide. A good example is Microsoft. In the 1990s, the U.S. government and several U.S. states brought

> Some think that the WTO is the proper avenue for such worldwide cooperation. Others believe an international antitrust authority would be appropriate.

*Civil liability calls for payment of money damages. Criminal liability may result in fines or imprisonment.

antitrust actions against Microsoft. The actions continued well into the early 21st century. The EU also brought several actions against Microsoft, one of which we mentioned above. In 2008 China began examining whether Microsoft has a monopoly position. The Microsoft case is a good example of how one company can get bogged down with antitrust laws in multiple jurisdictions. In light of the numerous countries that impose antitrust rules worldwide, many argue that greater worldwide cooperation in antitrust enforcement is needed. Some think that the WTO is the proper avenue for such worldwide cooperation. Others believe an international antitrust authority would be appropriate. Reaching such an agreement would be difficult because of the differing interests involved.[10] The U.S. government has proposed a world organization for the clearance of antitrust issues. If approved, the organization would probably take the form of a clearinghouse for merger filings. Calls for such an entity are increasing because of the multinational nature of most large mergers.

Tariffs, Quotas, and Other Trade Obstacles

Trade obstacles are legal forces as well as political and financial forces. For that reason, we mention them again here. Every country has laws on these subjects. The stated purpose of a tariff is to raise revenue for the government, but it may serve the additional objective of keeping certain goods out of a country. Quotas limit the number or amount of imports.

There are many other forms of protection or obstacles to trade in national laws. Some are health or packaging requirements. Others deal with language, such as the mandatory use of French on labels and in advertising, manuals, warranties, and so forth, for goods sold in France, including websites located on servers physically in France. When Vietnam catfish imports into the U.S. flooded the market, lawyers for the U.S. catfish industry successfully argued that the Vietnamese product was not catfish but a different family of fish. After this failed to stop the imports, they reversed themselves and alleged that these catfish were being "dumped" on the U.S. market.[11] Table 7.3 is a sampling of trade barriers.

In many countries, U.S. and EU exports may encounter weak patent or trademark protection, high tariffs, quarantine periods, and a variety of other obstacles.

The United States has many options in dealing with trade obstacles abroad. It can impose retaliatory barriers on products from countries imposing barriers against U.S. goods. It sometimes uses tariffs and quotas. It also uses a form of quota called by some "voluntary" restraint agreements (VRAs) and by others "voluntary" export restraints (VERs). *Voluntary* is in quote marks because these barriers are imposed by the U.S. government on the exporting

countries. The inevitable result is higher costs to American consumers, as exporters send only the higher-priced top of their lines and importers charge more for scarcer products.[12] The United States is not the only country that imposes VRAs and VERs on its trading partners—far from it. Japan, Canada, the EU countries, and many others require that countries exporting to them "voluntarily" limit the number or value of goods exported.

LO4   Explain the risk of product liability legal actions.

Torts

Torts are injuries inflicted on other people, either intentionally or negligently. Tort cases in the United States may result in awards of very large sums of money. Other countries have tort laws that restrict the amount of money that can be obtained in tort actions.

Product Liability   One important area of torts, especially in the international arena, is **product liability.** Product liability laws hold a company and its officers and directors liable and possibly subject to fines or imprisonment when its product causes death, injury, or damage. Such liability for faulty or dangerous products was a growth area for the U.S. legal profession beginning in the 1960s. Liability insurance premiums soared, and there were concerns that smaller, weaker manufacturing companies could not survive. In the 1980s that boom spread to Europe and elsewhere. As foreign firms buy or build U.S. plants, they are being hit by the same liability and insurance problems have long faced by U.S. companies.[13]

Manufacturers of products are often held to a standard of **strict liability,** which holds the designer/manufacturer

▼ **TABLE 7.3**   Worldwide Examples of Tariffs and Other Trade Barriers

Product	Destination	Barrier
U.S. apples	Japan	Orchard inspection, buffer zones
EU wines and spirits	India	Federal and state additional duties
Integrated computer circuits	China	Tax rebates for locally produced circuits give them unfair price advantage against imports
Internet gambling from EU providers	United States	Discriminatory legislation
U.S. grains	EU	EU moratorium on genetically modified grains
U.S. computer technology	Brazil	30% tariffs
U.S. poultry	Russia	Import restrictions (quotas)

Sources: Office of U.S. Trade Representative, Monitoring and Enforcement Press Releases, http://ustraderep.gov (accessed August 1, 2010); and European Commission, "Trade Issues," http://ec.europa.eu/trade/issues/respectrules/tbr/cases/usa_gam.html (accessed June 15, 2010).

cu_{in}ib

Jeremy Capdevielle: Sustainability Work in Ecuador

I graduated from Cal Poly–San Luis Obispo with a concentration in International Business with an emphasis in Entrepreneurship. My curiosity involving the intricacies of culture and relationships in the international context piqued my interest in IB, and a trip to New Zealand gave me a further glimpse into the world of limitless possibilities that further engaged my entrepreneurial spirit. Upon graduation, I had no idea as to the direction my life would lead, but one thing I was certain of was that I would embark on a trip to explore foreign lands for six months or longer.

Following graduation, I worked and saved money for four months, enjoyed many beautiful days upon the beaches of Southern California, read to my heart's desire, and reflected upon the topics of my choosing. It was the first time in a while when I took the time for myself to survey the wide and far stretching lands of my life and is probably one of the most important periods of my life. After methodically pulling pieces together, I discovered a direction that offered potential to fulfill my needs, both personally and professionally; that is, to work with and create organizations that are more conducive to people's happiness and personal well-being.

During that beautiful Southern California summer, I felt more strongly than ever that whatever the future had in store for me, traveling and experiencing foreign landscapes would be the best thing I could do for myself then. At the very least, I'd gain new insights, have my perspective and construction of the world challenged, and learn a new language. South America sparked my interest primarily due to its less-explored nature and my enthusiasm continued as I learned more about its highly diverse cultural and ecological landscapes. After making the necessary preparations and obtaining an insight into the cultural and political contexts in which I'd be traveling, I booked a flight to Panama and soon after travelled to South America.

After sailing through the San Blas Islands and seemingly endless seas from Panama to Cartagena, Colombia, I lived with a family for two months in Cali, Colombia. They introduced me to their incredibly warm and vibrant culture. I gained a further glimpse into the Cali lifestyle and the weekend life on the "fincas" (farms), learned to salsa (Cali is the "salsa capital of the world"), and independently taught English language courses. Cali is where I really experienced "culture shock." Some of it came from the different pace of culture and angles at which the world is viewed, but I attribute the majority of my culture shock to my lack of Spanish speaking abilities. I'm grateful to those who worked with me to communicate and connect out of sheer interest for me as a person, but when groups gathered, alienated is a good way to describe the way I felt. My basic Spanish wasn't nearly enough to keep up, and the pace of conversation swept over me like a wave—leaving me with only tones, vibrations and a feeling as to where the current of conversation was pulling. Although lacking the local language provides a different type of learning experience in itself, it also leads to missed opportunities for connecting and understanding. For those wishing to explore lands where a different language is spoken, I recommend at least an intermediate understanding of the language beforehand, scheduling home stays with locals, and arranging private language lessons upon arrival.

After leaving Cali, I headed south to the most ecologically diverse country in the world, Ecuador. What I expected to be a short trip through Ecuador's beautiful landscapes en route to Peru has evolved into a longer-term expedition and tremendous opportunity. Within days of arriving in Quito, I came across the coordinator of a volunteer program and soon after found myself volunteering with the charity, Great Aves [www.greataves.org/], teaching English and assisting with community development projects in rural communities of Amazonian Ecuador.

Great Aves' approach strives to enhance education throughout the communities with which it works in order to help develop sustainable businesses and implement more efficient agricultural methods, all the while maintaining a conscious mindset of the impacts each action has on the environment. After working at every level within the Great Aves organization, I increasingly became impassioned by the project and found myself in the role of Coordinator of the Amazon Conservation and Community Development project. Successful sustainable community development is a challenging endeavor that requires a deep understanding of the communities with whom we work, a clear picture of local resources available to help meet its needs, and the tact to develop this information into a working model that serves to bridge the gap between theory and implementation. I've learned it is extremely important to work ideas of progress and education around the ways of the community with which we work, rather than develop plans and attempt to mold the community to those.

liable for damages caused by a product without the need for a plaintiff to prove negligence in the product's design or manufacture. There are several reasons to believe that the impact of strict liability on product designers and manufacturers in Europe and Japan will not be as heavy or severe as it is in the United States. The EU allows companies to use "state-of-the-art" or "developmental risks" defenses, which allow the designer/manufacturer to show that at the time of design or manufacture, the most modern, latest-known technology was used. They also are permitted to cap damages. By comparison, damages awarded by American juries have been in the hundreds of millions of dollars.

Other differences in legal procedures in the United States compared with those in Europe and Japan will limit or prevent product liability awards by European and Japanese courts. As mentioned, in the United States, but not elsewhere, lawyers take many cases on a contingency fee basis whereby the lawyer charges the plaintiff no fee to begin representation and action in a product liability case. The lawyer is paid only when the defendant settles or loses in a trial, but then the fee is relatively large, running between one-third and one-half of the settlement or award. In addition, outside the United States, when the defendant wins a lawsuit, the plaintiff is often called upon to pay all the defendant's legal fees and other costs caused by the plaintiff's action.[14]

In the United States, product liability cases are heard by juries that can award plaintiffs actual damages plus punitive damages. As the name indicates, punitive damages have the purpose of punishing the defendant, and if the plaintiff has been seriously injured or the jury's sympathy can be otherwise aroused, it may award millions of dollars to "teach the defendant a lesson." Outside the United States, judges, not juries, hear product liability cases. Judges are less prone to emotional reactions than juries are, and even if the judge is sympathetic toward a plaintiff, punitive damages are not awarded by non-U.S. courts.

Punitive Damage Effects on Medicine

Multimillion-dollar punitive damage awards by U.S. courts have caused foreign firms to keep their products out of the United States. For instance, Axminster Electronics, a British firm whose devices help prevent crib death by monitoring a baby's breathing, does not sell in the United States because it cannot secure product liability insurance. Within the United States, every drug company knows that if a person uses a drug and subsequently gets ill, there is a chance that a jury somewhere in the United States may impose liability on the manufacturer and order it to pay damages.[15]

Miscellaneous Laws

Individuals working abroad must be alert to avoid falling afoul of local laws and police, army, or government officials. Some examples make the point.

A Plessey employee, a British subject, is serving a life sentence in Libya for "jeopardizing the revolution by giving information to a foreign company." Saudi Arabia may strictly enforce sanctions against importing or drinking alcohol and wearing revealing clothing. Foreigners in Japan who walk out of their homes without their alien registration cards (*gaikaku-jin Toroku*) can be arrested, as happened to one man while he was carrying out the garbage. An Australian writer was sentenced in Thailand to three years in jail for writing a novel (7 copies sold) that insulted the crown prince. Brunei has caned nearly 500 foreigners since 2004 for settling illegally in the sultanate.

A New York law firm, International Legal Defense Counsel (ILDC), has made a reputation dealing with countries where American embassies and consulates are of little legal help. One of its cases involved a Virginia photographer named Conan Owen, who agreed to transport a package of cocaine from Colombia to Spain, where he was arrested and slapped with a stiff prison sentence. The U.S. Attorney General personally interceded with no success, and Owen languished in prison for nearly two years. Then ILDC obtained his freedom through the use of a bilateral prisoner transfer treaty that permits American inmates in foreign jails to do their time in a facility back home. Once in the United States, Owen was quickly freed.

LO5 Discuss some of the U.S. laws that affect international business operations.

U.S. LAWS THAT AFFECT THE INTERNATIONAL BUSINESS OF U.S. FIRMS

Although every law relating to business arguably has some effect on international activities, some laws warrant special notice. We will look briefly at several U.S. laws. Although many U.S. laws affect activities of international firms, there has not been a successful effort to coordinate them. Some are even at cross-purposes, and some diminish the ability of U.S. businesses to compete with foreign companies.

Foreign Corrupt Practices Act

During the 1970s, revelations of **questionable or dubious payments** by American companies to foreign officials rocked governments in the Netherlands and Japan. Congress considered corporate bribery "bad business" and "unnecessary." As a result, the **Foreign Corrupt Practices Act (FCPA)** became law.

Uncertainties There are a number of uncertainties about terms used in the FCPA. An interesting case in point involves "grease." According to the FCPA's drafters, the act does not outlaw *grease*, which is facilitating payments made solely to expedite nondiscretionary official actions. Such actions as customs clearance and telephone calls have been cited. However there is no clear distinction between supposedly legal grease payments and illegal bribes. To confuse matters further, U.S. Justice Department officials have suggested that they may prosecute some grease payments anyway under earlier antibribery laws written to get at corruption in the United States.

Other doubts raised by the FCPA concern the accounting standards it requires for compliance. That matter is connected to questions about how far management must go to learn whether any employees, subsidiaries, or agents may have violated the act; even if management were unaware of an illegal payment, it could be in violation if it "had reason to know" that some portion of a payment abroad might be used as a bribe.*

The FCPA makes it unlawful to bribe foreign government officials to obtain or retain business. Facilitating payments for routine government actions such as visa issuance, import approvals, and the processing of government papers are permissible under the FCPA. In January 2010, nearly two dozen U.S. corporate executives were indicted in an undercover "sting" operation for bribing an African minister of defense.

Critics believed that the FCPA would harm American companies' competitiveness abroad because it would demand of American companies a higher standard of behavior than was common in the competitive environment. Congress decided that the potential economic damage to exports would be minimal and that the only companies that would be hurt would be those whose only means of competing was through the payment of bribes. The United States actively lobbied the international community to introduce similar legislation, which it did in 1997, with the OECD Convention on Bribery. There is also a UN Convention against Corruption, signed by more than 140 countries as of 2010.

You may wonder if U.S. laws on bribery place U.S. businesses at a disadvantage in international competition. What seems to have happened on the bribery front is interesting. The FCPA, along with the OECD convention and the UN initiative, have brought a discussion of bribery and transparency out into

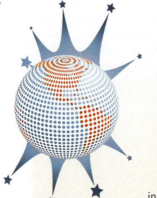

GLOBAL gauntlet

Barista Battles Over Patents

Nestlé has a new blockbuster product in Nespresso, an at-home brewing system for coffee. Their business model is based on selling the maker fairly cheaply and selling profitable single-serve capsules of coffee (5.5 billion capsules were sold in 2009). To protect their design, Nestlé filed 1,700 patents. Sara Lee claims to have found a gap in Nestlé's patent coverage that allows Sara Lee to market a compatible coffee capsule, a step Sara Lee took (in France) in 2010. Nestlé responded with a suit in France. A second firm, Ethical Coffee Co., has also begun selling compatible capsules in France but hasn't been sued.

What do you think? On the one hand, should Nestlé have had to file 1,700 patents to introduce a new coffee machine? On the other hand, Sara Lee has introduced a compatible capsule, which is less expensive and makes the capsules more available to consumers. What should we do, if anything?

Sources: http://www.businessweek.com/news/2010-06-15/nestle-takes-legal-action-on-sara-lee-coffee-capsules-update2-.html (accessed June 17, 2010); and Deborah Ball and Goran Mijuk, "Sara Lee Faces Nestlé Patent Suit," *The Wall Street Journal*, June 16, 2010, p. B3.

---

*Other words with similar connotations are *dash, squeeze, mordida, piston, cumshaw,* and *baksheesh.*

the open. Such discussions were further stimulated by the Asian financial crisis of 1997, one of whose causes was widely attributed to lack of transparency in financial dealings. Having an international reputation for transparency and being perceived as "aboveboard" have become increasingly important for global companies. There appears to be a strong move for company values that support integrity in the belief that integrity is better for business than are corrupt activities.

The organization Transparency International (www. transparency.org) publishes a bribe payers index (see Table 7.4). Its data for 2008 (the latest survey) are based on a survey of 2,742 respondents from 26 countries. Note that four more countries are now being tracked, South Africa (14), Brazil (17), India (19) and Mexico (20).

Accounting Law

Investor confidence in the integrity of financial reporting and corporate governance has been shaken by financial scandals worldwide. This crisis of confidence has substantially damaged the economic prospects of numerous companies, employees, retirees, customers, suppliers, and other stakeholders.

▼ **TABLE 7.4** Bribe Payers Index

Country	Rank		
	1999	2002	2008
Australia	2	1	8
Sweden	1	2	–
Switzerland	5	2	3
Austria	4	4	–
Canada	2	5	1
Netherlands	6	6	3
Belgium	8	6	1
United Kingdom	7	8	5
Germany	9	9	5
Singapore	11	9	9
Spain	12	11	12
France	13	12	9
Japan	14	13	5
United States	9	13	9
Malaysia	15	15	–
Hong Kong	n.a.	15	13
Italy	16	17	17
South Korea	18	18	14
Taiwan	17	19	14
China	19	20	21
Russia	n.a.	21	22

Sources: Transparency International, "Bribe Payers Index 2002," www. transparency.org/cpi/2002/bpi2002.en.html; http://www.transparency.org/news_room/latest_news/press_releases/2008/bpi_2008_en (accessed June 17, 2010).

U.S. accounting practice is guided by the Securities and Exchange Commission (SEC) and the Financial Accounting Standards Board (FASB) and follows standards known as generally accepted accounting principles (GAAP), while many other countries, including those in the EU, follow standards issued by the International Accounting Standards Board (IASB) known as the International Financial Reporting Standards (IFRS). These standards differ in many aspects, but a number of projects looking toward convergence are expected to be completed in 2015. ■

chapter eight

"The function of money is not to make money but to move goods. Money is only one part of our transportation system. It moves goods from man to man. A dollar bill is like a postage stamp: it is no good unless it will move commodities between persons. If a postage stamp will not carry a letter, or money will not move goods, it is just the same as an engine that will not run. Someone will have to get out and fix it."

—widely attributed to Henry Ford in a speech at the Ford Motor Company

the international monetary system
+financial forces

The international monetary system consists of institutions, agreements, rules, and processes that allow for the payments, currency exchange, and movements of capital required by international transactions.[1] To gain a sense of how the international monetary system has evolved, it's useful to build your understanding of how the institutions and arrangements that facilitate payments across national borders have evolved. So we begin this chapter with a review of the gold standard and the Bretton Woods system. We have already discussed the two institutions that were developed at the Bretton Woods meetings in 1944: the International Monetary Fund (IMF) and the World Bank (see Chapter 3). Here we examine one of them more closely, the IMF. The IMF plays a central role by providing the rules of the international monetary system "game." Then we consider the emergence of the current floating exchange rate system. We also look briefly at the Bank for International Settlements. After the international monetary system, we look at the major financial forces that shape the firm's international context. These forces include fluctuating currency values, currency exchange controls, taxation, and inflation and interest rates. We conclude with a focus on how the monetary exchanges among nations are recorded, the balance-of-payments accounts, and their relevance to the international manager.

LEARNING OBJECTIVES

After reading this chapter, you should be able to:

LO1 **Describe** the international monetary system's evolution and its importance to international business.

LO2 **Explain** the impact of fluctuating currency values.

LO3 **Discuss** the influence of currency exchange controls on international business.

LO4 **Summarize** the influences of differences in taxation and inflation rates on international business.

LO5 **Explain** the significance of the balance of payments (BOP) to international business decisions.

gold standard The use of gold at an established number of units per currency

Bretton Woods system The international monetary system in place from 1945 to 1971, with par value based on gold and the U.S. dollar

fixed exchange rate Specific currency exchange equivalence upheld by government

par value Stated value

LO1 Describe the international monetary system's evolution and its importance to international business.

THE INTERNATIONAL MONETARY SYSTEM

A Brief History: The Gold Standard

Based on its scarcity and easily assessed level of purity, gold has been trusted as a way for people to store value, exchange value, and measure value since ancient times. From about 1200 A.D. to the present, the price of gold has generally been going up.[2] From ancient times until the last part of the 19th century, international traders used bullion and gold and silver coins. However, as trade grew, carrying large amounts of gold became impractical. Think about it: gold is heavy, has transportation and storage costs, does not earn interest, and needs safekeeping. These drawbacks led to paper script that was backed by governments with a pledge to exchange it for gold at a fixed rate.

In 1717, Sir Isaac Newton, the great mathematician and master of the English mint, established the price of gold in terms of British currency at 3 pounds, 17 shillings, 10.5 pence per ounce, putting England de facto on the **gold standard.** Most trading or industrial countries followed England's move

and adopted the gold standard. Each country set a certain number of units of its currency per ounce of gold, and the ratios of their gold equivalence established the exchange rate between any two currencies on the gold standard. For example, if 5 British pounds were pegged at 1 ounce of gold and 10 French francs were pegged at 1 ounce, then the exchange rate would have been 2 French francs per British pound, or .5 pound per franc.

Except during the Napoleonic Wars, England stood willing to convert gold to currency, or vice versa, until 1914 and World War I. During those two centuries, more than 90 percent of world trade was financed in London.[3] The cost of World War I forced Britain to sell a substantial portion of its gold and suspend gold exchange. Other warring countries, including Germany, France, and Russia, suspended the exchange of paper money for gold and stopped exports of gold.

The simplicity of the gold standard was a large part of its appeal. When there were trade imbalances, they would be corrected by a flow of gold in the direction of the surplus. The money supply would rise or fall in direct relation to the gold flows. Although the gold standard has not been the international monetary system for many years, it continues to have some ardent advocates—most economists not among them—who call for a return to the gold standard and fixed exchange rates. The heart of their argument is expressed in one word: *discipline.* Under the gold standard, a government cannot create money that is not backed by gold. Therefore, no matter how great the temptation to create more money for political advantage, a government cannot do so without the required amount of gold.[4] Unfortunately, this discipline sacrifices a government's monetary flexibility. Increasing money supply to ward off a recession is not an option on the gold standard. Economist Paul Krugman points out that this flexibility is why the 1987 stock market crash did not cause a depression similar to that of 1929.[5]

Bretton Woods System

Allied government representatives met at Bretton Woods in 1944 to plan for post–World War II monetary arrangements. The consensus was that stable exchange rates were desirable but experience might dictate adjustments. They also agreed that floating or fluctuating exchange rates had proved unsatisfactory, although the reasons for this opinion were little discussed. These meetings established the IMF, which we have reviewed in our discussion of global institutions. The IMF Articles of Agreement contained the rules for a new international monetary system, the **Bretton Woods system,** also called the gold exchange standard and the fixed rate system, that served as the basis of the international monetary system from 1945 to 1971.

The new system set up **fixed exchange rates** among member-nations' currencies, with **par value** based on gold

Iranian currency trader counts gold coins, "Iranians' political hedge fund."

and the U.S. dollar, which was valued at $35 per ounce of gold. For example, the British pound's par value was US$2.40, the French franc's was US$.18, and the German mark's was US$.2732. There was an understanding that the U.S. government would redeem dollars for gold and that the dollar was the only currency to be redeemable for gold. This dollar-based gold exchange standard established the U.S. dollar as both a means of international payment and a reserve currency for governments to hold in their treasuries.

The Bretton Woods system supported substantial international trade growth during the 1950s and 1960s. Other countries changed their currency's value against the dollar

Agreements. Both times, however, banks, businesses, and individuals felt that the central banks had pegged the rates incorrectly, and the speculators were correct each time. In March 1973 the major currencies began to float in the foreign exchange markets, and the system of **floating currency exchange rates** still prevails. The agreement that established the rules for the

> " the flow of dollars out was greater than the flow in; the demand on dollars for holding outside the country was greater than those that flowed in as a result of export sales. "

and gold, but the U.S. dollar remained fixed. This meant that the United States, in order to satisfy the growing demand for reserves (because countries would hold dollars as a proxy for gold), had to run a balance-of-payments deficit. That is, in the United States the flow of dollars out was greater than the flow in; the demand on dollars for holding outside the country was greater than those that flowed in as a result of export sales. From 1958 through 1971, the United States ran up a cumulative deficit of $56 billion. The deficit was financed partly by use of the U.S. gold reserves, which shrank from $24.8 billion to $12.2 billion,[6] and partly by incurring liabilities to foreign central banks. During this period, those liabilities increased from $13.6 billion to $62.2 billion.[7] By 1971, the Treasury held only 22 cents worth of gold for each U.S. dollar held by those banks.

Floating Currency Exchange Rate System

After trade deficits in the late 1960s, President Charles de Gaulle pushed the Bank of France to redeem its dollar holdings for gold. In response, President Nixon announced in 1971 that the United States would no longer exchange gold for the paper dollars held by foreign central banks. This action took the U.S. dollar out of its role as a proxy for gold and a stabilizer for the international monetary system. The shock caused currency exchange markets to remain closed for several days, and when they reopened, they began developing a new system for which few rules existed. Ultimately, currencies floated against each other based on market forces.

Two attempts were made to agree on durable, new sets of fixed currency exchange rates, one in December 1971 and the other in February 1973, resulting in the Smithsonian

floating system was accepted by IMF members after the fact, at a meeting in Jamaica in 1976. Known as the **Jamaica Agreement,** it allows for flexible exchange rates among IMF members, while condoning central bank operations in the money markets to smooth out volatile periods. The Jamaica Agreement also demonetized gold; it was abandoned as a reserve currency.

Current Currency Arrangements

Initially the IMF recognized three types of currency exchange arrangements, but it later extended the categories to eight. The eight categories of exchange rate arrangements that the IMF now uses to describe how countries position their currencies in relation to other currencies are explained here, ranging from not having any legal tender to having fixed and then freely floating exchange rate arrangements.

- *Exchange arrangement with no separate legal tender:* one country adopts the currency of another or a group of countries adopt a common currency. An example of the first is the U.S. dollar's use in El Salvador and Ecuador. An example of the second is the European Union's euro being used as shared currency in 16 EU member-countries.

- *Currency board arrangement:* a legislated commitment to exchange domestic currency for a specific foreign currency at a fixed rate. The currency board arrangement commits the government to hold foreign reserves equal to its domestic currency supply, (e.g., Hong Kong and Bulgaria).

- *Conventional fixed peg arrangement:* a "peg," or fixed rate relationship where exchange rate fluctuations are allowed within a narrow band of less than 1 percent. The peg could be to one currency or to a basket of currencies. The Saudi riyal is, in effect, pegged in this way to the U.S. dollar.

- *Pegged exchange rate within a horizontal band:* a peg arrangement in which the exchange rate fluctuations are allowed to be greater than 1 percent around a central rate (e.g., Denmark's krone pegged to the euro).

- *Crawling peg:* a currency is readjusted periodically at a fixed, preannounced rate or in response to changes in indicators (e.g., at various times Mexico, Botswana, Costa Rica, and Iran).

- *Crawling band:* currency readjustment to maintain fluctuation margins around a central rate (Denmark to the euro).

- *Managed floating with no preannounced path for the exchange rate:* a monetary authority actively intervenes on the exchange market without specifying or making public its goals and targets. Algeria, India, Malaysia, and Singapore are examples of this approach. China relaxed a 10-year yuan peg in 2005 and allowed it to be managed against a basket of trading currencies. In May 2010, the Chinese government signaled a possible further relaxation of its control of the yuan exchange rate float.

- *Independently floating exchange rates:* rely on the market. There may be interventions, yet they are conducted to moderate the rate of change rather than to establish the currency's level. Examples of countries following this approach are the United States, Mexico, Japan, South Africa, Switzerland, Canada, India, and the United Kingdom.[8]

The floating exchange rate system, with its various approaches, seems to be meeting its recent challenges, several of which, including a central bank liquidity crisis in the spring of 2008, have been severe. In addition to economic policy,

coordination by the G8 countries (France, Germany, Italy, Japan, the United States, the United Kingdom, Canada, and Russia) has emerged as a key factor in the foreign exchange (FX) markets. As G8 central banks have become more adept at influencing currency movements, the explosive growth in the volume of currencies being traded in the world's foreign exchange markets challenges their efforts. From an annual volume of roughly $18 billion in 1979, foreign exchange transactions have been estimated at $3.2 trillion daily, up 71 percent since 2004.[9] This amount exceeds the reserves of the richest countries, such as China at $2.5 trillion in March 2010, so the market has increasing leverage to influence exchange rates. For example, if the foreign exchange market players believe the Japanese yen should be stronger in US$ terms, the yen will strengthen in spite of any government market intervention. The floating exchange system seems to be able to respond to market movements with flexibility and relative order. Figure 8.1 summarizes currency arrangements.

Floating currencies can move against one another quickly and in large swings. Such changes have many causes, including political events, expectations, and government economic policies, such as allowing trade imbalances and deficits. These changes create major uncertainties that managers protect against through a process called *hedging*, which is explained in Chapter 17, when we consider financial management in an international context.

Bank for International Settlements

One more institution that is an important, although often overlooked, part of the international monetary system, is the **Bank for International Settlements (BIS).** The BIS is known as the most discreet financial institution in the world. It is an international organization of central banks that exists to build cooperation among them to foster monetary and financial stability. Central bankers of major industrial countries meet at least seven times a year at the BIS to discuss the global financial system. BIS is the oldest international financial institution in the world, having been founded in 1930 to address war reparations imposed on Germany by the Treaty of Versailles. Today the BIS has four main functions: a banker for central banks, a forum for international monetary cooperation, a center for research, and an agent or trustee for governments in various international financial arrangements.

Having reviewed the basics of the international monetary system, we now are ready to focus on the financial forces external to the firm and largely uncontrollable that influence the context in which international managers make decisions. These forces include currency exchange

▼ FIGURE 8.1
Summary of Currency Arrangements

System	Gold	Bretton Woods Fixed Gold Exchange	Floating
Pros	Simplicity	Fixed rates	Flexibility (free/managed float, peg)
	Widely trusted	Supported trade growth	Reflects market forces
	Imposes monetary discipline		Handles huge volume
Cons	Impractical with large trade flows	Balance of payment deficit for U.S.	Wide swings in currency values
	Holding costs	U.S. government liabilities to foreign central banks Shrinking U.S. gold reserves	
Controlling Mechanism	Gold flows: price-specie-flow mechanism (Hume)	Government adjusted rates against dollar Dollar constant against gold	Market forces with some government intervention

rate fluctuation and its related exchange risk, as well as other financial forces that are external to the firm but have a great impact on the firm's management, such as currency exchange controls, taxation, inflation, and national-level balance-of-payments account balances. Although *uncontrollable* means that these financial forces originate outside the business and are beyond its influence, financial managers of a company are not helpless in the face of these forces. Possible ways to manage around them are discussed in Chapter 17, where we consider financial management.

LO2 **Explain** the impact of fluctuating currency values

FINANCIAL FORCES

We begin our review of financial forces with a focus on fluctuating currency values, examining foreign exchange (FX), FX quotation, causes of exchange rate movement, and exchange rate forecasting.

Fluctuating Currency Values

In a post–Bretton Woods monetary system, freely floating currencies fluctuate against each other. At times, central banks intervene in the foreign exchange markets by buying and selling large amounts of a currency in order to affect the supply and demand of the particular currency. Yet, for the most part, the major currencies (the U.S. dollar, the British pound sterling, the Japanese yen, and the euro) are allowed by their central banks to fluctuate freely against each other. These fluctuations may be quite large. For example, in January 1999, the euro rate was established at US$1.1667. In May 2000, the euro had sunk to US$.8895, a 23.75 percent drop. Then the trend reversed and by June 2006 the euro was trading at US$1.2644, an increase of 42.14 percent. Two years later, by early June 2008, the euro was trading at $1.5768. Yet, by May 2010 one euro was back to $1.28, as a result of the Greek economy's bailout problems encountered by the European Union that uncovered key flaws in the single European currency system.

Such fluctuations have considerable impact on financial transactions. This impact of exchange rate changes on the direction of trade was discussed in Chapter 2. Why these currency fluctuations occur—that is, what forces determine exchange rates—is our focus next. We begin with FX quotations and then move on to their causes.

FOREIGN EXCHANGE

People often like to do business in their own currency because, generally, they don't like to assume currency exchange risk. Foreign exchange quotations—the price of one currency expressed in terms of another—are reported in the world's currency exchange markets in terms of the U.S. dollar, and increasingly, the euro, and the local currency. Historically, the US$ has had a central role as a main **central reserve asset** of many countries, a **vehicle currency,** and an **intervention currency.** This role continues, yet the Japanese yen and the euro are increasingly joining the dollar in these functions.[10]

Exchange Rate Quotations

Table 8.1 is the listing of currency exchange rates from the foreign exchange site ONANDA on May 10, 2010. They are available at www.onanda.com. Depending on the transaction, you may want to convert from the US$ equivalent rate to the currency per US$ rate, or vice versa.

The exchange rate for a trade today for delivery within two days, as in Table 8.1, is known as the **spot rate.** The spot rate for the euro on May 23, 2010, in dollar terms, was $.79501.

The **forward currency market** allows managers to lock in purchases of currencies at known rates. The **forward rate** is the cost today for a commitment to buy or sell an agreed amount of a currency at a fixed, future date, usually on a 30-, 60-, 90-, or 180-day basis. The forward market rates can help you get a sense of where traders expect the currency to be headed. The *Financial Times* quotes forward rates for several currencies: the yen,

▼ **TABLE 8.1** OANDA: The Currency Site; May 23, 2010

	Bid	Offer
EUR/USD	1.25684	1.25784
USD/JPY	89.97	90.07
GBP/USD	1.44739	1.44839
USD/CAD	1.05922	1.06022
USD/CHF	1.14891	1.14991
EUR/JPY	113.12	113.22
EUR/GBP	0.86782	0.86882
EUR/CHF	1.44446	1.44546
GBP/CHF	1.66147	1.66347
GBP/JPY	130.23	130.43

Source: www.Oanda.com (accessed May 23, 2010)

the UK pound, the euro, and the U.S. dollar. Next, we discuss the reasons behind the direction and size of currency trends.

CAUSES OF EXCHANGE RATE MOVEMENT

Since 1973, the relative values of floating currencies and the ease of their convertibility have been set by market forces, influenced by many factors. These factors include such considerations as supply and demand forecasts for the two currencies; relative inflation in the two countries; relative productivity and unit labor cost changes; political developments such as expected election results; expected government fiscal, monetary, and currency exchange market actions; balance-of-payments accounts; and a psychological aspect.[11] Monetary and fiscal policies of the government, such as decisions on taxation, interest rates, and trade policies, and other forces external to the business, such as world events, all may play significant roles in this process. **Monetary policies** control the amount of money in circulation, whether it is growing, and, if so, at what pace. **Fiscal policies** address the collecting and spending of money by the government.

What determines exchange rates is a wide and complex variety of factors, such that economists have not yet developed an accepted theory to explain them. Economists have determined several *parity relationships,* that is, relationships of equivalence, among some of the various complex factors involved in exchange rate movements. We look now at two of these relationships, interest rate parity and purchasing power parity, because they are fundamental to our further consideration of exchange rates. They both rest on the **law of one price,** which states that in an efficient market, like products will have like prices. If price differences exist, the process of **arbitrage** (buying and selling to make a profit with no risk) will quickly close any gaps and the markets will be at equilibrium.

When the law of one price is applied to interest rates, it suggests that interest rates vary to take account of differing anticipated levels of inflation. The economic explanation of this relationship, which results in interest rate parity, is the **Fisher effect,** which states that the real interest rate will be the nominal interest rate minus the expected rate of inflation.

So an increase in the expected inflation rate will lead to an increase in the interest rate. A decrease in the expected inflation

> I think what we need to look at now is to find a greater voice in the management of international financial institutions, such as the World Bank and the IMF.
>
> —*People's Daily,* China,
>
> April 14, 2010

rate will lead to a decrease in the interest rate. An investor would want to earn more in a high-inflation environment to compensate for the effect of inflation on the investment.

The **international Fisher effect** says that the interest rate differentials for any two currencies reflect the expected change in their exchange rates.[12] For example, if the nominal interest rate in the United States is 5 percent per year and in the EU it is 3 percent, we would expect the dollar to decrease against the euro by 2 percent over the year.

A second parity relationship is **purchasing power parity (PPP).** PPP shows the number of units of a currency required to buy the same basket of goods and services in the foreign market that one dollar would buy in the United States. It is the result of the law of one price applied to a basket of commodity goods. PPP suggests that for a dollar to buy as much in the United Kingdom as in the United States, the cost of the goods in the UK should equal their U.S. cost times the exchange rate between the dollar and pound. Another way to think about what the PPP theory states is that currency exchange rates between two countries should equal the ratio of the price levels of their commodity baskets. For example, if a basket of goods costs $1,500 in the United States and £1,000 in the United Kingdom, the PPP exchange rate would be $1.50/£. If, in the trading market, the actual spot exchange rate was $2/£, the pound would be overvalued by 33 percent, or, equivalently, the dollar undervalued by 25 percent.

The Economist, a British weekly magazine, presents a playful application of PPP theory in its "Big Mac index" substituting a Big Mac for a basket of goods. This index suggests that, in the long term, many of the developing countries' currencies are undervalued and the euro and many European currencies are overvalued. The Big Mac PPP is the exchange rate that would have a Big Mac in other countries costing as it does in the United States. You can check the latest Big Mac index and view a video explaining *The Economist*'s efforts to make economics as simple as it ought to be at http://www.economist.com/markets/bigmac. So, for example, in May 2010 in China the Big Mac in U.S. dollars at the prevailing yuan-dollar exchange rate cost $1.83, whereas in the United States a four-city average price was $3.58. In effect, the yuan is 48.9 percent below the implied PPP exchange rate. That's a pretty inexpensive burger. *The Economist* claims that in the long run its Big Mac index performs pretty well, with many of the discounted and premium-fetching currencies correcting. Remember, too,

purchasing power parity (PPP). PPP shows the number of units of a currency required to buy the same basket of goods and services in the foreign market that one dollar would buy in the United Sates or other home market

efficient market approach Assumption that current market prices fully reflect all available relevant information

random walk hypothesis Assumption that the unpredictability of factors suggests that the best predictor of tomorrow's prices is today's prices

fundamental approach Exchange rate prediction based on econometric models that attempt to capture the variables and their correct relationships

technical analysis An approach that analyzes data for trends and then projects these trends forward

that the price of a Big Mac represents more than a basket of tradable goods, the situation PPP theory describes. For example, the McDonald's service level we may receive with our Big Mac can't be traded, nor can McDonald's brand image. Nevertheless, the Big Mac index is a helpful and playful way to get a quick sense of relative currency values and where they may be heading. Looking at the latest version of the Big Mac index might help you choose your next bargain vacation spot.

Now that we have looked at two parity relationships, interest rate parity and purchasing power parity, we can look more closely at exchange rate prediction.

Exchange Rate Forecasting

Because exchange rate movements are so important to all aspects of international business—production, sourcing, marketing, and finance—many business decisions take the risk of exchange rate movement into consideration. There are several

have surveyed the research on the various fundamental models and conclude that "the fundamental models failed to more accurately forecast exchange rates than either the forward rate model, which we have termed the efficient market model, or the random walk model."[14]

Technical analysis looks at history and then projects it forward. It analyzes historic data for trends and then, assuming that what was past will be future, projects these trends forward. Technical analysts think in terms of waves and trends. There is no theoretical underpinning to the technical approach and scholarly academic studies tend to dismiss it. Yet currency-trading marketing materials suggest that traders often use it.

As for the performance of these various approaches, recent research by Eun and Sabherwal on the exchange rate forecasts of major commercial banks indicates that the 10 banks in the study could not outperform the random walk model.[15] Their findings also suggest that the forward exchange rate and the spot rate were both about equal in value for predicting future

> "The fundamental models failed to more accurately forecast exchange rates than either the forward rate model, which we have termed the efficient market model, or the random walk model."

approaches to forecasting, and three of the main ones are the efficient market approach, the fundamental approach, and the technical approach. We briefly examine each.

The **efficient market approach** assumes that current prices fully reflect all available relevant information in the environment. That suggests that forward exchange rates are the best possible predictor of future spot rates because they will have taken into account all the available information. If interest rates are different between two countries, for example, the forward rate will reflect this (international Fisher effect). The efficient market approach does not suggest that the forward rates will be the future spot rates with perfect accuracy. Rather, the divergences will be random. A related approach is called the **random walk hypothesis,** and it holds because of the short-term unpredictability of factors, the best predictor of tomorrow's prices is today's prices.[13]

The **fundamental approach** to exchange rate prediction looks at the underlying forces that play a role in determining exchange rates and develops various econometric models that attempt to capture the variables and their correct relationships. Eun and Resnick, two noted international finance scholars,

exchange rates. The evidence available indicates that neither the technical nor the fundamental approach outperforms the efficient market approach.

We have examined a major financial force that international managers have to address, foreign exchange fluctuations, their causes and their prediction. How managers actually deal with the risk that such currency fluctuation exposure creates is a topic we address in Chapter 17. There are many other financial forces that confront international managers. Tariffs are a financial force because they represent increased costs and can change without notice. You can see the current U.S. tariff schedule at the U.S. International Trade Commission website (www.usitc.gov/tata/hts/bychapter/index.htm). One interesting aspect of the tariff schedule is how specific it is. For example, in Harmonized Tariff Schedule (HTS) category 0704.10.20, cauliflower, the tariff rate is 2.5 percent between June 5 and October 25, when the U.S. crop is being harvested. If the cauliflower is cut or sliced, the rate is 14 percent at any time. We now look at additional financial forces, beginning with currency exchange controls, and then move on to taxation, inflation and interest rates, and balance-of-payments effects.

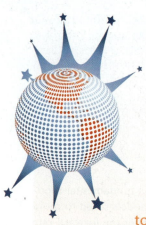

GLOBAL gauntlet

Most economists support the idea that floating exchange rates are beneficial for the world economy. A minority of experts advocate a return to the gold standard and fixed exchange rates. Let's further consider this choice.

In the early 1970s, the USA could not continue to guarantee that dollars floating around the world would be convertible to gold at the agreed rate. So, the USA decoupled the dollar from gold, with the immediate effect that the world's currency exchange rates were not fixed any more.[16]

Obstfeld and Rogoff[17] argue that the main reason exchange rates could not stay fixed was the rapid evolution of world capital markets since the 1950s. As the volume of global transactions started exceeding most countries' foreign exchange reserves, governments could no longer intervene effectively to sustain the value of their currency. Until the volume of trade grew, they would buy or sell significant amounts of their currencies in the global markets in an effort to sustain supply and demand equilibrium. At the same time, a speculative attack on a specific currency by the "market" could cause a run on a currency that a government could not counter. With the advent of the Internet, in less than 15 years the amount of *daily* foreign exchange transactions has increased from $1 trillion in 1994 to $3.2 trillion in 2008. So it is difficult to imagine the day when the main currency regimes around the world would be dominated by fixed rate relationships.

Even if a central bank could support its currency effectively, the impact on the rest of the economy could be considerable. In Chapter 8 we have discussed the relationship between exchange rates and interest rates. In an environment where currency A is becoming relatively stronger than currency B, the interest rates in country A are likely to be higher than those in country B. This increases the cost of doing business in country A versus country B. Moreover, interest rate movements, exchange rate values and inflationary pressures tend to be interlinked. Finally, the role of speculators cannot be overlooked. The currency market impressions of a currency's reputation can be enough to scare buyers away from a perceived weak currency toward a strong one. As with any other buying-selling relationship, this will weaken further the currency that buyers are fleeing from and strengthen the one they are going to. Then the strengthening currency has a negative impact on that country's ability to export.

The discussion up to here shows that we may not like "floating exchange rates" for whatever reasons, but is there an alternative in today's globalized economy and global capital markets? What are the key arguments for trying to "fix" exchange rates? Two are as follows:[18]

First, exchange rate changes increase the risk and cost of trade for industries that are based on producing goods. These industries have products that have to be shipped from one country to another. This process is associated with a time lag between the time when an order is placed, the time when the producer ships, and the time when the buyer receives a product. These three points in time may be associated with very different exchange rates among the currencies of the two countries involved. Whether it is the manufacturer or the buyer or both who bear the risk, there are ways to minimize foreign exchange risk related to timing. All these ways introduce a new cost to the transaction. Had the exchange rate been fixed, this cost would not arise.

Second, exchange rate fluctuations may lead to protectionist measures that can impede trade and deprive a country's people from trade benefits. Yet, fixing the exchange rate means that the government is also depriving itself of the ability to manage its monetary policy. Finally, fixed rate proponents say that fixed exchange rates impose monetary discipline on a government. A long, logical explanation shows, however, that this implies isolation from actions of other governments, an impossible option today.

Given the above discussion, what is your own broad conclusion about the viability of fixed or floating exchange rates?

LO3 **Discuss** the influence of currency exchange controls on international business

CURRENCY EXCHANGE CONTROLS

A government can limit the amount of its currency that can be exchanged for another currency in a particular transaction. Controls differ greatly from country to country and even within a country, depending on the type of transaction. In general, the developed countries have few or no currency exchange controls, but these nations are a minority of the world's countries. Many developing countries, though, such as Mexico, have reduced or eliminated such controls in order to encourage foreign investment. The international business manager must be aware of whether currency exchange controls exist both before and while doing business in any country, because the currency exchange control situation can change quickly.

Convertible currencies can be exchanged for other currencies without restrictions. These hard currencies include the Japanese yen, the U.S. dollar, the British pound, and the euro. When a currency is nonconvertible, its value is arbitrarily fixed, typically at a rate higher than its value in the free market. In such a case, the government imposes exchange controls to limit or prohibit the legal use of its currency in international transactions. The government also requires that all purchases or sales of other currencies be made through a government agency. Limitations might also restrict the amount of domestic currency transferred into foreign currency. Such restrictions may influence a firm's ability to repatriate their profits, that is, return their profits to the home country. A black market inevitably springs up alongside such currency restrictions, but it is of little use to the international manager who wants to abide by the laws.

Countries put limitations on the convertibility of their currency when they are concerned that their foreign reserves could be depleted. Foreign reserves are a source of currency for foreign debt service, import purchases, and other demands for foreign currency that domestic banks might encounter. An example of a country with exchange controls is China, whose currency is convertible in current accounts (accounts for day-to-day banking) but not capital accounts (longer-term accounts).

Often when a government requires the firm to have permission to purchase foreign currency, the exchange rates are above the free-market rate. If permission is not granted or if the cost of foreign currency is uneconomically high, the blocked currency can be used only within the country. Such repatriation limitations usually present international managers the problem of finding suitable products and investments within the country.

LO4 **Summarize** the influences of differences in taxation and inflation rates on international business

Taxation

We have just mentioned the legal aspects of taxation in Chapter 7. Taxation is also a financial force whose impact is significant. If a corporation can achieve a lower tax burden than its competitors have, it can lower prices to its customers or generate higher revenue with which to pay higher wages and dividends. Governments around the world widely use three types of taxation to generate revenue: income tax, value-added tax (VAT), and withholding tax. The *income tax* is a direct tax on personal and corporate income. Table 8.2 compares corporate taxation rates in selected countries.

A *value-added tax (VAT)* is a tax charged on the value added to a good as it moves through production from raw materials to final purchaser. It is really a sales tax whose payment documentation from one stage to another from production through to the final buyer becomes important for tax credits, because the seller collects the tax for the goods sold and then receives credits for VAT already paid earlier in the production process. Countries that levy value-added taxes are permitted by World Trade Organization (WTO) rules to rebate the value-added taxes to exporters, an incentive that makes the exports less expensive and thus more competitive.

The third general tax category is the *withholding tax.* This is an indirect tax levied on passive income (income such as dividends, royalties, and interest) that the corporation would pay out to nonresidents, people, or companies in another tax jurisdiction. Countries establish bilateral tax treaties to categorize passive-income withholding rates. For example, on interest the United States withholds 30 percent from residents of non–tax treaty countries. From UK residents it withholds nothing, while from residents of Pakistan it withholds 30 percent.

International companies need to understand tax laws in each country in which they operate and how those tax laws relate to tax laws in other countries. This additional tax burden can create financial risk, but it can also be an opportunity for savings, given good tax planning.

▼ **TABLE 8.2** Corporate Tax Rates

Country	Percent
Switzerland[a]	11.7– 24.10
Ireland	12.50
Singapore[b]	17.00
Russia	20.00
China[c]	25.00
Netherlands	25.50
Finland	26.00
Germany[d]	27.50– 37.50
United Kingdom	28.00
Peru[e]	30.00
Australia	30.00
Japan	30.00
France	33.33
United States[f]	35.00
Brazil	40.00
India	40.00

[a] These rates includes federal and canton taxes and vary by location.

[b] Rate for 2010; 18% up to 2009.

[c] Lower tax rate 15–20% for certain sectors/industries.

[d] This is the minimum based on location. The range includes: 15% corporation tax, 5.5% surcharge, and trade tax 7–17% based on location.

[e] On worldwide income.

[f] This is the federal tax rate. State and local tax rates range from 0 to 20%.

Source: Pricewaterhouse Coopers, 2010, http://www.taxsummaries.pwc.com/ (accessed May 22, 2010).

Inflation and Interest Rates

Inflation is a trend of rising prices. Some economists hold that it is caused by demand exceeding supply, while others view the cause as an increase in the money supply. All, however, agree that in an inflationary economy, prices increase. Table 8.3 shows inflation levels in selected countries. Japan, the EU, and the United States have had relatively good records in keeping inflation down in recent years. Historically, Latin American countries have had inflation troubles. However, these trends have been gradually reversed. Brazil experienced 3,118 percent inflation in 1990 and was able to decrease this to 4.2 percent in 2009. The overall highest inflation rate to date was found in Zimbabwe, where it reached 14.9 billion percent in July 2008. Most inflation is measured by a *consumer price index (CPI),* the price changes for a basket of consumer goods.

Inflation, a financial force external to companies, affects the firm in several major ways. First, the inflation rate determines the real cost of borrowing in capital markets. You'll recall the Fisher effect from our discussion of exchange rates. When the firm operates in multiple countries, it has multiple currency exposures, and the complexity of dealing with

inflation increases because inflation rates vary among countries. Should management raise capital, and if so, should this be done through equity or debt? In which capital markets? In what currency?

Further, increasing inflation rates encourage borrowing (debt) because the loan will be repaid with inflated, cheaper money. But high inflation rates bring high interest rates because banks have to offer more reward to draw in deposits. Then, inflation may discourage lending because lenders may fear that even with high interest rates, the amount repaid plus interest would be worth less than the amount lent. So there is a relationship between inflation and interest rates. And we have seen in our discussion of the international Fisher effect that there is a relationship between currency exchange rate trends and interest rates. So there is a relationship between inflation and currency exchange rates. Inflated currencies tend to weaken. In inflated economies, instead of lending, the money holder may buy something that is expected to increase in value, thereby

▼ **TABLE 8.3** World inflation Rates

Country	% Inflation 2009 (est.)	% Inflation 2008 (est.)
Afghanistan	30.5	20.7
Argentina	7.7	7.2
Australia	1.9	4.4
Brazil	4.2	5.9
Chile	1.7	8.7
China	−0.8	5.9
European Union	0.6	1.8
France	0.1	2.8
Germany	0	2.7
Greece	1.2	4.1
Ireland	−1.7	4.1
Italy	0.6	3.4
India	10.7	8.3
Japan	−1.3	1.4
Kenya	20.5	26.2
Korea, South	2.8	4.7
Nigeria	11.5	11.6
Russia	11.9	14.1
Spain	−0.8	4.1
Switzerland	0.1	−0.5
Turkey	6.5	10.1
United Kingdom	2.1	3.6
United States	−0.7	3.8
Venezuela	27.1	30.4
Zimbabwe	5.1	14.9 billion

Source: https://www.cia.gov/library/publications/the-world-factbook/ (accessed May 23, 2010).

CU_{in}ib

John Gallagher in China

When I entered college to study business, I knew that today's global economy would require me to have a global perspective. While I did not know how I was going to get a job overseas after graduation, I was drawn to the beauty and challenge of studying Chinese. So, I enrolled in the Chinese track of Northeastern University's Bachelor of Science degree in International Business (BSIB), which would include both study and coop abroad. The coop is similar to a corporate international assignment, with at least two work periods of approximately six months. My study abroad focused on my business discipline—finance—from an international perspective. Because I was going to study and work in China, I took Mandarin Chinese for three years in the U.S. By the fourth year when I was ready to go to Hong Kong, I knew enough Chinese to function in my daily life.

I arrived in Hong Kong to start my Junior year at Hong Kong University of Science and Technology. While my main curriculum focused on business subjects, I continued to study Chinese during my seven months there. In November of that year, I started interviewing for a cooperative education position with Chinese companies and with Chinese subsidiaries of foreign companies. The process of finding a job in China was a learning experience in itself. The practices are very different from those in the U.S. Position candidates have to be interviewed by managers from a very hierarchical society that expects young people to be deferential to their elders. Being forward can be seen as being rude. In the U.S. we are raised to value assertive action. Also, it was difficult to picture what the job content might likely be.

After much frustration with a few false starts, I found a job that was based in Beijing. I was to work with a management consulting firm. As soon as I accepted this job, I realized that when I got there in February, I would have to find a place to live for five months. The next stage of my adventure had crept up on me.

Well, I did find a place to live, and before I knew it, I was ready to return to the U.S. after my year in China to complete my senior year. The experience back home was interesting in a surprising way. I had changed enough in a year that I had to adapt to a new pace of life and study. My friends who were not in the international business program had finished their junior year in Boston and had not changed very much. Most did not have much of an interest in what I had done "over there" for a year. This was a "textbook" experience for a manager who returns from the overseas assignment: my friends and family had no real interest in listening to long stories of what I had done, where and how. I had to accept this and move on. What I did know, however, was that I was going to find a way to go back to China with a full-time job.

Back in the U.S. and two months before graduation, I was briefing the parents of a class of students two years behind me in the international business program. These students were scheduled to go overseas in the summer of 2010 and their parents were there to learn what their daughters and sons were going to be facing in the process of studying and working abroad. I was acting as the expert who could answer their questions from personal experience. Soon after I finished a lively question and answer session on the benefits and challenges of this program, the father of one of the students who was in the audience approached me. He offered me a job with his company on the spot! Three months later I was back in China working for his battery manufacturing company.

I am the only permanent American employee there. One of my primary responsibilities is to liaise between the subsidiary's Chinese managers and U.S. headquarters staff. This is a rewarding job because I am learning how the company functions, the expectations of the Chinese employees, the idiosyncrasies of the Chinese business environment, and the challenges of the business's supply chain all the way from raw materials to the end customer in the U.S. and elsewhere in the world. Every day, I use the Chinese I learned in my international business program, I have more responsibility than I ever imagined was possible in a first job, I am working between two cultures, and I am on the way to a very exciting career in the global economy.

Building my career in international business was not easy. It required single-minded determination, a willingness to work with a lot of ambiguity, and to take steps that may be considered risky to one's career. It has been worth it!

Central Bank or Country	End 2009 % Interest Rate
Bank of England	0.50
Bank of Japan	0.10
European Central Bank	1.00
Federal Reserve	0.25
Swiss National Bank	0.25
The Reserve Bank of Australia	4.25
Bank of Canada	0.25
Brazil	8.50
China	5.31
India	4.75
Korea, South	2.00
Mexico	4.50
Russia	8.75
Saudi Arabia	7.00
Turkey	6.50

Source: http://www.reuters.com/article/idUSGLOBAL20100219.

▼**FIGURE 8.2** Balance of Payments Major Accounts

I. Current Account

Net changes in exports and imports of goods and services—tangibles and intangibles.

    A. Goods or *merchandise account*—tangibles; net balance known as the *trade balance*

    B. *Services account*—intangibles

    C. *Unilateral transfers*—transfers with no reciprocity (gifts, aid, migrant worker earnings), to satisfy the needs of double-entry recording, entry made that treats the aid or gift as purchase of goodwill

II. Capital Account

Net changes in a nation's international financial assets and liabilities; credit entry occurs when resident sells stock, bonds, or other financial assets to non-resident. Money flows to resident, while resident's long-term international liabilities (debit entry) increase.

    A. *Direct investment*—located in one country and controlled by residents of another country

    B. *Portfolio investment*—long-term investments without control

    C. *Short-term capital flows*—such as currency exchange rate and interest rate hedging in the forward, futures, option, and swap markets; volatility and transaction privacy make this entry the least reliable measure

III. Official Reserves Account

    A. *Gold* imports and exports

    B. *Foreign exchange* (foreign currencies) held by government

    C. *Liabilities* to foreign central banks

further fueling inflation. In Brazil during a recent inflationary period, farmers would hoard their crops, not bring them to the market, and then use them in barter for imported farming equipment and Mercedes cars. Lenders have begun to use variable interest rates, which rise or fall with inflation, to shift financial risk to the borrower. This shift requires that the borrower be much more careful about borrowing. The original rate and any future changes are based on a reference interest rate, such as the U.S. prime rate (rate of interest banks lend to their best customers) or the London Interbank Offer Rate (the bank-to-bank interest rate in London—LIBOR).

As Table 8.4 suggests, year-end 2009 interest rates in the countries vary across a small range. This trend may be explained by the integration of financial markets as they become more globalized. In the table of 15 countries in Table 8.4, the average interest rate was 3.6 percent. A similar figure in 1993 was 6.9 percent.

Finally, inflation rates cause the cost of the goods and services produced in a country to rise, and thus the goods and services become less competitive globally. Producers in the high-inflation country find export sales more difficult. Such conditions may lead to balance-of-payments deficits in the trade account, so under these conditions management must be alert to government policy changes that attempt to correct these deficits. Such changes could include more restrictive fiscal or monetary policies, currency controls, export incentives, and import obstacles. We'll look now at the balance of payments account.

Balance of Payments

The **balance of payments (BOP)** is a record of a country's transactions with the rest of the world. BOP data are of interest to international businesspeople for several reasons. First, the balance of payments reveals demand for the country's currency. If a country is exporting more than it imports, there will be a high demand for the currency in other countries in order to pay for the exported goods. This demand may well create pressure on the exporter's currency, in which case it might be expected to strengthen. Conversely, when a country imports more than it exports, the currency might be expected to weaken, or if not a floating currency, to be devalued. Faced with a trade deficit, a government might lean toward restrictive monetary or fiscal policies. Currency or trade controls could be introduced. The BOP trend also helps managers predict what sort of changes in the economic environment might develop in the country. This prediction could impact their choice of strategic risks to take in a specific country.

balance of payments (BOP) Record of a country's transactions with the rest of the world

LO5 Explain the significance of the balance of payments (BOP) to international business decisions.

BOP Accounts

The BOP accounts are recorded in double-entry bookkeeping form. Each international transaction is an exchange of assets with a debit and a credit side. Payments *to* other countries, funds flowing out, are tracked as debits ($-$), while transactions that are payments *from* other countries, funds flowing in, are tracked as credits ($+$). The statement of a country's BOP is divided into several accounts and many subaccounts, as outlined in Figure 8.2.

Deficits and Surpluses in BOP Accounts

The BOP current account and capital account add up to the total account. A deficit in the current account is always accompanied by an equal surplus in the capital account, and vice versa. Let's see how this works. If you purchase a case of French wine in the United States for $200, your payment, as it heads out of the United States and to the French winery, will be recorded as a debit in the U.S. current account. Once the winery receives your dollars, it has to do something with them. If the treasurer of the winery decides to deposit your payment in a dollar account at a U.S. bank, the amount will show up as a credit in the U.S. capital account. If the winery exchanges your dollar payment for euros, then the bank receiving the dollars will have to make a decision about how to spend or invest the dollars. Sooner or later, these dollars will show up as a credit on the U.S. account.

Contrary to the commonly held belief, a current account deficit is not always a sign of bad economic conditions. It means that the country is importing capital. This is no more unnatural or dangerous than importing wine or cheese. The deficit is a response to conditions in the country. Among these conditions could be excessive inflation, low productivity, or inadequate saving. In the case of the United States, a current account deficit could occur because investments in the United States are secure and profitable. If there is a problem, it is in the underlying conditions and not in the deficit per se.[19] Countries with relatively high price levels, gross national products, interest rates, and exchange rates, as well as relatively low barriers to imports and attractive investment opportunities, are more likely to have current account deficits than are other countries.[20]

In recent years the United States has had a substantial deficit in its current account. Citizens of the United States are importing more goods than they are exporting, yet exporting more services than they are importing. There also is a surplus in the U.S. capital account. Those dollars that leave the United States to pay for imported goods come back into the United States in the form of foreign-owned investments (e.g., Treasury bills and investment property in New York City). So let's remember that a deficit or surplus in the current account cannot be explained or evaluated without simultaneously examining an equal surplus or deficit in the capital account.[21]

In our review of the monetary system and financial forces, we have briefly examined three currency arrangements: gold, the Bretton Woods system (which was a modified fixed rate system), and a floating system. We've also looked at our current monetary system and the Bank for International Settlements. Then we reviewed the major financial forces with which the firm has to work: fluctuating currency values, currency exchange controls, taxation, inflation, and interest rates. Finally, we reviewed the balance of payments accounts and their significance to the international manager. ■

"Globalization . . . means globalizing every activity of the company. . . . Globalization especially means finding and attracting the unlimited pool of intellectual capital—the very best people—from all around the globe."

—General Electric, "Key Growth Initiatives"

labor forces

Many of the labor conditions in an area are determined by social, cultural, religious, attitudinal, and other forces discussed throughout this text. Other determinants of labor conditions are political and legal forces, and in this chapter we expand on some of those. In particular, we will look at labor, the reasons for its availability or scarcity, the types of labor likely to be available or scarce under different circumstances, and employer–employee relationships. We will see how these relationships are affected by government and by employee organizations such as labor unions.

LEARNING OBJECTIVES

After reading this chapter, you should be able to:

LO1 Identify the forces that affect the quantity and quality of labor in a nation.

LO2 Discuss major factors that may impact employment policies in an international setting.

LO3 Discuss the differences and trends in labor unions from country to country and worldwide.

labor quality The skills, education, and attitudes of available employees

labor quantity The number of available employees with the skills required to meet an employer's business needs

LO1 Identify the forces that affect the quantity and quality of labor in a nation.

WORLDWIDE LABOR CONDITIONS AND TRENDS

The **quantity** and **quality** of labor vary across nations and regions of the world and also over time. A brief review of demographic data provides a starting point for examining labor conditions. This section then examines the impact of the current financial crisis on labor markets that has led to huge increases in global unemployment, the aging of populations, increasing migration from rural to urban areas, immigration, participation by children in the labor force, and forced labor.

Overall Size of the Workforce

We begin by looking at the overall situation in the world, in terms of some very macro demographic data. In 2010, the world had 6.8 billion inhabitants, 48 percent of whom were under the age of 25 and 31 percent under the age of 15.[1] Due to high birthrates and a decline in the rate of infant mortality, populations in the developing nations tend to be growing as well as becoming younger. Approximately 38 percent of the world's 15- to 24-year-olds, a key source of new workers during

▼**FIGURE 9.1**
Population by Region

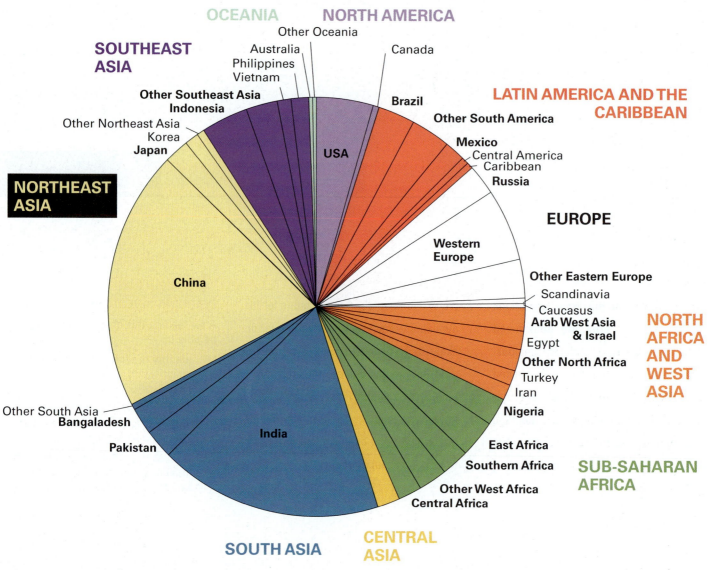

Source: http://en.wikipedia.org/wiki/File:World_population_pie_chart.PNG (June 24, 2010).

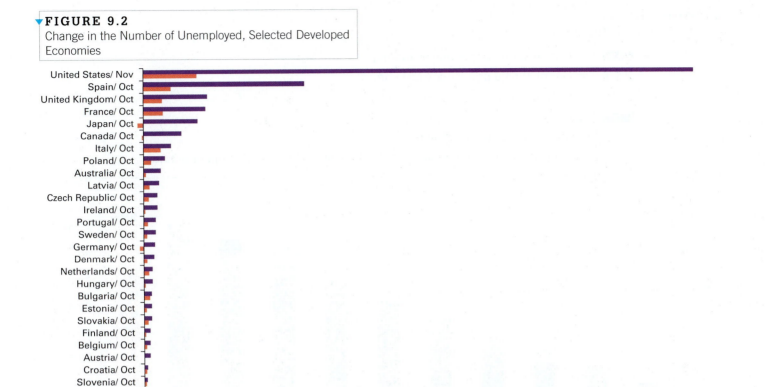

▼FIGURE 9.2
Change in the Number of Unemployed, Selected Developed Economies

Change in the number of unemployed ('000s)

■ Change between June 2008 and the most recent month in 2009
■ Change over the six most recent months in 2009

Source: Eurostat and OECD, online databases, accessed July 10, 2010.

the next decade, live in just two developing countries: India and China.[2]

In contrast, populations in many developed countries are projected to decline in the coming years, due to factors such as low birthrates and low levels of immigration. For example, between 2006 and 2050, Japan's population is projected to decline from 127.5 million to 99.9 million, Russia's from 142.9 million to 110.8 million, and Germany's from 82.4 million to 73.6 million. Countries that have admitted large numbers of immigrants—such as the United States, the United Kingdom, Canada, and Australia—are projected to have continued population growth due to the younger age and higher birthrates of their immigrant populations. For example, between 2010 and 2050, the U.S. population is projected to grow from 310 million to 439 million, and Canada's from 33 million to 37.5 million.

In addition to population, we need to consider the effects on the workforce of the 2009 financial crisis that began with the collapse of an American investment bank and led to near paralysis of the international financial system. The major effects of the crisis on labor have been widespread unemployment, underemployment, and less secure work situations.[3] Recent data indicate that the crisis may have bottomed out, with global growth rates for 2009 at minus 1.1 percent.[4]

Unemployment

The global unemployment rate is estimated to be at 6.6 percent, an increase of 34 million over the unemployed in 2007. Most of this increase occurred in 2009, and over two-thirds occurred in developed economies, which were hit much more severely than developing economies. Although recovery has begun, employment growth is projected to be slow in developed countries, with unemployment rates projected at 6.5 percent for 2010. Recovery in the labor markets is expected to lag behind the economic recovery and unemployment rates to reduce very slowly. The deterioration of the labor markets as a result of the financial crisis can also be seen in the growth of the vulnerable workforce. Figure 9.2 illustrates the change in unemployment during two periods of the financial crisis, while Figure 9.3 shows trends in global employment.

Vulnerable Workforce

The vulnerable workforce includes workers who work on their own account or as contributing family members. They are less likely to have a contract or other formal work arrangement, and their work is often characterized by inadequate earnings, low productivity, and difficult conditions that undermine workers' fundamental rights. Vulnerable workers are found

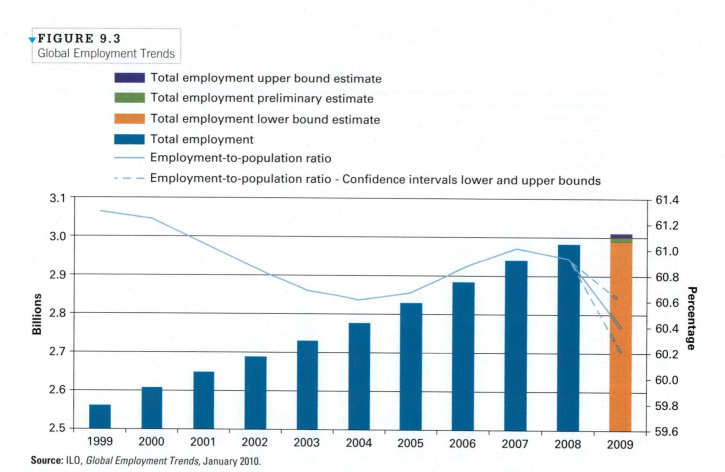

Legend:
- Total employment upper bound estimate
- Total employment preliminary estimate
- Total employment lower bound estimate
- Total employment
- Employment-to-population ratio
- Employment-to-population ratio - Confidence intervals lower and upper bounds

Source: ILO, *Global Employment Trends,* January 2010.

in all economies, and most frequently in the developing world. Before the economic crisis, the worldwide trend in vulnerable employment was downward, decreasing almost 4 percent between 1998 and 2008. But the vulnerable workforce has grown significantly since the economic crisis, and is estimated now to be about half the global workforce.[5] Data suggest that in Sub-Saharan Africa and South Asia, 80 percent of the employed are vulnerable workers.

Aging of Populations

The rapid increase in the proportion of the world's population that is age 65 or older has received much attention in recent years. In 2010, 7.6 percent of the world's population was 65 or older, versus 6.6 percent only a decade earlier. The proportion of those 65 or older is projected to increase to 8.4 percent of the world's population in 2015 and 16.4 percent by 2050, with the distribution illustrated in Figure 9.4.[6]

As Figure 9.4 illustrates, the aging of populations is more pronounced for the developed countries, in which the percentage of the population 65 and above grew from 10 percent in 1996 to 12 percent in 2010 and is projected to rise to 25.4 percent by 2050. An aging population in most of the developed countries has implications for labor force size and skill; for policies regarding immigration; for economic growth; and for a range of political issues related to pension plans, health care, and other key social, economic, and political factors in those nations. For example, the European Commission predicts that

Europe's share of world output could decline from its current 18 percent to 10 percent by 2050, and Japan's from 8 to 4 percent, unless major population-related policy changes are undertaken. In contrast, a more youthful United States could expand its world output share from 23 to 26 percent during the same time. Compared to developed countries, the developing countries will have only about one-half the proportion of people age 65 and older, at least through 2025. Take India for example. A much larger proportion of Indians will be of traditional working age (20 to 64) than will be the case for most of the rest of the world, especially the developed countries. That may have important implications for international companies considering where to locate production as well as those seeking markets for products that target working-age adults.

Urbanization of Workforce

The population and labor force worldwide have been shifting dramatically from rural to urban during the past century. Less than 29 percent of the world's population lived in urban areas in 1950. By 2010, more than half of the world's population was urban, and this proportion is projected to increase to 60 percent by the year 2030. Although the level of urbanization is higher in developed countries, the rate of urbanization was four times faster in developing countries from 1975 to 2009 as these nations experienced rapid increases in population as well as increasing economic development.

As populations migrate from rural areas to urban areas, particularly within developing nations, they also move from agriculturally based employment to employment in industry and service sectors. Often, this influx of labor from rural areas creates a pool of low-cost, low-skilled workers, a large portion of which may be classified as part of the vulnerable workforce. While labor trainers for international companies in developing nations have found that people learn industrial skills rapidly, a more difficult challenge is teaching new workers who come from farms and villages how to adjust socially and psychologically to work life in industry or service sectors. Figure 9.5 shows the occupations of national labor forces.

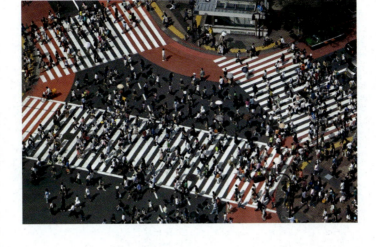

Immigrant Labor

Although classical economists assumed that labor was immobile, we now know that **labor mobility** does exist. For example, at least 60 million people left Europe to work and live overseas between 1850 and 1970. During part of that time, between the end of World War II and the mid-1970s, some 30 million workers from southern Europe and North Africa flowed into eight northern European countries where they were needed because of the economic boom there. When possible, people move to secure better economic situations, regardless of their socioeconomic level, and immigration is at least partly the result of the relative supply of and demand for labor as well as regulations influencing those factors.

▼**FIGURE 9.4**
Population Aged 65 and Above (2015)

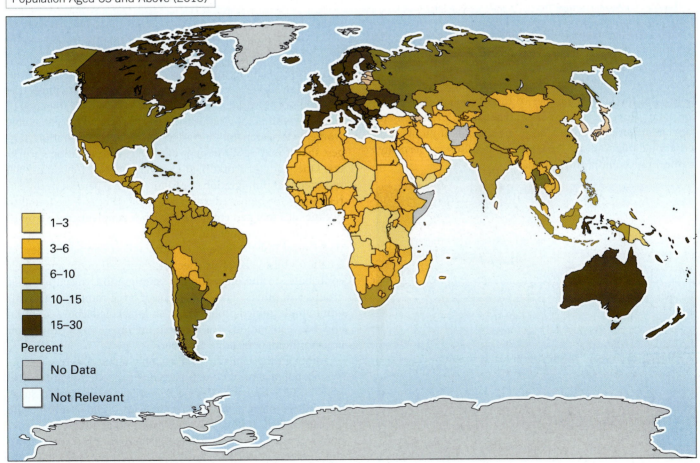

Percent

1–3
3–6
6–10
10–15
15–30

No Data

Not Relevant

Source: http://globalis.gvu.unu.edu/ (June 24, 2010).

▼**FIGURE 9.5** Primary Occupation of National Labor Force

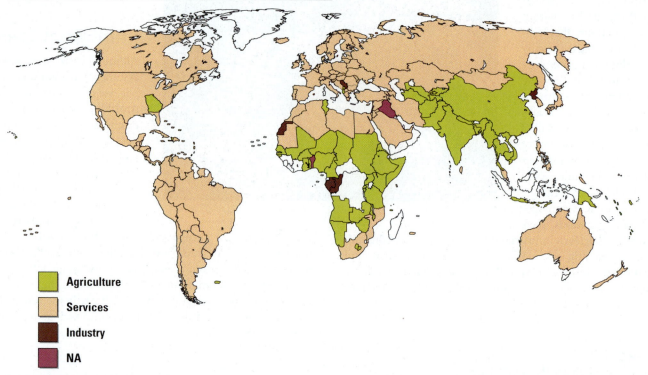

- ■ Agriculture
- ■ Services
- ■ Industry
- ■ NA

Source: Country reports from *The CIA World Factbook,* https://www.cia.gov/cia/publications/factbook/fields/2048.html (accessed March 11, 2010).

In 2005, there were at least 191 million people living outside their nation of birth, nearly three times the level in 1960. Sixty percent of the world's migrants live in developed countries, particularly the United States, Europe, and Australia.[7] The nations with the largest number of their people migrating to other nations are Mexico, Russia, India, China, Ukraine, Bangladesh, and Turkey. Nations receiving the largest numbers of international migrants are the United States, Russia, Germany, Ukraine, France, India and Canada.

Protest against the U.S. House of Representatives H4437, whose passage would make illegal immigration a felony.

Migrant labor ranges from highly skilled jobs such as in information technology and medicine to lower-skilled jobs in agriculture, cleaning, and domestic service. Many migrants are involved in "3-D" jobs—dirty, dangerous, and degrading—that a nation's own workers reject or for which there are not enough available workers. Many of these 3-D jobs employ vulnerable workers. Research on the wage effects of immigration suggest that it may result in depressed wages for a nation's workers. One study of workers in Canada between 1980 and 2000 reported that immigration contributed to a 7 percent decline in real wages for highly educated workers.[8] Wages were found to decline by 3 to 4 percent when the labor supply increased by 10 percent due to immigration. While immigration can be a net positive for inflation and international cost competitiveness of a nation's businesses, this effect of immigration on wage levels contributes to the opposition to immigration voiced by labor groups and others. The movement of large numbers of immigrants, both trained professionals and unskilled laborers, within and between nations has become an increasingly important issue for human resource managers.

Although the United States has only about 5 percent of the world's population, it has 20 percent of the world's migrants.[9] In 2008, 12.5 percent of the people residing in the United States were foreign-born, up from 5 percent in 1970, and over half of the increase in the U.S. population between 2000 and 2009 came from immigration.[10] About 58 percent of the new jobs created since 1995 have been filled with foreign-born workers, including more than 85 percent of new positions for mechanics and construction workers and more than 60 percent of service positions. Overall, more than 23 percent of the U.S. population either is foreign-born or has one or both parents who were foreign-born. Immigrants come to the United States from all over the world, with the largest number of foreign-born coming from Latin America (53 percent), Asia (25 percent), and Europe (14 percent).[11]

The International Labour Organization (ILO) reports that in 2008, workers sent home $338 billion. ILO estimates that remittances will have dropped 6.1 percent, to $317 billion in 2009,[12] due largely to the economic crisis. These remittances are a major influence on economic development for the country of origin; they exceed all official governmental assistance worldwide targeted for development. Immigrants also enhance home-country development by transferring skills and technology if they return home.

Child Labor

According to UNICEF, 158 million (one in six) of the world's children aged 5 to 14 work under conditions that fail to meet their basic needs and that are considered exploitative, hazardous, or illegal.[13] Often they work and live in dangerous or filthy conditions for miserable wages or no compensation at all. Child labor has the highest rates in Asia and Africa. **Child labor** also exists in developed countries, although the proportion is lower than is frequently found in developing countries. Overall, nearly 70 percent of child labor is in agriculture.

child labor The labor of children 14 years of age and below who are forced to work and usually receive little or no education

In developing countries, the child labor issue often is complex, because forcing children out of factories or fields and into schools may actually hurt them. Unless their families are compensated for the lost income, such a policy can worsen their poverty. The World Bank says that children's work can be in their own interests and that a family's survival may depend on it. UNICEF advocates banning only work that can harm children's development. With increased global awareness of the child labor issue, governments once reluctant to even admit child labor problems now are trying to solve them. Reports over the last several years suggest these efforts are beginning to have an effect.[14] One notable effort is UNICEF's Convention on the Rights of the Child (CRC), "the first legally binding international instrument to incorporate the full range of human rights—civil, cultural, economic, political, and social rights."[15] The CRC establishes basic standards that should be observed with respect to children worldwide. Its four core principles are (1) nondiscrimination; (2) devotion to the best interests of the child; (3) the right to life, survival, and development; and (4) respect for the views of the child. Countries that ratify the CRC commit themselves to protecting the rights of children and to holding themselves accountable internationally. All member countries of the United Nations

> "Forcing children out of factories or fields and into schools may actually hurt them"

▼**FIGURE 9.6**
Net Migration Rates, 2008

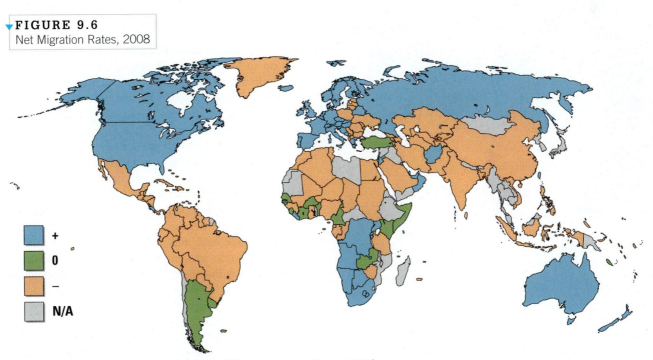

+
0
—
N/A

Source: *CIA Factbook* (accessed March 8, 2010), Wikipedia (accessed March 9, 2010).

have ratified the CRC, with the exception of Somalia and the United States. The United States has failed to ratify the CRC due to a combination of concerns about potential conflicts with the nation's Constitution voiced by some religious and political conservatives.[16]

Forced Labor

Forced labor, which is most common in South and East Asia, northern and western Africa, and parts of Latin America, also occurs in developed nations including the United States. It affects at least 12.3 million people today. Women, children, and

> If a child is not employed, it will beg or lie in the street, or use drugs.
>
> —owner of a Nepalese carpet factory

low-income men are typical victims of forced labor. The U.S. Secretary of State, Hillary Clinton, recently observed about the human trafficking that often accompanies forced labor that "because they live out of sight, that number (12.3 million) is almost certainly too low. More than half of all victims of forced labor are women and girls, compelled into servitude as domestics or sweatshop workers or . . . forced into prostitution. To some, human trafficking may seem like a problem limited to other parts of the world. In fact, it occurs in every country, including the United States, and we have a responsibility to fight it just as others do. It undermines our long-term efforts to promote peace and prosperity worldwide. And it is an affront to our values and our commitment to human rights."[17]

Forms of human trafficking in the United States State Department *Trafficking in Persons Report* included bonded labor, involuntary servitude, debt bondage, involuntary domestic servitude, forced child labor, child soldiers, sex trafficking and prostitution, children exploited for commercial sex, and child sex tourism. Some forms of prison labor are also considered forced labor, as is descent-based slavery in which people are forced to work for little or no pay due to their ethnicity or social status, such as the "untouchables" caste of Dalits in India.

Brain Drain

Record numbers of immigrants are moving to many OECD countries in search of jobs. The latest edition of the OECD's annual *Trends in International Migration* notes that even recent economic downturns in some OECD countries have not affected the upward trend in international migration that began in the mid-1990s.[18] When skilled workers migrate from developing economies, a phenomenon known as **brain drain,** they generally do so for professional opportunities and economic reasons. Brain drain has become a serious problem for developing countries, because it involves the loss of such skilled professionals as scientists, IT specialists, engineers, teachers, and health care professionals. In some Central American and Sub-Saharan African countries, over half of the college-educated population emigrates, often to seek adequate infrastructures in the area in which they have trained. For example, 90 percent of doctors trained in Kenya's public hospitals subsequently emigrate, leaving many areas of the country without adequate medical care.[19] UNESCO recently began "The Brain Drain Initiative," a program to provide Arab and African researchers access to global scientific networks and enabling computing power researchers to collaborate with experts around the world through grid and cloud computing in order to boost loyalty to the local science and technology effort in the developing nation.[20]

Traditionally, a major destination for these skilled workers has been the United States, due to factors such as top-quality universities; dynamic companies; an open, merit-based economic

Om Prakash Gurjar was born in Dwarapur village of Alwar district, Rajasthan, to a family of bonded laborers. For many years, he was forced to work on the farm of the landlord as a bonded laborer. After being liberated with the help of Bachpan Bachao Andolan in 2002, he was educated and trained at Bal Ashram. Om Prakash has helped liberate many of the children of his village from child servitude and helped them enroll for school. He has emerged as an unparalleled warrior for child rights and was awarded the International Child Peace Prize in 2006. At present, he is a young Bachpan Bachao Andolan activist and a student in the 11th grade.

system; the social environment; and the standard of living. Because of the salary and research opportunities available, the United States continues to attract scientists and engineers from other countries, and these immigrants have become an essential element for the health of the U.S. economy. For example, almost 25 percent of college-educated workers in the United States are foreign-born, as are more than 50 percent of workers with doctorates in engineering. Roughly 53 percent of foreign students remain in the United States after receiving doctorates in science.

Guest workers provide the labor that host countries need, which is desirable as long as the economies are growing. But when the economies slow, fewer workers are needed and problems develop. Unemployment increases among citizens, who then want the jobs held by guest workers. To appease their citizens, some countries

> ## almost 25 percent of college-educated workers in the United States are foreign-born, as are more than 50 percent of workers with doctorates in engineering

Reverse brain drain has recently become a concern of American educators and businesspeople. The return home of highly skilled immigrants who have made significant contributions in their adopted country is a trend related to the growth of outsourcing and a willingness of the federal government to allow "controversial" scientists to move to other countries.[21] Some developing countries whose scientists and engineers have gone to industrialized nations sponsor reverse-brain-drain programs. For example, Beijing has launched the Thousand Talents Program in a bid to capture talent that has emigrated from China. The program offers top scientists grants of 1 million yuan (about $146,000), high salaries, and generous lab funding. Brain drain has also been exacerbated by United States government limitations on the number of work visas and long queues for naturalization.[22] The growth of outsourcing in developing economies such as India is also pulling Indian talent back home. American firms contribute aggressively to this aspect of reverse brain drain as they outsource knowledge work—engineering, software, product design, and development—to such countries as China, India, and Russia. In some controversial areas of science where the American government has limited research efforts, such as stem cell research, scientists—both native and non-native—move to environments where such cutting-edge research is supported.

Guest Workers

Countries that receive many refugees or have high birthrates may have too many people for the available jobs, but there are also countries that have too few people. France, Germany, the Scandinavian countries, and Switzerland, all of which have low birthrates, have labor shortages. And to those countries have come the so-called **guest workers** to perform certain types of jobs, usually in service, factory, or construction work. Most of the guest workers in these countries are from such places as Turkey, Eastern Europe, and North Africa.

refuse to renew guest workers' permits. In other countries, where work is seasonal, guest workers are deported at the end of the season instead of being permitted to stay and take other work. The mere presence of people from another country can sometimes stimulate uneasiness in the host nation, and many times the guest workers are treated as a less desirable element of the social structure within the host country and with fewer protections.

LO2 Discuss major factors that may impact employment policies in an international setting.

CONSIDERATIONS IN EMPLOYMENT POLICIES

Companies considering doing business in international markets must consider a range of issues related to the employment policies to use. Some of these issues, such as social status, sexism, racism, the existence of minorities within traditional societies, and overall labor situations commonly encountered in developing nations, are discussed in this section.

Social Status

Chapter 4 discussed the importance of culture to international business. Culture is especially important with respect to the labor force, because culture so dominates human behavior and attitudes. Understanding social status is necessary to understanding cultures because in some cultures, social divisions are more extreme than in others. Employment practices need to take into account social status issues as they affect work relationships. For example, the class system in the United Kingdom may be eroding, but people there are still classified in a hierarchy, and one of the markers of place is the accents acquired at home and school. Although class differences do not cause riots in the United Kingdom, as caste differences have in India, a foreign employer should nevertheless be conscious of the possibilities for friction arising from lack of knowledge of those differences and their potential impacts.

Sexism

Acceptability of women as full participants in the workforce ranges from a trend toward improvement in the United States and Western Europe to limited acceptability in some other countries. Sexism, the denial of equal participation in a society for women, developed as an inherent part of many cultures, based as they are on patriarchal values. Greater awareness of the importance of providing equal opportunity for both genders and changing attitudes toward the roles of women in society in general and, more specifically, in business have made women's success in business possible in many parts of the world.

Culture and tradition, though, continue to make full and equal participation in business a challenge for women, especially in societies where laws, customs, and attitudes continue to act as barriers. For example, in Saudi Arabia and some other Middle Eastern countries, laws and traditional customs have prevented the commingling of men and women in the workplace, and women have been prohibited from driving vehicles. Yet, the role of women is changing in Saudi Arabia. The first coed university opened there in 2009. There is a vibrant women's business sector, too, though not a public one. In addition, programs have recently been set up to encourage women to start businesses, the range of sectors in which women can work has been expanded, and women managers can have males as their subordinates.[23]

Worldwide, less than a quarter of all senior management positions are held by women.[24] Over one-third of privately held companies have no women in senior management. Countries in which women hold a significant percentage of senior management positions are the Philippines (47%), Russia (42%), Thailand (38%), Poland (31%), and China (31%). As Figure 9.7 illustrates, the United States is below the 24 percent average, along with the United Kingdom, France, and Germany.

Women's education is an important aspect of the workforce, since studies show a persistent correlation between the length of women's schooling and birthrates, child survival, family health, and a nation's overall prosperity. Women's education is making marked improvements, with the rate of illiteracy declining significantly across all regions during the past two decades. An increasing number of countries are realizing the importance of educating females. For example, the Egyptian government is integrating a successful concept of girl-friendly community schools into the formal education system. These schools use female teachers, active learning, and child-centered class management. In one region of China, villages and households that send girls to school are given priority for loans or development funds.

> " BECAUSE THERE STILL EXISTS A SIGNIFICANT PAY GAP, WOMEN TEND TO EARN LESS THAN MEN OVER THE COURSE OF THEIR LIFETIMES. COMPOUNDING THE PROBLEM, WOMEN TEND TO SPEND LESS TIME IN THE WORKFORCE.

—Steve Israel "

Average percentage of women in the senior management of the business 2009		
	Philippines	47
	Russia	42
	Thailand	38
	Poland	32
	Mainland China	31
	Malaysia	31
	Taiwan	31
	Mexico	31
	Armenia	29
	Brazil	29
	Turkey	29
	Vietnam	28
	Hong Kong	28
	South Africa	28
	Canada	28
	Singapore	28
	New Zealand	27
	Botswana	25
Global average		
	Chile	24
	Finland	23
	Australia	23
	Greece	23
	Ireland	22
	Sweden	22
	Italy	21
	United Kingdom	21
	Spain	21
	United States	20
	France	18
	Argentina	17
	Germany	17
	Netherlands	15
	India	15
	Denmark	13
	Belgium	12
	Japan	7

Source: Grant Thornton IBR 2009

Source: www.grantthorntonibos.com/Press-room/2009/women_in_business.asp.

10 Countries with the Lowest Female Literacy Rates (2007)		
1	Chad	20.84
2	Burkina Faso	21.58
3	Sierra Leone	26.77
4	Benin	27.93
5	Mozambique	32.95
6	Yemen, Rep.	40.47
7	Morocco	43.22
8	Nepal	43.56
9	Bangladesh	48.05
10	Mauritania	48.28

Source: UNESCO Institute for Statistics in EdStats, Aug 2009

The statistics are still shocking, despite the improvements. In all of the countries listed in Figure 9.8, less than half the women are literate. Even in countries where women have made some strides, their progress is not necessarily secure. When the Taliban took power in Afghanistan, they closed education for girls and women and reinstated the custom of purdah, the practice of preventing women from being seen by men. When the fundamentalist Islamic government took control from the shah in Iran in 1979, it separated the sexes, ordering women to return to their strict traditional dress and roles. In recent years, women have regained some opportunities. Iran is a society with firm gender roles, as are Afghanistan, Iraq, and many other collectivist societies with high power distance on Hofstede's cultural dimensions.

A core, persistent gender-related problem in the labor markets is the issue of maternity and ensuing family responsibilities. Although in the United States there is much talk of "family-friendly" business practices, as Table 9.1 indicates, maternity leave arrangements do not parallel those in the EU or many other OECD countries. The challenges for American women who choose to be mothers and have professional careers are significant, largely because there is no public day care, and only the best employers make such support available. Private day care may be costly, and its standards vary greatly.

Then there is the issue of salary rates. Throughout most of the world, women on average still earn only a fraction of the level of pay that men earn for comparable positions, as shown in Figure 9.9 for the OECD nations. In all OECD countries, earnings of women are below those of men, with an average difference of about 20 percent. In Japan and Korea, men's earnings are over 30 percent higher. Unequal pay exists in part because women are more likely to work in lower-paid occupations than men. Women also are more likely than are men to have vulnerable jobs and part-time jobs.

▼ **TABLE 9.1** Maternity Leave Legislation, Selected Countries

Country	Maternity Leave			Parental Leave	
	Length (weeks)	Payment (% earnings)	Continuation of Payment by Employer	Length (months)	Payment (% earnings)
Austria	16	100	Low-wage workers	3–24	21
Canada	17	55	—	8.5	55
Denmark	18	100	Yes	8	90
Finland	18	65	Yes	6.5	60
France	16	100	Yes	39	25.8
Germany	14	100	No	26	11
Italy	21	80	—	4	80
Japan	14	60	—	—	Unpaid
Mexico	12	100	—	—	Unpaid
Netherlands	16	100	No	6	Unpaid
Norway	9	80	—	10	100
Sweden	15	80	—	12	80
United Kingdom	26	90	No	6	Unpaid
United States	12	Unpaid	No	—	Unpaid

Sources: Ghazala Azmat, Mara Güell, and Alan Manning, "Gender Gaps in OECD Countries," www.oecd.org (2004); and OECD, "Key Characteristics of Parental Leave Systems," http://www.oecd.org/dataoecd/45/26/37864482.pdf (accessed March 9, 2010).

Racism

Unfortunately, examples of racial conflicts and discrimination are found worldwide. There are black-versus-white conflicts in the United States, South Africa, Great Britain, and elsewhere and Arab-, Indian-, or Pakistani-versus-black conflicts in Africa. Racial friction exists related to the guest workers in parts of Europe. There has been bloody conflict in Sri Lanka between Tamils and Sinhalese. The list goes on: Bosnia, Kosovo, Zimbabwe, Rwanda, Burundi, the Sudan.

Because globalization increases individual contacts among quite different people, over time, it may work against racism. Some, it must be acknowledged, see the process of globalization in an opposite way, as a source of increased racism.

The reasoning for hope is that successful international managers develop a global mind-set, made up of cognitive complexity and a cosmopolitan attitude that, in its openness to the world and valuing of difference, leaves no room for racism.[25]

▼**FIGURE 9.9**
Gender Gap in Median Earnings

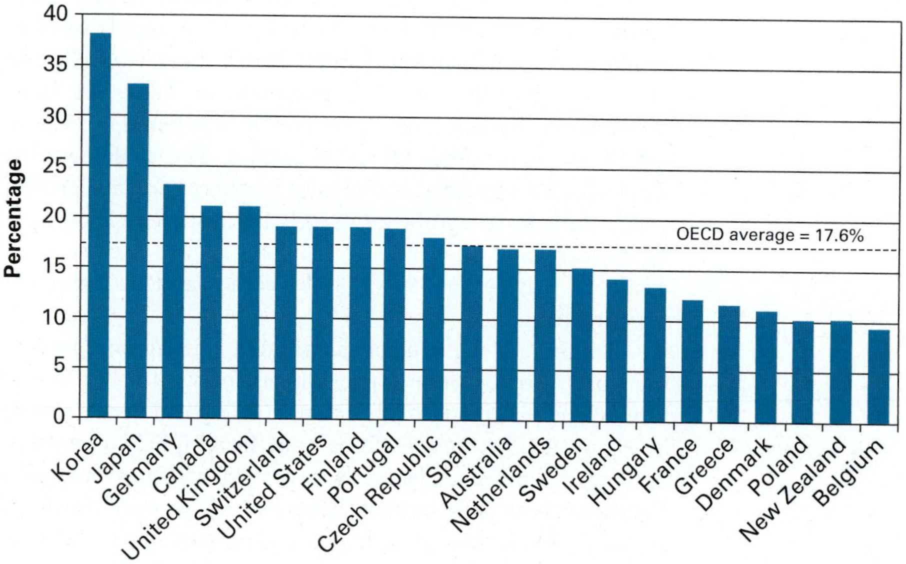

Source: GenderBrief, OECD Social Policy Division, March 2010, http://www.oecd.org/els/social.

Minorities in Traditional Societies

Traditional societies present opportunities as well as problems for employers. In some traditional societies, merchants, businesspeople, and bankers are looked down on, and people prefer political, religious, military, professional, or agricultural careers. In such societies, outsiders may dominate commercial and banking activities. Some examples are the Indians and Pakistanis in East Africa, the Chinese in Southeast Asia, and the Greeks in Turkey.

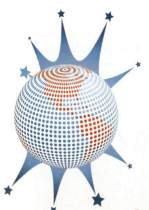

GLOBAL gauntlet

Are Harmonized Labor Standards a Good Idea or Is Labor Best a National-Level Concern?

Labor unions, human rights activists, and some developed country governments argue that access to their markets should be dependent on improved labor standards in developing countries and that trade sanctions should be imposed for violation of those standards (the so-called *social clause*). Other governments in both developed and developing countries see the social clause as protectionism. Yet even in trade agreements, governments argue for strict labor standards. NAFTA, which was negotiated among the United States, Canada, and Mexico, includes major sections involving labor matters.

According to the International Monetary Fund (IMF), the economic arguments for harmonizing labor standards are weak. In fact, well-intentioned attempts to impose higher labor standards on developing countries may actually be detrimental to workers, especially if they are enforced through trade sanctions. Low labor standards are not the primary source of developing countries' comparative advantage, while most labor standards—such as minimum wages—are not attainable in many poor countries.

Higher labor standards, the IMF points out, are primarily a consequence rather than a cause of economic growth, and the surest way to improve labor standards in poor countries is through economic growth, which international trade facilitates. This argument suggests that pursuing trade and labor market policies conducive to high growth rates will be far more effective in raising labor incomes than will be mandating levels of wages and benefits or imposing trade sanctions for perceived violations. What do you think? Is there a threshold level of labor conditions that all nations should follow, or are labor conditions a national-level issue?

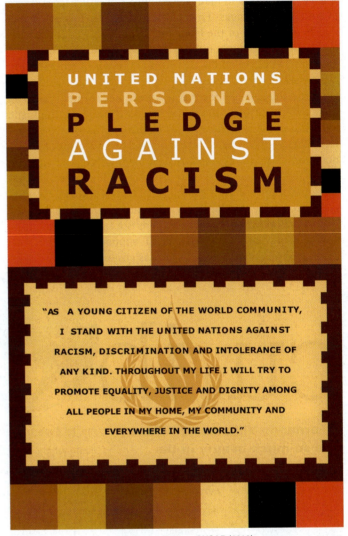

Source: Photo courtesy of UN, www.UN.org/WCAR (2010).

An advantage for a foreign employer moving into these societies is that such minorities may be immediately available, bringing financial and managerial skills to the employer. They speak the local language and usually one or more others, and they are less nationalistic than the majority. A disadvantage is that these minorities are often unpopular with the majority local population. Foreign employers can easily become too dependent on minority employees, thus becoming isolated and insulated from the world of the majority. Discrimination against such minorities has often occurred. In Uganda, for example, the government seized the property, shops, and land of people of Indian and Pakistani heritage, drove them out, and turned the seized assets over to native Ugandan citizens. In Zimbabwe, the government seized the land and assets of white farmers and gave these assets to black Zimbabweans, most of whom were supporters of President Mugabe's ruling party.

Labor in Developing Nations

The labor situation in many developing economies faces several formidable challenges. First are the effects of poverty, which affects the quality of the labor force due to low education levels. Many developing nations face this handicap, especially among females. In addition, with the growth of globalization, businesses in many developing nations face global-level competition. Increasingly, there is less tolerance in the globalizing marketplace for local inefficiencies. As if these developments were not enough in the way of challenge, the devastation of HIV/AIDS—exacerbated by local poverty, low levels of education, and social unrest—has created labor shortages that many developing nations will face for the foreseeable future. In these economies, up-skilling—training the local workforce to minimally acceptable standards—is a primary employer challenge.

In developing nations where there is a high level of education, outsourcing of production, IT support, and, increasingly, service functions such as customer service help lines and marketing lead follow-ups have been the recent trend. This has become a political issue in the United States, because it represents jobs transferred from the U.S. economy to a developing economy such as India. But from the developing country's point of view, it may be seen as one of the benefits of globalization.

EMPLOYER–EMPLOYEE RELATIONSHIPS

The relationship between employers and employees varies around the world. In some countries, employers must deal with strong labor unions; in others, with governments representing employees. In any case, a company seeking to employ people must be aware of the local employment context. Factors such as employee strikes can significantly affect business activity, and these factors often vary substantially across nations.

CU in ib

Fernando Villanueva: "There is so much beauty in the world"

Fernando Villanueva has advice for others wanting to join him in international business. He is from Palo Alto, California, completed a bachelor's degree in International Business at the California Polytechnic State University San Luis Obispo, and financed most of his own college education. Here's his advice:

My interest in obtaining a degree in International Business first arose after I travelled to France in 1998. I was 16 at the time. I had the opportunity to participate in a program called The Experiment in International Living. This program allowed me to experience the French culture by living with a French family and taking language courses with people from all over the world. Ever since then, I knew international business was the right place for me.

A year after graduating from Cal Poly, I was able to work and live in the Czech Republic thanks to an AIESEC traineeship with the Univerzita Pardubice. Some of my responsibilities were conducting research work for business related articles; coordinating and conducting presentations for professors in the European Union; coordinating events for students in the Erasmus program; and editing and reviewing articles being considered for publication. While working for the Univezita Pardubice, I was credited as one of the official translators/editors in two published books. I was also able to travel for work or leisure to Austria, Belgium, Czech Republic, Denmark, Egypt, England, Finland, France, Germany, Greece, Hungary, Italy, Luxembourg, Netherlands, Poland, Scotland, Slovakia, Spain, Sweden, Turkey, and Wales.

When traveling to new destinations, I always try to research the country and city I will be visiting. This allows me to have some basic knowledge of where I am going. My experience with locals has been that they appreciate my efforts to familiarize myself with their city beforehand. Knowing some basic words or phrases has always been helpful and equally appreciated. Another thing I try to do when in a new country is eat the traditional local dishes. I try to avoid spending a lot of time with other foreigners, interacting instead with the locals. I have found that this helps me adapt to the culture and people much more quickly.

The reason why I chose to be an AIESEC trainee was to obtain experience working

Importance of Proper Preparation When Entering a Market

When a foreign company arrives in a **labor market,** it must take what it finds. Of course, a prudent company will study the labor market when considering whether to invest in a country. Among the many information sources are *Foreign Labor Trends* and the *Handbook of Labor Statistics,* available from the U.S. Department of Labor in Washington, D.C., and the *Yearbook of Labor Statistics,* published by the United Nations International Labor Office in Geneva, Switzerland.

LO3 Discuss the differences and trends in labor unions from country to country and worldwide.

Labor Unions: Europe, United States, And Japan

Labor unions vary significantly from country to country. They tend to be more effective in developed countries, but even comparing Europe, the United States, and Japan, it is apparent that labor unions in various countries serve different purposes and influence

labor market The pool of available potential employees with the necessary skills within commuting distance from an employer

labor unions Organizations of workers

collective bargaining The process in which a union represents the interests of workers bargaining in negotiations with management

employee matters differently. European labor unions are usually identified with socialist and democratic political parties. A sense of worker identity is common in these unions, probably because European labor gained freedom from feudalism as well as various rights and powers through collective action. In the United States, by contrast, male laborers already possessed many civil rights, including the vote, by the time unions became important. Women won voting rights in 1920. As a result, unionism in the United States often has been viewed as more pragmatic than political and more concerned with the immediate needs of workers than with a political ideology.

Labor legislation in the United States has mostly confined itself to the framework of **collective bargaining.** Collective bargaining is the process in which a union represents the interests of everyone in a bargaining unit (which may include both union members and nonmembers) in negotiations with

internationally, thus making me a valuable asset for any company I choose to work for in the future. Having successfully completed my traineeship will show future employers that I am able to adapt to new environments and successfully function in complex situations. Thanks to my experience with AIESEC, I have learned how to communicate and work with people from all over the world.

Two of my biggest challenges while working abroad, and with people from various parts of the world, were adjusting to the different modes by which business was conducted and to bureaucracy. Ever since my first international experience, I have had to remind myself that business is not always conducted in the same mode in each country and that I must be able to adjust to new forms of business practices. Working with other government entities can be challenging; I have accepted this fact and I try to not let this discourage me from working with them. I have discovered that achieving good cooperation with other

government entities and learning to work with them can be beneficial for both me and the company I work for.

I have really enjoyed working abroad because it has allowed me to travel to various countries and it has also allowed me to acquire the ability to successfully function in nearly any business environment, both internationally and domestically. While in these countries, I have met many interesting and amazing people, and I have maintained a good relationship with many of the people I have met throughout this experience. I have learned a lot from the people I have met, both professionally and personally. Thanks to my international experience, I have learned that culturally we are all different yet we also share a lot in common. I have found this to be true no matter where I have travelled.

When you are visiting a country that you do not reside in, always remember that you are a guest of that country—no matter what your purpose for visiting may be. A recommendation I have for anyone who is,

or will be, working internationally is to not assume that the way things are done back home is always the way things are done everywhere else. Telling a person that he or she is doing a task wrong just because they are doing that task in a different way than it is done back home normally does not go well. Also, people do not like to hear what you believe is wrong about their country and what makes yours better. If you focus most of your energy on pointing out what is wrong, or what you hate, about the country you are visiting you will lose the opportunity to see what is great about it. There is so much beauty in the world; allowing yourself to have the opportunity to see a small part of it is truly amazing.

Fernando Villanueva
Born in Palo Alto, California, on July 3, 1981.
I have been dancing Mexican Folklore since the age of 15.
I financed most of my college education on my own.
I enjoy travelling and meeting new people.

management. In Europe, government's role is more active, with wages and working conditions frequently legislated. Many Latin American governments are also active in employer–employee relationships, frequently because the unions are weak and the union leaders inexperienced.

In Germany and France, the influences of law and government administrative actions on work conditions are extensive. Labor negotiations are conducted on national or regional levels, and in France, government representatives take part in the negotiations. In addition to national-level regulations, the European Union also enacts labor law, such as recent legislation limiting working time.

In contrast to the adversarial relationship usually found between unions and management in Europe and in the United States, Japanese unions tend to identify strongly with the interests of the company. For example, if Japanese unions are convinced a high wage increase would hurt the company's competitiveness, they tend to not ask for much of a pay raise. Japanese unions are also enterprise based rather than industrywide.

The level of union membership also varies substantially across countries, from single digits in some nations to more than 80 percent in others, as shown in Figure 9.11. For the past four decades, there has been a decline in the number of union members in most of the developed countries, especially among workers in industrial sectors. The reasons for this trend are several:

- Employers have made efforts to keep their businesses union-free, including putting employees on business boards and instituting profit-sharing plans. This co-optive approach has had its desired effect in many cases.

- More women and teenagers have joined the workforce, and because theirs are usually secondary incomes, they accept lower wages and have little loyalty toward organized labor.

- The unions have been successful. Their results have led to wage increases, which have led to higher costs and lower competitiveness of their employers, which have led to layoffs, downsizing, and movement of jobs to lower-cost locations. So in this sense, unions have been the victims of their own success.

- As developed countries transition to a knowledge economy, their industrial jobs that have formed the core of union membership are declining.

Despite a general decline in union members in industrial sectors, many developed nations have seen an increase in union membership in recent years. This trend is particularly prominent in those nations where unions have successfully organized workers in the expanding service sectors of their post-industrial economies.

Multinational Labor Activities

The internationalization of business has been under way for many years, and international companies have expanded rapidly since the 1950s. National unions have begun to perceive opportunities for companies to escape the organizing reach of unions through the relatively simple step of international outsourcing, transferring production to another country. Unions

FIGURE 9.11
Trade Union Membership (Most Recent) by Country

Rank	Countries	Amount
#1	Sweden:	82%
=2	Denmark:	76%
=2	Finland:	76%
#4	Norway:	57%
#5	Belgium:	53%
#6	Ireland:	45%
#7	Austria:	37%
#8	Italy:	35%
#9	Canada:	30%
#10	United Kingdom:	29%
#11	Germany:	26%
=12	Australia:	26%
=12	Netherlands:	22%
=14	Switzerland:	22%
=14	New Zealand:	22%
=14	Japan:	22%
#17	United States:	13%
#18	France:	9%
	Weighted average:	38.0%

Source: http://www.nationmaster.com/graph/lab_tra_uni_mem-labor-trade-union-membership.

see such steps as dangerous. To combat those dangers, national unions have begun to (1) collect and disseminate information about companies, (2) consult with unions in other countries, (3) coordinate with those unions' policies and tactics in dealing with some companies, and (4) encourage international company codes of conduct. Such multinational labor activity is likely to increase, although unions are divided by ideological differences and are frequently strongly nationalistic. Vastly more effort and money have been spent on lobbying for protection of national industries than on cooperating with unions in other countries.

An important first arena in which successful multinational unionism may develop is the European Union. The EU member-countries are steadily eliminating or harmonizing their tariffs, taxes, monetary systems, laws, and much more. As further progress is made in this harmonization process, the resulting atmosphere may be more hospitable for the cooperation of national unions. Also working in efforts to internationalize unions are two other organizations, the European Trade Union Confederation (ETUC) and the Union Network International (UNI). The ETUC is an umbrella organization representing 82 national union federations, representing 60 million members in 36 nations.[26] Some ETUC member-unions have begun cooperating across national borders in pursuit of common goals. UNI was formed in 2000 to promote global union efforts in response to the increasing level of globalization of industries and employers. Based in Switzerland, it includes 900 unions with more than 15.5 million members in more than 140 nations.

The United States union federation, the AFL-CIO, cooperates with labor organizations worldwide, including ETUC, UNI, the International Confederation of Free Trade Unions (ICFTU), the Asia Pacific Regional Organization (APROICFTU), and the Latin America Regional Organization (ORIT-ICFTU).

The United Nations also has a specialized agency, the International Labour Organization (ILO), whose purpose is to promote social justice and internationally recognized human and labor rights worldwide. The ILO was founded in 1919 and is the only surviving major creation of the Treaty of Versailles, which founded the League of Nations. It became the first specialized agency of the UN in 1946. Today, the ILO formulates international labor standards in the form of treaties and recommendations, setting minimum standards for basic labor rights: freedom of association, the right to organize, collective bargaining, abolition of forced labor, equality of opportunity and treatment, and other standards regulating working conditions. More information can be obtained at the ILO's website, www.ilo.org. The Organisation for Economic Cooperation and Development (OECD), an international organization designed to assist with economic development issues in its member-nations, also has a Trade Union Advisory Committee (TUAC). TUAC's role is to ensure that labor issues are considered in global markets.

In this chapter, we have examined worldwide labor conditions and trends, including the size of the workforce,

unemployment, the vulnerable workforce, the aging population, urbanization, immigrants, child labor, forced labor, the brain drain, and guest workers. We then looked at considerations firms should keep in mind when they development employment policies in cultures they are still learning about, including social status, sexism, racism, minorities in traditional societies, and labor in developing nations. Finally, we completed our review of employer–employee relations, including labor unions. This completes our focus on the major topics of labor as a part of the external environment. ■

coming up

In the preceding two sections, the primary focus has been on the broad environmental context in which international businesses compete. Section One introduced you to issues regarding the nature of international business, including international business, trade, investment, and the institutional context in which international business functions. Section Two discussed forces that affect international business and with which management must cope.

In Section Three, our attention shifts away from the external environment and focuses instead on the business itself, including actions that managers can take to help their companies compete more effectively as international businesses. In identifying potential management responses and solutions to problems caused or magnified by the foreign and international environments, this book is intended to be only an introduction to international business. Deeper discussions into specific areas can be found in textbooks specializing in those areas.

Chapter 10 deals with the concept of international competitive strategy and how companies use strategic planning techniques to address international business opportunities and challenges. Chapter 11 looks at organizational design and the different ways in which international companies can be structured. Chapter 12 deals with assessing and analyzing international markets. Chapter 13 explores ways in which a company can enter international markets, including practices and procedures for exporting and importing. Chapter 14 explores international marketing and ways in which it differs from domestic marketing. Chapter 15 deals with operations management in international companies, including management of international supply chains. Chapter 16 presents material on managing human resources in international businesses, particularly nonexecutive, technical, or sales employees. Chapter 17 covers management issues of a financial or accounting nature that arise in conjunction with international business activities. ■

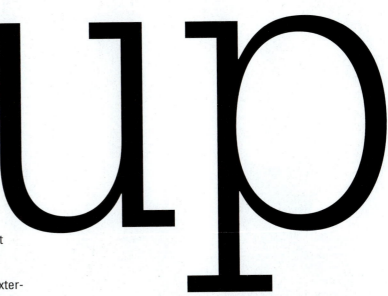

THE ORGANIZATIONAL ENVIRONMENT

international
competitive strategy

chapter ten

> "What business strategy is all about—what distinguishes it from all other kinds of business planning—is, in a word, competitive advantage. Without competitors there would be no need for strategy, for the sole purpose of strategic planning is to enable the company to gain, as effectively as possible, a sustainable edge over its competitors."
>
> —Kenichi Ohmae, McKinsey & Company consultant

In the preceding two sections of this book, the primary focus has been on the broad environmental context in which international businesses compete. This discussion has included the theoretical framework for international trade and investment; the international institutions that influence international business; and the sociocultural, political, legal, financial, economic, physical, and labor forces that influence the international business environment. Our attention now shifts away from the external environment, and we focus instead on the business itself, including the actions managers can take to help their companies compete more effectively as international businesses. In this chapter, we discuss the concept of international strategy and how companies use strategic planning and the analysis of competitive forces to improve their global competitiveness.

LEARNING OBJECTIVES

After reading this chapter, you should be able to:

LO1 **Explain** international strategy, competencies, and international competitive advantage.

LO2 **Describe** the steps in the global strategic planning process.

LO3 **Explain** the purpose of mission statements, vision statements, values statements, objectives, quantified goals, and strategies.

LO4 **Explain** home replication, multidomestic, global, and transnational strategies and when to use them.

LO5 **Describe** the methods of and new directions in strategic planning.

international strategy The way firms make choices about acquiring and using scarce resources in order to achieve their international objectives

competitive advantage The ability of a company to have higher rates of profits than its competitors

competencies Skills or abilities required in order to adequately complete a task

---

LO1 Explain international strategy, competencies, and international competitive advantage.

THE COMPETITIVE CHALLENGE FACING MANAGERS OF INTERNATIONAL BUSINESSES

In Chapter 1, we discussed some of the important reasons that motivate companies to pursue international business opportunities, including the potential to increase profits and sales through access to new markets; to protect existing markets, profits, and sales; and to help satisfy management's overall desire for growth. However, in order to succeed in today's global marketplace, a company must be able to quickly identify and exploit opportunities wherever they occur, domestically or internationally. To do this effectively, managers must fully understand why, how, and where they intend to do business, now and over time. This requires that managers have a clear understanding of the company's mission, a vision for how they intend to achieve that mission, and an understanding of how they plan to compete with other companies. To meet these challenges, managers must understand the company's strengths and weaknesses and be able to compare them accurately to those of their worldwide competitors. Strategic planning provides valuable tools that help managers address these global challenges.

> In order to succeed in today's global marketplace, a company must be able to quickly identify and exploit opportunities wherever they occur, domestically or internationally.

markets to enter, and how to compete. It deals with all the various functions and activities of a company and the interactions among them, not merely a single area such as marketing or production. To be effective, a company's international strategy needs to be consistent among the various functions, products, and regional units of the company (internal consistency) as well as with the variety of demands associated with operating in the international competitive environment (external consistency).

The goal of international strategy is to achieve and maintain a unique and valuable competitive position both within a nation and globally, a position that has been termed **competitive advantage.** This suggests that the international company must either perform activities different from those of its competitors or perform the same activities in different ways. To create a competitive advantage that is sustainable over time, the international company should try to develop skills, or **competencies,** that (1) create value for customers and for which customers are willing to pay; (2) are rare, since competencies shared among many competitors cannot be a basis for competitive advantage; (3) are difficult to imitate or substitute for; and (4) are organized in a way that allows the company to fully exploit and capture the value from the competitive potential of these valuable, rare, and difficult-to-imitate competencies.[2]

Managers of international companies that are attempting to develop a competitive advantage face a formidable challenge because resources—time, talent, and money—are always scarce.

There are many alternative ways to use these scarce resources (e.g., which nations to enter, which technologies to invest in, and which products or services to develop and offer to customers), and these alternatives are not equally attractive. A company's managers are forced to make choices regarding what to do and what *not* to do, now and over time. Different companies make different choices, and those choices have implications for each company's ability to meet the needs of customers and create a defensible competitive position internationally. Without adequate planning, managers are more likely to make decisions that do not make good sense competitively, and the company's international competitiveness may be harmed.

WHAT IS INTERNATIONAL STRATEGY, AND WHY IS IT IMPORTANT?

International strategy is concerned with the way firms make fundamental choices about developing and deploying scarce resources internationally.[1] International strategy involves decisions that deal with which products or services to offer, which

GLOBAL STRATEGIC PLANNING

Why Plan Globally?

As was discussed in the various chapters of Section Two, companies are confronting a set of environmental forces that are increasingly complex, global, and subject to rapid change. In response, many international firms have found it necessary to institute formal global **strategic planning** to provide a means for top management to identify opportunities and threats from all over the world, formulate strategies to handle them, and stipulate how to finance and manage the strategies' implementation. Strategic plans help ensure that decision makers have a common understanding of the business, the strategy, the assumptions behind the strategy, the external business environment pressures, and their own direction, as well as promote consistency of action among the firm's managers worldwide. Strategic plans also encourage participants to consider the ramifications of their actions in the firm's other geographic and functional areas. These plans provide a thorough, systematic foundation for raising key questions about what a business should become and for making decisions regarding what resources and competencies the company should develop, when and how to develop them, and how to use those competencies to achieve competitive advantage. This is intended to help the organization respond more effectively to challenges than its competitors. Strategic planning is also intended to increase the likelihood of strategic innovations, promoting the development, capture, and application of these new ideas in order to promote success in a challenging competitive environment. McKinsey's "Global Survey" revealed that 85 percent of respondents perceived their company's business environment to be "more competitive" or "much more competitive" than it was five years earlier, with the intensity of competition increasing for both small and large companies and across all industries.[3] Despite complaints about the challenges of effectively implementing planning efforts, especially within large and international companies, Bain & Company's "Management Tools and Trends" survey reported that strategic planning continues to be the most commonly used management tool among global executives, and it is the tool with the highest reported level of satisfaction.[4]

strategic planning The process by which an organization determines where it is going in the future, how it will get there, and how it will assess whether and to what extent it has achieved its goals

L02 **Describe** the steps in the global strategic planning process.

Global Strategic Planning Process

Global strategic planning is a primary function of a company's managers, and the ultimate manager of strategic planning and strategy making is the firm's chief executive officer. The process of strategic planning provides a formal structure in which managers (1) analyze the company's external environments, (2) analyze the company's internal environment, (3) define the company's business and mission, (4) set corporate objectives, (5) quantify goals, (6) formulate strategies, and (7) make tactical plans. For ease of understanding, we present this as a linear process, but in actuality there is considerable flexibility in the order in which firms take up these items. In company planning meetings that one of the authors attended, the procedure was iterative; that is, during the analysis of the environments, committee members could skip to a later step in the planning process to discuss the impact of a new development on a present corporate objective. They then often moved backward in the process to discuss the availability of the firm's assets to take advantage of the environmental change. If they concluded that the company had such a capability, the committee would try to formulate a new strategy. If a viable strategy was developed, the members would then establish the corporate objective that the strategy was designed to attain.

You will note that the global planning process, illustrated in Figure 10.1, has the same basic format as the planning process for a purely domestic firm. As you know by now, most activities of the two kinds of operations are similar. It is the variations in values of uncontrollable forces that make the activities in a worldwide corporation more complex than they are in a purely domestic firm.

Analyze Domestic, International, and Foreign Environments
Because a firm has little opportunity to control these forces, its managers must know not only what the present values of the forces are but also where the forces

FIGURE 10.1
The Global Strategic Planning Process

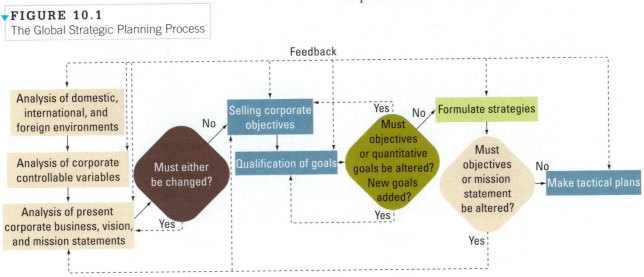

value chain analysis An assessment conducted on the chain of interlinked activities of an organization or set of interconnected organizations, intended to determine where and to what extent value is added to the final product or service

appear to be headed. An environmental scanning process similar to the market screening process described in Chapter 12 can be used for continuous gathering of information. Yet recognition of the nature and implications of the current and future domestic, international, and foreign environments is an essential input into the global strategic planning process.

While recognition of changes in key environmental forces is a necessary strategic task for managers of international companies, it is not sufficient. Management must also develop and implement appropriate responses to these changes. A study by the consulting company McKinsey & Company found that, worldwide, most executives agree that environmental, social, and business trends are more critical to company strategy than was the case five years ago.[5] Despite this, relatively few companies appear to act on key international trends that they observe, often due to a lack of the necessary skills and resources for addressing whether, how, and when to act in order to deal effectively with these environmental forces.

Analyze Corporate Controllable Variables

An analysis of the forces controlled by the firm will also include a situational analysis and a forecast. The managers of the various functional areas will either personally submit reports on their units or provide input to a planning staff that will prepare a report for the strategy planning committee.

Often management will analyze the firm's activities from the time raw materials enter the plant until the end product reaches the final user, what is frequently called a **value chain analysis.** As part of this process, management must address three key questions about the business:

1. Who are the company's target customers?

2. What value does the company want to deliver to these customers?

3. How will this customer value be created?

The value chain analysis itself focuses primarily on the third question, and it refers to the set of value-creating activities that the company is involved with, from sources for basic raw materials or components to the ultimate delivery of the final product or service to the final customer. A simplified value chain is shown in Figure 10.2. The goal of this analysis is to enable management to determine the set of activities that will comprise the company's value chain, including which activities the company will do itself and which will be outsourced. Management must also consider where to locate various value chain activities (e.g., should assembly be done in the company's home nation, located in a lower-cost location abroad, or located close to a customer abroad?). It is also necessary for management to examine the linkages among the activities in the value chain (e.g., between sales and product development, in order to ensure that customer needs are effectively communicated and incorporated in new products). Linkages must be examined not merely across activities within the company but also in terms of managing relationships with external entities such as suppliers, alliance partners, distributors, or customers within and across nations. The desired outcome of this analysis is the identification and establishment of a superior set of well-integrated value chain activities and the linkages among these activities, a

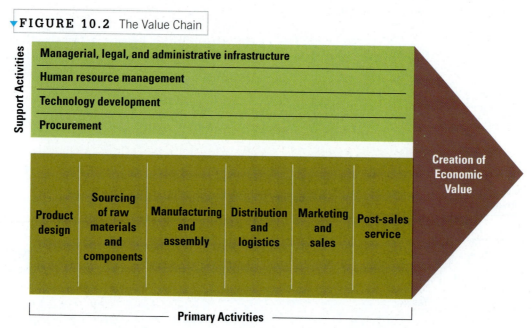

▼**FIGURE 10.2** The Value Chain

Source: Adapted from M. E. Porter, *Competitive Advantage* (New York: Free Press, 1985).

system that will permit the organization to more effectively and efficiently develop, produce, market, and sell the company's products and services to the target customers, thereby creating the basis for global competitive advantage.

Knowledge as a Controllable Corporate Resource

In today's highly competitive, rapidly changing, and knowledge-intensive economy, companies have the potential to achieve competitive advantage through leveraging their organizational knowledge across national boundaries. This organizational knowledge base includes the capabilities of employees (individually and in teams) as well as the knowledge that gets built into the overall organization through its various structures, systems, and organizational routines. As a valuable, scarce, and often unique organizational resource, knowledge is increasingly recognized as the basis for competitive advantage. As a result, managers are undertaking efforts to identify and evaluate the pool of knowledge that is contained within their companies on a global basis, including assessments of which knowledge and associated competencies will be the foundation for the company's future success. This process is frequently referred to as **knowledge management.** To help accelerate the acquisition, development, and exploitation of competitively valuable knowledge, managers are developing sets of techniques and practices to facilitate the flow of knowledge into and within their companies, to build knowledge databases, to transfer best practices within and across their international network of operations, and otherwise to create the foundation for a knowledge-based competitive advantage.

thinking of suppliers and customers located in that region and then transfer this knowledge back to their respective headquarters in Europe. Companies face an ongoing challenge of creating mechanisms that will systematically and routinely identify opportunities for developing and transferring knowledge and for ensuring that subsidiaries are willing and able both to share what they know and to absorb knowledge from other units of the company. They also must ensure that this proprietary knowledge is managed in a way that will protect it from diffusion to competitors, in order to help the company maintain its competitiveness over time.

After the analysis of corporate controllable variables, the planning committee must answer questions such as the following: What are our strengths and weaknesses? What are our human and financial resources? Where are we with respect to our present objectives? Have we uncovered any facts that require us to delete goals, alter them, or add

knowledge management The practices that organizations and their managers use for the identification, creation, acquisition, development, dispersion, and exploitation of competitively valuable knowledge

tacit knowledge Knowledge that an individual has but that is difficult to express clearly in words, pictures, or formulae, and therefore difficult to transmit to others

explicit knowledge Knowledge that is easy to communicate to others via words, pictures, formulae, or other means

mission statement A broad statement that defines the organization's purpose and scope

> ## "Knowledge is increasingly recognized as the basis for competitive advantage."

To effectively manage knowledge, companies must encourage individuals to work together on projects or somehow share their ideas. Much valuable knowledge is **tacit,** which means that it is known well by the individual but is difficult to express verbally or to document in text or figures. As a result, systems are needed in order to convey this tacit knowledge to others, possibly by converting it into **explicit,** codified knowledge and then making this knowledge accessible quickly and effectively to other employees who need it. In addition, to effectively design and deliver products that meet customers' needs, it is often necessary to gain access to valuable knowledge of suppliers, customers, and other partner organizations as well. In some cases, it is even necessary to establish company facilities in other locations in order to gain access to this knowledge. For example, Nokia and Ericsson, which are international leaders in telecommunications technology, both established offices in the Silicon Valley. Their objective was to tap into the latest

new ones? After completing this internal audit, the committee is ready to examine the company's mission, vision, and values statements.

LO3 **Explain** the purpose of mission statements, vision statements, values statements, objectives, quantified goals, and strategies.

Define the Corporate Mission, Vision, and Values Statements
These broad statements communicate to the corporation's stakeholders (employees, stockholders, governments, partners, suppliers, and customers) what the company is, where it is going, and the values that will guide the behavior of the organization's members. Some firms combine two or all three of these into a single statement, whereas others have separate statements. The **mission statement** defines the purpose for a company's existence, including its business,

vision statement A description of the company's desired future position if it can acquire the necessary competencies and successfully implement its strategy

values statement A clear and concise description of the fundamental values, beliefs, and priorities of the organization's members

competitive strategies Action plans to enable organizations to reach their objectives

support the development of others' potential, and (9) *Professionalism: To achieve and maintain high levels of expertise and skills.*[9]

After defining any or all of the three statements, management must then set corporate objectives.

objectives, and approach for reaching those objectives. A **vision statement** is a description of the company's desired future position, of what it hopes to accomplish if it can acquire the necessary competencies and successfully implement its strategy. In contrast, a **values statement** is intended to be a clear, concise description of the fundamental values, beliefs, and priorities of the organization's members, reflecting how they want to behave with each other and with the company's customers, suppliers, and other members of the global community. A Booz Allen Hamilton/Aspen Institute survey of corporations in 30 countries revealed that 89 percent of these organizations had explicit, written statements of corporate values and that greater success in linking a corporation's values to its operations was related to superior financial results.[6]

Set Corporate Objectives Objectives direct the firm's course of action, maintain it within the boundaries of the stated mission, and ensure its continuing existence. For example, Intel's mission is to "delight our customers, employees, and shareholders by relentlessly delivering the platform and technology advancements that become essential to the way we work and live." Its objectives are stated as (1) extend leadership in silicon and platform manufacturing, (2) deliver architectural innovation for market-driving platforms, and (3) drive worldwide growth.[10] How does Intel know whether it achieves these objectives? How will the company assess whether it has successfully delivered "architectural innovation for market-driving platforms," for example?

> # "To enhance a company's ability to develop and implement an effective strategy . . . it is important that efforts be made to quantify these objectives."

Some Examples Unilever states the following about its mission:

> *Unilever's mission is to add vitality to life. We meet the everyday needs for nutrition, hygiene, and personal care with brands that help people feel good, look good, and get more out of life.*[7]

Amazon.com states the following about the vision for that company:

> *Our vision is to be earth's most customer-centric company; to build a place where people can come to find and discover anything they might want to buy online.*[8]

Sumitomo Corporation of Japan states its nine basic values as being:

> *(1) Integrity and Sound Management: To comply with laws and regulations, while maintaining the highest ethical standards, (2) Integrated Corporate Strength: To create no boundaries within the organization; always to act with a company-wide perspective, (3) Vision: To create a clear vision of the future, and to communicate to share it within the organization, (4) Change and Innovation: To accept and integrate diversity in values and behavior, and to embrace change as an opportunity for action, (5) Commitment: To initiate, own, and achieve organizational objectives, (6) Enthusiasm: To act with enthusiasm and confidence, and to motivate to others through such action, (7) Speed: To make quick decisions and act promptly, (8) Human Development: To fully*

Quantify the Objectives To enhance a company's ability to develop and implement an effective strategy, one that will enable the company's objectives to be attained, it is important that efforts be made to quantify these objectives. Of course, strategic planning for international operations typically involves a range of qualitative as well as quantitative factors, which complicates efforts to quantify objectives. When objectives can be quantified in a relevant manner, they should be. However, despite the strong preference of most top managers for verifiable objectives, they frequently do have nonquantifiable or directional goals. Incidentally, objectives do tend to be more quantified as they progress down the organization to the operational level, because, for the most part, strategies at one level become the objectives for the succeeding level. Up to this point, only *what, how much,* and *when* have been stipulated. *How* these objectives are to be achieved will be determined in the formulation of strategies.

LO4 Explain home replication, multidomestic, regional, global, and transnational strategies and when to use them.

Formulate the Competitive Strategies

Generally, participants in the strategic planning process will formulate alternative **competitive strategies** and corresponding plans of action that seem plausible considering the directions the external environmental forces are taking and the company's strengths, weaknesses, opportunities, and threats (something that endangers the business, such as a merger of two competitors, the bankruptcy of a major customer, or a new product that appears to make the company's product obsolete).

When developing and assessing strategic alternatives, it is important to remember that companies competing in international markets confront two opposing forces: reduction of costs and adaptation to local markets. To be competitive, firms must do what they can to lower costs per unit so that customers will not perceive their products or services as being too expensive. This often results in pressure for some of the company's facilities to be located in places where costs are low, as well as for developing products that are highly standardized across multiple nations.

However, in addition to responding to pressures to reduce costs, managers also must attempt to respond to local pressures to modify their products to meet the demands of the local markets in which they do business. This modification requires that the company differentiate its strategy and product offerings from nation to nation, reflecting differences in distribution channels, governmental regulations, cultural preferences, and similar factors. However, modifying products and services for the specific requirements of local markets can involve additional expenses, which can cause the company's costs to rise.

As a consequence of these two opposing pressures, companies basically have four different strategies that they can use for competing internationally: home replication, multidomestic, global, and transnational. As suggested in Figure 10.3,

the strategy that would be most appropriate for the company, overall and for various activities in the value chain, depends on the amount of pressure the company faces in terms of adapting to local markets and achieving cost reductions. Each of these strategies has its own set of advantages and disadvantages, as summarized here, a factor that must be carefully considered when making decisions about the strategy an international company will choose to deploy.

Home Replication Strategy According to this typology, companies pursuing a home replication strategy typically centralize product development functions in their home country. After they develop differentiated products in the home market, these innovations are then transferred to foreign markets in order to capture additional value. To be successful, the company has to possess a valuable distinctive competency that local competitors lack in the foreign markets. The company's home-country headquarters usually maintains tight control over marketing and product strategy, and the primary responsibility of local subsidiaries is to leverage home-country capabilities. The extent of local customization of product offerings or marketing strategy tends to be limited. As a result, once local demand and circumstances justify such an investment, the company will tend to establish manufacturing and marketing functions in each major country in which it does business. This strategy can be appropriate if the company faces relatively weak pressures for local responsiveness and cost reductions. When there are strong pressures for local responsiveness, however, companies pursuing a home replication strategy will be at a disadvantage compared with competitors that emphasize customization of the product offering and market strategy for local conditions. Companies pursuing a home replication strategy may also face high operating costs, due to duplication of manufacturing facilities across the markets they serve.

Multidomestic Strategy A multidomestic strategy tends to be used when there is strong pressure for the company to adapt its products or services for local markets. Under these circumstances, decision making tends to be more decentralized in order to allow the company to modify its products and to respond quickly to changes in local competition and demand. Subsidiaries are expected to develop and exploit local market opportunities, which means that knowledge and competencies should be developed at the subsidiary level. By tailoring its products for specific markets, the company may be able to charge higher prices. However, local adaptation of products usually will increase the company's cost structure. To effectively adapt products, the company will have to invest

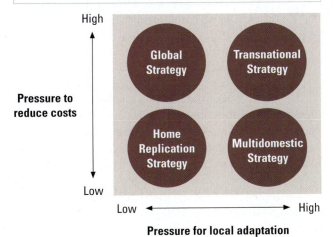

▼**FIGURE 10.3**
Cost and Adaptation Pressures and Their Implications for International Strategies

in additional capabilities and knowledge in terms of local culture, language, customer demographics, human resource practices, government regulations, distribution systems, and so forth. Adapting products too much to local tastes may also take away the distinctiveness of a company's products. For example, KFC's chicken outlets in China are highly popular because they are perceived to reflect American values and standards, something that might be lost if the company tried to adapt the stores and products to be more like other Chinese food outlets. The extent of local adaptation may also change over time, as when customer demands start to converge due to the emergence of global telecommunications, media, and travel, as well as reduced differences in income between nations.

The cost and complexity of coordinating a range of different strategies and product offerings across national and regional markets can also be substantial.

Global Strategy

A global strategy tends to be used when a company faces strong pressures for reducing costs and limited pressure to adapt products for local markets. Strategy and decision making are typically centralized at headquarters, and the company tends to offer standardized products and services. Overseas offices are expected to adopt the most efficient strategies found within the entire corporation. Value chain activities are often located in only one or a few geographic locations to assist the company in achieving cost reductions due to economies of scale. International subsidiaries are expected to transmit information to headquarters and to submit to centralized controls imposed by headquarters. There tends to be strong emphasis on close coordination and integration of activities across products and markets, as well as the development of efficient logistics and distribution capabilities. These strategies are common in industries such as semiconductors (e.g., Intel) or large commercial aircraft (e.g., Boeing). However, global strategies may also confront challenges such as limited ability to adjust quickly and effectively to changes in customer needs across national or regional markets, increased transportation and tariff costs for exporting products from centralized production sites, and the risks of locating activities in a centralized location (which can, for example, cause the firm to confront

> " Local adaptation of products usually will increase the company's cost structure. "

risks from political changes or trade conflicts, exchange rate fluctuations, and similar factors).

Transnational Strategy

A transnational strategy tends to be used when a company confronts simultaneous pressures for cost effectiveness and local adaptation and when there is a potential for competitive advantage from responding to both of these two divergent forces. The location of a company's assets and capabilities will be based on where it would be most beneficial for each specific activity, neither highly centralized as with a global strategy nor widely dispersed as with a multidomestic strategy. International subsidiaries are expected to contribute actively to the development of the company's capabilities, as well as to develop and share knowledge with company operations worldwide. Typically, "upstream" value chain activities, such as product development, raw materials sourcing, and manufacturing, will be more centralized, while the "downstream" activities, such as marketing, sales, and service, will be more decentralized, located closer to the customer. Of course, achieving an optimal balance in locating activities is a challenge for management, as is maintaining this balance over time as the company faces changes in competition, customer needs, regulations, and other factors. Management must ensure that the comparative advantages of the locations of the company's various value chain activities are captured and internalized, rather than wasted due to limitations of the organization's people, structures, and coordination and control systems. The complexity associated with the strategic decisions, as well as the supporting structures and systems of the organization, will be much greater with a transnational strategy. Caterpillar, for example, has tried to manufacture many of the standardized components of its products in a few locations worldwide. At the same time, the company has set up assembly operations in each major market, sometimes accompanied by specialized local production capability, thereby promoting its ability to tailor products to local needs.

Standardization and Planning

While the preceding discussion addressed basic strategic alternatives at a business or corporate level, it should be remembered that not all activities of an organization confront the same mix of globalization and localization pressures. For example, historically, more aspects of research and development and manufacturing have been standardized and coordinated worldwide by companies than has been the case for other value chain activities such as marketing. Many top executives believe marketing strategies are best determined locally because of differences among the various foreign environments. Yet there remains a desire within many international companies to achieve benefits from standardizing various elements of marketing strategies as well as the total product itself, which leads to their inclusion in the global strategic planning process. In making such strategic plans, however, companies must look beyond what makes sense under current circumstances and also consider how the situation may change in the future and the implications of these changes. This need to focus on the future helps explain companies' increasing use of scenarios in the planning process.

scenarios Multiple, plausible stories about the future

contingency plans Plans for the best- or worst-case scenarios or for critical events that could have a severe impact on the firm

Although the origins of scenario planning are unclear, the multinational company Royal Dutch Shell is widely recognized as a pioneer in popularizing the technique. Shell made scenario planning a staple of its strategic planning efforts more than 30 years ago, when it was confronted with a severe and unexpected global oil shortage. In dealing with such uncertainty and change, traditional strategic planning approaches based on extrapolation of historical conditions are of limited value. Managers find it difficult to break away from their existing view of the world, one that results from a lifetime of training and experience. Through presenting other ways of seeing the world, scenarios allow managers to envision alternatives that might lie outside their traditional frame of reference. Such an approach is particularly useful for international companies that face high levels of change and uncertainty regarding political, technological, competitive, and other forces because it allows management to anticipate and prepare for opportunities and threats that cannot be fully predicted or controlled.[11]

Scenarios Because of the rapidity of changes in the uncontrollable variables, many managers have become dissatisfied with planning for a single set of events. Instead, they have turned to **scenarios,** which are multiple, plausible stories for probable futures. Scenario analysis allows management to assess the implications for the company of various economic conditions and operating strategies. Scenarios integrate a variety of ideas about the future, including key certainties and uncertainties, and present these ideas in a useful and comprehensible manner. Managers can brainstorm various "what-if" scenarios, raising and challenging their assumptions and projected outcomes before committing to a specific course of action. Often, the what-if questions reveal weaknesses in current strategies. Some of the common kinds of subjects for scenarios are large and sudden changes in sales (up or down), sudden increases in the prices of raw materials, sudden tax increases, and a change in the political party in power.

Contingency Plans Many companies prepare **contingency plans** for worst- and best-case scenarios and for critical events as well. Every operator of a nuclear power plant has contingency plans, as do most producers of petroleum and hazardous chemicals since such ecological disasters as the *Valdez* oil spill and the Bhopal gas leak occurred. Because of the important impact on profits of changes in the prices of jet fuel, contingency planning is a common strategic activity for domestic and international airlines. The deadly terrorist attacks on the World Trade Center in New York and the Pentagon in Washington, D.C., on September 11, 2001, reminded many organizations of the importance of developing contingency plans to ensure the effective continuation of their operations in the event that their headquarters or other key locations are attacked or otherwise incapacitated for a period of time.

GLOBAL gauntlet

Google's Values and Strategy versus the China Opportunity

Google, the world's leader in the global Internet search engine business, with over two-thirds of global net searches, has actively promoted its ethical values—including its unofficial motto of "don't be evil"—as a foundation for its business activity. In 2006, Google entered the rapidly growing and potentially lucrative Internet search market in China. To obtain permission for entry, Google agreed to modify its operating approach to fit with Chinese requirements to censor Internet searches, particularly those involving certain socially or politically sensitive topics. Google's decision to engage in censorship, taken after much soul-searching, reflected a belief that the company's participation might contribute to a gradual loosening of Beijing's restrictions on free speech. The company included a disclosure on its site, stating that some search information had been removed, in an effort to raise awareness of censorship among Chinese Internet users. "I actually feel like things really improved" in the initial years after Google's entry, co-CEO Sergey Brin said. "We were actually able to censor less and less."[12]

By the end of 2009, Google had gained 36 percent of the Chinese market, second only to local company Baidu and far outdistancing rivals such as Microsoft and Yahoo. Google's Chinese revenues, estimated at $300 million in 2009 and projected at $600 million in 2010, had the potential to reach $5 billion to $6 billion by 2014.[13]

However, Google decided that its reputation for ethical behavior was more valuable than the potential returns from China's search engine market. In a highly publicized move on January 12, 2010, Google announced it would stop obeying censorship requirements on its Chinese site. This decision was triggered by increasingly strict government requirements to limit Internet freedom in that country, as well as a series of highly sophisticated

cyberattacks on its servers in the U.S., allegedly originating in China. Google's chief legal officer, David Drummond, asserted that these attacks were, "almost singularly focused on getting into Gmail accounts specifically of human-rights activities, inside China or outside." They were "all part of an overall system bent on suppressing expression, whether it was by controlling Internet search results or trying to surveil activists."[14] CEO Eric Schmidt stated, "We like what China is doing in terms of growth . . . we just don't like censorship."[15]

Despite a series of tense negotiations with the Chinese government, on March 22, 2010, Google shut down its Chinese search site. Google moved its Chinese-language search activities to Hong Kong, a special administrative region which has broader protection of free speech under the "one country, two systems" approach that was established in 1997, when the British handed over control of their former colony.

Mr. Brin, who was born in the Soviet Union and whose family experienced government repression prior to emigrating to the U.S., explained Google's move by stating, "in some aspects of their (China's) policy, particularly with respect to censorship, with respect to surveillance of dissidents, I see the same earmarks of totalitarianism (as in the former Soviet Union), and I find that personally quite troubling."[16] This argument ultimately prevailed over CEO Schmidt and others who believed that Google should maintain its presence in China. "One of the reasons I am glad we are making this move in China is that the China situation was really emboldening other countries to try and implement their own firewalls," said Mr. Brin.[17] "Ultimately, I guess it is where your threshold of discomfort is. So we obviously as a company crossed that threshold of discomfort."

Google's high-profile exit was applauded by many, both inside and outside the company. By positioning Google as a champion of free speech, it reinforced Google's well-publicized "don't be evil" motto and reputation for ethical values and behavior, a reputation that had been questioned as a result of the company's Chinese censorship activities. Mitch Kapor, a well-known Silicon Valley venture capitalist, stated that, "More businesses ought to follow 'gut principles' and shareholders and customers ought to support and encourage them to do so."[18] Google's decision to exit China was also expected to enhance customers' perceived trust in the company and its commitment to protect customers' personal information. This is a particularly important consideration, as Google's business model increasingly emphasizes cloud computing—an approach by which data that individuals and businesses currently keep on their own computers will instead be stored online, making it accessible from virtually any computer or wireless device. Implementation of such a model requires a high level of trust that a company such as Google will protect these data. As one of Google's former Chinese employees stated, "If what Google does in China makes its data seem unsafe, then Google's global strategy is gone."[19]

However, Google's decision to exit the Chinese search engine market was not without its detractors. The Chinese government expressed displeasure with Google's highly visible actions, stating, "Google has violated its written promise it made when entering the Chinese market by stopping filtering its searching service and blaming China in insinuation for alleged hacker attacks. This is totally wrong. We're uncompromisingly opposed to the politicization of commercial issues, and express our discontent and indignation to Google for its unreasonable accusations and conducts."[20] Li Yizhong, Minister of Industry and Information Technology, said, "I hope Google can respect Chinese rules and regulations. If you insist on taking this action that violates Chinese laws, I repeat: You are unfriendly and irresponsible, and you yourself will have to bear the consequences."[21] The highly publicized actions threatened Google's ability to compete in the world's largest and fastest growing Internet market, leaving the company exposed to the risk that the Chinese government could block access for users from the Chinese mainland. Although a complete blockage of access did not occur initially, repeated interruptions of Google searches initiated in China raised concerns about the reliability and long-term commercial viability of Google's services for China-based customers. Chinese Foreign Ministry spokesperson Qin Gang said, "The one whose reputation has been harmed isn't China, rather it is Google."[22]

Google's actions also potentially aided local Chinese competitors. Baidu saw its market share increase by nearly 10 percent, to 64 percent, in the 3 months after Google's announcement, along with a 60 percent increase in its stock price. International rivals also stood to benefit. Microsoft's senior manager for regulatory policy, Cornelia Kutterer, stated, "We have done business in China for over 20 years, and we intend to continue our business in China," reaffirming Microsoft's intention to adhere to local laws, including Chinese censorship requirements.[23] A Microsoft spokesperson said, "If we do a great job with the product, then we will hopefully attract more share."[24] A number of Google's partners terminated or sharply scaled back their involvement with the company. For example, Tom Group Ltd. removed Google's search service from its Chinese Internet portal and Motorola announced plans to provide links to other search engines on its phones in China. China's second largest wireless carrier, China Unicom, announced that it would drop Google as the company's default search engine for its newest smartphones. "We are open to cooperating with any handset makers and companies. But they must obey China's regulations," said Unicom president Lu Yimin.[25]

Did Google make a good decision to leave China? What do you think?

Prepare Tactical Plans

Because strategic plans are fairly broad, tactical (also called *operational*) plans are a requisite for spelling out in detail how the objectives will be reached. In other words, very specific, short-term means for achieving the goals are the objective of tactical planning. For instance, if the British subsidiary of an American producer of prepared foods has as a quantitative goal a 20 percent increase in sales, its strategy might be to sell 30 percent more to institutional users. The tactical plan could include such points as hiring three new specialized sales representatives, attending four trade shows, and advertising in two industry periodicals every other month next year. This is the kind of specificity found in the tactical plan.

Strategic Plan Features and Implementation Facilitators

Sales Forecasts and Budgets

Two prominent features of the strategic plan are sales forecasts and budgets. The

sales forecast A prediction of future sales performance

budget An itemized projection of revenues and expenses for a future time period

policies Broad guidelines intended to assist lower-level personnel in handling recurring issues or problems

procedures Specified ways of performing a particular task or activity

sales forecast not only provides management with an estimate of the revenue to be received and the units to be sold but also serves as the basis for planning in the other functional areas. Without this information, management cannot formulate the production, financial, and procurement plans. **Budgets,** like sales forecasts, are both a planning and a control technique. During planning, they coordinate all the functions within the firm and provide management with a detailed statement of future operating results and the resources required to achieve those outcomes.

Plan Implementation Facilitators Once the plan has been prepared, it must be implemented. Two of the most important plan implementation facilitators that management employs are policies and procedures.

Policies **Policies** are broad guidelines issued by upper management for the purpose of assisting lower-level managers in handling recurring problems. Because policies are broad, they permit discretionary action and interpretation. A policy is intended to economize managerial time and promote consistency among the various operating units. For example, if a company's distribution policy states that sales will be made through wholesalers, marketing managers throughout the world would know that they should normally use wholesalers and avoid selling directly to retailers. Similarly, publicity regarding the widespread occurrence of bribery in various international markets has prompted numerous companies to issue policy statements condemning this practice. Managers have thus been put on notice by these statements that they are not to offer bribes.

Procedures **Procedures** prescribe how certain activities will be carried out, thereby ensuring uniform action on the part of all corporate members. For instance, most international corporate headquarters issue procedures for their subsidiaries to follow in preparing annual reports and budgets. This assures corporate management that whether the budgets originate in Thailand, Brazil, or the United States, they will be prepared using the same format, which facilitates comparison.

Performance Measures A key part of strategic planning is measuring performance in order to assess whether the strategy and its implementation are proceeding successfully or whether modifications may need to be made. Companies need to consider at least three types of measures when assessing strategic performance: (1) measures of the company's success in obtaining and applying the required resources, such as financial, technological, and human resources; (2) measures of the effectiveness of the company's personnel, within and across the firm's international network of operations, in performing their assigned jobs; and (3) measures of the company's progress toward achieving its mission, vision, and objectives and doing so in a manner consistent with the company's stated values.[26] A range of concepts and tools, including the balanced scorecard and triple-bottom-line accounting, have been promoted as alternatives for helping to measure strategic performance. For example, the balanced scorecard approach is based on an integration of strategic planning with a company's budgeting processes, and short-term results from the balanced scorecard can serve as a means of monitoring progress in achieving strategic objectives across four dimensions: financial, customer, internal, and learning and growth.

Kinds of Strategic Plans

Time Horizon Although strategic plans may be classified as short, medium, or long term, there is little agreement about the length of these periods. For some businesses, long-range planning may be for a five-year period. For others, such as manufacturers of commercial aircraft, this would be the length of a medium-term plan; their long range might cover 15 years or more. Short-range plans are usually for one to three years; however, even long-term plans are subject to review annually or more frequently if a situation requires it. Furthermore, the time horizon will vary according to the age of the firm and the stability of its market. A new venture in a field such as social networking (e.g., Facebook) or Internet television (e.g., Brightcove) is extremely difficult to plan for more than three years in advance, but a five- or six-year horizon may be sufficient for a mature company in a steady market.

Level in the Organization Each organizational level of the company will have its level of plan. For example, if there are four organizational levels, as shown in Figure 10.4, there will be four levels of plans, each of which will usually be more specific than the plan that is at the level above. In addition, the functional areas at each level will have their own plans and sometimes will be subject to the same hierarchy, depending mainly on how the company is organized.

Methods of Planning

Top-Down Planning In **top-down planning,** corporate headquarters develops and provides guidelines that include the definition of the business, the mission statement, company objectives, financial assumptions, the content of the plan, and special issues. If there is an international division, its management may be told that this division is expected to contribute $350 million in profits, for example. The division, in turn, would break this total down among the affiliates under its control. The managing director in Germany would be informed that the German operation is expected to contribute $35 million; Brazil, $8 million; and so on. An advantage of top-down planning is that the home office, with its global perspective, should be able to formulate plans that ensure the optimal corporatewide use of the firm's scarce resources. This approach may also promote creativity, because a corporatewide perspective on market opportunities may yield insights that are not readily observable lower in the organization, such as by managers within individual national markets.

Disadvantages of top-down planning are that it restricts initiative at the lower levels and shows some insensitivity to local conditions, particularly within ethnocentric management teams. Furthermore, especially in an international company, there are so many interrelationships that consultation is necessary. Can top management, for example, decide on rationalization of manufacturing without obtaining the opinions of the local units as to its feasibility?

Bottom-Up Planning
Bottom-up planning operates in the opposite manner. The lowest operating levels inform top management about what they expect to do, and the total becomes the firm's goals. The advantage of bottom-up planning is that the people responsible for attaining the goals are formulating them. Who knows better than the subsidiaries' directors what and how much the subsidiaries can sell in their respective geographic regions? Because the subsidiaries' directors set the goals with no coercion from top management, they feel obligated to make their word good. Their hands-on perspective may allow them to recognize potentially innovative opportunities to create and leverage value within their local markets, thus serving as a basis for improved performance or even strategic experimentation. However, bottom-up planning has a disadvantage: because each affiliate is free to some extent to pursue the goals it wishes to pursue, there is no guarantee that the sum total of all the affiliates' goals will coincide with those of headquarters. When discrepancies occur, extra time must be taken at headquarters to eliminate them.

Iterative Planning
It appears that **iterative planning** (see Figure 10.4) is becoming more popular, especially in global companies that seek to have a single global plan while operating in many diverse foreign environments. Iterative planning combines aspects of both top-down and bottom-up

planning. An example of iterative planning is the approach used in 3M. In 2009, 3M generated over 63 percent of its $23 billion in sales from outside the United States, where it has operations in more than 60 nations and sales in more than 200. Strategic planning plays a key role in the company's resource allocation decisions and global expansion. Figure 10.4 illustrates how 3M's iterative planning process functions. Planning starts with the operating managers of the company's six operating business segments, who analyze strengths and weaknesses and external forces, such as new technology and government regulatory changes; perform a competitor analysis; and determine the company resources they will need to achieve their objectives. Their plans then go to the market group, in which from three to five business divisions are typically located. They are reviewed by the market group management and consolidated for presentation to the strategic planning committee, consisting of the 12 vice presidents at headquarters who represent the markets into which

top-down planning Planning process that begins at the highest level in the organization and continues downward

bottom-up planning Planning process that begins at the lowest level in the organization and continues upward

iterative planning Repetition of the bottom-up or top-down planning process until all differences are reconciled

▼**FIGURE 10.4**
3M Strategic Planning Cycle

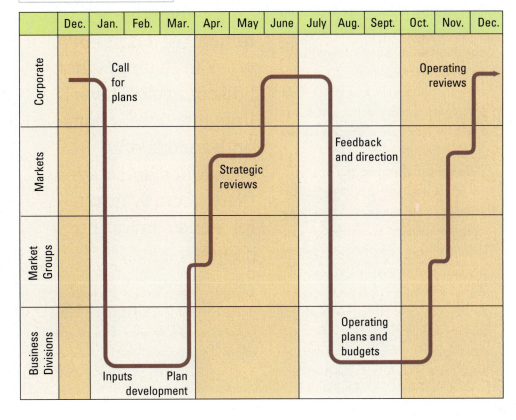

cu in ib

Eduardo Rangel: Growth in International through Experience

Eduardo Rangel was born in the U.S. and spent his preschool years in Tijuana, Mexico, where his family lived while his father commuted to work in the U.S. Here are some of his observations about how he got involved in international business:

Although I was born in San Diego, CA, my family continued living in Tijuana, Mexico. It made sense to my father to save money by living in Mexico and working in the U.S. When I was five years old, we moved together to San Diego. Without any academic guidance, I nearly skipped college altogether and joined the military, but I caved in to peer pressure in high school and applied to colleges like most of my friends. At this point, my life, including school, was a personal path of trial and error, a lot more wrong choices than right ones.

Following a three-year stint in community college, I transferred to California State University–Northridge to try my chances there, concentrating in international business. Then they canceled their International Business concentration, so I decided to transfer again to Cal Poly in San Luis Obispo, CA. Although I was taking general courses to satisfy graduation requirements for a business degree at Cal Poly, I directed most of my attention to the international business classes.

I was in search of an international position in business after graduation, rather than immediately finding a job in the U.S., in order to move outside of my comfort zone. As a result, I joined a student club, AIESEC, which gave me the opportunity to apply for international internships.[27] As a member of the Cal Poly chapter of AIESEC, a global youth organization that engages in international student exchange internships, I actively participated in club events and info sessions. I became aware of internship opportunities they offered in Asia, my first choice for working abroad. After much consideration, I selected Beijing, China, to participate in a 9-month internship during my senior year. China was

> " I vividly remember a dismal week in Beijing, when I disconnected myself from any interaction with friends and colleagues and stayed in my room waiting for some comforting advice. "

among the most discussed themes in my business classes, and by working in Beijing I figured I could learn about a new culture, beyond the popularized images presented in various mass market sources (e.g., *Lonely Planet, National Geographic, New York Times*). My decision-making process to take the initiative to go to China can best be described by Nike's slogan, "Just Do It."

I decided to arrive in Beijing three months before the beginning of my internship in order to take an intense Mandarin course at a local university during the first month, and then to travel around China. The point was to let the process of culture shock and jet lag take its course. Having a simple structure, like going to class and walking around the city, enabled me to improve my assimilation into the local culture.

Many of my colleagues were greatly affected by culture shock, and as a result, they became reluctant to accept their new standard of living in Beijing. Culture shock is a feeling of anxiety, loneliness, and confusion that people sometimes experience when living in another country. My friends struggled with the concept of accepting another country's values. Ultimately, some of them decided to leave the country and head back home. Being open minded is crucial in this instance.

I vividly remember a dismal week in Beijing, when I disconnected myself from any interaction with friends and colleagues and stayed in my room waiting for some comforting advice. I called one of my professors from Cal Poly, asking for help to regain the lost enthusiasm that existed when I first arrived in China. I began explaining to her I had been taking my time in China for granted by working long hours and ignoring invitations from friends to travel. She suggested I have fun and enjoy myself and return to feeling like a visitor again. She reminded me that I needed to maintain the perspective that I was a visitor and I needed to enjoy my time in China and continually be learning about the local culture.

In China, I worked with United Education Culture Exchange (UECE). Part of my role was to uphold and reflect an American image to our clients. UECE offers a vast array of programs for Chinese students who want to participate in a cultural exchange by either working or studying in the United States. UECE sponsors their U.S. visa and assists them with accommodations and obtaining their social security cards. I specifically dedicated most of my time to the Work & Travel USA program. Every Wednesday and Friday, we had students come in at 14:00 for a presentation I developed in English, followed by an on-site interview to assess their English fluency. Although many clients failed to understand my presentation in English, the intention was to give UECE credibility by having an American presence, a branding effort of sorts.

Near the end of my internship, UECE organized a press conference to commemorate the success of the Work & Travel USA program. Leading up to the event, we toured universities in China to present our program on campuses on a large scale. We interviewed over 5,000 students in 15 universities and accepted 700 students into the program, a 1000% increase from the previous year. Government officials, distinguished guests, and the local media were present for this lavish event, and I was at the center of it. I made the keynote presentation, in English, thanking everyone for attending and outlining the goal of the Work & Travel USA program. The press conference was a celebration of our achievements, a very satisfying culminating experience for my Beijing internship.

After returning to the U.S. from Beijing, I spent a quarter at Cal Poly completing my bachelor's degree. Then I returned to work for another two years in Beijing, China, exploring the culture and learning the language. The global recession served as a convenient excuse to stay longer in Beijing, as I was earning a good income and lived well there. Ultimately I returned to the States, and having traveled to over ten countries and lived in three of them already has fueled my desire to continue learning about other people.

Here's what Eduardo mentioned as important things he learned from his work in China:

Patience

Being productive in an international company does not necessarily equate to feeding or pushing ideas to your superiors immediately after beginning your new position in the company. Most companies in China are micromanaged and subordinates seldom approach their superiors about any dispute or concerns. Most foreigners mistakenly apply the same work habits from their home country to their host country. When they push their method onto their colleagues, the colleagues feel uncomfortable.

Theoretical vs. Experiential Learning

Reading about the importance of a business card in China cannot replace the physical exchange during a meeting with a prospective Chinese client. The concept of *guanxi,* literally translating to "relationships," continues after the card exchange with dinners and involves constant communication. At times, the managers and I would have dinners with high ranking school or government officials in order to maintain an already established relationship. This is perceived as a way to solidify friendships by proving a client's worth. Guanxi is a term that I learned about in my international business courses, but I did not realize its importance until I was partaking in such behavior in my internship.

Knowing Your Objective

Make a plan or outline of what you want to achieve from your trip, while also recognizing that there is always room to be flexible. I saw many foreigners stuck in China without any idea as to what their next objective would be. They stayed in China for work just because it was easy, it was all they knew to do. Being focused on one's career goals is necessary in order to have an international career in business, rather than merely a business career in China.

the market groups are divided. The plans are reviewed, and the results of this review are discussed with the market group management. Any differences between market and market group managements are reconciled.

Two months later (July), the corporate headquarters' management committee, to which the strategic planning committee vice presidents belong, reviews the plans and votes on spending priorities. Feedback and direction are given to the business divisions, which then prepare operating plans and budgets by December and submit them to headquarters. They are finalized with corporate worldwide plans. Then, a few days before the December operating reviews, the management committee holds brainstorming sessions to discuss trends and developments over the coming 15 years. The general manager of each business division presents the best picture possible for that industry for the period. The outcome of this meeting is a broad guide for strategic planning. Although operating managers do the planning, the director and staff of a planning services and development

Google headquarters in China.

unit provide an analysis of 3M's 20 principal competitors worldwide and any other information the divisions require. They also try to identify opportunities and new products.

LO5 Describe the methods of and new directions in strategic planning.

New Directions in Planning

Strategic planning, particularly in the more traditional, bureaucratic form that is still practiced in some corporations, has been described as a calendar-driven ritual, not an exploration of the company's potential. This traditional strategic planning approach commonly consists of a company's CEO and the head of planning getting together to devise a corporate plan, which would then be handed to the operating people for execution. Too frequently, companies' annual strategic planning processes have become ritualistic and devoid of discovery, with planners working "from today forward, not from the future back, implicitly assuming, whatever the evidence to the contrary, that the future will be more or less like the present."[28] Tending to generate projections based on historical conditions and performance, this traditional planning

approach tends to fall victim to collective—and frequently outdated—mind-sets about the competitive environment. Not surprisingly, the resulting strategic planning documents often fail to be implemented successfully.

Increasingly, the old process is being replaced by a *strategic management* approach, which combines strategic thinking, strategic planning, and strategic implementation and which is increasingly recognized as a fundamental task of line management rather than merely specialized planners in staff positions. Although still susceptible to problems such as groupthink, this more contemporary approach attempts to incorporate changes in three areas: (1) who does the planning, (2) how it is done, and (3) the contents of the plan.

Who Does Strategic Planning? Although CEOs report that they would like to spend about one-third of their workday on strategy, strategic planning is no longer something that only the company's most senior executives do.[29] Top management, at the urging of strategy consultants, is assigning strategic planning to teams of line and staff managers from different business, geographic, and functional areas, much as it has done with process-improvement task forces and quality circles. Frequently these teams include a range of ages—from junior staff members who have shown the ability to think creatively to experienced veterans near retirement age who will "tell it like it is." Another difference between the new and the old approaches: traditional planning is a company activity done in seclusion; now, the new approach often includes interaction with such parties as important customers, distributors, suppliers, and alliance partners, in order to gain firsthand experience with the firm's markets. Other important stakeholders such as governments or stakeholder activists are also relevant influences, if not necessarily direct participants, in this strategic planning process. Incorporating these diverse perspectives can help a company to identify creative and effective ways to address the challenge of increasingly uncertain and changing international competitive environments.

How Strategic Planning Is Done The rapid rise in the levels of uncertainty in many areas of international business, combined with the challenge of quantifying factors relating to sociopolitical and other worldwide developments associated with environmental forces such as those discussed in Section Two, made it clear to top managers of many affected companies that there was no point in making detailed five-year forecasts when various international crises were exposing the nonsense of many previous forecasts. Instead, many firms have moved toward less structured formats and much shorter documents. The top management of companies generally accepts the fact that, to be effective, strategic planning processes should permit ideas to surface from anywhere in the organization and at any time. As indicated earlier in Figure 10.1, objectives and strategies are intertwined, as are tactics and strategy. If the planning team is unable to come up with suitable tactics to implement a strategy, the strategy must be altered. In a similar fashion, if strategies cannot be formulated to enable the firm to reach the objective, the objective must be changed.[30]

Contents of the Plan The contents of the plan are also different. Many top managers say they are much more concerned now with focusing on issues, strategies, and implementation and with incorporating creative, forward-looking ideas that are essential to competitive success within a changing and uncertain international environment. In the contemporary global competitive environment, where firms often must place bigger bets on new technologies and other competitive capabilities, companies cannot afford to devote large amounts of money in one direction only to discover years later that this was the wrong direction for investing. Instead, competition in today's global competitive environment requires an approach to strategic planning that effectively incorporates a long-term perspective to strategic decision making and resource allocation decisions.

Summary of the International Planning Process

A good way to summarize the new direction in planning is to quote Frederick W. Gluck, from the consulting firm McKinsey & Co. Gluck says that if major corporations are to develop the flexibility to compete, they must make the following major changes in the way they plan:

1. Top management must assume a more explicit strategic decision-making role, dedicating a large amount of time to deciding how things ought to be instead of listening to analyses of how they are.

2. The nature of planning must undergo a fundamental change from an exercise in forecasting to an exercise in creativity.

3. Planning processes and tools that assume a future much like the past must be replaced by a mind-set that is obsessed with being first to recognize change and turn it into a competitive advantage.

4. The role of the planner must change from being a purveyor of incrementalism to being a crusader for action and an alter ego to line management.

5. Strategic planning must be restored to the core of line management responsibilities.[31]

CHECK IT OUT!

mhhe.com/GeringerM

for study materials
including quizzes,
iPod downloads,
and video

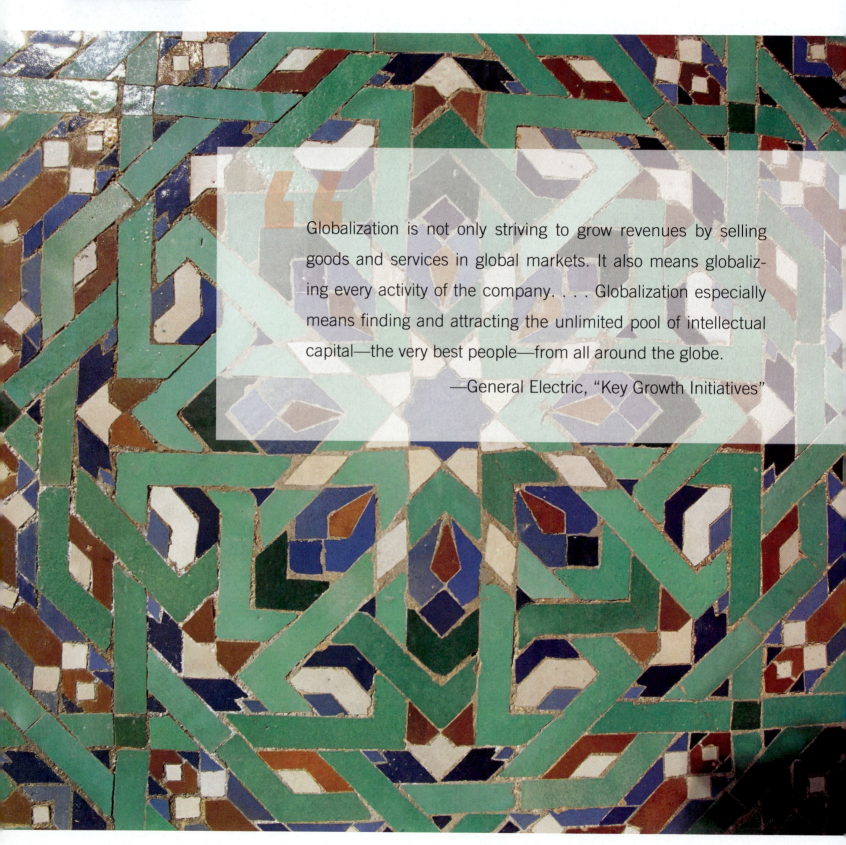

> Globalization is not only striving to grow revenues by selling goods and services in global markets. It also means globalizing every activity of the company. . . . Globalization especially means finding and attracting the unlimited pool of intellectual capital—the very best people—from all around the globe.
>
> —General Electric, "Key Growth Initiatives"

organizational design
+ control

Organizations exist for the purpose of enabling a group of people to effectively coordinate their collective activities and accomplish objectives.[1] **Organizational structure** refers to the way that an organization formally arranges its various domestic and international units and activities and the relationships among these organizational components. A company's structure helps determine where formal power and authority will be located within the organization, and this structure is what is typically presented in a company's organization chart.

Creating and evolving the structure of an international organization over time are fundamental tasks of senior management. Few executives except those in the senior levels of the organization are capable of establishing or changing the overall structure of an international company, because people at an organization's lower levels lack the broad perspective necessary for making the various trade-offs that will influence the organization as a whole. Nevertheless, all of the company's managers have to perform their job responsibilities within the context created by this structure. Further, most managers need to be able to effectively structure the various activities that are within their area of responsibility and to do so in a manner that is consistent with the company's overall structure. As a result, developing an understanding of the different ways in which international companies can be structured and the

LEARNING OBJECTIVES

After reading this chapter, you should be able to:

LO1 **Explain** why the design of organizational structure is important to international companies.

LO2 **Discuss** the organizational dimensions that must be considered when selecting organizational structures.

LO3 **Discuss** the various organizational forms available for structuring international companies.

LO4 **Explain** why decisions are made when they are among parent and subsidiary units of an international company.

LO5 **Discuss** how an international company can maintain control of a joint venture or of a company in which the IC owns less than 50 percent of the voting stock.

LO6 **List** the types of information an international company needs to have reported to it by its units around the world.

relative strengths and weaknesses of each of the various structural alternatives is an essential skill for managers.

In this chapter, we discuss the different organizational forms an international company can take and key strategic issues that managers must address in choosing among these various organizational designs. Included in the discussion will be the identification of concerns that managers have regarding their ability to control the international activities of their companies. ■

LO1 Explain why the design of organizational structure is important to international companies.

WHAT IS ORGANIZATIONAL DESIGN, AND WHY IS IT IMPORTANT FOR INTERNATIONAL COMPANIES?

Organizational design is a process that deals with how an international business should be organized in order to ensure that its worldwide business activities are able to be integrated in an efficient and effective manner. As suggested in Figure 11.1, in designing an international organization, it is essential that the structures and systems being implemented are not merely consistent with each other but also consistent with the environmental context in which the organization is operating and the strategy the company is using for competing in this international environment. The size of the organization and the complexity of its business operations must also be considered in the design of a company.

The structure of an international company (IC) must be able to evolve over time, to allow the organization to respond to change and to efficiently and effectively reconfigure the way in which its competencies and resources are integrated within and across the company's various units. This is a major challenge for international companies, especially as their activities are increasingly dispersed across the globe as well as subject to rapid and ongoing environmental and

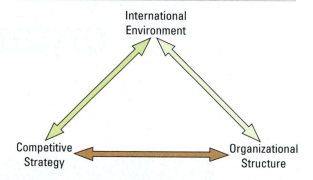

▼**FIGURE 11.1** The Relationship among International Environment, Competitive Strategy, and Organizational Structure

strategic change. Failure to successfully deal with this challenge threatens the organization's performance and, indeed, its long-term survival.

The international company's strategic planning process itself, because it encompasses an analysis of the firm's external environments as well as its strengths and weaknesses, often discloses a need to alter the organization. Changes in an international company's strategy may require changes in the organization, but the reverse is also true. For instance, a new CEO may join the firm, or the company may acquire a company in another nation or in another area of business activity. Strategic planning and organizing are so closely related that usually management treats the structure of the organization as an integral part of the strategic planning process.

LO2 Discuss the organizational dimensions that must be considered when selecting organizational structures.

Organizational Design Concerns

Two of the concerns that management faces in designing the organizational structure for an IC are (1) finding the most effective way to departmentalize to take advantage of the efficiencies gained from specialization of labor and (2) coordinating the activities of those departments to enable the firm to meet its overall objectives. As all managers know, these two concerns run counter to each other; that is, the gain from increased specialization of labor may at times be nullified by the increased cost of coordination. It is the search for an optimum balance between them that often leads to a reorganization of the international company's structure.

There are four primary dimensions that need to be considered when designing the structure of an international company:

1. *Product and technical expertise* regarding the different businesses that the company participates in.

2. *Geographic expertise* regarding the countries and regions in which the company operates.

3. *Customer expertise* regarding the similarity of client groups, industries, market segments, or population groups that transcend the boundaries of individual countries or regions.

4. *Functional expertise* regarding the various value chain activities that the company is involved with.

International companies vary with respect to the way these four dimensions are structured and integrated. No single structure is best for all companies and contexts. Rather, managers have to consider the nature of their company's international operating environment and strategy—both currently and how they are expected to change in the future—when deciding when and how to modify the company's organizational structure. In the following sections, we discuss the most common types of organizational designs for international companies. In reality, due to the complex nature of their operating environments and nuances of their historical origins and evolution, the structure of many ICs may deviate to some extent from these basic organizational designs. Nevertheless, understanding attributes associated with these basic designs can assist managers of international companies in selecting an organizational structure appropriate for their current and anticipated circumstances.

LO3 Discuss the various organizational forms available for structuring international companies.

Evolution of the International Company

As discussed in Chapters 2 and 13, companies often enter foreign markets first by exporting and then, as sales increase, by forming overseas sales companies and eventually setting up manufacturing facilities. As the firm's foreign involvement changes, its organization frequently changes as well. It might first have *no one* responsible for international business; the firm's marketing department might fill the export orders. Next, an export department might be created, possibly in the marketing department; and when the company begins to invest in various overseas locations, it could form an **international division** to take charge of all overseas involvement. Larger

> **INTERNATIONAL COMPANIES VARY WITH RESPECT TO THE WAY THESE FOUR DIMENSIONS ARE STRUCTURED AND INTEGRATED. NO SINGLE STRUCTURE IS BEST FOR ALL COMPANIES AND CONTEXTS.**

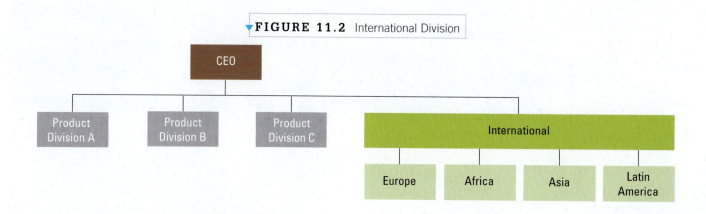

▼ FIGURE 11.2 International Division

CEO

Product Division A

Product Division B

Product Division C

International

Europe | Africa | Asia | Latin America

firms, such as Ford, IBM, and Wal-Mart, commonly organize their international divisions on a regional or geographic basis (Figure 11.2). Today, we still see companies—both those that are relatively modest in size and those that are some of the largest in the world—that are organized into a primary domestic division, supplemented by an international division to serve the rest of the world.

As their overseas operations increase in importance and scope, most managements feel the need to eliminate international divisions and establish worldwide organizations based on *product, region, function,* or *customer classes.* At secondary, tertiary, and still lower levels, these four dimensions—plus (1) process, (2) national subsidiary, and (3) international or domestic—provide the basis for subdivisions. As a result, as they grow over time, most international companies move away from the use of international divisions and instead

implement one of the global structures that we present in the subsequent sections of this chapter. The initial choice of organizational structure after discarding the international division is usually one based on either global product or global geographic factors. These alternative paths for the design and evolution of the international company are presented in the international stages model of organizational structures, as shown in Figure 11.3.[2]

Managements that change to these types of organizations feel they will (1) be more capable of developing competitive strategies to confront the increasing global competition, (2) obtain lower production costs by promoting worldwide product standardization and manufacturing rationalization, and (3) enhance technology transfer and the allocation of company resources.

Global Corporate Form—Product
Frequently, this structure represents a return to pre-export department times in that the domestic product division has been given responsibility for global line and staff operations. In the present-day global form, product divisions are responsible for the worldwide operations such as marketing and production of products under their control. Each division generally has regional experts, so while this organizational form avoids the duplication of product experts common in a company with an international division, it creates a duplication of area experts. Occasionally, to avoid placing regional specialists in each product division, management will have a group of managerial specialists in an international division who advise the product divisions but have no authority over them (see Figure 11.4). For example, all of General Electric's businesses are managed through a global line-of-business structure, and investment opportunities are identified and assessed on a global basis by managers within each of these business areas.

Global Corporate Form—Geographic Regions
Firms in which geographic regions are the primary basis for division put the responsibility for all activities under area managers who report directly to the chief executive officer. This

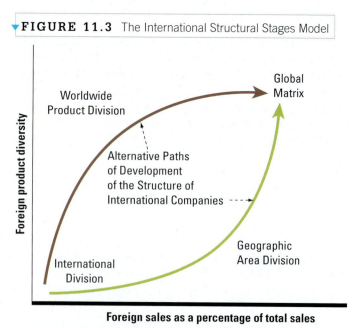

▼ FIGURE 11.3 The International Structural Stages Model

Foreign product diversity

Worldwide Product Division

Global Matrix

Alternative Paths of Development of the Structure of International Companies

Geographic Area Division

International Division

Foreign sales as a percentage of total sales

Source: Based on John M. Stopford and Louis T. Wells, *Strategy and Structure of the Multinational Enterprise* (New York: Basic Books, 1970).

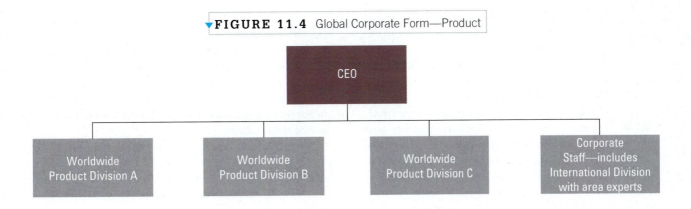

FIGURE 11.4 Global Corporate Form—Product

kind of organization simplifies the task of directing worldwide operations, because every country in the world is clearly under the control of someone who is in contact with headquarters (see Figure 11.5).

Of course, this organizational type is used for both multinational (multidomestic) and global companies. Global companies that use it consider the division in which the home country is located as just another division for purposes of resource allocation and a source of management

having different product requirements, competitive environments, and political risks. Many producers of consumer products, such as prepared foods, pharmaceuticals, and household products, employ this type of organization. The disadvantage of an organization divided into geographic regions is that each region must have its own product and functional specialists, so although the duplication of area specialists found in product divisions is eliminated, duplication of product and functional specialists is necessary.

> "The regionalized organization appears to be popular with companies that manufacture products with a rather low, or at least stable, technological content that require strong marketing ability."

personnel. Some U.S. global companies have created a North American division that includes Canada, Mexico, and Central American countries in addition to the United States, possibly in part to emphasize that the home country is given no preference.

The regionalized organization appears to be popular with companies that manufacture products with a rather low, or at least stable, technological content that require strong marketing ability. It is also favored by firms with diverse products, each

Production coordination across regions presents difficult problems, as does global product planning. To alleviate these problems, managements often place specialized product managers on the headquarters staff. Although these managers have no line authority, they do provide input to corporate decisions concerning products.

Global Corporate Form—Function Few firms are organized by function at the top level. Those that are obviously

FIGURE 11.5 Global Corporate Form—Geographic Regions

believe worldwide functional expertise is more significant to the firm than is product or area knowledge. In this type of organization, those reporting to the CEO might be the senior executives responsible for each functional area (marketing, production, finance, and so on), as in Figure 11.6. The commonality among the users of the functional form is a narrow and highly integrated product mix, such as that of aircraft manufacturers or oil refining companies.

Hybrid Forms
In a **hybrid organization,** a mixture of the preceding organizational forms is used at the top level and may or may not be present at the lower levels as well. Figure 11.7 illustrates a simple hybrid form. Such combinations are often the result

of a regionally organized company having introduced a new and different product line that management believes can best be handled by a worldwide product division. An acquired company with distinct products and a functioning marketing network may be incorporated as a product division even though the rest of the firm is organized on a regional basis. Later, after corporate management becomes familiar with the operation, it may be regionalized.

A mixed structure may also result from the firm's selling to a sizable, homogeneous class of customers. Special divisions for handling sales to the military or to original equipment manufacturers, for example, are often established at the same level as regional or product divisions.

Matrix Organizations
The **matrix organization** has evolved from management's attempt to mesh product, regional, and functional expertise while still maintaining clear lines of authority. It is called a matrix because an organization based on one or possibly two dimensions is superimposed on an organization based on another dimension. In an organization of two dimensions, such as area and product, both the geographic area managers and the product managers will be at the same level, and their responsibilities will overlap. An individual manager—say, a

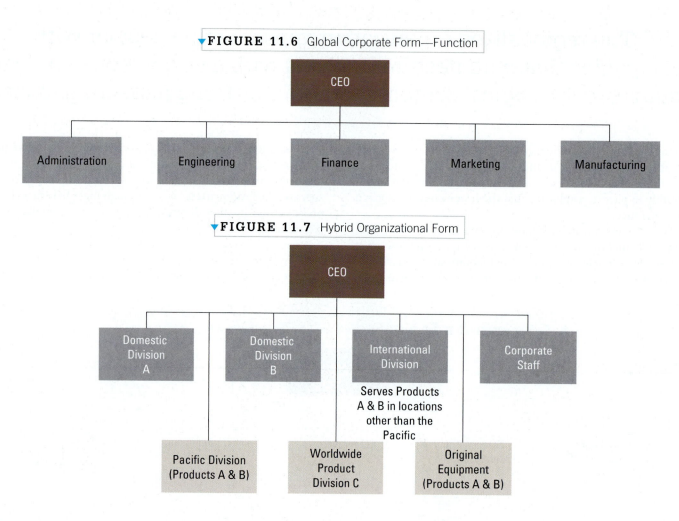

▼**FIGURE 11.6** Global Corporate Form—Function

CEO

Administration | Engineering | Finance | Marketing | Manufacturing

▼**FIGURE 11.7** Hybrid Organizational Form

CEO

Domestic Division A | Domestic Division B | International Division | Corporate Staff

Serves Products A & B in locations other than the Pacific

Pacific Division (Products A & B) | Worldwide Product Division C | Original Equipment (Products A & B)

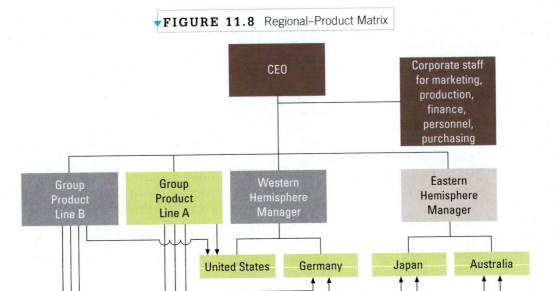

marketing manager in Germany—will have a multiple reporting relationship, being responsible to the manager overseeing the geographic area that includes Germany and in some instances to an international or worldwide marketing manager at headquarters. Figure 11.8 illustrates an extremely simple matrix organization based on two organizational dimensions. Note that the country managers are responsible to both the area managers and the product-line managers.

Problems with the Matrix Although at one time it seemed that the matrix organizational form would enable firms to have the advantages of the product, regional, and functional forms, the disadvantages of the matrix form have kept most worldwide companies from adopting it. One problem with the matrix is that the two or three managers (if it is a three-dimensional matrix) must agree on a decision. This can lead to less-than-optimum compromises, delayed responses, and power politics in which more attention is paid to the process

than to the problem. When the managers cannot agree, the problem goes higher in the organization and takes top management away from its duties. Dow Chemical Company, which has operations in more than 175 countries, changed its organizational structure from a geographic matrix to one of global business processes and 16 global business units that have individual global profit-and-loss responsibility.

Because of these difficulties associated with the matrix structure, many firms have maintained their original organizations based on product, function, region, or international divisions and have built into the structure accountability for the other organizational dimensions; this is called by some a **matrix overlay.**

Matrix Overlay The matrix overlay attempts to address the problems of the matrix structure by requiring accountability of all functions in the organization while avoiding the burdensome management stresses of a pure matrix structure.

> THE MATRIX ORGANIZATION HAS EVOLVED FROM MANAGEMENT'S ATTEMPT TO MESH PRODUCT, REGIONAL, AND FUNCTIONAL EXPERTISE WHILE STILL MAINTAINING CLEAR LINES OF AUTHORITY. IT IS CALLED A MATRIX BECAUSE AN ORGANIZATION BASED ON ONE OR POSSIBLY TWO DIMENSIONS IS SUPERIMPOSED ON AN ORGANIZATION BASED ON ANOTHER DIMENSION.

We have already mentioned how a firm organized by product may have regional specialists in a staff function with the requirement that they have input to product decisions. They may even be organized in an international division, as was mentioned previously. Conversely, a regional organization would have product managers on its staff who provide input to regional decisions.

Strategic Business Units

Strategic business units (SBUs) are an organizational form in which product divisions have been defined as though they were distinct, independent businesses. An SBU is defined as a self-contained business entity with a clearly defined market, specific competitors, the ability to carry out its business mission, and a size appropriate for control by a single manager. Most SBUs are based on product lines, such as Caterpillar's 31 autonomous profit center business units.[3] If a product must be modified to suit different markets, a worldwide SBU may be divided into a few product/market SBUs serving various markets or groups of countries. Shell Chemical Company's SBUs, which it calls product business units (PBUs), are global.[4] BP's business units, which it calls strategic performance units (SPUs), are also global.

Changes in Organizational Forms

The rapidly changing business environment caused by increased global competition, customer preference for custommade rather than mass-produced products, and faster technological change is pressuring companies to step up their search for organizational forms that will enable them to act more quickly, reduce costs, and improve the quality of product offerings. The ability to maintain alignment between the organization and its global and hypercompetitive environment has become a fundamental determinant of many organizations' ability to merely survive. As a result, change in organizational form has become an almost constant process. Not only are companies mixing older, established forms of organization; they are also changing to different forms, many of which are modified versions of long-established forms with new names.

The increasing acceptance by many companies of the need for frequent reorganization, called **reengineering** by many, is often accompanied by a significant reduction in the levels of middle management, restructuring of work processes to reduce the fragmenting of the process across functional departments, improvement in the speed and quality of strategy execution, empowerment of employees, and the use of computers for instant communication and swift transmittal of information. CEOs are striving to make their organizations lean, flat, fast to respond, and innovative.

Current Organizational Trends

Two organizational forms are now receiving the attention of many CEOs: the virtual corporation and the horizontal corporation.

Virtual Corporation A **virtual corporation,** also called a *network corporation,* is an organization that coordinates economic activity to deliver value to customers using resources outside the traditional boundaries of the organization. In other words, it relies to a great extent on third parties to conduct its business. Outsourcing once was used for downsizing and cost reduction, but now companies are using it to obtain specialized expertise that they don't have but need in order to serve new markets or adopt new technology.

The evolution of the technology infrastructure has made possible changes in the work force and working methods, such as teleworking, home offices, and flexible working practices. All these factors have contributed to the increase in virtual corporations. Global networking on the Internet has made worldwide outsourcing possible for firms of all sizes. Dell Computer is a well-known example of a company that has used tight integration with its global network of

> THE ABILITY TO MAINTAIN ALIGNMENT BETWEEN THE ORGANIZATION AND ITS GLOBAL AND HYPERCOMPETITIVE ENVIRONMENT HAS BECOME A FUNDAMENTAL DETERMINANT OF MANY ORGANIZATIONS' ABILITY TO MERELY SURVIVE, AND CHANGE IN ORGANIZATIONAL FORM HAS BECOME AN ALMOST CONSTANT PROCESS.

suppliers in order to assemble and deliver semi-customized computers to its international customers within days of receiving an order, and without carrying large volumes of expensive inventory that is prone to losing value through technological obsolescence.

Although the name is new, the virtual corporation concept has existed for decades. It has been extremely common for a group of construction firms, each with a special area of expertise, to form a consortium to bid on a contract for constructing a road or a sports stadium, for example. After finishing the job, the consortium would disband. Other examples of network organizations are the various clothing and athletic shoe marketers such as DKNY, Nike, and Reebok. The latter firms are also called *modular corporations.*

The virtual corporation concept has several potential benefits. In particular, it permits greater flexibility than is associated with more typical corporate structures. Rather than building competence from the ground up and incurring high start-up costs that could limit future production decisions, virtual corporations form a network of dynamic relationships that allow them to take advantage of the competencies of other organizations in order to respond rapidly to changing circumstances. However, this form of organization can have disadvantages, including the potential to reduce management's control over the corporation's activities (it is vulnerable to the opportunistic actions of partners, including cost increases, unintended "borrowing" of technical and other knowledge, and potential departure from the relationship at inappropriate times). From the standpoint of employees, the virtual corporation form of organization may replace the security of long-term employment and the promise of ever-increasing salaries with the insecurity of the market—a global market.

> **Small is not better; focused is better.**

Horizontal Corporation Another organizational form, the **horizontal corporation,** has been adopted by some large technology-oriented global firms in highly competitive industries such as electronics and computers. Firms such as 3M, General Electric, and DuPont have chosen this organizational form to give themselves the flexibility to respond quickly to advances in technology and be product innovators. In many companies, *teams* are drawn from different departments to solve a problem or deliver a product.

This organization has been characterized as "antiorganization" because its designers are seeking to remove the constraints imposed by the conventional organizational structures. In a horizontal corporation, employees worldwide create, build, and market the company's products through a carefully cultivated system of interrelationships. In a horizontal corporation, marketers in Great Britain speak directly to production people in Brazil without having to go through the home office in Germany, for example.

Proponents of the horizontal organization claim lateral relationships incite innovation and new-product development. They also state that this approach to organizing helps to place more decision-making responsibility in the hands of middle managers and other skilled professionals, who do not have to clear each detail and event with higher-ups. The objective is to substitute cooperation and coordination, which are in the interest of everyone, for strict control and supervision. Pursued effectively, this approach can help to develop international communities of skilled workers that create and exploit valuable intangible assets.[5]

Corporate Survival in the 21st Century

Managers in many international companies can expect to make greater use of the *dynamic network structure* that breaks down the major functions of the firm into smaller companies coordinated by a small-size headquarters organization. Business functions such as marketing and accounting may be provided by separate organizations—some of them owned partially or fully by the international company, some of them not—that are connected by computers to a central office. To attain the optimum level of vertical integration, a firm must focus on its core business. Anything not essential to the business can often be done cheaper, faster, and better by outside suppliers.[6]

As companies engage in the global battles of the 21st century, we must remember that organizations, like people, have life cycles. In their youth, they are small and fast growing. However, as they age, they often become big, complex, and out of touch with their markets. The firms of tomorrow must learn how to be both large and entrepreneurial. As one CEO put it, "Small is not better; focused is better."

CONTROL

Every successful company uses controls to put its plans into effect, evaluate their effectiveness, make desirable corrections, and evaluate and reward or correct executive performance. The challenges associated with achieving effective control are more complicated for an international company than for a one-country operation. In earlier chapters, we discussed several of the complicating causes. They include different languages, cultures, and attitudes; different taxes and accounting methods; different currencies, labor costs, and market sizes; different degrees of political stability and security for personnel and property; and many more. For these reasons, international companies need controls even more than do domestic ones.

Subsidiaries

The terms **subsidiaries** and **affiliates** sometimes are used interchangeably, and we first examine the control of those in which the parent has 100 percent ownership. This avoids for now the additional complications of joint ventures or subsidiaries in which the parent has less than 100 percent ownership. We deal with those later in the chapter.

LO4 **Explain** why decisions are made when they are among parent and subsidiary units of an international company.

Where to Make Decisions in Wholly-Owned Subsidiaries?

There are three possibilities. Theoretically, all decisions could be made either at the international company (IC) headquarters or at the subsidiary level. As common sense would indicate, they are not; instead, some decisions are made at headquarters, some are made at subsidiaries, and—the third possibility—some are made cooperatively. Many variables determine which decision is made where. Some of the more significant variables are (1) product and equipment, (2) the competence of subsidiary management and reliance on that management by the IC headquarters, (3) the size of the IC and how long it has been one, (4) the detriment of a

subsidiary for the benefit of the enterprise, and (5) subsidiary frustration. We discuss each of these variables in the sections that follow.

Product and Equipment As to decision location, questions of standardization of product and equipment and second markets can be important for international companies. In Chapter 15, we will discuss how large global manufacturers of consumer products, such as Procter and Gamble (P&G) and Colgate, are developing standardized products from the outset for global or at least regional markets. In these situations, the affiliates have to follow company policy. Of course, representatives of the affiliates may have an opportunity to take part in the product design, contrary to the way new products were typically introduced before the globalization strategy became so popular. Then, as we discussed in Chapter 2 on the international product life cycle, new products often have been introduced first in the home market. After the production process has been stabilized, the specifications are sent to the affiliates (second markets) for local production, where adaptations can be made if the local managements deem them necessary for their markets.

In a firm without a global product policy, the preference of the operations management people in the home office has always been to standardize the product or at least the production process in as many overseas plants as possible, as we will explain in Chapter 15. If, however, any subsidiary can demonstrate that the profit potential is greater for a product tailored for its own market than what the company would realize from global standardization, the subsidiary ordinarily is allowed to proceed. Of course, the decision in such a case is cooperative in that the parent has the power to veto or override its subsidiary's decision.

Competence of Subsidiary Management and Headquarters' Reliance on It Reliance on subsidiary management can depend on how well the executives know one another and how well they know company policies, on whether headquarters management feels that it understands host country conditions, on the distances between the home country and the host countries, and on how big and old the parent company is.

Moving Executives Around Many ICs have a policy of transferring promising management personnel between parent headquarters and subsidiaries and among subsidiaries. Thus, the manager learns firsthand the policies of headquarters and the problems of putting those policies into effect at subsidiary levels.

A result of such transfers, which is difficult to measure but nevertheless important, is a network of intra-IC personal relationships. This tends to increase the confidence of executives in one another and to make communication among executives easier and less subject to error. Another development is that

some ICs have moved their regional executives into headquarters to improve communications and reduce cost.

Understanding Host Country Conditions
One element in the degree of headquarters' reliance on subsidiary management is the familiarity of headquarters with conditions in the subsidiary's host country. The less familiar or the more different conditions in the host country are perceived to be, the more likely headquarters is to rely on subsidiary management.

How Far Away Is the Host Country?
Another element in the degree of headquarters' reliance on subsidiary management is the distance of the host country from home headquarters. Thus, an American parent is likely to place more reliance on the management of an Indonesian subsidiary than on the management of a Canadian subsidiary. This occurs for two reasons: American management typically perceives management conditions in Canada to be more easily understood than conditions in Indonesia, and Indonesia is much farther from the United States than Canada is—not merely geographically but also in terms of culture, politics, and other variables.

Size and Age of the IC
As a rule, a large company can afford to hire more specialists, experts, and experienced executives than can a smaller one. The longer a company has

to subsidiary managements in order to effectively sense pressures for adaptation, to serve as tools for developing and communicating innovation, and to promote effective execution of strategy.

Benefiting the Enterprise to the Detriment of a Subsidiary
An IC has opportunities to source raw materials and components, locate factories, allocate orders, and govern intrafirm pricing that are not available to a non-IC. Such activities may be beneficial to the enterprise yet may result in **subsidiary detriment.**

Moving Production Factors
For any number of reasons, an IC may decide to move factors of production from one country to another or to expand in one country in preference to another. In addition to the cost, availability, or skill levels of labor, other possible reasons include such factors as taxation, market, currency, and political stability issues.

The subsidiary from which factors are being taken would be unenthusiastic about giving up control over existing activities. Its management would be slow, at best, to cut the company's capacity or to downsize or eliminate local operations. Headquarters would typically have to make such decisions.

subsidiary detriment Situation in which a small loss for a subsidiary results in a greater gain for the total IC

> **"The less familiar or the more different conditions in the host country are perceived to be, the more likely headquarters is to rely on subsidiary management."**

been an IC, the more likely it is to have a number of experienced executives who know company policies and have worked at headquarters and in the field. Successful experience builds confidence. In most ICs, the top positions are at headquarters, and the ablest and most persistent executives will typically get positions there eventually. Thus, over time, the headquarters of a successful company is run by experienced executives who are confident of their knowledge of the business in the home and host countries and in combinations thereof.

It follows that in larger, older organizations, more decisions are made at headquarters and fewer are delegated to subsidiaries. Smaller companies, in business for shorter periods of time, tend to be able to afford fewer internationally experienced executives and will not have had time to develop them internally. Smaller, newer companies often have no choice but to delegate decisions to subsidiary managements. However, with the increasing pace of change and intensity of competition in many markets of the world, as well as continued differences across many markets, even large and experienced companies are finding the need to delegate at least some decision-making authority

Which Subsidiary Gets the Order?
Similarly, if an order—say, from an Argentine customer—could be filled from a subsidiary in France or another in South Africa or a third in Brazil, parent headquarters might decide which subsidiary gets the business. Among the considerations in the decision would be transportation costs, production costs, comparative tariff rates, customers' currency restrictions, comparative order backlogs, governmental pressures, and taxes. Having such a decision made by IC headquarters avoids price competition among members of the same IC group.

Multicountry Production
Frequently, the size of the market in a single country is too small to permit economies of scale in manufacturing an entire industrial product or offering a full range of services for that one market. An example is Ford's production of a light vehicle for the Asian market. In that situation, Ford negotiated with several countries to the end that one country would make one component of the vehicle for all the countries involved. Thus, one country makes the engine, a second country has the body-stamping plant, a

transfer pricing Pricing that is established for transactions between members of the enterprise

third makes the transmission, and so forth. In this fashion, each operation achieves the efficiency and cost savings of economies of scale. Of course, this kind of multinational production demands a high degree of IC headquarters' control and coordination.

Which Subsidiary Books the Profit?

In certain circumstances, an IC may have a choice of two or more countries in which to declare profits. Such circumstances may arise where two or more units of the IC cooperate in supplying components or services under a contract with a customer unrelated to any part of the IC. Under these conditions, there may be opportunities to allocate higher prices to one unit or subsidiary and lower prices to another within the global price to the customer.

If the host country of one of the subsidiaries has lower taxes than the other host countries, it would be natural to try to maximize profits in the lower-tax country and minimize them in the higher-tax country. Other differences between host countries could dictate the allocation of profit to or from the subsidiaries located there. Such differences could include currency controls, labor relations, political climate, and social unrest. It is sensible to direct or allocate as much profit as reasonably possible to subsidiaries in countries with the fewest currency controls, the best labor relations and political climate, and the least social unrest, for example.

The intrafirm transaction may also give a company choices regarding profit location. Pricing between members of the same enterprise is referred to as **transfer pricing,** and while IC headquarters could permit undirected, arm's-length negotiations between itself and its subsidiaries, this might not yield the most advantageous results for the enterprise as a whole.

Price and profit allocation decisions like these are usually best made at parent-company headquarters, which is supposed to maintain the overall view, looking out for the best interests of the enterprise. Naturally, subsidiary management does not gladly make decisions to accept lower profits, largely because its evaluation may suffer as a result of the apparent reduction in performance at the subsidiary level.

The following two tables illustrate how the total IC enterprise may profit even though one subsidiary makes less. Assume a cooperative contract by which two subsidiaries are selling products and services to an outside customer for a price of $100 million. The host country of IC Alpha levies company income taxes at the rate of 50 percent, whereas IC Beta's host country taxes its income at 20 percent. The customer is in a third country, has agreed to pay $100 million, and is indifferent to how Alpha and Beta share the money. The first table shows the enterprise's after-tax income if Alpha is paid $60 million and Beta is paid $40 million. Thus, after tax, the enterprise realizes $62 million.

GLOBAL gauntlet

Life in a Virtual Organization

Accenture Ltd. delivers a range of consulting, outsourcing, and technology services to clients around the world, harnessing its 177,000 employees to generate revenues of more than $21 billion in 2009. Yet, according to the company's senior management, Accenture has neither an operational headquarters facility nor any formal branch facilities. Instead, the company's approach to organizing its global operations might be termed *virtual*. Prior to 2000, Accenture had been the consulting arm of the now-defunct Arthur Andersen accounting company. During that time, the consulting operations had been managed for decades by the Swiss-based company, Andersen Worldwide. After consulting was split off from Andersen's accounting operations and subsequently became a separate organization under the name Accenture, the partners could not agree on a location for the new, Bermuda-incorporated company's headquarters. Because they typically spent a major portion of their time on the road, Accenture's executives decided to live where each of them wanted and forgo an organization built around a central headquarters. As a result, the chief financial officer lives in California's Silicon Valley, the chief technology officer lives in Germany, and many of the company's globally diverse workforce of consultants are traveling nearly nonstop to client sites worldwide. Even the company's Boston-based CEO, Bill Green, doesn't have a permanent desk or office location. Coordinating this geographically dispersed workforce is facilitated by technology. Employees log on to Accenture's intranet daily, either from home, from a hotel or airport, or from a temporary cubicle in one of the more than 110 locations that the company leases around the world. Every six weeks or so, the 23 members of the company's executive leadership team meet face-to-face for several days, with the location for the meetings rotating among different cities worldwide. Says Green, "We land somewhere, meet clients in the area, meet employees, then get together as a team to make decisions—and head out again." Says Adrian Lajtha, Accenture's Chief Leadership Officer, "Anyone who says managing this way is easy is lying."[7] What do you think might be the greatest strengths and weaknesses of working in a virtual organization like this?

	Receives ($ millions)	Tax ($ millions)	After Tax ($ millions)
Alpha	$60	$30	$30
Beta	40	8	32
			$62

The second table shows the after-tax income if Alpha is paid $40 million and Beta is paid $60 million. Thus, after taxes, the enterprise realizes $68 million.

	Receives ($ millions)	Tax ($ millions)	After Tax ($ millions)
Alpha	$40	$20	$20
Beta	60	12	48
			$68

These simple examples illustrate that the IC would be $6 million better off if it could shift $20 million of the payment from Alpha to Beta, while the customer is no worse off, as it pays $100 million in either case. Alpha, having received $20 million less in payment, is $10 million worse off after taxes, but Beta is $16 million better off—and the enterprise is $6 million ahead on the same contract. Given the number of countries and tax laws in the world, there are countless combinations for how such savings can be accomplished. Financial management awareness and control are the keys.

We do not mean to leave the impression that the host and home governments are unaware of or indifferent to transfer pricing and profit allocating by ICs operating within their borders. The companies must expect questioning by host and home governments and must be prepared to demonstrate that prices or allocations are reasonable. This may be done by showing that other companies charge comparable prices for the same or similar items or, if there are no similar items, by showing that costs plus profit have been used reasonably to arrive at the price. As to allocation of profits, the IC in our example would try to prove that the volume or importance of the work done by Beta or the responsibilities assumed by Beta—such as financing, after-sales service, or warranty obligations—justify the higher amount being paid to Beta. Of course, the questioning in this instance would come from the host government of Alpha if it got wind of the possibility of more taxable income for Beta and less for itself.[8]

Subsidiary Frustration An extremely important consideration for parent-company management is that the management of its subsidiaries be motivated and loyal. If all the big decisions are made, or are perceived to be made, at the IC headquarters, the managers of subsidiaries can lose incentive and prestige or face with their employees and the community. They may grow hostile and disloyal.

Therefore, even though there may be reasons for headquarters to make decisions, it should delegate as many as is reasonably possible. Management of each subsidiary should be kept thoroughly informed and be consulted seriously about decisions, negotiations, and developments in its geographic area. The trend for many ICs of shifting power away from subsidiaries toward the parent has caused predictable frustration to subsidiary management, sometimes followed by resignations.

L05 Discuss how an international company can maintain control of a joint venture or of a company in which the IC owns less than 50 percent of the voting stock.

Joint Ventures and Subsidiaries Less Than 100 Percent Owned

A *joint venture*, as defined in Chapter 13, may be a corporate entity between an IC and local owners or a corporate entity between two or more companies that are foreign to the area where the joint venture is located, or it may involve one company working on a project of limited duration (e.g., constructing a dam) in cooperation with one or more other companies. The other companies may be subsidiaries or affiliates, but they may also be entirely independent entities.

All the reasons for making decisions at IC headquarters, at subsidiary headquarters, or cooperatively apply equally in joint venture situations. However, headquarters will almost never have as much freedom of action and flexibility in a joint venture as it has with subsidiaries that are 100 percent owned.

Loss of Freedom and Flexibility The reasons for that loss of freedom and flexibility are easy to see. If shareholders outside the IC have control of the affiliate, they can block efforts of IC headquarters to move production factors away, fill an export order from another affiliate or subsidiary, and so forth. Even if outside shareholders are a minority and cannot directly control the affiliate, they can bring legal or political pressures on the IC to prevent it from diminishing the affiliate's profitability for the IC's benefit. Likewise, the local partner in a joint venture is highly unlikely to agree with measures that penalize the joint venture for the IC's benefit.

"With less than 50 percent of the voting stock and even with no voting stock, an IC can have control."

HOUSE

Saviors

Cameron enlists House's help in the case of an environmental activist who collapses at a protest.

watch now ▶

Popular Episodes

CC American Dad!: Oedipal Panties

Season 3 | Ep. 11 (21:53)

More: American Dad!

Channel: Comedy

CC The Simpsons: Eeny Teeny Maya Mo

Popular Clips

Saturday Night Live: Digital Short: Party...

Excerpt (01:35)

More: Saturday Night Live

Saturday Night Live: Digital Short: I'm O...

Featured Videos

CC The Office: Broke

Season 5 | Ep. 23 (21:50)

More: The Office

My Name is Earl: Gospel

Season 4 | Ep. 23 (21:34)

Hulu's Pick

Exclusive look at The Brothers Bloom, a comedy starring Rachel Weisz, Adrien Brody and Mark Ruffalo.

explore

Popular TV Shows

The popular video streaming Web site, Hulu, is a Joint Venture of NBC Universal + Fox Entertainment Group + ABC, Inc.

CU in ib

Isaac Rush in Tianjin: So Much More Fun when You Don't Understand Everything!

Isaac Rush was an international business major at Cal Poly–San Luis Obispo whose interest in international work began with trips to Mexico to help build homes for people who were homeless. When he started seeing how other people lived their lives and how it worked for them, it sparked his interest. In his own words, "I was intrigued by different cultures and people— how they ate different foods, had different hobbies, and had completely different ways of doing things that sometimes made sense to me and sometimes did not. I realized that there is so much more excitement and adventure when you don't understand everything; and that is why I chose to go international." He recently spent four months in China teaching English with AIESEC. Here's his report, which includes his advice:

Initially, I chose China because there were many teaching opportunities there and foreign teachers are in high demand. I went to China through the international business club, AIESEC, and they were able to provide internships connecting with another university in Tianjin, China. I knew that Mandarin Chinese is one of the hardest languages to learn and that living in China is really affordable. These two aspects were really appealing for me. Having just graduated from college, I was on a tight budget and looking for a new challenge that could really enhance my resume.

In order to prepare for my trip, I connected with students from China and gained some valuable advice: buy a map and make copies of your passport. I also got connected with a couple of Cal Poly students who were currently working abroad in China, and they helped me with many of the basics, for instance, what type of visa to apply for, the need for bringing basic medications, and to be picky about finding an apartment because cleanliness standards are much lower than in the U.S. I also bought some books on Chinese culture and travel, as well as a simple phrase book, and I went on YouTube to practice pronunciation of basic phrases.

One of the most valuable things that I did when I was in China was e-mail and talk on Skype to family and friends because then I didn't feel quite as removed from what was familiar. I also recommend getting involved in other activities to meet friends, because without a couple of good friends I don't know how I would have survived. I also kept up with some typical routines that I did when I was in the U.S. like running, reading,

and going to Starbucks for some coffee because instant coffee, which is dominant all over China, wouldn't cut it for me.

When I first began teaching, I was teaching a wide variety of students: primary school kids, high school students, college students, and even business professionals. I was traveling to several different companies in the city of Tianjin and changing up my lessons based on the audience. My main focus was oral English with all my students so that they could take an IELTS examination and pass. The IELTS would certify a student to study abroad, improve business opportunities, or simply provide evidence of being a better English speaker.

Some of my biggest challenges were ordering food in a restaurant because I didn't recognize any of the food, and navigating around the city because I would have to memorize landmarks and then get around in the city in a taxi without being able to speak Chinese. The way I managed was finding restaurants with pictures to point to, buying an English map, and every time I had to get into a taxi, I would have an address written down on a note card in case the driver didn't understand my accent, which was 95 percent of the time.

One surprising discovery that I found out by experience is that you have to carry around toilet paper in public places in China because many places don't supply it. This I found out the hard way, but never left home without paper in my pocket again.

Some of my greatest enjoyments in China were going to my Chinese friends' homes

and getting meals prepared by their parents. When I would arrive, they would offer me their best fruits, nuts, and snacks; then they would offer me cigarettes because most males in China smoke, and then they would bring out tons of food and would keep offering me more and more until I was absolutely full. The Chinese hospitality was amazing. I also really enjoyed the high value that Chinese place on family. Most Chinese have all of their relatives living in the same town and it has been that way for generations.

One thing that I would highly recommend is that, when you're in China or any other foreign country, try as hard as possible to follow the same habits as the local people: eating, dress, and hobbies. This shows the local people that you actually care about their culture and want to see things from their perspective. It will open up more opportunities.

Some major learning points I can share with you are: do your best to learn the local language because this is the most difficult but necessary tool to learn about the foreign culture. Be disciplined because it takes determination and intensity. I also learned that I have to throw out all my standards of hygiene because trash is thrown out on the streets and smoking indoors is completely legal.

I am currently working in sales for a moving company and may open up a franchise in Orange County in the next year or two. Eventually, I will head back abroad to work once I have some industry experience. Perhaps we'll meet up!

Control Can Be Had With less than 50 percent of the voting stock and even with no voting stock, an IC can have control. Some methods of maintaining control are:

- A management contract.
- Control of the finances.
- Control of the technology.
- Putting people from the IC in important executive positions.

As might be expected, ICs have encountered resistance to putting IC personnel in the important executive positions from their joint venture partners or from host governments. The natural desire of these partners and governments is that their own nationals have at least equality in the important positions and that they get training and experience in the technology and management.

LO6   List the types of information an international company needs to have reported to it by its units around the world.

Reporting

For controls to be effective, all operating units of an IC must provide headquarters with timely, accurate, and complete reports. There are many uses for the information reported. Among the types of reporting required are (1) financial, (2) technological, (3) market opportunity, and (4) political and economic.

Financial   A surplus of funds in one subsidiary should perhaps be retained there for investment or contingencies. On the other hand, such a surplus might be more useful at the parent company, in which case payment of a dividend is indicated. Or perhaps another subsidiary or affiliate needs capital, and the surplus could be lent or invested there. Obviously, parent headquarters must know the existence and size of a surplus to determine its best use.

Technological   New technology should be reported. New technology is constantly being developed in different countries,

market share and whether it is growing or shrinking, together with explanations.

Political and Economic   Not surprisingly, reports on political and economic conditions have multiplied mightily in number and importance over the past 20 or so years as revolutions—some bloody—have toppled and changed governments. Democracies have replaced dictatorships, one dictator has replaced another, countries have broken apart or reunited—changes have been occurring on almost every continent.

Managing in a World out of Control

The Internet may be the closest thing to a working anarchy the world has ever seen. Nobody owns it, nobody runs it, and most Internet users get along by dint of online etiquette, not rules and regulations. The Internet was built up without any central control because the U.S. Defense Department wanted to ensure that the Internet could survive a nuclear attack. The Internet has proved to be a paragon of hothouse expansion and constant evolution. Although it may be messier and less efficient than a similar system designed and run by an agency or company, this organically grown network is also more adaptable and less susceptible to a systemwide crash.

The consequence for management in a world out of control, such as the Internet, is a recipe developed at Massachusetts

---

> [**"For controls to be effective, all operating units of an IC must provide headquarters with timely, accurate, and complete reports."**]

---

and the subsidiary or affiliated company operating in such a country is likely to learn about it before IC headquarters hundreds or thousands of miles away does. If headquarters finds the new technology potentially valuable, it can gain competitive advantage by being the first to contact the developer for a license to use it.

Market Opportunities   The affiliates in various countries may spot new or growing markets for some product of the enterprise. This could be profitable all around, as the IC sells more of the product while the affiliate earns sales commissions. Of course, if the new market is sufficiently large, the affiliate may begin to assemble or produce the product under license from the parent company or from another affiliate.

Other market-related information that should be reported to IC headquarters includes competitors' activities, price developments, and new products of potential interest to the IC group. Also of importance is information on the subsidiary's

Institute of Technology for devising a system of distributed control: (1) do simple things first, (2) learn to do them flawlessly, (3) add new layers of activity over the results of the simple task, (4) don't change the simple things, (5) make the new layer work as flawlessly as the simple one, and (6) repeat ad infinitum. Many organizations would benefit by adopting organizing principles as deceptively simple as these.

Increasingly, the most successful companies, like the machines and programs so many of them now make, and the networks on which they all will rely will advance only by evolving and adapting in this organic, bottom-up way. Successful leaders will have to relinquish control. They will have to honor error because a breakthrough may at first be indistinguishable from a mistake. They must constantly seek disequilibrium.

Control: Yes and No   We have spoken of control within the IC family of parent, subsidiaries, affiliates, and joint ventures. This deals with where decisions are made on a variety of subjects under different circumstances. Timely and accurate reporting to the parent is necessary for success of the IC family. The trend in this area of control is toward centralized decision making, with more being done by the parent.

The other control of which we have spoken involves the design, production, and order-filling functions of companies. Here, the explosion of software, computer networks, and information technology, including the Internet, has tended to decentralize and de-job organizations. More and more, workers do evolving tasks with changing teams of other workers. Hierarchies dissolve and successful leaders relinquish control as workers are trained and encouraged to cope with evolving tasks and rewarded for coping well. ■

CHECK IT OUT!

mhhe.com/GeringerM

for study materials
including quizzes,
iPod downloads,
and video

"Think locally, offer value, and be patient. That last one is key: You can make an elephant dance. But it takes time to learn the right tune."

—Om Malik on marketing to India, *Business 2.0,* July 2004

chapter twelve

assessing international markets

A s described in Section Two of this book, international environmental forces can complicate management efforts to assess the attractiveness of expanding into foreign markets. Companies have used a broad range of approaches to assess international markets, some of them rather unsystematic and prone to error. We think that many international managers might prefer to use a more systematic approach, and in the following pages we describe in some detail a structured approach to the international market screening process.

LEARNING OBJECTIVES

After reading this chapter, you should be able to:

L01 **Discuss** environmental analysis and two types of market screening.

L02 **Explain** market indicators and market factors.

L03 **Describe** some statistical techniques for estimating market demand and grouping similar markets.

L04 **Discuss** the value to businesspeople of trade missions and trade fairs.

L05 **Discuss** some of the problems market researchers encounter in foreign markets.

L06 **Discuss** the different options for conducting survey-based research.

L07 **Explain** the difference between country screening and segment screening.

The first step in the market screening process is determining the basic need potential. We describe this process in the next section. **Market screening** is a modified version of environmental scanning in which the firm identifies markets by using the environmental forces to eliminate the less desirable markets. **Environmental scanning,** from which market screening is derived, is a procedure in which a firm scans the world for changes in the environmental forces that might affect it.[1] For some time, environmental scanning has been used by managers during the planning process to provide information about world threats and opportunities. Those who do environmental scanning professionally may belong to such organizations as the Society of Competitive Intelligence Professionals (www.scip.org). In addition, environmental scanning services are available from a number of private firms. Examples of such service providers include Smith Brandon International (www.smithbrandon.com) and Stratfor Inc. (www.stratfor.com).

LO1 Discuss environmental analysis and two types of market screening.

MARKET SCREENING

Market screening is a method of market analysis and assessment that permits management to identify a small number of desirable markets by eliminating those judged to be less attractive. This is accomplished by subjecting the markets to a series of screenings based on the environmental forces examined in Section Two. Although these forces may be placed in any order, the arrangement suggested in Figure 12.1 is designed to progress from the least to the most difficult analysis based on the accessibility and subjectivity of the data. In this way, the smallest number of candidates is left for the final, most difficult screening.

Market screening assists two different kinds of firms. One is the firm selling exclusively in the domestic market but with the belief it might increase sales by expanding into overseas markets. The other is the firm already a multinational, but wanting to avoid missing potential new markets. In both situations, managers require an ordered, relatively fast method of analyzing and assessing the nearly 200 countries (and multiple market segments within countries) to pinpoint the most suitable prospects.

Two Types of Market Screening: Country and Segment

In this chapter we will look at two types of market screening procedures. The first, which we call **country screening,** uses countries as the relevant unit of analysis. The second, which we call **segment screening,** is based on a subnational analysis of groups of consumers.

COUNTRY SCREENING

Initial Screening—Basic Needs Potential

Basic Needs Potential An initial screening based on the basic needs potential is a logical first step, because if the need is lacking, no reasonable expenditure of effort and money will enable the firm to successfully market its goods or services. For example, the basic need potential of certain goods is dependent on various physical forces, such as climate, topography, and natural resources. If the firm produces air conditioners, the analyst will look for countries with warm climates. Manufacturers of large farm tractors might not consider Switzerland a likely prospect because of its mountainous terrain. Manufacturers of large yachts might consider a landlocked country such as Paraguay to be an unattractive potential market, and only areas known to possess gold deposits are probable markets for gold-dredging equipment.

Generally, producers of specialized industrial materials or equipment experience little difficulty in assessing their basic

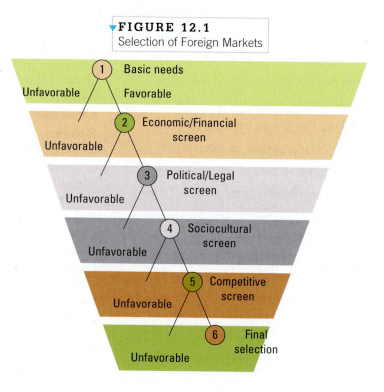

▼**FIGURE 12.1**
Selection of Foreign Markets

1 Basic needs
Unfavorable   Favorable

2 Economic/Financial screen
Unfavorable

3 Political/Legal screen
Unfavorable

4 Sociocultural screen
Unfavorable

5 Competitive screen
Unfavorable

6 Final selection
Unfavorable

need potential. A list of firms in an industry, often on a worldwide basis, is available either from the specific industry association for that industrial sector or from specialized trade journals. A builder of cement kilns, for example, can obtain the names and addresses of cement plants worldwide through the website of the Portland Cement Association. What about less specialized products that are widely consumed? For example, it is problematic to establish a basic need for chocolate and harder still to do so for MP3 players, consumer robots, or movies on Blu-ray discs. In these cases, we are moving from needs to wants.

Foreign Trade Analysts who want to know where American competitors are exporting their products can go to the website of the International Trade Administration (ITA), www.ita.doc.gov. The U.S. Department of Commerce also has the report *U.S. Exports of Merchandise* on the National Trade Data Bank (NTDB), which is available online for a subscription fee. This report's information is especially useful, as it includes both units and dollar values, permitting the analyst to calculate the average price of the unit exported. The Department of Commerce compiles and releases foreign trade statistics on a monthly and cumulative basis in its report *U.S. International Trade in Goods and Services,* commonly referred to as the FT900. It is published as a press release and can be found at http://www.census.gov/foreign-trade/Press-Release/current_press_release/index.html.

For help in their search for markets, analysts can obtain from the nearest Department of Commerce office numerous studies prepared by U.S. embassies. *Annual Worldwide Industry Reviews* and *International Market Research Reports* indicate major markets for many products.

Basic needs assessment might make Paraguay an unattractive market for a producer of yachts.

The *Country Market Surveys* indicate products for which there is a good, established market in a given country. We shall discuss these publications in greater detail in Chapter 14. Other countries publish similar data. For example, the data office of the European Union (Eurostat) publishes an annual, *External Trade,* and JETRO (the Japanese External Trade Organization) publishes a wide assortment of trade and industry data, many of which are put on its Internet site.

Imports Do Not Completely Measure Market Potential Even when a basic need is clearly indicated, experienced researchers will still investigate trade flows in order to have an idea of the magnitude of present sales. Of course, imports alone seldom measure the full market potential. Myriad reasons are responsible, among which are poor marketing, lack of foreign exchange, and high prices (e.g., from the effects of transportation, duties and markups). Nor can imports give much indication of the potential demand for a really new product.

Moreover, import data indicate only that a market has been buying certain products from abroad and are no guarantee that these imports will continue. A competitor may decide to produce locally, which in many markets will cause imports to cease. Change in a country's political structure also may reduce or eliminate imports, as we saw in the case of Iran after the revolution there, when orders worth billions of dollars were suddenly canceled. Nevertheless, import data do provide the firm with an indication of how much product is currently being purchased and provide managers with a conservative estimate of the immediate market potential at the going price. If local production is being considered and calculations show that goods

> "Import data indicate only that a market has been buying certain products from abroad and are no guarantee that these imports will continue."

market
indicators Economic
data used to measure
relative market strengths
of countries or geographic
areas

produced in the country could be sold at a lower price, the firm might reasonably expect to sell more than the quantity currently being imported.

Second Screening—Financial and Economic Forces

After the initial screening, the analyst will have a much smaller list of prospects. This list may be further reduced by a second screening based on the financial and economic forces. Trends in inflation, currency exchange rates, and interest rates are among the major financial points of concern. The analyst should consider other financial factors, such as credit availability, paying habits of customers, and rates of return on similar investments. It should be noted that this screening is not a complete financial analysis. That will come later if the market analysis and assessment disclose that a country has sufficient potential for capital investment.

Economic data may be employed in a number of ways, two measures of market demand based on them are especially useful. These are *market indicators* and *market factors*. Other methods for estimating demand that depend on economic data are *trend analysis* and *cluster analysis*.

L02   Explain market indicators and market factors.

Market Indicators Market indicators are economic data that serve as yardsticks for measuring the relative market strengths of various geographic areas. As an example, we developed an index of e-commerce potential for Latin America so that the countries in the region could be compared. The results appear in Table 12.1. In this methodology, we assembled data on 20 Latin American countries and then ranked the countries against each other. We wanted to include indicators of the strength and growth rate of the overall economy, as well as factors related more specifically to e-commerce or to

▼ **TABLE 12.1** E-Commerce Potential: Rankings for Latin America

Countries	Market Size	Market Growth Rate	E-Commerce Readiness	Overall E-Commerce Potential
South America				
Argentina	4	17	3	6
Bolivia	17	5	15	15
Brazil	5	12	3	4
Chile	1	5	1	1
Colombia	11	7	9	9
Ecuador	14	1	9	6
Paraguay	12	16	15	17
Peru	12	3	15	11
Uruguay	7	20	9	12
Venezuela	2	19	7	9
Caribbean				
Dominican Republic	10	9	9	9
Haiti	20	18	20	19
Jamaica	3	14	2	3
Central America				
Costa Rica	6	2	3	2
El Salvador	15	13	9	12
Guatemala	17	11	9	12
Honduras	15	4	19	15
Mexico	6	15	3	6
Nicaragua	17	10	15	17
Panama	5	6	7	4

Source: Michael S. Minor and Alexandra Brandt, "A Possible Index of E-Commerce Potential for Latin America," working paper, January 8, 2002, updated June 2006 by Adesegun Oyedele and October 2008 by Michael S. Minor. Reprinted with permission of the authors.

communications that would aid the growth of e-commerce. We developed three indices. Each indicator is given equal weight in each index.

Market size $=$ Size of urban population + Electricity consumption

Market growth rate $=$ Average growth rate in commercial energy use + Real growth rate in GDP

E-commerce readiness $=$ Mobile phones per 1,000 + Number of PCs per 1,000 + Internet hosts per million people

The rankings on these three indexes were then utilized to form a composite ranking. We called this composite ranking the "e-commerce potential." As you can see in Table 12.1, by utilizing our methodology, the countries with the most e-commerce potential appear to be Chile, Costa Rica, Jamaica, and Brazil, while Paraguay, Nicaragua, and Haiti appear to have the least potential.

Market Factors

Market factors are similar to market indicators except that they tend to correlate highly with the market demand for a given product. If the analyst of a foreign market has no factor for that market, he or she may be able to use one from the domestic market to provide an approximation for the foreign market. Moreover, an analyst who works for a multinational firm may be able to obtain market factors developed by comparable subsidiaries. To be able to transfer these relationships to the country under study, the analyst must assume that the underlying conditions affecting demand are similar in the two markets.

We can illustrate this process, which is called **estimation by analogy,** by using the following example. If a supplier of laptops knows that one-fifth of all laptops are replaced every year in the United Kingdom, he or she might use the same relationship to estimate demand for replacement computers

in a new overseas market. If there are 3 million existing laptops in the new market, the analyst might forecast that 3 million $\times$ 0.20, or 600,000, replacement laptops will be sold annually. The constant in the country under study may be somewhat different (it usually is), but with this approach, the estimates may represent a reasonable approximation and a base from which further analysis can be conducted. Many such factors exist, and generally research personnel, either at the home office or in foreign subsidiaries, are familiar with them.

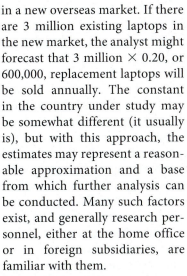

Trend Analysis

When the historical growth rates of either the pertinent economic variables or the imports of a product are known, future growth can be forecast by means of **trend analysis.** A time series may be constructed in a manner similar to the way a regression model is made, or the arithmetic mean of past growth rates may be applied to historical data. Caution is advised when using the second method because if the average annual growth rate is applied mechanically, in just a few years the dependent variable may reach an incredible size. For example, a 5 percent growth rate, compounded annually, will result in a doubling of the original value in only 15 years. Because trend analysis is based on the assumption that past conditions affecting the dependent variable will remain constant, analysts will generally modify the outcome to take into account any changes that can be foreseen or to create alternate scenarios for use in the company's analyses. Often there are obvious constraints that will limit growth. One of these constraints is the near certainty that competitors will enter the market if large increases in demand continue for very long.

cluster analysis Statistical technique that divides objects into groups so that the objects within each group are similar

LO3 Describe some statistical techniques for estimating market demand and grouping similar markets.

Cluster Analysis and Other Techniques

As multinationals extend their presence to more markets, managers are searching for ways to group countries and geographic regions by common characteristics. **Cluster analysis** divides objects (market areas, individuals, customers, and other variables) into groups so that the variables within each group are similar. For example, a team of college softball players sitting at a table in a restaurant might be a "cluster." Marketers, for example, use cluster analysis to identify a group of markets where a single promotional approach can be employed; attorneys can use it to group nations according to similarities in certain types of laws; and so forth. In other words, cluster analysis is used to classify a "mountain" of information into meaningful "piles."

Periodic Updating

If the estimates are altered appreciably in the periodic updating that all long-term forecasts undergo, managers may change the extent of the firm's involvement to be in line with the new estimates. Fortunately, the alternative forms of participation in a market permit the firm to become progressively more involved, with corresponding increases in investment. As discussed in Chapter 13, most companies can enter a market in stages, perhaps in this sequence: exporting, establishment of a foreign sales company, local assembly, and, finally, local manufacturing.

Even when the decision is whether to produce overseas, management may plan to assemble a combination of imported and domestically produced parts initially and then progressively to manufacture more components locally as demand rises. Automobile manufacturers have begun a number of foreign operations employing this strategy.

Third Screening—Political and Legal Forces

The elements of the political and legal forces that can eliminate a market from further consideration (or make it more attractive) are numerous.

Entry Barriers

Import restrictions can be positive or negative, depending on whether managers are considering whether to serve the market by exporting (can the firm's products enter the country?) or by setting up a foreign plant (will competitive imports be kept out?). If an objective is 100 percent ownership, will the nation's laws permit it, or is some local participation required? Will the government accept a minority local ownership, or must a minimum of 51 percent of the subsidiary be in the hands of nationals? Are there laws that reserve certain industries for either the government or its citizens?[2] Is the host government demanding that the foreign owner turn over technology to its proposed affiliate that the foreign owner prefers to keep at the home-country plant? Perhaps the host government has local content restrictions that the prospective investor considers excessive. There may be a government-owned company that would compete with the proposed plant. Depending on the circumstances and how strongly management wishes to enter the market, any one of these conditions may be sufficient cause to eliminate a nation from further consideration.

Profit Remittance Barriers

When there are no objectionable requisites for entry, a nation may still be excluded if there are what management believes to be undue restrictions on the repatriation of earnings. Limits linked to the amount of foreign investment or other criteria may be set, or the nation may have a history of inability to provide foreign exchange for profit remittances.

Policy Stability

Another factor of importance to management in studying the possibilities of investing in a country is the stability of government policy. Is there continuity in policy when a new leader takes office, for example? What is the political climate? Is the government stable, or is there infighting among government leaders? How about the public? Is there visible unrest? Do the armed forces have a history of intervention when there are public disturbances? Business can adapt to the form of government and thrive as long as the conditions are stable. But instability creates uncertainty, and this complicates planning. An often-heard complaint is, "They've changed the rules again."

It is important to make a distinction between *political stability* and *policy stability*. Rulers may come and go, but if the policies that affect businesses do not change very much, these political changes really may not be important. In fact, if one measures political stability in terms of changes in leadership at the top, the United States is politically unstable compared with many countries!

> IT IS IMPORTANT TO MAKE A DISTINCTION BETWEEN *POLITICAL STABILITY* AND *POLICY STABILITY*. RULERS MAY COME AND GO, BUT IF THE POLICIES THAT AFFECT BUSINESSES DO NOT CHANGE VERY MUCH, THESE POLITICAL CHANGES REALLY MAY NOT BE IMPORTANT.

Anti-government demonstrators in Bangkok, Thailand, in May of 2010.

Sources of analysis on political and policy stability are numerous. Some, such as Stratfor, have already been mentioned. In addition, Business Environment Risk Intelligence S.A. (www.beri.com) and Political Risk Services (www.prsgroup.com) publish rankings that compare countries on the issue of political risk.

Fourth Screening—Sociocultural Forces

A screening of the remaining candidates on the basis of sociocultural factors is often an arduous process. First, sociocultural factors are fairly subjective. Second, data are difficult to assemble, particularly from a distance. The analyst, unless he or she is a specialist in the country, must rely on the opinions of others. It is possible to hire consultants who typically are "old hands" with experience in the country or region. Others may have a particular methodology, such as Clotaire Rapaille, whose approach is mentioned in the Global Gauntlet box near the end of this chapter. Also, professional organizations and universities frequently hold seminars to explain the sociocultural aspects of doing business in a particular area or country.

Reading *Overseas Business Reports* (U.S. Department of Commerce), international business publications *(Business International, Financial Times, The Economist),* and specialized books will augment the analyst's sociocultural knowledge. The use of a checklist of the principal sociocultural components, as explained in Chapter 4, will serve as a reminder of the many factors the analyst must consider in this screening.

Although there are many difficulties, it is possible that recent immigrants or students from foreign countries may be used to shed light on potential sociocultural issues. A danger, of course, is that immigrants and students may not be "typical" representatives of their country, and there is also the prospect that they have been affected by their experience living abroad. Therefore, they are not necessarily reliable indicators of the reaction your product might receive from an audience "back home."

After the fourth screening, the analyst should have a list of countries for which an industry demand appears to exist. However, what management really wants to know is which of these markets seem to be the best prospects for the *firm's* products. A fifth screening based on the competitive forces will help provide this information.

Fifth Screening—Competitive Forces

In this screening, the analyst examines markets on the basis of such elements of the competitive forces as:

1. The number, size, and financial strength of the competitors.

2. Their market shares.

3. Their marketing strategies.

4. The apparent effectiveness of their promotional programs.

5. The quality levels of their product lines.

6. The source of their products—imported or locally produced.

7. Their pricing policies.

8. The levels of their after-sales service.

9. Their distribution channels.

10. Their coverage of the market. (Could market segmentation produce niches that are currently poorly served?)

Concerning item 10, it may be important to examine regional or ethnic subcultures in a particular foreign market. These subcultures may be natural or at least identifiable segments for which specific marketing programs may be successful. For example, there are sufficient Hispanic, Chinese, and other subcultures in the United States to merit the importation of Latin American and Chinese products into the United States.

Perhaps other countries have significant immigrant or subcultural populations whose needs you already understand and can serve. As an example, Japan has a small but growing population of immigrants from Latin America whose parents emigrated from Japan to Latin America in earlier times. These returnees tend to preserve their Latin heritage in Japan and might provide a market niche for firms whose strength is marketing to Latin Americans rather than to the Japanese.

Countries in which management believes strong competitors make a profitable operation difficult to attain are eliminated unless management (1) follows a strategy of being present wherever its global competitors are or (2) believes entering a competitor's home market will distract the competitor's attention from its home market, a reason for foreign investment that we discussed in Chapter 1.

Final Selection of New Markets

While much can be accomplished through analysis, there is no substitute for personal visits to markets that appear to have the best potential. An executive of the firm or a team of company representatives should visit those countries that still appear to be good prospects. Before leaving, this person or team should review the data from the various screenings along with any new information that the researcher can supply.

On the basis of this review and experience in making similar domestic decisions, the executive or team should prepare a list of points on which information they must obtain on arrival. Management will want the facts uncovered by the desk study (the five screenings) to be corroborated. Management will also expect a firsthand report on the market, including information on competitive activity and an appraisal of the suitability of the firm's present marketing mix and the availability of support services (warehousing, media agencies, credit, and so forth).

Field Trip The field trip should not be hurried; as much or more time should be allotted to this part of the study as would be spent on a similar domestic field trip. The point is to try to develop a "feel" for what is going on, and this cannot be accomplished quickly. For example, while Japanese youths model themselves after American basketball stars by wearing Nike sneakers, it appears that they change into off-brand sneakers when they actually play basketball. As another example, it seems to be relatively more common for men to shop in grocery stores in Chile, as compared with elsewhere in Latin America. And there is not much tradition in East Asia of men taking on the "do-it-yourself" projects for which Home Depot and similar brands are famous. This type of insight is not likely to develop without actual visits to the market.

LO4 **Discuss** the value to businesspeople of trade missions and trade fairs.

Government-Sponsored Trade Missions and Trade Fairs

When government trade specialists perceive an overseas market opportunity for an industry, they may organize a **trade mission.** The purpose is to send a group of executives from firms in the industry to a country or group of countries to learn firsthand about the market, meet important customers face-to-face, and make contacts with people interested in representing their products. Because of discounted airfares, hotels, and so forth, the cost to the firm may be less than it would pay if it arranged for its personnel to visit on their own. Moreover, the impact of a group visit is often greater than that of an individual company's visit. Before the mission's arrival, consulate or embassy officials will have publicized the visit and made contact with local companies they believe are interested. State governments, trade associations, chambers of commerce, and other export-oriented organizations also organize trade missions.

Probably every nation in the world holds a **trade fair** periodically. Usually each nation has a specifically marked area

> " While much can be accomplished through analysis, there is no substitute for personal visits to markets that appear to have the best potential. "

(Chinese pavilion, Argentine pavilion, etc.) at the fairgrounds where its exhibitors have their own booths staffed by company sales representatives. Trade fairs are open to the public, but during certain hours (generally mornings), entrance is limited to businesspeople interested in doing business with the exhibitors.

While most fairs in developing countries are general, with displays of many kinds of products, those in Europe are usually specialized. A famous example is the annual CeBIT computer and telecommunications trade fair—the largest computer-related trade fair in the world—held annually in Hannover, Germany. Up to 400,000 people made the trip to this show in 2010 to see exhibits from 4,157 exhibitors from 68 countries.[3]

Besides making contact with prospective buyers and agents (direct sales are often concluded during these meetings), most exhibitors use these fairs to learn more about the market and gather competitive intelligence. They not only receive feedback from visitors to their exhibits but also have the opportunity to observe their competitors in action.

> When a firm's research personnel have had no experience in the country, management should probably hire a local research group to do the work.

LO5 **Discuss** some of the problems market researchers encounter in foreign markets.

Sometimes Local Research Is Required

For many situations, the manager's field report will be the final input to the information on which the decision is based. Occasionally, however, the proposed human and financial resource commitments are so great that management will insist on gathering data in the potential market rather than depending solely on the desk and field reports.[4] This would undoubtedly be the position of a consumer products manufacturer that envisions entering a large competitive market of an industrialized country. It might also be the recommendation of the manager making the field trip if he or she discovered that market conditions were substantially different from those to which the firm was accustomed. Often, in face-to-face interviews, information is revealed that would never be written. In these situations, research in the local market not only will supply information on market definition and projection but also will assist in the formulation of an effective marketing mix.

Research in the Local Market

When a firm's research personnel have had no experience in the country, management should probably hire a local research group to do the work. Generally, home-country research techniques may be used,

though they may need to be adapted to local conditions. It is imperative, therefore, that the person in charge of the project have experience either in that country or in one that is culturally similar and preferably in the same geographic area.

If secondary data are unavailable, the researchers must collect primary data, and here they face other complications caused by *cultural problems* and *technical difficulties*.

Cultural Problems

If the researchers are from one culture and are working in another, they may encounter some cultural problems. When they are not proficient in the local language or dialect, the research instrument or the respondents' answers must be translated. As we learned in Chapter 4's discussion of sociocultural forces, a number of languages may be spoken in a country, and even in countries where only one language is used, a word's meaning may change from one region to another.

Other cultural problems plague researchers as they try to collect data. Low levels of literacy may make the use of mail questionnaires virtually impossible. If a husband is interviewed in a market where the wife usually makes the buying decisions, the data obtained from him may be worthless. Nor is it always clear who should be interviewed. Respondents sometimes refuse to answer questions because of their general distrust of strangers. In other instances, the custom of politeness toward everyone will cause respondents to give

Exhibitors and attendees at CeBIT Trade Fair.

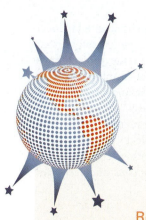

GLOBAL
gauntlet

Clotaire Rapaille: Charlatan or Code Breaker Extraordinaire in International Market Research?

Clotaire Rapaille is a charlatan—or possibly an adviser your company simply cannot do without. Originally a psychologist treating autistic children in Europe, Rapaille now operates from a mansion in upstate New York, where top management seek his advice on "the code" that will allow them access to the Indian, French, or Norwegian psyche. And from there, this insight should help them understand the motivations that will draw these people to buy their products.

Rapaille's earlier insights came when comparing French and American attitudes toward cheese. For the French, he says, cheese is alive, and the French would not put cheese in the refrigerator any more than one would put one's cat in the fridge. Both are "alive." But for Americans, Rapailles's insight is that cheese is "dead," so Americans seal it in a plastic "casket" and put it in a refrigerator, which is really a "morgue." Americans are more concerned about safety than taste: the French

reverse these preferences. So more French than American consumers die from eating cheese: but the Americans eat a relatively sterile and tasteless product, while the French enjoy a variety of cheeses that Americans cannot fathom.

Rapaille was also influential in the development of Chrysler's PT Cruiser, the retro car that has enjoyed great success. He has in total 50 of the Fortune 100 firms as clients. His claim is that teams under his direction have "broken the code" for

"anti-Americanism," "China," "seduction," the "teen Internet," and more. A recent excursion to India led him to pronounce that the caste system was simply a "practical" way of signaling to all their places in society. "It's not a problem, it's a solution," he summarizes.

Rapaille displays a certain confidence bordering on arrogance, and he follows a research method that is unusual, to say the least. Rather than relying on focus groups or surveys, he "breaks the code" of certain countries in roughly three-hour sessions. In these sessions, paid respondents first discuss the topic of interest; then they are asked to tap into their emotional reactions; and finally Rapaille explores, as he puts it, their "reptilian brain." It is the last that he finds useful. "Never believe what people say," Rapaille says. "I want to understand why people do what they do." Ultimately, he has respondents on the floor in the fetal position, reliving childhood memories.

From this process, he says, he discovers cultural archetypes, which are long lasting, although opinions may change more readily.

Former clients have scoffed at him, using "the cheese is dead" as a constant mantra, mocking his methods. For others, the idea that complex attitudes (such as the German code for Americans, which is "John Wayne") can be summarized in a word or phrase is, well, silly. Yet many of the same clients come back to him—P&G has come back 35 times.

As a manager, why would you—or why would you not—hire Clotaire Rapaille or his company to assist you in assessing and interpreting international market opportunities?

Sources: Danielle Sacks, "Crack This Code," *Fast Company,* April 2006, pp. 97–101, www.pbs.org/wgbh/pages/frontline/shows/persuaders/interviews/rapaille.html (accessed October 3, 2006); www.archetype discoveries.com (accessed June 9, 2010); "The Last Word: Clotaire Rapaille," *Newsweek,* international ed., www.msnbc.msn.com/id/4710897 (accessed October 4, 2006) and "Archetype Discoveries Worldwide," http://www.rapailleinstitute.com/ (accessed June 9, 2010).

answers calculated to please the interviewer; this is known as **social desirability bias.**

Often, people have practical reasons for not wanting to be interviewed. In some countries, income taxes are based on the apparent worth of individuals as measured by their tangible assets. In such countries, when asked if there is a stereo or TV in the household, the respondent may suspect the interviewer of being a tax assessor and refuse to answer. To overcome such a problem, experienced researchers often hire college students as interviewers because their manner of speech and their dress correctly identify them as what they are.

Technical Difficulties
As if the cultural problems were not enough, researchers may also encounter technical difficulties. First, up-to-date maps are often unavailable. The streets chosen for sampling may have three or four different names along their length, and the houses may not be numbered. In Japan, it is said, only cab drivers can find street addresses. Telephone surveys can be a formidable undertaking.[5]

Mail surveys can be troublesome too, as mail deliveries within a city may take weeks or are sometimes not made at all. For instance, the postal service in Italy has sometimes been so slow (two weeks for a letter to go from Rome to Milan) that some Italian firms have used private couriers to go to Switzerland to dispatch their foreign mail. The response to a mail survey is often low if the respondent must go to the post office to mail a letter. To increase returns, firms often offer such premiums as lottery tickets or product samples to persons who complete a mail questionnaire.

Research As Practiced
The existence of hindrances to marketing research does not mean it is not carried out in foreign markets. As you might surmise from the discussion of the availability of secondary data, marketing research is highly developed in many areas where markets are large and incorrect decisions are costly. Problems like the ones we have mentioned are prevalent in the developing nations, but they are well known to those who live there. It does not take long for the newcomer to become aware of them either, because longtime residents are quick to point them out.

Analysts tend to do less research and use simpler techniques in these nations because often the firm is in a seller's market, which means everything produced can be sold with a minimum of effort. Moreover, competition is frequently less intense

in developing nations because (1) there are fewer competitors and (2) managements are struggling with problems other than marketing, which keep them from devoting more time to marketing issues. Even in Mexico, an important market for American firms, marketing research is less popular.[6] Although the situation is changing, the most common technique continues to be a combination of trend analysis and the querying of knowledgeable persons such as salespeople, channel members, and customers. Researchers then adjust the findings on the basis of subjective considerations.

LO6 Discuss the different options for collecting survey-based research data.

Collecting Data Using Surveys

How can companies begin to get that elusive "feel" for a country from survey data? As we mentioned, one way is to do it yourself via surveys and personal visits. Two other methods involve the use of an outside firm. Under one scenario, you can hire an outside firm to do customized research for your firm's needs. The second involves using surveys that are administered only partially, or not at all, with your specific firm in mind.

Customized Research
Many firms that can do multicountry surveys on behalf of clients belong to ESOMAR (http://www.esomar.org), the European Society of Opinion and Marketing Research. Originally the member-firms were European, but there are now 5,000 members from more than 100 countries.

Consumer products firms often utilize ethnographic research techniques, sometimes referred to as "corporate anthropology," to develop detailed understanding. A number of firms specialize in this type of research. These firms do extensive "on-the-ground" research, watching consumers actually use products, rather than relying on surveys or focus groups. An example of these specialist firms is Point Forward (www.pointforward.com). In one project, Point Forward helped Wrigley examine attitudes toward breath-freshening aspects of

Social desirability bias The custom of politeness toward everyone that can cause respondents to give answers calculated to please the interviewer rather than to reflect the respondent's true beliefs or feelings

cu_{in}ib

Chad Henry: What Happened with an Internship to Croatia

I was born and raised in Sacramento, California, and went to Cal Poly–San Luis Obispo on a full scholarship to play college football. I initially intended to study architectural engineering, but switched into business administration with a concentration in finance.

After completing my degree and collegiate athletic career, I was searching for a direction that I should take with my career. I wanted to do something different with my life other than the traditional opportunities that were being offered. I didn't see myself as a traditional "finance" guy and was uncertain if these traditional careers paths would bring personal fulfillment. With the influence of my parents and sports, I had already traveled extensively throughout the United States and thought to myself, "why not take a step into a new frontier?" At the time, I didn't realize or think about the magnitude of such a decision. As a young man, to me it was an opportunity to work and live abroad.

I ended up applying for and accepting an AIESEC internship to Croatia, a place I knew almost nothing about. I tried to gather as much information as possible about Croatia before leaving. Due to a short time frame, approximately three weeks, I didn't place much thought into my travel. My main preparation focused on understanding exactly where I was going, ensuring that it was safe, and preparing information for my parents so they knew where I was going. The information I gathered was very general.

My internship was only for 12 months. However, I enjoyed the experience and ultimately became fluent with the language, took on a range of different jobs, and lived in Croatia for about 10 years. It was an exciting time in a country undergoing many changes. During this time, I lived in the cities of Split, Varazdin, and Zagreb. I also traveled to a number of countries, including the U.S., Canada, the UK, Netherlands, Denmark, Finland, Germany, Austria, Spain, Italy, France, Belgium, Luxembourg, Switzerland, Poland, Czech Republic, Slovakia, Slovenia, Romania, Bulgaria, Hungary, Croatia, Serbia, Bosnia and Herzegovina, Montenegro, Russia and the Ukraine.

Among the jobs that I pursued during my decade abroad, I had positions in export development, strategic development and management consulting (on issues of foreign direct investment, business zone development, organic farming cooperatives, and business process management), investment development (creating a food processing facility), commercial real estate development (for Arena Zagreb, a multi-functional sports hall with 16,000 seats; Arena Centar, a multi-functional shopping and entertainment center; and Ciovo tourist development), and start-up development. I also played professional baseball for a Croatian team and coached a team playing American football.

The keys to my successful adjustment while away from the U.S. included keeping a very open mind and maintaining my determination to succeed. This latter trait helped me deal with challenges as they presented themselves. The biggest challenges I confronted were learning to accept things as they are without making value judgments, remembering that things are more relative rather than absolute. While as individuals we are taught a certain way to do things or approach situations, this doesn't make it right or wrong. When you can learn to accept different viewpoints and see the value in them—even if not necessarily agreeing with them— then it allows you to enjoy and adapt to the culture in which you are immersed.

My greatest enjoyment from my time abroad included learning to successfully manage people who have intrinsically different values in regards to work; finding a way to work with people and get the most out of them; and being accepted by peers and friends in another culture. The greatest learning points from my international experience included developing my ability to see and understand things from multiple perspectives and learning to adapt and

chewing gum, leading to a new Wrigley campaign in China. Another firm is Envirosell (www.envirosell.com), which specializes in research on shopping. A third firm, QualiData Research Inc., found that in Islamic households, men's and women's clothing were usually washed separately.

General Surveys

General surveys are not done with a specific firm in mind. There are three types of general survey. The first is the *omnibus survey*. Omnibus surveys are regularly scheduled surveys conducted by research agencies with questions from different clients (i.e., they are wholly or partially "syndicated"). Because several firms contribute questions, the cost is spread across several users and the surveys are relatively fast. However, these surveys can ask only a limited number of questions that are directly relevant to a particular client, and the sample may not be representative of a particular firm's potential target market.

One example of a firm involved in administering omnibus surveys is A.C. Nielsen (www.acnielsen.com). Although we may know Nielsen best from the "Nielsen ratings," its TV-watching media measurement service, the firm offers services in more than 100 countries. Nielsen does an omnibus survey in China, among other countries. Another familiar firm—the Gallup Organization (www.gallup.com)—is also involved in this type of research in a variety of countries.

In the second type of noncustomized general survey, market research firms do surveys of their own design and whose results they then market to a variety of firms. An example is the Asian Pacific Consumer Confidence Poll in 13 Asian Pacific markets, a Nielsen survey. Nielsen can even track TV-watching habits in China and India. Another firm that does industry-level surveys spanning a number of countries for general sale is Frost & Sullivan (www.frost.com).

Nonprofit Surveys

The third type of survey is administered by a government or nongovernment agency, generally not for profit. The Eurobarometer surveys (http://ec.europa.eu/public_opinion/index_en.htm) are administered several times a year to thousands of respondents in European countries, under the auspices of the European Commission. Recent reports of Eurobarometer results with implications for consumer behavior include reports on attitudes toward vacations, food product safety, young people and drugs, and the family. Although these surveys are not specifically directed toward consumption issues, they are free and may be useful. A similar survey, called a *barómetro,* is conducted annually in 18 Latin American countries (www.latinobarometro.org).

The Internet

Internet research is increasingly an option, and we are gradually moving toward a time when the technology of Internet surveys may offer any firm the opportunity to do its own surveys anywhere in the world. For example, in 2007 Publicis Groupe used the Internet to tap into French voters' views on French presidential elections. The use of the Internet allowed the firm to set up a blog as a substitute for a three-hour focus group session. The blog allowed participants to discuss their opinions over a two-week period. By the end of the survey period, the consensus had changed: Nicolas Sarkozy moved from "scary" as an unknown to someone

> " INTERNET RESEARCH IS INCREASINGLY AN OPTION, AND WE ARE GRADUALLY MOVING TOWARD A TIME WHEN THE TECHNOLOGY OF INTERNET SURVEYS MAY OFFER ANY FIRM THE OPPORTUNITY TO DO ITS OWN SURVEYS ANYWHERE IN THE WORLD. "

articulating the need for change in France. Not only did the longer period result in a change of opinion, but 250 participants could be involved.

LO7 **Explain** the difference between country screening and segment screening.

SEGMENT SCREENING

As was mentioned earlier, when a company intends to do business in several countries, managers can choose two broad market screening approaches: country segments or market segments. In the first approach, Brazil may be viewed as a target market segment. Using the second approach, while Brazil is the physical location of a large group of consumers, the important variables for segmentation are commonalities in needs and wants among consumers *across nationalities*. These consumers may reside in different countries and speak different languages, but they have similar desires for a product or service. From this perspective, age, income, and psychographics (lifestyles) are the essential means of identifying market segments. The relevant marketing question is not where consumers reside but whether they share similar wants and needs. The targeted consumers may be global teens, middle-class executives, or young families with small children: each of these segments may share wants and needs across borders. An example comes from "phone surfers"—young Japanese who actively use their mobile phones to surf the Internet. The small phone screen and tiny keys may be a turnoff for older computer users in the West who have frequent and easy access to desktop or laptop PCs. But youngsters in the West have grown up with Nintendo DS devices, cell phone texting, and iPod nanos, and they readily

Because we usually organize the world mentally in terms of countries, we naturally tend to want to analyze markets as country segments. It is much more difficult to think of ourselves as market segments that extend across borders. Also, as was mentioned in the discussion of sociocultural differences, these data can be difficult to secure. Nonetheless, it is important to do this because this approach is the logical outgrowth of the marketing concept. And the fact that certain types of data are difficult to gather does not mean that the data can be ignored. There is an old saying about research: "If you can count it, that ain't it." In our context, the easy-to-generate data are not necessarily the important data.

Criteria for Identifying and Assessing Segments

Among the criteria managers should use when identifying and assessing segments, it is important that these segments be:

1. *Definable.* We should be able to identify and measure segments. The more we rely not on socioeconomic indicators but on lifestyle differences, the more difficult this becomes, but the more accurate the resulting analysis is likely to be.

2. *Large.* Segments should be large enough to be worth the effort needed to serve a segment. Of course, as we get closer to flexible manufacturing, the need to find large segments is beginning to recede. Further, the segments should have the potential for growth in the future.

3. *Accessible.* If we literally cannot reach our target segment for either promotional or distribution purposes, we will be unsuccessful.

4. *Actionable.* If we cannot bring components of marketing programs (the 4 Ps of product, promotion, place, and price) to bear, we may not be successful. For example, in Mexico, the price of tortillas was formerly controlled by the government.

> "There is an old saying about research: 'If you can count it, that ain't it.' In our context, the easy-to-generate data are not necessarily the important data."

adapt to the small screens and tiny buttons that are a part of using cell phones as an Internet device. On the other hand, baby boomers—whether in London, Los Angeles, or Lima, Peru—resist the thought of needing hearing aids. Swiss-based Phonak Group makes aids in 15 colors, fashions them like an ear phone, and calls them a "personal communication assistant" around the world. Also, because women around the world are buying similar clothing and cosmetics on the Internet, beauty regimens are becoming more universal.

Therefore, competition on the price variable was impossible. Foreigners could not penetrate the Mexican market for the standard tortilla by offering a lower price.

5. *Capturable.* Although we would love to discover market segments whose needs are completely unmet, in many cases these market segments are already being served. Nonetheless, we may still be able to compete. Where segments are completely "captured" by the competition, however, our task is much more difficult.[7]

Two Screening Methods, Reconsidered

In the final analysis, our view of the rest of the world is organized along national lines. However, it may be useful to attempt to leave that viewpoint behind when examining international markets.

With the increasing recognition of the existence of subcultures *within* nations and similarities between subcultures *across* nations, the international businessperson may wish to expand his or her horizon beyond the conventional view of the nation as the relevant "unit of analysis."

The next chapter takes up a series of related questions. Are our needs and desires becoming more and more alike, or are the differences in consumption preferences between us more relevant than the similarities? ▪

entry modes

"Our development strategy adapts to different markets addressing local needs and requirements. We currently use three business strategies: joint ventures, licenses, and company-owned stores."

—Starbucks Corporation

A cross industry after industry, market leaders rise, then plummet, sometimes disappearing completely. Compaq was once the undisputed leader in laptops and is now not even a minor player. Not all pioneers capitalize on their potential advantages, yet some evidence does suggest that pioneers gain and maintain a competitive edge in new markets. For instance, researchers have found that surviving pioneers hold a significantly larger average market share when their industries reach maturity than do firms that were either fast followers or late entrants in the product category.

On the other hand, as Compaq illustrates, pioneers can certainly fail. One recent study that took failed pioneers into account and averaged their performances with those of the more successful survivors found that, overall, pioneers did not perform as well over the long haul as followers. Of course,

LEARNING OBJECTIVES

After reading this chapter, you should be able to:

LO1 **Explain** the pros and cons of being a "market pioneer" versus being a "fast follower."

LO2 **Explain** the international market entry methods.

LO3 **Identify** two forms of piracy, and discuss how they both help and harm firms doing international business.

LO4 **Discuss** why firms export and the three challenges of exporting.

what measures are used can be important here: volume and market share are not the only dimensions by which success can be measured. The truth is that there really is little evidence one way or the other concerning the effect of the *timing* of a firm's entry into a new market on its ultimate profitability in that market or the value it generates for shareholders.

In many cases a firm entering into international markets becomes a follower by default, because a quicker competitor simply beats it by entering into the market first. But even when a company has the capability of being the first-mover, there are possible advantages to letting others go first and shoulder the initial risks while the follower observes the pioneers' shortcomings and mistakes.

A pioneering firm stands the best chance for long-term success in market-share leadership and profitability when (1) the pioneering firm is insulated from the entry of competitors (high entry barriers), at least for a while, by strong patent protection, proprietary technology (such as a unique production process), or substantial investment requirements; or (2) the firm has sufficient size, resources, and competencies to take full advantage of its pioneering position and preserve it in the face of later competitive entries. Indeed, some recent evidence suggests that organizational competencies such as R&D and marketing skills not only affect a firm's success as a pioneer but also influence the company's decision about whether to be a pioneer in the first place. Firms that lack the competencies necessary to sustain a first-mover advantage may be more likely to wait for another company to take the lead and then enter the market later.

On the other hand, a follower will most likely succeed when there are few legal, technological, cultural, or financial barriers to inhibit entry (low entry barriers) and when it has sufficient resources or competencies to overwhelm the pioneer's early advantage. The most successful fast followers tend to have the resources to enter the new market on a larger scale than the pioneer. Thus, they can quickly reduce their unit costs and offer lower prices than incumbent competitors.[1]

Thus, the evidence is not clear on whether the firm should be first—or nearly first—into a foreign market. Even after that decision, we have other decisions to make regarding which entry mode the firm should use in entering the market first (or not). ∎

ENTERING FOREIGN MARKETS

As you learned in Chapter 1, we can use a variety of names to identify large firms that operate on a multicountry scale: *global, multidomestic,* and *international* firm or company; *multinational enterprise (MNE)* or *multinational company (MNC); international company (IC); transnational company;* and even *multicultural multinational company.* Long before companies become any of these, however, they are usually smaller companies with only domestic experience. In this chapter we examine the very start—that is, the entry into international operations. We first examine nonequity modes of market entry, followed by equity-based modes.

Nonequity Modes of Entry

Most firms begin their involvement in overseas business by exporting—that is, selling some of their regular production overseas. This method requires little investment and is relatively free of risks. It is an excellent means of getting a feel for international business without committing a great amount of human or financial resources. If management does decide to export, it can choose between *direct* and *indirect* exporting. Management can also consider the use of nonequity options such as turnkey projects, licensing, franchising, management contracts, and contract manufacturing.

> **"The evidence is not clear on whether the firm should be first—or nearly first—into a foreign market."**

indirect exporting The exporting of goods and services through various types of home-country based exporters

direct exporting The exporting of goods and services by the firm that produces them

sales company A business established for the purpose of marketing goods and services, not producing them

licensing A contractual arrangement in which one firm grants access to its patents, trade secrets, or technology to another for a fee

Indirect Exporting

Indirect exporting is simpler than direct exporting because it requires neither special expertise nor large cash outlays. Exporters based in the home country do the work. Those exporters are called a number of different things, including (1) *manufacturers' export agents,* who sell for the manufacturer, (2) *export commission agents,* who buy for their overseas customers, (3) *export merchants,* who purchase and sell for their own accounts, and (4) *international firms,* which use the goods overseas (mining, construction, and petroleum companies are examples).

Indirect exporters, however, pay a price for such service: (1) they pay a commission to the first three kinds of exporters, (2) foreign business can be lost if exporters decide to change their sources of supply, and (3) firms gain little experience from these transactions. This is why many companies that begin in this manner generally change to direct exporting.

Direct Exporting

To engage in **direct exporting,** the export business is handled by someone within the firm. The simplest arrangement is to give someone, often the sales manager, the responsibility for developing the export business. Domestic employees may handle the billing, credit, and shipping initially, and if the business expands, a separate export department may be set up. A firm that has been exporting to wholesale importers in an area and serving them with visits from either home office personnel or foreign-based sales representatives frequently finds that sales have grown to a point that will support a complete marketing organization.

Management may then decide to set up a **sales company** in the area. The sales company imports in its own name from the parent and invoices in local currency. It may employ the same channels of distribution, although the new organization may permit the use of a more profitable arrangement. This type of organization can grow quite large, often invoicing several millions of dollars annually. Before building a plant in Mexico, for many years Eastman Kodak imported and resold cameras and photographic supplies while doing a large business in local film developing. Many firms that began with local repair facilities later expanded to produce simple components. Gradually, they produced more of the product locally until, after a period of time, they were manufacturing all the components in the country.

The Internet has made direct exporting much easier. For the beginning exporter, the possibility of making availability of your product or service known abroad is dramatically increased. And although it is likely that a substantial international presence on the Internet will require a significant investment, the cost of trial is now very low.

Turnkey Projects

A *turnkey project* is an export of technology, management expertise, and, in some cases, capital equipment. The contractor agrees to design and erect a plant, supply the process technology, provide the necessary suppliers of raw materials and other production inputs, and then train the operating personnel. After a trial run, the facility is turned over to the purchaser.

The exporter of a turnkey project may be a contractor that specializes in designing and erecting plants in a particular industry, such as petroleum refining or steel production. It may also be a company in the industry that wishes to earn money from its expertise by delivering a plant ready to run rather than merely selling its technology. Another kind of supplier of a turnkey project is the producer of a factory.

LO3 **Identify** two forms of piracy, and discuss how they both help and harm firms doing international business.

Licensing

Frequently, worldwide companies are called on to furnish technical assistance to firms that have sufficient capital and management strength. By means of a **licensing** agreement, one firm (the licensor) will grant to another firm (the licensee) the right to use any kind of expertise, such as manufacturing processes (patented or unpatented), marketing procedures, and trademarks for one or more of the licensor's products.

The licensee generally pays a fixed sum when signing the licensing agreement and then pays a royalty of 2 to 5 percent of sales over the life of the contract (five to seven years with an option for renewal is one common way to structure such agreements). The exact amount of the royalty will depend on the amount of assistance given and the relative bargaining power of the two parties. In 2009, the total paid to American firms in foreign royalties and license fees amounted to $84.4 billion, an actual decline of 7.8 percent from 2008.

In the past, licensing was not a primary source of income for international firms due to patent infringement, which can

> ## Most firms begin their involvement in overseas business by exporting—that is, selling some of their regular production overseas.

franchising A form of licensing in which one firm contracts with another to operate a certain type of business under an established name according to specific rules

management contract An arrangement by which one firm provides management in all or specific areas to another firm

contract manufacturing An arrangement in which one firm contracts with another to produce products to its specifications but assumes responsibility for marketing

be considered a form of piracy. Licensing has changed in recent years, however, especially in the United States, because (1) the courts began upholding patent infringement claims more than they used to, (2) patent holders became more vigilant in suing violators, and (3) the federal government pressed foreign governments to enforce their patent laws.

As a result, more companies at home and abroad began to obtain licenses instead of making illegal copies. Texas Instruments (TI), for example, sued nine Japanese electronics manufacturers for using its patented processes without paying licensing fees. The defendants have paid TI more than $1 billion since 1986. Although the company does not publish its royalty receipts in its income statements, here's an idea of the magnitude of the earnings from royalties associated with TI's 6,000 patents: TI announced 10-year agreements with both Hyundai Electronics and Samsung Electronics projected to yield royalty payments of more than $1 billion.

In addition to having to protect their property against patent piracy, the beginning exporter may find that real piracy, as in the movie *Pirates of the Caribbean,* is a threat to precious cargo as well as to sailors. Most ships are relatively defenseless: crews are small and seldom carry weapons. They rely instead on antipiracy devices, such as carpet tacks spread on decks, fire hoses, deck patrols, dummies set at the railings at night, brilliant deck lights, and new satellite tracking devices that can help the International Maritime Bureau and local navies locate hijacked ships. But it is nearly impossible to keep determined pirates off a ship, and it is best for a crew not to resist (as in many cases pirates do not kidnap or kill). Some shipping companies that have the resources have employed more high-tech and expensive measures, such as wiring decks to administer lethal electric charges, closed-circuit TV cameras to detect someone slipping aboard a ship, and, particularly in the case of cruise ships, armed mercenaries (some cruise lines are known to use Nepalese Gurkhas).

Piracy incidents rose in 2009, surpassing the previous record set in 2008 (406 registered cases compared with 293 in 2008). And they were more dangerous, with 35 percent of incidents involving guns. Pirates today can be anyone from highly trained guerrillas to rogue military units (such as in Indonesia) to international criminal gangs or cartels. Pirates might belong

to international terrorist organizations (particularly Abu Sayyaf out of the Philippines, which has strong links to al Qaeda as well as to Asian crime syndicates and the heroin trade), or they might simply be local down-and-out fishermen who see a rich prize steaming by and can't resist trying to capture it. Poverty has driven many to piracy in the Caribbean, Somalia, Nigeria, Bangladesh, and elsewhere. On a brighter note, a recent study finds that there hasn't been an increase in the connection between piracy and terrorism. Although both are rising, piracy for financial gain is rising faster.

The center of piracy has traditionally been Southeast Asia around Indonesia. However, while Indonesian incidents decreased from a high of 121 in 2003 to just 15 incidents in 2009, increases have been seen off the coast of Africa, particularly in Nigeria and Somalia. Somali pirates made 217 attacks in 2009 versus 111 in 2008.

Technology is not the only thing that is licensed to support a firm's market entry. In the fashion industry, a number of designers license the use of their names. Pierre Cardin, one of the largest such licensors, reported more than 900 licenses in more than 170 countries for everything from a broad range of clothing to such items as skis, frying pans, sardines, floor tiles, and silk cigarettes. These licenses have earned the company approximately $75 million annually. As Cardin himself commented, "If someone asked me to do toilet paper, I'd do it. Why not?"[2]

Are you giving Coca-Cola free advertising on your T-shirt? The company's manager for merchandise licensing expects the company to make millions from an agreement with the founder of Gloria Vanderbilt. He says the firm agreed to the arrangement because "clothes enhance our image. The money is not important."

Another industry, magazine publishing, is licensing overseas editions. For example, you can buy *Cosmopolitan* in more than 100 countries, and it is printed in 34 different languages.[3] *Playboy* is available in 20 different international editions, including in Indonesia.[4]

Despite the opportunity to obtain a sizable income from licensing, many firms, especially those that produce high-tech products, still will not grant licenses. They fear that a licensee will become a competitor upon expiration of the agreement or that the licensee will aggressively seek to market the products outside its territory. At one time, licensors routinely inserted a clause in the licensing agreement that prohibited exports, but most governments will not accept such a prohibition.

Franchising Firms have also gone overseas with a different kind of licensing—**franchising.** Franchising permits the franchisee to sell products or services under a highly publicized brand name and a well-proven set of procedures with a carefully developed and controlled marketing strategy. Of some 500 U.S. franchisers with approximately 50,000 outlets worldwide,

> " There hasn't been an increase in the connection between piracy and terrorism. Although both are rising, piracy for financial gain is rising faster. "

A woman sits beside her stall with Pierre Cardin shirts on a Hanoi street in June 2004. The shirts are made under French designer Pierre Cardin's firm license by a local garment factory. Each shirt sells for around 10 U.S. dollars.

fast-food operations (such as McDonald's, KFC, Subway, and Pizza Hut) are the most numerous—on one "Top 10 franchises" list, the franchise that has the greatest international presence is Japanese-owned 7-Eleven, with 26,680 foreign franchises, about one-third of them in Japan. Other types of franchisers are hotels (Intercontinental), business services (Muzak, The UPS Store), fitness (Curves, Jazzercise), building maintenance (Service-Master, Nationwide Exterminating), and real estate (ReMax).

Management Contract

The **management contract** is an arrangement under which a company provides managerial know-how in some or all functional areas to another party for a fee that typically ranges from 2 to 5 percent of sales. International companies make such contracts with (1) firms in which they have no ownership (e.g., Hilton Hotel provides management for nonowned overseas hotels that use the Hilton name, and Delta provides management assistance to foreign airlines), (2) joint venture partners, and (3) wholly owned subsidiaries. The last arrangement is made solely for the purpose of allowing the parent to siphon off some of the subsidiary's profits. This becomes extremely important when, as in many foreign exchange–poor nations, the parent firm is limited in the amount of profits it can repatriate. Moreover, because the fee is an expense, the subsidiary receives a tax benefit.

Contract Manufacturing

International firms employ **contract manufacturing** in two ways. One way is as a means of entering a foreign market without investing in plant facilities. The firm contracts with a local manufacturer to produce products for it according to its specifications. The firm's sales organization markets the products under its own brand.

The second way is to subcontract assembly work or the production of parts to independent companies overseas. Although the international firm has no equity in the subcontractor, this practice does resemble foreign direct investment. When the international firm is the largest or only customer of the subcontractors, it has in effect created in another country a new company that generates employment and foreign exchange for the host nation. Frequently, the international firm will lend capital to the foreign contractor in the same way that a global or multinational firm will lend funds to its subsidiary. Because of these similarities, this practice is sometimes called *foreign direct investment without investment.*

> "The international firm will lend capital to the foreign contractor in the same way that a global or multinational firm will lend funds to its subsidiary."

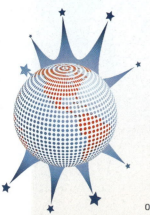

GLOBAL
gauntlet

Social Networking

With the increasing business being done on the Internet, it might seem that anyone can easily become an Internet entrepreneur. In reality, it might be a little more complicated.[5]

It's true that there is a worldwide presence on the Web. In the United States alone, some $1.5 billion worth of advertising will be done on social networking sites by 2012. MySpace, Facebook, and Hi5 have extensive foreign operations. For example, MySpace claims more than 93 million page views per month in Japan and has local operations in South Korea, India, and China. The French luxury company Cartier began featuring separate pages for its "Love by Cartier" product line on MySpace's UK, China, France, Italy, Spain, and Japan sites. Two things are interesting here. First, because MySpace is best known as a youth site, the advertising of luxury brands seems out-of-place—you wouldn't think the audience would be there. Love by Cartier, after all, also has a campaign on the elite, invite-only social network A Small World, which has a jet-set user base that seems a much more appropriate target for a pricey jewelry brand. But MySpace representatives say their image as a teen hangout is a bit misleading, citing ComScore statistics that estimate a quarter of its traffic comes from households with annual incomes greater than $100,000. Second, Cartier chose to enter MySpace's country-specific sites rather than stay with a single approach. Thus, for example, an Italian will see the site in Italian (written in Italian, not machine translated to Italian).

For deep penetration abroad, perhaps you also need to utilize localized or country-specific sites. This might give you a leg up when it comes to understanding the local environment, especially for younger citizens. In fact, of the 20 largest networking sites in the world, 10 of them are sites whose followers are primarily outside the U.S. Among these localized, country-, or regional-specific sites, are the following:

IN ASIA

In India, bigadda.com is popular. Bigadda has 5.5 million users. Hi5 is also popular in India (and Mongolia, Thailand, Romania, Jamaica, Central Africa and Latin America). In China, three social networks are popular: Renren.com, Kaixin001.com, and 51.com. Rumors periodically circulate that Facebook will enter China but it currently is not available there. MySpace does have a China site. In Korea, CyWorld.com is a major site, especially for young adults. There are 22 million registered users in South Korea, 6 million abroad in China and Vietnam. CyWorld has a major music component, and many Korean socialites and celebrities post their tours and news of their work on it.

IN EUROPE

MySpace.com proved to be the most popular social networking property in Germany, attracting 3.7 million unique visitors. But German site StudiVZalso recorded strong traffic, with 15 million visitors. Grono.net is popular in Poland, as is Vkontakte in Russia.

IN LATIN AMERICA

Several sites are well-established, including Orkut, Hi5, and Wamba. Another site that is important in Latin America is Sonico, based in Argentina. In addition, Peru is an Hi5 stronghold, Orkut is popular in Brazil, and Badoo is particularly strong in Venezuela.

Of course, the "just-around-the-corner" commercial battleground is mobile networking: 88 percent of Latin Americans own a mobile phone, versus the more than 60 percent worldwide average. And the largest single collection of cell phone users is in China.

Given the importance of appealing to local tastes, are the obstacles to exporting created by a two-tiered social networking structure, where many citizens access major worldwide sites such as Facebook and MySpace, but also access a local or regional network, significant enough that only the largest companies should attempt to do this?

Equity-Based Modes of Entry

When management does decide to make a foreign direct investment, it usually has several alternatives available, though not all of them may be feasible in a particular country:

1. Wholly owned subsidiary
2. Joint venture
3. Strategic alliances.

Wholly Owned Subsidiary A company that wishes to own a foreign subsidiary outright may (1) start from the ground up by building a new plant (greenfield investment); (2) acquire a going concern; or (3) purchase its distributor, thus obtaining a distribution network familiar with its products. In this last case, of course, production facilities will typically have to be built.

Historically, firms making a foreign direct investment have generally preferred wholly owned subsidiaries, but they have not had a marked preference for any of the three means of obtaining them. However, this has not been the case for foreign investors in the United States, who have demonstrated a general preference for acquiring going concerns for the instant access to the market they provide. Moreover, they also have one less competitor after the purchase. In 2007, 92 percent of the $276.8 billion that was invested in the United States was used to acquire existing companies, versus only $21.9 billion that was spent to create new businesses.

Sometimes it is not possible to have a wholly owned foreign subsidiary. The host government may not permit it, the firm may lack either capital or expertise to undertake the investment alone, or there may be tax and other advantages that favor another form of investment, such as a joint venture.

Joint Venture A **joint venture** may be (1) a corporate entity formed by an international company and local owners, (2) a corporate entity formed by two international companies for the purpose of doing business in a third market, (3) a corporate entity formed by a government agency (usually in the country of investment) and an international firm, or (4) a cooperative undertaking between two or more firms of a limited-duration project. Large construction jobs such as a dam or an airport are frequently handled by this last form.

Sometimes, forming a joint venture can allow the partners to avoid making expensive and time-consuming investments of their own, while simultaneously helping to avoid dangerous competition with another company.

When the government of a host country requires that companies have some local participation, foreign firms must engage in joint ventures with local owners to do business in that country. In some situations, however, a foreign firm will seek local partners even when there is no local requirement to do so.

joint venture A cooperative effort among two or more organizations that share a common interest in a business enterprise or undertaking

Strong Nationalism Strong nationalistic sentiment may cause the foreign firm to try to lose its identity by joining with local investors. Care must be taken with this strategy, however. Although a large number of people in many developing countries dislike multinationals for "exploiting" them, they still believe, often with good reason, that the products of the foreign companies are superior to those of purely national firms. One solution to this ambivalence has been to form a joint venture in which the local partners are highly visible, give it an indigenous name, and then advertise that a foreign firm (actually the partner) is supplying the technology. Even wholly owned subsidiaries have followed this marketing strategy.

Expertise, tax, and other benefits Other factors that influence companies to enter joint ventures are the ability to acquire expertise that is lacking, the special tax benefits some governments extend to companies with local partners, and the need for additional capital and experienced personnel.

Some firms, as a matter of policy, enter joint ventures to reduce investment risk. Their strategy is to enter into a joint venture with either native partners or another worldwide company. Still others have joined together to achieve economies of scale. Incidentally, any division of ownership in a joint venture is possible unless there are specific legal requirements.

Disadvantages of joint ventures Although a joint venture arrangement offers the advantage of a smaller commitment of financial and managerial resources and thus less risk, there are some disadvantages for the foreign firm. One, obviously, is that profits must be shared. Furthermore, if the law allows the foreign investor to have no more than 49 percent participation, it may not have control. If the stock markets in these countries are small or nonexistent, it is generally impossible to distribute the shares widely enough to permit the foreign firm with its 49 percent to be the largest stockholder.

Lack of control over the joint venture is the reason many companies resist making such arrangements. They feel that they must have tight control of their foreign subsidiaries to obtain an efficient allocation of investments and production and to maintain a coordinated marketing plan worldwide. For example, local partners might wish to export to markets that the global company serves from its own plants, or they might want to make the complete product locally when the global company's strategy is to produce only certain components there and import the rest from other subsidiaries.

In the recent past, numerous governments of developing nations have passed laws requiring local majority ownership for the purpose of giving control of firms within their borders to their own citizens. Despite these laws, control with a minority ownership may still be feasible.

strategic alliances Partnerships between or among competitors, customers, or suppliers that may take one or more of various forms, both equity and nonequity

Control of joint ventures through management contracts
Management contracts, which were discussed earlier in this chapter under nonequity-based modes of entry, can enable the global partner to control many aspects of a joint venture even when holding only a minority position. If it supplies key personnel, such as the production and technical managers, the global company can be assured of the product quality with which its name may be associated. It may also be able to earn additional income by selling the joint venture inputs manufactured in the home plant. This is possible because the larger global company is more vertically integrated. A local paint factory, for example, might have to import certain semiprocessed pigments and driers that the foreign partner produces in its home country for domestic operations. If these can be purchased elsewhere at a lower price, the local majority could insist on other sources of supply. This rarely happens, because the production and technical

managers can argue that only inputs from their employer will produce a satisfactory product. They are the experts, and they generally have the final word.

Strategic Alliances Faced with expanding global competition; the growing cost of research, product development, and marketing; and the need to move faster in carrying out their global strategies, many firms are forming **strategic alliances** with customers, suppliers, and competitors. In fact, in a 12-country study, consultants Ernst & Young found that 65 percent of non-U.S. and 75 percent of U.S. companies are engaged in some form of strategic alliance.[6] The aim of these companies is to achieve faster market entry and start-up; gain access to new products, technologies, and markets; and share costs, resources, and risks. Alliances include various types of partnerships and may or may not include equity. Companies wanting to share technology may cross-license their technology, with each licensing its technology to the other. If their aim is to pool research and design resources, they may form an R&D partnership.

CUinib

Vadim Rozhkov: International All the Way!

I was born in Ekaterinburg, Russia. I enjoy active sports, surfing, rally, boxing, and hiking. My hobbies include history, travel, applied science, and listening to classical music. I have a B.S. degree in mechanical engineering from Ural State University in Russia, then earned a B.S. in electrical engineering, M.S. in industrial technology, and M.B.A. from California Polytechnic State University in San Luis Obispo.

My interest in international business came up a bit unexpectedly, a result of my interest in global heavy industries and their involvement in international trade

and politics. Studying for my M.B.A. gave me a better understanding of global trade, including knowledge about the economic aspects of manufacturing and production, price formation, and cross-border tariffs.

> "My interest in international business came up a bit unexpectedly, a result of my interest in global heavy industries and their involvement in international trade"

I am a sales manager, involved directly in business-to-business sales. Sales managers at my company are given different countries of responsibility, and my assigned countries include Italy, Germany, and Mexico.

My job is to identify and contact a circle of potential customers, namely, companies that purchase tooling for operating large-scale metallurgical mills. I use an information-based approach to identifying customers. First, I trace metals prices on the LME (London Metal Exchange), and I usually have a good idea of the average price for my product in my assigned countries. Then I contact and visit representatives from these companies' technical maintenance, engineering, and purchasing departments. After the initial meeting, where I am given drawings and

Alliances May Be Joint Ventures Other companies carry the cooperation further by forming joint ventures in manufacturing and marketing.

Pooling versus Trading Alliances A useful distinction can be made between pooling and trading alliances. *Pooling alliances* are driven by similarity and integration, while *trading alliances* are driven by the logic of contributing dissimilar resources. These two types are typically different in their goals (common vs. compatible goals), optimal structures (many vs. few partners), and managerial challenges (low vs. high coordination needs).[7]

Alliances versus Mergers and Acquisitions Generally mergers and acquisitions are not considered alliances. However, both may be ways for firms to get their hands on new technology, by either acquiring or working with smaller, innovative firms. For example, the merger between Canadian brewer Molson and U.S. brewer Coors was analyzed by many as a union of two "struggling" mid-sized beer companies. The merged company in 2008 was part of a joint venture with the U.S. operations of SABMiller plc, the maker of Miller beer. Sandoz, a Swiss pharmaceutical manufacturer, acquired Gerber for $3.7 billion in order to double the size of its food products division. Two years later, because of the increased global competition and the

specifications of the product they are interested in, I work with my company's accounting department to calculate manufacturing costs, and I determine logistics and insurance expenses (I am in constant contact with different shipping companies). It usually takes a few days to come up with a final quote for the product and a delivery option. Most of my customers request CIF Incoterms, which means my company as the seller pays the cost, insurance and freight associated with shipping goods to the destination port. Then this quote is sent to my customer. If my customer accepts the price and delivery options, a purchasing/manufacturing contract is signed.

I visit a potential customer only once I am sure that I am well prepared for the trip, that the customer is expecting me, and that the topic of the visit is clearly laid out and ready for discussion. I usually have phone conversations in advance with the people I am intending on meeting during my visit. Not only do I know the financial aspect of

a possible deal, I also come very well prepared technically. I study the products my customers use. I know how my products are installed and operated within complex, large-scale metallurgical mills. It is very important that my customers see that I have deep technical understanding of products I am selling. I also study my competitors. I know the strong and weak points of their products, and I am knowledgeable about their business policies.

The biggest challenge of my job is coming to agreement with my international customers on common terms for the purchase. Cultural differences play a big role in dealing with people overseas and understanding the ways that people conduct their business in a particular country is crucially important. For example, as a result of my numerous business trips to Mexico, I have learned to respect the local pace of life. Sometimes rushing things will not necessarily make things happen more quickly!

The greatest enjoyment of my job, so far, was signing my first contract for supplying tooling to a company in Mexico. Actually, I was ecstatic, as it took me two years of work and relationship-building effort before this contract finally came through.

Doing business internationally teaches you a few great things. Patience is one of them. After all, you are a guest and a foreign business representative. Simply put, you are asking for a part of their business and you need them more than they need you.

In my opinion, to be successful in international business, you need common sense, cultural respect, and extensive knowledge of the subject or business area in which you are working. As for what NOT to do: never leave your customer aggravated, despite how ridiculous their suggestions or demands may seem. Even if you don't sign a deal today, make sure you will be able to come back tomorrow and have a friendly conversation with your potential customer.

mounting cost of technology, Sandoz and Ciba Geigy, another Swiss drug company, merged to form Novartis, which became the second-largest pharmaceutical firm in the world. In 2007, Novartis sold Gerber to Nestlé.

Future of Alliances Many alliances fail or are taken over by one of the partners. The existence of two or more partners—which are often competitors as well as partners and typically have differences in strategies, operating practices, and organizational cultures—often causes alliances to be difficult to manage, particularly in rapidly changing international competitive environments.[8] Alliances can also allow a partner to acquire the firm's technological or other competencies, thereby raising important competitive concerns. The management consulting firm McKinsey & Co. surveyed 150 companies whose alliances with Japanese partners had been terminated. It found that three-quarters of the alliances had been taken over by Japanese partners.

Despite the challenges involved with forming and managing alliances successfully, there is no question that some alliances have accomplished what they set out to accomplish. CFM International, the alliance between General Electric and France's Snecma (Société Nationale d'Étude et de Construction de Moteurs d'Aviation), has been producing jet engines for

some of their foreign markets by exporting because no firm, no matter how large, can afford to manufacture a complete product line in every country where its goods are sold. Markets without local factories are supplied through exports from the home country or from a foreign affiliate. In markets of sufficient size to justify the production of some but not all of the product mix, the affiliate will supplement local production with imports. A car plant in a developing nation may produce the least expensive cars and import luxury models. Also, the more vertically integrated plants may export semifinished products that are inputs for the less integrated subsidiaries.

- To satisfy a host government's requirement that the local subsidiary have exports. Governments of developing nations often require that the local affiliate export, and some require that it earn sufficient foreign exchange to cover the cost of its imports. This is why Ford located a radio plant in Brazil that exports to Ford's European assembly plants.

- To remain price competitive in the home market. Many firms import labor-intensive components produced in their foreign affiliates, or export components for assembly in countries where labor is less expensive and import the finished product.

- To test foreign markets and foreign competition inexpensively. This is a common strategy for firms that want to test a product's acceptance before investing in local production

> ## P&G began to introduce products on a worldwide basis early in their development to avoid giving competitors time to react in other markets.

more than two decades. Airbus SAS, an alliance among British, French, German, and Spanish aircraft manufacturers, is now a leading commercial aircraft producer. It seems that alliances in their various forms will continue to be used as important strategic and tactical weapons, particularly given the financial, technological, political, and other challenges facing companies involved in increasingly competitive international marketplaces.

L04 **Explain** why firms export.

THE CHALLENGES OF EXPORTING

Although this chapter has mentioned many obstacles to exporting, many firms, both large and small, do engage in exporting. Among the reasons:

- To serve markets where the firm has no or limited production facilities. Many large multinationals, like DuPont, supply

facilities. Exports may also enable firms to test market strategies and make adjustments with reduced risk in a smaller market. If the strategy or product fails, the firm can withdraw without having a costly and sometimes damaging failure to the entire firm. There is, however, a downside to this strategy: whatever the firm does in the foreign market may be seen by a competitor. This is especially true for large, global firms such as Unilever and Procter & Gamble (P&G). Former P&G CEO Edwin Artzt changed the company's strategy for introducing new products. Rather than postpone a global launch until the firm accumulated marketing experience in a country, P&G began to introduce products on a worldwide basis early in their development to avoid giving competitors time to react in other markets.

- To meet actual or prospective customer requests for the firm to export. This type of accidental exporting is fairly common. A foreign buyer often will search for something it cannot find locally by consulting the Internet or Thomas Net, a website listing North American producers for thousands of products.

- To offset cyclical sales in the domestic market.

- To achieve additional sales, which will allow the firm to use excess production capacity to lower per-unit fixed costs.

- To extend a product's life cycle by exporting to currently unserved markets where the product will be at the introduction stage of the life cycle.

- To respond strategically to foreign competitors that are in the firm's home market by entering their home market.

- To achieve the success the firm's management has seen others achieve by exporting.

- To improve the efficiency of manufacturing equipment, which usually works better at or near full capacity. ■

> "A global company should always go about its business in a way that's responsive to the major differences from one country to another, in terms of, for example, how retailing or distribution or payment systems work. But the core product or service should remain unchanged . . . since that is what is 'globalized.'"
>
> —Theodore Levitt, author of the landmark *Harvard Business Review* article on standardization, "The Globalization of Markets"

fourteen

marketing internationally

Whether a policy or technique is first designed for global use and then adapted for local market differences or the idea comes from the home country and then is used overseas, marketers must know where to look for possible differences between marketing domestically and marketing internationally. Marketers everywhere must know their markets; develop products or services to satisfy their customers' needs; price the products or services so that they are readily acceptable in the market; make them available to buyers; and inform potential customers, persuading them to buy.

LEARNING OBJECTIVES

After reading this chapter, you should be able to:

L01 **Explain** the differences between domestic and international marketing.

L02 **Discuss** why international marketing managers may wish to standardize the marketing mix.

L03 **Explain** why it is often impossible to standardize the marketing mix worldwide.

L04 **Explain** why consumer products generally require greater modification for international sales than do industrial products or services.

L05 **Discuss** some of the effects the Internet may have on international marketing.

L06 **Explain** "glocal" advertising strategies.

ADDED COMPLEXITIES OF INTERNATIONAL MARKETING

Although the basic functions of domestic and international marketing are the same, international markets served often differ widely because of the great variations in the uncontrollable environmental forces—sociocultural, resource and environmental, economic and socioeconomic, legal, financial, and labor—that we examined in Section Two. Moreover, even the forces we think of as controllable vary across markets within wide limits. For example, distribution channels to which the marketer is accustomed may be unavailable. Certain aspects of the product may need to be different, for a number of reasons that range from taste and aesthetic preferences to voltage patterns and altitude issues. Then, too, the promotional mixes often must be dissimilar. Finally, distinct cost structures of specific markets may require that different prices be set.

The international marketing manager's task is complex. She or he frequently must plan a variety of marketing strategies, rather than a single unified and standardized one, and then coordinate and integrate those strategies into a single marketing program. Even marketing managers of global firms who may want to use a single worldwide strategy realize that doing so is impossible. They must know enough about the uncontrollable variables to be able to make quick and decisive implementation changes when necessary.

THE MARKETING MIX (WHAT TO SELL AND HOW TO SELL IT)

The *marketing mix* is a set of strategy decisions made in the areas of product, promotion, pricing, and distribution in order to satisfy the needs and desires of customers in a target market.

The number of variable factors included in these four marketing areas is large, making possible hundreds of combinations. Often a company's domestic operation has already established a successful marketing mix, and the temptation to follow the same strategies and tactics overseas is strong. Yet, as we have seen, important differences between the domestic and foreign environments are likely to make a wholesale transfer of the mix—its standardization—impossible, however desirable such a transfer may be from a business viewpoint. The question that the international marketing manager must resolve for each market is, "Can we standardize worldwide, should we make some changes, or should we formulate a completely different marketing mix?"

Standardize, Adapt, or Formulate Anew?

Often, top management would prefer to standardize the marketing mix globally; that is, the strategic decision makers would prefer to use the same marketing mix in all of the firm's markets because standardization can produce significant cost savings. If the product sold in the domestic market can be exported, regardless of where the product is made, there can be longer production runs, which lower manufacturing costs. In addition to these economies of scale, the longer experience curve, or learning curve, can create economies as well: the more experience we have doing something, the better we get at that activity, usually. Both of these economies, scale and experience, apply to marketing. A standardized approach can result in significant savings.

When advertising campaigns, promotional materials (catalogs, point-of-purchase displays), and sales training programs can be standardized, the expensive creative work and artwork need be done only once. A standardized corporate visual identity (CVI -firm name, slogan, and graphics) can help project a consistent image for a multinational with publics dispersed across geographic locales.[1] Standardized pricing strategies for firms that serve markets from several different subsidiaries prevent the embarrassment of having an important customer receive two different price quotations for the same product. In summary, in addition to the cost benefits from standardizing the marketing mix, control and coordination are easier, and

> **BUT WHEN IT COMES TO QUESTIONS OF TASTE AND, ESPECIALLY, AESTHETIC PREFERENCE, CONSUMERS DO NOT LIKE AVERAGES. . . . THE LURE OF A UNIVERSAL PRODUCT IS A FALSE ALLURE.**
>
> —Kenichi Ohmae

time spent preparing the marketing plan is reduced significantly. Example: In 2009 Levi's standardized the fit of its 501 jeans worldwide, rather than have the fit vary by country, and launched its first global ad campaign.

In spite of the advantages of standardization, almost all firms find that the nearby quote by Kenichi Ohmae is accurate for them: standardization is seldom as easy as it seems. Many firms find it necessary to modify the present marketing mix or develop a new one. The extent of the changes depends on the type of product, the environmental forces, and the degree of market penetration desired. Further, given that the very concept of standardization is in a state of tension with the marketing principle—which centers on the needs of the buyer, not the seller—we probably should not be too disappointed that the economies that would come with complete standardization are seldom available to the seller, especially the seller of consumer goods.

Choosing not to market locally, Levi's 501 jeans are cut to fit the same way in every country.

Product Strategies

The product is the central focus of the marketing mix. If it fails to satisfy the needs of consumers, no amount of promotion, price cutting, or distribution will persuade people to buy. Consumers will not repurchase a detergent if the clothes do not come out as clean as commercials say they will. They will not be deceived by advertisements announcing friendly service if their own experience demonstrates otherwise.

In formulating product strategies, international marketing managers must remember that the product is more than a physical object. The **total product** is what the customer buys, including the physical product, brand name, accessories, after-sales service, warranty, instructions for use, company image, and package. The total product may present the company with product adaptation opportunities that are less expensive and easier than would be the case if every adaptation had to alter the product's physical characteristics. Different package sizes and promotional messages, for example, can create a new total product for a distinct market. The relative ease of creating a new total product without changing the manufacturing process explains why there is more physical product standardization internationally than one might expect. Remember that a product can be localized by adaptation of the package, brand name, accessories, after-sales service, warranty, instructions for use, company image, or any combination of these.

total product What the customer buys, including the physical product, brand name, accessories, after-sales service, warranty, instructions for use, company image, and package.

LO4 Explain why consumer products generally require greater modification for international sales than do industrial products or services.

Type of Product The amount of change to be made in a product is affected by whether it is a consumer or industrial product or service and by the foreign environmental forces. Generally, consumer products require greater adaptation than do industrial products. If the consumer products are stylish or the result of a fad, they are especially likely to require changes. These product types form a sensitivity continuum ranging from insensitive to the foreign environment to highly sensitive, as shown in Figure 14.1.

Industrial products As Figure 14.1 suggests, many industrial products can be sold unchanged worldwide. Memory chips, for example, are used wherever computers are manufactured. If product changes are required, they may be cosmetic—many shoes and other clothing items now provide information on sizes in a variety of systems.

When actual product adaptations are necessary, they may be relatively simple ones, such as lengthening pedals and changing seat positions to compensate for consumer preferences among markets. However, somewhat more drastic modifications in the physical product may be necessary. Adaptations are occasionally necessary to meet local legal requirements, such as those that govern noise, safety, or exhaust emissions. To avoid the need to change the product, some manufacturers design it to meet the most stringent laws even though it will be overdesigned for the rest of its markets. In some instances, governments have passed strict laws with the intent of protecting a local producer from import competition. When this occurs, the

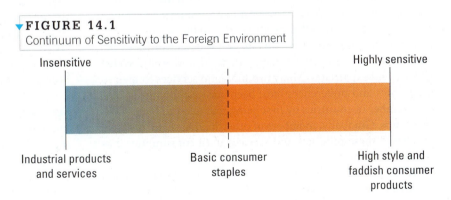

▼**FIGURE 14.1**
Continuum of Sensitivity to the Foreign Environment

Insensitive   Highly sensitive

Industrial products and services   Basic consumer staples   High style and faddish consumer products

company may prefer to design the product for the country with the next most stringent laws and stay out of the first market. Of course, this may be what the government had in mind when it passed the law. However, a word of caution based on one of the author's experiences: the company in this situation would be advised to test the local manufacturer's product before giving up on the market. On occasion, the local product also has failed to meet the specifications. When confronted with this evidence, the government has had to change its laws.

Consumer products Although consumer products generally require greater modification to meet local market requirements than do industrial products, some can be sold unchanged to certain market segments that have similar characteristics across countries. Consumer products of this kind include many luxury items, such as automobiles and perfumes. Every country contains a market segment that is more similar to the same segment in other countries with respect to economic status, buyer behavior, tastes, and preferences than it is to the rest of the segments in the same country. This market segment includes the cosmopolitan consumers: foreign-educated and well-traveled citizens and expatriates. Many products and services foreign to local tastes and preferences have been successfully introduced in a number of countries by first being marketed to these similar groups. Gradually, members of other market segments have purchased these products and services until consumption has become widespread.

While "jet-setters" may share much in common across countries, marketers tend to find greater dissimilarities in social and cultural values as they go down the economic strata in each country. It follows from this that, in general, the deeper the desired immediate market penetration is, the greater must be the product modification. Remember that this observation does not suggest that for deeper market penetration, the physical product has to be changed. Perhaps a modification of one of the other elements of the total product is sufficient—a different size or color of the package, a change in the brand name, or a new positioning, if the product is consumed differently. Different emphasis in after-sales service is also important.

An example illustrates the repositioning and repackaging possibilities. Mars, one of the largest privately owned and family operated companies, faced a drop in Bahrain's imports of candy when it was ready to launch M&M's. Fortunately, its marketing research discovered that Bahrainis consider the peanut to be healthy, so Mars repositioned its peanut M&M's as a health food. The company also was able to turn the hot Gulf climate to its advantage by emphasizing the packaging through its traditional slogan, "M&M's melt in your mouth, not in your hand." As you will see later in this chapter, Mars followed promotional strategy number 2, same product—different message, although even part of the message (the slogan) remained the same.

Services The marketing of services, like the marketing of industrial products, is generally less complex globally than is the marketing of consumer products. The consulting firm Accenture has over 190,000 employees in 52 countries offering the same kinds of business expertise as the firm provides in the United States.[2]

However, laws and customs sometimes do mandate that providers alter their services. For example, Manpower cannot operate in some markets because in those countries, private employment agencies are against the law. Accounting laws vary substantially among nations, but the large accounting firms operate globally, making local adaptations where necessary. PricewaterhouseCoopers has 163,545 professionals in 151 countries.[3]

A perfectly good brand name may have to be scrapped because of its unfavorable connotations in another language. An American product failed to survive in Sweden because its name translated to "enema." In Latin America, a product had to be taken off the market when the manufacturer found that the name meant "jackass oil." Of course, this problem occurs in both directions, as a Belgian brewery found when it tried to introduce its Delerium Tremens lager to the U.S. market.

"
Laws and customs sometimes do mandate that providers alter their services.
"

Foreign Environmental Forces

In Section Two we examined the foreign environmental forces extensively, so here we limit our discussion to a few concrete examples of how some of these forces might affect product offerings.

Sociocultural forces Dissimilar cultural patterns often require changes, either in the physical product or in aspects of the total product, in food and other consumer goods. Heinekin beer accounts for less than 20 percent of the total volume of beer sold by the company. The other 230 local brands—Tiger in Singapore, Star in Nigeria, Christal in Chile—are referred to by the CEO as "local treasures."

While some international firms, such as Campbell's, have been extremely successful in employing the same brand name, label, and colors worldwide, other firms learn they must change names, labels, or colors because of cultural differences. Gold appears frequently on packages in Latin America because Latin Americans view it as a symbol of quality and prestige. Procter & Gamble found that a gold package has value in Europe, too, after it launched its silver-boxed Crest Tartar Control Formula in the United Kingdom, which was followed two months later by Colgate's equivalent in a gold box. P&G officials agreed that Colgate's choice of gold was better than their silver. They explained that silver was how the product was packaged in the United States.[4] The meaning that colors have for people in different cultures is also a marketing consideration. For example, in the Netherlands blue is considered warm and feminine, but the Swedes consider it masculine and cold.

Even if the colors can remain the same, instructions on labels must be translated into the language of the market. Firms selling in areas where two or more languages are spoken, such as Canada, Switzerland, Belgium, and the United States, may need to use multilingual labels. Where instructions are not required, as in the case of some consumer or industrial products whose use is well known, there is an advantage to printing the label in the language of the country best known for the product. A French label on a perfume helps strengthen the product's image in the United States.

American authorities told the company the name was an incitement to drinking.[5] Sometimes a firm will not use a perfectly good name because the firm makes assumptions about the impact of the name on foreign locals and doesn't test these assumptions with locals. This is what happened with the Nova. As the story goes, Chevrolet couldn't sell Novas in (the storyteller picks a Spanish-speaking country) because Nova means *no va* ("doesn't go") in Spanish. But the two words are pronounced very differently—*Nova* has the accent on the first syllable, whereas the accent for *no va* falls on the *va*. Therefore, to someone speaking Spanish, the words have very different meanings. Native Spanish-speaking people would be likely to connect *nova* with "star," which is probably what General Motors had in mind. You may be surprised to learn that Pemex, the government-owned petroleum monopoly in Mexico, once called its regular gasoline *Nova*.

An important difference in social forces to which American marketers are not accustomed is people's preference in other nations for making daily visits to small neighborhood specialty shops and large, open markets where they can socialize while shopping. More frequent buying involves smaller packages, which is important to a shopper who has no automobile in which to carry purchases. However, this custom is changing in Europe, where consumers are demanding the kinds of assortments that only a large store can offer. Shopping frequency is also slowing as European women are finding that they have less shopping time than previously. The solution has been the huge combination supermarket–discount house (*hypermarché* in France) with ample parking, located in the suburbs.

Legal forces Legal forces can be a formidable constraint in the design of products because if the firm fails to adhere to a country's laws governing the product, it will be unable to do business in that country. Laws concerning pollution, consumer protection, and operator safety have been enacted in many parts of the world and limit the marketer's freedom to standardize the product mix internationally. For example, American machinery makers exporting to Sweden have found that Swedish operator safety requirements are stricter than those required by the

promotion Any form of communication between a firm and its publics

Occupational Safety and Health Act (OSHA), so if they wish to market in Sweden, they must produce a special model. Of course, product standards set ostensibly to protect a nation's citizens can be effective in protecting local industry from foreign competitors.

Foods and pharmaceuticals are especially influenced by laws concerning purity and labeling. Food products sold in Canada, whether imported or produced locally, are subject to strict rules that require both English and French on the labels as well as metric and inch/pound units. The law even dictates the space permitted between the number and the unit—"16 oz." is correct, but "16oz." is not. The Venezuelan government has decreed that the manufacturer or the importer must affix to the package the maximum retail price at which many products can be sold. Because of Saudi Arabians' concern about avoiding food containing pork, the label of any product containing animal fat or meat that is sold in Saudi Arabia must identify the kind of animal used or state that no swine products were used.

Legal forces may also prevent a worldwide firm from employing its brand name in all its overseas markets. Managements accustomed to the American law, which establishes the right to a brand name by priority in use, are surprised to learn that in code law countries, a brand belongs to the person registering it first. Thus, the marketer may go into foreign markets expecting to use the company's long-established brand name only to find that someone else owns it. The name may have been registered by someone who is employing it legitimately for his or her own products, or it may have been pirated, that is, registered by someone who hopes to profit by selling the name back to the originating firm.

To avoid this predicament, the firm must register its brand names in every country in which it might want to use them in

> ## "Foods and pharmaceuticals are especially influenced by laws concerning purity and labeling."

Pemex gasoline "doesn't go."

the future. And this must be done rapidly. The Paris Convention grants a firm that has registered a name in one country only six months' priority to register it elsewhere. To be certain that it has enough names for new products, Unilever, the English-Dutch manufacturer of personal care products, has more than 100,000 trademarks registered throughout the world, most of which are kept in reserve.

Economic forces The disparity in income throughout the world is an obstacle to worldwide product standardization. Some products are priced too high for some consumers in developing nations, and so the firm must adjust to the consumers' ability to pay. Such adjustments may include simplification or repackaging. Procter & Gamble sells shampoo for individual use in India, in addition to the regular bottle quantity. In addition, many consumers throughout the world buy cell phone airtime by purchasing prepaid cards worth only a few dollars or even by renting cell phones by the call from intermediaries.

In some cases, the foreign subsidiary cannot afford to produce as complete a product mix as does the parent. Most automobile manufacturers assemble the less expensive and higher-volume line locally and broaden the local product mix by importing the luxury cars. International firms practice this marketing technique whenever possible because a captive foreign sales organization is available to promote the sales of the home organization's exports and because the revenue derived helps pay the subsidiary's overhead. Yet GM has been successful with its Buick in China by introducing the Buick as a premium brand and then moving to mid-range and economy

Cooking at high altitudes requires companies to post alternative instructions on food packaging.

vehicles. Thanks to Buick, GM has 13.4 percent of the market in China and may sell more cars in China than in the U.S. in the future.[6]

Physical forces Physical forces, such as climate and terrain, also militate against international product standardization. Manufacturers of clothes washers have found success in India by "hardening" their machines against heat, dirt, and power outages. Consumer goods that are affected by moisture must be specially packaged to resist its penetration. Thus, pills are wrapped individually in foil and baked goods are packaged in tin boxes to prevent their degradation by moisture.

High altitudes frequently require product alteration. Food manufacturers have found that they must change their cooking instructions for people who live at high altitudes because at such altitudes cooking takes longer. The thinner atmosphere requires that producers of cake mixes include less yeast as well. Gasoline and diesel motors generate less power at high altitudes, so the manufacturer must often supply a larger engine.

Promotional Strategies

Promotion, one of the basic elements of the marketing mix, is communication that secures understanding between a firm and its publics to bring about a favorable buying action and achieve long-lasting confidence in the firm and the product or service it provides. Note that this definition employs the plural *publics,* because the seller's promotional efforts must be directed to more than just the ultimate consumers, including retailers and other members of the distribution channel.

Promotion both influences and is influenced by the other marketing mix variables. Nine distinct promotion strategies are possible, by combining the three alternatives of (1) marketing the same physical product everywhere, (2) adapting the physical product for foreign markets, and (3) designing a different physical product with (*a*) the same, (*b*) adapted, or (*c*) different messages.[7] Here we examine the six strategies most commonly used:

1. *Same product–same message.* When marketers find that target markets vary little with respect to product use and consumer attitudes, they can offer the same product and use the same promotional appeals in all markets. Avon, Maidenform, and A.T. Cross follow this strategy.

2. *Same product–different message.* The same product may satisfy a different need or be used differently elsewhere. This means the product may be left unchanged but a different message is required. Honda's early "You meet the nicest people on a Honda" campaign appealed to Americans who used their motorcycles as pleasure vehicles, but in Brazil Honda stressed the use of motorcycles as basic transportation.

3. *Product adaptation–same message.* In cases where the product serves the same function but must be adapted to different conditions, the same message is employed with a changed product. In Japan, Lever Brothers puts Lux soap in fancy boxes because much of it is sold as gifts.

4. *Product adaptation–message adaptation.* In some cases, both the product and the promotional message must be modified for foreign markets. In Latin America, Tang is specially sweetened, premixed, and ready to drink in pouches. In China, Tang comes in a box of single-serve powder sticks with a "Tang makes water more exciting" tagline.

5. *Different product–same message.* In some markets the potential customers cannot afford the product as manufactured for developed markets. To overcome this obstacle, companies frequently produce a very distinct product for these markets. Substituting a low-cost plastic squeeze bottle for an aerosol can and a manually operated washing machine for an automated one are two examples. The promotional message, however, can be very similar to what is used in the developed markets if the product performs the same functions.

6. *Different product for the same use–different message.* Frequently, the different product requires a different message as well. The governments of developing countries faced with high unemployment would be persuaded by a message emphasizing the job-creating possibilities of labor-intensive processes rather than the labor saving of highly automated machinery.

The tools for communicating these messages—the promotional mix—are advertising, personal selling, sales promotion, public relations, and publicity. None of these tools are inherently superior to the others, although circumstances in a given situation may dictate that one of them be emphasized more than the others. Just as in the case of the product strategies, the composition of the promotional mix will depend on the type of product, the environmental forces, and the amount of market penetration desired.

Advertising

advertising Among all the promotional mix elements, advertising may be the one with the greatest similarities worldwide. U.S. ad agencies have followed their corporate customers into the global realm through wholly owned subsidiaries, joint ventures, and working agreements with local agencies. The decision to go global, as Apple has with the iPod, or to go either local or regional, as P&G and McDonald's have, is not an easy one. One commentator observes that the trend is toward localization, at least for a while.[8]

Global or national The debate continues among international marketers about using global, regional, or national brands. Companies that acquired successful regional or national brands on purchasing the original owner have been extremely cautious about converting them to their global brands. Nestlé is an example of a large global firm that uses both. Nestlé tries to achieve consumer familiarity and marketing efficiency by using two brands on a single product, a local brand that may be familiar and appeal only to a small group of consumers and a corporate strategic brand such as Nestlé or Nescafé. In Asian markets, for example, product quality across many categories is suggested by a shared brand. This developed from the *keiretsu* structure as evidenced by Mitsubishi, C. Itoh, and Mitsui.

Private brands Private brands have become serious competitors for manufacturers' brands and are responsible for a shift in power from manufacturers to retailers. Private labels have flooded Japan's large supermarket chains, capturing one-third

of the British and Swiss food markets and one-fifth of the French and German markets. The trend toward private labels also has caught on in Spain and the Netherlands. The Swedish food group Axfood AB notes that it profits twice from private-label manufacturing: first when it sells the product (such as ketchup) at a lower price to its stores, and then when the profit margin is higher when selling to the ultimate consumer.[9]

LO5 Discuss some of the effects the Internet may have on international marketing.

Internet advertising Among the appealing factors of online advertising in the international sphere are the following:

1. The Internet provides an affluent, reachable audience. A high number of users in a wide variety of countries read English or other common languages well. Native-language sites are strongly preferred, though.

2. Unlike TV or newspaper ads, Internet communications can be interactive. They are cheap. And they are possibly less regulated than other advertising forms. In Europe, where direct advertising of prescription drug products is banned, Internet sites are a way to provide potential consumers with product information. The disclaimer that the information is for U.S. audiences only may be ignored.

3. The possibility exists of involving customers in determining which messages and information they receive. For this reason, there is some possibility that company Web offerings will be tailor-made by the user. This customization increases the application of the marketing concept.

4. Although the Internet doesn't reach all possible groups, for some groups it may be among the best media choices. For teenagers in particular, Internet advertising can be important because teenagers spend less time watching TV than any other demographic group, preferring to spend time on the Internet or to play computer games.

Type of product Buyers of industrial goods and luxury products usually act on the same motives the world over; thus, these products lend themselves to a standardized approach. Such standardization enables manufacturers of capital goods, such as General Electric and Caterpillar, to prepare international campaigns that require very little modification in their various markets. Certain consumer goods markets are similar, too. Another set of characteristics also permits firms to use the same appeals and sales arguments worldwide: when the product is low-priced, is consumed in the same way, and is bought for the same reasons. Examples of such products are gasoline, soft drinks, detergents, cosmetics, and airline services. Firms such as ExxonMobil, Coca-Cola, Apple, and Avon have used the international approach successfully. Generally, the changes they have made are a translation into the local language and the use of indigenous models.

Foreign environmental forces Foreign environmental forces act as deterrents to the international standardization of advertising, and as you would expect, among the most influential of these forces are the *sociocultural* forces, which we examined in Chapter 4.

A basic cultural decision for the marketer is whether to position the product as foreign or local. Which way to go seems to depend on the country, the product type, and the target market. In Germany, for example, consumers are not at all impressed by the carmaker that announces it has American know-how. At the same time, such purely American products as bourbon, fast-food restaurants, and blue jeans have made tremendous inroads there and in the rest of Europe.

Similarly, in Japan and elsewhere in Asia, the national identity of some consumer products enhances their image. The rage among Chinese and Japanese teenagers is anything from Korea, to the extent that some Japanese have learned Korean in order to follow Korean trends. The influence of American-style fast-food restaurants on Japanese youth was emphasized in a survey taken by the Japanese Ministry of Agriculture, which found that more than 50 percent of the country's teenagers would rather eat Western foods than the traditional dishes. U.S.-based

Because a nation's laws generally reflect public opinion, the cultural forces tend to be closely allied to the legal forces, which exert a strong and pervasive influence on advertising. We have seen how laws affect media availability; they also restrict the kinds of products that can be advertised and the copy employed in the advertisements.

Advertisers in the Islamic countries face limitations, although these vary widely. A recent study shows that women appear about as often in Lebanese and Egyptian TV ads as in U.S. ads, although only half as often in Saudi ads. The women are just as likely to be dressed "immodestly" in Lebanese as in U.S. ads, although less often in Egyptian and never in Saudi ads.[11] In Japan, images of Western women in suggestive poses were acceptable, while similar images of Japanese women were not.

Globalization versus localization With so many obstacles to international standardization, what should be the approach of the international advertising manager? The opinion of some experts is that good brands and good product

> ## "18-year-olds in Paris have more in common with 18-year-olds in New York than with their own parents."

fast-food restaurants such as McDonald's (Japan's largest restaurant business), KFC (the third largest), Dairy Queen, and Mister Donut account for half the total restaurant business. And KFC is zeroing in on an even larger Asian market—it had well over 2,500 restaurants in China in 2008 and is expanding by more than 200 units a year.[10]

The experience of suppliers to the youth market indicates that this, too, is an international market segment, much like the market for luxury goods. A former director of MTV Europe observed that "18-year-olds in Paris have more in common with 18-year-olds in New York than with their own parents. They buy the same products, go to the same movies, listen to the same music, sip the same colas. Global advertising merely works on that premise." This similarity suggests that marketers can formulate global advertising campaigns for these consumers that will require little more than a translation into the local language, unless the product strategy goes with a foreign identity. That decision should be made with local input.

Because communication is impossible if the language is not understood, translations must be made into the language of the consumers. Unfortunately for the advertiser, almost every language varies from one country to another. The same word may be perfectly apt in one country while connoting something completely different in another. To avoid errors in translation, the experienced advertising manager will use a back translation and plenty of illustrations with short copy.

ideas can cross international borders but each may have to be adjusted for the local market. Let's examine this situation more closely.

A global product and a global brand, such as Dell computers, reaches many markets unchanged or virtually unchanged. An ability to standardize both the product and the brand can

Are these teens in Japan or the United States? Japan. But, like teens in the United States, they wear Levi's and carry American skateboards.

lead to valuable cost savings.[12] Such products tend to be innovations. A global product with a local brand is often the result of mergers. Germany's Henkel, owner of Right Guard, Dial Soap, and other consumer products, has kept local packaging and standardized the physical product. Such a combination of localization of the product packaging and standardization of the contents makes manufacturing efficiencies possible.

The final option, a local product with a local brand, is the most localized approach and is appropriate when, for perhaps cultural reasons, the product that sells well in one country will not transfer to another, or does so for quite a different set of purposes. Dish soaps that are adjusted for the hardness of local water and sell under local names are an example. P&G's Fairy Liquid, a dishwashing soap that is a leading brand in the United Kingdom similar to Joy in the U.S. market, is one example of localization of the product on both brand and content.

LO6 **Explain** "glocal" advertising strategies.

Neither purely global nor purely local You probably have already gathered from this discussion that for most firms neither a purely global nor a purely local campaign is the best way to handle international advertising. In fact, companies at either end of the global–local spectrum, with purely global campaigns or only local campaigns, tend to be moving toward the middle, with a "glocal" approach. Advertisers have followed glocalization to reduce costs. It allows them to develop a common strategy for large regions.[13] Coca-Cola says simply, "Think globally, but act locally."

Programmed-management approach The **programmed-management approach** is a middle-ground advertising strategy in which the home office and the foreign subsidiaries agree on marketing objectives, after which each subsidiary puts together a tentative advertising campaign. This is submitted to the home office for review and suggestions. The campaign is then market-tested locally, and the results are submitted to the home office, which reviews them and offers comments. The subsidiary then submits a complete campaign to the home office for review. When the home office is satisfied, the budget is approved and the subsidiary begins implementing the campaign. The result may be a highly standardized campaign for all markets or one that has been individualized to the extent necessary to cope with local market conditions. The programmed-management approach gives the home office a chance to standardize those parts of the campaign that can be standardized but still permits flexibility in responding to different marketing conditions.

Personal selling Along with advertising, personal selling constitutes a principal component of the promotional mix. The

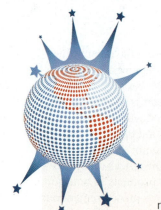

GLOBAL gauntlet

An Ethical Situation*

The Swiss pharmaceutical global corporation Hoffman-La Roche has made a major breakthrough in the relief of a serious disabling disease that affects 3 percent of the world's population. Its new product, Tigason, is the first product that effectively controls severe cases of psoriasis and dyskeratoses, skin disorders that cause severe flaking of the skin. Sufferers from these diseases frequently retreat from society because of fear of rejection, thus losing their families and jobs. Tigason does not cure the diseases, but it causes the symptoms to disappear.

There is one potential problem. Because of the risk of damage to unborn babies, women should not take the drug for one year before conception or during pregnancy. Hoffman-La Roche is well aware of the potential for harm to the company if the product is misused. It has seen the problems of another Swiss firm, Nestlé. After much discussion, the company has decided the product is too important to keep off the market. It is, after all, the product that gives the greatest relief to sufferers.

The marketing department is asked to formulate a strategy for disseminating product information and controlling Tigason's use. As the marketing manager, what do you recommend?

*This is an actual situation.

---

importance of this promotional tool compared with advertising depends to a great extent on the relative costs, the funds available, media availability, and the type of product sold.

Manufacturers of industrial products rely more on personal selling than on advertising to communicate with their overseas markets. However, producers of consumer products may also emphasize personal selling overseas, especially in the developing countries, because this may be more effective in the local environment.

Personal selling and the internet Evidence suggests that the Internet, when used to build trust (through consumer orientation, competence, dependability, candor, and likability),[14] can be an effective tool in personal selling. It may be enhanced by face-to-face communication as well. There are evolving approaches to trust building in a virtual environment that seem to be working, such as the eBay community and other sales and social sites.

International standardization By and large, the organization of an overseas sales force, sales presentation, and training methods are very similar to those employed in the home country, whenever possible. Avon was following the same plan of person-to-person selling in its major markets when, without notice, China outlawed door-to-door selling in 1998. The Chinese government claimed to be concerned about consumer safety and fraudulent pyramid schemes.[15] Avon had begun in China in 1990 with a $40 million manufacturing base in Guangzhou. To comply with Chinese law, Avon China shifted to a retail model and provided products through a network of 6,000 beauty boutiques and 1,000 beauty counters. In mid-2006, China approved Avon for person-to-person selling in China. It resumed the successful model, and by 2008 had some 600,000 sales promoters. Meanwhile, during the same period in Venezuela and Russia, Avon was extremely successful with the same personal selling approach it uses in the United States.

Other firms also follow their home-country approach. Missionary salespeople from pharmaceutical manufacturers such as Pfizer and Upjohn introduce their products to physicians, just as they do in the United States. Salespeople calling on channel members perform the same tasks of informing middlemen, setting up point-of-purchase displays, and fighting for shelf space as do their American counterparts.

Recruitment Recruiting salespeople in foreign countries is at times more difficult than recruiting them at home because sales managers may have to cope with the stigma attached to selling that exists in some areas. There is also the need to hire salespeople who are culturally acceptable to customers and channel members. This can be difficult and costly in an already small market that is further subdivided into several distinct cultures with different customs and languages.

Sales Promotion

Sales promotion provides the selling aids for the marketing function and includes activities such as the preparation of point-of-purchase displays, contests, premiums, trade show exhibits, money-off offers, and coupons.

The international standardization of the sales promotion function is not difficult, because experience has shown that what is successful in the United States generally proves effective overseas, although often at a diminished rate. Couponing is a good example. A Nielsen report surveyed consumers on cost-saving measures that would move them to increased coupon use. In the United States, 46 percent of consumers stated that they would increase coupon use, while the global average was 19 percent.[16] One major difference in coupon use among markets is the method of distribution. In the United States, the free-standing insert is most frequently used, while in Europe coupons are distributed in stores, usually on the package itself. In some European countries couponing is illegal because price discrimination among consumers is illegal. In other countries, the selling price of specific goods is set within a narrow range.

When marketers are considering transferring sales promotion techniques to other markets, they must consider some cultural constraints.

Sociocultural and economic constraints Cultural and economic constraints influence sales promotions. For example, a premium used as a sales aid for the product must be meaningful to the purchaser. A kitchen gadget might be valued by an American but will not be particularly attractive to a Latin American of similar economic status with two maids. Putting a prize inside the package is no guarantee that it will be there when the purchaser takes the package home, either. While living in Mexico, one of this book's authors bought a product for the plastic toy it contained. When he opened the package at home, there was no toy. Examining the package closely, he found that a small slit had been made in the top. Where labor costs and store revenues are low, the income from the sale of these premiums is an extra profit for the retailer.

Contests, raffles, and games have been extremely successful in countries where people love to play the odds. If Latin Americans or the Irish will buy a lottery ticket week after week, hoping to win the grand prize playing against odds of 500,000 to 1, why shouldn't they participate in a contest that costs them nothing to enter? Point-of-purchase displays are well accepted by retailers, although many establishments are so small that there is simply no place to put all the displays that are offered to them. The marketing manager who prepares a well-planned program after studying the constraints of the local markets can expect excellent results from the time and money invested.

Public Relations

Public relations is the firm's communications and relationships with its various publics, including

> " INTERNATIONAL PHARMACEUTICAL MANUFACTURERS ARE VIEWED WITH SUSPICION BY THE PUBLIC IN DEVELOPING NATIONS BECAUSE, ALTHOUGH THEIR PRODUCTS MAY ALLEVIATE SUFFERING, THEY DO SO AT A PROFIT "

cu in ib

Mark Haupt: A Central California–based International Career

Mark Haupt graduated from Cal Poly with a business degree, concentrating in international business. He loved the area where he went to university and wanted to continue living there, so he put together a career that is both international and allows him to work near home. Here's his story:

I think my interest in international business started when I was little. My father had a job with IBM and he was constantly traveling domestically and internationally. I'm also a big soccer fan and soccer is such a global sport that you start learning more and more about different countries, cities, cultures, etc. . . . and that has always been fascinating to me. I grew up with a lot of different ethnicities and cultures around and it's the differences—and sometimes similarities—that make things interesting to me.

After graduation, I wanted to remain in the Central Coast region of California, near the ocean, but also have international business opportunities. Despite the rural nature of this area, I was able to find a position with a local sporting goods company. I am in charge of our specialty/sporting goods division and my title is "Specialty Sales Manager." I manage a network of sales representatives, domestic and international, as well as select independent accounts and key accounts.

In less than two years with the company, I have worked with customers in over 30 different nations, including Australia, New Zealand, Canada, Mexico, Colombia, Brazil, Chile, Venezuela, Ireland, England, Germany, Italy, France, the Benelux Region (Belgium, Netherlands, Luxemburg), Scandinavia (Iceland, Sweden, Norway, Finland, Denmark), Romania, Latvia, Belarus, China, Japan, Singapore, Australia, New Zealand, South Africa, Egypt and Russia. My business association with most of these customers is a distribution arrangement. Companies in these countries distribute my company's products as well as those of other firms.

To prepare for travel, I always like to research the country I am visiting. I start by finding out a little about that country's sport of choice. For me, that's always an easy conversation starter and something that almost everyone has an opinion on. Then I like to find out about popular venues, sights, etc. Finally, I find out what to do or not to do. I research online and talk to people who have already visited the country. I pack light because I never seem to need much besides a few business outfits and some casual clothes. English has been the accepted business language for all my travels, but I like to learn at least a few words of the native language. For me, that shows that I am interested in the country and people seem to appreciate that. I don't have any routines for when I return from travel. I always seem to take way too long to unpack to the point where I run out of clothes. I am working on that.

To help myself adjust to being away, I always make sure I'm exhausted before I get on the plane. I sleep amazingly well on planes, probably because I have been flying ever since I was little. Usually, I wake up completely refreshed when I arrive.

To make my U.S. location convenient for my international counterparts, I have kept some odd hours. I rely on e-mail, but that usually creates a one-day delay and sometimes doesn't deliver the message effectively. If I use phone or video chat, I try to make the hours work for my customers, which isn't always easy. I have fielded calls as early as 5 a.m. and as late as midnight. That's all part of the job.

My biggest challenge to date has been working on a special order from one of my customers in Asia. Our factory is located in Taiwan, and I have encountered endless complications with molds, materials, packaging, etc. It's easy enough to say you can make a special product and give pricing. It is much more complicated once this actually comes to fruition. For big special orders, it's important that you get everything right. Errors that you might not think about can ruin a project and, potentially, a business relationship.

My greatest international-related enjoyment was going to New Zealand. I loved it over there. The scenery, people, and activities are all amazing. My greatest international business-related enjoyment was starting a relationship with what I first considered to be a mid-sized customer internationally and watching them blossom into one of our biggest customers. In sales, you don't always see your efforts pay off. Sometimes you work extra hours and put your heart and soul into something and get nothing out of it. It's extremely satisfying when you put in the extra effort, work extra hours, and it all pays off.

My greatest learning point from my international experience is that I have

> It's easy enough to say you can make a special product and give pricing. It is much more complicated once this actually comes to fruition.

learned to assume nothing. I have become so incredibly detailed in everything I do because I can never assume that a customer or client understands something exactly the way I do, especially when

English isn't their native language. It is much easier to go over something twice in the beginning rather than look back and try to correct a misunderstanding.

My advice for others who are interested in going abroad or working with others who are abroad is the following: If you have the chance, learn any language you can. This is an invaluable asset. Spend some time learning about the countries you are visiting or doing business with, and be extremely inquisitive. Do not act as if you already know everything. It's good to be knowledgeable and worldly, but people love talking about their country and culture and love it when you ask questions and are curious about their lifestyles. Be curious, but not ignorant. Make sure you don't ask anything that might bring up a sore subject.

the governments where it operates, or as one writer has put it, "Public relations is the marketing of the firm." Although American internationals have had organized public relations programs for many years in the United States, they have paid much less attention to this important function elsewhere. Informing the local public of what they are doing has been overlooked by some U.S. corporations.

Nationalism and anti-multinational feeling in many countries have made it imperative that companies with international operations improve their communications to their nonbusiness publics with more effective public relations programs. International pharmaceutical manufacturers are viewed with suspicion by the public in developing nations because, although their products may alleviate suffering, they do so at a profit, made from the poor. To improve their images, major pharmaceuticals have begun global programs related to disease. Their AIDS campaigns in Africa have received much public attention.

One of the most vexing problems for firms is how to deal with critics of their operations and motives. Some try to defuse criticism by holding regularly scheduled meetings at which topics of interest are debated. Others prefer to meet with critics privately, although they may find themselves caught in a never-ending relationship in which the critics continually escalate their demands.

Another alternative is to do nothing. If the criticism receives no publicity, it may die from lack of interest. Yet

sometimes a libeled company chooses to defend its reputation in court. McDonald's was the victim in London when Helen Steel and Dave Morris distributed leaflets accusing the company of starving the Third World, exploiting children in its advertising, and destroying the Central American rain forests. It was also cruel to animals, they alleged, because at times chickens were still conscious when their throats were cut. McDonald's sued Steel and Morris in 1994. It became the longest libel trial in English history. McDonald's was awarded $98,000 in damages in a case it had spent $16 million to pursue. Despite the award, which McDonald's has never collected, there is now a major anti-McDonald's website (www. McSpotlight.org) dedicated to protests against McDonald's, and October 16 has become established as Worldwide Anti-McDonald's Day.[17]

Pricing Strategies

Pricing, the third element of the marketing mix, is an important and complex consideration in formulating the marketing strategy. Pricing decisions affect other corporate functions, directly determine the firm's gross revenue, and are a major determinant of profits. Most pricing research has been done on North Americans, and this raises serious problems for its generalizability.[18] Americans like sales, for example, while consumers in countries where goods are more scarce may attribute sales to low quality rather than to a desire to gain market share. There is some evidence that perceived price–quality relationships are quite high in Britain and Japan. Thus, discount stores have had difficulty in both these markets. In developing countries, there is less trust of outsiders in the market. Cultural differences may influence the effort a buyer puts into evaluating deals in these markets, where buy decisions rest on relationships. That consumers in some economies are usually paid weekly rather than biweekly or monthly may influence the effectiveness of framing attempts as well. "A dollar a day" is a much bigger chunk from a weekly than a monthly paycheck.

Pricing, a Controllable Variable

Effective price setting consists of more than mechanically adding a standard markup to a cost. To obtain the maximum benefits from pricing, management must regard pricing in the same manner as it does other controllable variables. Pricing is one element of the marketing mix that can be varied to achieve the marketing objectives of the firm.

For instance, if the marketer wishes to position a product as a high-quality item, setting a relatively high price will reinforce promotion that emphasizes quality. However, combining a low price with a promotional emphasis on qual-

Foreign national pricing Some foreign governments fix prices on just about everything, while others are concerned only with pricing on essential goods. In nations with laws on unfair competition, the minimum sales price may be controlled rather than the maximum. The German law is so comprehensive that under certain conditions even premiums and cents-off coupons may be prohibited because they violate the minimum price requirements.

Prices can vary because of cost differentials on opposite sides of a border. One government may levy higher import duties on imported raw materials or may subsidize public utilities, while another may not. Differences in labor legislation cause labor costs to vary. Competition among local suppliers may be intense in one market, permitting the affiliate to buy inputs at better prices than those paid by an affiliate in another market.

Competition on the selling side may be diverse also. Frequently, an affiliate in one market will face heavy local competition and be limited in the price it can charge, while in a neighboring market a lack of competitors will allow another affiliate to charge a higher price. As regional economic groupings reduce trade barriers among members, such opportunities are becoming fewer because firms must meet regional as well as local competition.

International pricing International pricing involves the setting of prices for goods produced in one country and sold in another. A special kind of exporting, *intracorporate sales,* is common among large companies as they attempt to require that subsidiaries specialize in the manufacture of some products

> ## "Increasingly the Internet is redefining pricing options. It is a tremendous tool for comparing prices"

ity could result in a contradiction that would adversely affect credibility with the consumer. Pricing can also be a determinant in the choice of middlemen, because if the firm requires a wholesaler to take title to, stock, promote, and deliver the merchandise, it must give the wholesaler a much larger trade discount than would be demanded by a broker, whose services are much more limited.

Standardizing Prices

Companies that pursue a policy of unified, global corporate pricing know that pricing is subject to the same forces that work against the international standardization of the other marketing mix components. Pricing for the overseas markets is more complex because managements must be concerned with two kinds of pricing: **foreign national pricing,** which is domestic pricing in another country, and **international pricing** for exports.

and import others. Their imports may consist of components that are assembled into the end product, such as computer chips made in one country that are mounted on boards built in another, or they may be finished products imported to complement the product mix of an affiliate. In either case, judgment is needed in setting a **transfer price.**

It is possible for the firm as a whole to gain while both the buying and the selling subsidiaries "lose," that is, receive prices that are lower than would be obtained through an outside transaction. The tendency is for transfer prices to be set at headquarters so that the company may obtain a profit from *both* the seller and the buyer or locate its profit in lower-tax environments. The selling affiliate would like to charge other subsidiaries the same price it charges all customers, but when combined with transportation costs and import duties, such a price may make it impossible for the importing subsidiary to compete in its market. If headquarters dictates that a lower-than-market transfer price be charged, the seller will be unhappy because its profit-and-loss statement suffers. This can be problematic for managers whose promotion bonuses depend on the bottom line.

Increasingly the Internet is redefining pricing options. It is a tremendous tool for comparing prices—already sites can scan hundreds of outlets for prices on certain goods—and so national boundaries may mean less and less. In a sense, world prices for consumers may be on the way to being achieved. The effect extends to business-to-business pricing as well. ■

chapter fifteen

global operations
+ supply chain management

> "Creating a national company is like rocket science . . . but creating an international company is like proton physics."
>
> —John Strand, Strand Consulting

As firms continue to enter global markets, global competition increases. This forces management of both international and domestic companies to search for ways to lower costs while improving their products or services in order to remain competitive. Sometimes the desired results are obtained through improvements within existing operations. Other times, improved competitiveness is pursued by having the company open new—or transfer existing—operations abroad or find alternative outside sources for the labor, raw materials, or other inputs that it is currently sourcing from other organizations. A third option involves **outsourcing,** that is, hiring others to perform some of the noncore activities and decision making in a company's value chain, instead of continuing to do them in-house. Commonly, outsourcing firms provide key components of data processing, logistics, payroll, and accounting, although any activity in the value chain can be outsourced. It is common that management will pursue some combination of these different options in their efforts to enhance their company's international competitiveness. The efforts to improve the efficiency and effectiveness of a firm's international operations are often referred to as **supply chain management.** In this chapter, we discuss the topics of global supply chain management and critical issues in the management of global operations, including global sourcing, manufacturing systems, productivity and performance of international manufacturing operations, and issues associated with global standardization versus localization of international operations.

LEARNING OBJECTIVES

After reading this chapter, you should be able to:

LO1 **Understand** the concept of supply chain management.

LO2 **Recognize** the relationship between design and supply chain management.

LO3 **Describe** the five global sourcing arrangements.

LO4 **Understand** the increasing role of electronic purchasing for global sourcing.

LO5 **Appreciate** the importance of the added costs of global sourcing.

LO6 **Explain** the potential of global standardization of production processes and procedures, and identify impediments to standardization efforts.

LO1   **Understand** the concept of supply chain management.

MANAGING GLOBAL SUPPLY CHAINS

Supply chain management has become an increasingly popular and strategically important topic in international business in recent years. *Supply chain* refers to the activities that are involved in producing a company's products and services and how these activities are linked together. The concept of supply chain management involves the applications of a total systems approach to managing the overall flow of materials, information, finances, and services within and among companies in the value chain—from raw materials and components suppliers through manufacturing facilities and warehouses and on to the ultimate customer.[1] Supply chains are an integral part of global quality and cost management initiatives, because a typical company's supply chain costs can represent more than 50 percent of assets and more than 80 percent of revenues.[2] Figure 15.1 illustrates a global supply chain for an American laptop computer company. This example broadly illustrates the activities and linkages involved in transforming initial designs into the finished goods and support services delivered to the consumer. These include product design, suppliers that provide the various inputs, assembly and testing activities, warehousing and distribution of finished goods, and the sales and technical support operations.

Because inventory is carried at each stage in the supply chain, and because inventory ties up money, it has been argued that the ultimate goal of effective supply chain management systems is to reduce inventory, consistent with the prerequisites that the company's products be available when needed and

at the desired level of quality and quantity. For that reason, it is critical that the operations at each stage in the supply chain are synchronized in order to minimize the size of these buffer inventories. Shorter, less predictable product life cycles, as well as the impact of unplanned economic, political, and social events, have placed further emphasis on the achievement of effective supply chain performance.[3] New technologies, including Web-enabled tools for supply chain planning, execution, and optimization, have enhanced the availability of data and integration with suppliers and customers, helping to enhance the international competitiveness of companies that have adopted and mastered these technologies.

Global supply chain management has been receiving increasing attention because many companies have achieved significant international competitive advantage as a result of the manner in which they have configured and managed their global supply chain activities. Some organizations, such as the computer and information technology company Dell, have reconfigured their international supply chains to substantially reduce or eliminate activities such as finished goods warehousing and retail stores, thus reducing costs and increasing effectiveness.[4] Other companies, such as the Hong Kong export trading company Li and Fung, have transformed their operations to enter into new, value-adding activities in an industry's value chain.[5] Effective supply chain management can also enhance a company's ability to manage regulatory, social, and other environmental pressures, both nationally and globally.

LO2   **Recognize** the relationship between design and supply chain management.

DESIGN OF PRODUCTS AND SERVICES

An important factor in the structure and management of a company's global supply chain is the issue of design. The design of a company's products and services has a fundamental

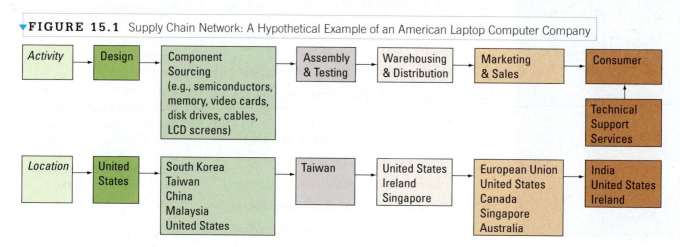

▼**FIGURE 15.1**   Supply Chain Network: A Hypothetical Example of an American Laptop Computer Company

Activity	Design	Component Sourcing (e.g., semiconductors, memory, video cards, disk drives, cables, LCD screens)	Assembly & Testing	Warehousing & Distribution	Marketing & Sales	Consumer	Technical Support Services
Location	United States	South Korea Taiwan China Malaysia United States	Taiwan	United States Ireland Singapore	European Union United States Canada Singapore Australia	India United States Ireland	

relationship with the type of inputs that the company will require, including labor, materials, information, and financing. As we discussed in Chapter 14, an important consideration in design is the extent to which the international company's products and services will be standardized across nations or regions or adapted to meet the different needs of various markets. The decision on standardization versus localization of designs is affected by a range of competitive, cultural, regulatory, and other factors and is an important strategic consideration for a company.

A traditional approach to product design has been termed the "over-the-wall" approach. This involves a sequential approach to design: an initial step in which the designers prepare the product's design, followed by sending the newly created design to the company's manufacturing engineers, who must then address the production-related problems that often result from their exclusion from the initial design activity.

An alternative approach to design is to promote cross-functional participation in the design stage, thereby helping to identify and avoid many of the potential sourcing, manufacturing, and other difficulties that can be associated with a particular design. Many companies also involve key customers

improvement idea or another. Other companies such as Nike are finding that such activities also help to engage the customer, possibly increasing loyalty.[6]

SOURCING GLOBALLY

Reasons for Sourcing Globally

Although the primary reason for sourcing globally is to obtain lower prices, there are other reasons. Perhaps certain products the company requires are not available locally and must be imported. Another possibility is that the firm's foreign competitors are using components of better quality or design than those available in the home country. To be competitive, the company may have to source these components or production machinery in foreign countries. The term **offshoring** is commonly used for a company's decision to relocate activities to foreign locations.

When deciding to source internationally, companies can either set up their own facilities or outsource the production

ANY PART OF THE VALUE CHAIN CAN BE OUTSOURCED, INCLUDING PRODUCT DESIGN, RAW MATERIAL OR COMPONENT SUPPLY, MANUFACTURING OR ASSEMBLY, LOGISTICS, DISTRIBUTION, MARKETING, SALES, SERVICE, HUMAN RESOURCES, OR OTHER ACTIVITIES.

in the design activities, to ensure that designs are consistent with the customers' needs. Using this type of concurrent engineering approach allows the proposed designs to be subjected to earlier assessments on cost, quality, and manufacturability dimensions, thereby enhancing the efficiency and effectiveness of subsequent manufacturing and supply chain management activities. Indeed, design decisions must often be integrated with assessment of the various supply chain considerations, such as whether and where the company can obtain the inputs needed for the company's operations, whether the firm will source locally or from foreign locations, and whether the company has the capability to produce and deliver the product or service in a competitively viable manner.

A recent change in the approach to design is the penchant to solicit very broad input, increasingly from general customers, into the process. Examples of customer solicitation of input include Dell's IdeaStorm site and Starbucks' suggestion site. Within a week of Starbucks' opening of their MyStarbucksIdea .com site, more than 100,000 votes had been cast for one

to other companies. Outsourcing has become an increasingly common option for companies, as they try to focus scarce resources on their core competencies and leverage the skills of other companies to reduce costs and capital investments, improve flexibility and speed of response, enhance quality, and provide other strategic benefits. The activities can be outsourced either to another company in the same country or to a company in another country (the latter would constitute "offshore outsourcing"). Any part of the value chain can be outsourced, including product design, raw material or component supply, manufacturing or assembly, logistics, distribution, marketing, sales, service, human resources, or other activities.

Outsourcing decisions, including the decision to use global sources of supply, are extensions of the make-or-buy decisions of earlier eras. The pros and cons of these decisions usually include comparisons of costs as well as managerial control of confidential product design specifications, delivered quantity, quality, design, and delivery time and method. Other

> ## THE ABILITY TO EFFECTIVELY AND EFFICIENTLY USE GLOBAL SOURCES HAS BEEN ENHANCED BY THE PLUMMETING COST OF COMMUNICATIONS, WIDESPREAD USE OF STANDARDIZED INTERFACES SUCH AS WEB BROWSERS, AND THE INCREASING PACE AT WHICH COMPANIES ARE AUTOMATING AND DIGITIZING DATA.

considerations include the manufacturing expertise required to make the raw material or components as well as the added cost of not being able to take advantage of the scale or larger volumes a vendor may have. In global purchasing, these issues are exacerbated by such factors as distance, different languages of buyers and sellers, and different national laws and regulations. Over time, many organizations have developed the ability to manage these obstacles fully or in part, thus enabling global outsourcing to become a viable option for an increasing number of firms. When possible, it is better for companies to initially outsource simple activities and gradually outsource more complex activities as both the outsourcer and the service provider gain experience.

The lure of global sourcing is the existence of suppliers with improved competitiveness in terms of cost, quality, timeliness, and other relevant dimensions. For example, certain nations may provide access to lower-cost or better-quality minerals or other important raw materials or components compared to what might be available domestically (such as bauxite in Jamaica or dynamic random-access memory chips in South Korea). In addition, the existence of industrially less developed countries with inexpensive and abundant unskilled labor may provide an attractive source of supply for labor-intensive products with low skill requirements. This helps explain why many relatively standardized and labor-intensive operations (such as the assembly of athletic shoes or men's dress shirts) have moved away from the more industrialized countries, where labor is more expensive. The international product life cycle theory, which was discussed in Chapter 2, helps explain this migration of operations from the developed to the developing areas of the world. These emerging economies have moved on the product and process continuum from high-labor-content products made with light, unsophisticated process equipment, to sophisticated processes and more complex, lower-labor-content machinery, or skill-intensive engineering and design services.

The ability to effectively and efficiently use global sources has been enhanced by the plummeting cost of communications, widespread use of standardized interfaces such as Web browsers, and the increasing pace at which companies are automating and digitizing data. As more of a company's operational activities are automated, it becomes easier and more economical to outsource these activities. Increasing numbers of companies have begun to compete for outsourcing business, and customers have become more accustomed to using these services.

LO3 **Describe** the five global sourcing arrangements.

Global Sourcing Arrangements

As was suggested in Chapter 13, any of the following arrangements can provide a firm with foreign products:

1. *Wholly owned subsidiary.* May be established in a country with low-cost labor to supply components to the home country plant, or the subsidiary may produce a product that either is not made in the home country or is of higher quality.

2. *Overseas joint venture.* Established where labor costs are lower, or quality higher, than in the home country to supply components to the home country.

3. *In-bond plant contractor.* Home-country plant sends components to be machined and assembled or only assembled by an independent contractor in an in-bond plant.

4. *Overseas independent contractor.* Common in the clothing industry, in which firms with no production facilities, such as DKNY, Nike, and Liz Claiborne, contract with foreign manufacturers to make clothing to their specifications with their labels.

5. *Independent overseas manufacturer.*

Importance of Global Sourcing

A strong relationship exists between global sourcing and ownership of the foreign sources. *Intrafirm trade,* which includes trade between a parent company and its foreign affiliates, accounts for 30 to 40 percent of exports of goods and 35 to 45 percent of imports in the case of the United States.[7]

In U.S. industry, the proportion of purchased materials in the overall cost of goods sold has been rising for several decades, from an average of 40 percent in 1945 to 50 percent in 1960 and 55 to 79 percent today.[8] There are several reasons for this phenomenon, including greater complexity of products and increasing pressure for firms to focus on their core business and outsource other activities in which they lack strong competitive ability.

In addition, competitive pressures and reduced concept-to-market cycle times in many product and service sectors have resulted in a rapid increase in the number of new products that are made available to the market. It has been estimated that at least 50 percent of products currently on the market were not available five years ago. This development has created additional pressure to locate suppliers worldwide that can provide inputs at competitive prices and quality and with quick responsiveness to market changes.

LO4 Understand the increasing role of electronic purchasing for global sourcing.

The Increasing Use of Electronic Purchasing for Global Sourcing

Simply entering "exporter" and the name of the product in a search engine will bring up the websites of dozens of exporters around the world that have online catalogs and information on how to order their products. There are also buyers, some of them from large companies, looking for products. In recent years, many firms have set up electronic procurement (e-procurement) exchanges, individually or in conjunction with other firms, to identify potential suppliers or customers and facilitate efficient and dynamic interactions among these prospective buyers and suppliers.

Ambitious B2B e-procurement projects have been announced in automobile manufacturing (e.g., Covisint.com), chemicals (e.g., ChemConnect.com), steel (e.g., e-steel.com), insurance, petroleum, and hospital supplies. There is even a similar initiative in the advertising industry called NuIdea-EXchange, where marketers looking for advertising suggestions can connect with "creatives" who may have a good idea that has not found a home. In many companies, the purchasing function has been neglected for many years and is often viewed as a prime candidate for outsourcing to other firms. However, purchasing is increasingly being considered a strategic function, a trend encouraged by rapid developments in e-procurement.

While direct production–oriented goods have been the focus of management attention for many years, the purchasing of goods and services that are not part of finished goods—termed *indirect procurement*—is also critical. Including such items as maintenance, repair, operating supplies, office equipment, and other services and supplies, indirect procurement can account for as much as 70 percent of the total purchasing expenditures in a company. Although many organizations have continued to rely on traditional paper-based processes for indirect procurement despite their cost and inefficiency, new technologies are quickly encouraging change in this approach, even for small and mid-sized companies.

Options for Global Electronic Procurement

Among the most basic transactions that can occur over electronic purchasing exchanges are catalog purchases. Suppliers will provide a catalog of the products available, and buyers can access, review, and place orders for desired items at a listed price. The supplier can keep the catalog updated in real time, adjusting prices according to inventory levels and the need to move particular products. Electronic exchanges can also permit buyers and suppliers to interact through a standard bid/quote system in which buyers can post their purchasing needs online for all prospective suppliers to view and the suppliers can then submit private quotes to the buyer. The buyer can then select among the submitted quotations on the basis of price, delivery times, or other factors. Industry-sponsored exchanges can also facilitate obtaining letters of credit, contracting for logistics and distribution, and monitoring daily prices and order flows, among other services.

Benefits of Global Electronic Procurement
Systems The benefits of electronic purchasing initiatives can be quite substantial. For example, Oracle Corporation announced that it would save $2 billion annually from companywide e-business initiatives that have allowed the company to streamline operations, cut costs, and improve productivity in supply chain management and customer response.[9] Research found that suppliers cut invoice and ordering errors by an average of 69 percent when using an e-marketplace, enhancing efficiency and reducing costs.[10] Websites like Exostar help companies simplify and standardize procurement processes, streamline supply chains, reduce costs, improve productivity, and reach new markets.

Smaller companies are also using the Internet to purchase raw materials as well as to sell their products to customers, often on a worldwide basis. Developments such as e-procurement exchanges have opened the door for many smaller suppliers, which now have to spend very little to get into the market, lowering barriers to entry to domestic and international market opportunities. As asserted by Amanda Mesler, managing director of KPMG Consulting in Houston, Texas, "The promise of an exchange is that it allows them [smaller companies] to leverage their size further and get into more markets, especially globally and internationally, than they ever have before."[11]

Overall, emerging industry-based B2B exchanges can help optimize the supply chain across an entire network of organizations, not merely within a single company. These exchanges can create value by aggregating the purchasing power of buyers, improving process efficiency, integrating supply chains, enhancing content dissemination, and improving overall market efficiency within and across nations.

LO5 Appreciate the importance of the added costs of global sourcing.

Problems with Global Sourcing
Although global sourcing is a standard procedure for half of the U.S. firms with sales greater than $10 million, it does have some disadvantages.[12] Inasmuch as lower price is the primary reason

costing" to analyze purchasing decisions through the life of the purchased item, including trade-in or future estimated salvage value. Even on components, firms are increasingly including full costing, including the use of activity-based costing systems, to ensure that all the costs associated with foreign sourcing (e.g., transportation, insurance, increased inventory levels to insulate against delays in delivery) are fully recognized when they make purchasing decisions.[13] It is essential that global sourcing decisions be closely linked to the organization's strategy and that explicit objectives for suppliers (such as delivery times and cost objectives) be defined and incorporated in contracts, ideally with incentives for meeting or exceeding them. Cross-company teams should also be developed in order to enhance the likelihood that best practices can be effectively shared between the organization and its suppliers, in order to avoid supply problems.

Added Costs The buyer must understand the terms of sale because international freight, insurance, and packing can add as much as 10 to 12 percent to the quoted price, depending on the sales term used. The following is a list of the costs of importing, with an estimate of the percentage of the quoted price that each cost adds:

1. International freight, insurance, and packing (10–12%).
2. Import duties (0–50%).
3. Customhouse broker's fees (3–5%).
4. Transit or pipeline inventory (5–15%).
5. Cost of letter of credit (1%).
6. International travel and communication costs (2–8%).
7. Company import specialists (5%).
8. Reworking of products out of specification (0–15%).

Other Disadvantages One disadvantage an importer should not have to face is an increase in price because the home currency has lost value as a result of exchange rate fluctuation. For example, if an American importer requires that the exporter quote dollar prices, the importer has no exchange rate risk. However, if the firm has a large volume of imports and

> "Emerging industry-based B2B exchanges can help optimize the supply chain across an entire network of organizations, not merely within a single company."

companies make foreign purchases, they may be surprised that what initially appeared to be a lower price is not really lower once all the costs connected to the purchase are considered.

For purchases of capital goods such as manufacturing equipment, many U.S. buying organizations now use "life-cycle

the dollar is unstable, management may want a quotation in foreign currency. In that case, the chief financial officer of the importing company probably will protect the company from exchange rate risk by using one of the hedging techniques discussed in Chapter 17. Hedging has been used for many years by companies that operate internationally, particularly if their raw materials include one or more of the commodities traded on established commodities markets. In most cases, such hedging has been done not for speculative reasons but as a means of protecting the company from the risk of rapid price fluctuations.

The emergence of e-procurement has also been accompanied by problems. E-procurement and electronic commerce as a whole cannot be isolated from the company's overall business system. Many early efforts at developing e-procurement systems have been made in isolation and have subsequently failed to deliver on their potential. Successful electronic commerce initiatives include connections to traditional systems for fulfilling procurement and other value chain activities, as well as considerations on how to manage the transition to new, electronic approaches. The traditional functions of purchasing—supplier determination, analysis, and selection—still have to be accomplished before the actual purchasing via e-procurement. In most instances, a company may be able to use the Internet for quicker data acquisition about possible suppliers and generally from a much broader information base than was previously available in a timely manner. Ensuring that a supplier is selected that can meet all of the company's conditions for its raw material in terms of quality, delivery, price, and so forth, remains a challenge, particularly in a broadscale e-procurement network involving suppliers with which the company is not familiar. Suppliers located in emerging nations may also encounter difficulty in accessing and supporting sophisticated IT infrastructures, which can affect e-procurement performance.

Security also is often a significant concern for e-procurement. For B2B electronic commerce to achieve its full potential, access to the company's internal systems from outside is critical. Companies are wary of opening up the details of their business—including pricing, inventory, or design specifications—to competitors, to avoid risking the loss of brand equity and margins. In addition, exposing internal business systems to access via the Internet can expose the firm to a wide range of potential security issues, such as unauthorized entry ("hacking") and fraudulent orders. Although extensive research and development efforts have been undertaken in encryption technology and other technology and processes to ensure integrity, much progress still remains to be achieved before these systems can be considered fully secure. Different country standards are also of concern in attempting to implement international e-procurement systems. Governmental concerns with potential anticompetitive effects of collaboration among competitors may also cause problems for industry-wide B2B exchanges.

MANUFACTURING SYSTEMS

Since international firms maintain manufacturing facilities in countries at various levels of development—facilities utilizing factors of production that vary considerably in cost and quality from one country to another—it is understandable that manufacturing systems will also vary considerably, even within the same company. A single company may have a combination of plants that range from those with the most advanced production technology to those with far less advanced technology. The manufacturing systems in place within and across a company's international operations can have important implications for the way in which the company's global supply chain is set up and managed.

> " E-procurement and electronic commerce as a whole cannot be isolated from the company's overall business system. "

Advanced Production Techniques can Enhance Quality and Lower Costs

Growing international competition requires increasing efforts from companies to achieve efficiency and effectiveness in their international production activities. As a result, companies all over the world have pursued ways to improve their competitiveness, putting into place advanced production systems such as just-in-time supply chains or highly synchronized manufacturing systems. Others have installed computer-integrated manufacturing (CIM), utilizing computers and robots to further improve productivity and quality. Although these innovations can be a major challenge to implement successfully, their impact on international companies' competitiveness can be impressive.

LO6 Explain the potential of global standardization of production processes and procedures, and identify impediments to standardization efforts.

LOGISTICS

Logistics refers to managerial functions associated with the movement of materials such as raw materials, work in progress, or finished goods. The effectiveness of supply chain management efforts is strongly influenced by how a company manages the interface of logistics with sourcing and manufacturing, as

Use of robots alongside humans within an auto assembly plant

well as with other activities such as design, engineering, and marketing.[14] Given the strong emphasis on minimization of inventory and handling in supply chains, the way a product (or the components and materials that will go into a product) is designed can significantly influence the cost of delivering the product. For example, packaging and transportation requirements for a product can significantly influence logistics costs, and these factors should be addressed during design as well as in other steps in the value chain.

Many companies have chosen to outsource their logistics needs to outside specialists, particularly for managing international logistics activities. Companies such as Federal Express, DHL, and UPS have developed expertise in handling and tracking materials within and across nations, including sophisticated computer technology and systems for tracking shipments. For example, FedEx's website (www.fedex.com) allows a company to arrange pickups and then monitor the status of each item being transported, including information on the time the shipment was picked up; when and where

it has been transferred within FedEx's network; and delivery location, time, and recipient. Many of these logistics companies have developed systems whereby their customers' in-house information systems are integrated with the logistics company's shipping and tracking systems. It is also common for logistics companies to offer a broad range of services beyond shipping, including warehousing, distribution management, and customs and brokerage services.

STANDARDIZATION AND THE MANAGEMENT OF GLOBAL OPERATIONS

Standards are documented agreements containing technical specifications or other precise criteria that will be used consistently as guidelines, rules, or definitions of the characteristics of a product, process, or service.

Benefits of Standardization of Global Operations

Standards help ensure that materials, products, processes, and services are appropriate for their purpose. Credit cards and phone cards are produced to an accepted standard, including an optimal thickness of 0.76 mm, so that these cards can be used worldwide. The same symbols for automobile controls are displayed in cars throughout the world, no matter where the vehicles are produced.

In most countries, standards have been developed across product lines and for various functions. In the United States, for example, the standards developed by the American Society for Testing and Materials (ASTM) and other organizations are used in lieu of specific detailed requirements to ensure an expected level of use and quality. In Europe, the most used standard for quality is ISO 9000. This is a set of five universal standards for a quality assurance system that has been agreed to by the International Organization for Standardization (ISO), a federation of standards bodies from approximately 157 countries. The intention is that ISO 9000 standards will be applicable worldwide, avoiding technical barriers to trade attributable to the existence of nonharmonized standards between countries. If a product or service is purchased from a company that is registered to the appropriate ISO 9000 standard, the buyer will have important assurances that the quality of what was received will be what was expected. Indeed, registered companies have reported dramatic reductions in customer complaints as well as reduced operating costs and increased demand for their products and services. The United States has adopted the ISO 9000 series verbatim as the ANSI/AQC900 series.

The most comprehensive of the standards is now ISO 9001. It applies to industries involved in the design, development, manufacturing, installation, and servicing of products and services. The standards apply uniformly to companies, regardless of their size or industry. In general, companies that want to do business in Europe must have at least ISO 9000 registration, and many companies also require registration by their suppliers to provide further assurance of compliance.

Although it has been widely adopted as a standard for quality, not all quality "experts" agree that ISO 9000 is superior to other alternatives: "The focus of the standards is to establish quality management procedures, through detailed documentation, work instructions, and record keeping. These procedures . . . say nothing about the actual quality of the product—they deal entirely with standards to be followed." Phil Crosby, a noted quality expert and the author of several books on quality, states, "It is a delusion that sound management can be replaced by an information format. It is like putting a Bible in every hotel room with the thought that occupants will act according to its contents."[15]

In addition to those just mentioned, there are other important, although perhaps less obvious, reasons for global standardization. The following sections discuss some of these reasons.

Organization and Staffing

Some of the reasons for the global standardization of a firm's manufacturing systems are the effects on organization and staffing.

Simpler and Less Costly When Standardized

The standardization of production processes and procedures simplifies the manufacturing organization at headquarters because their replication enables the work to be accomplished with a smaller staff of support personnel. Fewer labor hours in plant design are involved because each new plant is essentially a scaled-up or scaled-down version of an existing one. The permanent group of experts that international companies maintain to give technical assistance to overseas plants can be smaller. Extra technicians accustomed to working with the same machinery can be borrowed from the domestic operation as needed.

Worldwide uniformity or standardization in manufacturing methods also increases headquarters' effectiveness in keeping the production specifications current. Every firm has hundreds of specifications, and those specifications are constantly being changed because of new raw materials or manufacturing procedures. If all plants, domestic and foreign, possess the same equipment, notice of a change can be given with one indiscriminate notification (e.g., an e-mail); there is no need for highly paid engineers to check each affiliate's list of equipment to see

> **standards**
> Documented agreements containing technical specifications or other precise criteria that will be used consistently as guidelines, rules, or definitions of the characteristics of a product, process, or service

> THE FOCUS OF THE STANDARDS IS TO ESTABLISH QUALITY MANAGEMENT PROCEDURES, THROUGH DETAILED DOCUMENTATION, WORK INSTRUCTIONS, AND RECORD KEEPING. THESE PROCEDURES . . . SAY NOTHING ABOUT THE ACTUAL QUALITY OF THE PRODUCT— THEY DEAL ENTIRELY WITH STANDARDS TO BE FOLLOWED.

which ones are affected. Companies whose manufacturing processes are not unified have found that maintaining a current separate set of specifications for each of 15 or 20 affiliates is both more costly (larger staff) and more error-prone.

Logistics of Supply

As we discussed at the beginning of this chapter on the value of a supply chain management orientation, management has become increasingly aware that greater profits may be obtained by organizing all of its companies' production facilities into one logistical supply system that includes all the activities required to move raw materials, parts, and finished inventory from vendors, between enterprise facilities, and to customers. The standardization of processes and machinery provides a reasonable guarantee that parts manufactured in the firm's various plants will be interchangeable. This assurance of interchangeability enables management to divide the production of components among a number of subsidiaries in order to achieve greater economies of scale and take advantage of the lower production costs in some countries.

Rationalization

Manufacturing rationalization, as this production strategy is called, involves a change from a subsidiary's manufacturing only for its own national market to its producing a limited number of components for use by all subsidiaries.

For manufacturing rationalization to be possible, the product mix must first be rationalized; that is, the firm must elect to produce products that are identical worldwide or region-wide. Once this has been done, each subsidiary can be assigned to produce certain components for other foreign plants, thus attaining a higher volume with a lower production cost than would be possible if it manufactured the complete product for its national market only. Obviously, this strategy is not viable when consumers' tastes and preferences differ markedly among markets. For less differentiated products, however, manufacturing rationalization permits economies of scale in production and engineering that would otherwise be impossible.

Purchasing

When foreign subsidiaries are unable to purchase raw materials and machinery locally, they generally look for assistance from the purchasing department at headquarters. Because unified processes require the same materials everywhere, buyers can handle foreign requirements by simply increasing their regular orders to their usual suppliers and passing on the volume discounts to the subsidiaries. However, when special materials are required, purchasing agents must search out new vendors and place smaller orders, often at higher prices.

Control

All the advantages of global standardization cited thus far also pertain to the other functions of management. Three aspects of

control—quality, production, and maintenance—merit additional discussion.

Quality Control

When production equipment is similar, home office control of quality in foreign affiliates is less difficult because management can expect all plants to adhere to the same standard. The home office can compare the periodic reports that all affiliates submit and quickly spot deviations from the norm that require remedial action, such as a large number of product rejects. Separate standards for each plant because of equipment differences are unnecessary.

Production and Maintenance Control

A single standard also lessens the task of maintenance and production control. The same machinery should produce at the same rate of output and have the same frequency of maintenance no matter where it is located. In practice, deviations will occur because of the human and physical factors (dust, humidity, temperature), but at least similar machinery permits the home office to establish standards by which to determine the effectiveness of local managements. Furthermore, the maintenance experience of other production units in regard to the frequency of overhauls and the stock of required spare parts will help plants avoid costly, unforeseen stoppages from sudden breakdowns.

Planning

When a new plant can be built that is a duplicate of others already functioning, the planning and design will be both simpler and quicker because they are essentially a repetition of work already done:

1. Design engineers need only copy the drawings and lists of materials that they have in their files.

2. Vendors will be requested to furnish equipment that they have supplied previously.

3. The technical department can send the current manufacturing specifications without alteration.

4. Labor trainers experienced in the operation of the machinery can be sent to the new location without undergoing special training on new equipment.

5. Reasonably accurate forecasts of plant erection time and output can be based on experience with existing facilities.

In other words, the duplication of existing plants greatly reduces the engineering time required in planning and designing the new facilities and eliminates many of the startup difficulties inherent in any new operation. Just how important the savings from plant duplication are was emphasized in a study of the chemical and refining industries that indicated that the cost of technology transfer was lowered by 34 and 19 percent for the second and third startups, respectively.[16]

If the case for global standardization of production is so strong, why do differences among plants in the same company persist?

IMPEDIMENTS TO STANDARDIZATION OF GLOBAL OPERATIONS

Generally, it is easier for international corporations to standardize the concepts of total quality management and synchronous manufacturing in their overseas affiliates than it is to standardize the actual manufacturing facilities. Units of an international multiplant operation differ in size, machinery, and procedures because of the intervention of the foreign environmental forces, especially the economic, cultural, and political forces.

Environmental Forces

Let us examine the impact of the three kinds of forces just mentioned.

Economic Forces The most important element of the economic forces that impede production standardization is the wide range of market sizes, discussed in Chapter 12.

To cope with the great variety of production requirements, the designer generally has the option of selecting either a *capital-intensive process* incorporating automated, high-semimanual-output machinery or a *labor-intensive process* employing more people and general-purpose equipment with lower productive capacity. The automated machinery is severely limited in flexibility (variety of products and range of sizes), but once set up, it will turn out in a few days what may be a year's supply for some markets.[17] For many processes, this problem may be resolved by installing one machine of the type used by the hundreds in the larger home plant. However, sometimes this option is not available; some processes use only one or two large machines, even in manufacturing facilities with large output, as we mentioned in the discussion of standardized manufacturing. Until recently, when the option was not available, plant designers had to choose between the high-output specialized machinery and the lower-output, general-purpose machines mentioned earlier. The major difference is that general-purpose machines require skills that are built into a special-purpose machine. The general-purpose machine usually produces a product of lower quality and higher per-unit costs than does the special-purpose machine.

A third alternative is available: computer-integrated manufacturing (CIM), which many international firms are using. However, its cost and high technological content generally limit its application to the industrialized nations and the more advanced developing nations. CIM systems enable a machine to make one part as easily as another in random order on an instruction from a bar code reader of the kind used in supermarkets. This reduces the economic batch quantity to one—the minimum number of a part that can be made economically by a factory—and it facilitates the potential for mass customization that we discussed earlier in this chapter. There is a limit, nevertheless, to the variety of shapes, sizes, and materials that can be accommodated.

Another economic factor that influences the designer's selection of processes is the *cost of production*. Automation tends to increase the productivity per worker because it requires less labor and results in higher output per machine. But if the desired output requires that the machines be operated only a fraction of the time, the high capital costs of automated equipment may result in excessive production costs even though labor costs are low. In situations where production costs favor semimanual equipment, the designer may be compelled to install high-capacity machines instead because of a lack of floor space. Generally, the space occupied by a few high-capacity machines is less than that required for the greater number of semimanual machines needed to produce the same output. However, because the correct type and quality of process materials are indispensable for specialized machinery, the engineers cannot recommend this equipment if such materials are unobtainable either from local sources or through importation. Occasionally, management will bypass this obstacle by means of **backward vertical integration;** that is, manufacturing capacity to produce essential inputs will be included in the plant design even though it would be preferable from an economic standpoint to purchase those materials from outside vendors. For example, a textile factory might include a facility for producing nylon fibers.

The economic forces we have described are fundamental considerations in plant design, yet elements of the cultural and political forces may be sufficiently significant to override decisions based on purely economic reasoning.

Cultural Forces When a factory is to be built in an industrialized nation that has a sizable market and high labor costs, capital-intensive processes will undoubtedly be employed. However, such processes may also be employed in developing

backward vertical integration
Arrangement in which facilities are established to manufacture inputs used in the production of a firm's final products

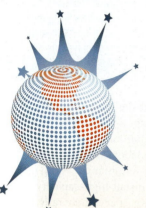

GLOBAL Gauntlet

Is Offshore Outsourcing Ending Its Run?

In 2003, nearly 900 workers at a cookware factory in Manitowoc, Wisconsin, switched off their machines. Their company was moving operations to Mexico. Now, however, many of the same workers are back, this time making pots and pans for Brazilian cookware maker Tramontina. In Japan, Sharp Corporation is building a $9 billion factory complex that is the largest LCD and solar panel plant in the world. When plans for the plant were first announced, the trend in Japan was to build manufacturing offshore in places like China. But Sharp's chairman wanted to manufacture at home, and even included factories for many of its suppliers in its plans for the site. Sharp is bucking current trends in two directions. First, it is concentrating on manufacturing, rather than outsourcing production and concentrating on design and marketing. Second, it is building new production facilities in a high-cost country rather than in a low-cost area. So it is running against both the trend to outsource production and to "off-shore" that production. In many economically developed countries, governments are offering a range of incentives to attract and retain jobs in manufacturing and other sectors of the economy.

This may represent a trend toward HCCS—high-cost country sourcing. The idea here is that being "at home," or in some cases "closer to home," may provide advantages, or at least make off-shore production less attractive. First, as the cost of transportation increases, staying closer to home may become more economical. Second, while the labor costs of LCCS (low-cost country sourcing) will probably always be a reason to offshore, producing closer to home allows better control of quality and service. One furniture maker in Manitowoc says he can offer 150 different colors of furniture, a variety that is possible because he does not have to produce months in advance in order to bring product from offshore. As manufacturing moves from make-to-stock, repetitive production to more flexible approaches, other industries may find themselves in this situation.

In 2009, the cumulative value of outsourcing contracts was more than $200 billion, and developments such as cloud computing, increased used of multiple-source supply systems, and risk management provide indications that extensive outsourcing and offshoring activity will continue. But only about 35 percent of outsourcing proposals directly met buyers' objectives in 2009, a sharp decline from prior years, and outsourcing contracts generally appear to be decreasing in terms of average duration and contract value.

What factors will determine whether or not more manufacturing and other activities will remain in—or come back to—high-cost countries such as the United States in coming years? What are the implications of your analysis for economic prosperity—and job creation—in these countries?

Sources: David Jacoby and Bruna Figueiredo, "The Art of High-Cost Country Sourcing," *Supply Chain Management Review,* May/June 2008, pp. 32–38; Yukari Iwatani Kane, "Sharp Focuses on Manufacturing," *The Wall Street Journal,* July 9, 2008, p. B1; "Global Oursourcing Contract Volume Set to Climb in 2010," *PR Newswire,* March 18, 2010, http://www.prnewswire.com/news-releases/global-outsourcing-contract-volume-set-to-climb-in-2010-88404022.html (accessed June 12, 2010); John Hill, "Manitowoc Plant Gets Second Chance to Make Cookware," *Corporate Report Wisconsin,* November 1, 2006, http://www.allbusiness.com/north-america/united-states-wisconsin/4104370-1.html (accessed June 12, 2010); Linda Wertheimer, "Are Outsourced Jobs Coming Back?" National Public Radio, February 2, 2009, http://www.npr.org/templates/story/story.php?storyId-100131296 (accessed June 12, 2010); Stephanie Overby, "Multi-billion-dollar Outsourcing Deals Turn Bad," *ITWorldCanada,* March 31, 2010, http://www.itworldcanada.com/news/multi-billion-dollar-outsourcing-deals-that-went-bad/140342 (accessed June 12, 2010); and Timothy Aeppel, "Export Boom Fuels Factory Town's Revival," *The Wall Street Journal,* July 18, 2008, pp. A1, A14.

countries, which commonly lack skilled workers despite their abundant supply of labor. This situation favors the use of specialized machines. Although a few highly skilled persons are needed for maintenance and setup, the job of *attending* these machines (starting, feeding stock) can be performed by unskilled workers after a short training period. In contrast, general-purpose machinery requires many more skilled operators.

These operators could be trained in technical schools, but the low prestige of such employment, a cultural characteristic, affects both the demand for and the supply of vocational education. Students do not demand it, and the traditional attitude of educational administrators in many developing nations causes resources to be directed to professional education instead of to the trades.

These economic and cultural variables, important as they are, are not the only considerations of management; the requirements of the host government must be met if the proposed plant is to become a reality.

Political Forces

When planning a new manufacturing facility in a developing country, management is frequently confronted by an intriguing paradox. Although the country desperately needs new job creation, which favors labor-intensive processes, government officials often insist on the most modern equipment. Local pride may be the cause, or it may be that these officials, wishing to see the new firm export, believe that only a factory with advanced technology can compete in world markets. They not only may be reluctant to take chances on "inferior" or untried alternatives, but also may feel that low-productivity technology will keep the country dependent on the industrialized countries. In some developing countries, this fear has been formalized by laws prohibiting the importation of used machinery.

Some Design Solutions

More often than not, after consideration of the environmental variables, the resultant plant design will be a hybrid or one using intermediate technology.

Hybrid Design Commonly, in designing plants for developing countries, engineers will use a hybrid of capital-intensive processes when they are considered essential to ensure product quality and labor-intensive processes to take advantage of the abundance of unskilled labor. For example, they may stipulate machine welding rather than hand welding but then use semimanual equipment for the painting, packaging, and materials handling.

Intermediate Technology In recent years, the press of a growing population and the rise in capital costs have forced the governments of developing nations to search for something less than highly automated processes. They are becoming convinced that there should be something midway between the capital- and labor-intensive processes that will create more jobs, require less capital, but still produce the desired product quality. Governments are urging investors to consider an **intermediate technology,** which, unfortunately, is not readily available in the industrialized nations. This means that international companies cannot transfer the technology with which they are familiar but must develop new and different manufacturing methods. It is also possible that the savings in reduced capital costs of the intermediate technology may be nullified by higher startup costs and the greater expense of its transfer.

LOCAL MANUFACTURING SYSTEM

Basis for Organization

Except for plants in large industrialized nations, the local manufacturing organization is commonly a scaled-down version of that found in the parent company. If the firm is organized by product companies or divisions (tires, industrial products, chemicals) in its home nation, the subsidiary will be divided into product departments. Manufacturing firms that use process organizations (departmentalized according to production processes) in the domestic operation will set up a similar structure in their foreign affiliates. In a paper-box factory, separate departments will cut the logs, produce the paper, and assemble the boxes. The only noticeable difference between the foreign and domestic operations is that in the foreign plant all these processes are more likely to be at one location because of the smaller size of each department.

Horizontal and Vertical Integration

The local manufacturing organization is rarely integrated either vertically or horizontally to the extent that the parent is. Some vertical integration is traditional, as in the case of the paper-box factory, and some will occur if it is necessary to ensure a supply of raw materials. In this situation, the subsidiary might be more

cu_{in}ib

Rory Burdick: Career Launch in International

Rory Burdick graduated from California Polytechnic State University with a business major and economics minor, both with an international concentration. Then he traveled, just for the adventure of it all.

After completing my courses at Cal Poly, I joined a group of friends who were traveling to South Africa from East Asia. I went on to travel through London, Amsterdam, Berlin, and Prague. After emptying my bank accounts, I returned to San Francisco to work in various technology startups.

I joined a successful startup whose customer base eventually grew to a size that required 24/7 customer support, and the decision was made to implement follow-the-sun coverage across the United States, Europe, India and China. This decision led to my first international work experience, managing the training of these offshore support groups. During this project I learned how to overcome cultural, communication and time zone issues. A college friend moved to Paris, which was a good excuse for a road trip originating in Amsterdam, through Paris, Marseille, Barcelona, back to Paris through the Pyrenees and returning to Amsterdam.

Shortly after that road trip, I was approached with an opportunity to interview for a position at Google. Once a part of Google, I joined a small global team and traveled on assignment to Atlanta, New York, and Frankfurt. A director visiting my group in Mountain View mentioned he was looking for someone to take a position in Brazil. Knowing very little about the country or the opportunity, I expressed interest and arranged an interview with the hiring manager, which led to a six-month assignment in Sao Paulo that included a short assignment in Buenos Aires. Since returning to the United States, I have spent time with my family in British Columbia and Nuevo Vallarta, and I am writing this profile from Sardinia, Italy.

I'd like to tell you my personal travels have been well thought out cultural excursions, but in reality I've chosen my destinations for surfing (South Africa, Mexico), snowboarding (Canada, Santiago), festivals (Europe, Jamaica), and the opportunity to travel with good friends in countries with favorable exchange rates! After joining Google, I worked hard to establish myself with local management as an ambitious self-starter who could be trusted with difficult projects where individual contributors would have minimal support from management. Once established as a strong individual contributor and leader, I was asked to travel to locations that were short-handed or needed project-specific burst labor. My travels enabled me to interface with employees from different locations around the world, which helped me make a name for myself. This strategy allowed me to make a case for taking the position in Brazil for a related group in a position I had never before performed.

Roughly four months passed between initially expressing my interest and being offered the position in Brazil, but I only had three weeks to prepare for departure! After the initial interview, I was given the names of several people who had worked or were currently working in South America. Some were Americans like me, and others were Brazilians who had grown up in or around Sao Paulo. I conducted a series of informational interviews with these staff members to hear what they had to say about their experiences. I asked about the culture of Brazil, personal safety, cost of living, and what the city of Sao Paulo had to offer. All of them had insightful comments, but nothing would fully prepare me for my assignment.

I can honestly say my time in Brazil was both the most challenging and most rewarding experience of my life. Sao Paulo has one of the most ethnically diverse populations in the world, and because of this I blended in with everyone else. I inherited a project that was behind schedule and suffered from various vendor and contractor issues, as well as internal customer issues. I had to quickly find solutions despite my language shortcomings, while maintaining a positive relationship with our Brazilian business partners. I managed this by closely watching the cultural norms of those around me and maintaining a positive attitude with a quiet confidence. By demonstrating my desire to perform well and my interest in establishing positive relationships, my Brazilian counterparts were extremely interested in working with me to find mutually beneficial solutions to the hurdles we faced.

There were many amazing aspects of my trip, but three stand out from the rest. Portuguese is a beautiful language with

vertically integrated than the parent, which depends on outside sources for many of its inputs. However, the additional investment is a deterrent to vertical integration, as are the extra profits gained by supplying inputs to these captive customers from the home plants. Some countries prohibit vertical integration for certain industries. In Mexico, for example, severe restrictions on private investment (Mexican or foreign) in the petroleum and petrochemical industry still exist and keep producers of products that use petrochemicals from achieving backward vertical integration. In contrast, some countries require a percentage of local content in finished products. When the subsidiary cannot meet the requirement by local sourcing, it may be forced to produce components that its parent does not.

Horizontal integration is much less prevalent in foreign subsidiaries, although restaurant chains, banks, food-processing plants, and other industries characterized by small production units often will, of course, integrate horizontally in the manner of the domestic company. Overseas affiliates themselves become conglomerates when the parent acquires a multinational. ■

"Paradoxically, in spite of the opportunities for [human resource management, or HR] to contribute to globalization in added-value ways, the HR function is not perceived in many companies as a full partner in the globalization process. Sometimes it is viewed as an obstacle, slowing down the process through bureaucratic central procedures. The ethnocentric and parochial HR systems and policies inherited from the past, focused on the parent company and projected onto the rest of the world, are all too often a barrier to the implementation of effective global organizational processes."

—Paul Evans, Vladimir Pucik, and Jean-Louis Barsoux,
The Global Challenge, 2002

sixteen

managing human resources in an international context

The effectiveness of every organization depends to a great extent on the nature of its workforce and how well its human resources are utilized. Their effective use depends on management's policies and practices. Management of a company's human resources is a shared responsibility. The day-to-day supervision of people on the job is the duty of the operating managers, who must integrate human, financial, and physical resources into an efficient production system. However, the formulation of policies and procedures for (1) estimation of workforce needs, (2) recruitment and selection, (3) training and development, (4) motivation, (5) compensation, (6) discipline, and (7) employment termination is generally the responsibility of personnel managers working in cooperation with executives from marketing, production and operations, and finance as well as the firm's lawyers.

global mind-set Combines an openness to and an awareness of diversity across markets and cultures with a propensity and ability to synthesize across this diversity

ethnocentric As used here, related to hiring and promoting employees on the basis of the parent company's home-country frame of reference

polycentric As used here, related to hiring and promoting employees on the basis of the specific local context in which the subsidiary operates

regiocentric As used here, related to hiring and promoting employees on the basis of the specific regional context in which the subsidiary operates

geocentric As used here, related to hiring and promoting employees on the basis of ability and experience without considering race or citizenship

Finding the right people to manage an organization can be difficult under any circumstances, but it is especially difficult to find good managers of overseas operations. Such positions require more and different skills than do purely domestic executive jobs. The right persons need to be bicultural, with knowledge of the business practices in the home country plus an understanding of business practices and customs in the host country. And to fully understand a culture, any culture, it is usually necessary to speak the language of its people. Only with a good grasp of the language can one understand the subtleties and humor and know what is really going on in the host country. Although difficult to locate, such managers do exist, and they may be found in (1) the home country, (2) the host country, or (3) a third country. ■

L01 Discuss the importance of creating a company "global mind-set."

Research indicates that many CEOs feel that developing a company **global mind-set** is a "prerequisite for global industry dominance."[1] Global mind-set is defined as "one that combines an openness to and awareness of diversity across cultures and markets with a propensity and ability to synthesize across this diversity." Percy Barnevik, who served as the leader for the merger of Swedish Asea with Swiss Brown Boveri to create the global engineering and manufacturing giant ABB, aptly observed, "Global managers have exceptionally open minds. They respect how different countries do things, and they have the imagination to appreciate why they do them that way. But they are also incisive; they push the limits of the culture. Global managers don't passively accept it when someone says, 'You can't do that in Italy or Spain because of the unions,' or 'You can't do that in Japan because of the Ministry of Finance.' They sort through the debris of cultural excuses and find opportunities to innovate."[2]

L02 Explain the relationship between competitive strategies (international, multidomestic, global, and transnational) and international human resource management approaches (ethnocentric, polycentric, regiocentric, and global).

THE INTERNATIONAL HUMAN RESOURCE MANAGEMENT APPROACH

Chapter 10 explained that two competing forces—the pressure to achieve global integration and reduce costs and the pressure to respond to local differentiation—determine which of four alternative competitive strategies (home replication, multidomestic, global, or transnational) a company should adopt. A company's competitive strategy should, in turn, drive the organization's approach to international human resource management (IHRM).

Heenan and Perlmutter developed a model that considers these four competitive strategies to determine whether the organization's approach to IHRM should be **ethnocentric, polycentric, regiocentric,** or **geocentric.**[3] Further, along with this decision, the employees used in the organization may be classified into one of three categories: (1) **home-country nationals** or **parent-country nationals (PCNs),** (2) **host-country nationals (HCNs),** or (3) **third-country nationals (TCNs).** These relationships are illustrated in Table 16.1.

RECRUITMENT AND SELECTION OF EMPLOYEES

The recruitment and selection of employees, frequently referred to as *staffing,* should be determined in a manner consistent with one of the four IHRM approaches the organization is pursuing, as discussed next.[4]

Ethnocentric Staffing Policy

Companies with a primarily international strategic orientation (characterized by low pressures for cost reduction and low pressures for local responsiveness) may adopt an ethnocentric staffing policy. In this approach, most decisions are made at headquarters, using the home country's frame of reference. International

home-country national Same as parent-country national

parent-country national (PCN) Employee who is a citizen of the nation in which the parent company is headquartered; also called *home-country national*

host-country national (HCN) Employee who is a citizen of the nation in which the subsidiary is operating, which is different from the parent company's home nation

third-country national (TCN) Employee who is a citizen of neither the parent company nation nor the host country

expatriate A person living outside his or her country of citizenship

companies (ICs) utilize citizens of their own countries, or PCNs, in key foreign management and technical positions.

At first, PCNs usually are not knowledgeable about the host-country culture and language. Many such **expatriates** have adapted, learned the language, and become thoroughly accepted in the host country, although it is also common that such managers encounter difficulty both in overcoming the biases of their own cultural experience and in being able to understand and perform effectively within the new operating context.

Labor negotiators and other specialists may be sent to troubleshoot such problems as product warranty, international contracts, taxes, accounting, and reporting. Teams may be sent from the home country to assist with new plant startup, and they would probably stay until subsidiary personnel were trained to run and maintain the new facilities.

An advantage to using home-country citizens abroad is to expand their experience in preparation for becoming high-level

▼ **TABLE 16.1** Strategic Approach, Organizational Concerns, and the International Human Resource Management Approach to Be Used

Aspects of the Enterprise	Orientation			
	Ethnocentric	**Polycentric**	**Regiocentric**	**Geocentric**
Primary strategic orientation/stage	Home replication	Multidomestic	Regional	Transnational
Perpetuation (recruiting, staffing, development)	People of home country developed for key positions everywhere in the world	People of local nationality developed for key positions in their own country	Regional people developed for key positions anywhere in the region	Best people everywhere in the world developed for key positions everywhere in the world
Complexity of the organization	Complex in home country, simple in subsidiaries	Varied and independent	Highly interdependent on a regional basis	"Global Web," complex, independent, worldwide alliances/network
Authority, decision making	High in headquarters	Relatively low in headquarters	High regional headquarters and/or high collaboration among subsidiaries	Collaboration of headquarters and subsidiaries around the world
Evaluation and control	Home standards applied to people and performance	Determined locally	Determined regionally	Globally integrated
Rewards	High in headquarters, low in subsidiaries	Wide variations, can be high or low rewards for subsidiary performance	Rewards for contribution to regional objectives	Rewards to international and local executives for reaching local and world-wide objectives based on global company goals
Communication, information flow	High volume of orders, commands, advice to subsidiaries	Little to and from headquarters, little among subsidiaries	Little to and from corporate headquarters, but may be high to and from regional headquarters and among countries	Horizontal, network relations
Geographic identification	Nationality of owner	Nationality of host country	Regional company	Truly global company, but identifying with national interests ("glocal")

Source: Adapted from David A. Heenan and Howard V. Perlmutter, *Multinational Organization Development* (Boston: Addison-Wesley, 1979).

managers at headquarters. Firms earning a large percentage of their profits from international sources require top executives who have a worldwide perspective, both business and political. It is difficult to impossible to acquire that sort of perspective without living and working abroad for a substantial period of time.

If new technology for the subsidiary is involved, the parent company will probably station at least one of its technologically qualified experts at the subsidiary until its local personnel learn the technology. In this way, the home office can be confident that someone is immediately available to explain headquarters' policies and procedures, see that they are observed, and interpret what is happening locally for the IC's management. Positions that an IC must take or demands that it must make are sometimes not popular with a host government. It can seem unpatriotic for a host-country national to do such things, whereas the host government can understand, and sometimes accept, such positions or demands from a foreigner.

more skilled and managerial slots must be given to the local people. If foreign-owned firms in Indonesia fail to hire enough *pribumi* (indigenous Indonesians), those firms are likely to encounter difficulties with reentry permits for foreign employees as well as with other government licenses and permits that they need. Bribery requests have been known to increase until more pribumi were hired and promoted.

A disadvantage of hiring local managers is that they are often unfamiliar with the home country of the IC and with its corporate culture, policies, and practices. As Liu Zhengrong, head of human resources for the German chemical group Lanxess, said of hiring local managers, "You lose something in terms of communication with the headquarters, but you get more hints about the local marketplace."[6] Differences in attitudes and values, as discussed in Chapter 4, can cause these locally hired managers to act in ways that surprise or displease headquarters. Also, local managers may create their own upward immobility

> ["If you look at capital investment strategy, marketing, research and development, those types of activities are international. But if you talk about people, humans, it is quite local in nature."]

LO3 **Compare** home-country, host-country, and third-country nationals as international company executives.

Polycentric Staffing Policy

When the company's primary strategic orientation is multi-domestic, with low pressures for cost reduction and high pressures for local responsiveness, a polycentric approach may be used. Polycentric staffing involves human resource policies that are created at the local level for the specific context of the local operations. Companies primarily hire HCNs for subsidiaries and PCNs for headquarters' positions; movement from the local subsidiaries to headquarters' positions is uncommon.

When HCNs are employed at the subsidiary level, there is no problem of their being unfamiliar with local customs, culture, and language. Furthermore, the first costs of employing them are generally lower (compared with the costs of employing home-country nationals and paying to move them and their families to the host country), although considerable training costs are sometimes necessary. If there is a strong feeling of nationalism in the host country, having nationals as managers can make the subsidiary seem less foreign. As Fujio Mitarai, chairman and CEO of Canon, said, "If you look at capital investment strategy, marketing, research and development, those types of activities are international. But if you talk about people, humans, it is quite local in nature."[5]

The government development plans and laws of some countries demand that employment in all sectors and at all levels reflect the racial composition of the society. In other words,

if, because of strong cultural or family ties, they are reluctant to accept promotions that would require them to leave the country to work at parent headquarters or at another subsidiary.

Foreign-owned companies that hire and train local, host-country people frequently experience a common, and disruptive, IHRM problem. The best of these people may be pirated away by local firms or other IC subsidiaries, as local executive recruiters are constantly on the lookout to make raids and entice the most talented employees to leave the original IC and join another firm that is seeking to overcome its own shortage of skilled personnel.

Finally, there can be a conflict of loyalty between the host country and the employer. For example, the host-country national may give preference to a local supplier even though imported products may be less expensive or of better quality. Local managers may oppose headquarters' requests to set low transfer prices in order to lower taxes payable to the host government.

Regiocentric Staffing Policy

Companies with a regional strategic approach (with slightly higher pressures for cost reduction and slightly lower pressures for local responsiveness than the multidomestic strategy) can employ a regiocentric staffing approach. In this approach, regional employees are selected for key positions in the region, employing a variety of HCNs and TCNs.

The disadvantages often encountered when using employees from the home or host country can sometimes be avoided by sending third-country nationals to fill management posts. A Chilean going to Argentina may have little cultural or language difficulty, but IC headquarters should be careful not to

264 SECTION 3 | The Organizational Environment

rely too heavily on similarities in language as a guide to similarities in other aspects of cultures. Mexicans, for example, may have to make considerable adjustments if they are transferred to Argentina, and they would find a move to Spain even more difficult. This is because the Mexican culture, in general, differs considerably from that of both Argentina and Spain. Although Argentina and Chile are certainly not identical, they do have many similarities. A fair generalization is that after an executive has adapted once to a new culture and language, a second or succeeding adaptation is easier.

may first be assigned to the international division at the firm's headquarters, where they handle problems submitted by foreign affiliates and meet visiting overseas personnel.

If the company feels that it probably will send PCNs abroad, it will frequently encourage them to study the language and culture of the country to which they are going. Such employees will probably be sent on short trips abroad to handle special assignments and to be exposed to foreign surroundings. Newly hired PCNs with prior overseas experience may undergo similar but shorter training periods.

> ## Training and development involve efforts to facilitate the acquisition of job-related knowledge, behavior, and skills.

An employer should not count on cost savings in using third-country nationals. Although they may come from countries where salary scales are lower, in such countries as Brazil and most of the nations of northwestern Europe, salaries may be higher than American companies are paying at comparable position levels.

Geocentric Staffing Policy

Companies with a transnational strategic orientation, driven simultaneously by high pressures for cost reduction and high pressures for local responsiveness, follow a geocentric staffing policy. These organizations select the best person for each job without considering national origin and can therefore capitalize on the advantages of each staffing policy. With a geocentric staffing policy, HRM strategy tends to be consistent across all subsidiaries, borrowing best practices from wherever they may be found across the company's worldwide network of operations rather than showing preference only to the practices used at headquarters within a local context.

TRAINING AND DEVELOPMENT

Training and development involve efforts to facilitate the acquisition of job-related knowledge, behavior, and skills. The training and development of managers and other key IC employees vary somewhat, depending on whether the candidate is from the home country, the host country, or a third country.

Home- or Parent-Country National

Relatively few recent college graduates are hired for the express purpose of being sent overseas. Usually they spend a number of years in the domestic (parent) company, and they may get into the company's international operations by design and persistence, by luck, or by a combination of those elements. They

It is increasingly possible for American ICs to supplement their in-house training for overseas work with courses in American business schools. In recognition of the growing importance of international business, those schools are expanding the number and scope of international business courses they offer. In addition, a number of university-level business schools are now operating in other countries.

A major concern for employers involves families of executives transferred overseas. Even though the employee may adapt to and enjoy the foreign experience, the family may not, and an unhappy family may sour the employee on the job or even split up the marriage. In such cases, the company may have to ship the family and its possessions back home at great expense. Consequently, many companies try to assess whether the executive's family can adapt to the foreign ambience before assigning the executive abroad. This is part of the subject of expatriates that is dealt with later in this chapter.

Host-Country National

The same general criteria for selecting home-country employees apply to host-country nationals. Usually, however, the training and development activities undertaken for HCNs will differ from those used for home-country nationals in that host-country nationals are more likely to lack knowledge of advanced business techniques, particularly those that are specific to business applications and operations of the IC, and knowledge of the company as a whole.

HCNs Hired in the Home Country Many multinationals try to solve the business technique problem by hiring host-country students upon their graduation from home-country business schools. After being hired, these new employees are usually sent to IC headquarters to receive indoctrination in the firm's policies and procedures as well as on-the-job training in a specific function, such as finance, marketing, or production.

HCNs Hired in the Host Country Because the number of host-country citizens graduating from home-country universities is limited, multinationals must also recruit locally for their management positions. To impart knowledge of business techniques, the company may do one or more things. It may set up in-house training programs in the host-country subsidiary, or it may utilize business courses in the host-country's universities. The IC may also send new employees to home-country business schools or to home-country training programs offered by the parent company. In addition, employees who show promise will be sent repeatedly to the parent-company headquarters, divisions, and other subsidiaries to observe the various enterprise operations and meet the other executives with whom they will be communicating during their careers. Such visits are also learning opportunities for the home office and the other subsidiaries.

Third-Country National

Hiring personnel who are citizens of neither the home country nor the host country is often advantageous. TCNs may accept lower wages and benefits than will employees from the home country, and they may come from a culture similar to that of the host country. In addition, they may have worked for another unit of the IC and thus be familiar with the company's policies, procedures, and people. This can simplify the training and development requirements for such recruits.

The use of TCNs has become particularly prevalent in the developing countries because of shortages of literate, not to mention skilled, locals. It can be an advantage to get someone who already resides in the country and has the necessary work permits and knowledge of the local languages and customs.

Host-Country Attitudes If the host government emphasizes employment of its own citizens, third-country nationals will not be welcomed any more than will home-country people. Actually, third-country nationals could face an additional obstacle in obtaining necessary work permits. For example, the host government can understand that the German parent company of a subsidiary would want some German executives to look after its interests in the host country. It may be harder to convince the government that a third-country native is any better for the parent than a local executive would be.

Generalizations about TCNs Are Difficult We must be careful with generalizations about third-country personnel, partly because people achieve that status in different ways. They may be foreigners hired in the home country and sent to a host-country subsidiary either because they have had previous experience there or because that country's culture is similar to their own. Third-country nationals may have originally been home-country personnel who were sent abroad and became dissatisfied with the job but not with the host country. After leaving the firm that sent them abroad, they take positions with subsidiaries of multinationals from different home countries. Another way in which TCNs can be created is by promotion within an IC. For instance, if a Spanish executive of the Spanish subsidiary of an Italian multinational is promoted to be general manager of the Italian firm's Colombian subsidiary, the Spanish executive is then a third-country national.

As multinationals increasingly take the *geocentric* view toward promoting (according to ability and not nationality), we are certain to see greater use of TCNs. This development will be accelerated as more executives of all nationalities gain experience outside their native lands. Another, and growing, source for third-country nationals is the heterogeneous body of international agencies. As indicated in Chapter 3, these agencies deal with virtually every field of human endeavor, and all member-countries send their nationals as representatives to the headquarters and branch office cities all over the world. Many of those people become available to, or can be hired away by, international companies.

LO4 Explain what an expatriate is, and identity some of the challenges and opportunities of an expat position.

EXPATRIATES

In Chapters 1 and 2, we discussed that international markets are becoming increasingly important to success for even small and medium-sized companies. To exploit these international opportunities, staffing of positions in international operations is an important strategic issue. Although many of the employees may be hired in the host country (sometimes called *inpatriates*), ICs have continued to send employees on foreign assignments. Some of the international positions, especially

> " ABOUT 80 PERCENT OF MEDIUM- AND LARGE-SIZED COMPANIES HAVE EMPLOYEES WORKING ABROAD, AND 65 PERCENT OF SURVEYED COMPANIES SAID THEY WERE PLANNING TO INCREASE THE USE OF EXPATS. "

those that deal with addressing a specific technical problem or transferring specialized knowledge, will be staffed with home- or third-country employees who are on short-term assignments (called *flexpatriates*). Yet companies will continue to staff many key positions with expatriates, employees who are relocated to the host country from the home country or a third country, with the assignment lasting for an extended period of time (two to four years is a common length of time for an expatriate assignment). In fact, about 80 percent of medium- and large-sized companies have employees working abroad, and 65 percent of surveyed companies said they were planning to increase the use of expats.[7] The average age of expats is getting somewhat younger, with 54 percent now being between 20 and 39 years, versus the historical average of 41 percent.[8] In addition, a higher proportion of expatriates are women, reaching 21 percent versus the historical average of 15 percent.

Why use expatriates rather than just hire local employees? Expatriates can bring technical or managerial skills that are scarce in the host country; they can help transfer or install companywide systems or cultures; they may provide a trusted connection for facilitating oversight or control over foreign operations, whether it is a new endeavor or an operation that is already in existence; or the international assignment may enable the expat to develop the skills and experiences that will allow a subsequent promotion into leadership positions of greater scope and responsibility within the IC. The most effective leaders in an increasingly complex and internationalizing world tend to be those who can understand and interact effectively with a variety of stakeholders, despite differences in culture or location. Expat assignments can demonstrate such skills, and these assignments have been reported to lead to faster promotions.[9]

The costs of using expatriates are substantial, estimated at about $50 billion annually for U.S. companies, so the performance of expatriates is an important issue for ICs.[10] Yet various studies report that failure rates for expatriate assignments—including failing to achieve performance targets for an international assignment or prematurely returning from the assignment—range from 25 to 45 percent.[11] Approximately one-quarter of expats leave their firms during the course of their overseas assignment, and an additional 28 percent leave their companies within a year of their return from abroad, hindering the IC's ability to retain and leverage the skills and experience that the expatriate has gained from the international assignment.[12]

One important cause of expatriate performance problems is **culture shock,** which is the anxiety people often experience when they move from a culture that they are familiar with to one that is entirely different.[13] Because familiar signs and symbols are no longer present in the new culture, a person experiencing culture shock tends to feel lack of direction or inadequacy from not knowing what to do or how things are done in the new culture. Physical and emotional discomfort and feelings of disorientation and confusion are a common experience for people who go to other nations to work, live, or

culture shock The anxiety people often experience when they move from a culture that they are familiar with to one that is entirely different

study. Many expatriates and members of their families are affected by culture shock, sometimes to a very great degree. Once a person has grown accustomed to a new culture, returning to one's home culture can produce the same experiences as described in the preceding phases, referred to as *reverse culture shock.*

Researchers have identified three different dimensions associated with cross-cultural adjustment.[14] The first is associated with the work context, such as the extent of job clarity, inherent conflict in the person's role, and amount of discretion associated with completing the job tasks. Adjustment to the general environment, the second dimension, is associated with reacting to differences in housing, food, education, health, safety, and transportation. The third dimension, interaction with local nationals, involves adjusting to differences in behavioral norms, ways of dealing with conflict, communication patterns, and other relationship issues that can produce anger or frustration. An expatriate can experience some degree of culture shock associated with any or all of these three dimensions.

To enhance expatriate performance, ICs should consider the support that they provide to the employee during predeparture, while away on assignment, and upon repatriation.[15] Preassignment, the focus of support efforts should be on ensuring that the expatriate has the skills needed for successful performance in the foreign assignment, including language and cultural training, career counseling, and any needed technical or other skill development. Support during assignment includes the use of mentors (both home- and host-country), career counseling, and communication strategies to ensure that the expatriate remains connected to the IC's strategy, people, policies, and culture. Repatriation support, including management of the relocation to the home or

other nation and reintegration into the company, is discussed later in this section. Organizational support has been shown to be a predictor of the success of expatriates' adjustment to their international postings.[16]

The Expatriate's Family

It has been suggested that as many as 9 out of 10 expatriates' failures are family related, and 81 percent of the employees who declined relocations in a recent study cited family concerns as the basis for their decision. In contrast to immigrants, who typically commit themselves to becoming part of their new country of residence, expats usually are only living temporarily in the new nation, so they often fail to adopt the host country's culture and seldom attempt to gain citizenship in that nation. The cultural adaptation pressures may be particularly great for the accompanying spouses, especially because they often are unable to work in the host country and may experience more challenges with regard to their personal identity. Spouses also typically need to interact more extensively with the local host community than do their expatriate partners, for such things as shopping, schools, and the management of domestic help, and related issues exacerbate adjustment pressures.[17] The stress an overseas move places on spouses and children will ultimately affect employees no matter how dedicated they may be to the company. Even worse, if the employee asks to go home early, the company is losing a "million-dollar corporate-training investment" in the executive. On the other hand, expatriates tend to have better satisfaction and performance when their spouses and other family members are able to adjust well to the new host country context.[18] Although a recent study reported that 77 percent of companies considered that cross-cultural training was highly valuable, only 21 percent of the companies required such training for their expats or their families.[19]

> **It has been suggested that as many as 9 out of 10 expatriates' failures are family related.**

LO5 Discuss the increasing importance of accommodating the trailing spouse of an expatriate executive.

Trailing Spouses in Two-Career Families

While 82 percent of expats are accompanied by a spouse or partner, the number of two-career families is growing. That is a major factor affecting expatriate adjustment and performance, and it can complicate matters when one spouse is offered a juicy job abroad.[20] In many countries, the employee's spouse does not have the legal right to work, as work permits for foreigners may be difficult or nearly impossible to acquire. Even though 60 percent of the partners were employed before their spouse's international assignment began, as few as 8 percent were employed during the course of the assignment, which can increase financial pressures and strain relationships before, during, and after the expatriate assignment.[21] The trailing spouse must often make major adjustments in lifestyle, family balance of power, and self-image. They often experience stages of grief from derailment of their careers that is similar to the loss of a loved one—going through shock, denial, and anger—and sometimes fail to reach the reconciliation stage of adjustment.[22] Indeed, concern about the implications of an international assignment for the employee's partner and the partner's career prospects represented the second highest reason for refusing an expatriate assignment, behind family concerns (such as children's education, family adjustment, resistance by the partner, difficult location for assignment, cultural adjustments, length of the assignment, and language).

In efforts to ease the problem, some companies are starting programs that give trailing spouses more help in adjusting. Such help may take the form of assisting with job hunting in the host country, writing résumés, providing language and cultural training, identifying career opportunities, or giving tips on local interview techniques. A reported 30 percent of companies provide education or training assistance to spouses, 36 percent sponsor work permits, and 69 percent provide language training to spouses. Many companies have made greater use of shorter international assignments, under the belief that this can be less disruptive to the expatriate family's lives while still permitting benefits from the international assignment of personnel. "People are going on assignments for 12, 9, even 6 months in much more dynamic arrangements than used to be the case," said Scott Sullivan, senior vice president at GMAC. "What it is to be an expatriate is changing."

Another option many companies apparently are pursuing is to hire people for expat assignments who are single and often younger as well, with over 40 percent of such positions being filled by unmarried personnel.[23] It should be noted that hiring of single people for expatriate positions is not without its own set of potential concerns.

Expatriate Children May Suffer the Most

Children are an important but often overlooked consideration when planning for an international move, particularly because 45 percent of expats have children between the ages of 5 and 12.[24] Although an overseas stint may be seen as critical for career advancement of a parent, it can wreak havoc upon children's lives. Children are seldom involved in the initial decision-making process associated with a move abroad. This can result in the children experiencing many feelings (such as insecurity, frustration, and powerlessness) from being uprooted from friends and many of the sources of their own identity. A move does not merely involve changing schools; there are also new systems, new learning styles, new language, and so forth that the child must contend with. Sometimes these children are referred to as *third-culture kids* (or *TCKs*) because they often speak several different languages, hold passports from more than one country, and have difficulty explaining where they are from (where "home" is). As a consequence of these challenges, companies are increasing their focus on easing the disruptions faced by children.

Preparation for the Transition: Language Training

The English language has become the *lingua franca* of the world; in effect, it is everybody's second language. Nevertheless, foreign language skill has been shown to be a critical factor influencing effective adjustment of expatriates and their family members within the host country. When you are trying to sell to potential customers, it is much better to speak their language. As English speakers try to sell abroad, it is far more likely that their customers will speak English than that the English speakers will be able to speak the customers' language. Customers can then hide behind their language during negotiations. If your career involves international business—and few can avoid at least some exposure to it—it is likely to suffer if you speak English only.

Expatriate Services

Although most U.S. expatriates currently continue health coverage with their company's domestic plans, we can expect that to change in the near future as expatriate health care programs are being created to assist companies and expatriates with claims administration, language translations, currency conversions, and service standardization.[25] Similarly, banks are developing expatriate services, allowing expatriates to sign up for services

teach you the social norms and where to shop and not to shop. Expats can teach you where to get things only expats want. Websites that focus on expatriate issues and can assist you in preparing for, adjusting to, or returning from an expatriate assignment include www.ExpatExpert.com and www.branchor.com.

Repatriation—The Shock of Returning Home

There is often reverse culture shock when an expatriate returns to the home company and country. The expatriate will have gained new skills and knowledge, and the company's attitudes and people will have changed. Expatriates who have become accustomed to high levels of autonomy while abroad often struggle with the more restrictive work context when they return home, as well as experiencing the common frustration of failing to be promoted or have their job expectations fulfilled after repatriation. If fully utilized, the repatriate can provide the company with rare, difficult to imitate, and competitively valuable knowledge and skills.

That is why planning for an expat's return should start well before the overseas assignment even begins. The person and the employer should discuss up front how the assignment will fit the employee's long-range career goals and how the company will handle the return. Challenges of repatriation should be discussed even before departure, and a mentor program should be considered between the expat and a mentor back home. During the assignment, expats should be encouraged to make regular visits back to the home country offices to help "stay in the loop" and feel part of the organizational network. When expats come back, companies have to understand that they are going to be different and should try to harness their new knowledge.[26] Efforts should be made to help the repatriates find appropriate positions that use their newly

> **"Planning for an expat's return should start well before the overseas assignment even begins."**

online and providing 24-hour assistance to their customers, regardless of where in the world the expatriate is working.

In recognition of expatriate family issues, some companies have begun to prepare and assist these families. Assistance may take the form of realistic job previews for expatriates (and sometimes for their family members), training in the culture and language of the host country, assistance in finding suitable schools or medical specialists, or even arranging for long-distance care for elderly relatives or parents while the family is living abroad. House-hunting help may be given, and the new transplants should be taken on grocery and hardware shopping trips with locals and expats who have been in the host country for a while. Locals can

developed skills and to help the expat and the family members re-acculturate, including access to counseling and other forms of support in order to promote adjustment success and build company loyalty. Nevertheless, only 49 percent of ICs have repatriation programs, and 68 percent of expatriates report that they do not have any guaranteed position in their IC after the end of their international assignment.[27] "We are seeing rapid globalization, and it's going to become a real problem to find people who are willing and qualified to go overseas if everyone hears about people who were not satisfied" after they are repatriated, said Lisa Johnson, the director of consulting services for Cendant Mobility.[28]

COMPENSATION

Establishing a compensation plan that is equitable and consistent and yet does not overcompensate the overseas executive is a challenging, complex task, especially since a "one-size-fits-all" approach does not match up well with the reality of diverse company and country assignments. Rebecca Powers of Mercer Human Resource Consulting said, "More companies are now sending employees on expatriate assignments, so there is a greater need to keep pace with the cost of living changes. Employers need to be proactive in managing their expatriate programs to ensure they receive a proper return on their investment and employees are compensated fairly."[29] If ICs are not able to compensate in a manner that is perceived to be fair and attractive, it will become ever more difficult to attract the quantity and quality of potential expatriates needed to satisfy the company's international requirements. This can also fundamentally affect the extent to which a company's future leaders are shaped by such experiences and have developed the skills and experiences needed to lead effectively in an increasingly complex and internationalizing business environment.

The method favored by the majority of American ICs has been to pay a base salary equal to that paid to a domestic counterpart and then, in the belief that no one should be worse off for accepting foreign employment, to add a variety of allowances and bonuses. Table 16.2 provides an example of some of the compensation costs for sending an American manager on a two-year assignment to Russia. Many international assignments will entail significantly higher levels of additional costs, when compared with those in the home country, than suggested by this example.

▼ **TABLE 16.2** Total Compensation Costs for Sending an Expatriate American Manager to Russia

The following compensation costs are illustrative of those an IC might encounter annually when sending an American manager and his or her family (spouse, two children) to Russia for a two-year assignment.

Compensation Component	Annual Cost (US$)
Base salary	$160,000
Incentive plan	16,000
Location differential (hardship premium)	7,000
Housing allowance	78,400
Cost-of-living allowance	8,500
Automobile allowance	36,500
Home leave	12,000
Educational assistance	24,000
Relocation/repatriation expenses	25,000
Total compensation before tax	**$367,400**
Tax assistance	54,200
Total compensation expense	**$421,600**
Other Expenses	
Preparation services (passports, visas, language training, etc.)	$ 3,800
Settling-in services	4,500
Emergency leave	6,700
Total annual cost for expatriate	**$436,600**

Source: Author estimates and "U.S. Firms Extend Global Reach," *Workforce Management,* December 2004, p. 142.

Because of the high cost typically associated with expatriate assignments, some companies have attempted various schemes to help reduce these costs. In terms of salaries and other benefits, some companies have localized their workforce, replacing expatriates with qualified but lower cost locals if such personnel are available. In other instances, an expatriate may begin with a higher salary and benefit package, but then have some but not all of this extra "expatriate package" phased out over time, creating a hybrid compensation scheme (e.g., key benefits such as children's schooling or housing subsidies may be maintained while other perks are eliminated). Another approach is to eliminate all expatriate compensation and benefits premiums, substituting a "local terms" package identical to what would be paid to an indigenous manager. This latter approach may be used from the point of initial recruitment, or be applied after a certain trigger point is reached (such as time since initial appointment of the expat).[30]

Salaries

The practice of paying home-country nationals the same salaries as their domestic counterparts permits worldwide consistency for this part of the compensation package. Because of the increasing use of third-country nationals, those personnel are generally treated in the same way.

Some firms take the equal-pay-for-equal-work concept one step further and pay the same base salaries to host-country nationals. In countries that legislate yearly bonuses and family allowances for their citizens, a local national may receive what appears to be a higher salary than is paid the expatriate, although companies usually make extra payments to prevent expatriates from falling behind in this regard. In the United Kingdom, it is a common practice to pay executives relatively lower salaries and to provide them with expensive perquisites, such as chauffeured automobiles, housing, and club memberships.

Allowances

Allowances are payments made to compensate expatriates for the extra costs they must incur to live as well abroad as they did in the home country. The most common allowances are for housing, cost of living, tax differentials, education, and moving.

Housing Allowances Housing allowances are designed to permit executives to live in houses as good as those they had at home. A common rule of thumb is for the firm to pay all of the rent that is in excess of 15 percent of the executive's salary.

Cost-of-Living Allowances

Cost-of-living allowances are based on differences in the prices paid for food, utilities, transportation, entertainment, clothing, personal services, and medical expenses overseas compared with the prices paid for these items in the headquarters' city. Many ICs use the U.S. Department of State index, which is based on the cost of these items in Washington, D.C., but have found it is not altogether satisfactory. For one thing, critics claim this index is not adjusted often enough to account for either the rapid inflation in some countries or the changes in relative currency values. Another objection is that the index does not include many cities in which the firm operates. As a result, many companies take their own surveys or use data from the United Nations, the World Bank, the International Monetary Fund, or private consulting firms. Figures and comparisons on costs of living, prices, and wages can also be found in private publications. Table 16.3 provides a ranking of the 20 cities with the highest cost of living, as of 2009, as well as a ranking of quality of living.

allowances Employee compensation payments added to base salaries because of higher expenses encountered when living abroad

▼ **TABLE 16.3** Cost-of-Living and Quality-of-Living Rankings of 20 Cities, from Highest to Lowest

Cost-of-Living Rank	City	Country	Quality-of-Living Rank	City	Country
1	Tokyo	Japan	1	Vienna	Austria
2	Osaka	Japan	2	Zurich	Switzerland
3	Moscow	Russia	2	Geneva	Switzerland
4	Geneva	Switzerland	4	Vancouver	Canada
5	Hong Kong	Hong Kong	5	Auckland	New Zealand
6	Zurich	Switzerland	6	Dusseldorf	Germany
7	Copenhagen	Denmark	7	Frankfurt	Germany
8	New York City	United States	7	Munich	Germany
9	Beijing	China	9	Bern	Switzerland
10	Singapore	Singapore	10	Sydney	Australia
11	Milan	Italy	11	Copenhagen	Denmark
12	Shanghai	China	12	Wellington	New Zealand
13	Paris	France	13	Amsterdam	Netherlands
14	Oslo	Norway	14	Ottawa	Canada
15	Caracas	Venezuela	15	Brussels	Belgium
16	London	United Kingdom	16	Toronto	Canada
17	Tel Aviv	Israel	17	Berlin	Germany
18	Rome	Italy	18	Melbourne	Australia
19	Helsinki	Finland	19	Luxembourg	Luxembourg
20	Dubai	United Arab Emirates	20	Stockholm	Sweden

Note: Cost-of-living index includes cost of housing. Base City, New York City, USA = 100. Cost-of-living index is for 2009. Quality-of-living index is for 2010.

Sources: Mercer Human Resource Counsulting, *2009 Cost-of-Living Survey,* http://www.mercer.com/costoflivingpr#Top_50 (accessed June 8, 2010); Mercer Human Resource Consulting, *2010 Quality of Living Survey,* http://www.mercer.com/qualityoflivingpr#City_Ranking_Tables (accessed June 8, 2010).

bonuses Expatriate employee compensation payments in addition to base salaries and allowances because of hardship, inconvenience, or danger

Allowances for Tax Differentials

ICs pay tax differentials when the host-country taxes are higher than the taxes that the expatriates would pay on the same compensation and consumption at home. The objective is to ensure that expatriates will not have less after-tax take-home pay in the host country than they would at home. This can create a considerable extra financial burden on an American parent company because, among other things, the U.S. Internal Revenue Code treats tax allowances as additional taxable income. There are other tax disincentives for Americans to work abroad.

Education Allowances

Expatriates are naturally concerned that their children receive educations at least equal to those they would get in their home countries, and many want their children taught in their native language. Primary and secondary schools with teachers from most industrialized home countries are available in many cities around the world, but these are private schools and therefore charge tuition. ICs either pay the tuition or, if there are enough expatriate children, operate their own schools. For decades, petroleum companies in the Middle East and Venezuela have maintained schools for their employees' children.

Moving and Orientation Allowances

Companies generally pay the total costs of transferring their employees overseas. These costs include transporting the family, moving household effects, and maintaining the family in a hotel on a full expense account until the household effects arrive. Some firms find it less expensive to send the household effects by air rather than by ship because the reduction in hotel expenses more than compensates for the higher cost of air freight. It has also been found that moving into a house sooner raises the employee's morale.

Companies may also pay for some orientation of the employees and their families. Companies frequently pay for language instruction, and some will provide the family with guidance on the intricacies of everyday living, such as shopping, hiring domestic help, and sending children to school.

Bonuses

Bonuses (or *premiums*), unlike allowances, are paid by firms in recognition that expatriates and their families undergo some hardships and inconveniences and make sacrifices while living abroad. Bonuses include overseas premiums, contract termination payments, and home leave reimbursement.

Overseas Premiums

Overseas premiums are additional payments to expatriates and are generally established as a percentage of the base salary. They typically range from 10 to 25 percent. If the living conditions are extremely disagreeable, the company may pay larger premiums for hardship posts. The U.S. Department of State maintains a list of hardship differential pay premiums that is often used as a reference by ICs and expats. Table 16.4 shows the hardship differentials for 25 selected cities as of June 2010.

Contract Termination Payments

These payments are made as inducements for employees to stay on their jobs and work out the periods of their overseas contracts. The payments are made at the end of the contract periods only if the employees have worked out their contracts. Such bonuses are used in the construction and petroleum industries and by other firms that have contracts requiring work abroad for a specific period of time or for a specific project. They may also be used if the foreign post is a hardship or not a particularly desirable one.

Home Leave[31]

ICs that post home-country—and sometimes third-country—nationals in foreign countries make it a practice to pay for periodic trips back to the home country by such employees and their families. The reasons for this are

▼ **TABLE 16.4** Hardship Differential Pay Premiums for Selected Cities and Countries, 2010

City and Country	Differential Pay Premium (%)
Kabul, Afghanistan	35
Sarajevo, Bosnia-Herzegovina	20
São Paulo, Brazil	10
Phnom Penh, Cambodia	25
Guangzhou, China	25
Bogotá, Colombia	5
Cairo, Egypt	15
Tbilisi, Georgia	25
Port-au-Prince, Haiti	35
Kolkata, India	25
Jakarta, Indonesia	25
Baghdad, Iraq	35
Kingston, Jamaica	15
Nairobi, Kenya	30
Mexico City, Mexico	15
Peshawar, Pakistan	35
Karachi, Pakistan	30
St. Petersburg, Russia	20
Riyadh, Saudi Arabia	20
Johannesburg, South Africa	10
Bangkok, Thailand	10
Istanbul, Turkey	10
Kiev, Ukraine	20
Caracas, Venezuela	20
Harare, Zimbabwe	30

Source: U.S. Department of State, "Post (Hardship) Differential," June 6, 2010, http://aoprals.state.gov/Web920/location.asp?menu_id=95 (accessed June 8, 2010).

GLOBAL gauntlet

Are Women Appropriate for International Assignments?

Although women make up about 47 percent of the workforce in the United States, they represent a relatively small (albeit growing) fraction of the population of expatriates. Why this difference, especially with the pressing need for finding and developing competent global leaders? Adler examined three myths about women in international management:

Myth 1: **Women do not want to be international managers.**

Myth 2: **Companies refuse to send women abroad.**

Myth 3: **Foreigners' prejudice against women renders them ineffective.**

When Adler tested these myths empirically, neither the first nor the third was supported, but the second one was. Adler's research suggested that 70 percent of her sample of international companies were hesitant to select women for expatriate assignments. Why? Among the reasons expressed were that women in dual-career relationships would experience problems with international assignments, that gender-based prejudice would limit women's performance in many challenging countries or cultures, that women might feel lonely and isolated in an international assignment or be subjected to sexual harassment, or that the men making selection decisions regarding international assignments were themselves biased by traditional views and stereotypes regarding the appropriateness of assigning women to expatriate positions.

Is this hesitancy by companies regarding selecting women for international assignments justified? Research has shown that women are just as eager to go abroad as are men, sometimes more so. Additional research has shown that gender is unrelated to the performance ratings of expatriates, with the adjustment of expatriates to the host-country context, or with the intention of expatriates to leave their ICs. Recent studies have even suggested that the skills and identity typically associated with women (e.g.,

attentiveness to personal aspects of business and skill in building interpersonal relationships) may actually give women an edge over men for some expatriate assignments. In addition, rather than cultural attributes serving as a barrier to the effectiveness of women expats (e.g., a women-unfriendly environment in some host-country cultures), as has sometimes been argued in explaining why women could not or should not be assigned to international positions, these structural aspects may serve as an advantage for women in international roles.

Indeed, women may be able to divert attention from gender by demonstrating individualized sources of legitimacy and power, such as functional expertise and experience, and thereby enhance their effectiveness in international assignments. Similarly, although studies have reported that women assigned to countries where females have lower social status often have a more difficult time adjusting, they are nevertheless rated as being equally effective as men at their jobs. Some Japanese even refer to female expats as "the third gender" because they are accorded a different role and status than local women. A recent Australian study showed that childless single women were most likely to take expatriate roles because they did not encounter the same role conflicts and social pressures that married women or women with children might face. Women expatriates who are married are much less likely to take a partner overseas with them than is the case for male expatriates. Only 16 percent of women bring partners, versus 57 percent for male expatriates.

So should ICs select more women for expatriate assignments? Are there circumstances in which you believe that the use of women expatriates should be most strongly considered, or perhaps not considered at all?

Sources: Nancy J. Adler, "Women Do Not Want International Careers: And Other Myths about International Management," *Organizational Dynamics* 13, no. 2 (1984), pp. 66–80; Paula M. Caligiuri and Wayne Cascio, "Can We Send Her There? Maximizing the Success of Western Women on Global Assignments," *Journal of World Business* 33 (1998), pp. 394–417; Rosalie Tung, "Female Expatriates: The Model Global Manager?" *Organizational Dynamics*, August 2004, pp. 243–53; Phyllis Tharenou, "Disruptive Decisions to Leave Home: Gender and Family Differences in Expatriation Choices," *Organizational Behavior and Human Decision Processes*, March 2008, pp. 183–200; Ann Pomeroy, "Outdated Policies Hinder Female Expats," *HR Magazine*, December 2006, p. 16; and Jeremy Smerd, "More Women, Young Workers on the Move," *Workforce Management*, August 2007, pp. 9–10.

cu in ib

Laura Gunderson

I first caught the travel bug at age 6, as a result of growing up in Jakarta, Indonesia, as part of an expatriate family. Upon return to the U.S., I spent my life traveling, living, and studying all over the country, and then the world in places such as Australia, Mexico, New Zealand, and the United Kingdom. I had no idea that I could actually satisfy this craving for travel and international perspective while actually earning a living. I decided to attend Cal Poly–San Luis Obispo as a Business Administration major, but frankly at that point I really didn't even know what I wanted to do with my life.

It quickly became apparent that regardless of what level you were as a student taking business courses such as finance, accounting, economics, business law, or marketing, a common thread appeared amongst them all. This commonality was the incredible complications that arose when a business wanted to expand in any way internationally. This realization really struck me, and I wanted to understand how *do* all these aspects of business work together to create the best solutions . . . beyond just the United States. When it came time to select a concentration, I distinctly remember thinking, "How could I *not* do international business?"

I embarked on my newfound educational course, taking all classes related to how to resolve the issues posed by doing business internationally. International human resource management (IHRM), in particular, captured my interest. Although I didn't know how, I knew I wanted to work with a company to leverage their greatest assets, their people, to achieve business success. I could combine my passion for people with my passion for business success (dating back to my childhood summer sidewalk lemonade café business venture). As I was graduating at one of the most difficult economic times the country had seen in decades, making this dream a reality seemed near to impossible. However, after much hard work and preparation, I have now worked in IHRM for a little over a year coordinating expatriate, repatriate and host-to-host assignees on three different continents for a Fortune 100 company. My experience has been working with assignees, business leaders and HR colleagues across all functions and located around the country and globe. Throughout my experience, I faced numerous challenges specific to IHRM supporting business success, including but not limited to:

- Relocation: How do we coordinate an employee's immigration and tax considerations? How do we prepare them for the cultural differences they will experience?
- Talent management: How do we best leverage the experiences and knowledge of individuals who have gone

on assignment? How do we avoid the dreaded "out of sight, out of mind" experience felt by many assignees upon repatriation?

- Recruitment: What criteria are we selecting candidates based on?
- Employee development: Are we a culture that supports assignments as a career steppingstone? How do we ensure that assignees are still receiving an equivalent access to HR programs and support as domestic employees?
- Compensation: How can we properly incentivize employees to live and work in less desirable areas, especially if they have a family?
- Labor relations: Does a union-represented environment affect an employee's ability or desire to go on an assignment?
- Information systems: How are we managing employee data in countries where our typical infrastructure or software systems may not exist?

Considering the economic climate, cost considerations were a huge component of every single decision: What is the best option to balance what is best for the company strategically and what is best for the assignee personally, while keeping the bottom line in mind. In addition, many of these challenges were completely unique, and our team had to stretch to use all resources available to take action, usually on a short timeframe. I learned the best way to resolve these situations was to ask as many questions as possible, and to continuously learn from my own and others' experience. As an entry level professional, no one will expect you to be an expert, otherwise they would have hired one, and you don't get to be an expert without starting somewhere. A large majority of the lessons learned during my college courses were directly applicable from my first day on the job, so believe it or not, it was incredibly helpful to keep my course notes and textbooks available.

An inspiring mentor of mine explained to me that luck was nothing more than being prepared for an opportunity when it arises, which allows you to make the most of any situation. I have found this to be absolutely true in every situation, which is why as an HR professional and as someone who recently went through the long and exhausting job search process, my strongest advice is simply to be prepared. This doesn't mean you have to have a dozen internships abroad or speak five languages, because I definitely didn't, though it certainly wouldn't hurt. I suggest that you apply and interview for as many positions as possible in order to gain comfort and experience speaking with recruiters. Send your resume to everyone, including teachers, mentors, alumni, family, and friends for editing and review; it may even open unexpected doors and networks. If you are currently employed and an IHRM position is not readily available, volunteer or suggest HR projects related to your international business and learn as much as possible about your firm's international programs. Continue to build your networks and communicate your interests to as many people as possible; there is always an opportunity out there. It is imperative to advertise yourself and your interests while doing as much as possible to prepare for when that great IHRM job does present itself.

Although challenging and sometimes stressful, working in IHRM has always been incredibly rewarding. I feel I am truly helping people and program success by finding the best solutions for both the company and the individual employee. By stretching me in so many ways, both personally and professionally, working in IHRM has given me a great international business foundation because I truly understand how HR directly supports international business ventures. Everyone can gain from this experience and take their careers as far as possible—the sky is the limit, and I hope to see you there!

twofold. One, companies do not want employees and their families to lose touch with the home country and its culture. Two, companies want to have employees spend at least a few days at company headquarters to renew relationships with headquarters' personnel and catch up with new company policies and practices.

Some firms grant three-month home leaves after an employee has been abroad about three years, but it is a more common practice to give two to four weeks' leave each year. All transportation costs are paid to and from the executive's hometown, and all expenses are paid during the executive's stay at company headquarters.

Compensation Packages Can Be Complicated

One might think from the discussion to this point that **compensation packages,** while costly—the extras frequently total 50 percent or more of the base salary—are fairly straightforward in their calculation. Nothing could be further from the truth.

What Percentage? All allowances and a percentage of the base salary are usually paid in the host-country currency. What should this percentage be? In practice, it varies from 65 to 75 percent, with the remainder being banked wherever the employee wishes. One reason for such practices is to decrease the local portion of the salary, thereby lowering host-country income taxes and giving the appearance to government authorities and local employees that there is less difference between the salaries of local and foreign employees than is actually the case. Another reason is that expatriate employees have various expenses that must be paid in home-country currency. Such expenses may include professional society memberships, purchases during home leave, payments on outstanding debts in the employee's home country (e.g., mortgage, school loans), and tuition and other costs for children in home-country universities.

What Exchange Rate? Inasmuch as most of the expatriate's compensation is usually denominated in the host-country currency but established in terms of the home-country currency to achieve comparable compensation throughout the enterprise, a currency exchange rate must be chosen. In countries whose currencies are freely convertible into other currencies, this presents no serious problem, although the experienced expatriate will argue that an exchange rate covers only international transactions and may not represent a true purchasing power parity between the local and home-country currencies. For instance, such items as bread and milk are rarely traded internationally, and living costs and inflation rates may be much higher in the host country than in the home country. International companies attempt to compensate for such differences in the cost-of-living allowances.

More difficult problems must be solved in countries that have exchange controls and nonconvertible currencies. Without exception, those currencies are overvalued at the official rate, and if the firm uses that rate, its expatriate employees are certain to be short-changed. Reference may be made to the free market rate for the host-country currency in free currency markets in, for example, the United States or Switzerland or to the black market rate in the host country, but these do not give the final answers. In the end, all companies must pay their expatriate employees enough to enable them to live as well as others who have similar positions in other firms, regardless of how the amount is calculated.

A common compensation component at many American companies is a stock plan that gives employees opportunities to acquire the company's stock on favorable terms. Such programs are designed to increase loyalty and productivity, but they sometimes run into problems outside the United States. Share ownership is unknown or restricted in numerous countries. DuPont, for example, discovered it could not give stock options in 25 of 53 nations, primarily because those countries' laws ban or limit ownership of foreign shares.

Compensation of Third-Country Nationals

Although some companies have different compensation plans for third-country nationals, there is a trend toward treating them the same as home-country expatriates. In either event, there are areas in which problems can arise. One of these areas is the calculation of income tax differentials when an American expatriate is compared with an expatriate from another country.[32] This results from the unique American government practice of taxing U.S. citizens even though they live and work abroad and treating tax differential payments made to those citizens as additional taxable income. No other major country taxes its nationals in those ways.

Another possible problem area is the home leave bonus. The two purposes of home leave are to prevent expatriates from losing touch with their native cultures and to have them visit IC headquarters. A third-country national must visit two countries instead of only one to achieve both purposes, and the additional costs can be substantial. Compare the cost of sending an Australian employee home from Mexico with that required to send an American from Mexico to Dallas.

Regardless of problems, the use of third-country nationals is growing in popularity. As businesses race to enlarge their ranks of qualified international managers, third-country nationals are in greater demand. They often win jobs because they speak several languages and know an industry or country well.

As the number of TCNs employed as executives by ICs continues to grow, the possible combinations of nationalities and host countries are virtually limitless, further complicating compensation efforts.

International Status

In all of this discussion, we have been describing compensation for expatriates who have been granted **international status.** Merely being from another country does not automatically qualify an employee for all the benefits we have mentioned. A subsidiary may hire home-country nationals or third-country nationals and pay them the same as it pays host-country employees. However, managements have found that although an American, for example, may agree initially to take a job and be paid on the local scale, sooner or later bad feeling and friction will develop as that person sees fellow Americans enjoying international status perquisites to which he or she is not entitled.

Sometimes firms promote host-country employees to international status even without transferring them abroad. This is a means of rewarding valuable people and preventing them from leaving the company for better jobs elsewhere.

Thus, international status means being paid some or all of the allowances and bonuses we have discussed, and there can be other sorts of payments as individual circumstances and people's imaginations combine to create them. Compensation packages for expatriates and other international executives are sufficiently important and complicated to have become a specialization in the personnel management field; at one firm, the title is "international employee benefits consultant." Help is also available from outside the IC. From time to time, the large consulting firms publish pamphlets advising about the transfer of executives to specific countries.

Perks

Perks originated in the perquisites of the medieval lords of the manor, whose workers paid parts of their profits or produce to the lords to be allowed to continue working. Today, perks

> WHEN CONSIDERING A RELOCATION ABROAD, WHETHER FOR A FEW MONTHS OR MANY YEARS, IT IS IMPORTANT FOR YOU TO CONSIDER WHAT ELEMENTS OF COMPENSATION AND BENEFITS ARE IMPORTANT FOR YOU.

are symbols of rank in the corporate hierarchy and are used to compensate executives while minimizing taxes. Among the most common perks are:

Cars, which may include chauffeurs, especially for executives higher up the organization ladder.

Private pension plan.

Retirement payment.

Life insurance.

Health insurance.

Emergency evacuation services (for medical or other reasons).

Kidnapping, ransom and extortion insurance.

Company house or apartment.

Directorship of a foreign subsidiary.

Seminar holiday travel.

Club memberships.

Hidden slush fund (such funds may be illegal, but some corporations are said to have them).

What's Important to You?

When considering a relocation abroad, whether for a few months or many years, it is important for you to consider what elements of compensation and benefits are important for you. Common considerations include cost of living, safety of personnel, medical facilities, housing, and schools. They may also include availability of good restaurants, sports facilities, shopping facilities, and quality theatre or other entertainment venues. See Table 16.3 again for a ranking of the top 20 cities in the world for quality of life; none of these cities is located in an emerging country. Also important to many employees may be the number of vacation days they are likely to receive annually. For example, the average number of vacation days in Japan is 25 per year, versus 35 in Germany, 37 in France, and 42 in Italy. In the United States, the average is 13 days, half of what Canadians enjoy.[33]

Also of importance in decisions on where to locate a business operation are considerations such as cost of living, business environment, and office rents. Despite labor market problems and less attractive market opportunities, the quality of the business environment in western European and North American countries remains higher than that in most emerging markets because those countries possess sophisticated institutions, such as advanced financial sectors, reliable legal systems, and political stability, that companies value. See again Table 16.3 for cost-of-living comparisons for a number of the world's cities. The survey compares the prices of goods and services typically consumed by the families of executives being sent abroad. You will note that not many of the cities ranked in the top 20 are located in emerging countries. ■

CHECK IT OUT!

mhhe.com/GeringerM

for study materials
including quizzes,
iPod downloads,
and video

"Quick decisions are unsafe decisions."

—Sophocles, 496–406 B.C.

international accounting
+financial management

chapter seventeen

In Chapter 8, we reviewed some of the major financial forces international managers face in their daily operations. Now we look at how managers deal with these forces. Because accounting is a fundamental tool of financial management, and because accounting practices and standards change across national borders, we begin with a look at these differences and the move toward convergence of standards in international accounting. In our discussion, when we describe specific practices, we use the U.S. multinational company (MNC) for the sake of simplicity, remembering that MNCs can be any nationality and increasingly are headquartered in emerging-market economies such as China, India and Brazil. Our review of financial management begins with how the company's capital is structured and then moves to cash management, including techniques such as multilateral netting and approaches to currency fluctuations. Finally, we discuss some aspects of taxation.

INTERNATIONAL ACCOUNTING

The purpose of accounting in all countries is to provide managers with financial data for use in their decision making and to provide external constituencies (investors, governments, lenders, suppliers, and others) the quantitative information they seek to inform their decisions. Accounting also provides the data governments need to levy taxes. As you can well imagine, the idea of what constitutes useful data, separate from their reliability, varies from country to country. For example, in Germany, the primary users of financial information historically have been creditors, so accounting focuses on the balance sheet and the company's assets. By contrast, in the United States, investors are major users of financial information, and they look to the income statement as a sign of the company's future.[1] An international company such as the Indian Tata Group, the Chinese household appliance company Haier Group, or the American consumer goods company Procter & Gamble has to address transactions in foreign currencies, with an obvious impact on the practice of accounting. But the differences do not end there. Different needs of varying constituencies in different countries have led to large variations in financial statements across the globe. Assumptions that underlie the country's legal, political, and economic systems, as well as the country's history, influence the commonly shared understanding of the purpose of accounting. That is to say, culture plays a significant role in the practice of accounting. In this section, we examine both transactions in foreign currencies and the role of culture in accounting, and then we go on to look at possible convergence among these various approaches.

LO1   Identify the major international accounting issues that international firms face.

Accounting and Foreign Currency

There are two points at which operating in a foreign currency raises issues from an accounting perspective: when transactions are made in foreign currencies and when branches and subsidiaries operate in foreign currencies and their results need to be made a part of the parent company's financial reports. We look first at transactions and then at translation and consolidation, the two processes involved in merging subsidiary financial results with those of the parent company.

When the U.S.-based company has foreign currency–based transactions such as sales, purchases, and loans (made and taken), they need to be recorded as revenues, expenses, assets,

or liabilities. Suppose the U.S.-based company buys Swiss watches in Geneva for 25,000 Swiss francs (CHFs) on June 1. Because the company's books are in U.S. dollars, the transaction is entered in dollars at the exchange rate on June 1. Let's say it's $0.963149/CHF. That is, 1 CHF buys $0.963149. The purchase entry would be $24,078.73. Accounts payable would also be $24,078.73 and the exchange rate notation "CHF 25,000 @ $0.963149" would be made. Now, if the payment is immediate or stipulated in US$, that would be fine. But suppose there is a time lag, the payment is made on August 1 and the exchange rate has changed. If the transaction is stipulated in CHF, the underlying dollar value of the purchase would change. Let's say the Swiss franc weakens against the dollar, moving to $0.94300/CHF on August 1, when the payable is due. Now the U.S. company has to pay $23,575. The $503.73 difference constitutes a foreign exchange gain. In this case, the journal entries would remain the same, and the gain (or loss) would be recorded in the income statement. This process is described by the U.S. Financial Accounting Standards Board Statement 52 (FASB 52), which requires that companies record foreign currency–based transactions at the spot rate at the time of the transaction. Any gains or losses from changes in exchange rates for items carried as payables or receivables are posted in the income statement. The International Accounting Standards Board (IASB), the international accounting standards organization that we'll soon discuss when we look at the convergence of accounting standards, has the same rule.

Now to our second concern about foreign currencies in accounting operations. When a U.S. MNC's foreign subsidiary reports results, these results need to be translated into the parent company's operating currency, in this case, dollars, and made to conform to U.S. generally accepted accounting principles (GAAP). Then these various results are aggregated into one financial report. This process is called **consolidation.** The two basic approaches to translation, the current rate method and the temporal method, have as their objectives to accurately reflect business results. By the **current rate method,** assets and liabilities are translated at the rate in effect the day the balance sheet is produced. By the **temporal method,** monetary items such as cash, receivables, and payables are translated at the current exchange rate. Fixed assets and long-term liabilities are translated at the rates in effect the date they were acquired or incurred.

Choice of translation method depends on the **functional currency** of the foreign operation. The functional currency is the primary currency of the operation, the currency in which cash flows, pricing, expenses, and financing are denominated. This translation process is set out in FASB 52 and IASB 21. Figure 17.1 summarizes implications of using the local or parent company currency as the functional currency.

Accounting and Culture

We know that accounting follows different patterns in different parts of the world. Sidney Gray suggests that differences in accounting measurement and disclosure practices, that is, how companies value assets and what information companies provide, are influenced by culture. His study classified countries on two dimensions, secrecy-transparency and optimism-conservatism.[2]

The dimension of secrecy-transparency measures the degree to which companies disclose information to the public. Germany, Japan, and Switzerland tend to value secrecy or privacy over transparency. In the United Kingdom and the United States, there is more disclosure and less privacy. The dimension of optimism-conservatism measures the degree to which a company is cautious in its valuing of assets and measuring of income. Accounting reports in countries with more conservative asset-valuing approaches tend to understate assets and income, while those in countries whose asset-valuing approach is more optimistic tend toward overstatement. In France, Germany, and Japan, public companies' capital structure tends to depend more on debt rather than equity, with banks being a major source of the debt. Banks are concerned with liquidity. A conservative statement of profits may reduce tax exposure and dividend payouts, contributing to cash reserves that can be tapped for debt service. On the optimism measure, U.S. and, in a more restrained way, U.K. companies want to show impressive earnings that will attract investors.

▼ **FIGURE 17.1** Functional Currency and Translation Methods

When Functional Currency is:	Local Currency	Parent Company Currency
Translation method is:	Current method	Temporal method
Assets are translated at:	Spot rate on date balance sheet prepared	Spot rate for monetary assets Historic cost for fixed assets
Income statement is translated at:	Average exchange rate for reporting period	Cost of goods sold and depreciation at historic rates Average exchange rate for reporting period Other items at average rate for period
Owner's equity is translated at:	Rates in effect when stock issued	Rates in effect when stock issued
Retained earnings are translated at:	Rates in effect when earnings posted	Rates in effect when earnings posted

▼ **FIGURE 17.2** Cultural Differences in Measurement and Disclosure for Accounting Systems

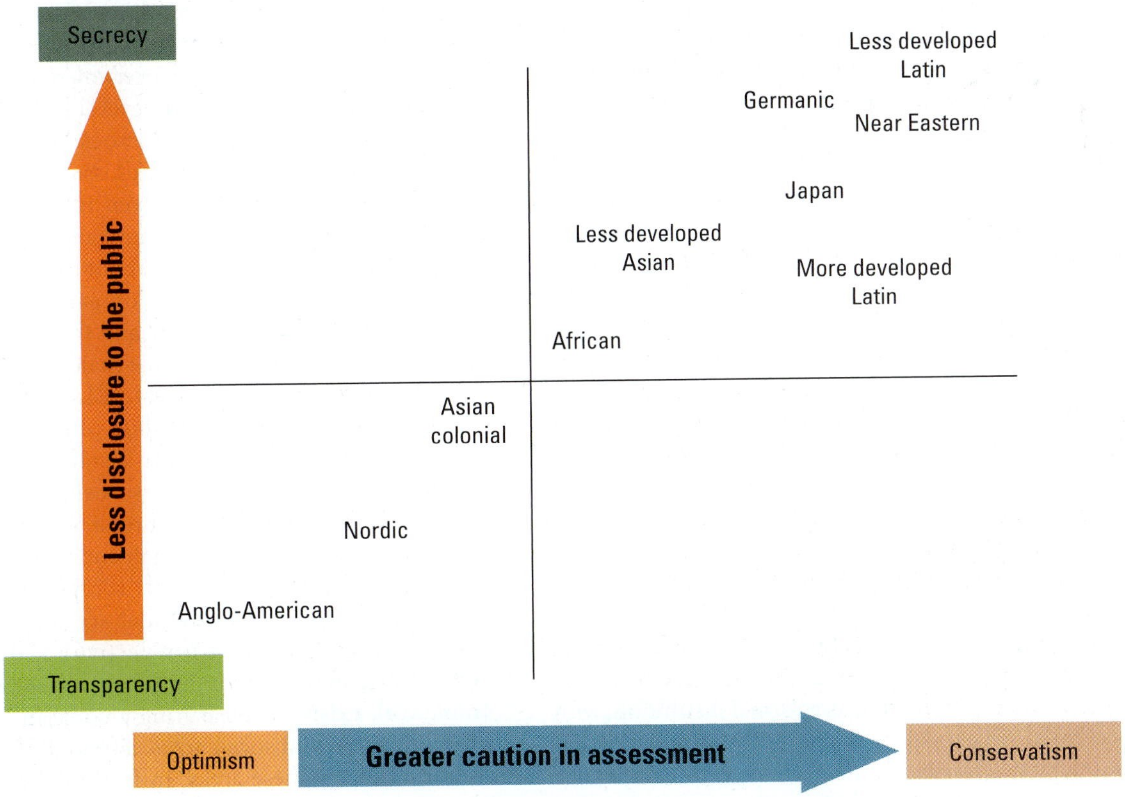

Source: Adapted from Lee Radebaugh and Sidney J. Gray, Accounting and Multinational Enterprises, 5th ed. (New York: John Wiley & Sons, 2002).

Convergence of Accounting Standards

Largely due to globalization and MNCs' desire to list stock in foreign markets to tap into their potential as a source of shareholders, a process known as *cross-listing,* there is a growing movement toward convergence of accounting standards. The body that establishes accounting standards in the United States is a private organization, the Financial Accounting Standards Board (FASB). The more international body is the International Accounting Standards Board (IASB). In 2002, FASB and IASB agreed in principle on harmonization of standards and convergence. The FASB's standards are the U.S. generally accepted accounting principles (U.S. GAAP), while the IASB's standards are the International Financial Reporting Standards (IFRS). Significant progress has been made on this commitment by a negotiating group, with a target date of June 2011, a date later extended to 2015. There is general agreement to move towards the principles-based IASB standards (IFRS) from the rules-based FASB standards. With so many important and heavily detailed aspects of specific standards to be reconciled, the progress toward convergence is impressive.

LO2 Describe the international accounting standards' convergence process and its importance to international firms.

On the path of convergence, the EU Parliament and the Council of Europe decided to require IASB standards for financial reporting as of 2005. Australia and New Zealand have joined the EU in this step forward. The transition seems to have gone smoothly. Presently there are more than 90 countries that require public companies to list using IFRS and another 30 permit it. Many other countries, including those in the EU, have adopted IFRS with minor modifications, called carve-outs, on the path to full IFRS acceptance. As of 2007, the U.S. Securities and Exchange Commission (SEC) decided that foreign companies listing their shares in the United States no longer needed to restate their financial statements to comply with FASB standards. Incidentally, in 2002, when the U.S. Congress passed the Sarbanes-Oxley Act (SOX), in response to a series of corporate scandals in which accounting practices were at the center (Tyco, Enron, and WorldCom among them), it also noted in the legislation its desire for convergence in accounting standards. SOX named the SEC as the responsible party for recognizing the IASB. The SEC anticipates that by 2015 U.S. public companies will be required to use IFRS. This suggests that the SEC has recognized the higher standards of IFRS.

One of the largest differences between GAAP and the IFRS has to do with their general approach. GAAP relies on rules and regulations; we can think of it as a formal institution, with compliance based on expedience. The IFRS has greater reliance on principles, a normative institution, with compliance based on social obligation. Shared principles suggest the need for reasoned judgment because they allow for interpretations, unlike the application of rules, so accountants with GAAP approaches will have to get used to a new way of thinking. At this point, the United States is the only major nation that follows GAAP.

With convergence, financial markets around the world will become more integrated because the statements will be directly comparable. Investors and other interested parties will be able to see company performance across borders, companies will no longer have to restate their financials, and the complex process of consolidation will be much less so. These features of standardization mean substantial cost reductions for companies and better information for everyone.

Triple-Bottom-Line Accounting

Increasingly, companies have made efforts to report on their environmental, social, and financial results. Such a reporting framework has been termed **triple bottom line (3BL),** a term credited to John Elkington in his 1997 book, *Cannibals with Forks: The Triple Bottom Line of 21st Century Business.*[3] The book's argument is that capitalism can become civilized; capitalists can be taught to eat with forks, due to consumer pressure and other social forces. Corporate capitalism can become sustainable capitalism. Elkington describes seven drivers of this transformation: markets, values, transparency, life-cycle technology, partnerships, time, and corporate governance. This approach supports sustainability, as discussed in Chapter 5, and corporate social responsibility (CSR). As we have seen in our earlier discussion, sustainability is a systems concept that has three major aspects: the environmental or ecological, the social, and the economic. Currently, we measure at the economic level and, where required by government or social pressure, we measure at the environmental level (as with emission controls and hazardous waste) and at the social level (as with the Equal Employment Opportunity Commission's enforcement of the federal civil rights laws). Yet even in the environmental and social areas, we tend to know more about the problems—what is reported in the media—than about the company-level thinking on these important issues. Companies should measure and make public the environmental and social effects of their decisions. These are, in summary, the major argument for 3BL.

The major argument against 3BL is neither a substantive disagreement with the desirability of ecologically responsible business practices that support sustainability nor a disagreement with the idea of business being socially responsible; rather, it is the claim that measurement will not get us closer to the desired state. Wayne Norman and Chris MacDonald argue that social performance and environmental impact cannot be objectively measured in ways that are comparable to our economic measurements of a firm's activities.[4] They point out that the rhetoric may be appealing, but no widely implementable framework exists for measuring a company's performance in environmental and social areas, although there are high levels of consulting in these areas. In fact, they suggest that a focus on the measurement of these activities may well detract from efforts to figure out ways to combine sustainability and social responsibility with positive economic results, which is a more difficult challenge. There is a parallel with codes of ethics: what matters is what a company actually does, not whether a code of ethics is hanging on the wall of every office. The poster is rhetoric. Posting it is not ethical action. Decisions in the field that have to do with implementation are what matter, as well as how the organization's members understand the company's values and what those values say about their duties to stakeholders.

Perhaps such reporting requires a reframing of how we think about organizational outcomes, a process that is incremental and subtle. Notable efforts to develop a framework that supports substantive reporting on the environmental, social, and financial aspects of business have been made by the Global Reporting Initiative (GRI), an international network of stakeholders from thousands of organizations, including private sector businesses, nongovernmental organizations, and government organizations, both local and international. There are more than 20,000 stakeholders from more than 80 countries. GRI is independent and collaborates with the United Nations Environmental Program (UNEP). Details can be accessed at www.globalreporting.org.

INTERNATIONAL FINANCIAL MANAGEMENT

We now look at how the firm manages funds across borders. This process of transferring value internationally is interesting and complex because it involves many variables, among them, exchange rates among currencies, varying restrictions on the movement of funds, differing tax systems, and differing economic environments. We begin our financial management review with a focus on the capital structure of the firm, and then move on to cash flow management across borders, looking at both the financial flows themselves and the techniques used to move them. Foreign exchange (FX) risk management follows. We also look at taxation issues.

LO3 Explain the capital structure choices open to firms and their significance.

CAPITAL STRUCTURE OF THE FIRM

We have seen that firms are becoming increasingly international in their markets and their sourcing in order to exploit attractive opportunities. Such an opportunity is also available for the capital structure of the firm, and, increasingly, chief financial officers (CFOs) have been tapping international financial markets, both public and private. Because financial markets are not globally integrated though they are increasingly interconnected, varying opportunities arise among them

with varying costs. So if a CFO can raise capital in a foreign market at a lower cost than in the home market, such an opportunity may be attractive as a way to increase shareholder value.

The firm raises capital internally through its retained earnings and then, externally, through either equity, the issuing of shares, or debt (leveraging). Many firms choose to issue stocks in foreign markets, in part to tap into a broader investor pool, which can raise the stock price and reduce the cost of capital. Participation in local finance also may have a significant marketing advantage, raising the profile of the brand name abroad. Foreign companies that have issued shares in the United States include Unilever, Fuji Film, Canadian Pacific, KLM, Sony, Toyota, and Cemex. Sometimes, foreign shares are directly traded in the American stock markets, but many times, they are traded in the form of **American depository receipts (ADRs).** These receipts represent shares that are held by the custodian, usually an American bank, in the stock's home market. They are denominated in dollars and traded on the U.S. exchange, eliminating the need to have a broker in the country of issue and the need for currency exchange. If there is concern about foreigners having control of domestic assets, there may be restrictions on foreign ownership of equity. These restrictions are more prevalent in developing countries. For example, in India, Mexico, and Indonesia, foreign ownership in specific sectors is limited. Some sectors in developed nations are also protected from foreign ownership, often through an approval process. Such an example in the United States is found with airlines, which must be directed and operationally controlled by a U.S. citizen.[5]

Debt markets are the other source of capital for the firm, and increasingly the tendency is to tap local markets first. That may mean that a foreign subsidiary of the Japanese firm Toyota would look first to its market in the United States for funds to use in the U.S. operations. Multinational corporations, in addition to obtaining funds at the corporate level, can explore borrowing in their domestic and international debt markets, increasing the opportunities to reduce the cost of capital. They also have access to **offshore financial centers,** locations that specialize in financing by nonresidents, where the taxation levels are low and the banking regulations are slim. Switzerland, the Cayman Islands, Hong Kong, and the Bahamas are examples of offshore financial centers.

Debt financing is thought to be less expensive than is equity financing, because the interest paid on the debt is usually tax-deductible, while dividends paid out to investors are not. Yet the choice of debt or equity financing is also influenced by local practice. Companies in the United States, the United Kingdom, and Canada tend to rely on equity more heavily than

American depository receipts (ADRs) Foreign shares held by a custodian, usually a U.S. bank, in the issuer's home market and traded in dollars on the U.S. exchange

offshore financial center Location that specializes in financing nonresidents, with low taxes and few banking regulations

do companies in many other countries. In both Japan and Germany, banks traditionally play a more central role than do the stock markets in the financing picture. In Japan, we find the interlocking relationships of the *keiretsu*, where related companies in a larger family, such as Mitsubishi, Sumitomo, or C. Itoh, are connected with interlocking ownership of stocks and bonds, with the company bank at their center. Essentially, this structure eliminates the stakeholder conflicts between bondholders and stockholders, an appropriate characteristic for a national culture where harmony is an important cultural value.

In addition to differing tax treatments and local practices, other country-level policies may influence the firm's capital structure. Exchange controls may limit dividend payments to foreign equity holders, and national policies designed to encourage local reinvestment may control the remission of dividends.

Decisions a financial manager would make in the process of raising capital are as follows:

1. In what currency should the capital be raised, considering an estimate of its long-term strength or weakness?

2. How should the capital raised be structured between equity and debt?[6]

3. What are the sources of capital available? Should money be borrowed from a commercial bank by an ordinary loan; a bank as part of a swap; another company as part of a swap; another part of the MNC; or a public offering in one of the world's capital markets, for example, in the New York or eurobond market?

4. If the decision is made to use one of the world's capital markets, management must then decide in which of those markets it can achieve its objectives at the lowest cost.

5. Are there other sources of money available? For example, a joint venture partner, private capital, or a host government may be some sources. A host government may be a source of funds or tax abatement if the move is expected to bring the MNC's technology, management knowledge, or the jobs that will be created.

▼**FIGURE 17.3** Capital Structure Percentages for Selected Countries

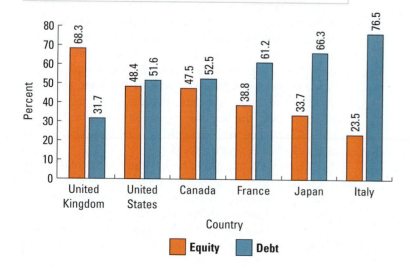

Equity ▪ Debt

6. How much money does the company need and for how long? For instance, if the company is moving into a new market or product, there will probably be a period during product introduction or plant construction when the new venture will need more capital than it can generate.

LO4 Describe the process of cash flow management in the international firm.

CASH FLOW MANAGEMENT

The management of cash flows is an important part of international financial management that differs from the management of cash and cash flows in a purely domestic firm, although there are some basic commonalities. For example, all firms would want to source funds in low-cost markets and place excess funds where they would get the best return. The global cash management picture is more complex than that of a domestic firm due to the number of national locations in which the firm has subsidiaries. Operating in 25 local currencies is not uncommon for the international firm. The overall goal of cash flow management is to reduce risks and position the firm so it can benefit from opportunities. Some of the sources of these risks and opportunities are foreign exchange (FX) movements, interest rates, inflation, government regulation, and taxes. We first look at the major reasons for which an international company moves funds and then at its international finance center's activities.

Why Funds are Moved

Firms move funds for many reasons, among them dividends, royalties and fees from the subsidiary to the parent company, loans from the parent to the subsidiary or among subsidiaries, and transfer pricing of sales between subsidiaries and the parent company. Dividends result from the parent company's equity interest in the subsidiary, while royalties and fees are payments made for the use of company assets such as trade names, technology, consulting, and management systems. These payments, important to the business in and of themselves, additionally are useful in cash flow management in several ways. They may serve as vehicles for moving profits from subsidiaries in high-tax environments to lower-tax environments. They may be a way to move profits out of countries where repatriation of profits is blocked or limited. They may also be a way to reduce FX risk by moving currency from environments that have a high risk of devaluation to lower risk ones. Note, too, that these payments are business expenses, so they may be used to impact tax liability.

Loans also may be useful in cash flow management. Parent companies may loan funds directly to the subsidiary, yet these direct loans face some risk because the host government is able to restrict the subsidiary's remittances, including the loan payments, back to the parent. A **fronting loan** is an approach that achieves the same objective for the firm, with much less risk. In a fronting loan, the parent company deposits money in an international bank, which then lends to the subsidiary, *fronting* for the parent company. The host government is not inclined to restrict subsidiary loan payments, especially to a major international bank. There is a small cost to the parent company, while the bank has no risk because it is holding a fully collateralized loan. If the deposit is made from a tax haven, there will be tax advantages as well. Such loans may also be a way to get around blocked funds in general. Such funds may be the result of a host government's effort to protect their balance of payments position. These blocked funds may affect the firm's ability to repatriate profits or royalties.

One additional method of transferring funds within the firm that has cash management value is transfer pricing. The **transfer price** is the bookkeeping cost of goods transferred from one unit of a business to another in another country. Such transfers are common with globally dispersed firms, making up 60 percent of world trade. Because the sale that creates the transfer is internal, its cost can be seen as somewhat flexible. In this flexibility lies the potential to move funds from high-tax, weak-currency environments in ways that are beneficial to the firm. Transfer pricing may also be used to circumvent host-country currency transfer controls and tariffs. Because it may often represent lost tax revenues for host governments, transfer pricing is carefully reviewed by host-government authorities. Transfer pricing can be seen to raise ethical issues, because the maneuvers, although they may be legal, are often not in the spirit of the host-country tax and monetary laws. The OECD and the U.S. Internal Revenue Service have issued guidelines on transfer pricing, and some firms now voluntarily agree in advance with the host country on their approach to internal pricing. Such agreements, in addition to offering ethical guidelines to decision makers, reduce the firm's legal and tax audit risks.

International Finance Center

The increasing complexity of global financing, combined with increasing global competition, has encouraged firms to pay more attention to financial management. In many firms, the finance operation has become centralized and established as a profit center, a bit like a company bank. Developments leading to the establishment of finance centers are (1) floating exchange rates, whose fluctuations are sometimes volatile; (2) growth in the number of capital and foreign exchange markets, where the firm can shop for lower interest costs and better currency rates; (3) different and changing inflation rates from country to country; (4) advances in electronic cash management systems; (5) realization by financial managers that through innovative management of temporarily idle cash balances of the subsidiaries, they can increase yields and, thereby, profit; and (6) the explosive growth of derivatives to protect against commodity, currency, interest rate, and other risks. These centralized finance centers can balance and hedge currency exposures, tap capital markets, manage inflation rate risk, manage cash management technological innovation, manage derivatives use, handle internal and external invoicing, help a weak-currency subsidiary, and strengthen subsidiary evaluation and reporting systems. We look at multilateral netting and leading and lagging as two approaches the firm's finance center uses to manage cash flows.

Multilateral Netting

There are many possible types of cash flows between subsidiaries and the parent company and among subsidiaries: loans from the parent to the subsidiary and increased investment in the form of equity capital and then, in the other direction, cash from sales, dividends, royalties, and fees. One common strategy finance centers use to manage and optimize these flows is **multilateral netting.** This is a centralized approach in which subsidiaries transfer their net cash flows within the company to a cash center that disperses cash to net receivers. A single transaction to or from each member settles the net result of all cashflows.

Why do companies consider multilateral netting? First of all, the transfer of funds has a cost attached to it, the *transaction cost,* and at the same time, the funds while in transit present an opportunity cost: they are not working for the company. In addition, FX costs are incurred. By reducing the transfer transactions, there is less inactive time for funds, the actual transfer costs are reduced, and there are fewer FX transactions, as well. Netting among, for example, the European and Middle Eastern subsidiaries of a firm would require each subsidiary with a

fronting loan A loan made through an intermediary, usually a bank, from parent company to subsidiary

transfer price The bookkeeping cost of goods transferred from one unit of a business to another in another country

multilateral netting Strategy in which subsidiaries transfer net intracompany cash flows through a centralized clearing center

> " IN OUR VIEW, DERIVATIVES ARE FINANCIAL WEAPONS OF MASS DESTRUCTION CARRYING DANGERS THAT, WHILE LATENT, ARE POTENTIALLY LETHAL.
>
> —WARREN BUFFETT "

net payable position to transfer its funds to a central account once a month, where the central account manager would then transfer funds to the net receivers. Compare the two approaches in Figure 17.4. Without netting, reconciling the positions would require eight transactions and $1.2 million in transit. With netting, there are four transactions, and $600,000 in transit. Plus, the foreign exchange transaction costs are reduced.

Leading and Lagging

The floating of currency exchange rates creates a risk for the multinational firm. To minimize such a risk, one useful technique is **leading and lagging,** which involves the timing of payments. A *lead* approach is to collect receivables early when the foreign currency is expected to weaken and fund payables early when the foreign currency is expected to strengthen. A *lag* approach is to collect receivables late when the currency is expected to strengthen and fund payables late when the currency is expected to weaken. Leading and lagging can be coordinated among MNC subsidiaries to reposition funds and help to compensate for blocked funds or funds about to be blocked.

FOREIGN EXCHANGE RISK MANAGEMENT

When operating across different currencies, MNC managers regularly encounter currency exchange rate movements. These unanticipated shifts present risks to the international business because they represent unplanned-for changes in the value of assets and liabilities. These significant risks are usually categorized into three types: transaction exposure, translation exposure, and economic exposure. These exposures result in positions that are either uncovered or covered, that is, hedged.

LO5 Categorize foreign exchange risks faced by the international firm into transaction exposure, translation exposure, and economic exposure.

Transaction Exposure

Transaction exposure occurs when the firm has transactions denominated in a foreign currency. The exposure is due to currency exchange rate fluctuations between the time the commitment is made and the time it is payable. For example, an order for German diesel truck engines is placed by a Massachusetts company, for payment in 180 days in euros, €150,000 (US$189,000 at the then-prevailing exchange rate of $1.26 per euro). If the euro strengthens against the dollar to $1.38 when the company converts its dollars to euros, the engines' price in dollar terms would increase by $18,000 to US$207,000. In this case, there would be a cash flow effect for the importer but no effect

▼**FIGURE 17.4** Advantages of Multilateral Netting

US$-000			
Subsidiary	**Receivable**	**Payables**	**Net**
Chinese	350	450	(100)
German	250	300	(50)
Indian	150	300	(150)
Mexican	450	150	300

MNC, Inc. intra-subsidiary cash positions

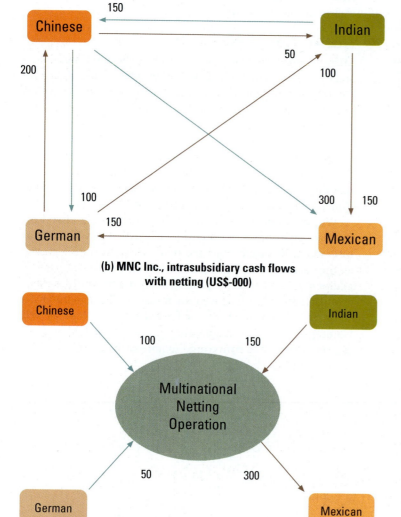

(a) MNC Inc., intrasubsidiary cash flows (US$-000)

(b) MNC Inc., intrasubsidiary cash flows with netting (US$-000)

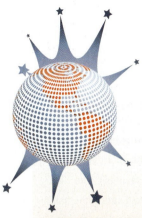

GLOBAL gauntlet

Microloan Bankers: Charity or For-Profit Business Model?

You might think it would be utter folly to lend money to the poor in a developing country. What about a loan to a new small business or entrepreneur such as a vegetable peddler, tailor, or candle maker? Worldwide, development organizations are finding that some of the world's poorest entrepreneurs repay their debts at rates approaching 100 percent. To encourage grassroots private business in Latin America, Asia, and Africa, microlending organizations are expanding programs that already lend thousands of small entrepreneurs amounts ranging

This is Sophia Maimu, a melon stand owner and microloan client of ACCION Tanzanian partner, Akiba Commercial Bank.

from $50 to several hundred dollars. Tiny businesses in developing countries commonly repay these microloans faithfully because of community pressure and the security of a favorable credit rating. Microloans give them small spurts of working capital when they need it, allow them to establish credit, and let them borrow again in hard times. The money helps them start or expand their businesses—selling vegetables, sewing, repairing shoes, making furniture, and the like—and boosts the local economy.

The microcredit concept was developed by Professor Muhammad Yunus, a U.S.-trained Bangladeshi PhD economist, through the Grameen Bank in Bangladesh (which he established to administer his program), and ACCION, a U.S. microcredit organization. Dr. Yunus was awarded the Nobel Peace Prize in 2006 for his work fighting poverty.

The microloan repayment performance shines when compared with that of some sovereign nations. It also looks very good compared with a default rate of 5.4 percent among U.S. recipients of federally guaranteed student loans. ACCION reports a repayment rate over the life of its program of 97 percent. A Mexican program, Compatramos, reports a 1 percent default rate.

Critics point out, though, that one microloan is not going to pull a budding entrepreneur out of poverty, let alone a whole country. When Tufts University received an endowment to set up a microloan program, specialists were ready to warn Tufts of the ethical aspects of

microloans: its program needs to be much more than banking. A series of loans is probably necessary, combined with training and support.

Recently, several not-for-profit microloan operations have changed. Because of their success, they have become banks, and in one case, Mexico's Banco Compartamos sold 30 percent of its shares to the public, with the IPO share price moving up 34 percent. Their 2007 IPO also brought a lot of difficult issues forward. Compartamos began as a charity grant program, then became a bank, and then a publicly listed bank. It is the move to private ownership seeking return on investment that changes the business model substantially, from *charity* to *business*. The charity model uses donated funds and funds from international financial institutions such as the World Bank and the European Bank for Reconstruction and Development, and they have low interest rates. Some of the microcredit organizations even make profits, but they are cooperatives, such as Grameen Bank, so their profit moves back into their stakeholder community. Compartamos, in contrast, now charges its credit customers in the range of 100 percent (on an annualized basis) to cover loan interest, fees, and taxes. That is three times the cost of borrowing from other microcredit lenders. To make matters a little more complicated, many of the shareholders who profited greatly from the Compartamos IPO are themselves microlenders, such as ACCION.

Is it right to profit from loans to the poor? Dr. Yunis thinks definitely not, and "refuses to mention the words *Compartamos* and *microfinance* in the same breath."[7] At the same time, here's an explanation from the two friends who founded Compartamos in 1990. They suggest that, much like food crisis and famine, the issue isn't the existence of the needed good; both food and money exist. The issue is one of distribution: the food and money frequently are not where they are needed most desperately. The argument is that a profit potential brings private capital in touch with the people who need it, the world's poor, quickly and efficiently. It is a way to align the world's wealth with the world's poor. Big investment firms and banks have begun to participate in profitable microlending. Firms such as CITI Group, Morgan Stanley, TIAA-CREF, and Deutsche Bank are active in the sector now. With returns like Compartamos has, at 53 percent, investors are interested. Here's how the loans work: they are small, usually to women, guaranteed by peers, paid off on time, and often followed immediately by another loan.[8,9] So, what do you think? Is profiting from microloans to the poor ethical? View a PBS video that explores this issue further at http://www.pbs.org/now/enterprisingideas/Compartamos.html.

CU in ib

Bryan Goldfinger: Microfinance in Latin America with Kiva

I was born and raised in San Diego, California, surfing, playing soccer and generally living a pretty stereotypical California life. My first two years at Cal Poly, San Luis Obispo, I was a business administration major with an undeclared concentration. I spent my third year of university studying abroad in Puntarenas, Costa Rica, where I lived with a Spanish-speaking host family and completed primarily Spanish classes. During this year I became infatuated with travel, the Latin people and culture, gained fluency in Spanish and a desire to in some way help those less fortunate. Upon my return, I declared a concentration in International Business Management and later that same year, also declared a concentration in Accounting. I graduated in June 2007 with a minor in Spanish and a contract to begin auditing with KPMG in January of 2008. The months between graduation and entering the "real world" I spent taking an overland trip from Nicaragua to Argentina. This travel experience proved to be more valuable than I could have imagined.

I began my time at KPMG with high hopes of completing the CPA examinations, spending a minimum of two years auditing and hopefully being able to complete an international rotation at one of their overseas offices. My time at KPMG was extremely valuable, although not quite what I had expected. I had the opportunity to work on clients in the roofing and construction industry, real estate, telecommunications, insurance and agriculture. However, at the end of my first year, I began feeling as though the work I was doing did not satisfy my goals of helping others, and the lifestyle of public accounting was not consistent with one I desired to live. Just after completing my first year, I left KPMG.

During this time, a friend asked me what my ideal dream job would entail. The dream job that I conjured up would involve international business travel, allow me to utilize my Spanish skills, involve more time in the field and less in an office, and be more socially fulfilling than my previous work. Two days later he sent me an e-mail about a friend who was currently working in Paraguay with a company called Kiva, and included a link to the website (www.kiva.org). Kiva's mission is to connect people through lending to help alleviate poverty. Individuals like you or me provide funds in increments of $25, via the organization's website, to entrepreneurs in developing countries and the United States. Kiva then sends the funds to their partner microfinance institutions (MFIs), which provide loans to the selected entrepreneurs.

The work of a Kiva Fellow varies greatly, depending on their experience, skill set and which partner institution they are assigned to work with. Kiva Fellows are volunteers who work closely with the partner institutions to help them implement Kiva policies, meet and interview borrowers and complete verifications of the information the MFIs provide to Kiva. Essentially, the Kiva Fellows are Kiva's eyes and ears in the field and connect all four stakeholders involved with Kiva: the borrowers, the lenders, the MFIs and Kiva headquarters.

I completed two placements as a Kiva Fellow, the first as a roaming Fellow in Peru, and the second in Managua, Nicaragua. The primary objective of my placement in Peru was borrower verification. I would select a small sample of loans from several MFIs, visit the borrowers, and verify that the information Kiva had on the website was consistent with what was actually taking place in the field. During these visits, I would also write a short journal entry on the progress of the borrowers. This journal entry would then be uploaded to the Kiva website and sent out to everyone who had lent money to that particular borrower. In Nicaragua, I worked primarily with one MFI to complete a review of their social performance. Social performance monitoring is a new and growing subject in microfinance. There are a variety of tools and companies whose sole purpose is social performance monitoring. The goal is to review and identify strengths and weaknesses of an MFI's social performance. More specifically, what is the mission statement of the MFI and is the mission being applied in the field? Kiva has recently begun administering social performance questionnaires to many of its partner MFIs and utilizing Kiva Fellows to assist MFIs in filling out and reviewing the questionnaires.

Due to the vastly different locations and duties Kiva Fellows are assigned, each Fellow tends to have wildly different experiences, challenges and rewards. In my opinion, the most rewarding part of being a Kiva Fellow was visiting and interviewing borrowers and having the opportunity to witness, firsthand, the effects of microfinance. To trek out into the field with a loan officer to a place you would likely never go otherwise, meet a person who you would likely never meet otherwise, ask them in-depth questions about their business and life, and at the end ask, "what are your hopes and dreams?" is quite a unique and rewarding experience.

Aside from the small frustrations of working in and learning the work culture of a new country and MFI, I was lucky to have very few, if any, difficulties in relation to my work as a Kiva Fellow. Reflecting on both of my placements as a Kiva Fellow, the biggest challenge I experienced, particularly during my placement in Peru and the first half of my placement in Nicaragua, was loneliness and lack of a social network. Although an incredibly rewarding and equally valuable experience, work travel is not the same as tourist travel or a study abroad experience. One does not necessarily have the built-in support group that is often present in a study abroad program, or the free time and lodging situations that "tourist" travel provides which are helpful in facilitating social interactions. That said, by the end of each placement, I found myself wishing I did not have to leave so soon. In my experience, the most important thing to do when in such a situation is to not resort to crawling into a ball and secluding yourself. The Internet and comforts of home can easily become a crutch to lean on, which ultimately serve no purpose in alleviating the situation. Go out by yourself, put your pride on the line, meet random people and be willing to experience situations you normally would never dream of.

As far as Kiva is concerned, one of the most important aspects of an applicant is their experience living, working, studying and traveling abroad. Obviously, work experience and study background weigh in heavily, but with no experience abroad, Kiva will likely not even consider your application. The reasoning behind this is that there are a multitude of applicants who are qualified to do the work of a Kiva Fellow. The reality is that Kiva trains the Fellows on what they need to know once in the field. They realize that cultural sensitivity, adaptability, and general decision making when abroad is knowledge primarily gained through experience and travel, and cannot be taught in a classroom at Kiva Headquarters.

My advice to anyone who wishes to pursue international work opportunities is to get as much international experience as possible before entering the "work force." Whether it is through study abroad, international internships, small jobs abroad like working at a restaurant, bar or hostel, or just flat out travel, one gains knowledge and experience that cannot be taught in any classroom.

for the exporter. Had the exporter quoted the engines' price in U.S. dollars, the situation would have been reversed.

An initial observation is that the company could avoid transaction exposure by refusing to enter into foreign currency contracts. Yet the desire to conduct business across currency borders suggests a willingness to accept this risk. One party will always have to, and doing so might be a part of the contract negotiation strategy. There are other approaches to dealing with eliminating the risk of a transaction exposure, or **hedging,** at the operations level. Remember our discussion of leading and lagging? Let's look at an example.

The U.S. company Nucor is exporting to Spain a €20 million boutique steel order, made from recycled steel, payable in euros. Nucor has accepted the foreign exchange risk as a part of its marketing strategy. It may also have factored a currency shift expectation into its euro pricing. Here are the foreign exchange and interest data:

EU interest rate:	4.00
U.S. interest rate:	5.00
Spot rate	$1.534
Forward rate	$1.527 (one year forward)

Nucor would like to lead its receivable, because the market indicates that the dollar may well strengthen against the euro. That suggests that Nucor will be able to buy more dollars for its receivable now than in the future. The Spanish customer may well want to lag the payment, though, if there is no incentive for early payment.

In another way to hedge on transaction exposure through company actions, many multinationals follow a centralized practice similar to multilateral netting: *exposure netting*. The firm will run a centralized clearing account that matches and nets out foreign exchange exposures across currencies or across currency families. Working with currency families recognizes that some currencies tend to move in lockstep with one another.

There are also ways to hedge foreign currency exposure by engaging in contracts known as *hedges* and *swaps*. A **forward market hedge** involves a quite simple transaction: the company sells forward its foreign currency receivables for its home currency, matching the time forward to the due date of the receivables. When the Spanish company pays, Nucor will deliver the amount to its bank, the partner in the forward market hedge contract. Nucor will not have been exposed to currency risk in

forward market hedge Foreign currency contract sold or bought forward in order to protect against foreign currency movement

currency option hedge An option to buy or sell a specific amount of foreign currency at a specific time in order to protect against foreign currency risk

money market hedge A method to hedge foreign currency exposure by borrowing and lending in the domestic and foreign money markets

swap contract A spot sale/purchase of an asset against a future purchase/sale of an equal amount in order to hedge a financial position

translation exposure Potential change in the value of a company's financial position due to exposure created during the consolidation process

the Spanish sale. Because the forward market hedge is a way to cover the complete exposure in a given transaction, it is the most widely used approach. Yet because the forward market hedge assumes all of the foreign exchange risk, it eliminates the chance of gaining from a currency move in the company's favor.

An approach to hedging an exposure but not losing the opportunity to gain from a currency appreciation is a *foreign currency option*. With a **currency option hedge,** you purchase an option to buy or sell a specific amount of currency at a specific time, but the option can be exercised or not. These hedges are *calls*—or contracts with an option to buy—for foreign currency payables and *puts*—or contracts to sell—for foreign currency receivables. Because these are options, if the market works against you, you can exercise the contract. If the market works for you, you don't need to exercise the option.

The money markets also afford an opportunity to hedge a foreign transaction. In a **money market hedge,** Nucor would borrow euros in the European money market in the amount of the receivables from the Spanish sale. The basic idea here is to match the balance sheet asset with a liability in the same currency. Here's how the money market hedge works: Nucor borrows the equivalent of $20 million in euros, or €13,035,300, for a period that matches the receivable's due date. Nucor then converts the euros to dollars at the spot rate and then invests them. The euros that are received from the Spanish company will be used to close out the euro loan. Then the invested dollars plus their interest provide Nucor the dollar amount for the Spanish sale.

Swap contracts are also used to hedge foreign currency exposure. This is an agreement to exchange currencies at specified rates and on a specified date or sequence of dates. Swaps are quite flexible and may be undertaken for long periods, much longer than in the forward market. So if Nucor had a series of sales in the EU over the next 10 years, all denominated in euros, it could enter into a series of swaps so that the exchange rate or series of exchange rates would be known in advance.

Translation Exposure

Translation exposure occurs when subsidiary financial statements are consolidated at the corporate level for the companywide financial reports. Because the foreign subsidiaries operate in nondollar currencies, there is a need to translate subsidiary financial reports to the parent company's currency during the corporate consolidation process. Exchange rate movements can have substantial impact on the value of these financial statements, which may affect per-share earnings and stock price. Take a U.S. company that has subsidiaries in Brazil, Japan, Spain, and the United Kingdom. The subsidiary financial reports will be prepared in their own currency, so amounts in four currencies will be translated. Any changes in the exchange

rates will affect the dollar values. Such changes, either gains or losses, are not reflected in cash flow; they are paper or unrealized changes.

The key issue related to translation exposure is what currency exchange rate to use for the translation. The two basic approaches to translation, the current rate method and the temporal method, and their exchange rate use rules are discussed earlier in this chapter. Approaches to translation exposure differ by country.

Many organizations do not hedge translation exposure because hedging a translation exposure can actually increase transaction exposure. If the translation exposure is hedged through a matching foreign exchange liability, such as a debt, then that debt is an exposure at the transaction level. Transaction exposure is fundamental to a corporation's value.

Economic Exposure

Economic exposure occurs at the operations level and results from exchange rate changes on projected cash flows. Unlike transaction exposure, which addresses the individual transaction, economic exposure is firmwide and long term. For example, when the dollar strengthens, as it did in the 1990s, U.S. export prices increased in terms of other currencies, and so sales plummeted. U.S. exported goods became less price-competitive in foreign markets. Yet when the dollar weakens, as it has recently, U.S. export prices become more attractive in foreign markets. These changes are examples of the possible effects of economic exposure. Economic exposure can affect both the dollar value of the company's foreign assets and liabilities and the company's cash flow, because it has an impact on foreign sales. Asset exposure includes the fixed assets as well as the financial assets. The exposure of cash flow to currency fluctuation is known as *operating exposure*. Operating exposure is difficult to measure because it involves both the cash flows and the larger commercial context, the competitive conditions connected to obtaining inputs and selling. The management of economic exposure draws on the hedging and swap contracts we have discussed as ways to manage transaction exposure, on flexibility in sourcing, and on a portfolio approach to foreign market involvement.

TAXATION

In Chapter 8, we discussed taxation as a financial force and outlined three major types of taxation that governments around the world use—income tax, value-added tax, and withholding tax. **Income tax** is a direct tax levied on earnings. **Value-added tax (VAT)** is an indirect tax, in that the tax authority collects it from the person or firm that adds value during the production and marketing process, not from the owner of the item taxed. The ultimate user of the product pays the full amount of tax that is rebated to the others in the value chain. Thus, the government is collecting the tax on the value added in the process. The **withholding tax** is also an indirect tax, in that it is paid not by the person whose labor generates the income but by the business that makes the payment for the labor. Usually the withholding tax is levied on passive income such as royalties, dividends, and interest. Governments follow two approaches to the jurisdiction of their taxes, either worldwide or territorial. A worldwide approach is to tax residents of the country on their worldwide income. The United States follows a policy of worldwide taxation, and it can be argued convincingly that, despite tax treaties, such taxation puts U.S. firms operating foreign subsidiaries at a disadvantage compared with their foreign domestic competitors.[10] A territorial taxation policy taxes income earned within the nation's borders. There are tax credits, based on treaties that reduce or eliminate double taxation for U.S. residents and companies, as long as the foreign tax liability is less than the U.S. equivalent would be.

How the foreign operations of a company are organized is key to its U.S. tax liability on foreign earnings. If the operation is a **branch,** that is, an extension of the parent company, not a separate legal entity incorporated in the foreign country, its losses may be deducted by the parent company from its U.S. taxable income. If the foreign entity is a **subsidiary,** that is, a separate legal entity incorporated in the foreign country, its ownership by the MNC may be minority, that is, between 10 and 50 percent. Such minority company income, both active and passive, is taxed only when it is remitted to the parent company. If the foreign subsidiary is actually controlled by the parent company, with more than 50 percent ownership, it is known as a *controlled foreign corporation (CFC),* and its active income is taxed in the United States when that income is remitted to the parent company, but its passive income (royalties, licensing fees, dividends, service fees) is taxed as it occurs. When deciding where to locate and how to structure a foreign operation, MNC managers would want to review the tax rates of possible locations and also consider what legal form their operations should take. Often, startups have several years of losses, so establishment of a branch rather than a subsidiary might generate valuable losses, from a tax point of view, for the parent company. Transfer pricing, which we discussed earlier, offers international businesses a way to reduce tax liability.

In Chapter 17 we have examined two basic areas that are fundamental to the financial management of an international business, international accounting and the process of financial management. Our review of accounting looked at accounting issues related to foreign currency, culture, convergence of accounting standards and 3BL accounting efforts. In financial management, we reviewed the capital structure of the international firm, cash flow management, FX risk, and taxation. Financial management is becoming increasingly central to capturing efficiencies in the international firm. The green eyeshades are passé—it's an exciting area in which to develop a career. ■

notes

CHAPTER 1

1. For example, see Cornelis A. de Kluyver and John A. Pearce II, *Strategy: A View from the Top,* 2nd ed. (Upper Saddle River, NJ: Pearson Prentice Hall, 2006), p. 38; *InvestorDictionary. com,* "Multinational Corporation" http://investordictionary. com/definition/multinational-corporation.aspx (May 2, 2010); and "Multinational Corporation," http://en.wikipedia.org/wiki/ Multinational_corporation (May 2, 2010).

2. UNCTAD, "Transnational Corporations Statistics," www. unctad.org/templates/Page.asp?intItemID=3159&lang=1 (May 2, 2010).

3. Anil K. Gupta, Vijay Govindarajan, and Haiyan Wang, *The Quest for Global Dominance,* 2nd ed. (San Francisco: Jossey-Bass, 2008); Yves Doz, Jose Santos, and Peter Williamson, *From Global to Metanational* (Boston, MA: Harvard Business School Press, 2001); Anne-Wil Harzing, "An Empirical Analysis and Extension of the Bartlett and Goshal Typology of Multinational Corporations," *Journal of International Business Studies,* First Quarter 2000, pp. 101–19; and C. A. Bartlett and S. Goshal, *Managing across Borders: The Transnational Solution* (Boston: Harvard Business School Press, 1989).

4. "The Black Death," www.insecta-inspecta.com/fleas/bdeath/ bdeath.html (May 2, 2010); and Robbie Robertson, "Globalization Is Not Made in the West," www.globalpolicy.org/globaliz/define/ 2005/0413notmadeinthewest.htm (May 2, 2010).

5. "A Quick Guide to the World History of Globalization," www. sas.upenn.edu/~dludden/global1.htm (May 2, 2010); "Dutch East India Company," http://en.wikipedia.org/wiki/Dutch_ East_India_Company#History (May 2, 2010); BBC News, "Globalization: What on Earth Is It About?" http://news.bbc. co.uk/1/hi/special_report/1999/02/99/e-cyclopedia/711906. stm (May 2, 2010); and "The Growth of Global Industry," *The Wheel Extended,* no. 4 (1989), p. 11.

6. "Multinationals Come into Their Own," *Financial Times,* December 6, 2000, p. 16.

7. Bayer, "History," www.bayer.com/bayer-group/history/page701. htm (May 2, 2010).

8. Alfred D. Chandler Jr. and Bruce Mazlish, eds., *Leviathans: Multinational Corporations and the New Global History* (New York: Cambridge University Press, 2005), pp. 66, 88–89.

9. UNCTAD, "Development and Globalization: Facts and Figures," http://globstat.unctad.org/html/index.html (May 16, 2008).

10. *Fortune,* "2009 Global 500," http://money.cnn.com/magazines/ fortune/global500/2009/snapshots/6388.html (May 2, 2010); The World Bank, "GNI, Atlas Method (current US$)," http://data. worldbank.org/indicator/NY.GNP.ATLS.CD (May 2, 2010).

11. Calculation based on information found in the Consolidated Financial Statements Royal Dutch Shell, *"Annual Report 2008,"* http://www.shell.com/home/content/investor/financial_ information/annual_reports/2009/2009_annual_reports.html (May 2, 2010).

12. United Nations Conference on Trade and Development (UNCTAD), "FDI Stock, by Region and Economy, 1990, 2000, 2008," *World Investment Report 2009* (New York: United Nations, 2009), p. 251.

13. "Total Merchandise Trade," World Trade Organization, http:// stat.wto.org/StatisticalProgram/WsdbExport.aspx?Language=E (May 2, 2010).

14. "Trade in Commercial Services," World Trade Organization, http://stat.wto.org/StatisticalProgram/WSDBStatProgramSeries. aspx?Language=E (May 2, 2010).

15. Fred W. Riggs, "Globalization Is a Fuzzy Term But It May Convey Special Meanings," The Theme of the IPSA World Congress 2000, July 1999, www2.hawaii.edu/fredr/ipsaglo. htm (May 11, 2008); and "Globalization," http://en.wikipedia. org/wiki/Globalization (May 2, 2010).

16. Theodore Levitt, "The Globalization of Markets," *Harvard Business Review* 61, no. 3 (May–June 1983), pp. 92–93.

17. "Running a Global Company Well Poses Major Operational Challenges," http://knowledge.wharton.upenn.edu (July 4, 2006), p. 2.

18. "ICC Brief on Globalization," www.iccwbo.org/home/commercial_ practice/case_for_the_global_economy/globalization%20brief/ globalization_brief.asp (July 5, 2006); Paul Krugman, "The Good News," *New York Times,* November 28, 2003, p. A31; Horst Kohler and James Wolfensohn, "We Can Trade Up to a Better World," *Financial Times,* December 12, 2003, p. 19; and Martin Wolf, *Why Globalization Works* (New Haven, CT: Yale University Press, 2004).

19. "The Case for Open Trade," World Trade Organization, http:// www.wto.org/english/thewto_e/whatis_e/tif_e/fact3_e.htm (May 2, 2010).

20. Kohler and Wolfensohn, "We Can Trade Up to a Better Financial World."

21. Gary Burtless, Robert Z. Lawrence, Robert E. Litan, and Robert J. Shapiro, *Globaphobia: Confronting Fears about Open Trade* (Washington, D.C.: Brookings Institution Press, 1998); Alan Tonelson, *The Race to the Bottom: Why a Worldwide Worker Surplus and Uncontrolled Free Trade Are Sinking American Living Standards* (Boulder, CO: Westview Press, 2002); Daniel Seligman, "On NAFTA's Tenth Anniversary, Americans Demand Safe, Clean and Fair Trade," Sierra Club, San Francisco, www.sierraclub.org/pressroom/releases/ pr2003-12-23a.asp (May 2, 2010); John-Thor Dahlburg, "Protesters Tell a Different Tale of Free Trade," *Los Angeles Times,* November 20, 2003, p. A3; *Human Development Report 2003,* United Nations Development Program, New York, http://hdr.undp.org/en/reports/global/hdr2003/ (May 2, 2010); *World Development Indicators 2004,* World Bank, http://www.worldbank.org/data/countrydata/countrydata.html (July 15, 2004); and John Audley, Sandra Polaski, Demetrios G. Papademetriou, and Scott Vaughan, *NAFTA's Promise and Reality: Lessons from Mexico for the Hemisphere* (Washington, D.C.: Carnegie Endowment for International Peace, 2003).

22. Wolf, *Why Globalization Works.*

23. Tonelson, *The Race to the Bottom.*

24. Burtless et al., *Globalphobia: Confronting Fears about Open Trade.*

25. John Audley, Sandra Polaski, Demetrios G. Papademetriou, and Scott Vaughan, *NAFTA's Promise and Reality: Lessons from Mexico for the Hemisphere* (Washington, DC: Carnegie Endowment for International Peace, 2003).

26. United Nations Development Programme (UNDP), "Economy and Inequality," *Human Development Report 2009* (New York: United Nations Development Programme, 2009), pp. 195–98.

CHAPTER 2

1. World Exports of Merchandise and Commercial Services, by Selected Region and Nation (FOB values; billions of current U.S. dollars). Sources: *Monthly Bulletin of Statistics* (New York: United Nations, June 1997), pp. 92–102, 266–71; and World Trade Organization, 2009, *World Trade Report 2009,* (Geneva, Switzerland: World Trade Organization).

2. United Nations Industrial Development Organization, *International Yearbook of Industrial Statistics 2010* (Vienna Austria: UNIDO, 2010); and UNIDO, IDSB 2008 statistical database, "World—MVA Share of Country Groups," http://www. unido.org/index.php?id_o3474 (July 7, 2008).

3. "International Merchandise Trade—World Exports by Provenance and Destination," *Monthly Bulletin of Statistics,* July 2009, Table 40, http://unstats.un.org/unsd/mbs/table_list.aspx (May 15, 2010); *Monthly Bulletin of Statistics* (New York: United Nations), July 2001, pp. 266–71, July 2000, pp. 258–61, June 1997, pp. 255–62, June 1993, pp. 266–71; and *Statistical Yearbook* (New York: United Nations, 1969), pp. 376–83.

4. U.S. Census Bureau, Foreign Trade Statistics, "Trade in Goods (Imports, Exports and Trade Balance) with Canada," http://www.census.gov/foreign-trade/balance/c1220.html (May 15, 2010).

5. U.S. Census Bureau, Foreign Trade Statistics, "Trade in Goods (Imports, Exports and Trade Balance) with Mexico," http://www.census.gov/foreign-trade/balance/c2010.html (May 15, 2010).

6. World Trade Organization, "Merchandise Trade of Selected Regional Trade Agreements, 2000–2008," *International Trade Statistics 2009,* http://www.wto.org/english/res_e/statis_e/its2009_e/its09_appendix_e.htm (May 15, 2010).

7. Internet URLs are as follows:

   a. Office of Industry Analysis, www.ita.doc.gov/td/industry/otea (May 15, 2010).

   b. *U.S. Foreign Trade Highlights,* www.ita.doc.gov/industry/otea/usfth (May 15, 2010).

   c. *U.S. Commodity Trade with 80 Largest U.S. Trading Partners,* www.ita.doc.gov/td/industry/otea/usfth/top80cty/top80cty.html (May 15, 2010).

8. Government administrators involved in project evaluation are increasingly applying socioeconomic rather than purely financial criteria. For example, social rates of discount and opportunity costs are considered rather than the pure costs of borrowing money. Although marketing managers do not have to be development economists any more than they need to be specialists in marketing research, they should have knowledge of the basic concepts.

9. Peter Navarro, *Report of "The China Price Project"* (Irvine, CA: Merage School of Business, University of California, January 2007), https://webfiles.uci.edu/navarrop/public/00%20fixed%20ChinaPriceReportFinal0107.pdf?uniq=11vxzr (June 1, 2008).

10. David Ricardo, "The Principles of Political Economy and Taxation," in *International Trade Theory: Hume to Ohlin,* ed. William R. Allen (New York: Random House, 1965), pp. 62–67.

11. Ibid., *International Trade Theory,* pp. 174–77.

12. Gerard Tellis and Peter Golder, "First to Market, First to Fail? Real Causes of Enduring Marketing Leadership," *Sloan Management Review* 37, no. 2, cited in "Why First May Not Last," *The Economist,* March 16, 1996, p. 65.

13. Alfred Marshall, *Principles of Economics,* 8th ed. (London: Macmillan, 1920).

14. Michael E. Porter, *The Competitive Advantage of Nations* (New York: Free Press, 1990).

15. U.S. Department of Commerce, Bureau of Economic Analysis, "International Investment Position of the United States at Yearend, 1976–2008," http://www.bea.gov/international/index.htm#iip (May 15, 2010).

16. Ibid.

17. UNCTAD, *World Investment Report 2009,* "Annex table B.2. FDI stock, by region and economy, 1990, 2000, 2008," http://unctad.org/en/docs/wir2009_en.pdf (May 15, 2010).

18. Murray Weidenbaum and Samuel Hughes, "Asia's Bamboo Network," http://www.taemag.com/issues/articleid.16299/article_detail.asp (July 8, 2008); and Joe Quinlan, "China's Capital Finds New Targets across South-East Asia," *Financial Times,* November 14, 2007, p. 24.

19. Bob Davis, "International Finance: Sovereign-Wealth Funds Seek Control," *The Wall Street Journal,* June 6, 2008, p. C2; Ben Hall, "France Warms to Sovereign Wealth," *Financial Times,* May 23, 2008, p. 4; Ernest Zedillo, "Governments as Global Investors," *Forbes,* May 19, 2008, p. 25; International Financial Services London, "Sovereign Wealth Funds 2010," March 2010, http://www.ifsl.org.uk/output/ReportItem.aspx?NewsID=20 (May 15, 2010).

20. Various "Country Fact Sheets," *World Investment Report 2001,* United Nations Conference on Trade and Development, Geneva, October 2001; and "Annex table B.1. FDI flows, by region and economy, 2006–2008," *World Investment Report 2009,* United Nations Conference on Trade and Development, Geneva, http://unctad.org/en/docs/wir2009_en.pdf (May 15, 2010).

21. Ibid.

22. UNCTAD, *Developing Countries in International Trade 2005: Trade and Development Index* (New York: United Nations, 2005), p. 11, http://www.unctad.org/templates/webflyer.asp?docid=6443&intItemID=1397&lang=1&mode=downloads (May 15, 2010).

23. UNCTAD, *Developing Countries in International Trade 2005: Trade and Development Index* (New York: United Nations, 2005), http://www.unctad.org/templates/webflyer.asp?docid=6443&intItemID=1397&lang=1&mode=downloads (May 15, 2010); and UNCTAD, *Developing Countries in International Trade 2007: Trade and Development Index* (New York: United Nations, 2007), http://www.unctad.org/Templates/Page.asp?intItemID54388&lang51 (May 15, 2010).

24. Charles Kindleberger, *American Business Abroad* (New Haven, CT: Yale University Press, 1969), pp. 43–44.

25. Stephen Hymer, *The International Operations of International Firms: A Study in Direct Investment* (Cambridge, MA: MIT Press, 1976).

26. E. M. Graham, "Transatlantic Investments by Multinational Firms: A Rivalistic Phenomenon," *Journal of Post-Keynesian Economics,* Fall 1978, pp. 82–99.

27. P. Buckley and M. Casson, *The Future of Multinational Enterprise* (New York: Macmillan, 1976); D. Teece, *The Multinational Corporation and the Resource Cost of International Technology Transfers* (Cambridge MA: Ballinger, 1986); and A. M. Rugman, *Inside the Multinationals: The Economics of International Markets* (New York: Columbia University Press, 1986).

28. John H. Dunning, *International Production and the Multinational Enterprise* (London: George Allen & Unwin, 1981), pp. 109–10.

CHAPTER 3

1. W. Richard Scott, *Institutions and Organizations,* 3rd ed. (Thousand Oaks, CA: Sage, 2008) p. 48.

2. Talcott Parsons, "Prolegomena to a Theory of Social Institutions," *American Sociological Review* 55 (1934/1990), pp. 319–39, as referenced by Scott (2008), p. 14.

3. Douglass North, *Institutions, Institutional Change and Economic Performance* (Cambridge: Cambridge University Press, 1990) p. 4, as quoted in Scott (2008). Also see Gerry Everding, "Douglass North Prizes Economic History," *Washington University Record,* October 21, 1993, p. 3.

4. Scott, *Institutions and Organizations.*

5. Ibid., p. 100, referencing John Boli and George M. Thomas, "World Culture in the World Polity: A Century of International Nongovernmental Organization," *American Sociological Review* 62, pp. 171–90.

6. Geert Hofstede, *Cultures and Organizations: Software of the Mind* (San Francisco: Jossey Bass, 1991).

7. M. W. Peng, "How Entrepreneurs Create Wealth in Transition Economies," *Academy of Management Executive* 15 (2001), pp. 95–108, as cited in M. W. Peng, *Global Business* (Mason, OH: South-Western Cengage, 2009), p. 33.

8. Martin Wolfe, "Why Washington and Beijing Need Strong Global Institutions," *Financial Times,* April 19, 2006, p. 13.

9. See http://www.un.org/partners/business/index.asp (accessed January 15, 2010).

10. See http://www.un.org/partners/business/otherpages/factsheets/fs2.htm (accessed January 14, 2010).

11. See http://www.un.org/en/peacekeeping/currentops.shtml (accessed January 15, 2010).

12. See http://www.icj-cij.org/docket/index.php?p1=3&p2=1 (accessed January 14, 2010).

13. A. Acheson et al., *Bretton Woods Revisited* (Toronto: University of Toronto Press, 1972).

14. See www.imf.org/external/np/sec/memdir/eds.htm (accessed January 15, 2010).

15. IMF, "Articles of Agreement," www.imf.org/external/pubs/ft/aa/aa01.htm (accessed January 15, 2010).

16. World Bank Annual Report 2009. See www.worldbank. org; http://siteresources.worldbank.org/EXTAR2009/Resources/World_Bank_Lending_Presentation.ppt (accessed January 15, 2010).

17. http://us.ft.com/ftgateway/superpage.ft?news_id=fto030220081417540944 (accessed February 3, 2010).

18. See www.wto.org/english/thewto_e/whatis_e/tif_e/fact2_e.htm (accessed January 30, 2010).

19. *A Fair Globalization,* International Labour Organization (2004), www.ilo.org/public/english/wcsdg/docs/report.pdf (accessed January 31, 2010).

20. See Yale Center for the Study of Globalization, at http://www.ycsg.yale.edu/ for resources on issues related to globalization and equity.

21. WTO, Regional trade agreements, http://www.wto.org/english/tratop_e/region_e/region_e.htm (accessed January 16, 2010).

22. See "NAFTA: Myth Versus Fact," http://www.ustr.gov/Trade_Agreements/Regional/NAFTA/Section_Index.html (accessed January 18, 2010).

23. Amber Waves, USDA, http://www.ers.usda.gov/AmberWaves/September07/Findings/NAFTA.htm (accessed January 18, 2010).

24. See www.uschamber.com/issues/index/international/drcafta.htm and John Murphy, "DR-CAFTA: The Record So Far," November 2007 (accessed January 18, 2010).

25. See www.aseansec.org/64.htm (accessed January 20, 2010).

26. See the EU website for further information on accession: http://europa.eu (accessed January 23, 2010).

27. http://epp.eurostat.ec.europa.eu (accessed January 23, 2010).

28. "Eurozone Should Get Seat in G20, IMF: EU's Rehn," *Eurobusiness,* January 11, 2010, http://www.eubusiness.com/news-eu/economy-budget-g20.27l (accessed January 23, 2010).

CHAPTER 4

1. "How to Win Friends and Influence Clients," *The European,* January 21–27, 1994, p. 11.

2. I. Brady and B. Isaac, *A Reader in Cultural Change,* vol. 1 (Cambridge, MA: Schenkman Publishing, 1975), p. x.

3. Hy Mariampolski, *Ethnography for Marketers: A Guide to Consumer Immersion* (Thousand Oaks, CA: Sage Publications, 2005), p. 123.

4. "What Is Culture?" Center for Advanced Research on Language Acquisition, University of Minnesota, http://www.carla.umn.edu/culture/definitions.html (accessed June 4, 2010).

5. Vern Terpstra and Kenneth David, *The Cultural Environment of International Business* (Cincinnati, OH: South-Western, 1985), p. 7.

6. See self-reference criterion in Chapter 1. The influence of the self-reference criterion leads to ethnocentric behavior.

7. E. T. Hall, *Beyond Culture* (Garden City, NY: Doubleday, 1977), p. 54.

8. C. Kluckhohn and K. Strodtbeck, *Variations in Value Orientations* (Westport, CT: Greenwood, 1961).

9. E. T. Hall, *The Silent Language* (New York: Doubleday, 1959); *The Hidden Dimension,* 1966; *Beyond Culture,* 1976.

10. Robert J. House et al., *Culture, Leadership and Organizations: The Globe Study of 62 Societies* (Thousand Oaks, CA: Sage, 2004).

11. Geert Hofstede, *Culture and Organizations: Software of the Mind* (London: McGraw-Hill, 1991).

12. Fons Trompenaars, *Riding the Waves of Culture* (Burr Ridge, IL: Irwin, 1993).

13. E. T. Hall and Mildred Hall, *Hidden Differences: Doing Business with the Japanese* (Garden City, NY: Anchor Press/Doubleday, 1987).

14. Carol Kaufman-Scarborough and Jay D. Lindquist, "Time Management and Polychronicity: Comparisons, Contrasts, and Insights for the Workplace," *Journal of Managerial Psychology,* ttp://crab.rutgers.edu/~ckaufman/polychronic.html (accessed June 9, 2010). VOl. 14, Numbers 3-4, 288-312, 1999.

15. Hofstede's work has received considerable critical commentary, which centers on methodological survey issues; his analysis done on one level (organization) and then extrapolated to another (national); his dated data; and oversimplification, that five dimensions are not robust enough to describe a culture. While these are important issues, managers have found his work helpful. We look forward to continued work in the area.

16. Geert Hofstede, "Cultural Dimensions in Management and Planning," *Asia Pacific Journal of Management,* January 1984, pp. 81 and 84.

17. The source of the descriptions of the dimensions is Hofstede's website, which is well worth a visit because it has the raw

scores for the countries against the five dimensions: www.geert-hofstede.com (accessed June 5, 2010).

18. Modified from Ting-Toomey, Table 3.5.

19. Stella Ting-Toomey and others use Confucian dynamism to describe this dimension: *Communicating Across Cultures* (New York: Guilford Press, 1999).

20. Fons Trompenaars and Charles Hampden-Turner, *Riding the Waves of Culture* (New York: McGraw-Hill, 1997); John Bing, "The Use and Misuse of Questionnaires in Intercultural Training," ITAP International, http://www.itapintl.com/facultyandresources/articlelibrarymain/the-use-and-misuse-of-questionnaires-in-intercultural-training.html (accessed June 6, 2010); David Thomas, *Essentials of International Management: A Cross-Cultural Perspective* (Thousand Oaks, CA: Sage, 2002); vas Taras et al., "Half a Century of Measuring Culture: Review of Approaches, Challenges, and Limitations Based on the Analysis of 121 Instruments for Quantifying Culture," *Journal of International Management* 15(2009) pp. 357–373.

21. Joyce S. Osland and Allan Bird, "Beyond Sophisticated Stereotyping: Cultural Sense-Making in Context," *Academy of Management Executive* 14, no. 1 (2000), p. 65.

22. Anita Snow, "Ad Featuring 'Che' Guevara Sparks Furor," *The Monitor,* August 10, 2000, p. 8a.

23. E. T. Hall, *The Hidden Dimension* (Garden City, NY: Doubleday, 1969), pp. 134–35.

24. Internet resources may be helpful, such as Neil Payne, "International Gift Giving Etiquette," http://www.buzzle.com/editorials/10-23-2004-60743.asp (accessed June 6, 2010).

25. Herskovits, *Man and His Works,* p. 303. (New York: A. A. Knopf, 1967).

CHAPTER 5

1. Rhoads Murphey, *The Scope of Geography,* 2nd ed. (Skokie, IL: Rand McNally, 1973), pp. 65–67.

2. M. E. Porter, *The Competitive Advantage of Nations* (New York: Free Press, 1990).

3. *Daily Yomiuri Online,* January 28, 2010, http://www.yomiuri.co.jp/dy/business/T100127006823.htm (accessed February 7, 2010).

4. Federal Research Division, Library of Congress, "Afghanistan," Country Studies/Area Handbook Series, http://countrystudies.us/afghanistan/32.htm (accessed February 13, 2010).

5. "Facts about Afghanistan," *World Facts,* http://worldfacts.us/Afghanistan.htm (accessed February 13, 2010).

6. "Spain's Regions," *The Economist,* November 16, 1996, pp. 55–56.

7. United Nations Population Information Network, http://www.un.org/popin/data.html (accessed February 13, 2010).

8. Fiona Harvey, "Analysis: A Costly Thirst," *Financial Times,* April 4, 2008, p. 7. See www.ft.com/cms/s/0/71ea7cce-01e1-11dd-a323-000077b07658.html?nclick_check=1 (accessed February 20, 2010).

9. WaterAid is a nonprofit organization based in London, United Kingdom, whose mission is to help poor communities establish sustainable water supplies and latrines. It is referenced in Fiona Harvey's *Financial Times* piece, "Analysis: A Costly Thirst."

10. Murphey, *The Scope of Geography,* pp. 188–89.

11. Jared Diamond, *Guns, Germs, and Steel: The Fates of Human Societies* (New York: W. W. Norton 1997).

12. Andrew M. Karmack, *The Tropics and Economic Development* (Washington, D.C.: World Bank, 1976), p. 5.

13. Kenneth Deffeyes, *Hubbert's Peak: The Impending World Oil Shortage* (Princeton, NJ: Princeton University Press, 2001), p. 146; Peter Jackson, "What Are the Real Decline Rates for Global Oil Production?" Cambridge Energy Research Associates, 2007.

14. Cambridge Energy Research Associates, "The Future of the Global Oil Supply: Understanding the Building Blocks," November 4, 2009, www.cera.com/aspx/cda/client/report/report.aspx?KID=5&CID=10720 (accessed February 20, 2010).

15. Association for the Study of Peak Oil and Gas, www.peakoil.net (accessed February 20, 2010).

16. Energy Information Administration, "Annual Energy Outlook 2010," www.eia.doe.gov/ (accessed February 20, 2010).

17. *The Oil Drum,* Update November 2009, http://www.theoildrum.com/node/5979 (accessed February 21, 2010).

18. Russell Gold, "As Prices Surge, Oil Giants Turn Sludge into Gold," *The Wall Street Journal,* March 27, 2006, p. 1; PennWell Corporation, Oil & Gas Journal, Vol. 105.48 (December 24, 2007).

19. Sasol, "Sasol Oil-from-Coal Process," www.sasol.com/sasol_internet/downloads/SASOL_global_force_March07_1172224987155.pdf (accessed February 27, 2010).

20. Carola Hoyos, "Running on Empty? Fears Over Oil Supply Move into the Mainstream," *Financial Times,* May 20, 2008, p. 9

21. Carol Kopp, "The US Air Force Synthetic Fuels Program," Technical Report APA-TR-2008-0102, http://www.ausairpower.net/APA-USAF-SynFuels.html (accessed February 27, 2010).

22. On April 25, 1986, the world's worst nuclear power accident so far occurred at Chernobyl in Ukraine. The Chernobyl nuclear power plant, 80 miles north of Kiev, had four reactors, and while testing reactor number 4, personnel disregarded safety procedures. At 1:23 a.m. the chain reaction in the reactor became out of control, creating explosions and a fireball that blew off the reactor's heavy steel and concrete lid. See http://www.un.org/ha/chernobyl/history.html (accessed February 28, 2010).

23. International Atomic Energy Agency, http://www.iaea.org/programmes/a2/ (accessed February 28, 20010).

24. http://www.world-nuclear.org/info/inf63.html (accessed February 28, 2010).

25. http://www.nei.org/keyissues/newnuclearplants (accessed February 28, 2010).

26. World Nuclear Association, "Nuclear Power in France, 2008," http://www.world-nuclear.org/info/inf40.html (accessed February 28, 2010).

27. U.S. Energy Information Administration, "International Energy Outlook 2009," May 2009, www.eia.doe.gov/oiaf/ieo/coal.html (accessed February 28, 2010).

28. Ibid.

29. http://tonto.eia.doe.gov/energyexplained/index.cfm?page=coal_reserves (accessed February 28, 2010).

30. Renewables Global Status Report 2009, http://www.ren21.net/globalstatusreport/g2009.asp (accessed February 28, 2010).

31. Global Wind Energy Council, February 3, 2010, http://www.gwec.net/index.php?id=30&no_cache=1&tx_ttnews[tt_news]=247&tx_ttnews[backPid]=4&cHash=1196e940a0 (accessed February 28, 2010).

32. Gideon Rachman, "The World Has Two Energy Crises but No Real Answers," *Financial Times,* July 10, 2007, p. 11, www.ft.com/cms/s/0/0a97e57e-2e34-11dc-821c-0000779fd2ac.html (accessed March 5, 2010).

33. Phillip Sutton, "Sustainability, What Does It Mean?" *Green Innovations* homepage, August 28, 2000, www.green-innovations.asn.au/sustblty.htm (accessed March 6, 2010).

34. Ibid.

35. Paul Hawken, *The Ecology of Commerce* (New York: HarperCollins, 1994), p. 139.

36. Brundtland Commission, *Our Common Future: From One Earth to One World,* World Commission on Environment and Development (Oxford: Oxford University Press, 1987).

37. Economics Network, UK Higher Education Academy, "Development Survey on Definitions: Sustainable," www.economicsnetwork.ac.uk/projects/esd/def_survey.pdf (accessed March 6, 2010).

38. "Oil Firms in Nigeria Cut Output," *BBC News,* www.vanityfair.com/politics/features/2007/02/nigeria_photoessay200702 (accessed March 6, 20100); Dino Mahtani, "Nigerian Oil Industry Helpless as Militants Declare War on Obasanjo," *Financial Times,* February 21, 2006. For Michael Kamber's photographs of the Nigerian issue, see http://www.vanityfair.com/politics/features/2007/02/nigeria_slide0702 (accessed March 6, 2010); Amnesty International, March, 2010 (accessed March 6, 2010).

39. Francesco Guerrera and Richard Waters, "IBM Chief Wants End to Colonial Companies," *Financial Times,* June 12, 2006, p. 1; Samuel Palmisano, "Multinationals Have Been Superseded," *Financial Times,* June 12, 2006, p. 15.

40. R. Edward Freeman, *Strategic Management: A Stakeholder Approach* (Boston: Pitman, 1984).

41. R. Edward Freeman, Andrew C. Wicks, and Bidhan Pamar, "'Stakeholder Theory' and the Corporate Objective Revisited," *Organizational Science* 15, no. 3 (May–June 2004), pp. 364–69.

42. "Our Goals: Sustainability Overview," Interface Inc., http://www.interfaceinc.com/goals/sustainability_overview.html (accessed March 6, 2010).

43. "Environmentalism: What We Do," Patagonia.com, http://www.patagonia.com/web/us/patagonia.go?assetid=2329 (accessed April 4, 2010).

44. Y. Chouinard, *Patagonia: The Next Hundred Years* (1995), p. 8, http://uwsustainability.com/ (accessed March 6, 2010).

CHAPTER 6

1. John Lancaster, "U.S. Arms Sales in Gulf Risk Being Eroded by China and Others," *International Herald Tribune,* July 17, 1997, p. 6.

2. "The Price of Paying Ransoms," *The Economist,* September 2, 2000, p. 17.

3. Sarah Butcher, "No Hostages to Fortune," *Financial Times,* March 4, 2002, p. 10.

4. Joann S. Lublin, "Keeping the CEO Safe Can Be Costly," *The Wall Street Journal,* June 9, 2008, p. B.1.

5. See Chapter 2 for more on the growth of FDI.

6. www.duke/edu/~charvey/Country_risk/pol.htm; and http://www.polrisk.com/products.htm (both accessed July 21, 2002).

7. "Footwear Industry Tells Congress 'Shoe Gap' Threatens U.S. Defense," *The Wall Street Journal,* August 24, 1984, p. 21; and Thomas A. Pugel, *International Economics,* 13th ed. (New York: McGraw-Hill Irwin, 2007), pp. 197–98.

8. Lance Davis and Stanley Engerman, "History Lessons: Sanctions: Neither War nor Peace," *Journal of Economic Perspectives* 17, no. 2 (Spring 2003), p. 187.

9. Gary C. Hufbauer, "Economic Sanctions: America's Folly," in *Economic Casualties: How U.S. Foreign Policy Undermines Trade, Growth and Liberty,* ed. S. Singleton and D.T> Griswold (Washington D.C.: Cato Institute, 1999), pp. 90–99; and Askari et al., "Measuring Vulnerability."

10. "How to Lower Price of Ethanol; Kill the Tariff, Help Consumers," *Rocky Mountain News,* May 14, 2006, p. 5E; Scott Learn, "Rice University Analysis Questions Ethanol Subsidies," http://www.oregonlive.com/environment/index.ssf/2010/01/rice_university_analysis_quest.html (accessed June 15, 2010).

11. Robert Anderson, "Slovakia's 'Soviet' Skills Set to Create Car World-Beater," *Financial Times,* April 20, 2006, p. 4; John Gapper, "It Is Time for the Big Three to Shut Up," *Financial Times,* October 20, 2005, p. 19; "The New Rules of Trade," *National Review,* April 18, 1994, pp. 40–44; and Marc Champion and Adam Z. Horvath, "EU Expansion Fuels Debate on Taxes," *The Wall Street Journal,* May 3, 2004, p. A18.

12. World Trade Organization, *Annual Report 2003* (Lausanne, Switzerland: WTO, 2003); OECD, *Farm Household Income, Issues and Policy Responses* (Paris: OECD, 2003).

13. *Report on United States Barriers to Trade and Investment* (Brussels: European Commission, December 2003).

14. Office of the Foreign Trade Representative, *2006 National Trade Estimate Report on Foreign Trade Barriers.*

15. Ibid.

16. Ibid.

17. http://en.wikipedia.org/wiki/International_trade_of_genetically_modified_foods (accessed June 21, 2010).

CHAPTER 7

1. "Shanghai Sees Law as Key to Being Commercial Hub," *Financial Times,* July 1, 2002, p. vi.

2. A. H. Herman, "Growth in International Trade Law," *Financial Times,* March 30, 1989, p. 10.

3. Avery Johnson, "Pfizer Buys More Time for Lipitor," *The Wall Street Journal,* June 19, 2008, p. B1: "Avorastatin," http://en.wikipedia.org/wiki/Lipitor (accessed June 15, 2010).

4. Chester Yung, "Hong Kong's Antitrust Law Proposal Is Rapped for Lacking Punch," *The Wall Street Journal,* June 19, 2008, p. A10.

5. The Lex Column, *Financial Times (London),* June 16–17, 2001, p. 24.

6. Pierre Verkhhovsky and Clifford Chance, "Advising Japanese Clients on EU Competition Law," *International Journal of Competition Policy and Regulation,* www.global competition-review.com/apar/jap_eu.cfm (accessed July 30, 2004); and http://www.tradingmarkets.com/news/press-release/lgepf_-lead-japan-s-antitrust-watchdog-fines-samsung-sdi-ex-lg-affiliate-for-price-rigging-889764.html (accessed June 17, 2010).

7. *The Economist,* June 9, 1979, pp. 91–92.

8. Molly S. Boast and Hannah M. Pennington, "Extraterritorial Applications of U.S. Antitrust Laws: An Overview," http://www.abanet.org/antitrust/at-committees/at-ic/pdf/spring/05/boast.pdf (accessed June 12, 2010).

9. "Brussels Clears AOL–Time Warner Merger," *Financial Times,* October 12, 2000, p. 24; and Stephen Castle, "EU Fine Sends Message to Microsoft and Others," http://www.nytimes.com/2008/02/27/technology/27iht-msft.4.10498942.html (accessed June 15, 2010).

10. "Caught in a Web of Jurisdiction," *Financial Times,* May 15, 2002, p. 13.

11. "Alan Beattie, "From a Trickle to a Flood—How Lawsuits Are Coming to Dictate the Terms of Trade," *Financial Times,* March 20, 2007, p. 11.

12. Thomas G. Donlan, "Not So Free Trade: U.S. Preaches What It Doesn't Always Practice," *Barron's,* June 27, 1988, pp. 70–71.

13. Harvey Kaplan and Jon Strongman, "United States: Developments in U.S. Product Liability Law and the Issues Relevant to Foreign Manufacturers," http://www.mondaq.com/unitedstates/article.asp?articleid=89684 (accessed June 12, 2010).

14. Sandra N. Hurd and Frances E. Zollers, "Desperately Seeking Harmony: The European Community's Search for Uniformity in Product Liability Law," *American Business Law Journal* 30 (1992), pp. 35–68.

15. "Product Liability," *The Economist,* May 25, 1996, p. 67; and Katherine Dowling, "Wide-Ranging Suits against Manufacturers May Keep Lifesaving Medical Devices on the Shelf and out of Reach," *The Wall Street Journal,* August 19, 1997, p. A4.

CHAPTER 8

1. Cheol S. Eun and Bruce G. Resnick, *International Financial Management,* 4th ed. (Burr Ridge, IL: McGraw-Hill Irwin, 2007), p. 25.

2. Charles N. Henning, William Pigott, and Robert Haney Scott, *International Financial Management* (New York: McGraw-Hill, 1978), p. 149.

3. Albert C. Whitaker, *Foreign Exchange,* 2nd ed. (New York: Appleton-Century-Crofts, 1933), p. 157.

4. Jacques Rueff, *La réforme du système monétaire international* (Paris: Plon, 1973).

5. Paul Krugman, "The Gold Bug Variations," November 1996, www.pkarchive.org/ (accessed May 23, 2010).

6. *Federal Reserve Bulletin,* September 1969 and January 1974.

7. *Federal Reserve Bulletin,* December 1971 and January 1974.

8. The Japanese Ministry of Finance has a good site for exchange rate agreements, as well. See http://www.mof.go.jp/english/if/if043k.htm (accessed May 23, 2010).

9. Bank for International Settlements, "Central Bank Survey of Foreign Exchange and Derivatives Market Activity in 2007," December 19, 2007, http://www.bis.org/press/p071219.htm (accessed May 23, 2010).

10. Michael B. Devereux and Shouyong Shi, "Vehicle Currency," No. 10, Globalization and Monetary Policy Institute Working Paper from Federal Reserve Bank of Dallas, 2008.

11. Susie Gharib, "Slowing Global Growth May Energize the Dollar," February 28, 2008, PBS, *Nightly Business Report,* http://www.pbs.org/nbr/site/onair/transcripts/080208a/ (accessed May 23, 2010).

12. Eun and Resnick, *International Financial Management,* pp. 147–48. The technical explanations here are clearly described and well illustrated.

13. Ibid., p. 149.

14. Ibid., p. 151.

15. Cheol Eun and Sanjiv Sabherwal, "Forecasting Exchange Rates: Do the Banks Know Better?" *Global Finance Journal,* 2002, pp. 195–215.

16. M. Obstfeld and K. Rogoff, "The Mirage of Fixed Exchange Rates," *Journal of Economic Perspectives* 9, no. 4 (1995), pp. 73–96.

17. Ibid.

18. P. B. Kenen, "Fixed versus Floating Exchange Rates," *Cato Journal* 20, no. 1 (2000), pp. 109–13.

19. Herbert Stein, "Balance of Payments," in *The Concise Encyclopedia of Economics,* David R. Hendersen, ed., 1993, www.econlib.org/library/Enc/BalanceofPayments.html (accessed May 23, 2010).

20. Ibid.

21. Ibid.

CHAPTER 9

1. U.S. Census Bureau, International, www.census.gov/ipc/www/idb/region.php (accessed March 7, 2010).

2. Ibid.

3. *Global Employment Trends Brief* (Geneva: International Labour Office, January 2010).

4. Ibid.

5. Ibid.

6. U.S. Census Bureau, International, "Midyear Population, by Age and Sex," U.S. Population Reference Bureau, www.prb.org/Datafinder/Topic/Map.aspx?variable=119 (accessed March 8, 2010).

7. *Costs and Benefits of International Migration* (New York: Council on Foreign Relations, September 2005).

8. Eric Beauchesne, "Immigration Cuts Wages; StatsCan Study Finds 7% Slide at Top of Pay Scale," *National Post,* May 26, 2007, p. FP7.

9. *Costs and Benefits of International Migration.*

10. Aaron Terrazas and Jeanne Batalova, *Migration Information Source* (Washington, DC: Migration Policy Institute, 2009); www.migrationpolicy.org (accessed March 10, 2010).

11. The most recent immigration data from the U.S. Census Bureau can be accessed at www.census.gov/population.

12. *Workers' Remittances Fall* (Washington, DC: The World Bank, November 2009).

13. *The Convention on the Rights of the Child,* UNICEF, 2009. www.unicef.org (accessed March 9, 2010).

14. Ibid.

15. UNICEF, "Convention on the Rights of the Child," http://www.unicef.org/crc/ (accessed March 10, 2010).

16. "Convention on the Rights of the Child," http://en.wikipedia.org/wiki/Convention_on_the_Rights_of_the_Child (accessed March 10, 2010).

17. U.S. Department of State, *Trafficking in Persons Report 2009,* www.state.gov/g/tip/rls/tiprpt/2009/index.htm (accessed March 9, 2010).

18. OECD, "Migration and the Brain Drain Phenomenon," www.oecd.org/document/16/0,3343,en_2649_33935_39269032_1_1_1_1,00.html (accessed March 9, 2010).

19. "Africa Economy: EU Foreign Ministers Bid to Stop Africa's Brain-Drain," *EIU ViewsWire,* New York, March 30, 2006.

20. "UNESCO Fights Brain Drain with Computing Gain," *NGO News Africa,* December 31, 2009, http://www.ngonewsafrica.org/2009/12/continental-unesco-fights-brain-drain.html (accessed March 9, 2010).

21. Alan M. Webber, "Reverse Brain Drain Threatens U.S. Economy," *USA Today,* February 23, 2004, http://www.usatoday.com/news/opinion/editorials/2004-02-23-economy-edit_x.htm (accessed March 11, 2010).

22. Vivek Wadhwa, "The Reverse Brain Drain," *BusinessWeek Online,* August 23, 2007, http://www.businessweek.com/smallbiz/content/aug2007/sb20070821_920025.htm (accessed March 9, 2010).

23. Neil Heathcote, "Saudi Women Break into Business," *BBC News,* February 27, 2006, http://news.bbc.co.uk/1/hi/world/middle_east/4754430.stm (accessed March 9, 2010).

24. "Women Still Hold Less than a Quarter of Senior Management Positions in Privately Held Businesses," Grant Thornton, 2009, www.grantthorntonibos.com/Press-room/2009/women_in_business.asp (accessed March 9, 2010).

25. N. Boyacigiller, S. Beechler, S. Taylor, and O. Levy, "The Crucial Yet Illusive Global Mindset," in *The Blackwell Handbook of Global Management: A Guide to Managing Complexity*, ed. H. W. Lane, M. Maznevski, M. Mendenhall, and J. McNett (Oxford, UK, and Malden, MA: Blackwell, 2004).

26. European Trade Union Confederation, "Our Members," www.etuc.org/r/13 (accessed March 10, 2010).

CHAPTER 10

1. For a discussion of strategy, see Michael E. Porter, "What Is Strategy?" *Harvard Business Review*, November–December 1996, pp. 61–78.

2. Jay B. Barney, "Looking Inside for Competitive Advantage," *Academy of Management Executive* 9 (1995), pp. 49–61; M. A. Peteraf, "The Cornerstones of Competitive Advantage: A Resource-based View," *Strategic Management Journal* 14, no. 3 (1993), pp. 179–91; B. Wernerfelt, "A Resource-based View of the Firm," *Strategic Management* Journal 5, no. 2 (1984), pp. 171–80; and Jay Barney, *Gaining and Sustaining Competitive Advantage*, 2nd ed. (Upper Saddle River, NJ: Prentice Hall, 2002).

3. "An Executive Takes on the Top Business Trends: A McKinsey Global Survey," *The McKinsey Quarterly*, April 2006, www.mckinseyquarterly.com/article_print.aspx?L2=21&L3=114&ar=1754 (accessed May 22, 2010).

4. Darrell Rigby and Barbara Bilodeau, "Management Tools and Trends 2007," Bain & Company, http://www.bain.com/management_tools/Management_Tools_and_Trends_2007.pdf (accessed May 22, 2010), p. 10

5. "How Companies Act on Global Trends: A McKinsey Global Survey," *The McKinsey Quarterly*, March 2008, pp. 1–9.

6. Reggie Van Lee, Lisa Fabish, and Nancy McGaw, "The Value of Corporate Values," *Strategy + Business*, www.strategy-business.com/article/05206?gko=7869b-1876-9176155&tid=230&pg=all (accessed May 22, 2010).

7. Unilever, "Our Mission," http://www.unilever.com/ourcompany/ (accessed June 25, 2008).

8. Amazon.com, "Does Amazon.com Have a Mission or Vision Statement?" http://phx.corporate-ir.net/phoenix.zhtml?c=97664&p=irol-faq#14296 (accessed May 22, 2010).

9. Sumitomo Corporation, "SC Values," http://www.sumitomocorp.co.jp/english/company/principles/index.html (accessed May 22, 2010).

10. "Intel's Mission Statement, Values, and Objectives," www.intel.com/intel/company/corp1.htm (accessed May 22, 2010).

11. Jeroen van der Veer, "Shell Energy Scenarios to 2050," http://www.shell.com/home/content/aboutshell/our_strategy/shell_global_scenarios/shell_energy_scenarios_2050/shell_energy_scenarios_02042008.html (accessed May 22, 2010).

12. Ben Worthen, "Soviet-born Brin Has Shaped Google's Stand on China," *Wall Street Journal Online*, March 13, 2010 (accessed May 24, 2010).

13. Tim Bradshaw, David Gelles and Richard Waters, "Realism Lies behind Decision to Quit," *Financial Times*, March 24, 2010, p. 6.

14. L. Gordon Crovitz, "Google Search Result: Hong Kong; The Company Had to Maintain the Trust of Its Users," *Wall Street Journal Online*, March 29, 2010 (accessed May 24, 2010).

15. Rebecca Blumenstein and Stephen Fidler, "Google Takes Aim at Beijing Censorship; CEO Schmidt Hopes to 'Apply Some Pressure,' as Business Leaders Voice Concerns about Growing China-U.S. Tension," *Wall Street Journal Online*, January 30, 2010 (accessed May 24, 2010).

16. Jessica E. Vascellaro, "Google Brin Talks about China Gamble, *Wall Street Journal Online*, March 24, 2010 (accessed May 24, 2010).

17. Jessica E. Vascellaro, "Brin Drove Google Pullback," *The Wall Street Journal*, March 25, 2010, p. A1.

18. Ibid.

19. Matthew Forney and Arthur Kroeber, "Google Business Reason for Leaving China: Of Reputation and Revenue," *Wall Street Journal Online*, April 6, 2010 (accessed May 24, 2010).

20. Anonymous, "China Calls Google's Actions 'Wrong,'" *Informationweek Online*, March 23, 2010 (accessed May 24, 2010).

21. Jason Dean, Geoffrey A. Fowler, and Aaron Back, "China Threatens Google; Beijing Raises Tension in Censorship Spat: 'You Are Unfriendly and Irresponsible,'" *Wall Street Journal Online*, March 13, 2010 (accessed May 24, 2010).

22. Loretta Chao, "Google Braces for Fallout in China," *The Wall Street Journal*, March 24, 2010, p. B1.

23. Sharon Gaudin, "Google, China Play Game of Cat and Mouse," *Computerworld*, April 5, 2010, p. 8.

24. Geoffrey A. Fowler and Loretta Chao, "Google Exit Would Open a Door for Microsoft," *Wall Street Journal Online*, March 16, 2010 (accessed May 24, 2010).

25. Aaron Back and Loretta Chao, "Google Weaves a Tangled Chinese Web," *Wall Street Journal Online*, March 25, 2010 (accessed May 24, 2010).

26. Cornelius A. de Kluyver and John A Pearce II, *Strategy: A View from the Top*, 2nd ed. (Upper Saddle River, NJ: Pearson Prentice Hall, 2006), p. 9.

27. www.aiesec.org.

28. Gary Hamel, "Strategy as Revolution," *Harvard Business Review*, July–August 1996, p. 70.

29. Eric D. Beinhocker and Sarah Kaplan, "Tired of Strategic Planning?" *The McKinsey Quarterly*, 2002 (special edition on risk and resilience), www.mckinseyquarterly.com/article_print.aspx?L2=21&L3=37&ar=1191 (accessed May 22, 2010).

30. Andrew Campbell and Marcus Alexander, "What's Wrong with Strategy?" *Harvard Business Review*, November–December 1997, p. 46.

31. Frederick W. Gluck, "A Fresh Look at Strategic Management," *Journal of Business Strategy*, Fall 1985, p. 6.

CHAPTER 11

1. Nitin Nohria, *Note on Organization Structure* (Boston: Harvard Business School, 1991).

2. John M. Stopford and Louis T. Wells, *Strategy and Structure of the Multinational Enterprise* (New York: Basic Books, 1972).

3. Caterpillar Inc., *2007 Annual Report*, http://www.cat.com/cda/files/887773/7/AR_2007_final.pdf (accessed May 30, 2010).

4. Shell Chemicals, "Glossary & Trademarks," http://www.shellchemicals.com/glossary/1,1098,1159,00.html#P (accessed May 30, 2010).

5. Lowell L. Bryan and Claudia Joyce, "The 21st-Century Organization," *The McKinsey Quarterly*, no. 3 (2005),

www.mckinseyquarterly.com/article_print.aspx?L2=18&L3=30&ar=1628 (accessed April 27, 2006).

6. Remo Häcki and Julian Lighton, "The Future of the Networked Company," *The McKinsey Quarterly,* no. 3 (2001), pp. 26–39.

7. Accenture, "Fact Sheet," http://accenture.tekgroup.com/section_display.cfm?section_id=160 (accessed May 30, 2010); "Have Advice, Will Travel," *The Wall Street Journal,* June 5, 2006, pp. B1, B3; Yongsun Paik and David Y. Choi, "The Shortcomings of a Standardized Global Knowledge Management System: The Case Study of Accenture," *Academy of Management Executive* 19, no. 2 (2005), pp. 81–84; and Glenn Simpson, "The Economy: Consultants Accenture, Monday Take Steps That May Reduce Taxes," *The Wall Street Journal,* eastern ed., July 3, 2002, p. A2.

8. Glenn R. Simpson, "Wearing of the Green: Irish Subsidiary Lets Microsoft Slash Taxes in U.S. and Europe," *The Wall Street Journal,* November 7, 2005, p. A1.

CHAPTER 12

1. A good introduction to scanning the environment is "Environmental Scanning," http://en.wikipedia.org/wiki/Environmental_scanning (accessed June 9, 2010).

2. Virtually all governments have barriers to foreign direct investment and at the same time offer a variety of incentives to potential foreign investors. For example, Mexico currently restricts foreign investment in the petroleum industry. See, for example, UNCTAD's series of *World Investment Reports,* published in an annual edition: http://www.unctad.org/Templates/Page.asp?intItemID=1485&lang=1 (accessed June 9, 2010).

3. "CeBIT 2010 Has Been Very Impressive," http://www.cebit.de/end_of_show_report_2010 (accessed June 9, 2010).

4. Secondary data and sometimes primary data will be gathered on a field trip, but the visitor rarely has the time or ability to conduct a complete field study.

5. Yuezhi Zhao, "The 'People's Phone' on Hold," *Foreign Policy,* July–August 2002, pp. 83–85.

6. For a sophisticated example in Mexico, see http://www.pearson-research.com/english/informacion-america-latina-mexico.phtml (accessed June 9, 2010).

7. Carol Hymowitz, "Marketers Focus More on Global 'Tribes' than on Nationalities," *The Wall Street Journal,* December 10, 2007, p. B1. The segment screening approach was inspired by Masaaki Kotabe and Kristiaan Helsen, *Global Marketing Management* (New York: Wiley, 2008).

CHAPTER 13

1. This discussion owes a great deal to Orville C. Walker Jr., John Mullins, and Harper W. Boyd Jr., *Marketing Strategy: A Decision-Focused Approach* (Burr Ridge, IL: Irwin/McGraw-Hill, 2011).

2. Thayne Forbes, "Set the Right Royalty Rate," www.intangiblebusiness.com (accessed June 30, 2010).

3. "Cosmopolitan," http://www.hearst.com/magazines/cosmopolitan.php (accessed June 30, 2010).

4. "Is *Playboy* Available Outside North America?" www.playboy.com/worldofplayboy/faq/subscribing.html#4 (accessed June 30, 2010).

5. Sources: Nyay Bhushan, Berwin Song, and Mark Russell, "Rising in the East: A Guide to the Key Asian Social Networking Services," *Billboard,* May 24, 2008, p. 20; "List of Social Networking Sites," *Wikipedia,* http://en.wikipedia.org/wiki/List_of_social_networking_websites (accessed June 30, 2010); "German Social Networking Community Reaches

14.8 Million," http://www.comscore.com/press/release.asp?press=1737 (accessed June 30, 2010); Eric Eldon, "The Latin American Social Networking Wars," June 3, 2008, http://venturebeat.com/2008/06/03/the-latin-american-social-networking-wars-market-leader-hi5-has-been-growing-but-so-has-facebook-and-sonico/ (accessed June 30, 2010); http://www.wired.com/gadgetlab/2009/03/report-60-of-wo/ (accessed June 20, 2010); http://blog.euromonitor.com/2010/05/regional-focus-latin-america-enjoys-mobile-telephone-boom.html (accessed June 18, 2010); and http://en.wikipedia.org/wiki/List_of_social_networking_websites (accessed June 22, 2010).

6. Frank Tian Xie and Wesley J. Johnston, "Strategic Alliances: Incorporating the Impact of E-Business Technological Innovations," *Journal of Business and Industrial Marketing* 19, no. 3 (2004), pp. 208–22.

7. Edward J. Zajac, "Creating an Academic Framework for Strategic Alliances," www.kellogg.northwestern.edu/kwo/sum02/indepth/theory.htm (accessed June 30, 2010).

8. For discussion of challenges in managing international joint ventures and alliances, see Colette A. Frayne and J. Michael Geringer, "Challenges Facing General Managers of International Joint Ventures," in *Readings and Cases in International Human Resource Management,* 2nd ed., ed. M. Mendenhall and G. Oddou (Cincinnati, OH: South-Western, 1995), pp. 85–97; J. Michael Geringer and C. Patrick Woodcock, "Agency Costs and the Structure and Performance of International Joint Ventures," *Group Decision and Negotiation* 4, no. 5 (1995), pp. 453–67; and Colette A. Frayne and J. Michael Geringer, "Joint Venture General Managers: Key Issues in Research and Training," in *Research in Personnel and Human Resources Management,* ed. K. M. Rowland, B. Shaw, and P. Kirkbride (Greenwich, CT: JAI Press, 1993), supplement 3, pp. 301–21.

CHAPTER 14

1. T. C. Melewar and John Saunders, "International Corporate Visual Identity: Standardization or Localization?" *Journal of International Business Studies,* Third Quarter 1999, pp. 583–98; and Adesegun Oyedele, Osama J. Butt, and Michael S. Minor, "The Extent of Global Visual Identity as Expressed in Web Sites: An Empirical Assessment," working paper, 2004.

2. "Accenture," http://newsroom.accenture.com/fact+sheet/ (accessed June 24, 2010).

3. "PricewaterhouseCoopers Global," http://www.pwc.com/gx/en/about-pwc/facts-and-figures.jhtml (accessed June 24, 2010).

4. "A Global Comeback," *Advertising Age,* August 20, 1987, p. 146.

5. "Belgium's Strong Drinks," *International Management,* June 1992, p. 65; and http://en.wikipedia.org/wiki/Delirium_Tremens_(beer) (accessed June 29, 2010).

6. GM Worldwide site, www.gm.com/company/corp_info/global_operations/asia_pacific/chin.html (accessed October 10, 2006); and Peter Whoriskey, "GM Sales in China Surge 67 percent in 2009," http://www.washingtonpost.com/wp-dyn/content/article/2010/01/04/AR2010010403160.html (accessed June 29, 2010).

7. Warren J. Keegan, "Multinational Product Planning Strategic Alternatives," *Journal of Marketing,* January 1969, pp. 56–62, combines these strategies to formulate five product and promotional strategies.

8. Geoffrey Fowler, "Intel's Game: Play It Local but Make It Global," *The Wall Street Journal,* September 30, 2005.

9. "About Axfood: Strategic Matters," www.axfood.se/showdoc.asp ?docId=3&channelId=103&folderid=22&objectname=Strate gi&selectedchannelId=103&priority=2&startfolderid=22&setl anguageid=4 (accessed August 2, 2004).

10. "KFC and McDonald's: A Model of Blended Culture," *China Daily,* June 1, 2004, www.chinadaily.com.cn/english/doc/2004-06/01/content_335488.htm (accessed October 10, 2006); and Yum Brands, *Annual Report, 2006,* www.yum.com (accessed October 10, 2006).

11. Morris Kalliny, Grace Dagher, Michael S. Minor, and Gilberto de los Santos, "Television Advertising in the Arab World: A Status Report," *Journal of Advertising Research,* June 2008, pp. 215–23.

12. "Brands That Stop at the Border," *Financial Times,* October 6, 2006, p. 10.

13. "World Brands," *Advertising Age,* February 2, 1992, p. 33.

14. Stephen X. Doyle and George Thomas Roth, "Selling and Sales Management in Action: The Use of Insight and Coaching to Improve Relationship Selling," *Journal of Personal Selling & Sales Management,* Winter 1992, p. 62.

15. Melissa Campanelli, "Avon's Calling in China," *DM News,* March 10, 2006. www.dmnews.com/cms/dm-news/international/36010.html (accessed October 12, 2006).

16. "Our Social Lives and Personal Image the First to Suffer When the Going Gets Tough," ACNielsen, April 25, 2006, www2.acnielsen.com/news/20060425.shtml (accessed October 13, 2006).

17. "McDonald's Wins Its Libel Case against Two Activists in the UK," *The Wall Street Journal,* June 20, 1997, p. B2; and http://www.google.com/search?q=worldwide+Anti-McDonald%27s+Day&rls=com.microsoft:en-us&ie=UTF-8&oe=UTF-8&startIndex=&startPage=1 (accessed June 30, 2010).

18. Lars Perner, "International Marketing," www.consumerpsychologist.com/international_continued.htm (accessed October 14, 2006). These observations draw closely on his work.

CHAPTER 15

1. Donald J. Bowersox, David J. Closs, and M. Bixby Cooper, *Supply Chain Logistics Management,* 2nd ed. (Burr Ridge, IL: McGraw-Hill Irwin, 2007), pp. 2–18.

2. Robert D'Avanzo, "The Reward of Supply-Chain Excellence," *Optimize,* December 2003, p. 68.

3. David Demers and Priya Sathyanarayanan, "Charting the Supply Chain DNA," *Supply Chain Management Review,* November–December 2003, pp. 48–58.

4. Joan Magretta, "The Power of Virtual Integration: An Interview with Dell Computer's Michael Dell," *Harvard Business Review,* March–April 1998, pp. 73–84.

5. Joan Magretta, "Fast, Global, and Entrepreneurial: Supply Chain Management, Hong Kong Style—An Interview with Victor Fung," *Harvard Business Review,* September–October 1998, pp. 3–14.

6. http://www.dellideastorm.com/about; and Elizabeth M. Gillespie, "Online Starbucks Suggestion Box Is a Hit," April 10, 2008, http://www.mailtribune.com/apps/pbcs.dll/article?AID=/20080410/BIZ/804100332 (accessed June 12, 2010).

7. William J. Zeile, "U.S. Affiliates of Foreign Companies: Operations in 2000," *Survey of Current Business,* August 2002, p. 161.

8. L. J. Krajewski and L. P. Ritzman, *Operations Management,* 5th ed. (Boston: Addison-Wesley, 1999), p. 456; J. Heizer and B.

Render, *Principles of Operations Management,* 4th ed. (Upper Saddle River, NJ: Prentice Hall, 2001), p. 436, table 11.2; and Bowersox, Closs, and Bixby Cooper, *Supply Chain Logistics Management,* p. 81.

9. Sam Jaffe, "Oracle: A B2B Rebirth That Few Foretold," *BusinessWeek,* April 6, 2000, http://www.businessweek.com/ebiz/0004/es0406.htm (accessed June 12, 2010).

10. Sam Fortescue, "Companies Warm to Doing Deals on e-Marketplaces," *Supply Management,* June 10, 2004, p. 10.

11. Ibid.

12. Richard B. Chase, F. Robert Jacobs, and Nicholas J. Aquilano, *Operations Management for Competitive Advantage,* 11th ed. (Burr Ridge, IL: McGraw-Hill Irwin, 2006), chap. 10.

13. Ronald C. Ritter and Robert A. Sternfels, "When Offshore Manufacturing Doesn't Make Sense," *The McKinsey Quarterly,* no. 4 (2004), www.mckinseyquarterly.com/article_print.aspx?L2=1&L3=106&ar=1510 (accessed June 12, 2010).

14. Chase, Jacobs, and Aquilano, *Operations Management for Competitive Advantage,* pp. 413–14.

15. Heizer and Render, *Principles of Operations Management,* p. 173.

16. D. J. Teece, "Technology Transfer by Multinational Firms," reprinted in M. Casson, ed., *The International Library of Critical Writings in Economics I* (London, UK: Edward Elgar, 1990), pp. 185–204.

17. A highly automated machine may make only one or two sizes or types of a product, whereas a general-purpose machine may be capable of producing not only all sizes of a product but other products as well. Its output, however, may be as little as 1 percent of that of a specialized machine.

CHAPTER 16

1. Vijay Govindarajan and Anil Gupta, *The Quest for Global Dominance: Transforming Global Presence into Global Competitive Advantage* (San Francisco: Jossey-Bass, 2001), p. 106.

2. Ibid., p. 111.

3. David A. Heenan and Howard V. Perlmutter , *Multinational Organization Development* (Boston: Addison-Wesley, 1979).

4. Consistency between mind-set and IHRM practices was reported in Linda K. Stroh and Paula M. Caligiuri, "Strategic Human Resources: A New Source for Competitive Advantage in the Global Arena," *International Journal of Human Resource Management* 9, no. 1 (1998), pp. 1–17.

5. David Pilling and Francesco Guerrera, "We Are a Mixture: Western Style in Management but with an Eastern Touch," *Financial Times,* September 26, 2003, p. 13.

6. Geoff Dyer, "A Tale of Two Corporate Cultures," *Financial Times,* May 23, 2006, p. 8.

7. GMAC Global Relocation Services, *Global Relocation Trends 2007 Survey Report,* www.gmacglobalrelocation.com/2007survey (accessed July 10, 2008); and Mary G. Tye and Peter Y. Chen, "Selection of Expatriates: Decision-Making Models Used by HR Professionals," *Human Resource Planning* 28, no. 4 (2005), pp. 15–20.

8. "Expatriate Workforce Demographics," *HR Magazine* 51, no. 5 (May 2006), p. 16.

9. GMAC Global Relocation Services, *Global Relocation Trends 2007 Survey Report.*

10. John C. Beck, "Globalization: Don't Go There . . .," www.accenture.com/Global/Research_and_Insights/ (accessed June 8, 2010).

11. Juan I. Sanchez, Paul E. Spector, and Cary L. Cooper, "Adapting to a Boundaryless World: A Developmental Expatriate Model," *Academy of Management Executive* 14, no. 2 (May 2000), pp. 96–106.

12. GMAC Global Relocation Services, *Global Relocation Trends 2007 Survey Report.*

13. Lalervo Oberg, "Culture Shock and the Problem of Adjustment to New Cultural Environments," www.worldwide.edu/travel_planner/culture_shock.html (accessed June 6, 2010).

14. Margaret A. Shaffer, David A. Harrison, and K. Matthew Gilley, "Dimensions, Determinants, and Differences in the Expatriate Adjustment Process," *Journal of International Business Studies* 30, no. 3 (1999), pp. 557–81.

15. Deirdre McCaughey and Nealia S. Bruning, "Enhancing Opportunities for Expatriate Job Satisfaction: HR Strategies for Foreign Assignment Success," *Human Resource Planning* 28, no. 4 (2005), pp. 21–29; and Jie Shen, "International Training and Management Development: Theory and Reality," *Journal of Management Development* 24, no. 7 (2005), pp. 656–66.

16. Shaffer, Harrison, and Gilley, "Dimensions, Determinants, and Differences in the Expatriate Adjustment Process."

17. Margaret A. Shaffer and David A. Harrison, "Forgotten Partners of International Assignments: Development and Test of a Model of Spouse Adjustment," *Journal of Applied Psychology* 86, no. 2 (2001), pp. 238–54.

18. Riki Takeuchi, Seokhwa Yun, and Paul E. Tesluk, "An Examination of Crossover and Spillover Effects of Spousal and Expatriate Cross-Cultural Adjustment on Expatriate Outcomes," *Journal of Applied Psychology* 87, no. 4 (August 2002), p. 655.

19. GMAC Global Relocation Services, *Global Relocation Trends 2007 Survey Report.*

20. GMAC Global Relocation Services, *Global Relocation Trends 2003/2004 Survey Report,* www.nftc.org/default/hr/GRTS_2003-4.pdf (accessed September 19, 2008); and GMAC Global Relocation Services, *Global Relocation Trends 2007 Survey Report.*

21. Michael Harvey, "Dual-Career Expatriates: Expectations, Adjustment and Satisfaction with International Relocation," *Journal of International Business Studies* 28, no. 3 (1997), pp. 627–58; and Perri Capell, "What 'Trailing Spouses' Can Do," *The Wall Street Journal,* May 2, 2006, p. B6.

22. Alison Langley, "Always Beginning Again: The Opportunity to Make a Home Abroad Can Sound Exciting but the Spouses of Overseas Workers Face Particular Challenges," *Financial Times,* November 4, 2006, p. 1.

23. Jeremy Smerd, "More Women, Young Workers on the Move," *Workforce Management,* August 2007, pp. 9–10.

24. Expatica, "Helping Families Meet the Challenge of Moving Abroad," http://www.expatica.com/hr/story/helping-families-meet-the-challenge-of-moving-abroad-10453.html (accessed June 8, 2010); and Expatica, "How Children View Moving Abroad," http://www.expatica.com/hr/story/how-children-view-moving-abroad-10567.html (accessed June 8, 2010).

25. Joanne Wojcik and Sarah Veysey, "Expatriate Health Coverage Often Hard to Coordinate," *Crain Communications,* 2004, p. 10.

26. Annette Haddad and Scott Doggett, "Road Home Hard after Working Overseas," *Los Angeles Times,* March 13, 2000, p. C2; and Leslie Gross Klaff, "The Right Way to Bring Expats Home," *Workforce,* July 2002, pp. 40–44.

27. GMAC Global Relocation Services, *Global Relocation Trends 2003/2004 Survey Report;* and Kathryn Tyler, "Retaining Repatriates," *HR Magazine* 51, no. 3 (March 2006), pp. 97–102.

28. Tyler, "Retaining Repatriates."

29. "Worldwide Cost of Living Survey 2006—City Rankings," www.mercerhr.com/pressrelease/details.jhtml/dynamic/idContent/1142150 (accessed July 23, 2006).

30. Tess Lyons, "Betting Big on 'Internationalising' Local Employees," *China Staff,* May 2005, pp. 12–14.

31. Some writers regard paid home leave as an allowance, but our experience convinces us that it is a bonus, because ICs consistently give more frequent or longer home leaves to employees working in less desirable assignments.

32. Tom Herman, "Americans Working Overseas May See Big Jump in Tax Bill," *The Wall Street Journal,* May 20, 2006, p. B4.

33. World Tourism Organization, "Average Number of Vacation Days around the World per Year," http://www.infoplease.com/ipa/A0922052.html (accessed June 8, 2010).

CHAPTER 17

1. John Daniels, Lee Radebaugh, and Daniel Sullivan, *International Business: Environments and Operations,* 11th ed. (Upper Saddle River, NJ: Pearson, 2007), p. 639.

2. Sidney J. Gray, "Towards a Theory of Cultural Influence on the Development of Accounting Systems Internationally," *Abacus* 24, no. 1 (1998), pp. 1–15.

3. John Elkington, *Cannibals with Forks: The Triple Bottom Line of 21st Century Business* (Gabriola Island, BC, Canada: New Society Publishers, 1997).

4. Wayne Norman and Chris MacDonald, "Getting to the Bottom of 'Triple Bottom Line,'" *Business Ethics Quarterly,* April 2004, www.businessethics.ca (accessed June 12, 2008).

5. James Oberstar, House Transportation and Infrastructure Committee testimony before the U.S. Senate Committee on Commerce, Science and Transportation, May 9, 2006.

6. When equity securities (stock shares) are issued, part of the ownership is being sold. No money is being borrowed that must be repaid, as is the case when debt securities (bonds) are issued.

7. "Yunus Blasts Compartamos," *BusinessWeek,* December 13, 2007, www.businessweek.com/magazine/content/07_52/b4064045920958.htm (accessed June 16, 2008).

8. www.ACCION.org (accessed June 16, 2008); Maria Otero, "Microfinance at the Crossroads," *Forbes.com,* May 19, 2008, http://www.forbes.com/opinions/2008/05/19/micro-finance-accion-oped-cx_mot_0519accion.html (accessed June 16, 2008).

9. Haley Dillan, November 4, 2009, www.globalenvision.org/2009/10/20/microfinance-update-interview (accessed May 20, 2010).

10. Daniel Mitchell, "Job Creation and the Taxation of Foreign Earned Income," *Executive Memorandum 911,* The Heritage Foundation, 2004.

Photo Credits

CHAPTER 1

Page 2: © Glow Images/SuperStock; **4:** © Stockbyte/Getty Images; **6:** © McGraw-Hill Companies, Inc./Gary He, photographer; **14:** © Getty Images; **19:** © Bloomberg via Getty Images

CHAPTER 2

Page 24: © Royalty-Free/Corbis; **Page 29:** © Royalty-Free/Corbis; **34:** © Andrzej Gorzkowski/Alamy; **36:** © Image Source/Getty Images; **40:** © Photolink/Getty Images

CHAPTER 3

Page 44: © Nick Koudis/Getty Images; **48:** © AFP/Getty Images; **57:** © Photodisc/Getty Images

CHAPTER 4

Page 60: © Royalty-Free/Corbis; **62:** © Punchstock/Digital Vision; **67 left:** © Jack Hollingsworth/Corbis; **67 right:** © Image 100/Corbis; **72:** © Ryan McVay/Getty Images

CHAPTER 5

Page 78: © Joeseph Sohm-Visions of America/Getty Images; **82:** © Getty Images/Photodisc; **83:** © Royalty-Free/Corbis; **87:** © 1997 IMS Communications Ltd/Capstone Design. All Rights Reserved; **92:** © Royalty-Free/Corbis; **98:** © Royalty-Free/Corbis; **99:** © Lynn Bendickson/Cutcaster

CHAPTER 6

Page 104: © Royalty-Free/Corbis; **108:** © AP Photo/Visar Vryeziu; **111:** © Getty Images

CHAPTER 7

Page 118: © Getty Images; **122:** © Erica Simone Leeds; **123:** © PRNewsFoto/Netflix, Inc.

CHAPTER 8

Page 130: © Brand X Pictures/Jupiter Images; **132:** © Photographer's Choice/Getty Images; **139:** © Getty Images

CHAPTER 9

Page 144: © Imagestate Media (John Foxx); **149:** © Getty Images; **150:** © The McGraw-Hill Companies, Inc./John Flournoy, photographer; **153:** © The McGraw-Hill Companies, Inc./Barry Barker, photographer

CHAPTER 10

Page 162: © Chris George/Alamy; **164:** © Royalty-Free/Corbis; **172:** © Comstock Images/Jupiterimages; **173:** © Comstock; **180:** © Bobby Yip/Reuters/Landov

CHAPTER 11

Page 182: © Atamu Rahi/Icontec; **185:** © Bloomberg via Getty Images; **192:** © M. Scott Brauer/Onasia.com; **196 top:** © Mike Margol/PhotoEdit

CHAPTER 12

Page 200: © Stockbyte/Getty Images; **203:** © Jennifer Thermes/Getty Images; **205:** © Digital Vision/Getty Images; **207:** © Getty Images; **209:** © 2010 Deutsche Messe AG – All Rights Reserved; **210:** © Imagesource/PictureQuest; **211:** © Digital Vision/Alamy

CHAPTER 13

Page 216: © James Hardy/PhotoAlto; **221:** © AFP/Getty Images

CHAPTER 14

Page 228: © Erica Simone Leeds 2007; **231:** © Redfx/Alamy; **232:** Kerry-Edwards 2004, Inc./Sharon Farmer, photographer; **234:** © Victoria Ball; **235:** © Blend Images/Getty Images; **237:** © Catherine Karnow/Woodfin Camp

CHAPTER 15

Page 244: © Comstock Images/Alamy; **249:** © PRNewsFoto/Apple; **252 top:** © 1998 EyeWire, Inc.; **252 bottom:** The McGraw-Hill Companies, Inc./Jill Braaten, photographer; **255:** © Getty Images; **256:** © Creative Crop/Getty Images; **257:** © Hill Street Studios

CHAPTER 16

Page 260: © Design Pics/PunchStock; **263:** © arabianEye/PunchStock; **267:** © Stockbyte/Getty Images; **270:** © Digital Vision/Getty Images

CHAPTER 17

Page 278: © Stockbyte/PunchStock; **287:** © John Rae for ACCION International

"Check it Out" Photo: © BLOOM Image/Getty Images

name/company index

Fair competition argument, 110
Fair-trade certification, 115
Fair-Trade Labeling Organizations International, 115
Families of expatriates
    adjustment problems, 268
    children, 268–269
    two-career families, 268
Family, 75
Faster-growing markets, 17
FAS terms of sale, 121
Fast-food restaurants, Japan, 237
Federation of International Trade Associations, 21
Femininity, 68
Field trip, 208
Finance, cultural differences, 65
Financial Accounting Standards Board, 129
    functions, 282
    Statement 52, 280
Financial crisis of 2008, 147
Financial forces
    balance of payments, 142–143
    causes of exchange rate movements, 136–137
    in country screening
        cluster analysis, 206
        estimation by analogy, 205
        market factors, 205
        market indicators, 204–205
        periodic updating, 206
        trend analysis, 205
    currency exchange controls, 139–143
    definition, 7
    exchange rate forecasting, 137
    fluctuating currency values, 135
    foreign exchange, 135–136
    inflation and interest rates, 140–142
    international monetary system, 131–135
    taxation, 139–140
    uncontrollable, 135
Financial management
    and capital structure, 283–284
    cash flow management, 284–286
    company finance centers, 285
    debt vs. equity finance, 283–284
    decisions by financial managers, 284
    economic exposure, 290
    foreign exchange risk management, 287–290
    hedging, 289–290
    leading and lagging technique, 286
    microloan bankers, 287–289
    multilateral netting, 285–286
    offshore financial centers, 283
    organization of foreign operations, 291
    raising capital, 283–284
    swap contracts, 290
    and taxation, 290–291
    translation exposure, 290
Financial markets
    debt markets, 283
    integrated, 282
    stock markets, 283
Financial reporting, 280
    Global Reporting Initiative, 283

Financial reports, 198
Financial scandals, 129
Financial services dumping, 112
Financial statements, variations worldwide, 280
Financial Times, 14, 21, 47, 51, 136, 207
Finland
    corporate tax rates, 140
    gender gap in pay, 156
    maternity leave policy, 156
Firm strategy, structure, and rivalry, 33
First-movers, 217–218
Fiscal policy
    and balance of payments, 142
    and currency market, 136
Fischer-Tropsch process, 92
Fisher effect, 136, 140
Fixed exchange rates
    in Bretton Woods system, 132–133
    debate on, 138
    and Smithsonian Agreements, 133
Fixed peg arrangement, 133
Flexpatriate, 267
Floating exchange rates, 131
    after Bretton Woods, 133
    debate on, 138
    and hedging, 134
    independently floating, 134
    Jamaica Agreement, 133
    managed, 134
    pros and cons, 134
    success of, 134
Fluctuating currency values, 135
Folklore, 71
Food laws, 234
Forced labor, 152
Forecasting
    exchange rates, 137
    by trend analysis, 205
Foreign business, 6
Foreign Corrupt Practices Act
    case study, 76
    definition, 128
    grease payments vs. bribery, 128
    provisions, 128
    and Transparency International, 129
    uncertainties about, 128
Foreign currency, and accounting, 280
Foreign currency options, 290
Foreign direct investment, 25
    annual inflows, 38
    annual outflows, 37–38
    bamboo network, 35–37
    critics of, 15
    definition, 11, 35
    effect on economic and social development, 39–40
    international trade leading to, 40–41
    level and direction of, 38–39
    for mergers and acquisitions, 38
    outstanding stock of, 35
    selected countries, 35
    theories of
        dynamic capabilities, 41
        eclectic theory of international production, 41–43
        internalization, 41

        monopolistic advantage, 41
    in wholly owned subsidiaries, 223
    world stock in 2008, 11
Foreign direct investment without investment, 221
Foreign environment
    analysis of, 167–168
    decision making in, 9
    definition, 8
    differing values, 8
    difficulty in accessing, 8
    interactions in, 8–9
    International Organizations, 9
    interrelated environmental forces, 8
Foreign environmental forces
    and advertising, 236–237
    product strategies, 233–235
Foreign exchange, 142
    lack of, 18
Foreign exchange controls, 18
Foreign exchange market
    amount of daily transactions, 138
    annual volume, 134
    arbitrage, 136
    effect of capital markets, 138
    effect of ending Bretton Woods, 133
    exchange rate forecasting, 137
    exchange rate quotations, 135–136
    explosive growth in trading, 134
    forward market, 135
    forward rate, 135
    and G8 countries, 134
    ONANDA website, 135
    speculators in, 138
    spot rate, 135
Foreign exchange risk, in cash flow management, 284
Foreign exchange risk management
    economic exposure, 290
    operating exposure, 290
    reasons for, 286
    transaction exposure, 286–290
    translation exposure, 290
Foreign investment; *see also* Foreign direct investment
    direct, 35
    portfolio, 35
Foreign Labor Trends, 159
Foreign markets, 209; *see also* International marketing
    aids in selecting
        field trips, 208
        surveys, 211–214
        trade fairs, 208–209
        trade missions, 208
    challenges of exporting, 226–227
    chance for success in, 218
    channels of distribution, 219
    equity-based modes of entry
        joint ventures, 223–224
        strategic alliances, 224–226
        wholly owned subsidiaries, 223
    fast-growing, 17
    local research
        cultural problems, 209–211
        research practice, 211
        social desirability bias, 211
        technical difficulties, 211
    market screening for
        country screening, 202–214

        environmental scanning, 202
        segments screening for, 214
    motives for entering
        acquire know-how, 19
        attack competitor's home market, 18
        downstream markets, 19
        faster-growing markets, 17
        geographic diversification, 19
        greater profits, 17
        greater revenue, 17
        improved communication, 17
        investment opportunity, 18
        lack of foreign exchange, 18
        local production by competitors, 19
        lower costs of goods sold, 17–18
        lower costs of production, 18
        management desire for expansion, 19
        new market creation, 16–17
        protect domestic market, 18
        protect foreign markets, 18
        protectionism issue, 19
        raw materials supply, 19
    nonequity-based modes of entry
        contract manufacturing, 221
        direct exporting, 219
        franchising, 220–221
        indirect exporting, 219
        licensing, 219–220
        management contracts, 221
        sales company, 219
        social networking, 222
        turnkey projects, 219
    pioneers vs. followers, 218
    protection of, 18
    reason for exporting to, 226–227
    sales company, 219
    timing of entry, 217–218
Foreign national pricing, 242
Foreign ownership restrictions, 283
Foreign Service oral exam, 20
Formal institutions
    definition, 46
    major rule-setters, 46
Forward currency market, 135
Forward market hedge, 289–290
Forward rate, 135, 137
Fossil fuel crisis, 93
Four Ps of marketing, 214
France
    capital structure, 284
    collective bargaining, 160
    corporate tax rates, 140
    foreign direct investment outflows, 38
    gender gap in pay, 156
    inflation rate 2008–9, 140
    maternity leave policy, 156
    nuclear power in, 94
    rank in international trade, 27
Franchising, to enter foreign markets, 220–221
Free association, 75
Free trade
    critics of, 15
    and socioeconomic development, 14
Free trade areas, 3, 53
Fronting loans, 285
Functional divisions, 188

Functional expertise, 185
Fundamental approach, 137
Future-oriented cultures, 70–71

G

Hindukush, 82
HIV/AIDS, 54, 158
Hofstede's dimensions of culture, 66–69
Home-country nationals
  definition, 263
  salary, 270–271
  training for, 265
Home leave bonus, 272–275, 276
Home market, protecting, 18
Home replication strategy, 171
Hong Kong
  legal tradition, 120
  rank in international trade, 27
Horizontal corporation, 191
Horizontal integration, 257–259
Host country
  distance from headquarters, 193
  employer conflict of loyalty, 264
  exporting requirements, 226
  host-country nationals hired in, 266
  in joint ventures, 223
  understanding conditions in, 193
Host-country nationals
  definition, 263
  hired in home country, 265
  hired in host country, 266
  in polycentric staffing, 264
  regiocentric staffing, 264–265
  for subsidiaries, 264
  training for, 265–266
Housing allowance, 271
Human developmental differences, 89
Human Development Report (UN), 16–17
Human resource management; *see* International human resource management
Human resources, cultural differences, 65
Hungary, gender gap in pay, 156
Hybrid design, 257
Hybrid organization, 188
Hypermarché, 233

I

Ijaw tribe, 99
Immigrant labor
  brain drain, 152–153
  departures from Africa 1945–1970, 150
  departures from Europe 1850–1970, 149–150
  dirty, dangerous, and degrading jobs, 150
  effect on wages, 150
  range of skills, 150
  remittances home, 151
  and reverse brain drain, 153
  size of workforce, 150
  sources and destination, 150
  in United States, 150–151
Import controls, 18
Importers
  Asian, 29
  lack of foreign exchange, 18
  world leaders, 27
Importing, 11
Import restrictions, 30, 206

Imports
  in current account, 142
  government data on, 29
  laws against, 231–232
  as measure of market potential, 203–204
  of minerals by U.S., 97
  of raw materials, 19
In-bond plant contractors, 248
Income, understated or overstated, 281
Income disparities, 234–235
Income inequality, 15
Income statement, translation method, 281
Income tax, 290
Incoterms, 121
Independent contractors, 248
India
  caste differences, 154
  coal use in, 94
  corporate tax rates, 140
  Dalits, 152
  decline in poverty, 52
  inflation rate 2008–9, 140
  information technology industry, 36
  jobs offshored to, 36–37
  nuclear power in, 94
  size of workforce, 36
  software companies, 17
  statistics on, 53
  violation of intellectual property rights, 52
  working age population, 148
Indirect exporting, 219
Indirect procurement, 249
Individualism, 67, 70
  country scores, 69
Indo-malayan people, 81
Indonesia
  mining operations, 99
  piracy incidents, 220
  pribumi, 263
Industrial products
  advertising, 236
  in marketing mix, 231–232
Industry-sponsored exchanges, 249
Inequality, and power distance, 67
Infant industries, 17
Infant industry argument, 110
Inflation
  and balance of payments deficits, 142
  and currency exchange controls, 140–142
  definition, 140
  effect on borrowing and lending, 140
  and interest rates, 136
  world rates 2008–2009, 140
Informal institutions, 46
  characteristics, 47
  cognitive, 46–47
  definition, 47
  guanxi, 47
  normative, 46
  United Nations, 47–49
Inland waterways
  Amazon Basin, 87
  in Asia, 87–89
  ocean outlets, 89
  Parana and Paraguay Rivers Trade Corridor, 89, 90

Rhine-Main-Danube Canal, 87, 88
  Rhine waterway, 87
Innovation, from adverse conditions, 80
Inpatriates, 266
Inputs for product design, 247
Instability, 108
Institutions
  definition, 46
  formal, 46
  informal, 46
  new institutional theory, 46
  rules of the game image, 46
  social agreements, 47
Intellectual property
  copyrights, 122, 123
  definition, 122
  patents, 122–123
  trade names, 122, 123
  trade-related aspects, 122, 123
  trade secrets, 122
  and World Intellectual Property Organization, 121
Intellectual property rights, 52
Interchangeability, 254
Interdependence, 99
Interest rate parity, 136
Interest rates
  and currency exchange controls, 140–142
  and exchange rates, 138
  Fisher effect, 136
  international Fisher effect, 136
  and law of one price, 136
  London Interbank Offered Rate, 142
  national comparisons, 142
  prime rate, 142
Intermediate technology, 257
Internalization, 43
Internalization theory, 41
Internal Revenue Code, 272
Internal Revenue Service, on transfer pricing, 285
International accounting; *see* Accounting
International Accounting Standards Board, 129
  functions, 282
  Statement 21, 280
International Association of Business Communicators, 21
International Atomic Energy Agency, 94
International Bank for Reconstruction and Development, 50; *see also* World Bank
International business
  adapting to culture, 64
  career information sources, 20–21
  careers in China, 141
  competitive challenges, 166
  contrasted with domestic business, 7
  controllable forces, 7
  definition, 6
  drivers of globalization, 12–13
  effects of culture, 64–65
    accounting and finance, 65
    human resources, 65
    leadership styles, 65
    marketing, 65
    production, 65

environmentally sustainable practices
  equity in distribution, 99
  interdependence, 98–99
  limits, 98
expanding number of companies, 10–11
exporting, 11
external environmental forces, 7
foreign direct investment growth, 11
getting a job in, 57, 112
history of, 9–10
impact of European Union on, 58–59
importance of exchange rate movements, 137
internal environmental forces, 7
and legal forces worldwide, 119
manager knowledge of, 6
role of United Nations, 47–48
terminology for, 6
uncontrollable forces, 7
United Nations rules, 48
women as expatriate managers, 273
International careers, 21
International Center for the Settlement of Investment Disputes, 50, 123
International Chamber of Commerce, 21
  Uniform Rules and Practice on Documentary Credits, 121
International Civil Aviation Organization, 48
International companies
  based on product, region, function, or customer classes, 186
  changes in form, 190
  changes over time, 184
  control in
    centralized vs. decentralized, 198–199
    distributed control, 198
    joint ventures, 195–198
    less than wholly owned subsidiaries, 195–198
    reports required of subsidiaries, 198
    wholly owned subsidiaries, 192–195
  corporate form
    functional divisions, 187–188
    geographic regions, 186–187
    product divisions, 186, 187
  countermeasures against terrorism, 107
  country screening by, 202–214
  current organizational trends
    horizontal corporation, 191
    modular corporation, 191
    virtual corporation, 190–191
  definition, 6
  dynamic network structure, 191
  evolution of, 185–190
  expanding number of, 10–11
  exporting by, 11
  foreign direct investment by, 11
  as global customers, 13
  versus gross national incomes, 11
  hybrid organization, 188

Patents—*Cont.*
  and patent trolls, 122
  in pharmaceutical industry, 122
Patent trolls, 123
Patent violations, 52
Patron, 65
Pegged exchange rate
  crawling peg, 134
  fixed arrangement, 133
  within horizontal band, 134
People's Daily, China, 136
Performance measures, 176
Periodic updating, 206
Perks, 276–277
Per se concept, 124
Personal selling
  and Internet, 238
  legal forces, 239
  in promotional mix, 238
  recruiting salespeople, 239
  standardization of, 239
Personnel managers, 261
Peru, corporate tax rates, 140
Petroleum
  depleted supplies, 90
  estimates of reserves, 90–91
  and fossil fuel crisis, 93
  present production, 91
  projected consumption, 91
  reserves by country in 2010, 91
  unconventional sources
    coal, 92
    heavy oil, 92
    natural gas, 92–93
    oil sands, 91
    shale, 91–92
  worldwide proven reserves
    and investment risk, 92
    and political risk, 92
Pharmaceutical industry
  patents, 122
  patent violations, 52
Phone surfers, 214
Physical forces, 7
  product strategies, 235
Pioneering firms, 218
Piracy
  and patent infringement,
    219–220
  traditional type, 220
Plague, 9–10
Plain plateaus, 81
Planning, in global standardization,
  254
Plant design
  backward vertical integration, 255
  for capital-intensive processes,
    255
  cost of production and, 257
  and cultural forces, 255–257
  design solutions, 257
  and economic forces, 255
  hybrid design, 257
  intermediate technology, 257
  for labor-intensive processes, 255
  local manufacturing, 257–259
  planning, 254
  and political forces, 257
  replication, 254
Plant layout, 65
Point-of-sale displays, 239
Poland, gender gap in pay, 156
Policies, 176

Policy stability, 206–207
Political forces
  country risk assessment,
    108–109
  in country screening
    entry barriers, 206
    policy stability, 206–207
    profit remittance barriers, 206
  definition, 7
  for globalization, 12
  government ownership, 106
  government protection, 106–107
  government stability, 108
  impediment to global standardiza-
    tion, 255
  and international companies, 108
  privatization, 106
  and staffing policies, 263
  trade restrictions, 109–117
Political reports, 198
Political risk, and proven oil reserves,
  92
Political stability vs. policy stability,
  206–207
Pollution, from burning coal, 94–95
Polycentric staffing policy, 262,
  264
Polychronic cultures, 66
Pooling alliances, 225
Population
  age 65 and above, 149
  aging of, 148
  areas of decline, 147
  areas of increase, 147
  concentration in Australia, 86
  foreign-born in U.S., 151
  global, 146
  major trading nations, 53
  near bodies of water, 87
  rural vs. urban, 148–149
  world map, 88
Population density, for selected
  countries, 86
Portfolio investment, 35, 142
Portugal, gender gap in pay, 156
Poverty
  decline in China and India, 52
  in developing countries, 158
  worldwide decline 1981–2001, 14
Power distance, 67
  country scores, 69
  plot of selected nations, 70
Preassignment support, 267
Predatory dumping, 111
Predictability in business, 51
Preferential trading arrangements, 12
Pribumi, 263
Price(s)
  and cost differentials, 242
  in efficient market hypothesis,
    137
  reason for local sourcing, 250
  standardized, 242–243
  in supply decision, 46–47
  transfer price, 194, 242–243,
    264, 285, 291
Price-quality relationships, 242
Pricing
  and choice of middlemen, 242
  and competition, 242
  controllable variable, 242
  cost differentials, 242
  cultural differences, 242

  effective, 242
  effect of Internet, 243
  foreign national, 242
  international, 242–243
  in international marketing,
    241–243
  intracorporate sales, 242
  research on, 241–242
  standardized, 230
  standardizing, 242–243
  transfer pricing, 242–243
  varied methods, 242
Prime rate, 142
Principles-based accounting standards, 282
Private brands, 236
Privatization
  definition, 106
  and globalization, 12
  by region, 106
Procedures, 176
Procurement
  cultural differences, 65
  electronic, 249–251
  high-cost country sourcing, 256
  indirect, 249
Product(s)
  global, 237–238
  local adaptation
    global strategy, 172
    home replication strategy, 171
    multidomestic strategy,
      171–172
    transnational strategy, 172
  national identity of, 237
Product business units, 190
Product decisions, 192
Product design
  broad input for, 247
  concurrent engineering, 247
  cross-functional participation, 247
  global standardization, 247
  in marketing mix, 231–232
  over-the-wall approach, 247
  and supply chain management,
    246–247
Product development, in home replication strategy, 171
Product differentiation, 33
  in home replication strategy, 171
Product divisions, managerial specialists, 186
Product division strategic business
  units, 190
Product expertise, 184
Production; *see also* Cost of
  production
  automated, 255
  capital-intensive, 255
  computer-integrated manufactur-
    ing, 255
  coordination across regions, 187
  cultural differences, 65
  labor-intensive, 255
  local, by competitors, 19
  multicountry, 193–194
Production control, 254
Production specifications, 253–254
Production technique, 251
Product liability
  cap on damages, 127
  defenses in European Union, 127
  definition, 125

  in European Union, 127
  insurance for, 125
  in Japan, 127
  punitive damages, 127
  strict liability, 125–127
  in United States, 125–127
Product life cycle
  reason for exporting, 227
  and supply chain management,
    246
Product mix
  rationalization, 254
  of subsidiaries, 234–235
Product strategies
  foreign environmental forces
    economic, 234–235
    legal, 233–234
    physical, 235
    sociocultural, 233
  in marketing mix, 231–233
  total product, 231
  type of product
    consumer products, 232
    industrial products, 231–232
Profit
  motive for entering foreign mar-
    kets, 16–19
  overseas investment motive, 18
  shared in joint ventures, 223
  of subsidiaries
    decision on disbursing, 194
    examples, 194–195
    and transfer pricing, 194
Profit remittance barriers, 206
Programmed management approach
  to advertising, 238
Promotion
  definition, 235
  factors limiting standardization,
    236–238
  recruiting salespeople, 239
Promotional strategies
  advertising in, 236–238
  different product-different mes-
    sage, 236
  different product-same message,
    236
  personal selling in, 238–239
  product adaptation-message adap-
    tation, 235
  product adaptation-same message,
    235
  public relations, 239–241
  sales promotion, 239
  same product different message,
    235
  same product-same message, 235
Promotion (job)
  cultural differences, 264
  geocentric view, 266
Property rights, and World Trade
  Organization, 52
Proprietary knowledge, 169
Protectionism, 19, 231–232; *see
  also* Trade restrictions
  Buy America Act, 116
  and exchange rate fluctuations,
    138
  and new market creation, 17
Protocols, 120
Proximity, geographical, 81
Public relations
  dealing with critics, 241

definition, 239–241
and nationalism, 241
Punitive damages, 127
Purchasing
global standardization, 254
local manufacturing, 257–259
Purchasing power parity
Big Mac index, 136–137
definition, 136
and exchange rate movements, 136–137
Putonghua, 84
Puts, in hedging, 290
Pyrenees, 82

Q

Qatar, proved oil reserves, 91
Quality control, 254
Quality management procedures, 253
Quality of labor, 146
Quality of living, city rankings, 272
Quality of work life, 68
Quality standards, 253
Quantitative nontariff barriers, 114–116
Quantity of labor, 146
Questionable or dubious payments, 128
Quotas
absolute, 114
definition, 114
global, 114
as legal forces, 125
transshipping to evade, 114–116
voluntary restraint agreements, 125

R

Race to the bottom, 15
Racism
and employment, 156
and globalization, 156
kinds of conflicts, 156
Random walk hypothesis, 137
Raw materials; *see also* Natural resources
costs, 248
guaranteed supply of, 19
Recycling, in European Union, 58–59
Red Army Faction, Germany, 107
Reengineering, 190
Reformulate, in marketing mix, 230–231
Regiocentric staffing policy, 262, 264–265
Regional brands, 236
Regional clusters of industry, 33
Regionalized organizations, 186–187
Regional trade agreements, 28
Central America, 54–55
South America, 54–55
and World Trade Organization, 52
Regional trading blocs, table of, 53
Related and supporting industries, in Porter's theory, 33
Religion
component of culture, 71–72
world map, 73
Remittances from immigrant labor, 151

Renewable Energy Policy Network, 96
Renewable energy sources
biomass, 95–97
power capacities worldwide, 95
Repackaging, 232
Repatriation, 269
Repatriation limitations, 139
Repatriation support, 267–268
Reporting
financial, 198
on market opportunities, 198
political and economic conditions, 198
technological, 198
Repositioning, 232
Republic of Congo, oil sands, 91
Research and development partnership, 224
Resource endowments, 32
Resources, scarce, 166
Retained earnings
for raising capital, 283
translation method, 281
Retaliation argument, 110–111
Reuters, 21
Revenue
India's information technology industry, 36
motive for entering foreign markets, 17
Reverse brain drain, 153
Reverse culture shock, 267, 269
Rhine-Main-Danube Canal, 87, 88
Rhine Waterway, 87
Rich vs. poor nations, 15, 52
Riley Guide, 20
Risks
in country risk assessment, 108–109
economic exposure, 290
operating exposure, 290
transaction exposure, 286–290
translation exposure, 290
Roger and Me, 99
Royalties
in cash flow management, 284
from licensing, 219
Rule of law, 120
Rules-based accounting standards, 282
Rules of the game, 46, 48
Rules vs. relationships, 69–70
Russia
corporate tax rates, 140
expatriate costs in, 270
inflation rate 2008–9, 140
nuclear power in, 94
projected population decline, 147
proved oil reserves, 91
statistics on, 53

S

Sahara Desert, 81
Salaries, 270–271
Sales
intracorporate, 242
motive for entering foreign markets, 16–19
reason for exporting, 226–227
Sales company, 219
Sales forecasts, 175–176

Salespeople, recruiting, 239
Sales promotion
contests and games, 239
couponing, 239
definition, 239
economic forces, 239
in marketing mix, 239
point-of-sale displays, 239
sociocultural forces, 239
standardization of, 239
Sales tax, VAT as, 139
Sanctions, 110
Sarbanes-Oxley Act, 282
Satellite TV, 13
Saudi Arabia
changing role of women, 154
labeling law, 234
oil reserves, 93
proved oil reserves, 91
sanctions against alcohol, 127
Scenario analysis, 173
Scenarios, 173
Scientific tariff, 110
Secrecy-transparency in accounting, 281
Secretariat of the United Nations, 49
Secretary-general of the United Nations, 49
Securities and Exchange Commission, 129, 282
Security, in electronic procurement, 251
Segment screening
across nationalities, 214
criteria for, 214
definition, 202
relevant marketing questions, 214
Self-reference criterion, 9
Senior management, women in, 154, 155
Services
design of, 246–247
in marketing mix, 232–233
offshored to India, 36–37
Services account, 142
Services trade
percentage of Gross domestic product, 26
volume in 2008, 26
world leaders, 27
Severe acute respiratory syndrome (SARS), 9
Sexism
acceptability of women in workforce, 154
and culture, 154–156
definition, 154
education of women, 154–155
family responsibility, 155
gender gap in median earnings, 156
maternity leave laws, 155–156
salary rates, 155
women in management, 154, 155
Shale, 91–92
Shopping frequency, 233
Short-range planning, 176
Short-term capital flow, 142
Sierra Leone, women's literacy rates, 155
Singapore
corporate tax rates, 140
foreign direct investment in, 38

Skilled workers, immigrant labor, 150
Slovakia, tax dumping, 112
Small and medium-sized businesses
electronic procurement by, 250
in global competition, 13
Smithsonian Agreements, 133
Smoot-Hawley Tariff Act of 1930, 113
Social clause, 157
Social desirability bias, 211
Social development, effect of trade and investment, 39–41
Social dumping, 112
Social networking, to enter foreign markets, 222
Social networks, 75–77
Social status, and employment practices, 154
Societal organization, 75–77
Sociocultural, 64
Sociocultural forces
and advertising, 237
aesthetics, 71
in country screening, 207, 210
country screening for, 207
definition, 7
gift giving, 72–75
and human resources, 65
language, 72, 74
material culture, 72
product strategies, 233
religion, 71–72, 73
and sales promotion, 239
societal organization, 75–77
Socioeconomic forces, 7
Somalia, piracy incidents, 220
South Africa, apartheid boycott, 92
South African Customs Union, 53
South Asia, population statistics, 146
Southeast Asia, population statistics, 146
Southern African Development Community, 54
South Korea
earnings of men vs. women, 155
gender gap in pay, 156
inflation rate 2008–9, 140
rank in international trade, 27
Soviet bloc collapse, 81
Spain
gender gap in pay, 156
inflation rate 2008–9, 140
languages, 82–84
regional map, *83*
Specialization
in absolute advantage, 31
in comparative advantage, 31
Specific vs. diffuse, 70
Speculators, 138
Spot rate, 135, 280
Stability, 108
Staffing
compensation plans, 270–277
effects of standardization, 253–254
ethnocentric policy, 262–264
expatriate managers, 266–269
geocentric policy, 265
global mind-set, 262
international human resource management, 262–265
polycentric policy, 264

in a nutshell

International business, which involves activities carried out across national borders, has become such an important issue that all managers must have a basic knowledge of it. Effective managers understand the key drivers that are leading firms to internationalize their operations, the reasons underlying firms' decisions to enter foreign markets, and how to determine the extent to which their companies should globalize different dimensions of their operations. Managers must also understand the arguments supporting, and opposing, globalization of business.

The following questions will test your take-away knowledge from this chapter. How many can you answer?

LO1 What is international business and why is it important?

LO2 Why and how does international business differ from domestic business?

LO3 Can you summarize international business's long and important history in the world's development?

LO4 Can you discuss the dramatic internationalization that has occurred in the world's markets?

LO5 What are the five kinds of drivers, all based on change, which are leading firms to internationalize their operations?

LO6 Can you summarize the key arguments for and against the globalization of business?

LO7 Can you explain the reasons underlying firms' decisions to enter foreign markets?

LO8 Can you identify the seven dimensions of a firm that can be globalized, and can you explain how the extent of a firm's globalization can vary across these dimensions?

Did your answers include the following important points?

LO1 What is international business and why is it important?

- International business is business whose activities are carried out across national borders. International business is important because of the increasing scale and scope of activities that occur across national borders.

LO2 Why and how does international business differ from domestic business?

- International business differs from its domestic counterpart in that it involves three environments—domestic, foreign, and international—instead of one. Although the kinds of forces are the same in the domestic and foreign environments, their values often differ. The international environment is defined as the interactions (1) between the domestic environmental forces and the foreign environmental forces and (2) between the foreign environmental forces of two countries when an affiliate in one country does business with customers in another.

LO3 Can you summarize international business's long and important history in the world's development?

- International business has a long and important history, extending thousands of years into the past. Politics, the arts, agriculture, industry, public health, and other sectors of human life have been profoundly influenced by the goods and ideas that have come with international trade.

LO4 Can you discuss the dramatic internationalization that has occurred in the world's markets?

- Global competition is mounting as the number of international companies expands rapidly. The huge increase in import penetration, plus the massive amounts of overseas investment, means that firms of all sizes face competitors from everywhere in the world. This increasing internationalization of business is requiring managers to have a global business perspective gained through experience, education, or both.

LO5 What are the five kinds of drivers, all based on change, which are leading firms to internationalize their operations?

- The five major kinds of drivers that are leading international firms to globalize their operations are: (1) political, (2) technological, (3) market, (4) cost, and (5) competitive.

LO6 Can you summarize the key arguments for and against the globalization of business?

- Key arguments in support of the globalization include: (1) free trade enhances socioeconomic development, and (2) free trade promotes more and better jobs. Key concerns with the globalization of business include: (1) globalization has produced uneven results across nations and people, (2) globalization has had deleterious effects on labor and labor standards, and (3) globalization has contributed to a decline in environmental and health conditions.

LO7 Can you explain the reasons underlying firms' decisions to enter foreign markets?

- Companies enter foreign markets (exporting to and manufacturing in) to increase sales and profits and to protect markets, sales, and profits from being eroded by competitors.

LO8 Can you identify the seven dimensions of a firm that can be globalized, and can you explain how the extent of a firm's globalization can vary across these dimensions?

- The seven dimensions along which management can globalize (standardize) when organizing their international activities are: (1) product, (2) markets, (3) promotion, (4) where value is added to the product, (5) competitive strategy, (6) use of non-home-country personnel, and (7) extent of global ownership in the firm. The possibilities range from zero standardization (multidomestic) to standardization along all seven dimensions (completely global). A firm can have, and usually does have, an international strategy that is partially multidomestic in some dimensions and partially global in others.

Practical Application

LO1

- _____ _____ is business whose activities are carried out across national borders.
- A _____ company is an organization that attempts to standardize and integrate operations worldwide in most or all functional areas.

LO2

- International business differs from domestic business in that a firm operating across borders must deal with the forces of three kinds of environments—_____, _____, and _____.
- The external forces influencing the life and development of the firm are commonly called _____ forces.

LO3

- _____ was the world's leading manufacturing country for about 1,800 years, until it was replaced by Britain in about 1840.

LO4

- _____ _____ account for approximately 25 percent of total global output and two-thirds of world trade.
- _____ is the transportation of any domestic good or service to a destination outside a country or region.

LO5

- Five major kinds of drivers, all based on change, that are leading international firms to globalize their operations are: (1) _____, (2) _____, (3) _____, (4) _____, and (5) _____.

LO6

- The issue of the impact of globalization on _____ standards has become an oft-mentioned concern of workers in the United States and other nations.

LO7

- The reasons international firms enter foreign markets are all linked to either (1) the desire to increase _____ and _____ or (2) the desire to protect these from being eroded by _____.

LO8

- The seven dimensions along which management can globalize (standardize) when organizing their international activities are: (1) _____, (2) _____, (3) _____, (4) where value is added to the product, (5) competitive strategy, (6) use of non-home-country personnel, and (7) extent of global ownership in the firm

nutshell

The magnitude of both international trade and foreign investment has been increasing rapidly in recent years, strongly impacting the competitiveness and prosperity of nations. To understand these developments, managers—and key government officials—must understand the key theories that help to explain international trade and investment.

The following questions will test your take-away knowledge from this chapter. How many can you answer?

LO1 Can you discuss the magnitude of international trade and how it has grown?

LO2 Can you identify the direction of trade, or who trades with whom, and trends in such trade?

LO3 Can you describe the theories that attempt to explain why certain goods are traded internationally?

LO4 Can you discuss the size, growth, and direction of foreign direct investment?

LO5 Can you identify and explain some of the theories of foreign direct investment?

Did your answers include the following important points?

LO1 Can you discuss the magnitude of international trade and how it has grown?

- The volume of international trade in goods and services measured in current dollars exceeded $19.5 trillion in 2008. Merchandise exports, at $15.8 trillion, were nearly five times what they were in 1990. Services exports were only $3.7 trillion in 2008, but their rate of growth since 1980 has been faster than that of merchandise exports.

LO2 Can you identify the direction of trade, or who trades with whom, and trends in such trade?

- Developed countries tend to trade with developed countries and they account for a majority of the exports worldwide. More than half of the exports from developed countries also go to developed countries, although this proportion has been declining. The results for services exports are similar to those found for merchandise exports. The rise of regional trade agreements, as well as other factors, is transforming the volume and direction of world trade in merchandise and services.

LO3 Can you describe the theories that attempt to explain why certain goods are traded internationally?

- Why do nations trade? Mercantilists did so to build up storehouses of precious metals. Later, Adam Smith's theory of absolute advantage showed that a nation will export goods that it can produce with less labor than can other nations. Ricardo then proved that even though a country is less efficient than other nations, that country can still profit by exporting goods if it holds a comparative advantage in the production of those goods.

  Newer explanations for the direction of trade include the idea that a nation tends to export products requiring a large amount of a resource that is relatively abundant in that nation. In contrast to resource endowments, Linder theorized that because customers' tastes are strongly affected by income levels, a nation's income level per capita determines the kinds of goods they will demand. The kinds of goods produced to meet this demand reflect the country's income per capita. International trade in manufactured goods will be greater between nations with similar levels of per capita income. Porter helped to explain how nations can achieve competitive advantage through the emergence of regional clusters, claiming that four classes of variables are critical in this regard: demand conditions; factor conditions; related and supporting industries; and firm strategy, structure, and rivalry. Competitiveness can also be affected by government and by chance.

LO4 Can you discuss the size, growth, and direction of foreign direct investment?

- The book value of FDI was $16.2 trillion at the end of 2008. Although the largest source of this FDI, the proportion of global foreign direct investment accounted for by the United States has been declining, while the proportion accounted for by the European Union has risen. The proportion of FDI originating in the developing nations has also been increasing. On an annual basis, over 81 percent of FDI flows came from developed countries in 2008. Overall, an average of nearly 70 percent of annual FDI investments have been going into developed countries in recent years, although the proportion is declining, with a majority of this investment occurring in the form of acquisitions of existing companies. The direction of FDI follows the direction of foreign trade; that is, developed nations invest in each other just as they trade with each other.

LO5 Can you identify and explain some of the theories of foreign direct investment?

- International investment theory attempts to explain why FDI takes place. Product and factor market imperfections provide firms, primarily in oligopolistic industries, with advantages not open to indigenous companies. The internalization theory states that firms will seek to invest in foreign subsidiaries, rather than license their superior knowledge, to receive a better return on the investment used to develop that knowledge. The dynamic capabilities perspective suggests that firms must have not only ownership of specific knowledge or resources but also the ability to dynamically create and exploit capabilities in order to achieve success in FDI. The eclectic theory explains an IC's choice of its overseas production facilities. The firm must have location and ownership advantages to invest in a foreign plant. It will invest where it is most profitable to internalize its monopolistic advantage.

Practical Application

LO1
- A measure of the significance of international trade is that _____-_____ of everything grown or made in the world is now exported.

LO2
- Approximately 70 percent of exports from developed economies go to _____ nations.
- The three largest trading partners of the United States in 2009, for both exports and imports, were _____, _____, and _____.

LO3
- _____ is an economic philosophy based on the belief that (1) a nation's wealth depends on accumulated treasure, usually gold, and (2) to increase wealth, government policies should promote exports and discourage imports.

- The theory of _____ _____ explains trade when a country can produce a larger amount of a good or service for the same amount of inputs as can another country or when it can produce the same amount of a good or service using fewer inputs than could another country.

LO4
- _____ countries have dramatically increased their share of FDI stock, from 1 percent in 1980 to nearly 15 percent in 2008.
- The vast proportion of outward FDI, more than 81 percent in 2008, originates from the _____ countries.

LO5
- The eclectic theory of international production states that for a firm to invest overseas it must have three kinds of advantages: _____ specific, _____, and _____ specific.

ANSWERS LO1•one-fourth LO2•industrialized (or developed) •Canada •Mexico •China LO3•Mercantilism •absolute advantage LO4•Developing •developed LO5•ownership •internalization •location

chapter three

active review card
International Institutions from an
International Business Perspective

 in a
nutshell

International institutions are important to international business decision makers because they regulate the relations of individuals one to another. They are organized collections of basic rules and unwritten codes of conduct that limit and direct the decisions firms can make. The United Nations, IMF, World Bank, WTO and EU all influence the conduct of business in significant ways.

The following questions will test your take-away knowledge from this chapter. How many can you answer?

LO1 Can you explain the general importance of international institutions to business decision makers and their firms?

LO2 Can you outline the United Nations as an institution and its relevance to international business?

LO3 Can you describe the purposes of the two global monetary institutions, the IMF and the World Bank?

LO4 Can you discuss the purpose of the World Trade Organization and its impact on international business?

LO5 Can you identify the levels of economic integration?

LO6 Can you discuss the EU and its impact?

Did your answers include the following important points?

LO1 Can you explain the general importance of international institutions to business decision makers and their firms?

- International institutions limit and direct the decisions available to business decision makers.

LO2 Can you outline the United Nations as an institution and its relevance to international business?

- The United Nations, dedicated to the promotion of peace and stability of the world, is composed of five organs, the General Assembly, the Security Council, the Economic and Social Council, The International Court of Justice and the Secretariat. The impact of the UN on the conduct of business can be extremely specific, because UN committees negotiate the global "rules of the game" for the international exchanges of goods, services, money, and information.

LO3 Can you describe the purposes of the two global monetary institutions, the IMF and the World Bank?

- The purpose of the IMF is to coordinate multilateral monetary rules and their enforcement. The purpose of the World Bank is to lend money for development projects.

LO4 Can you discuss the purpose of the World Trade Organization and its impact on international business?

- The purpose of the WTO is to establish and help implement rules of trade between nations. It has been markedly successful in doing so, judging by increasing trade flows, but presently faces the challenge of bringing the benefits of increased trade to poorer countries.

LO5 Can you identify the levels of economic integration?

- Economic integration begins with a free trade area, may move on to a customs union, and then to a common market. A common market may move toward complete economic integration.

LO6 Can you discuss the EU and its impact?

- The EU is a body of 27 European countries committed to economic and political integration. The EU has harmonized national standards, labeling laws, testing procedures, and consumer protection measures, eliminated customs and tax formalities within the EU, and introduced the euro. It has reduced the cost of doing business within the EU, set highly regarded ecological and sustainability standards, and greatly impacted business through its regulations.

Practical Application

LO1

- New institutional theory suggests institutions are a collection of _____ that "regulate the relations of individuals to each other."
- Institutions strive to reduce _____ in the firm's external environment.
- Based on the way they influence behavior, institutions can be either _____ or _____.

LO2

- UN agreements set technical standards and norms that function as the _____ for the global economy.
- UN agreements negotiate the global _____ for the international exchanges of goods, services, money, and information.
- The General Assembly is the UN's the main deliberative body, in which each nation has _____.

LO3

- Each of the IMF members contributes funds, known as _____, determined by the nation's relative size in the world economy, which in aggregate form a pool of money from which the IMF can lend.
- As the IMF struggles today with core issues related to its purpose in a changing world, some economists think that _____ may be an area for renewed IMF focus.
- The World Bank was established at the Bretton Woods meeting in order to address _____ issues.

LO4

- The first WTO principle or norm on which the global trade system rests is that trade should be without discrimination, a principle also known as _____.
- Although the WTO is known as the "free trade organization," many of its agreements support _____.
- The WTO's current conference on trade, _____, has seen discord on many issues connected to the trading needs of developing nations.

LO5

- In a free trade area (FTA), each member-nation maintains its own _____.
- A common market is essentially a single market, so all of the _____ become common.
- NAFTA is an example of a _____ in North America.

LO6

- The EU is a _____ body that has become a regional government.
- _____ has power to impose sanctions on individuals, companies, and member-nations that are found to violate EU agreements.
- EU regulations have _____ impact in the United States, Japan, China, and elsewhere.

ANSWERS LO1•norms •uncertainty •formal or informal LO2•soft infrastructure •rules of the game •one vote LO3•quotas •exchange rates •development LO4•the most-favored nation (MFN) principle •fair competition •the Doha Development Agenda LO5•external tariffs •barriers to trade •free trade area LO6•supranational •The European Court of Justice •major

in a nutshell

Culture, the way groups of people give meaning and order to their lives, matters in core ways to all aspects of IB. To analyze culture differences, frameworks are helpful. Hall sees the context of communication as central to cultural attributes. Hofstede has developed five dimensions to capture cultural attributes, and Trompenaars, seven. The sociocultural aspects of culture are revealed in all human activity.

The following questions will test your take-away knowledge from this chapter. How many can you answer?

LO1 Can you describe in a general way what culture is?

LO2 Can you explain the significance of culture differences for international business, in general, and also for several of the functional areas?

LO3 Can you describe Hall's concept of high and low context and how it applies to cultures?

LO4 Can you describe Hofstede's framework?

LO5 Can you outline Trompenaars' dimensions?

LO6 Can you discuss the sociocultural aspects of culture?

Did your answers include the following important points?

LO1 Can you describe in a general way what culture is?

- Culture is the beliefs, rules, techniques, institutions, and artifacts that characterize human populations. In other words, culture consists of the "individual worldviews, social rules, and interpersonal dynamics characterizing a group of people set in a particular time and place." It is learned, interrelated, shared, constructed through social interaction, and defines the boundaries of groups.

LO2 Can you explain the significance of culture differences for international business, in general, and also for several of the functional areas?

- Culture affects everything we do; it affects international business because crossing borders is elemental to IB. In marketing, culture may require different marketing mixes for different cultures. In HR, culture influences the processes of motivation and evaluation. Culture may influence production through plant layout. In accounting, culture contributes to whether the controls are tight or loose. In finance, borrowing is influenced by culture. Desirable leadership traits are also greatly influenced by culture.

LO3 Can you describe Hall's concept of high and low context and how it applies to cultures?

- Hall's HC LC concept is a classification of cultures based on the amount of context the culture's communication patterns rely on.

In HC cultures, communication tends to be implicit, whereas in LC cultures, communication is explicit.

LO4 Can you describe Hofstede's framework?

- Hofstede's framework is concerned with work values across cultures and has five dimensions. They are: individualism-collectivism, power distance, uncertainty avoidance, masculinity-femininity, and long-term orientation (aka Confucian Dynamism).

LO5 Can you outline Trompenaars' dimensions?

- Trompenaars' dimensions number seven, and the first five address the culture's patterns for relationships among people, while the final two have to do with time and nature. The dimensions are: Universalism vs. Particularism (rules vs. relationships), Individualism vs. Communitarianism, Neutral vs. Affective (unemotional vs. emotional), Specific vs. Diffuse, and Achievement vs. Ascription; and then Attitudes toward Time and Attitudes toward the Environment.

LO6 Can you discuss the sociocultural aspects of culture?

- The sociocultural aspects of culture are how a society's culture manifests or shows itself. Culture shows itself through all parts of a society; aesthetics, religion, material culture, language, and social organization are some of the major sociocultural categories. The text has a special focus on gift giving across cultural borders.

Practical Application

LO1

- Because culture cannot be _____, we learn about it by observing its social world.
- _____ is considering one's own culture superior to others.
- Hall suggests that to understand a culture you must _____ or have intensive training in it.

LO2

- Production manager know that the cultural attitude toward _____ can influence the local acceptance of new production methods.
- Culture influences others and _____.
- Leadership styles vary _____.

LO3

- Context is _____.
- Hall's approach is based on _____.
- LC culture is _____.

LO4

- In Hofstede's approach, _____ describes how the culture copes with inequality.

- Individualism-collectivism measures the degree to which people are _____.
- The masculinity-femininity dimension measures _____ gender roles in the culture.

LO5

- Most of Trompenaars' dimensions are based on the specific culture's patterns of _____.
- Trompenaars' Individualism-Communitarianism dimension is similar to _____'s Individual-Collectivism dimension.
- Trompenaars' past focused culture uses history to understand the _____.

LO6

- _____ context cultures tend to use the nonspoken language more intensively.
- Gestures (are, are not) _____ universal.
- Material culture includes all the _____ of a given culture.

in a nutshell

A nation's geographical features and natural resources are significant external forces that influence the firm. Awareness and consideration of these forces leads to the practice of sustainable business. One approach to sustainable business is through the stakeholder model, where the circle of involved parties is wide.

The following questions will test your take-away knowledge from this chapter. How many can you answer?

LO1 How do the geographical features of a country or region create contextual differences that contribute to economic, cultural, political, and social conditions important to international business?

LO2 What nonrenewable and renewable energy options are available, and what are their broad business implications?

LO3 What is environmental sustainability and what is its potential influence on business?

LO4 Explain the major characteristics of sustainable business.

LO5 How is the stakeholder model useful for achieving sustainable business practice?

Did your answers include the following important points?

LO1 How do the geographical features of a country or region create contextual differences that contribute to economic, cultural, political, and social conditions important to international business?

- Geographical features such as location, topography, and climate form the basis of the inherited context for business. Location influences access to ports and water ways, potential trade and political relationships. Topography influences available land use, accessibility and ease of transport. Climate controls where populations are. Porter's diamond is a good way to analyze how these endowments contribute to a nation's competitive advantage.

LO2 What nonrenewable and renewable energy options are available, and what are their broad business implications?

- The nonrenewable energy options are the fossil fuels: petroleum, coal and natural gas. Nuclear energy is also a nonrenewable energy source, but on a vastly different scale than the others. The renewable energy sources include at least eight sources: hydroelectric, solar, wind, geothermal, waves, tides, biomass fuels such as ethanol, and ocean thermal energy conversion. Renewable energy sources will replace fossil fuels, either due to price or depletion. There also is growing concern about the impact of carbon emissions produced by coal and oil on climate change. So there are many possible impacts on business, depending on the business positioning with renewable sources.

LO3 What is environmental sustainability and what is its potential influence on business?

- Environmental sustainability is an approach that takes care of the present needs of the business and the needs of future generations at the same time. Such approaches usually consider the ecological, social, and economic systems in which a business functions, its natural world, social world, and economic world.

LO4 Explain the major characteristics of sustainable business.

- Sustainability suggests limits, interdependence and equity in distribution for businesses. The business recognizes the limits to their actions when they recognize that environmental resources are exhaustible and that their business has a responsibility to sustain them. Interdependence describes the relationship among the ecological, social, and economic systems of the business. Equity suggests that for interdependence to work, there cannot be vast inequities in the distribution of gains from the value-adding activities of the business.

LO5 How is the stakeholder model useful for achieving sustainable business practice?

- Stakeholder theory involves consideration of the network of tensions caused by competing demands within which any business exists. Stakeholder theory forces a business to address *underlying values and principles.* It "pushes managers to be clear about how they want to do business, specifically, what kind of relationships they want and need to create with their stakeholders to deliver on their purpose."[i] Stakeholder theory also suggests that the tensions among the varying stakeholders in a business environment can be balanced. Business then becomes about relationships in the larger context and the responsibilities that develop from them. In stakeholder theory, profits are a *result* of value creation rather than the primary driver in the process, as in the economic model.

Practical Application

LO1

- Switzerland has built competitive advantage based on its geographical _____.
- More than _____ of the earth's surface consists of arid and semiarid regions.
- _____ is described as the world's most important inland waterway system.

LO2

- The term _____ describes unconventional sources of petroleum.
- The process that puts coal under pressure at high temperature to convert it to crude gas is the _____ process.
- Nuclear power is a _____ energy source.

LO3

- Sustainability is _____ and _____ at the same time.
- By its nature, sustainability is a _____ concept.

- A sustainable business operates so that the _____ is not damaged for future generations.

LO4

- _____ have to do with the recognition that environmental resources are exhaustible.
- With our open _____, vast inequities may lead to unrest and violence.
- Political tensions related to equity in distribution have been seen in _____ and _____ oil businesses.

LO5

- Stakeholder theory forces businesses to figure out what kind of _____ they want with their stakeholders.
- Interface produces Flor, a carpet product made from _____, in its attempts to move towards sustainability.
- Stakeholder theory suggests that the tensions among the varying stakeholders in a business environment can be _____.

[i]R. Edward Freeman, Andrew C. Wicks, and Bidhan Pamar, "'Stakeholder Theory' and the Corporate Objective Revisited," *Organizational Science* 15, no. 3 (May–June 2004), pp. 364–69.

ANSWERS LO1•constraints •one-third •Europe's Rhine waterway LO2•heavy oil •Fischer-Tropsch •renewable LO3•local and global •systems •environment LO4•Limits •communication •Venezuela's and Bolivia's LO5•relationships •petroleum •balanced

in a nutshell

International institutions are important to international business decision makers because they regulate the relations of individuals one to another. They are organized collections of basic rules and unwritten codes of conduct that limit and direct the decisions firms can make. The United Nations, IMF, World Bank, WTO and EU all influence the conduct of business in significant ways.

The following questions will test your take-away knowledge from this chapter. How many can you answer?

LO1 Can you discuss expropriation and privatization?

LO2 Can you explain how terrorism affects international business?

LO3 Can you evaluate the importance to business of government stability and policy continuity?

LO4 Can you explain country risk assessment by international business?

LO5 Can you discuss types of trade restrictions?

Did your answers include the following important points?

LO1 Can you discuss expropriation and privatization?

- From time to time governments take firms or organizations out of private and into government hands. When this is done without compensation, it is called expropriation. Governments sometimes sell government assets to private parties or contract with private firms to perform functions usually performed by governments. That is called privatization.

LO2 Can you explain how terrorism affects international business?

- Terrorism introduces instability into a country, making it difficult for businesses to know what the political environment will be in the future. In some cases terrorism is also personally hazardous to firm employees and to their families.

LO3 Can you evaluate the importance to business of government stability and policy continuity?

- Businesses can operate under almost any set of rules as long as those rules don't change often, so that businesses can make plans. When policy (tax rates is an example) changes frequently, businesses have difficulty complying with the rules, as well as difficulty setting prices, employment policies, etc.

LO4 Can you explain country risk assessment by international business?

- Country risk assessment is a form of assessment which includes political risks, but also others, such as difficulties in remitting profits, local content requirements, possible terrorist action, and the like. Businesses may choose to have CRA done inside the firm, the firm may hire outsiders, or even both.

LO5 Can you discuss types of trade restrictions?

- Trade restrictions include tariff barriers and nontariff barriers. There are a variety of tariff barriers, such as official prices and variable levies. Nontariff barriers include quotas, orderly marketing arrangements, customs and administrative procedures, and standards that aren't meant to protect citizens, but make trade more difficult.

Practical Application

LO1

- Margaret Thatcher was an early leader of the _____ movement.
- In Peru, the President is threatening to take over oil wells owned by foreign firms. This is not an example of _____.
- In the early 1990s a former Eastern German factory was offered to a similar Western Germany business for the cost of 1 mark. This is an example of _____.

LO2

- Is al Qaeda the only terrorist organization in the world? _____
- KRE insurance is insurance against _____, _____, and _____.
- Aum Shin Rikyo is a Japanese rock star. _____

LO3

- A government that can't maintain itself in power, or makes sudden, radical policy changes, might be called _____.
- If one measures only the number of regime changes (how often the top leader changes), is the U.S. a stable or unstable country?

- Should Zimbabwe be considered a stable or unstable country? _____

LO4

- Country risk assessment may be performed within the firm, or by _____ experts.
- A good source of CRA personnel might include veterans of the Department of _____.
- The CRA function in a firm is performed by _____.

LO5

- If a country doesn't allow the importation of cosmetics because "their skin is different," some may suspect that this is a _____ to trade.
- An _____ price is sometimes used to be sure that a minimum import duty will be paid.
- If a nation sets a numerical limit to the number of a specific type of good that can be imported without restrictions, that is generally called a _____.

in a nutshell

International business participants should understand the breadth and depth of laws in various jurisdictions worldwide. The size and variety of these forces complicate the task of understanding these laws. Laws enacted by governments at all levels on virtually any subject affect international business.

The following questions will test your take-away knowledge from this chapter. How many can you answer?

LO1 Can you discuss the complexity of the legal forces that confront international business?

LO2 Can you explain possibilities for international dispute settlement?

LO3 Can you recognize the need and methods to protect intellectual property?

LO4 Can you explain the risk of product liability legal actions?

LO5 Can you discuss some of the U.S. laws that affect international business operations?

Did your answers include the following important points?

LO1 Can you discuss the complexity of the legal forces that confront international business?

- International business is affected by thousands of laws and regulations issued by states, nations, and international organizations. Some are at cross-purposes, and some diminish the ability of firms to compete with foreign companies.

LO2 Can you explain possibilities for international dispute settlement?

- International disputes can be settled by litigation and arbitration. Litigation often raises issues of whose laws should apply and where the litigation should occur. Arbitration is often less expensive, faster and less formal.

LO3 Can you recognize the need and methods to protect intellectual property?

- Intellectual properties consist of patents, trademarks, trade names, copyrights, and trade secrets. Pirating of IP is common and can be difficult to prevent.

LO4 Can you explain the risk of product liability legal actions?

- Product liability refers to the civil or criminal liability of the designer or manufacturer of a product for injury or damages it causes.

LO5 Can you discuss some of the U.S. laws that affect international business operations?

- Many U.S. laws affect the international business operations of U.S. and even foreign corporations. For example, the Foreign Corrupt Practices Act applies to U.S. businesses in their foreign operations and to foreign businesses that conduct operations in the U.S.

Practical Application

LO1

- The U.S. government imposes taxes on U.S. citizens and U.S. permanent residents regardless of either the _____ or the residence of the taxpayer. Laws and regulations affecting international business can be issued by states, nations, and _____.
- Some of these laws are at _____.

LO2

- Two possibilities for international dispute settlements are _____.
- Of the two, _____ is usually less expensive.
- On the other hand, _____ is usually more formal.

LO3

- Two of the several types of intellectual property include _____ and _____.
- The prescription drug industry relies heavily on _____.

- The World Trade Organization administers TRIPS, which is not a travel agency but an _____.

LO4

- _____ hold a company and its officers and directors liable and possibly subject to fines or imprisonment when its product causes death, injury, or damage.
- Outside the United States, _____, not juries, hear product liability cases.
- Under the doctrine of _____ a designer or manufacturer is liable for damages caused by a product without the need for a plaintiff to prove negligence in the product's design or manufacture.

LO5

- The Foreign Corrupt Practices Act makes it _____ to bribe foreign government officials to obtain or retain business.
- The FCPA regulates the behavior of _____ and _____.
- Transparency International publishes a _____ index.

in a nutshell

The international monetary system consists of institutions, agreements, rules, and processes that allow for the payments, currency exchange, and movements of capital required by international transactions. These transactions are influenced by many factors, and awareness of their general movement is important in the conduct of international business. Taxation and inflation rates are among these factors.

The following questions will test your take-away knowledge from this chapter. How many can you answer?

LO1 How has the international monetary system evolved and what is its importance to international business?

LO2 What is the impact of fluctuating currency values?

LO3 How do currency exchange controls influence international business?

LO4 How do differences in taxation and inflation rates affect international business?

LO5 What is the significance of the balance of payments (BOP) to international business decisions?

Did your answers include the following important points?

LO1 How has the international monetary system evolved and what is its importance to international business?

- The international monetary system has evolved from a gold standard to a floating system, to the Bretton Woods System (gold, fixed rate), to a managed floating system.

LO2 What is the impact of fluctuating currency values?

- Fluctuating currency values, from a business perspective, create one more uncertainty or risk because they may affect the cost of doing business. Hedging is commonly used to protect against this risk.

LO3 How do currency exchange controls influence international business?

- Currency exchange controls influence international business because the business cannot exchange local currency for hard currency in order to move it out of the country.

LO4 How do differences in taxation and inflation rates affect international business?

- Differences in taxation and inflation rates do affect the costs of doing business. Taxation is an added business cost, and rising inflation leads to rising prices. Producers in high-inflation economies are less globally competitive than those in lower inflated economies. Lending is constrained in high-inflation economies, as well. International firms might expect the host governments of inflated economies to take corrective action, which may include exchange controls, export incentives, and more restrictive monetary and fiscal policies. The significance of these factors at the international level is the added complexity of many more governments and economies to deal with and to plan around.

LO5 What is the significance of the balance of payments (BOP) to international business decisions?

- The BOP trend helps managers predict what sort of changes in the economic environment might develop in the country. It may also indicate exchange rate movements.

Practical Application

LO1

- In 1717, _____, master of the English mint, established the price of gold in terms of British currency at 3 pounds, 17 shillings, 10.5 pence per ounce.
- The international monetary system in place from 1945 to 1971, with par value based on gold and the U.S. dollar, was the _____.
- A _____ exchange rate is one upheld by the government.

LO2

- _____ exchange rates are determined by market forces.
- _____ allows flexible exchange rates among IMF members.
- The currency arrangement when the government actively intervenes on behalf of its currency but does not make its intervention known is a _____.

LO3

- A developing country might put controls on currency exchange in order to limit the use of its currency in _____.
- _____ currencies are convertible.
- Exchange controls could be used to limit a firm's ability to _____ profits.

LO4

- The three types of taxes governments use to raise revenue are _____, _____, and _____.
- The highest inflation rate to date was found in _____ at 14.9 billion %.
- Inflation is usually measured by the _____.

LO5

- A current account deficit in the BOP means a country is _____ capital.
- The U.S. runs a deficit in its BOP _____.
- The BOP is a record of a country's _____ with the rest of the world.

ANSWERS LO1•Sir Isaac Newton •Bretton Woods system •fixed LO2•Floating •The Jamaica Agreement •managed float (with no pre-arranged path) LO3•international markets • Hard •repatriate LO4•income tax •VAT, and withholding tax •Zimbabwe •CPI LO5•importing •current account transactions

in a nutshell

Labor conditions are determined by social, cultural, religious, attitudinal, political and legal forces. Knowing the quality and quantity of available labor is critical for the firm. Social status, sexism, and racism are among the forces that may affect employment policy. Labor union activities vary by country.

The following questions will test your take-away knowledge from this chapter. How many can you answer?

LO1 What are the forces that affect the quantity and quality of labor in a nation?

LO2 What are the major factors that may impact employment policies in an international setting?

LO3 What are the differences and trends in labor unions from country to country and worldwide?

Did your answers include the following important points?

LO1 What are the forces that affect the quantity and quality of labor in a nation?

- Forces that affect the quantity and quality of labor in a nation include social, cultural, religious, attitudinal, political and legal forces. The characteristics of the population (age, education, location, mobility), immigrant and guest worker labor availability, and social, political and legal values related to labor all impact the quantity and quality of available labor.

LO2 What are the major factors that may impact employment policies in an international setting?

- Employment policies in international markets must take into account a range of issues related to the local environment. Some of these issues are social status, sexism, racism, the existence of minorities within traditional societies, and overall labor situations commonly encountered in developing nations.

LO3 What are the differences and trends in labor unions from country to country and worldwide?

- **Labor unions** vary significantly from country to country. They tend to be more effective in developed countries. European labor unions are usually identified with socialist and democratic political parties. In the U.S., unionism has been more pragmatic than political, more concerned with the immediate needs of workers than with a political ideology. The international union movement has been slow to develop, but is beginning to emerge with the EU.

Practical Application

LO1

- Workers without a contract or other formal work arrangement, whose work is underpaid and undertaken in difficult conditions with low productivity, may be classified as a part of the _____ workforce.
- More than _____ the world's population is urban.
- Child labor has the highest rates in _____ and _____.

LO2

- _____ is important with respect to the labor force, because it so dominates human behavior and attitudes.

- Women hold less than _____ of all senior management positions, worldwide.
- Studies show a correlation between the length of _____ and a nation's overall prosperity.

LO3

- Labor unions tend to be more effective in _____ countries.
- In the U.S., labor legislation is mostly concerned with _____.
- Adversarial relationships are not usually found between unions and management in _____.

in a nutshell

Managers should take those actions necessary to help their companies compete more effectively as international businesses. They must be able to quickly identify and exploit attractive opportunities, whether domestically or internationally. This requires managers to clearly understand their company's mission, vision, and strategy, and to understand the company's strengths and weaknesses compared to those of their worldwide competitors. Strategic planning is a key tool to help managers in these tasks.

The following questions will test your take-away knowledge from this chapter. How many can you answer?

LO1 Can you explain the concepts of international strategy, competencies, and international competitive advantage?

LO2 Can you describe the steps in the global strategic planning process?

LO3 What is the purpose of each of the following: mission statements, vision statements, values statements, objectives, quantified goals, and strategies?

LO4 Can you explain home replication, multidomestic, global, and transnational strategies and when to use each of them?

LO5 Can you describe the methods of and new directions in strategic planning?

Did your answers include the following important points?

LO1 Can you explain the concepts of international strategy, competencies, and international competitive advantage?

- International strategy is concerned with the way in which firms make fundamental choices about developing and deploying scarce resources internationally. Competencies are skills or abilities that are required in order to adequately complete a task. International competitive advantage is the ability of a company to have higher rates of profit than its international competitors. The goal of international strategy is to create a competitive advantage that is sustainable over time. To do this, the international company should try to develop skills, or competencies, that are valuable, rare, and difficult to imitate and that the organization is able to exploit fully.

LO2 Can you describe the steps in the global strategic planning process?

- Global strategic planning provides a formal structure in which managers (1) analyze the company's external environment, (2) analyze the company's internal environment, (3) define the company's business and mission, (4) set corporate objectives, (5) quantify goals, (6) formulate strategies, and (7) make tactical plans.

LO3 What is the purpose of each of the following: mission statements, vision statements, values statements, objectives, quantified goals, and strategies?

- Statements of the corporate mission, vision, and values communicate to the firm's stakeholders what the company is and where it is going, as well as the values to be upheld among the organization's members in their behaviors. A firm's objectives direct its course of action, quantification of goals allows progress to be verified, and strategies provide the action plans that enable management to reach the company's objectives.

LO4 Can you explain home replication, multidomestic, global, and transnational strategies and when to use each of them?

- When developing and assessing strategic alternatives, companies competing in international markets confront two opposing forces: reduction of costs and adaptation to local markets. As a result, companies basically have four different strategies that they can use for competing internationally: home replication, multidomestic, global, and transnational. The most appropriate strategy, overall and for various activities in the value chain, depends on the amount of pressure the company faces in terms of adapting to local markets and achieving cost reductions. Each of these four strategies has advantages and disadvantages.

LO5 Can you describe the methods of and new directions in strategic planning?

- Strategic planning is traditionally done in a top-down, a bottom-up, or an iterative process. Operating managers, rather than dedicated staff planners, now have assumed a primary role in planning. Firms use less structured formats and much shorter documents. Managers are more concerned with issues, strategies, and implementation.

Practical Application

LO1

- _____ _____ is the way firms make choices about acquiring and using scarce resources in order to achieve their international objectives.
- _____ _____ refers to the ability of a company to have higher rates of profits than its competitors.
- The process by which an organization determines where it is going in the future, how it will get there, and how it will assess whether and to what extent it has achieved its goals is known as _____ _____.

LO2

- _____ _____ _____ is an assessment conducted on a chain of interlinked activities of an organization or set of interconnected organizations, intended to determine where and to what extent value is added to the final product or service.
- The practices that organizations and their managers use for the identification, creation, acquisition, development, dispersion, and exploitation of competitively valuable knowledge are known as _____ _____.
- Knowledge that an individual has but that is difficult to express clearly in words, pictures, or formulae, and therefore difficult to transmit to others, is known as _____ knowledge.

LO3

- A _____ _____ is a broad statement that defines the organization's purpose and scope.

- The _____ _____ is a description of the company's desired future position if it can acquire the necessary competencies and successfully implement its strategy.
- To enhance a company's ability to develop and implement an effective strategy, one that will enable the company's objectives to be attained, it is important that efforts be made to _____ these objectives.

LO4

- A _____ strategy tends to be used when there is strong pressure for the company to adapt its products or services for local markets.
- A _____ strategy tends to be used when a company faces strong pressures for reducing costs and limited pressure to adapt products for local markets.
- _____ are multiple, plausible stories for probable futures.

LO5

- A planning process that begins at the highest level in the organization and continues downward is known as _____-_____.
- A _____ _____ approach to planning combines strategic thinking, strategic planning, and strategic implementation and is increasingly recognized as a fundamental task of line management rather than merely specialized planners in staff positions.
- Top management, at the urging of strategy consultants, is assigning strategic planning to teams of _____ and _____ managers from different business, geographic, and functional areas

in a nutshell

Organizations exist for the purpose of enabling a group of people to effectively coordinate their collective activities and accomplish objectives. Organizational structure refers to the way that an organization formally arranges its various domestic and international units and activities and the relationships among these organizational components. A company's structure helps determine where formal power and authority will be located within the organization, and this structure is what is typically presented in a company's organization chart.

The following questions will test your take-away knowledge from this chapter. How many can you answer?

LO1 Why is the design of organizational structure important to international companies?

LO2 What are the organizational dimensions that must be considered when selecting organizational structures?

LO3 Can you discuss the various organizational forms available for structuring international companies?

LO4 Why are decisions made where they are among parent and subsidiary units of an international company?

LO5 How can an international company maintain control of a joint venture or of a company in which the IC owns less than 50 percent of the voting stock?

LO6 What are the types of information an international company needs to have reported to it by its units around the world?

Did your answers include the following important points?

LO1 Why is the design of organizational structure important to international companies?

- The structure of an international organization involves how the domestic and international units and activities are arranged and where formal power and authority will be located inside the company. It helps determine how efficiently and effectively the organization will be able to integrate and leverage its competencies and resources within and across various units of the enterprise, and thus contribute to successful implementation of the company's strategy.

LO2 What are the organizational dimensions that must be considered when selecting organizational structures?

- The organizational structure selected for a company must be consistent with the organization's capabilities and resources, as well as with the environmental context in which the organization operates and with its strategy. In selecting an organizational structure, managers of an international company must consider the requirements for expertise in terms of product and technology, geography, customer, and function.

LO3 Can you discuss the various organizational forms available for structuring international companies?

- Companies may (1) have an international division; (2) be organized by product, function, or region; or (3) have a mixture of them (hybrid form). To attain a balance between product and regional expertise, some companies have tried a matrix form of organization. Its disadvantages, however, have caused many companies to put a matrix overlay over a traditional product, regional, or functional form instead of using the matrix.

LO4 Why are decisions made where they are among parent and subsidiary units of an international company?

- Several considerations govern where decisions are made in an IC family of organizations. They include the desirability of standardizing products as opposed to differentiating them for different markets, the competence of organization managements, the size and age of the IC, the benefit of one part of the company to the detriment of another, and building confidence or avoiding frustration of management.

LO5 How can an international company maintain control of a joint venture or of a company in which the IC owns less than 50 percent of the voting stock?

- Control can be maintained over a joint venture or a company in which the IC owns less than 50 percent of the voting stock by several devices, including a management contract, control of the finances, control of the technology, and putting people from the IC in key executive positions.

LO6 What are the types of information an international company needs to have reported to it by its units around the world?

- Subsidiaries should report to the IC information about financial conditions, technological developments, market opportunities and developments, and economic and political conditions.

Practical Application

LO1

- The way that an organization formally arranges its domestic and international units and activities, and the relationships among these various organizational components is known as _____ _____.
- In designing an international organization, it is essential that the structures and systems being implemented are not merely consistent with each other but also consistent with the _____ context in which the organization is operating and the _____ the company is using for competing in this international environment.

LO2

- The four primary dimensions that need to be considered when designing the structure of an international company include _____ and technical expertise, _____ expertise, _____ expertise, and _____ expertise.

LO3

- An _____ division is a division in the organization that is at the same level as the domestic division and is responsible for all non-home-country activities.
- A structure organized by more than one dimension at the top level is known as a _____ _____.
- A _____ _____ is an organizational structure composed of one or more superimposed organizational structures in an attempt to mesh product, regional, functional, and other expertise.
- A _____ _____ is an organization that coordinates economic activity to deliver value to customers using resources outside the traditional boundaries of the organization.

LO4

- Decisions in wholly-owned subsidiaries can be made at the IC _____, at the _____ level, or _____.
- In a firm without a global product policy, the preference of the operations management people in the home office has always been to _____ the product or at least the production process in as many overseas plants as possible.
- In larger, older organizations, more decisions are made at _____ and fewer are delegated to _____.
- _____ _____ refers to the situation in which a small loss for a subsidiary results in a greater gain for the total IC.

LO5

- Even if an IC has less than 50 percent of the voting stock of a joint venture, it may have control through such mechanisms as a _____ contract, control of the _____ or the _____, and putting people from the IC in important executive positions.

LO6

- For controls to be effective, all operating units of an IC must provide headquarters with timely, accurate, and complete reports, including information of the following types: _____, _____, _____ opportunity, and _____ and economic.

in a nutshell

International environmental forces can complicate management efforts to assess the attractiveness of expanding into foreign markets. Companies have to develop and apply appropriate approaches for assessing international markets.

The following questions will test your take-away knowledge from this chapter. How many can you answer?

LO1 Can you discuss environmental analysis and the two types of market screening?

LO2 Can you explain market indicators and market factors?

LO3 What are some statistical techniques for estimating market demand and grouping similar markets?

LO4 What is the value to businesspeople of trade missions and trade fairs?

LO5 What are some of the problems market researchers encounter in foreign markets?

LO6 What are the different options for conducting survey-based research?

LO7 Can you explain the difference between country screening and segment screening?

Did your answers include the following important points?

LO1 Can you discuss environmental analysis and the two types of market screening?

- A complete market analysis and assessment would be made by a firm that either is contemplating entering the foreign market for the first time or is already a multinational but wants to monitor world markets systematically to avoid overlooking marketing opportunities and threats. Many of the data requirements for a foreign decision are the same as those for a similar domestic decision, but it is likely that additional information about some of the international and foreign environmental forces will be needed. Essentially, the screening process consists of examining the various forces in succession and eliminating countries at each step. Screening based on (1) basic need potential, (2) financial and economic forces, (3) political and legal forces, (4) sociocultural forces, (5) competitive forces, and (6) personal visits is sequenced so as to have a successively smaller number of prospects to consider at each of the successively more difficult and expensive stages.

LO2 Can you explain market indicators and market factors?

- Market indicators are economic data used to measure relative market strengths of countries or geographic areas. Market factors are economic data that correlate highly with the market demand for a product.

LO3 What are some statistical techniques for estimating market demand and grouping similar markets?

- Some statistical techniques for estimating market demand and grouping similar markets are trend analysis and cluster analysis.

LO4 What is the value to businesspeople of trade missions and trade fairs?

- Trade missions and trade fairs enable businesspeople to visit a market inexpensively, make sales, obtain overseas representation, and observe competitors' activities.

LO5 What are some of the problems market researchers encounter in foreign markets?

- Cultural problems, such as a low level of literacy and distrust of strangers, complicate the data-gathering process, as do technical difficulties, such as a lack of maps, telephone directories, and adequate mail service. These hindrances to marketing research do not prevent the work from being done. There is a tendency in some markets, however, to do less research and use simpler techniques.

LO6 What are the different options for conducting survey-based research?

- Data collection via surveys can be done through the use of such options as customized research, general surveys, nonprofit surveys, and the Internet.

LO7 Can you explain the difference between country screening and segment screening?

- If we utilize country screening, we assume that countries are homogeneous units (i.e., "everyone living in Mexico or Chad is essentially the same"). In segment screening, we focus our attention not on the nation as a homogeneous unit but on groups of people with similar wants and desires (market segments) across as well as within countries.

Practical Application

LO1

- The first step in the market screening process is determining the _____ _____ _____.
- The second step in the market screening process is based on the _____ and _____ forces.

LO2

- _____ _____ are economic data that serve as yardsticks for measuring the relative market strengths of various geographic areas.
- _____ _____ are economic data that correlate highly with market demand for a product.

LO3

- When the historical growth rates of either the pertinent economic variables or the imports of a product are known, future growth can be forecast by means of _____ _____.
- _____ _____ divides objects (market areas, individuals, customers, and other variables) into groups so that the variables within each group are similar.

LO4

- The purpose of a _____ _____ is to send a group of executives from firms in the industry to a country or group of countries to learn firsthand about the market, meet important customers face-to-face, and make contacts with people interested in representing their products.

- A _____ _____ is a large exhibition, generally held at the same place and same time periodically, at which companies maintain booths to promote the sale of their products.

LO5

- If secondary data on a potential market are unavailable, the researchers must collect primary data, and here they face other complications caused by _____ problems and _____ difficulties.
- The custom of politeness toward everyone that can cause respondents to give answers calculated to please the interviewer rather than reflecting the respondent's true beliefs or feelings is known as _____ _____ _____.

LO6

- General surveys, which are not done with a specific firm in mind, have three different types: _____ surveys, _____ general surveys, and _____ surveys.
- The _____ is increasingly an option that may offer any firm the opportunity to do its own surveys anywhere in the world.

LO7

- The important issue for market segmentation is not where consumers reside but whether they share similar _____ and _____.
- Among the criteria managers should use when identifying and assessing segments, it is important that these segments be _____, _____, _____, _____, and _____.

in a nutshell

When most businesses begin they are focused on the domestic market and gradually become international in scope. International institutions are important to international business decision makers because they regulate the relations of individuals one to another. They are organized collections of basic rules and unwritten codes of conduct that limit and direct the decisions firms can make. The United Nations, IMF, World Bank, WTO, and EU all influence the conduct of business in significant ways.

The following questions will test your take-away knowledge from this chapter. How many can you answer?

LO1 Can you explain the pros and cons of being a "market pioneer" versus being a "fast follower"?

LO2 Can you explain the international market entry methods?

LO3 Can you identify two forms of piracy, and discuss how they both help and harm firms doing international business?

LO4 Can you discuss why firms export ?

Did your answers include the following important points?

LO1 Can you explain the pros and cons of being a "market pioneer" versus being a "fast follower"?

- Market pioneers and fast followers may both become "tops" in their industry, depending on a variety of factors.

LO2 Can you explain the international market entry methods?

- Firms may enter via nonequity (such as exporting or licensing) or equity modes (such as joint ventures).

LO3 Can you identify two forms of piracy, and discuss how they both help and harm firms doing international business?

- One form of piracy is literally piracy at sea, an increasing threat. Another is counterfeiting, which is also perceived to be increasing.

The first is always harmful, but the second may introduce new software or musical artists to potential future customers.

LO4 Can you discuss why firms export?

- Among many reasons firms export are: Exporting allows firm to serve markets where they have no production facilities, and it allows firms to "test the waters" in a foreign market with relatively little commitment.

Practical Application

LO1

- Market pioneers are _____ into a market.
- Compaq is an example of a market _____.
- High entry barriers help _____ a pioneering firm.

LO2

- Exporting is an example of a _____ international market entry method.
- Pierre Cardin makes a considerable amount of money by _____ the use of his name in foreign markets.
- An example of direct exporting is _____.

LO3

- "Pirates of the Caribbean" is a fictional movie, but why is it somewhat realistic? _____

- One barrier to selling software is the inability to provide a "sample" of the product. This function is sometimes provided by _____ _____.

LO4

- One reason firms begin exporting is to _____.
- Firms may also export to _____.
- When the U.S. economy is not expanding, exporters may be able to continue growing by exporting to another market that is currently vibrant. This is called _____ _____ sales in the domestic market.

in a nutshell

International business is both similar to, and can be quite different from, doing business domestically. A key issue is standardization of product (which is an economic advantage) versus product adaptation (which is at the heart of the marketing concept). Generally, industrial products can be more easily standardized than consumer products. The Internet has had an important effect on international business.

The following questions will test your take-away knowledge from this chapter. How many can you answer?

LO1 Can you explain why there are differences between domestic and international marketing?

LO2 Can you discuss why international marketing managers may wish to standardize the marketing mix?

LO3 Can you explain why it is often impossible to standardize the marketing mix worldwide?

LO4 Can you explain why consumer products generally require greater modification for international sales than do industrial products or services?

LO5 Can you discuss some of the effects the Internet may have on international marketing?

Did your answers include the following important points?

LO1 Can you explain why there are differences between domestic and international marketing?

- Sometimes there are no differences between domestic and international marketing, but often the differences are great enough for the marketing program to need changing.

LO2 Can you discuss why international marketing managers may wish to standardize the marketing mix?

- A standardized marketing mix can produce significant cost savings. In addition, it is easier to control, and less time may be spent in developing marketing plans.

LO3 Can you explain why it is often impossible to standardize the marketing mix worldwide?

- Customers in different cultures or countries often have different preferences, and marketing managers need to respond to those differences.

LO4 Can you explain why consumer products generally require greater modification for international sales than do industrial products or services?

- Industrial products (say, a bolt or a roll of cotton fabric) are generally more standardized across the globe than final products sold to end-users.

LO5 Can you discuss some of the effects the Internet may have on international marketing?

- The Internet offers a new advertising tool, providing an affluent audience with two-way communications possible. Groups such as teenagers, who are watching less TV, are spending more time on the Internet.

Practical Application (fill in the blank)

LO1

- Doing business internationally is _____ more complicated than doing business in one's own market.
- While weekly shopping trips may be the norm in the U.S., in other countries, shopping trips are often made _____.
- Differences in the legal environment often require _____ of the marketing plan.

LO2

- A standardized marketing mix is usually _____ costly than a marketing program which takes cultural differences into account.
- Gasoline is an example of a product which (cannot, can probably) _____ be standardized across markets.
- A standardized marketing plan usually takes _____ time to develop than a plan for each market.

LO3

- Coca-Cola eventually found that it could not standardize its _____ around the world.
- An _____ product may be easier to standardize than a consumer product.

- Theodore Levitt argued (for, against) _____ standardization of products.

LO4

- A product may be successfully standardized when the product is _____, is _____, and is _____.

LO5

- Teenagers are now watching _____ TV than they did in the past.
- Unlike TV, communication via the Internet can be _____.
- A (small, large) _____ number of Internet users read a common language such as English, Spanish or Chinese.

ANSWERS LO1•usually •daily •adaptation LO2•less •can probably •less LO3•marketing mix •industrial •for LO4•low-priced •consumed in the same way •is bought for the same reasons LO5•less •two-way •large

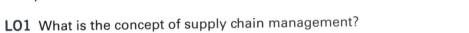

in a nutshell

As firms continue to enter global markets, global competition increases. This forces management of both international and domestic companies to search for ways to lower costs while improving their products or services in order to remain competitive. As a result, it has become increasingly critical to understand the topics of global supply chain management and the management of global operations, including global sourcing, manufacturing systems, productivity and performance of international manufacturing operations, and issues associated with global standardization versus localization of international operations.

The following questions will test your take-away knowledge from this chapter. How many can you answer?

LO1 What is the concept of supply chain management?

LO2 What is the relationship between design and supply chain management?

LO3 What are the five global sourcing arrangements?

LO4 Why is electronic purchasing playing an increasing role in global sourcing?

LO5 Can you explain the importance of the added costs of global sourcing?

LO6 Can you explain the potential of global standardization of production processes and procedures, and identify impediments to standardization efforts?

Did your answers include the following important points?

LO1 What is the concept of supply chain management?

- Supply chain management is the process of coordinating and integrating the flow of materials, information, finances, and services within and among companies in the value chain, from suppliers to the ultimate consumer. It is integral to cost and quality objectives and to achieving international competitiveness.

LO2 What is the relationship between design and supply chain management?

- The design of a company's products and services has a fundamental relationship with the types of inputs the company will require. Concurrent engineering approaches allow proposed designs to be subjected to earlier assessments on cost, quality, and manufacturability dimensions, enhancing the efficiency and effectiveness of supply chain management.

LO3 What are the five global sourcing arrangements?

- A firm may (1) establish a wholly owned subsidiary in a low-labor-cost country to supply components to the home-country plant or to supply a product not produced in the home country, (2) establish an overseas joint venture in a country where labor costs are lower to supply components to the home country, (3) send components to be machined and assembled by an independent contractor in an in-bond plant, (4) contract with an independent contractor overseas to manufacture products to its specifications, or (5) buy from an independent overseas manufacturer.

LO4 Why is electronic purchasing playing an increasing role in global sourcing?

- The establishment of electronic purchasing systems on a company or industry basis can influence the number and type of suppliers available internationally to firms. Electronic purchasing systems can produce significant reductions in the costs of inputs, both direct and indirect products and services. These systems can also permit the optimization of supply chains across networks of organizations.

LO5 Can you explain the importance of the added costs of global sourcing?

- International freight, insurance, and packing may add 10 to 12 percent to the quoted price, depending on the sales term used. Import duties, customhouse broker's fees, cost of letter of credit, cost of inventory in the pipeline, and international travel are some of the other added costs.

LO6 Can you explain the potential of global standardization of production processes and procedures, and identify impediments to standardization efforts?

- Standards help ensure that materials, products, processes, and services are appropriate for their purpose, helping companies meet market and competitive demands. Standardization of activities helps simplify organization and control at headquarters because replication enables work to be accomplished with a smaller staff of support personnel and internal best practices can more readily be applied across an IC's operations. However, differences in foreign environmental forces, especially economic, cultural, and political forces, cause units of an international multiplant operation to differ in size, machinery, and procedures, complicating efforts to achieve standardization of processes and procedures.

Practical Application

LO1

- The process of coordinating and integrating the flow of materials, information, finances, and services within and among companies in the value chain from suppliers to the ultimate consumer is known as _____ _____ _____.

- Hiring others to perform some of the noncore activities and decision making in a company's value chain, rather than having the company and its employees continue to perform those activities, is known as _____.

LO2

- The _____ of a company's products and services has a fundamental relationship with the type of inputs that the company will require, including labor, materials, information, and financing.

LO3

- The five arrangements that can provide a firm with foreign products are _____ _____ _____, overseas _____ _____, in-bond _____ contractor, overseas independent _____, and independent overseas _____.

LO4

- While direct production–oriented goods have been the focus of management attention for many years, the purchasing of goods and services that are not part of finished goods—termed _____ _____ is also critical.

- Emerging industry-based B2B exchanges can help _____ the supply chain across an entire _____ of organizations, creating value by aggregating the purchasing power of buyers, improving process efficiency, integrating supply chains, enhancing content dissemination, and improving overall market efficiency within and across nations.

LO5

- For purchases of capital goods such as manufacturing equipment, many U.S. buying organizations now use "_____-_____ _____" to analyze purchasing decisions through the life of the purchased item, including trade-in or future estimated salvage value. Even on components, firms are increasingly including _____ _____, including the use of activity-based costing systems, to ensure that all the costs associated with foreign sourcing are fully recognized when they make purchasing decisions.

LO6

- _____ are documented agreements containing technical specifications or other precise criteria that will be used consistently as guidelines, rules, or definitions of the characteristics of a product, process, or service.

- The standardization of production _____ and _____ simplifies the manufacturing organization at headquarters because their replication enables the work to be accomplished with a smaller staff of support personnel.